SOMETHING ABOUT THE AUTHOR

SOMETHING ABOUT THE AUTHOR

Facts and Pictures about Authors
and Illustrators of Books for Young People

ANNE COMMIRE

VOLUME 31

GALE RESEARCH COMPANY
BOOK TOWER
DETROIT, MICHIGAN
48226

Editor: Anne Commire

Associate Editors: Agnes Garrett, Helga P. McCue

Assistant Editors: Dianne H. Anderson, Joyce Nakamura, Linda Shedd, Cynthia J. Walker

Sketchwriters: Barbara G. Farnan, Rachel Koenig, Eunice L. Petrini, Michael G. Williston

Researcher: Kathleen Betsko

Editorial Assistants: Carolyn Brudzynski, Lisa Bryon, Susan Pfanner, Elisa Ann Sawchuk

Production Supervisor: Carol Blanchard

Production Associates: Cynthia G. La Ferle, Mary Beth Trimper

Text Layout: Vivian Tannenbaum

Cover Design: Arthur Chartow

Special acknowledgment is due to the members of the *Contemporary Authors* staff
who assisted in the preparation of this volume.

Frederick G. Ruffner, *Publisher*

James M. Ethridge, *Editorial Director*

Adele Sarkissian, *Senior Editor*

Also Published by Gale

CONTEMPORARY AUTHORS

*A Bio-Bibliographical Guide to Current Writers in
Fiction, General Nonfiction, Poetry, Journalism,
Drama, Motion Pictures, Television,
and Other Fields*

(Now Covers More Than 71,000 Authors)

Library of Congress Catalog Card Number 72-27107

ISBN 0-8103-0057-5

ISSN 0276-816X

Table of Contents

Introduction 9   **Acknowledgments 15**

Forthcoming Authors 13   **Illustrations Index 201**

Author Index 217

A

Alcorn, John   1935- 21

Allen, Adam [Joint Pseudonym]
see Epstein, Beryl 64
see Epstein, Samuel 66

Anderson, Brad   1924-
Brief Entry 22

Andrews, Benny   1930- 22

Antell, Will D.   1935- 26

B

Bahti, Tom
Brief Entry 26

Barker, Carol   1938- 26

Bennett, Dorothea
see Young, Dorothea Bennett 191

Blackton, Peter
see Wilson, Lionel
Brief Entry 186

Blume, Judy   1938- 28

Brady, Esther Wood   1905- 35

Briggs, Peter   1921-1975
Obituary Notice 36

Brink, Carol Ryrie   1895-1981 36

Briquebec, John
see Rowland-Entwistle, Theodore 145

Bröger, Achim   1944- 42

Brown, Conrad   1922- 43

Bryan, Ashley F.   1923- 44

Bushmiller, Ernie   1905-1982
Obituary Notice 45

C

Camp, Charles Lewis   1893-1975
Obituary Notice 46

Campbell, Bruce
see Epstein, Samuel 66

Cary, Barbara Knapp   1912(?)-1975
Obituary Notice 46

Cavanah, Frances   1899-1982 46

Chandler, Edna Walker   1908-1982
Obituary Notice 48

Charlot, Jean   1898-1979
Obituary Notice 48

Clyne, Patricia Edwards 49

Coe, Douglas [Joint Pseudonym]
see Epstein, Beryl 64
see Epstein, Samuel 66

Collins, Pat Lowery   1932- 51

Colt, Martin [Joint Pseudonym]
see Epstein, Beryl 64
see Epstein, Samuel 66

Conover, Chris   1950- 52

Cox, William R.   1901-
Brief Entry 53

Craft, Ruth
Brief Entry 53

Crane, Barbara J.   1934- 53

Cros, Earl
see Rose, Carl
Brief Entry 144

D

Dank, Milton   1920- 54

Davis, Hubert J.   1904- 55

De Groat, Diane   1947- 57

Dekker, Carl
see Laffin, John 111

Denzer, Ann Wiseman
see Wiseman, Ann 186

De Roussan, Jacques   1929-
Brief Entry 59

Dirks, Rudolph   1877-1968
Brief Entry 60

Dixon, Franklin W.
see McFarlane, Leslie 133

Dixon, Jeanne   1936- 60

Dolan, Edward F., Jr.   1924-
Brief Entry 61

Dottig
see Grider, Dorothy 75

E

Edwards, Audrey 1947-
Brief Entry 62

Edwards, Dorothy 1914-1982
Obituary Notice 62

Eisner, Will 1917- 62

Ellis, Anyon
see Rowland-Entwistle, Theodore 145

Ellis, Herbert
see Wilson, Lionel
Brief Entry 186

Epstein, Beryl 1910- 64

Epstein, Samuel 1909- 66

Erikson, Mel 1937- 69

Erwin, Will
see Eisner, Will 62

F

Fenwick, Patti
see Grider, Dorothy 75

Ferris, James Cody
see McFarlane, Leslie 133

Fleur, Anne 1901-
Brief Entry 70

Floyd, Gareth 1940-
Brief Entry 70

Ford, George 70

Foster, Hal
see Foster, Harold Rudolf
Obituary Notice 72

Foster, Harold Rudolf 1892-1982
Obituary Notice 72

Fraser, Betty
see Fraser, Elizabeth Marr 72

Fraser, Elizabeth Marr 1928- 72

Frimmer, Steven 1928- 74

G

Garbutt, Bernard 1900-
Brief Entry 74

Gardner, John Champlin, Jr. 1933-1982
Obituary Notice 74

Glaser, Dianne E. 1937-
Brief Entry 74

Greisman, Joan Ruth 1937- 74

Grider, Dorothy 1915- 75

H

Hale, Nancy 1908- 77

Hall, Borden
see Yates, Raymond F. 189

Hall, Brian P. 1935- 78

Hall-Clarke, James
see Rowland-Entwistle, Theodore 145

Hancock, Mary A. 1923- 78

Harding, Lee 1937-
Brief Entry 78

Harper, Mary Wood
see Dixon, Jeanne 60

Hautzig, Deborah 1956- 79

Hefter, Richard 1942- 80

Heinemann, George Alfred 1918-
Brief Entry 83

Henry, T.E.
see Rowland-Entwistle, Theodore 145

Hermes, Patricia 1936- 83

Hill, Robert W. 1919-1982
Obituary Notice 84

Houselander, Caryll 1900-1954
Brief Entry 84

Hughes, Thomas 1822-1896 85

Hunt, Joyce 1927- 91

Hunter, Edith Fisher 1919- 93

Hürlimann, Ruth 1939-
Brief Entry 93

Hutchens, Paul 1902-1977 94

I

Ishmael, Woodi 1914- 99

J

Janson, Dora Jane 1916- 100

Johnson, James Weldon
see Johnson, James William 101

Johnson, James William 1871-1938 101

Johnson, Milton 1932- 107

Jones, Penelope 1938- 108

Jordan, E.L. 1900-
Brief Entry 109

K

Kadesch, Robert R. 1922- 109

Keene, Carolyn
　see McFarlane, Leslie 133

Kelleam, Joseph E.　1913-1975　. 109

Kelley, Leo P.　1928-
　Brief Entry 109

Klaperman, Libby Mindlin　1921-1982
　Obituary Notice 110

Klug, Ron　1939-　. 110

Krahn, Fernando　1935-
　Brief Entry 111

L

Laffin, John　1922-　. 111

Laite, Gordon　1925-　. 112

Lamb, Elizabeth Searle　1917-　. 113

Lavine, David　1928-　. 114

Lawrence, J.T.
　see Rowland-Entwistle, Theodore 145

Levy, Elizabeth　1942-　. 115

Lippman, Peter J.　1936-　. 119

Lisowski, Gabriel　1946-
　Brief Entry 120

M

MacKenzie, Garry　1921-
　Brief Entry 120

Manniche, Lise　1943-　. 120

Marokvia, Artur　1909-　. 122

Marriott, Alice Lee　1910-　. 123

Marshall, Percy
　see Young, Percy M. 191

Marston, Hope Irvin　1935-　. 124

Martin, Rupert　1905-　. 125

Mazer, Harry　1925-　. 126

McClure, Gillian Mary　1948-　. 131

McFarlane, Leslie　1902-1977 133

McLeod, Emilie Warren　1926-1982
　Obituary Notice 142

McPharlin, Paul　1903-1948
　Brief Entry 142

McWhirter, A. Ross　1925-1975
　Obituary Notice 143

Meriwether, Louise　1923-
　Brief Entry 143

Miller, Albert G.　1905-1982
　Obituary Notice 143

Moser, Don
　see Moser, Donald Bruce 143

Moser, Donald Bruce　1932-　. 143

Moss, Elaine Dora　1924-
　Brief Entry 144

N

Napier, Mark
　see Laffin, John 111

Nye, Harold G.
　see Harding, Lee
　Brief Entry 78

O

Old Boy
　see Hughes, Thomas 85

P

Pioneer
　see Yates, Raymond F. 189

Powers, Bill　1931-
　Brief Entry 144

R

Reeve, Joel
　see Cox, William R.
　Brief Entry 53

Rensie, Willis
　see Eisner, Will 62

Robinson, Nancy K.　1942-
　Brief Entry 144

Rockwood, Roy
　see McFarlane, Leslie 133

Rose, Carl　1903-1971
　Brief Entry 144

Rowland-Entwistle, Theodore　1925-　. 145

S

Sabre, Dirk
　see Laffin, John 111

Salzer, L.E.
　see Wilson, Lionel
　Brief Entry 186

Sari
　see Fleur, Anne
　Brief Entry 70

Saville, Malcolm 1901-1982
   Obituary Notice 146

Schatzki, Walter 1899-
   Brief Entry 146

Schick, Joel 1945- 147

Schiller, Justin G. 1943-
   Brief Entry 149

Scott, Jack Denton 1915- 149

Seaman, Augusta Huiell 1879-1950 153

Sitomer, Harry 1903- 155

Sitomer, Mindel 1903- 157

Smith, Elva S. 1871-1965
   Brief Entry 157

Sobol, Donald J. 1924- 157

Stein, R. Conrad 1937- 159

Stine, Jovial Bob
   see Stine, Robert Lawrence 160

Stine, Robert Lawrence 1943- 160

Stone, Josephine Rector
   see Dixon, Jeanne 60

Strong, Charles [Joint Pseudonym]
   see Epstein, Beryl 64
   see Epstein, Samuel 66

Sutton, Ann 1923- 161

Sutton, Felix 1910(?)- 162

Sutton, Myron Daniel 1925- 165

T

Teague, Bob
   see Teague, Robert
   Brief Entry 166

Teague, Robert 1929-
   Brief Entry 166

Thomson, Peggy 1922- 166

Tichy, William 1924- 168

Tripp, Wallace 1940- 169

Turska, Krystyna 1933- 172

Tworkov, Jack 1900-1982
   Obituary Notice 176

V

Vass, George 1927-
   Brief Entry 176

Viator, Vacuus
   see Hughes, Thomas 85

Vlahos, Olivia 1924- 176

W

Walker, Alice 1944- 177

Walther, Thomas A. 1950- 179

Walther, Tom
   see Walther, Thomas A. 179

Weissenborn, Hellmuth 1898-1982
   Obituary Notice 179

Weller, George 1907- 179

Wharf, Michael
   see Weller, George 179

Whitlock, Pamela 1921(?)-1982
   Obituary Notice 181

Wilkie, Katharine E. 1904-1980 181

Wilkoń, Józef 1930- 182

Williams, Beryl
   see Epstein, Beryl 64

Wilson, Dagmar 1916-
   Brief Entry 186

Wilson, Lionel 1924-
   Brief Entry 186

Wiseman, Ann 1926- 186

Wittels, Harriet Joan 1938- 187

Wolitzer, Hilma 1930- 188

Wood, Esther
   see Brady, Esther Wood 35

Wynants, Miche 1934-
   Brief Entry 189

Y

Yates, Raymond F. 1895-1966 189

Young, Dorothea Bennett 1924- 191

Young, Percy M. 1912- 191

Introduction

If you have ever been asked to write a report or a paper, you probably know that writing can be hard work, even lonely and frustrating work at times. Have you ever wondered, then, what it takes to be a writer—someone who makes a profession of this demanding work? Is he or she someone provided at birth with special talents, someone who can be recognized by the easy flow of words from his or her pencil even in grade school? Maybe you've even asked yourself, "Could *I* be a writer?"

Writers themselves probably have the best answers to questions like these. And *Something about the Author* offers you a unique opportunity to tap into the experience and advice of more writers than you could ever meet face to face—writers of today and of the past, writers from countries around the globe, writers of stories, plays, poems, biographies, histories, novels, films, science and social science books, writers whose work is funny, sad, serious, informative, daring, and delightful. In this volume of *SATA*, and in the entire series, these diversely talented people tell you in their own words what made them the authors of the books that you are reading today.

As you may already suspect, the answers are likely to be as varied as the authors themselves. Some people, indeed, seem to have been "born" writers. Enid Bagnold, the writer of *National Velvet* whom you'll find in Volume 26, considered herself "a writer from the age of nine." Adele De Leeuw, a pioneer in teen novels, was ten years old when her first poem was published in her hometown newspaper, and by the age of fourteen she was producing a "literary magazine," with the help of her younger sister, for a list of ten subscribers. Her entry in Volume 30 details still other of her youthful accomplishments. But even young writers have to face disappointment. Julia Cunningham, the author of *Dorp Dead,* recalls in her Volume 26 entry that she received her first rejection slip at the age of twelve.

But not every writer you'll meet in *SATA* was born with pen in hand. Many authors didn't experience an urge to write until their adult years. For example, Harry Mazer, the author of *The War on Villa Street* who is profiled in Volume 31, began his first book when he was in his mid-thirties. Already a husband and a father, he had put in years of work as a longshoreman, railroad worker, welder, and iron worker before he gave his full time to writing. As Mazer describes it, he writes in spite of the fact that he doesn't feel articulate or fluent; in fact, he feels he has no "natural talent" as a writer. Another late-blooming writer is Marguerite de Angeli who produced an impressive body of writing and illustration for young people even though she was married and the mother of three children before she seriously embarked on her career. You'll find her entry in Volume 27.

Still other people became writers by accident rather than deliberate aim. Evaline Ness, for example, was a successful artist and illustrator when her editor suggested that she try supplying the words as well as the pictures for a book. As you'll see in Volume 26, that suggestion was a good one. Teacher and minister Paul Hutchens, who appears in this volume of *SATA,* took up writing when illness forced him into a long convalescence in bed. Eventually, his Christian novels became a cornerstone of his ministry. Among other "accidental authors," you may be surprised to find some that candidly admit they were somewhat less than star pupils in school and even poor spellers!

As you look through *SATA* you may find some special types of writers that you hadn't considered before. There are joint authors, for example, like Beryl and Samuel Epstein. If writing a book by yourself seems difficult enough, how do you suppose two people do it together? The Epsteins know: they've collaborated on successful fiction and nonfiction for more than forty years, and remain married. They tell how they do it in this volume of *SATA.*

Another special kind of writer is a "ghost writer," someone who writes anonymously or under a pseudonym without revealing his or her real name. The name Leslie McFarlane is probably unfamiliar to you even though he is the same "Franklin W. Dixon" who wrote the first volumes of the famous "Hardy Boys" series. McFarlane's entry in Volume 31 describes how he produced what he calls "hack work" and yet managed to bring creativity and quality to it.

We invite you to explore widely in *SATA*. Read for yourself what these and many more people reveal about what made each of them a writer. Perhaps you'll even see some reflection of yourself along the way. But even if you don't see yourself as a fledgling writer, *SATA* can open the door to information that will help you prepare a project like a book report, a story hour, or a book talk, or simply help you select your next reading venture.

What a *SATA* Entry Provides

In every *SATA* entry the editors attempt to give as complete a picture of the person's life and work as possible. In some cases that full range of information may simply be unavailable, or a biographee may choose not to reveal complete personal details. The information that the editors attempt to provide in every entry is arranged in the following categories:

1. The "head" of the entry gives

   —the most complete form of the name,
   —any part of the name not commonly used, included in parentheses,
   —birth and death dates, if known; a (?) indicates a discrepancy in published sources,
   —pseudonyms or name variants under which the person has had books published or is publicly known, in parentheses in the second line.

2. "Personal" section gives

   —date and place of birth and death,
   —parents' names and occupations,
   —name of spouse, date of marriage, names of children,
   —educational institutions attended, degrees received, and dates,
   —religious and political affiliations,
   —agent's name and address,
   —home and/or office address.

3. "Career" section gives

   —name of employer, position, and dates for each career post,
   —military service,
   —memberships,
   —awards and honors.

4. "Writings" section gives

   —title, first publisher and date of publication, and illustration information for each book written; revised editions and other significant editions for books with particularly long publishing histories; genre, when known.

5. "Adaptations" section gives

   —title, major performers, producer, and date of all known reworkings of an author's material in another medium, like movies, filmstrips, television, recordings, plays, etc.

6. "Sidelights" section gives

   —commentary on the life or work of the biographee either directly from the person (and often written specifically for the *SATA* entry), or gathered from biographies, diaries, letters, interviews, or other published sources.

7. "For More Information See" section gives

   —books, feature articles, films, plays, and reviews in which the biographee's life or work has been treated.

How a *SATA* Entry Is Compiled

A *SATA* entry progresses through a series of steps. If the biographee is living, the *SATA* editors try to secure information directly from him or her through a questionnaire. From the information that the biographee supplies, the editors prepare an entry, filling in any essential missing details with research. The author or illustrator is then sent a copy of the entry to check for accuracy and completeness.

If the biographee is deceased or cannot be reached by questionnaire, the *SATA* editors examine a wide variety of published sources to gather information for an entry. Biographical sources are searched with the aid of Gale's *Biography and Genealogy Master Index*. Bibliographic sources like the *National Union Catalog*, the *Cumulative Book Index, American Book Publishing Record*, and the *British Museum Catologue* are consulted, as are book reviews, feature articles, published interviews, and material sometimes obtained from the biographee's family, publishers, agent, or other associates.

For each entry presented in *SATA*, the editors also attempt to locate a photograph of the biographee as well as representative illustrations from his or her books. After surveying the available books which the biographee has written and/or illustrated, and then making a selection of appropriate photographs and illustrations, the editors request permission of the current copyright holders to reprint the material. In the case of older books for which the copyright may have passed through several hands, even locating the current copyright holder is often a long and involved process.

Other Information Features in *SATA*

Brief Entries, first introduced in Volume 27, are now a regular feature of *SATA*. Brief Entries present essentially the same types of information found in a full entry, but do so in a capsule form and without illustration. The editors hope that these entries will give you useful and timely information while the more time-consuming process of attempting to compile a full-length entry continues. Among the Brief Entries in Volume 31 you'll find Tom Bahti, who earned the Caldecott Medal for his illustration of Byrd Baylor's *When Clay Sings;* Rudolph Dirks, the creator of the "Katzenjammer Kids" cartoons; Fernando Krahn, the Chilean-born author/illustrator of books like *The Journey of Sebastian* and *Here Comes Alex Pumpernickel;* and Bob Teague, former star halfback at the University of Wisconsin, the first Black newsman hired by the NBC network, and now the author of *Agent K-Thirteen the Super Spy.*

Obituaries are another regular feature of *SATA*. An obituary in *SATA* is intended not only as a death notice, but also as a concise view of a person's life and work. Obituaries appear not only for persons listed in *SATA* prior to their death, but also for people who have not yet appeared in the series. Recent deaths noted in Volume 31 include those of Hal Foster, the creator of "Prince Valiant" in cartoons and books; John Gardner the eminent author and critic whose children's books include *Dragon, Dragon* and *A Child's Bestiary;* and Emilie McLeod, not only an author but a children's book editor and publisher under her own imprint, Unicorn Books.

Revised entries became a regular element in the *SATA* series with Volume 25. For each succeeding volume the editors select from among the early *SATA* listees those authors and illustrators who remain of interest to today's young readers and who have been active enough to require extensive revision of their earlier entry. The entry for a given biographee may be revised as often as there is substantial new information to provide. In Volume 31 you'll find revised entries for Judy Blume, Carol Ryrie Brink, Frances Cavanah, Beryl and Samuel Epstein, and Donald J. Sobol.

Highlights of This Volume

These are some of the people in Volume 31 that you may find particularly interesting:

JUDY BLUME......one of the most popular and highly-acclaimed writers for young people today. Books like *Are You There God? It's Me, Margaret, Tales of a Fourth Grade Nothing,* and *Blubber* have won Blume a long list of awards that includes the Charlie May Simon Award, Pacific Northwest Young Readers Choice Award, Sequoyah Children's Book Award, and state-wide awards in Georgia, South Carolina, Massachusetts, Arizona, and Indiana. In her newly-revised *SATA* entry Blume recalls that, as the mother of two young children, she turned to writing as a creative outlet. She stayed with it, even though her early efforts were poor imitations of Dr. Seuss and earned as many as six or seven rejection slips in a single week. The key to her success, she feels, is that she writes what she knows. The ideas, situations, and settings for her books come directly from her experience as a young girl. Blessed with "total recall," she can put herself right back in the third grade and *be* nine years old again.

CAROL RYRIE BRINK......was orphaned at the age of eight and raised by her grandmother and a maiden aunt. Much later in her life she looked back to that childhood as a happy though lonely time when she began to "lay up those riches" that would serve as the inspiration for her writing. Having to devise her own amusements, young Carol found animal friends all around her and vicariously relived the exciting childhood her grandmother described in stories about the Wisconsin frontier of her youth. Years later Brink recounted her grandmother's story in *Caddie Woodlawn,* earning both a Newbery Medal and a Lewis Carroll Shelf Award. Writing and the experience of living went hand in hand for Brink; and she continued to do both into her eighties. She once observed, "What you have fully experienced will enrich your writing, and what you have fully imagined will enrich your living."

DONALD J. SOBOL......whose books cover a broad range of topics from historical books, biographies, and even a book on stock and bonds. His preference, however, is writing fiction for young people. And young readers have shown a decided preference for his "Encyclopedia Brown" series. The little detective with the fact-filled memory is just as popular today as when he debuted in 1963—and still ten years old.

KRYSTYNA TURSKA......is the noted illustrator of children's books like Elizabeth Coatsworth's *Marra's World* and William Mayne's *The Mouse and the Egg;* but she is also an accomplished reteller of tales like *Pegasus,* which was nominated for a Greenaway Medal, and *The Woodcutter's Duck,* which was a Greenaway Medal winner. Turska, now a British citizen, fled Poland when she was a young child, only to be imprisoned in Russia and later to endure a journey through Persia, Iraq, Palestine, and Egypt before she and her family found a permanent home in England.

ALICE WALKER......kept a notebook of her poems from the time she was eight years old—not quite what you might expect from the youngest of eight children in a share-cropping family. But then, Alice always felt that she was somehow different than the rest of her family, needing more peace and quiet, more time to be by herself. She recently won both an American Book Award and a Pulitzer Prize for her book *The Color Purple,* which probably qualifies her as an "overnight success," by some standards. In fact, she has devoted some fifteen years to being a teacher of Black literature and a writer of numerous novels, poems, and essays.

HILMA WOLITZER......isn't what you'd expect in a writer: she never went to college; she hasn't had any exciting adventures to draw upon; she doesn't even write from her own experience as all good advice to writers prescribes. All she claims for glamour is that she went to the same high school as Maurice Sendak! Even when she did make a false start with adolescent poetry at the age of ten, her one published poem only went as far as *The Junior Inspectors' Club Journal* of the New York City Department of Sanitation. Even she isn't quite sure what brought her back to writing at the age of thirty-five, but it was lucky for young readers that she did. They can now enjoy *Introducing Shirley Braverman, Out of Love,* and *Toby Lived Here.*

These are only a few of the authors and illustrators that you'll find in this volume. We hope you find all the entries in *SATA* both interesting and useful. Please write and tell us if we can make *SATA* even more helpful for you.

A Partial List of Authors and Illustrators
Who Will Appear in Forthcoming Volumes of
Something about the Author

Abels, Harriette S.
Adrian, Mary
Ahlberg, Allan
Ahlberg, Janet
Aldridge, Alan   1943(?)-
Allard, Harry
Allen, Agnes B.   1898-1959
Allen, Jeffrey
Andrist, Ralph K.   1914-
Armitage, Ronda
Armstrong, Louise
Arneson, D.J.   1935-
Ashley, Bernard   1935-
Axeman, Lois
Ayme, Marcel   1902-1967
Baker, Olaf
Balderson, Margaret   1935-
Bang, Betsy
Barber, Richard   1941-
Barkin, Carol
Barnett, Moneta   1922-1976
Bartlett, Margaret F.   1896-
Batherman, Muriel   1926(?)-
Batson, Larry   1930-
Bauer, Caroline Feller   1935-
Bauer, John Albert   1882-1918
Becker, May Lamberton   1873-1958
Beckman, Delores
Beim, Jerrold   1910-1957
Beim, Lorraine   1909-1951
Bernheim, Evelyne   1935-
Bernheim, Marc   1924-
Birnbaum, Abe   1899-
Bjorklund, Lorence F.   1915(?)-
Blumberg, Rhoda   1917-
Boegehold, Betty   1913-
Boning, Richard A.
Bonners, Susan
Bowden, Joan C.   1925-
Bowen, Gary
Bracken, Carolyn
Brewton, Sara W.
Bridgman, Elizabeth P.   1921-
Brock, C(harles) E(dmond)   1870-1938
Broekel, Ray   1923-
Bromley, Dudley   1948-
Bronin, Andrew   1947-
Bronson, Wilfrid   1894-
Brooks, Ron(ald George)   1948-
Brown, Fern G.   1918-
Brown, Roy Frederick   1921-
Brownmiller, Susan   1935-
Buchanan, William   1930-
Buchenholz, Bruce
Budney, Blossom   1921-
Burchard, Marshall

Burke, David   1927-
Burns, Marilyn
Burstein, Chaya
Butler, Dorothy   1925-
Butler, Hal   1913-
Calvert, Patricia
Camps, Luis
Carey, M. V.   1925-
Carmer, Carl   1893-1976
Carroll, Ruth R.   1899-
Cauley, Lorinda B.
Charles, Donald
Cline, Linda   1941-
Cohen, Joel H.
Cole, Brock
Cole, Joanna
Cooper, Elizabeth Keyser   1910-
Cooper, Paulette   1944-
Cosgrove, Margaret   1926-
Coutant, Helen
Craik, Dinah M.   1826-1887
Dabcovich, Lydia
Darley, F(elix) O(ctavius) C(arr)
   1822-1888
D'Aulnoy, Marie-Catherine
   1650(?)-1705
David, Jay   1929-
Davies, Peter   1937-
Dean, Leigh
Degens, T.
DeGoscinny, Rene
Deguine, Jean-Claude   1943-
Deweese, Gene   1934-
Ditmars, Raymond   1876-1942
Dodd, Lynley
Duggan, Maurice (Noel)   1922-1975
Dumas, Philippe   1940-
East, Ben
Eastman, Philip D.   1909-
Edelson, Edward   1932-
Ehlert, Lois Jane   1934-
Eisenberg, Lisa
Elder, Lauren
Elgin, Kathleen   1923-
Elwood, Roger   1943-
Erwin, Betty K.
Etter, Les   1904-
Everett-Green, Evelyn   1856-1932
Falkner, John Meade   1858-1932
Farmer, Penelope   1939-
Fender, Kay
Filson, Brent
Fischer, Hans Erich   1909-1958
Flanagan, Geraldine Lux
Folch-Ribas, Jacques   1928-
Fox, Thomas C.

Frame, Paul   1913-
Frascino, Edward
Freschet, Berniece   1927-
Gans, Roma   1894-
Garcia-Sanchez, S.L.
Gardner, John Champlin, Jr.   1933-1982
Garrison, Christian   1942-
Gathje, Curtis
Gault, Clare   1925-
Geer, Charles   1922-
Gelman, Rita G.   1937-
Gemme, Leila Boyle   1942-
Gerber, Dan   1940-
Gerson, Corinne
Giff, Patricia R.
Gobbato, Imero   1923-
Goldstein, Nathan   1927-
Gordon, Shirley
Gould, Chester   1900-
Grabianski, Janusz   1929(?)-1976
Graboff, Abner   1919-
Graeber, Charlotte Towner
Gregor, Arthur S.
Gridley, Marion E(leanor)   1906-1974
Gross, Ruth B.
Gruelle, Johnny   1880(?)-1938
Gutman, Bill
Hague, Michael
Halacy, Daniel S., Jr.   1919-
Harris, Marilyn   1931-
Hayman, LeRoy   1916-
Healey, Larry
Heide, Florence Parry   1919-
Heine, Helme   1941-
Henty, George Alfred   1832-1902
Herzig, Alison Cragin
Hicks, Clifford B.   1920-
Hill, Douglas Arthur   1935-
Hirshberg, Albert S.   1909-1973
Hollander, Zander   1923-
Hood, Thomas   1779-1845
Horwitz, Elinor L.
Hudson, Kirsty   1947-
Hull, Jessie Redding
Hunt, Clara Whitehill   1871-1958
Ingelow, Jean   1820-1897
Isadora, Rachel
Jackson, Anita
Jackson, Robert   1941-
Jacobs, Francine   1935-
James, Elizabeth
Jameson, Cynthia
Janssen, Pierre
Jaspersohn, William
Jewell, Nancy   1940-
Johnson, Harper

Joyner, Jerry 1938-
Kahl, Virginia 1919-
Kahn, Joan 1914-
Kalan, Robert
Kantrowitz, Mildred
Kasuya, Masahiro 1937-
Keith, Eros 1942-
Kessler, Ethel
Kirn, Ann (Minette) 1910-
Koenig, Marion
Kohl, Herbert
Kohl, Judith
Kraske, Robert
Kredenser, Gail 1936-
Krensky, Stephen 1953-
Kullman, Harry
Kurland, Michael 1938-
Laure, Jason
Lawson, Annetta
Leach, Christopher
Leckie, Robert 1920-
Lerner, Carol
LeRoy, Gen
Le-Tan, Pierre 1950-
Levoy, Myron
Lewis, Naomi
Lindblom, Steve
Lines, Kathleen
Livermore, Elaine
Lubin, Leonard
MacDonald, George 1824-1905
MacKinstry, Elizabeth A. d. 1956
Mali, Jane Lawrence
Manes, Stephen
Marryat, Frederick 1792-1848
Mayakovsky, Vladimir 1894-1930
McCannon, Dindga
McKee, David 1935-
McKim, Audrey Margaret 1909-
McLenighan, Valjean
McLoughlin, John C.
McNaught, Harry 1897-1967
McNaughton, Colin
McPhail, David 1940-
Melcher, Frederic G. 1879-1963
Mendoza, George 1934-
Mezey, Robert
Molesworth, Maria L. 1839(?)-1921
Molly, Anne S. 1907-
Moore, Lilian
Moore, Patrick 1923-
Morgenroth, Barbara
Mozley, Charles 1915-
Murdocca, Sal
Murphy, Shirley Rousseau 1928-
Myers, Elisabeth P. 1918-
Nickl, Peter
Nostlinger, Christine 1936(?)-
Obligado, Lillian Isabel 1931-
O'Hanlon, Jacklyn
Oleksy, Walter 1930-
Olson, Gene 1922-
Oppenheim, Shulamith (Levey) 1930-
Orr, Frank 1936-
Orton, Helen Fuller 1872-1955
Overbeck, Cynthia
Owens, Gail 1939-

Packard, Edward 1931-
Parenteau, Shirley L. 1935-
Parker, Robert Andrew 1927-
Pascal, Francine
Paterson, A(ndrew) B(arton) 1864-1941
Paterson, Diane 1946-
Patterson, Sarah 1959-
Pavey, Peter
Pelgrom, Els
Peretz, Isaac Loeb 1851-1915
Perkins, Lucy Fitch 1865-1937
Peterson, Esther Allen
Peterson, Jeanne Whitehouse 1939-
Phillips, Betty Lou
Pinkney, Jerry 1939-
Plotz, Helen 1913-
Plowden, David 1932-
Plume, Ilse
Poignant, Axel
Pollock, Bruce
Polushkin, Maria
Pontiflet, Ted 1932-
Pope, Elizabeth M. 1917-
Porter, Eleanor Hodgman 1868-1920
Poulsson, Emilie 1853-1939
Powers, Richard M. 1921-
Prager, Arthur
Prather, Ray
Preston, Edna Mitchell
Pursell, Margaret S.
Pursell, Thomas F.
Pyle, Katharine 1863-1938
Rabinowitz, Solomon 1859-1916
Rae, Gwynedd 1892-
Rappoport, Ken 1935-
Rees, David 1936-
Reich, Hanns
Reid, Alistair 1926-
Reidel, Marlene
Reiff, Tana
Reynolds, Marjorie 1903-
Rice, Eve H. 1951-
Robison, Nancy 1934-
Rock, Gail
Rockwell, Anne 1934-
Rockwell, Harlow
Rockwood, Joyce 1947-
Rosier, Lydia
Ross, Pat
Ross, Wilda 1915-
Roughsey, Dick 1921(?)-
Roy, Cal
Roy, Ron
Ruby, Lois 1942-
Rudstrom, Lennart
Rush, Peter 1937-
Ryder, Joanne
Sargent, Sarah
Sauer, Julia Lina 1891-
Schindelman, Joseph 1923-
Schneider, Leo 1916-
Schoenherr, John C. 1935-
Sebestyen, Ouida
Seidler, Rosalie
Sewall, Helen 1881-
Sewell, Marcia 1935-
Shapiro, Milton J. 1926-

Shea, George
Shreve, Susan
Slater, Jim
Slepian, Jan(ice B.)
Smith, Alison
Smith, Catriona (Mary) 1948-
Smith, Ray(mond Kenneth) 1949-
Smollin, Michael J.
Sobol, Harriet L. 1936-
Spencer, Zane 1935-
Steiner, Charlotte
Steiner, Jorg
Steiner-Prag, Hugo 1880-1945
Stevens, Leonard A. 1920-
Stevenson, James
Stine, R. Conrad 1937-
Stong, Phil 1899-1957
Stubbs, Joanna 1940-
Sullivan, Mary Beth
Suteev, Vladimir Grigor'evich
Sutherland, Robert D.
Sweet, Ozzie
Taback, Simms 1932-
Taylor, Ann 1782-1866
Taylor, Jane 1783-1824
Thaler, Mike
Thomas, Ianthe
Thompson, Brenda 1935-
Thurman, Judith 1946-
Timmermans, Gommaar 1930-
Todd, Ruthven 1914-
Tourneur, Dina K. 1934-
Treadgold, Mary 1910-
Van Steenwyk, Elizabeth
Velthuijs, Max 1923-
Villiard, Paul 1910-1974
Waber, Bernard 1924-
Wagner, Jenny
Walker, Charles W.
Walsh, Anne Batterberry
Waterton, Betty
Watson, Aldren A. 1917-
Watson, Nancy D.
Watts, Franklin 1904-1978
Wayne, Bennett
Wellman, Alice 1900-
Werner, Herma 1926-
Weston, Martha
Whelen, Gloria
White, Wallace 1930-
Whitlock, Ralph 1914-
Wild, Jocelyn
Wild, Robin
Wilson, Edward A. 1886-1970
Winn, Marie
Winter, Paula 1929-
Winterfeld, Henry 1901-
Wolde, Gunilla
Wolf, Bernard
Wong, Herbert H.
Wormser, Richard
Wright, Betty R.
Yagawa, Sumiko
Zaidenberg, Arthur 1908(?)-
Zelinsky, Paul O.
Zimelman, Nathan
Zistel, Era

In the interest of making *Something about the Author* as responsive as possible to the needs of its readers, the editor welcomes your suggestions for additional authors and illustrators to be included in the series.

GRATEFUL ACKNOWLEDGMENT

is made to the following publishers, authors, and artists for
their kind permission to reproduce copyrighted material.

HARRY N. ABRAMS, INC. Jacket illustration from *The Story of Painting for Young People* by H. W. and Dora Jane Janson. Reprinted by permission of Harry N. Abrams, Inc.

ATHENEUM PUBLISHERS, INC. Illustration by Ashley Bryan from *The Dancing Granny,* retold by Ashley Bryan. Copyright © 1977 by Ashley Bryan. Reprinted by permission of Atheneum Publishers, Inc.

AUGSBURG PUBLISHING HOUSE. Illustration by Jim Roberts from *My Christmas ABC Book* by Ron and Lyn Klug. Copyright © 1981 by Augsburg Publishing House. Reprinted by permission of Augsburg Publishing House.

BRADBURY PRESS, INC. Jacket illustration by Larry Raymond from *Holding Together* by Penelope Jones. Jacket illustration copyright © 1981 by Larry Raymond. Text copyright © 1981 by Penelope Jones./ Jacket illustration by Eros Keith from *Are You There God? It's Me, Margaret* by Judy Blume. Copyright © 1970 by Judy Blume. Both reprinted by permission of Bradbury Press, Inc.

CHILDRENS PRESS. Illustration by Tom Dunnington from *The Story of the Golden Spike* by R. Conrad Stein. Copyright © 1978 by Regensteiner Publishing Enterprises, Inc. Reprinted by permission of Childrens Press.

THOMAS Y. CROWELL CO., PUBLISHERS. Illustrations by Richard Cuffari from *Zero Is Not Nothing* by Mindel and Harry Sitomer. Text copyright © 1978 by Mindel and Harry Sitomer. Illustrations copyright © 1978 by Richard Cuffari./ Cover illustration by Lise Manniche from *How Djadja-Em-Ankh Saved the Day: A Tale from Ancient Egypt,* translated by Lise Manniche. Copyright © 1976 by Lise Manniche./ Illustration by Don Miller from *Langston Hughes, American Poet* by Alice Walker. Text copyright © 1974 by Alice Walker. Illustrations copyright © 1974 by Don Miller. All reprinted by permission of Thomas Y. Crowell Co., Publishers.

COWARD, McCANN & GEOGHEGAN, INC. Illustration by Joseph Scrofani from *Dr. Beaumont and the Man with the Hole in His Stomach* by Sam and Beryl Epstein. Text copyright © 1978 by Sam and Beryl Epstein. Illustrations copyright © 1978 by Joseph Scrofani./ Illustration by Victor Juhasz from *She Never Looked Back: Margaret Mead in Samoa* by Sam and Beryl Epstein. Text copyright © 1980 by Sam and Beryl Epstein. Illustrations copyright © 1980 by Victor Juhasz./ Illustration by Wallace Tripp from *Casey at the Bat: A Ballad of the Republic, Sung in the Year 1888* by Ernest Lawrence Thayer. Illustrations copyright © 1978 by Wallace Tripp./ Photograph from *West Virginia* by Felix Sutton. Copyright © 1968 by Felix Sutton. All reprinted by permission of Coward, McCann & Geoghegan, Inc.

CROWN PUBLISHERS, INC. Illustration by John Wallner from *A January Fog Will Freeze a Hog and Other Weather Folklore,* compiled and edited by Hubert Davis. Text copyright © 1977 by Hubert J. Davis. Illustrations copyright © 1977 by John Wallner./ Illustration by Diane de Groat from *Alligator's Toothache* by Diane de Groat. Copyright © 1977 by Diane de Groat./ Jacket illustration by Richard Cuffari from *The Toad on Capitol Hill* by Esther Wood Brady. Copyright © 1978 by Esther Wood Brady. All reprinted by permission of Crown Publishers, Inc.

DELACORTE PRESS. Illustration by Mordicai Gerstein from *Nice Little Girls* by Elizabeth Levy. Text copyright © 1974 by Elizabeth Levy. Illustrations copyright © 1974 by Mordicai Gerstein./ Illustration by John Wallner from *Lizzie Lies a Lot* by Elizabeth Levy. Text copyright © 1976 by Elizabeth Levy. Illustrations copyright © 1976 by John Wallner. Both reprinted by permission of Delacorte Press.

DELL PUBLISHING CO., INC. Illustration by Amy Aitken from *The One in the Middle Is the Green Kangaroo* by Judy Blume. Text copyright © 1981 by Judy Blume. Illustrations copyright © 1981 by Amy Aitken. Reprinted by permission of Dell Publishing Co., Inc.

J. M. DENT & SONS LTD. Illustration by S. Van Abbé from *Tom Brown's School Days* by Thomas Hughes. Reprinted by permission of J. M. Dent & Sons Ltd.

ANDRÉ DEUTSCH LTD. Illustration by Gillian McClure from *What's the Time, Rory Wolf?* by Gillian McClure. Copyright © 1982 by Gillian McClure. Reprinted by permission of André Deutsch Ltd.

DILLON PRESS, INC. Sidelight excerpts and photograph from *Judy Blume's Story* by Betsy Lee. Copyright © 1981 by Dillon Press, Inc. Both reprinted by permission of Dillon Press, Inc.

DODD, MEAD & CO. Illustration by Ted Lewin from *Ghostly Animals of America* by Patricia Edwards Clyne. Copyright © 1977 by Patricia Edwards Clyne./ Photograph by Ira Mandelbaum from *What Does a Senator Do?* by David Lavine. Copyright © 1967 by David Lavine and Ira Mandelbaum. Both reprinted by permission of Dodd, Mead & Co.

DOVER PUBLICATIONS, INC. Illustrations by Edward Ardizzone from *Ding Dong Bell* by Percy Young and Edward Ardizzone. Copyright © 1957 by Percy Young and Dobson Books Ltd. Both reprinted by permission of Dover Publications, Inc.

E. P. DUTTON, INC. Illustration by Roy Doty from *Tales of a Fourth Grade Nothing* by Judy Blume. Text copyright © 1972 by Judy Blume. Illustrations copyright © 1972 by E. P. Dutton, Inc./ Illustration by Lillian Brandi from *Encyclopedia Brown and the Case of the Midnight Visitor* by Donald J. Sobol. Text copyright © 1977 by Donald J. Sobol. Illustrations copyright © 1977 by Thomas Nelson, Inc. Both reprinted by permission of E. P. Dutton, Inc.

FARRAR, STRAUS & GIROUX, INC. Illustration by George Ford from "Queen Cora," in *The Singing Turtle and Other Tales from Haiti* by Philippe Thoby-Marcelin and Pierre Marcelin. Translation by Eva Thoby-Marcelin. Copyright © 1971 by Farrar, Straus & Giroux, Inc./ Jacket illustration by Ruth Bowen from *Introducing Shirley Braverman* by Hilma Wolitzer. Copyright © 1975 by Hilma Wolitzer. Both reprinted by permission of Farrar, Straus & Giroux, Inc.

FOUR WINDS PRESS. Illustration by Sonia O. Lisker from *Freckle Juice* by Judy Blume. Copyright © 1971 by Judy Blume. Illustrations copyright © 1971 by Sonia O. Lisker./ Illustration by Chris Conover from *Where Did My Mother Go?* by Edna Mitchell Preston. Text copyright © 1978 by Edna Mitchell Preston. Illustrations copyright © 1978 by Chris Conover./ Illustration by Betty Fraser from *Giraffe: The Silent Giant* by Miriam Schlein. Text copyright © 1976 by Miriam Schlein. Illustrations copyright © 1976 by Betty Fraser. All reprinted by permission of Four Winds Press.

GARRARD PUBLISHING CO. Illustration by Gordon Laite from *The Adventures of Hiawatha* by Virginia Frances Voight. Copyright © 1969 by Virginia Frances Voight./ Illustration by E. Harper Johnson from *Daniel Boone: Taming the Wilds* by Katharine E. Wilkie. Copyright © 1960 by Katharine E. Wilkie. Both reprinted by permission of Garrard Publishing Co.

GROSSET & DUNLAP, INC. Illustration by J. Clemens Gretter from *The Sinister Signpost* by Franklin W. Dixon. Copyright 1936 by Grosset & Dunlap, Inc. Copyright renewed © 1964 by Harriet S. Adams and Edna C. Squier./ Illustration by Walter S. Rogers from *The Tower Treasure* by Franklin W. Dixon. Copyright 1927 by Grosset & Dunlap, Inc. Copyright renewed 1955 by Harriet S. Adams./ Illustration by Walter S. Rogers from *The Missing Chums* by Franklin W. Dixon. Copyright 1928 by Grosset & Dunlap, Inc. Copyright renewed © 1956 by Harriet S. Adams and Edna C. Squiers./ Illustration by Walter S. Rogers from *The House on the Cliff* by Franklin W. Dixon. Copyright 1927 by Grosset & Dunlap, Inc. Copyright renewed 1955 by Harriet S. Adams./ Illustration by James Schucker from *The Book of Clowns* by Felix Sutton. Copyright 1953 by Grosset & Dunlap, Inc. All reprinted by permission of Grosset & Dunlap, Inc.

HAMISH HAMILTON LTD. Illustration by Krystyna Turska from *The King of the Golden River* by John Ruskin. Illustrations copyright © 1978 by Krystyna Turska. Reprinted by permission of Hamish Hamilton Ltd.

HARCOURT BRACE JOVANOVICH, INC. Jacket illustration by Bonnie Dann from *Nobody's Fault?* by Patricia Hermes. Copyright © 1981 by Patricia Hermes./ Illustration by Woodi Ishmael from *Lone Journey: The Life of Roger Williams* by Jeanette Eaton. Copyright 1944 by Harcourt, Brace & World, Inc. Copyright renewed © 1972 by Winifred K. Eaton. Both reprinted by permission of Harcourt Brace Jovanovich, Inc.

HARPER & ROW, PUBLISHERS, INC. Illustration by Louis Rhead from *Tom Brown's School Days* by an "Old Boy" (pseudonym of Thomas Hughes). Copyright 1911 by Harper & Brothers. Reprinted by permission of Harper & Row, Publishers, Inc.

HAWTHORN PROPERTIES. Illustration by C. M. Relyea from *The Sapphire Signet* by Augusta Huiell Seaman. Copyright 1915, 1916 by The Century Co. Reprinted by permission of Hawthorn Properties.

HOLIDAY HOUSE, INC. Illustration by Artur Marokvia from *I Caught a Lizard* by Gladys Conklin. Text copyright © 1967 by Gladys Conklin. Illustrations copyright © 1967 by Artur Marokvia. Reprinted by permission of Holiday House, Inc.

HOLT, RINEHART & WINSTON. Illustration by Richard Hefter from *Goose Goofs Off* by Jacquelyn Reinach. Copyright © 1977 by Ruth Lerner Perle and Jacquelyn Reinach. Reprinted by permission of Holt, Rinehart & Winston.

THE HORN BOOK, INC. Sidelight excerpts from an article "On Poetry and Black American Poets," by Ashley Bryan, February, 1979, in *The Horn Book Magazine.* Copyright © 1979 by The Horn Book, Inc./ Sidelight excerpts from *Illustrators of Children's Books: 1967-1976,* edited by Lee Kingman and others. Copyright © 1978 by The Horn Book, Inc. All reprinted by permission of The Horn Book, Inc.

HOUGHTON MIFFLIN CO. Illustration by Bea Holmes from *Sue Ellen* by Edith Fisher Hunter. Copyright © 1969 by Edith Fisher Hunter./ Illustration by Milton Johnson from *The Black Pearl* by Scott O'Dell. Copyright © 1967 by Scott O'Dell. Both reprinted by permission of Houghton Mifflin Co.

HUMAN SCIENCES PRESS, INC. Illustrations by Jerry McConnel from *Things I Hate!* by Harriet Wittels and Joan Greisman. Copyright © 1973 by Human Sciences Press, Inc. Both reprinted by permission of Human Sciences Press, Inc.

INTERNATIONAL CHILDREN'S BOOK SERVICE. Cover illustration by Lise Manniche from *How Djadja-Em-Ankh Saved the Day: A Tale from Ancient Egypt* translated by Lise Manniche. Copyright © 1976 by Lise Manniche. Reprinted by permission of International Children's Book Service.

J. B. LIPPINCOTT CO. Illustration by John Alcorn from *Wonderful Time* by Phyllis McGinley. Text copyright © 1965, 1966 by Phyllis McGinley. Illustrations copyright © 1966 by John Alcorn./ Jacket illustration by Paul Bacon from *The Dangerous Game* by Milton Dank. Text copyright © 1977 by Milton Dank. Jacket design and illustration copyright © 1977 by Paul Bacon./ Photograph by Jonathan Rutland from *Looking at Spain* by Rupert Martin. Copyright © 1969 by A. & C. Black Ltd./ Illustration by Joel Schick from *Santaberry and the Snard* by Alice and Joel Schick. Copyright © 1976, 1979 by Pongid Productions./ Illustration by Joel Schick from *The Gobble-uns'll Git You Ef You Don't Watch Out!* by James Whitcomb Riley. Illustrations and illustrator's note copyright © 1975 by Pongid Productions. All reprinted by permission of J. B. Lippincott Co.

LITTLE, BROWN & CO. Jacket illustration by Doris Reynolds from *Dear Beast* by Nancy Hale. Copyright © 1959 by Nancy Hale./ Illustration by Wallace Tripp from *A Great Big Ugly Man Came Up and Tied His Horse to Me,* compiled by Wallace Tripp. Illustrations copyright © 1973 by Wallace Tripp./ Jacket illustration by Tom Walther from *Make Mine Music: How to Make and Play Instruments and Why They Work* by Tom Walther. Copyright © 1981 by the Yolla Bolly Press./ Illustration by Ann Wiseman from *Making Things* by Ann Wiseman. Copyright © 1973 by Ann Wiseman. All reprinted by permission of Little, Brown & Co.

MACMILLAN, INC. Illustration by Benny Andrews from "The Hope of Your Unborn," in *I Am the Darker Brother* edited by Arnold Adoff. Copyright © 1968 by Macmillan, Inc./ Illustration by Trina Schart Hyman from *Caddie Woodlawn* by Carol Ryrie Brink. Copyright 1935, renewed © 1963 by Carol Ryrie Brink. Copyright © 1973 by Carol Ryrie Brink. Copyright © 1973 by Macmillan Publishing Co., Inc./ Illustration by Marguerite Davis from *Magical Melons* by Carol Ryrie Brink. Copyright 1939, 1940, 1944 by Macmillan Publishing Co., Inc. Copyright renewed © 1967, 1968, 1972 by Carol Ryrie Brink./ Illustration by Fermin Rocker from *Winter Cottage* by Carol Ryrie Brink. Copyright 1939, 1940, © 1968 by Carol Ryrie Brink. Copyright © 1968 by Macmillan Publishing Co., Inc./ Illustration by Trina Schart Hyman from *The Bad Times of Irma Baumlein* by Carol Ryrie Brink. Copyright © 1972 by Carol Ryrie Brink. Copyright © 1972 by Macmillan Publishing Co., Inc./ Sidelight excerpts from "Author's Note," in *Caddie Woodlawn* by Carol Ryrie Brink. Copyright © 1973 by Carol Ryrie Brink. All reprinted by permission of Macmillan, Inc.

MACMILLAN & CO. LTD. (London). Illustration by Edmund J. Sullivan from *Tom Brown's School Days* by Thomas Hughes./ Illustration by Richard Doyle from *The Scouring of the White Horse; or, The Long Vacation Ramble of a London Clerk* by Thomas Hughes. Both reprinted by permission of Macmillan & Co. Ltd. (London).

McGRAW HILL, INC. Illustration by Richard Hefter from *One Bear Two Bears* by Richard

Hefter. Copyright © 1980 by One Strawberry, Inc. Reprinted by permission of McGraw Hill, Inc.

JULIAN MESSNER. Sidelight excerpts from the book jacket of *Big Game Hunter, Carl Akeley* by Felix Sutton. Copyright © 1960 by Felix Sutton. Reprinted by permission of Julian Messner.

METHUEN & CO. LTD. Sidelight excerpts from *Ghost of the Hardy Boys: An Autobiography* by Leslie McFarlane. Copyright © 1976 by Methuen Publications. Reprinted by permission of Methuen & Co. Ltd.

WILLIAM MORROW & CO., INC. Illustration by Ronald Himler from *Bruno* by Achim Bröger. Translated by Hilda van Stockum. English translation copyright © 1975 by William Morrow & Co., Inc./ Illustration by Muriel Batherman from *The Handsomest Father* by Deborah Hautzig. Text copyright © 1979 by Deborah Hautzig. Illustrations copyright © 1979 by Muriel Batherman./ Illustration by Krystyna Turska from *The King of the Golden River* by John Ruskin. Illustrations copyright © 1978 by Krystyna Turska./ Illustration by Krystyna Turska from *The Magician of Cracow* by Krystyna Turska. Copyright © 1975 by Krystyna Turska. All reprinted by permission of William Morrow & Co., Inc.

OXFORD UNIVERSITY PRESS, INC. Illustration by Carol Barker from *Arjun and His Village in India* by Carol Barker. Copyright © 1979 by Carol Barker. Reprinted by permission of Oxford University Press, Inc.

PRENTICE-HALL, INC. Illustration by Howard Berelson from *My Friend Andrew* by Pat Lowery Collins. Text copyright © 1981 by Patricia Lowery Collins. Illustrations copyright © 1981 by Howard Berelson./ Jacket illustration by Mel Erikson from *The Endocrine System* by Alvin Silverstein and Virginia B. Silverstein. Text copyright © 1971 by Alvin Silverstein and Virginia B. Silverstein. Illustrations copyright © 1971 by Prentice-Hall, Inc./ Illustration by Joseph Low from *Museum People, Collectors and Keepers at the Smithsonian* by Peggy Thomson. Copyright © 1977 by Peggy Thomson. All reprinted by permission of Prentice-Hall, Inc.

PUBLICATIONS ESTOUP ET ROY SÀRL. Sidelight excerpts from the preface to *Music Makers of Today* by Percy M. Young. Reprinted by permission of Publications Estoup et Roy Sàrl.

G. P. PUTNAM'S SONS. Photograph by Ozzie Sweet from *Return of the Buffalo* by Jack Denton Scott. Text copyright © 1976 by Jack Denton Scott. Photographs copyright © 1976 by Ozzie Sweet./ Photograph by Ozzie Sweet from *Island of Wild Horses* by Jack Denton Scott. Text copyright © 1978 by Jack Denton Scott. Photographs copyright © 1978 by Ozzie Sweet./ Photograph by Ozzie Sweet from *The Book of the Pig* by Jack Denton Scott. Text copyright © 1981 by Jack Denton Scott. Photographs copyright © 1981 by Ozzie Sweet./ Illustration by Wallace Tripp from *Pleasant Fieldmouse's Halloween Party* by Jan Wahl. Text copyright © 1974 by Jan Wahl. Illustrations copyright © 1974 by Wallace Tripp. All reprinted by permission of G. P. Putnam's Sons.

RANDOM HOUSE, INC. Illustration by Marilyn Miller from *Hurricane Guest* by Sam and Beryl Epstein. Copyright © 1964 by Sam and Beryl Epstein./ Illustration by Peter Lippman from *Busy Boats* by Peter Lippman. Copyright © 1977 by Random House, Inc./ Illustration by Peter Lippman from *Peter Lippman's Great Mix or Match Book* by Peter Lippman. Copyright © 1980 by Peter Lippman./ Illustration by Peter Lippman from *The Pigs' Book of World Records* by Bob Stine. Text copyright © 1980 by Robert L. Stine. Illustrations copyright © 1980 by Peter Lippman./ Illustration by W. T. Mars from *The Story of the Paratroops* by George Weller. Copyright © 1958 by George Weller. All reprinted by permission of Random House, Inc.

SCHOLASTIC, INC. Sidelight excerpts from *Books Are by People* by Lee Bennett Hopkins. Copyright © 1969 by Scholastic, Inc./ Illustration by Don Sibley from *Abe Lincoln Gets His Chance* by Frances Cavanah. Copyright © 1959 by Rand McNally & Co. Copyright © 1959 under International Copyright Union by Rand McNally & Co. Both reprinted by permission of Scholastic, Inc.

CHARLES SCRIBNER'S SONS. Illustration by Diane de Groat from *Antrim's Orange* by Sylvia Sunderlin. Text copyright © 1976 by Sylvia Sunderlin. Illustrations copyright © 1976 by Diane de Groat. Reprinted by permission of Charles Scribner's Sons.

STURGIS & WALTON CO. Illustration by George Wharton Edwards from *Little Mamselle of the Wilderness: A Story of La Salle and His Pioneers* by Augusta Huiell Seaman. Copyright 1913 by Sturgis & Walton Co. Reprinted by permission of Sturgis & Walton Co.

THE VANGUARD PRESS. Illustration by Paul Frame from *Jenny Lind and Her Listening Cat* by Frances Cavanah. Copyright © 1961 by Frances Cavanah. Reprinted by permission of The Vanguard Press.

VIKING PENGUIN, INC. Illustration by Betty Fraser from *A House Is a House for Me* by Mary Ann Hoberman. Text copyright © 1978 by Mary Ann Hoberman. Illustrations copyright © 1978 by Betty Fraser./ Sidelight excerpts and photograph from *Along This Way: The Autobiography of James Weldon Johnson* by James Weldon Johnson./ Illustration by Aaron Douglas from "The Judgment Day," in *God's Trombones* by James Weldon Johnson. Copyright 1927 by The Viking Press, Inc. Copyright renewed 1955 by Grace Nail Johnson./ Illustration by George Ford from *Far Eastern Beginnings* by Olivia Vlahos. Copyright © 1976 by Olivia Vlahos. Illustrations copyright © 1976 by Viking Penguin, Inc./ Sidelight excerpts from "Author's Note," in *Far Eastern Beginnings* by Olivia Vlahos. Copyright © 1976 by Olivia Vlahos. All reprinted by permission of Viking Penguin, Inc.

WALKER AND CO. Sidelight excerpts from *Breakthrough: Women in Writing* by Diana Gleasner. Copyright © 1980 by Diana Gleasner./ Illustration by Harriet Springer from *A First Look at Animals with Backbones* by Millicent E. Selsam and Joyce Hunt. Text copyright © 1978 by Millicent E. Selsam and Joyce Hunt. Illustrations copyright © 1978 by Harriett Springer. Both reprinted by permission of Walker and Co.

WARWICK PRESS. Cover illustration by Graham Allen from *Animal Homes* by Theodore Rowland-Entwistle. Copyright © 1978 by Grisewood & Dempsey Ltd. Reprinted by permission of Warwick Press.

Sidelight excerpts from an article "New Fire on the Mountain," by Don Moser, September, 1974, in *Audubon*. Copyright © 1974 by Audubon. Reprinted by permission of *Audubon*./ Sidelight excerpts from an article "Meet Your Author," by Achim Bröger, July, 1977, in *Cricket Magazine*. Copyright © 1977 by Open Court Publishing Co. Reprinted by permission of *Cricket Magazine*./ Jacket illustration by Troy Howell from *Lady Cat Lost* by Jeanne Dixon. Copyright © 1981 by Jeanne Dixon. Jacket painting copyright © 1981 by Troy Howell. Reprinted by permission of Dilys Evans./ Sidelight excerpts from an article "Writing for Kids Without Kidding Around," by Kathleen Hinton-Braaten, May 14, 1979, in *Christian Science Monitor*. Reprinted by permission of Kathleen Hinton-Braaten./ Illustration by Harriet Springer from *A First Look at Animals with Backbones* by Millicent Selsam and Joyce Hunt. Text copyright © 1978 by Millicent Selsam and Joyce Hunt. Illustrations copyright © 1978 by Harriett Springer. Reprinted by permission of Joyce Hunt./ Sidelight excerpts from an article "Comic Books in the Library," by Will Eisner, October 15, 1974, in *Library Journal*. Copyright © 1974 by Xerox Corp. Reprinted by permission of *Library Journal*./ Jacket photograph from *Big Rigs* by Hope Irvin Marston. Copyright © 1979 by Hope Irvin Marston. Reprinted by permission of Mack Trucks, Inc./

Illustration by Muriel Batherman from *The Handsomest Father* by Deborah Hautzig. Text copyright © 1979 by Deborah Hautzig. Illustrations copyright © 1979 by Muriel Batherman. Reprinted by permission of McIntosh & Otis, Inc./ Cover illustration from *Sugar Creek Gang: The Runaway Rescue* by Paul Hutchens. Copyright © 1960 by Paul Hutchens. Reprinted by permission of Moody Bible Institute of Chicago./ Sidelight excerpts from an article "Her Mother's Gift," by Mary Helen Washington, June, 1982, in *Ms.* magazine. Reprinted by permission of *Ms.* magazine./ Sidelight excerpts from an article "Do You Know This Woman? She Knows You: A Profile of Alice Walker," by Gloria Steinem, June, 1982, in *Ms.* magazine. Reprinted by permission of *Ms.* magazine./ Sidelight excerpts from *National Education Association of the United States Journal*, Vol. 25, No. 8, November, 1936. Reprinted by permission of National Education Association of the United States Journal./ Sidelight excerpts from an article "Growing Up with Judy," by Linda Bird Francke with Lisa Hartman, October 9, 1978, in *Newsweek*. Reprinted by permission of *Newsweek*./ Sidelight excerpts from an article "Coming of Age with Judy Blume," December 3, 1978, in *The New York Times Magazine*. Copyright © 1978 by The New York Times Co. Reprinted by permission of The New York Times Co./ Sidelight excerpts from an article "Judy Blume," by Sybil Steinberg, April 17, 1978, in *Publishers Weekly*. Copyright © 1978 by Xerox Corp. Reprinted by permission of *Publishers Weekly*./

Photograph by Ozzie Sweet from *Return of the Buffalo* by Jack Denton Scott. Text copyright © 1976 by Jack Denton Scott. Photographs copyright © 1976 by Ozzie Sweet. Reprinted by permission of Raines & Raines./ Illustration by Harriet Springer from *A First Look at Animals with Backbones* by Millicent E. Selsam and Joyce Hunt. Text copyright © 1978 by Millicent E. Selsam and Joyce Hunt. Illustrations copyright © 1978 by Harriet Springer. Reprinted by permission of Millicent Selsam./ Engraving from a drawing by George Back from *Journey into Ice: Sir John Franklin and the Northwest Passage* by Ann and Myron Sutton. Copyright © 1965 by Ann and Myron Sutton. Copyright 1965 under International Copyright Union by Ann and

Myron Sutton. Reprinted by permission of Ann and Myron Sutton./ Sidelight excerpts from *My Life and I* by Paul Hutchens. Copyright © 1962 by Paul Hutchens. Reprinted by permission of Pauline Hutchens Wilson./ Sidelight excerpts from an article "The Gold Mine of Experience," by Carol Brink, August, 1977, in *The Writer*. Copyright © 1977 by The Writer, Inc. Reprinted by permission of The Writer, Inc./ Sidelight excerpts from *Library Journal,* February 1, 1969. Copyright © 1969 by Xerox Corp. Reprinted by permission of Xerox Corp./ Sidelight excerpts from an article "Hilma Wolitzer," by Jean F. Mercier, July 17, 1978, in *Publishers Weekly*. Copyright © 1978 by Xerox Corp. Reprinted by permission of Xerox Corp.

PHOTOGRAPH CREDITS

Judy Blume: Charles William Bush; Carol Ryrie Brink: De Whit Studio; Ashley F. Bryan: Matthew Wysocki; Milton Dank: Tana Hoban; Will Eisner: Gershid Bharucha; Deborah Hautzig: Susan Hirschman; James Weldon Johnson: Carl Van Vechten; Penelope Jones: Rocco Nunno; Ron Klug: Alys Brockway; Harry Mazer: Ruth Putter; Joel Schick: Pongid Productions; Peggy Thomson: Jan Brown; Alice Walker: L.A. Hyder; Józef Wilkoń: Jerzy Jawczak.

something about the author

ALCORN, John 1935-

PERSONAL: Born February 10, 1935, in Corona, Long Island, N.Y.; married wife, Phyllis in 1955; children: four sons. *Education:* Graduated from Cooper Union, 1955. *Residence:* Ossining, N.Y. 10562.

CAREER: Commercial artist and designer, illustrator of children's books. Early in career, worked variously in the art department of *Esquire,* New York City, at Push Pin Studios, New York City, and for a pharmaceutical advertising agency; Columbia Broadcasting System, Inc., New York City, art department, radio and television promotion, 1958-59; free-lance artist, 1959—; has created numerous book jackets and paperback covers, and work has appeared in major exhibits, including the Push Pin Studios Retrospective Show at the Louvre, March, 1970. *Awards, honors:* New York Times Choice of Best Illustrated Children's Books of the Year, 1962, for *Books!,* 1966, for *Wonderful Time;* Fifty Books of the Year, American Institute of Graphic Arts, 1963, for *Books!;* first prize, Bologna Children's Book Fair, 1968; Augustus St. Gaudens Medal, Cooper Union, 1970.

ILLUSTRATOR—All for children, except as indicated: Murray McCain, *Books!* (nonfiction), J. Cape, 1962; Al Hine, *Where in the World Do You Live?* (fiction), Harcourt, 1962; Mary Kay Phelan, *The Circus,* Holt, 1963; Ogden Nash, *Everyone but Thee and Me* (adult poems), Dent, 1963; Hine, *Money Round the World,* Harcourt, 1963; Stella Standard, *The Art of Fruit Cookery,* Doubleday, 1964; Sesyle Joslin, *La petite famille* (French language reader), Harcourt, 1964; *Television Note Book: 1964,* Columbia Broadcasting System, Inc., 1964; McCain, *Writing!* (nonfiction), Ariel, 1964.

JOHN ALCORN

3. NINE and THREE
Are easy to see.
The Big Hand's up
As high as can be,
Straight as a soldier,
Guarding a town.

At THREE
The Little Hand's
Halfway down,
Like the soldier's gun
Before he drops it.

But NINE O'CLOCK
Is exactly opp'site.
Perhaps you're at school
Perhaps at play
Or else in bed
At the end of day,
But it's NINE O'CLOCK
Upon the crack
When the Brave Little Hand
Climbs halfway back.

(From *Wonderful Time* by Phyllis McGinley. Illustrated by John Alcorn.)

Hine, *A Letter to Anywhere* (nonfiction), Harcourt, 1964; Marie Winn and Allan Miller, *The Fireside Book of Children's Songs,* Simon & Schuster, 1966; Phyllis McGinley, *Wonderful Time* (poems), Lippincott, 1966; Joslin, *La Fiesta* (Spanish language reader), Harcourt, 1967; Jan Wahl, *Pocahontas in London* (fiction), Delacorte, 1967; Martin Gardner, *Never Make Fun of a Turtle, My Son* (poems), Simon & Schuster, 1969; *One, Two, Three,* Hallmark, 1970; *The Great Book of Puzzles and Perplexities,* Lyceum, 1978.

Has also illustrated and designed numerous book jackets and paperback covers, two printing catalogs, and contributed illustrations to many periodicals, including *McCall's, Playboy,* and *Sports Illustrated.*

SIDELIGHTS: A native New Yorker, John Alcorn was born in Corona, Long Island in 1935, and educated in local schools. He studied graphic arts at Cooper Union. During his first two years at Cooper, he studied drawing, caligraphy, architecture, the mechanics of typography, and dimensional design. In his last year his studies consisted of illustration, graphics, and advertising design.

Following graduation from Cooper Union, Alcorn married and settled in Ossining, New York, where he still lives with his wife, Phyllis, and their four sons. His early career included work in the art department of *Esquire* magazine, a brief stint

with a pharmaceutical advertising agency and sound training at The Push Pin Studios, a cooperative art studio. In 1958 Alcorn joined the CBS-TV art department, but a year later he decided to free-lance exclusively. In 1962 Alcorn designed and illustrated *Books* by Murry McCain, which was selected as one of the best fifty books of the year by the American Institute of Graphic Arts. Besides book illustrations, Alcorn has designed numerous paperback covers, jackets, and promotion materials and has received awards from the New York Art Directors Club, the New York Type Directors Club, the Society of Illustrators, and Cooper Union. In 1968 he won first prize at the Bologna Children's Book Fair.

Alcorn's works are included in the Kerlan Collection at the University of Minnesota.

FOR MORE INFORMATION SEE: American Artist, September, 1958; *Graphics,* November, 1958, Vol. 27, 1971-72; *Newsweek,* June 10, 1963; *Publishers Weekly,* June 1, 1964; Lee Kingman and others, compilers, *Illustrators of Children's Books, 1957-1966,* Horn Book, 1968; Doris de Montreville and Donna Hill, editors, *Third Book of Junior Authors,* H. W. Wilson, 1972.

ANDERSON, Brad(ley Jay) 1924-

BRIEF ENTRY: Born May 14, 1924, in Jamestown, N.Y. Cartoonist and author. Anderson has been a free-lance cartoonist since 1950. Between 1952-53, he worked as an art director for Ball & Grier, a public relations firm in Utica, N.Y. Anderson is best known as the creator of two cartoons ''Marmaduke'' and ''Grandpa's Boy,'' which have both been syndicated newspaper features since 1954. His work has been included in a number of exhibitions, including the *Punch* magazine British-American Exhibition in 1954, Selected Cartoons of Fourteen *Saturday Evening Post* Cartoonists in 1958, and at the San Francisco Museum of Fine Arts in 1977. Anderson is a member of the National Cartoonists' Society, the Magazine Cartoonist Guild, and the Newspaper Comics Council. His books for young people include *Marmaduke, Marmaduke Rides Again, Down, Marmaduke,* and *The Marmaduke Treasury. Home:* 1439 Pebble Beach, Yuma, Ariz. 85364. *FOR MORE INFORMATION SEE: National Geographic World,* May, 1979.

ANDREWS, Benny 1930-

PERSONAL: Born November 13, 1930, in Madison, Ga.; son of George (a day laborer) and Viola Andrews; married Mary Ellen Jones Smith in 1957; children: Christopher, Thomas Michael, Julia Rachael. *Education:* Attended Fort Valley State College, 1948-50; University of Chicago, 1956-58; Chicago Art Institute, B.F.A., 1958. *Home:* New York, N.Y.

CAREER: Artist and illustrator. New School for Social Research, New York City, instructor in art, 1967-68; Queens College, City University of New York, New York City, instructor of art, 1968—. Visiting artist, California State College, Hayward, 1969. Co-chairman of the Black Emergency Cultural Coalition, 1969—. Lecturer at the various colleges; visiting critic at Cornell University, Ithaca, N.Y., 1971, 1977, Yale, New Haven, Conn., 1974.

Benny Andrews. Drawing by Alice Neel. ■ (From *Between the Lines* by Benny Andrews.)

(From "The Hope of Your Unborn," in *I Am the Darker Brother*, edited by Arnold Adoff.
Illustrated by Benny Andrews.)

EXHIBITIONS—One-man shows: Paul Kessler Gallery, Provincetown, Mass., 1960; Forum Gallery, New York City, 1962, 1964, 1966; Studio Museum in Harlem, New York City, 1971; ACA Galleries, New York City, 1972, 1973, 1975; Aronson Gallery, Atlanta, Ga., 1973, 1976; High Museum of Art, Atlanta, Ga., 1975; Ankrum Gallery, Los Angeles, Calif., 1975; Gallery of Sarasota, Fla., 1975, 1976, 1978; Herbert F. Johnson Museum, Ithaca, N.Y., 1975; National Center of Afro-American Art, Boston, Mass., 1975; National Academy of Design, New York City, 1976; Lerner-Heller Gallery, New York City, 1976-78; Whitney Museum of American Art, New York City, 1976; Ulrich Museum, Wichita, Kan., 1977; Pelham-Stoffler Gallery, Houston, Tex., 1977.

Group Shows: Detroit Institute of Art, Mich., 1959; Philadelphia Academy of Art, Pa., 1960; American Academy of Arts and Letters, New York City, 1966; American Greeting Gallery, New York City, 1968; Minneapolis Institute of American Art, Minn., 1968; Museum of Modern Art, New York City, 1968, 1971, 1977; Boston Museum of Fine Arts, Mass., 1970, 1975; Carnegie Institute, Pittsburg, Pa., 1971; Studio Museum in Harlem, New York City, 1971; High Museum of Art, Atlanta, Ga., 1971; Lerner-Heller Gallery, New York City, 1973; Baltimore Museum of Art, Md., 1974; National Academy of Art, New York City, 1975; Oakland Museum, Calif., 1975; San Jose Museum, Calif., 1976; National Academy of Design, New York City, 1976; Whitney Museum of American Art, New York City, 1976; Museum of Modern Art, Tokyo, Japan, 1976; James Yu Gallery, New York City, 1976; National Museum of Sports, New York City, 1977; Everson Museum, Syracuse, N.Y., 1977.

Permanent collections: Butler Institute of American Art, Youngstown, Ohio; Detroit Institute of Art, Mich.; High Museum of Art, Atlanta, Ga.; Joseph H. Hirshhorn Museum, Washington, D.C.; Joslyn Museum of Art, Neb.; La Jolla Museum, Calif.; Museum of African Art, Washington, D.C.; Museum of Modern Art, New York City; New Jersey State Museum; Norfolk Museum, Va.; Wadsworth Atheneum, Hartford, Conn.; Ulrich Museum, Wichita, Kan.

MILITARY SERVICE: U.S. Air Force, 1950-54. *Awards, honors:* John Hay Whitney fellowship, 1965; University of Bridgeport Professor award, 1970; New York State Council Creative Arts Program award, 1971; Negro Art Collection award, Atlanta University, 1971, for "Educational Arts"; received Certificate of Merit from the City of New York, 1972; MacDowell fellowship, 1973, 1974, 1975, 1978; awarded a National Endowment for the Arts grant, 1974.

WRITINGS: (Editor, with Rudolf Baranik) *The Attica Book,* Custom Communications Systems, circa 1972; *Between the Lines: Seventy Drawings and Seven Essays,* Pella Publishing, 1978.

Illustrator: Arnold Adoff, editor, *I Am the Darker Brother: An Anthology of Modern Poems by Negro Americans* (ALA Notable Book), Macmillan, 1968.

Contributor of articles on black art and culture to professional journals.

SIDELIGHTS: "Drawing was the thing I took advantage of to survive, even in elementary school. I found out that I could literally work my way through the year—doing Santa Clauses and Thanksgiving turkeys and all that kind of stuff. And I was getting an advantage with the other kids by drawing cowboys for them. Then, when I went to high school, I had to do

something to offset the loss of time when I went to plant or pick cotton. I never got more than four or five months in and fell behind. So I drew all the biology and plane geometry projects and everything the teachers asked me to draw. My drawing had become a necessity. Now I think to draw, but mine was always a reality—it was very functional.

"I got a 4-H Club scholarship to go to Fort Valley State College. The Southern Iron Company gave out two scholarships in the state, one for a black person and one for a white person. I was the black winner and we were the first two, whoever that white person was, to win these 4-H Club scholarships. Poorly prepared as I was, they didn't dare throw me out of school. Eventually, I managed to catch up and then I went on to Chicago and later to New York, but basically the part of my life that made the most impression on me was those first eighteen years in Georgia. How I saw things and my ideas about things were formed there. When I went away to schools and other parts of the world, those impressions were sharpened and I got new references in terms of how to do things, but those first years were critical. Whatever I do is really kind of geared to that.

"My family was one of the poorest in Morgan County. We were probably as poor as people can be as far as any kind of money or physical possessions are concerned. We were sharecroppers. So racism was just one of the many problems I had. I had a class problem that was just as severe. We also had the problem of living in the country, so we were not included in the tokenism going on at the high school for example. There were so many difficulties. It was not just a fight being a black person in a white society; it was also a fight being a poor person in a rich society and a fight being a rural person in an urban society. When someone like me came out of the country to go to high school, there was a struggle to be one of the small number of blacks allowed to attend. My high school class at Burney Street High School (1948) graduated with a record number of students, 39, the sum total for the entire county. For me, success has always meant doing what I want to do." [Benny Andrews, "Sources," in *Black Artists on Art,* Volume 2, edited by Samella S. Lewis and Ruth G. Waddy, Contemporary Crafts, Inc., 1971.]

"The 24-Hour Life of Benny Andrews," directed by John Wise and produced by Nafarsi Productions, was screened at the Studio Museum in Harlem in 1974.

FOR MORE INFORMATION SEE: New York Times Book Review, November 3, 1968; Samella S. Lewis and Ruth G. Waddy, editors, *Black Artists on Art,* Volume 2, Contemporary Crafts, Inc., 1971; *Art News,* April, 1971, October, 1975.

Know you what it is to be a child? It is to be something very different from the man of today. It is to have a spirit yet streaming from the waters of baptism; it is to believe in love, to believe in loveliness, to believe in belief; it is to be so little that the elves can reach to whisper in your ear; it is to turn pumpkins into coaches, and mice into horses, lowness into loftiness, and nothing into everything, for each child has its fairy godmother in its soul.

—Francis Thompson

ANTELL, Will D. 1935-

PERSONAL: Born October 2, 1935, in White Earth, Minn,; married, 1958; children: three. *Education:* Bemidji State College, B.S., 1959; Mankato State College (now University), M.S., 1964; University of Minnesota, Ed.D., 1973. *Office:* Minnesota Department of Education, 550 Cedar St., St. Paul Minn. 55101.

CAREER: Teacher at public schools in Janesville, Minn., and Stillwater, Minn., 1959-68; Minnesota Department of Education, St. Paul, human relations consultant, 1968-69, director of Indian education, 1969-73, assistant commissioner of education, beginning in 1974. Regent of Institute of American Indian Art, 1971—; chairman of Special Committee on Indian Education of National Council for Indian Opportunity, 1970-72; visiting professor of educational administration at Harvard University, 1973-74; National Advisory Council on Indian Education, vice-chairman, 1973-74, chairman, beginning in 1974. *Member:* American Association of School Administrators, American Education Research Association, National Indian Education Association (president, 1970-72). *Awards, honors:* National Defense Education Act fellowship, Northern Michigan University, 1965, University of Minnesota, 1968; Bash Foundation fellowship, 1972.

WRITINGS: (Editor) *American Indians: An Annotated Bibliography of Selected Library Resources,* University of Minnesota, 1970; *William Warren* (juvenile biography), Dillon, 1973; *Culture, Psychological Characteristics, and Socioeconomic Status in Educational Program Development for Native Americans,* National Educational Laboratory Publishers, 1974.

BAHTI, Tom

BRIEF ENTRY: Author of several books on the crafts and tribes of Southwestern American Indians, Bahti graduated from the University of New Mexico with a degree in anthropology. His writings, which reflect his interest in the cultural aspects of man, include *An Introduction to Southwestern Indian Arts and Crafts,* 1964, *Southwestern Indian Tribes,* 1968, and *Southwestern Indian Ceremonials,* 1970. For children, he illustrated Byrd Baylor's *Before You Came This Way,* 1969. In 1973, he was awarded the Caldecott Medal for *When Clay Sings,* also written by Baylor.

BARKER, Carol (Minturn) 1938-

PERSONAL: Born February 16, 1938, in London, England; married; children: two sons. *Education:* Attended Bournemouth College of Art, Chelsea Polytechnic, and Central School of Arts and Crafts (London); private study at father's studio. *Residence:* England.

CAROL BARKER

One man stands at the well-head. He lowers the leather pouch into the well, lets it fill with water, and then winds it up by pulley. The other man guides the two pairs of bullocks up and down the ramp, sitting on the rope. ∎ (From *Arjun and His Village in India* by Carol Barker. Illustrated by the author.)

CAREER: Free-lance author and illustrator, beginning in 1958.

WRITINGS—All for children; all self-illustrated: (With Terence Milligan) *The Bald Twit Lion,* Dobson, 1968; *The Boy and the Lion,* Dobson, 1968; *The Boy and the Lion on the Wall,* Watts, 1969; *Carol Barker's Birds and Beasts,* Watts, 1972; *King Midas and the Golden Touch,* Watts, 1972; *The Alphabet,* Hamlyn Publishing Group, 1973; *How the World Began,* Abelard, 1974; *An Oba of Benin,* Macdonald & Jane's, 1976, published in America as *Worlds of Yesterday: An Oba of Benin,* Addison, 1978; *A Prince of Islam,* Macdonald & Jane's, 1976, published in America as *Worlds of Yesterday: A Prince of Islam,* Addison, 1977; *Arjun and His Village in India,* Oxford University Press, 1979.

Illustrator; all for children: Herbert Bates, *Achilles the Donkey,* Watts, 1962; Norman Wymer, *Gilbert and Sullivan,* Methuen, 1962; Aileen L. Fisher, *I Wonder How, I Wonder Why,* Abelard, 1962; H. Bates, *Achilles and Diana,* Watts, 1963; Eileen Colwell, editor, *A Storyteller's Choice: A Selection of Stories with Notes on How to Tell Them,* Bodley Head, 1963, published in America as *A Storyteller's Choice: Tales by Oscar Wilde, Hans Christian Andersen, Tolstoy, and Others,* Walck, 1964; H. Bates, *Achilles and the Twins,* Watts, 1964; Geoffrey Palmer, *Quest for Prehistory,* John Day, 1965; John A. Cunliffe, *Farmer Barnes and Bluebell,* Deutsch, 1966; *Rain and Shine: Nursery Rhymes for the Four Seasons,* Blackie & Son, 1966; Rumer Godden, *The Kitchen Madonna,* Viking, 1967; J.A. Cunliffe, *Farmer Barnes Buys a Pig,* Lion, 1968; Margaret Mahy, *Pillycock's Shop,* Watts, 1969; M. Mahy, *The Princess and the Clown,* Watts, 1971; Helen Hoke, compiler, *Dragons,*

Dragons, Dragons, Watts, 1972; Sandie Oram, *The Sun People,* Macdonald & Co., 1972; Nicholas Fisk, *Emma Borrows a Cup of Sugar,* Heinemann, 1973; Margaret Mayo, compiler, *If You Should Meet a Crocodile,* Kaye & Ward, 1974; H. Hoke, compiler, *Devils, Devils, Devils,* Watts, 1975; Richard Parker, *Lost in a Shop,* Macmillan, 1978; Janet McNeill, *It's Snowing Outside,* Macmillan, 1979.

SIDELIGHTS: Barker credits her father's influence, more than her art training, as the major influence in her work. "My father was a painter and designer and worked at home, so there was a very creative atmosphere throughout my childhood. I began drawing and painting early and started my first sketch book at the age of ten in Paris." [Lee Kingman and others, compilers, *Illustrators of Children's Books: 1957-66,* Horn Book, 1968.[1]]

While attending the School of Art in Chelsea, London, she also studied graphic design with her father. "This meant I was able to attain a solid training in abstract design and typography and have the freedom of self expression in painting as well."[1]

Beginning in 1958 as a free-lance illustrator, Barker has illustrated numerous children's books as well as her own stories. She was commended for the Kate Greenaway Medal in 1972 for her book, *King Midas and the Golden Touch.*

FOR MORE INFORMATION SEE: John Ryder, *Artists of a Certain Line,* Bodley Head, 1960; Lee Kingman and others, compilers, *Illustrators of Children's Books: 1957-1966,* Horn Book, 1968.

JUDY BLUME

BLUME, Judy (Sussman) 1938-

PERSONAL: Born February 12, 1938, in Elizabeth, N.J.; daughter of Rudolph (a dentist) and Esther (Rosenfeld) Sussman; married John M. Blume (an attorney), August 15, 1959 (divorced, 1975); children: Randy Lee (daughter), Lawrence Andrew. *Education:* New York University, B.A., 1960. *Religion:* Jewish. *Residence:* New York, N.Y. and Santa Fe, N.M. *Agent:* Harold Ober Associates, Inc., 40 East 49th St., New York, N.Y. 10017.

CAREER: Writer of juvenile and adult fiction. *Member:* Society of Children's Book Writers, Authors League, and Authors Guild.

AWARDS, HONORS: Are You There God?, It's Me, Margaret, chosen one of the best books for children by the *New York Times,* 1970, Nene Award, 1975, and Young Hoosier Award, 1976; Golden Archer Award, 1974; Charlie May Simon Children's Book Award, Pacific Northwest Young Readers Choice Award, and Sequoyah Children's Book Award, all 1975, and Georgia Children's Book Award, South Carolina Children's Book Award, and Massachusetts Children's Book Award, all 1977, all for *Tales of a Fourth Grade Nothing;* Arizona Young Readers Book Award, 1977; Pacific Northwest Young Readers Choice Award, 1977, for *Blubber;* South Carolina Children's Book Award, 1978, for *Otherwise Known as Sheila the Great.*

Superfudge was selected for Texas Bluebonnet List, 1980, Michigan Young Reader's Award, 1981, International Reading Association Children's Choice, 1981, Colorado Children's Book Award, First Buckeye Children's Book Award, Nene Award, 1982, Tennessee Children's Choice Book Award, 1982, Outstanding Mother Award, 1982, Utah Children's Book Award, 1982, Arizona Young Readers Award, 1982, United States Army in Europe Kinderbuch Award, 1982.

WRITINGS—All of interest to young people, except as noted: *The One in the Middle Is the Green Kangaroo* (illustrated by Lois Axeman), Reilly & Lee, 1969, reissued, illustrated by Amy Aitken, Bradbury, 1981; *Iggie's House,* Bradbury, 1970; *Are You There God?, It's Me, Margaret* (ALA Notable Book), Bradbury, 1970; *Then Again, Maybe I Won't,* Bradbury, 1971; *Freckle Juice* (illustrated by Sonia Lisker), Four Winds, 1971; *Tales of a Fourth Grade Nothing* (illustrated by Roy Doty), Dutton, 1972; *It's Not the End of the World,* Bradbury, 1972; *Otherwise Known as Sheila the Great,* Dutton, 1972; *Deenie,* Bradbury, 1973; *Blubber,* Bradbury, 1974; *Forever. . .*(young adult), Bradbury, 1975; *Starring Sally J. Freedman as Herself,* Bradbury, 1977; *Wifey* (adult), Putman, 1978; *Superfudge,* Dutton, 1980; *The Judy Blume Diary: The Place to Put Your Own Feelings,* Dell, 1981; *Tiger Eyes,* Bradbury, 1981.

Contributor to *Free to Be . . . You and Me,* for the *Ms.* Foundation, 1974.

ADAPTATIONS: Television film, "Forever," CBS-TV, February 6, 1978.

WORK IN PROGRESS: My Brother, My Sister and *Daddy Doesn't Live Here Anymore.*

SIDELIGHTS: **February 12, 1938.** Born in Elizabeth, New Jersey. Blume, whose rich memories of her youth are one key to her popularity among young people, reminisces about her childhood. "My mother was shy and quiet and very well organized. She loved to read. When I came home from school in the afternoon she was always there, waiting, curled up in her favorite chair, reading a book. My father was outgoing, fun, vital, vibrant. I was very close to him. He was a dentist but spent as much time as he could in his basement shop, working with his hands. He built me a beautiful desk and was proud of the fact that there wasn't one nail in it. When I was small he would sit me up on the workbench, with a hammer and nails so that I would feel I was included, and sharing something special with him. My brother was four years older than me and very clever, very mechanically inclined. He built radios and other electronic equipment. He spent even more time than my father in the workshop. He was shy and quiet, like my mother. I was an entertainer, more like my father.

"And yet, like most children, I sometimes felt alone. We didn't talk about problems in our family. We kept our feelings to ourselves. My father said that we could talk about anything, but somehow, we didn't. I hated family secrets. I had a lot of questions but I was afraid to ask them. I was curious about sex but no one gave me any information. My father gave me a brief, but totally confusing explanation about menstruation when I was nine, and then, at ten, tried to tell me where babies came from. Again, the explanation was confusing. Besides, I already knew, more or less. My friends at school had told me, but much of the information I picked up that way was incorrect. One of my friends had a book. Her parents had given it to her. She and I would read it again and again. But it wasn't as straightforward as we would have liked.

"I was a somewhat fearful child. Perhaps imaginative children always are. I was afraid of the dark, afraid of strange noises, afraid of dogs, afraid of my brother when he walked into my bedroom with a sheet over his head, calling 'Oooooohhhhh. . . .' and thunderstorms terrified me. They still do.

"I liked radio shows, movies, and going to the children's room at the public library in Elizabeth, New Jersey. I would sit on the floor with the books, sniffing them. My favorite was *Madeleine*. When I was older I liked the Betsy-Tacy books by Maud Hart Lovelace, and the Oz books, and Nancy Drew mysteries. But I didn't find real satisfaction in reading until I was older. Because there weren't any books with characters who felt the way I felt, who acted the way I did, with whom I could identify. I think I write the kinds of books I would have liked to read when I was young.

"I loved to dance. I took dancing lessons from the age of three. I still love to dance and take tap dancing lessons every day."

"As I grew older, I had a lot of tensions and problems. As a teenager, I'd get eczema over tests at school. I was a good girl, had to do well, please everyone. That was my role in life. Perhaps it was because my brother was a rebel. He kicked his kindergarten teacher in the stomach." ["Judy Blume," *Parents* Magazine, May, 1979.[1]]

Blume attended Battin High School in New Jersey, where she sang in the chorus, studied modern dance, and worked on the school newspaper. "There was no such thing as sexism at our school. We ran the show. The paper, the yearbook, the clubs, the politics." [Betsey Lee, *Judy Blume's Story*, Dillon Press, 1981.[2]]

Graduating with high honors, Blume chose Boston University, but after losing her first year to illness, transferred to New York University. "That was the beginning of my troubles with illness. I had mononucleosis then and for the next ten years a variety of other illnesses.

"Now I'm convinced that many of my problems were caused by emotions. It bothers me that no doctor was ever wise enough to suggest that maybe some therapy or counselling was needed." [Diana Gleasner, *Breakthrough: Women in Writing*, Walker and Co., 1980. Amended by Judy Blume.[3]]

July, 1959. Father died. In August of the same year she married John Blume, a lawyer. "My father always encouraged me to get out there and catch the moon. But after a few years of marriage I began to think, *Well, kid, this is where it's at for you. He does whatever he wants, and you stay home and make sure everything runs smoothly.* As a young child, I had missed the traditional female brainwashing. Maybe that's why I was so resentful later on. . . . As a young woman my mother prepared me for marriage and motherhood, but it wasn't enough. I needed something of my own. Perhaps it would have been different if I had chosen a marriage partner who encouraged me to have a career."[3]

1961. Daughter, Randy, born.

1963. Son, Larry, born. The responsibility of rearing her children kept her from beginning a teaching career, but did not entirely satisfy her creative needs. For a year she made felt banners for children's rooms which she sold to Bloomingdale's in New York.

(From *Are You There God? It's Me, Margaret* by Judy Blume. Jacket illustration by Eros Keith.)

1966. Tired of the banners, she began writing children's stories. "It was an accident. My kids were about three and five and I wanted to do something, but I didn't want to go back to classroom teaching, which is what I was qualified for. I read my kids a lot of books, and I guess I just decided—Well, I could do that too. So when I washed the dinner dishes at night I would do imitation Dr. Seuss rhyming books; and each night by the time I'd done the dishes I would have a whole book. I would send some of them in to publishers and they would be rejected. They were terrible. That's how I started.

"Then I thought it would be fun to do a longer book. . . . New York University . . . used to send me these brochures on courses they ran for graduates. One of these was a course on how to write for children. I thought that must be an omen, so I tried it. I didn't believe anybody could teach one to write, but I needed professional encouragement, as I was on the point of stopping altogether. My low point was when I had six or seven rejections in one week." [Justin Wintle and Emma Fisher, *The Pied Pipers*, Paddington Press, 1975.[4]]

"Then it occurred to me that what I really loved most was to read novels. I thought it would be fun to write books for young people—the kinds of books I'd wished I'd had to read when I was young. Books about real life. I had about two years of rejections. I can see now that those books were learning ex-

The young Judy Blume.

periences. . . . Actually, I'm glad that I didn't have success instantaneously. I think it was healthy for me—made me really define my ideas.'' [Sybil Steinberg, ''Judy Blume,'' *Publishers Weekly,* April 17, 1978. Amended by Judy Blume.[5]]

Attended a graduate class in writing at New York University. ''One day a week I'd leave the kids home and take a train into New York. I had supper alone at a restaurant and then I went to my class. It was the first time in my life I ever really felt independent. When the course was over, I took it again.'' [Joyce Maynard, ''Coming of Age with Judy Blume,'' *New York Times Magazine,* December 3, 1978.[6]]

''What I did was write like crazy so I had something to turn in every week. My teacher gave me a lot of encouragement. She would write me little notes telling me I would get published one day. I don't know what the other people did. We never did our writing in class. Class-time was divided between the teacher lecturing on things that really didn't mean too much to me, and letting us in on the professional world—things like how to prepare a manuscript, how to write a covering letter, and about agents. Occasionally we had guests come in and talk to us—established writers or publishers. It just made me feel that in this field I was suddenly developing an interest, for at least I was getting to know what's going on. I loved it. I even went back. I took the course twice because I didn't want to

lose that contact. I still had no other contacts as regards other writers or editors. But before I left the course, after two semesters of basically the same thing, I had sold a couple of stories to magazines, and I had written at least a version of *The One in the Middle Is the Green Kangaroo,* and finished my first longer book, *Iggie's House.* I wrote that chapter by chapter, week by week, the second semester that I took the course. It was like homework.''[4]

1969. *The One in the Middle is the Green Kangaroo* was published by Reilly and Lee. ''I was overjoyed, hysterical, unbelieving! I felt like such a celebrity.''[2]

Iggie's House was published as a serial by *Trailblazer* magazine, but was criticized as being too simplistic. ''It was very painful. If I hadn't already finished another book, I don't know if I could have gone on.''[2]

Bradbury Press was interested in the story, but not in its present form. ''I labored over that book for a month. Finally, when I had done all I could do, I sent it back to them. They called with the great news that they were accepting the book for publication.''[3]

About these publications she admitted: ''They aren't very good. They were imitations of books I'd admired, but I learned something from them. The most important lesson was that until you pull it out of your own heart, it doesn't really work.''[3]

1970. *Are You There God? It's Me, Margaret* published by Bradbury Press was named one of the outstanding children's books of 1970 by the New York *Times.* ''That was the first time I felt, 'I really can do this! These people are taking me seriously! It's not just pretend.'

''I just let go and wrote what I wanted to write and told the truth about what I felt.''[2]

Asked why she only writes about middle-class America, she replied: ''Because that's what I know best. That's how I was raised and that's how I live, and I think we write best about the things we really do know about. I set most of my [early] books in suburban New Jersey because this is where I grew up. And I think that when it's very real to you it's very real to your readers. I like to see something before I can write about it. I think I am a very visual person. Specifically I can run down the books and tell you exactly where the ideas came from visually. *Margaret* came right out of my own sixth-grade life, except for the family situation. Her feelings, her actions, her friends, her concerns—they were all the things we were interested in in sixth grade. I never wrote it thinking it would be widely accepted as the way kids think today, but apparently they do.''[4]

Although successful, the book stirred controversy among parents and schools because it dealt with such topics as menstruation. Nevertheless, many lauded her for breaking with tradition in children's literature by being frank about ''taboo'' subjects. ''I don't care about rules and regulations of writing for children.

''They say you mustn't write in the first person; they say you must never leave loose ends. I said I was going to do it my way anyway.''[2]

''I think that a lot of adults in our society are uncomfortable with their own sexuality, and therefore their children's sexuality is a threat to them. That's not true of everyone of course. I have had some very negative responses from adults, but I've

He had terrible dreams. A big green monster made him drink two quarts of freckle juice, three times a day. ■(From *Freckle Juice* by Judy Blume. Illustrated by Sonia O. Lisker.)

Mr. Denberg and Mr. Vincent gathered around him, along with the cameraman and Janet. They looked like a bunch of football players huddled together talking about the next play. ■ (From *Tales of a Fourth Grade Nothing* by Judy Blume. Illustrated by Roy Doty.)

also had some very wonderful ones. The negative responses don't usually come to me directly, but through a librarian or some other intermediary who tells me about some parent who comes in carrying a book of mine demanding that it be removed. . . .

"[My editor and I] talk a lot over each book. When I finish a manuscript I send it in to [him] and he reads it, and hopefully he'll like it and want to publish it. One time he really didn't like the book and asked me not to publish it. It's in the bottom of the closet now. I'm glad it's there now—he was right. Anyway, after he's read the manuscript I go to his office and we sit together all day and talk about it. First we talk about general ideas—the plot and the characters. I take notes furiously. Then we go over the book page by page, scribbling all over it. After that I take it home with me and work on it for several weeks at least. I usually wind up rewriting at least half. In *Margaret (Are You There God? It's Me, Margaret)* I think there were seventy-five pages that I totally rewrote. But a book grows. I love the rewriting—that's the best part of it. The hardest part is the first draft—that's torture, and always takes the longest. And when it's done I think I'll never be able to do it again, I'll never get another idea. The second draft is lots of fun, because it's all there, and all I have to do is get it right."[4]

1974. Published *Blubber*. ". . . The one thing I wanted desperately to do in *Blubber*, which is about fifth graders, was to let them use the language they really use. I think kids reach their peak of nastiness in fifth grade: they're very cruel to each other. Up until that point I hadn't really tackled language as kids use it. Publishers would have been frightened by it. But in *Blubber* they do talk the way I feel they talk to each other. Children in America who ride school buses use all the four-letter-words freely. I've tried to show that in *Blubber*. We had a little problem over that. The solution was that if the language was not important to the character or the plot we would use another word. If it showed characterization then it stayed, so there are a couple of 'phrases' in *Blubber*. I'm afraid it's a book that's going to make a lot of adult readers uncomfortable because it shatters the myth that kids are sweet and innocent. They just aren't. But I'm writing for the kids, and the only problem is that they're not the ones who buy their own books, or usually even choose them. What is available to them in the libraries is there because an adult has selected it. It is only with paperback books that they can get what they want.

". . . In . . . *Blubber* . . . the parents are very nice; . . . I don't think it was deliberate, what I did. For instance, I liked Margaret's parents. I thought they were nice people and I thought of her as having a happy home life. She was secretive about all those things because that's how I was. Most kids are that way. In *Then Again Maybe I Won't* the boy has a lousy mother, sure; and in *Deenie* my feeling was that if she had very warm, accepting, understanding parents, the story that I wanted to tell wouldn't have been there. It was not just about what was happening to her, but about the feelings and reactions of everyone around her as well. But I think it's a mistake to think that I always make adults come out that way."[4]

1974. Published *Deenie*. " . . . I start with the character. I don't know everything about the character when I start the book. I'm surprised along the way myself. *Deenie* of course, was a deliberate idea, to write a book about a child with scoliosis, because I met a kid with scoliosis. That required a lot of research, while all my other books required none. That was a very special experience, and I couldn't write about it until I'd seen it, the way I said. I went to the hospital and watched

these kids being molded and fitted for body-braces, because I couldn't visualize it on my own. My favorite scene in the book is the scene in the plaster-room. All of the dialogue in that is real. I sat in there with a pencil and a paper and wrote down everything the nurse and the doctor said. The children were very frightened and said nothing basically. Then I had to become Deenie. . . . "[4]

1975. Divorced John Blume. "To the outside world it seemed to be a nice marriage, but inside I was dying. When a marriage is about to dissolve the children want to know why and they have a right to know. They're thinking, 'How is this going to mess up my life?' 'What's going to happen to me?'"

"I don't know the answer for my generation. I think that for our children it's going to be different. I know Randy's growing up feeling without question that she will have to work. And her work will be as important as her mate's work, if she chooses to have a mate. Young men seem to understand that more and more. But there are still a lot of the old values around. I originally saw my role as being a perfect wife and mother."[3]

1977. On *Starring Sally J. Freedman as Herself*, largely an autobiographical novel, Blume commented: "I think that *Starring Sally J. Freedman* is primarily a warm and funny and loving family story. I laughed and I cried while writing it. But some of the reviews made me come close to throwing away my typewriter.

"My treatment of the Holocaust is absolutely accurate from the point of view of an American child growing up in the 1940s. At that time, we didn't really *know* anything. We hadn't seen the pictures, we couldn't even imagine the realities. So that kind of fantasy about the war is what went on in a lot of kids' heads, especially those who were Jewish and who heard their families talking about things they really didn't understand."[5]

" . . . *Starring Sally J. Freedman as Herself* [was] a very important book to me. I thought it was my best effort and that I had done something that I hadn't done before."[3]

1978. *Wifey,* her first adult novel, published. "It's really my younger children's books that have brought me my audience. I wrote *Wifey* because I felt a great need for change." [Kathleen Hinton-Braaten, "Writing for Kids Without Kidding Around," *Christian Science Monitor,* May 14, 1979.[7]]

"Yes—but now I will continue to write for both young people and adults. I need to explore experiences and feelings of all ages in my work."

"I'm very proud of *Wifey*. It was difficult, but it's something I very much wanted to do.

"I think I've written about the kind of person I was and could have remained if I had not met up with the good fortune of finding my career."[3]

"There's been an awful lot made of the explicit sex in *Wifey*, and I find that peculiar. I see my book as being very realistic, and as ludicrous as many of Sandy's thoughts are, people have ludicrous thoughts, and I think we should write about it more—so that people who have these thoughts can read it and say, 'ah-h-h-h, I'm not the only one. I'm so glad.'"[7]

"I just refuse to write another book in which a woman becomes liberated, slams the door and walks out. There are three women

The play began. Freddy did his big and little jumps. Every few minutes one of the fifth or sixth graders in the play said to him, "And who are you?" ■ (From *The One in the Middle Is the Green Kangaroo* by Judy Blume. Illustrated by Amy Aitken.)

I called when my first husband and I were splitting up, and they all cried. 'Oh God, you're so lucky,' they said. 'You have a way of getting out.' So this book is for them. They just continue to live lives of quiet desperation and at least saying it, getting it out in the open, is a step." [Linda Bird Francke with Lisa Hartman, "Growing Up With Judy," *Newsweek*, October 9, 1978.[8]]

"I am a loving person and I love hard. When you do love that intensely, you open yourself up to be hurt, but it's worth it. You can't be afraid to make mistakes. You can't spend your life saying, 'What if.'"[2]

Blume defined her thoughts about her readers and her work: "Kids live in the same world as adults do. They see things and hear things. Problems only get worse when there are secrets, because what kids imagine is usually scarier than the truth.

"Kids have a right to read about themselves. They've been denied that right for a long time....

"Being a kid is a universal joy and a universal problem."[2]

"I think I write about sexuality because when I was young, that's what I most wanted to know about. I identify very strongly with kids. Twelve- and thirteen-year-olds feel things very intensely. They need to know about what they are feeling, and more than anything else, they want reassurance that their feelings are normal. Besides, sex is very interesting."[3]

"I write about people, their relationships to each other and their feelings."

"If I could have read *Deenie* at 12, I could have known other kids masturbated and God, I would have been relieved. I was making deals up there. It was, 'Hey, listen, I'll only do it twice this week, if you'll make sure this happens and that happens.'"[8]

"My responsibility to be honest with my readers is my strongest motivation. I am offended by dishonest books. I hate the idea we should always protect children. They live in the same world we do. They see and hear things. Secrets are terrible because what they imagine and have to deal with alone is usually scarier than the truth."[3]

"I am frightened about not having kids around anymore. There is a very real possibility I will lose the inspiration to write for children if I am not living with them. I would not be the first person that has happened to.

"I used to think my inspiration come from within—from the child I was. Maurice Sendak does not live with children; it all comes from within himself! I felt I could write books like *Blubber* and *Tales of a Fourth Grade Nothing* because I could project myself back and *be* nine or ten years old. I could remember the smells, how things felt, what I thought. I think now that an awful lot of my inspiration comes from living with kids. . . . "[7]

"I feel, at age 44, that I am finally grown up. Not completely, of course, because we never stop growing and changing. But for the first time I feel in control of my own life. And that is a very good feeling."

"I look at the kids, the ages they are and the age I am, all the things we enjoy together, and I say, terrific, I like this. I'm so glad I had them when I did."[3]

Blume divides her time between her homes in New York City and Sante Fe, New Mexico.

"I'm a people person. One of the things that's difficult for me (when I am in Sante Fe) in a small community is that I don't have the contacts with people that I need and want. The biggest drawback to being a writer in the first place is that it's a lonely occupation."[5]

Blume's works are included in the Kerlan Collection at the University of Minnesota.

FOR MORE INFORMATION SEE: Library Journal, December, 1969, September, 1970, December, 1970; *New York Times Book Review,* May 24, 1970, December 9, 1970; *Publishers Weekly,* January 11, 1971, April 17, 1978; *Boston Globe,* January 30, 1971; *Elementary English,* September, 1974; Justin Wintle and Emma Fisher, *The Pied Pipers,* Paddington Press, 1975; *Children's Literature Review,* Volume 2, Gale, 1976; Doris de Montreville and Elizabeth D. Crawford, editors, *Fourth Book of Junior Authors,* H. W. Wilson, 1978; *Newsweek,* October 9, 1978; *People,* October 16, 1978, August 16, 1982; *New York Times Magazine,* December 3, 1978, August 23, 1982; *Top of the News,* Spring, 1978; *Writer's Digest,* February, 1979; *Parents Magazine,* May, 1979; *Christian Science Monitor,* May 14, 1979; *Seventeen,* August, 1979; Diana Gleasner, *Breakthrough: Women in Writing* (juvenile), Walker, 1980; Betsey Lee, *Judy Blume's Story,* Dillon Press, 1981; *New York Times,* October 3, 1982; *Teen,* October, 1982.

BRADY, Esther Wood 1905-
(Esther Wood)

PERSONAL: Born August 24, 1905, in Akron, N.Y.; daughter of Lawrence A. (a minister) and Ida (Eby) Wood; married George W. Brady (an aeronautical engineer), July 29, 1933; children: Caroline F., Barbara (Mrs. William A. Beeker). *Education:* Attended University of Rochester and Denison University; Boston University, B.A., 1928. *Religion:* Presbyterian. *Home:* 3023 44th St. N.W., Washington, D.C. 20016.

CAREER: Woman's Foreign Mission Society, New York, N.Y., editor, 1928-32; writer, 1936—. Past member of board of directors of Montclair Art Museum, Montclair Guidance Center and Montclair Junior League (all in New Jersey). *Member:* Authors Guild of Authors League of America, Daughters of the American Revolution, Columbia Historical Society, Children's Book Guild of Washington, D.C.

WRITINGS—Children's books; under name Esther Wood: *Great Sweeping Days,* Longmans, Green, 1936; *Pedro's Coconut Skates,* Longmans, Green, 1938; *Silk and Satin Lane,* Longmans, Green, 1939; *Pepper Moon,* Longmans, Green, 1940; *Belinda Blue,* Longmans, Green, 1940; *The House in the Hoo,* Longsman, Green, 1941; *Silver Widgeon,* Longmans, Green, 1942.

Children's books; under name Esther Wood Brady: *Toliver's Secret* (illustrated by Richard Cuffari), Crown, 1976; *The Toad on Capitol Hill* (illustrated by R. Cuffari), Crown, 1978.

WORK IN PROGRESS—Children's books: A historical novel set in Washington, D.C. in 1930; a mystery story set in old New York.

SIDELIGHTS: "I must have been born with wandering feet and a compulsion to see what was beyond the next hill. In school I loved to read about children in foreign countries and always dreamed that someday I'd find a lost wallet or a pot of gold to pay for a trip around the world.

"I never found the pot of gold, but I did earn enough money to travel if I didn't mind traveling on a shoestring. After college I worked for several years in New York, then went with friends for a foot-loose summer of wandering around Europe.

"Two years later, in 1933, I found that a favorable rate of exchange made it possible to go around the world on a series of German freighters. Away from the port cities I found the colorful old China and old Japan and tropical Philippines I had dreamed of. My most valuable insights and knowledge came from going with missionary nurses as they made their house calls on all classes of people. At length I came back with volumes of notes, a suitcase full of sketches, and a dozen ideas for children's stories.

"A month later I married, and happily put away my passport. We had two little girls and in the next seven years I produced seven books as well. But when the war disrupted our lives and my growing children needed more attention I gave up writing—for a while, I thought. It was thirty years before I got back to it.

"The life of a suburban housewife was a happy one. When our children were in college we moved to Washington, D.C., for the Space Age was upon us and my husband became part of that great venture.

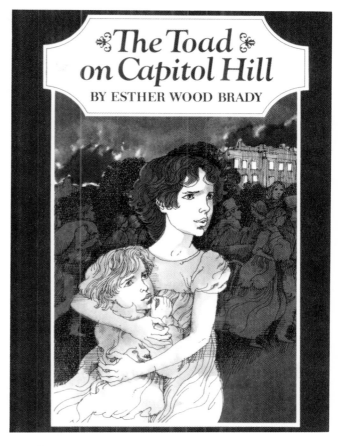

(From *The Toad on Capitol Hill* by Esther Wood Brady. Jacket illustration by Richard Cuffari.)

"Because I had discovered that my very slow reading ability was due to dyslexia, I became interested in children with that handicap. For ten years I did volunteer tutoring in public schools, and hunted constantly for easy books of high quality for my reluctant readers. This brought me back to my own writing career.

"*Toliver's Secret* was originally much shorter and simpler than it turned out to be when published. The editors at Crown urged me to enlarge it, and I found myself researching more details and absorbed in my second love—history.

"I had grown up with a feeling for history from my grandparents, whose ancestors were early colonists. Because no one in my husband's family ever threw away a letter, our attic has tin boxes crammed with letters from many generations. In addition there are boxes of shawls and mitts and shoebuckles and tall combs and steel-rimmed glasses. I feel I know all the people who wore them because of their intimate letters. The characters in my books are imaginary, but their times and lifestyles seem very real to me.

"I still love to travel, but have not seen the Orient again. We have traveled in Turkey and Greece and several times in Italy, my favorite, as well as other European countries. In the summers we go to a cottage in Leland, Michigan, where I write."

FOR MORE INFORMATION SEE: Stanley J. Kunitz and Howard Haycraft, editors, *Junior Book of Authors,* H. W. Wilson, 2nd edition, 1951.

BRIGGS, Peter   1921-1975

OBITUARY NOTICE: Born April 15, 1921, in St. Paul, Minn.; died July 18, 1975, in New York, N.Y. Editor and author of books for young readers. Briggs spent several years as promotion manager for various book publishing companies, including G.P. Putnam's Sons and John Day Co., Inc., before becoming nonfiction editor for *Ladies Home Journal* in 1951. Beginning in 1963, he was employed as a full-time free-lance writer. *Water: The Vital Essence* was published in 1967, the first of over a dozen books on the subject of oceanography. For *Laboratory at the Bottom of the World,* Briggs traveled to the Antarctica to conduct personal research. His other books include *Mysteries of the Sea, 200,000,000 Years Beneath the Sea,* and *What is the Grand Design?: The Story of Evolving Life and the Changing Planet on Which It Is Lived. For More Information See: Contemporary Authors,* Permanent Series, Volume 2, Gale, 1978. *Obituaries: AB Bookman's Weekly,* August 4, 1975.

BRINK, Carol Ryrie   1895-1981

PERSONAL: Born December 28, 1895, in Moscow, Idaho; died August 15, 1981, in La Jolla, Calif.; daughter of Alexander (first mayor of Moscow, Idaho) and Henrietta (Watkins) Ryrie; married Raymond Woodward Brink (a mathematics professor), July 12, 1918 (deceased); children: David Ryrie, Nora Caroline Brink Hunter. *Education:* Attended University of Idaho, 1914-17; University of California (Berkeley), B.A., 1918. *Religion:* Presbyterian. *Home:* San Diego, Calif.

CAREER: Self-employed author of books for both children and adults. *Member:* National League of American Penwomen, Authors' League of America, Women in Communications, Authors Guild, Society of Children's Book Writers, P.E.N., California Writers Guild, Southern California Council on Literature for Children and Young People, Faculty Women's Club (University of Minnesota), Phi Beta Kappa, Gamma Phi Beta. *Awards, honors:* John Newbery Medal, 1936, and Lewis Carroll Shelf Award, 1959, for *Caddie Woodlawn;* Friends of American Writers award, 1956, for *The Headland;* McKnight Family Foundation medal and National League of American Pen Women award, 1966, both for *Snow in the River;* Southern California Council on Literature for Children and Young People award, 1966; Irvin Kerlan Award, 1978, for *Four Girls on a Homestead;* D. Litt., University of Idaho, 1965.

WRITINGS—All published by Macmillan, except as indicated; juvenile: *Anything Can Happen on the River* (illustrated by W.W. Berger), 1934; *Caddie Woodlawn* (illustrated by Kate Seredy), 1935, new edition (illustrated by Trina Schart Hyman), 1973; *Mademoiselle Misfortune* (illustrated by Seredy), 1936; *Baby Island* (illustrated by Helen Sewell), 1937, new edition illustrated by Helen Sewell, Macmillan, 1966; *All Over Town* (illustrated by Dorothy Bayley), 1939, reprinted, 1968; *Lad with a Whistle* (illustrated by Robert Ball), 1941; *Magical Melons: More Stories about Caddie Woodlawn* (illustrated by Marguerite Davis), 1944, reprinted, 1963; *Narcissa Whitman: Pioneer to the Oregon Country* (illustrated by Samuel Armstrong), Row, Peterson, 1946; *Lafayette,* Row, Peterson, 1946; *Minty et Compagnie,* Casterman, 1948; *Family Grandstand* (Junior Literary Guild Selection; illustrated by Jean McDonald Porter), Viking, 1952; *The Highly Trained Dogs of Professor Petit* (Children's Book Club Selection; illustrated by Robert Henneberger), 1953; *Family Sabbatical* (Junior Literary Guild selection; illustrated by Susan Foster), Viking, 1956; *The Pink*

CAROL RYRIE BRINK

Motel (illustrated by Sheila Greenwald), 1959; *Andy Buckram's Tin Men* (Junior Literary Guild selection; illustrated by W.T. Mars), Viking, 1966; *Winter Cottage* (illustrated by Fermin Rocker), 1968; *Two Are Better Than One* (illustrated by Rocker), 1968; *The Bad Times of Irma Baumlein* (illustrated by Trina Schart Hyman), 1972; *Louly* (illustrated by Ingrid Fetz), 1974; *Four Girls on a Homestead,* Latah County (Idaho) Historical Society, 1977.

Plays: *The Cupboard Was Bare,* Eldridge Publishing, 1928; *The Queen of the Dolls,* Eldridge Publishing, 1928; *Caddie Woodlawn* (first produced in Minneapolis, 1957), Macmillan, 1945.

For adults; all novels except as indicated: *Buffalo Coat,* 1944; *Harps in the Wind* (biography), 1947, reprinted, Da Capo Press, 1980; *Stopover,* 1951; *The Headland,* 1955; *Strangers in the Forest,* 1959; *The Twin Cities* (non-fiction), 1961; *Chateau Saint Barnabé,* 1962; *Snow in the River,* 1964; *The Bellini Look,* Bantam, 1976.

Editor; both published by Row, Peterson: *Best Short Stories for Children,* 1935; *Best Short Stories for Boys and Girls,* 1936-39.

Also contributor of short stories and poems to magazines.

SIDELIGHTS: **December 28, 1895.** ''I was born in Moscow, Idaho. . . . When I was in France, the officials who inspected my card of identification always put me down as a Russian because they had never heard of Idaho, and thought that there was only one Moscow. But this one is a beautiful little university town among blue hills and checkered fields and I am glad that I grew up there.

"My father came from Scotland when he was about twenty and went West, as all young men did in those days. He settled in Idaho when it was not yet a state, and married the daughter of the pioneer doctor. My mother's people were of New England and English stock and had been on the move westward for a generation. My father died when I was five and my mother, when I was eight. I went to live with my grandmother and an unmarried aunt in a comfortable old house, surrounded by a large garden with fruit trees, barns, chicken yard, and all the pleasant elements of a farm encompassed in a part of a town block." [Carmen Nelson Richards and Genevieve Rose Breen, *Minnesota Writes: A Collection of Autobiographical Stories by Minnesota Writers*, Lund Press, 1945.[1]]

"Much of my childhood was lonely, but it was not unhappy—just enough unhappiness to make me think and appreciate. Because I was lonely, I learned a most valuable thing—how to make my own amusements by reading, writing, drawing, making things with my hands, and spending many happy hours on horseback. I always had animal friends—dogs, cats, and pet chickens. My grandmother and aunt were both great storytellers, and I lived vicariously the exciting childhood that my grandmother had lived on the Wisconsin frontier. Her stories were one of the delights of my earlier years." [Lee Bennett Hopkins, *More Books by More People*, Citation, 1974.[2]]

"My aunt was a second mother to me and spoiled and petted me. But my grandmother was always a bulwark of common sense and one whose judgment I could rely upon even when the balance was not in my favor. She had the rather masculine qualities of tolerance, impartiality, and a detached philosophical attitude toward life which have always endeared her to me. She was also a good story teller. How I loved the stories of her pioneer childhood in Wisconsin! Although the only member of her family whom I had ever seen besides herself was her sister, Hetty, I felt that I knew each one of them intimately. I knew her father's quiet wisdom and strength, and her mother's quick temper and longing for the home in Boston. I knew Nero and Uncle Edmund and the Indians. Sometimes she would sing the old-fashioned songs they had learned at school or recite the old pieces which they had spoken on holidays, and she could almost always be induced to tell the wonderful tale of Pee Wee.

"I had all sorts of pets, as a child, but dearest of all was a Shetland Pony who took me all over the country, summer and winter, from the time I was six until I was graduated from college and went away to be married. We had a good many troubles in those days: death, disaster, and loneliness; and yet I had a very happy childhood. I often think that my own children, who have known neither death, disaster, nor loneliness, have also somehow missed the especial kind of happiness that I had.

"I was not a very sturdy child, and we spent several winters in California and also lived for several years with an uncle in Spokane, Washington. My two last years of high school were spent in the fine old Portland Academy, which used to flourish in Portland, Oregon, but is now extinct.

"It was during my high-school years that I became tremendously interested in writing. As a child I had always said that

Instantly the schoolroom was in an uproar. Obediah lurched forward and caught hold of Caddie's curls. . . . ■ (From *Caddie Woodlawn* by Carol Ryrie Brink. Illustrated by Trina Schart Hyman.)

I wanted to write books and illustrate them myself; but I soon found that it was the writing and not the illustrating which appealed most keenly to me. During my last two years of high school I wrote a number of stories for the magazine which the students of the Academy brought out every month, and all through college I worked in one way or another on the college newspaper or other publications.

"For my college work I returned to the University of Idaho at Moscow and spent three years there. These were extremely important years to me, not only in the things I learned or worked out for myself, but also in the friendships I formed. For my senior year my best friend and I went to the University of California at Berkeley, and I was graduated from there. . . .

"Some years before this Raymond Brink, who was then nineteen and out in the world for his first job, had come to the University of Idaho to teach. During the years that I was growing up and he was at Harvard working for his Ph.D., we kept in touch with each other. During my junior year he had a traveling fellowship from Harvard, and on his return he came West to see me. The following summer, just after graduation from college, we were married and came to Minnesota where he was teaching mathematics at the state university.

"A little more than a year later he had an invitation to go to the University of Edinburgh as a lecturer. It was a wonderful opportunity and adventure; and we started off with a six-week-old baby boy, knowing practically nothing about babies or the dangers of traveling with them. We didn't even take a book on the care and feeding of infants with us, but some good angel who looks after the young and reckless saw us through without mishap. I met my Scotch relatives for the first time, and, besides seeing a great deal of Scotland (from behind a perambulator), we had a month in London at Christmas and six weeks in Paris at Easter. My husband had spent his student year in France and not only loved it but spoke the language very well, so that my introduction to France was a very happy one, and I have been fond of it ever since.

"Twice since this first visit there together, we have spent a year in France. . . ."[1]

"One year when we were in France, my husband, small son, and I bought a small motor boat and drove it up the Seine and Yonne rivers from Neuilly to Sens. We had intended to go much further, but the river locks took time, the weather turned cold, and motor trouble developed. But it was a great adven-ture, and I fictionalized this trip for children in my first book, *Anything Can Happen on the River.*"[2]

"The last time we were there we drove our own car; and the characters, places, and many of the events in *Mademoiselle Misfortune* originated in this third year abroad. We have also spent a summer touring Norway, Sweden, Denmark, and England."[1]

"I always wanted to write books, and at first I wrote and published some poetry. I have written poetry all my life but after I began writing prose, I no longer tried to publish the poems. When my two children, David and Nora, were small, they brought home Sunday school papers for me to read aloud. As I read the stories, I said to myself, 'If I can't do better than that, it is too bad.' So I sent my first children's stories to the Sunday school papers, and they were kindly received by friendly editors. I learned more in this humble field than I ever learned from creative writing courses in college." [*National Education Association of the United States Journal* (Washington, D.C.), Volume 25, Number 8, November, 1936.[3]]

"The stories appeared in several of the children's magazines and the story papers—about 130 of them in all. There were also several plays for children which were written for special occasions and produced by the Drama Section of the Minnesota Faculty Women's Club. Two of these were later published. For six years I edited a collection of best short stories for boys and girls, selected from the children's magazines and papers over a period of twelve months and published annually by Row, Peterson and Company."[1]

1934. First juvenile published. "Now that I have begun writing books for young people, I find it much more enjoyable than writing short stories. I like the opportunity for leisurely character development which the short story does not allow, and I feel that children are as much interested in character development as adults. For a number of years it had been the fashion to leave adults entirely out of stories for children or to make them the merest lay figures. In real life, children are surrounded by adults, and they are very quick to see their peculiarities and good or bad points. So in my books I like to try to draw real people, using adults as well as children, but trying always to see them from the child's point of view."[1]

"I feel very strongly that one can put as much sincerity, beauty, and understanding of life into juvenile books as into adult books and that we owe good writing to children perhaps even more than to adults since children's tastes and characters are in the forming process."[3]

1935. *Caddie Woodlawn*, Brink's second book for children, was published and won the Newbery Award the following year. "Of my juvenile books I suppose that *Caddie [Woodlawn]* is my favorite."[2]

"[*Caddie Woodlawn*] is my grandmother's story, and I loved hearing it as a child. I find that children are always delighted to know that the story is true. Also, *Caddie* has made me so many friends all over the world that I must always be grateful to it—to her. Winning the Newbery Award made me very proud and happy, and it has certainly done much to make the book well-known and popular. The medal is one of my prized possessions, and I shall always be thankful for it."[2]

"Caddie Woodlawn was my grandmother. Her real name was Caddie Woodhouse. All of the names in the book, except one, are changed a little bit. The names are partly true, partly made

. . . They joined Grandpa, who was sitting by the dining-room stove knitting purple wool into afghan squares. Hetty had never seen a gentleman knit—even such a very old gentleman as Grandpa. ▪ (From *Magical Melons* by Carol Ryrie Brink. Illustrated by Marguerite Davis.)

"Well, mouse or hamster, whatever it is, take it back tomorrow, child. We can't have it running loose, scaring the servants into fits." ■ (From *The Bad Times of Irma Baumlein* by Carol Ryrie Brink. Illustrated by Trina Schart Hyman.)

up, just as the facts of the book are mainly true but have sometimes been slightly changed to make them fit better into the story. The one name that remains unchanged is that of Robert Ireton. I liked the name and I thought that, since hired men often moved from place to place for seasonal work, no one was likely to remember him.

"It was many years later that I remembered these stories of Caddie's childhood, and I said to myself, 'If I loved them so much, perhaps other children would like them, too.' Caddie was still alive while I was writing, and I sent many letters to her, asking about the details that I did not remember clearly. She was pleased when the book was done. 'There is only one thing that I do not understand,' she said. 'You never knew my mother and father and my brothers—how could you write about them exactly as they were?'

"'But, Gram,' I said, 'you told me.'"[Carol Ryrie Brink, "Author's Note," *Caddie Woodlawn*, Macmillan, 1973.[4]]

"Before I began writing *Caddie Woodlawn* I had not thought very much about the duty we owe our children in regard to the past. . . . I talked with a number of old pioneers when I was forming my background for the story, and the more I talked with them the more convinced I became that we are about to lose a most precious contact with something that has vanished."[3]

Summers spent in the family's cottage in Wisconsin provided the setting for *Caddie Woodlawn*. "When we are at home, our summers have largely been spent in a little cottage in northern Wisconsin which has been in my husband's family for years and which has seen some very happy times. This knowledge of the backwoods of Wisconsin was of great value to me in recreating my grandmother's pioneer childhood for *Caddie Woodlawn*."[1]

". . . This gave me my background and the old stories gave me a foundation for my plot. Weaving the two together was really great fun."[3]

They cleared the snow off the ice in front of the cottage, and Joe taught the girls to skate. ■
(From *Winter Cottage* by Carol Ryrie Brink. Illustrated by Fermin Rocker.)

". . . I also made a pilgrimage to the real district from which she came, and found the very house in which she had lived as a child. Because of the lapse of river traffic and the fact that the railroad never came to Dunnville, this region is almost exactly as it was in 1860, and many of the same people are still living quietly on the same farms."[1]

1959. About her book, *The Pink Motel*, Brink commented: "Some of my books, such as *The Pink Motel*, have been creations of my fancy; but even in these books I like to preserve a core of reality and some sort of tie-in with my own personal experience. This first-hand element gives satisfaction to both author and reader in any fictional re-creation. Books which lack the author's own experience of living rarely move the reader."

1964. Besides her well-known children's books, Brink wrote several books for adults during her long career. ". . . Of all my twenty-four books, *Snow in the River* (an adult novel) is my favorite. Although it is freely fictionalized, it is probably

as near to an autobiography as I shall ever write. I put great feeling into it.

"I like to start with something that I know—a place, a person, an experience—something from which I have had an emotional reaction. Then I enjoy fictionalizing to various degrees and try to recreate my feelings for my readers. I write in the mornings and usually I can put things down in fairly final shape at the first writing. This is because much of the preliminary work has been done in my head as I do other tasks. I used to try out my stories on my own children, particularly my daughter who was a good little critic. Now, after many years experience, I know pretty well what children will like. Perhaps I am still something of a child myself and if I please myself, the children are likely to be pleased.

"But I am first a housewife and homemaker. My husband, a professor of mathematics and writer and editor of college math texts, has always been very helpful and understanding of my writing career. We have the same work habits; all we need are a couple of desks, plenty of paper and sharp pencils, and a free time to be happily content. The only advantage he has over me is that he can read and criticize what I write. His writing is as incomprehensible to me as Greek!''[2]

In 1974, she wrote: ''I think that I am probably what you would call a nice, old lady with grey hair, grey eyes, slightly over-weight, and reasonably wholesome and harmless. I have a happy disposition and enjoy my life. I like people, almost all kinds, and I like animals. I belong to the Humane Society because I feel that I owe animals a great debt. My husband and I have traveled and lived abroad a good deal. We have a very primitive cabin on a lake in northern Wisconsin where we go in the summer; we enjoy nature and the outdoors. Know-ing the wild flowers and trees has been a hobby of mine. For many years I also collected old children's books. I am still an amateur painter. Each of my children has four children of their own and, naturally, we think that the eight grandchildren pos-sess all possible charms, talents, and delights.''[2]

1978. As an octogenarian Brink continued to write books. Her last book, *Four Girls on a Homestead,* was also self-illustrated. ''Everyone, whether he writes it or not, has a novel in him, for no life is so completely dull and uneventful that it will not make a story. But we all know the one-novel writer, who, when he has told what happened to him, has exhausted his little vein of gold and can produce no more.

''The trick of longevity in writing is to begin laying up riches in childhood and never to cease learning and experiencing and storing away, so that the older the writer becomes, the richer the hidden mine will be. The next trick is to learn how to bring out a very little bit of gold at a time and spin and beat and carve it into something precious. The person who can do this will not be a one-novel author, but can continue to create as long as his mind remains clear and he has the gumption to use a typewriter.

''What have I already stored up? It is a good question for any writer to ask himself. He should take stock of his mind and see what it will yield. If he learned in childhood to use his senses and observe the world around him, he was fortun-ate. . . . Many of us . . . learned in childhood to amuse our-selves by observing and storing away details that the happy and extroverted child often misses.

''The more the writer stores away in the cells of memory, the more wealth he can pull out and use some day when he is sitting at a desk in a small room with a blank page of paper before him. The details, with which he surrounds his characters and rounds out his plot, leaven his story and make it come alive for his reader.

''Thomas Wolfe, in *Look Homeward, Angel,* has a long pas-sage which is merely a catalogue of smells. But close your eyes and let yourself go with him: '. . . the exciting smell of chalk and varnished desks; the smell of heavy bread sandwiches of cold fried meat and butter; the smell of new leather in a saddler's shop, or of a warm leather chair; of honey and of unground coffee; of barrelled sweet-pickles and cheese and all the fragrant compost of the grocers'. . . .' *Compost!* What a wonderful word to use in this connection! But we don't care to write so lavishly these days. What we aim for now is more compact writing, the spare, the lean, the elegant. We are con-tent to leave the catalogues and rivers of sensation to Wolfe and Walt Whitman. Yet the writer must never miss an oppor-tunity to appeal, however briefly, to his reader's senses, so

that the reader may experience vicariously the sensations which the writer has stored up for him.

''The writer must also use conscious selection in choosing material. Sometimes I think that the difference between good and bad writing depends entirely on the wisdom the author has used in selecting his material. Out of all the possibilities in the world, he has selected these characters, these events, these charmed words, and in the end he is either a good writer or a poor one. More than likely, it is the richness of his own ex-perience that will tip the scale in favor of good writing.

''We must open our senses to the mood of a new place. Change can stimulate the sensibilities, and I find myself most creative at the turn of the season or when seeing new places or meeting new people. It is not always about the new places or the new people that I want to write, but they may remind me of some-thing in my past, and, when I am in Europe, I may want to write about Idaho, and, when I am in America, I think back to Europe with creative nostalgia.

''The best fiction writing, it seems to me, arises out of the emotions. Most of my books, both for adults and children, start with a *feeling* for a person or a place. Plot comes harder for me, and it has to grow naturally out of the emotional feeling for the people or the place. I like my characters to grow and change as the book progresses. . . .

''Conversation should always be lively and interesting, and it should unobtrusively explain a situation or a character, or ad-vance the plot, but do not try to reproduce ordinary conver-sation verbatim. Selection is the keynote. Let the characters reveal themselves, but never let them become tiresome. When you feel bored with your writing, your reader is going to feel twice as bored in reading what you have written. Get up then and feed the cat or walk around the block or take a hot bath. If you have established good writing habits, you will soon want to go back to your desk, reread the last few pages, erase the dull part, and go on. If necessary just leave a blank line and proceed to the part that interests you. There is great virtue in the blank line. You need not say, 'Day followed day' or 'Came the dawn,' you just skip along to something more interesting, and your reader will be right with you instead of asleep in his chair.

''I have learned that a wealth of conscious experience not only makes a good writer, but it makes a sympathetic reader. What you have fully experienced will enrich your writing, and what you have fully imagined will enrich your living.'' [Carol Brink, ''The Gold Mine of Experience,'' *The Writer*, August, 1977.[5]]

August 15, 1981. Died in La Jolla, California. ''A lonely or unhappy childhood may be the greatest blessing for a writer.''[5]

HOBBIES AND OTHER INTERESTS: Painting, traveling and cooking. ''I can't think of many things I do not enjoy in the line of creative and constructive work. Most of all I enjoy being with and studying people.''

FOR MORE INFORMATION SEE: National Education As-sociation of the United States Journal [Washington, D.C.], Volume 25, Number 8, November, 1936; C.N. Richards and G.R. Breen, *Minnesota Writes: A Collection of Autobiograph-ical Stories by Minnesota Writers,* Lund Press, 1945; Elizabeth Rider Montgomery, *The Story Behind Modern Books,* Dodd, 1949; Stanley J. Kunitz and Howard Haycraft, *Junior Book of Authors,* second edition, H.W. Wilson, 1951; *Saturday Review of Literature,* March 10, 1951; Bertha Mahony Miller and

Elinor Whitney Field, editors, *Newbery Medal Books: 1922-1955,* Horn Book, 1955; *Horn Book,* August, 1967, Norah Smaridge, *Famous Modern Storytellers for Young People,* Dodd, 1969; Lee Bennett Hopkins, *More Books By More People,* Citation, 1974; *The Writer,* August, 1977; *Twentieth Century Children's Writers,* St. Martin's, 1978; *Contemporary Authors New Revision Series,* Volume 3, Gale, 1981; *The Writers Directory, 1982-84,* Gale, 1981.

Filmstrips: ''Meet the Newbery Author: Carol Ryrie Brink,'' Miller-Brody, 1977.

Obituaries: *Chicago Tribune,* August 19, 1981; *New York Times,* September 1, 1981; *Publishers Weekly,* September 11, 1981; *AB Bookman's Weekly,* September 14, 1981; *School Library Journal,* October, 1981.

BRÖGER, Achim 1944-

PERSONAL: Born May 16, 1944, in Erlangen, Germany; son of Arnold and Anneliese (Möhrenschlager) Bröger; married Elisabeth Zeeck, October 4, 1975; children: Jonas, Gunda, Olat. *Home and office:* Wilhelm-Raabe-Weg 3, 3300 Braunschweig Bienrode, Federal Republic of Germany.

CAREER: Writer, 1971—. *Member:* P.E.N. *Awards, honors:* Selected for best European children's books list, 1976; Schallplattenpreis der Deutschen Phonoakademie for *Der Ausreden-Erfinder;* nominated for the Mildred L. Batchelder Award for *Good Morning, Whale,* 1977; best German juvenile book list for *Moritzgeschichten,* 1979.

WRITINGS: Raupengeschichte (juvenile; illustrated by Katrin Brandt), Atlantis (Zurich), 1971, published as *The Caterpillers,* Scroll Press, 1973; *Doppelte Ferien sind am schönsten,* Thienemanns (Shuttgart), 1974; *Guten Tag,lieber Wal* (juvenile; illustrated by Gisela Kalow), Thienemanns, 1974, translation by Elizabeth Shub published as *Good Morning, Whale,* Macmillan, 1974; *Der Ausreden-Erfinder* (juvenile; illustrated by Ronald Himler), 1974, translation by Hilda van Stockum published as *Bruno,* Morrow, 1975; *Das wunderbare Bettmobil* (illustrated by G. Kalow), Thienemanns, 1975, translation by Caroline Gueritz published as *The Wonderful Bedmobile,* Hamish Hamilton, 1976; *Steckst du dahinter, Kasimir?* (juvenile; illustrated by Susan Jeschke), Thienemanns, 1975, translation by H. van Stockum published as *Outrageous Kasimir,* Morrow, 1976; *Der Saurier aus der Heinrichstrasse* (illustrated by Karl Meiler), Kinderbücher, 1976; *Mensch, wär das schön!,* Thienemanns, 1977; *Kurzschluss,* 1976, translation by Patricia Crampton published as *Running in Circles,* Morrow, 1977; *Bruno verreist* (juvenile; illustrated by G. Kalow), Thienemanns, 1978, translation by C. Gueritz published as *Bruno Takes a Trip,* Morrow, 1978 (published in England as *Bruno's Journey,* Hamish Hamilton, 1978); *Moritzgeschichten,* Thienemanns, 1979, translation by Elizabeth D. Crawford published as *Little Harry* (illustrated by Judy Morgan), Morrow, 1979; *The Happy Dragon* (illustrated by G. Kalow), Thienemanns, 1980, Methuen, 1981; *Meyers Grosses Kinderlexikon,* Bibliographisches Institute Mannheim, 1981; *In Wirklichkeit ist alles ganz anders,* Thienemanns, 1982; *Pizza und Oskat,* Arena-Verlag (Würzburg), 1982.

SIDELIGHTS: ''If you'd like to visit me, you may want to get a map. First cross the Atlantic Ocean (your finger can do that easily), then swim through the narrow channel between England and France, and finally drop anchor on the beach of West

Germany. You'll have to hike south a bit until you arrive in the city of Braunschweig. On the outskirts you'll find a rather small house, and you'll see a black dog running around the front garden. He is ours. There are five of us altogether—three children, my wife, and I. And we have lots of animals. I'm always complaining that we're on our way to becoming a zoo. But nobody listens to me.

''Ring the doorbell and climb the stairs to the second floor, where I usually write my books. If you ask me what I'm writing, I'll probably not tell you, because if I did, the story couldn't surprise me any more while I write it down. And I like to surprise myself and others.

''What do I like to write best? Sometimes funny, crazy fantasies, sometimes interesting, breath-taking cliff-hangers, sometimes everyday books, or sometimes all these things mixed together in one book. Mainly I want to write about things that I am interested in myself.

''I wish I could paint, because I think of pictures and then describe them. Either a word or sentence makes a picture appear in my mind, and it's followed by other pictures which then change into words, sentences, stories. And these stories are followed by new stories. All I have to do is write them down.

ACHIM BRÖGER

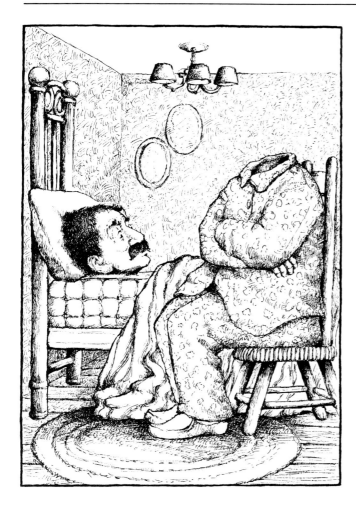

"What are you doing there without me?" he asked. "Did you have a bad night?" ■ (From *Bruno* by Achim Bröger. Illustrated by Ronald Himler.)

"It's great fun to write for you—or read my books to you. Here in Germany I often get together with children your age. We tell each other stories we make up or find new endings for old fairy tales. And some children send me stories they write themselves. I love to get them!" [Achim Bröger, "Meet Your Author," *Cricket*, July, 1977.]

Bröger writes his books exclusively for children. He has also worked on scripts for television as well as plays.

FOR MORE INFORMATION SEE: Cricket, July, 1977.

BROWN, Conrad 1922-

PERSONAL: Born in 1922, in Oregon. *Education:* Graduate of Brown University, R.I.

CAREER: Author and ski instructor. Employed as a ski instructor at Mad River Glen in Vermont; co-director of a ski school in East Madison, New Hampshire. *Military service:* Army ski trooper and ambulance driver during World War II.

WRITINGS: Skiing for Beginners: A Complete and Simple Method for Children and Their Parents (photographs by Nancy

Graham), Scribner, 1951; (with Bruce Gavett) *Skiing for Beginners* (photographs by Kim Massie), Scribner, 1971; (with Sidney Margolius) *How to Cope with the High Cost of Living* (adult), Meredith Corp., 1976.

SIDELIGHTS: Early in his career, Brown wrote *Skiing for Beginners,* a very helpful book of instructions for children and new skiers. As stated in the *Chicago Sunday Tribune,* "The young ski enthusiast, or the older beginner for that matter, who doesn't know much about this sport except that he'd like to enjoy it, will find this detailed book of instruction very helpful."

Much later in his career, Brown collaborated with another ski instructor on a new version of *Skiing for Beginners. Library Journal* claimed, "America's ski boom should flourish all the

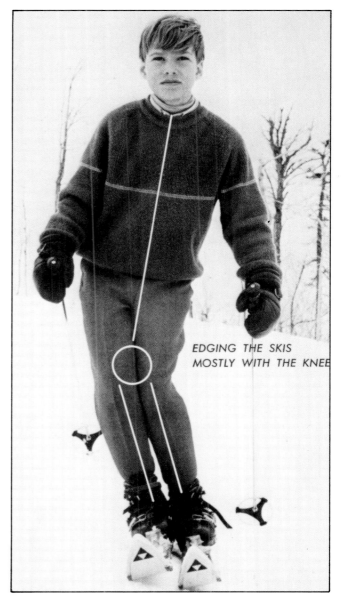

EDGING THE SKIS MOSTLY WITH THE KNEE

This is how the traverse position looks straight on. ■ (From *Skiing for Beginners* by Bruce Gavett and Conrad Brown. Photograph by Kim Massie.)

more thanks to *Skiing for Beginners.* Written by current ski instructor Bruce Gavett and former instructor Conrad Brown, the text is as graceful and precise as a good stem christie.''

FOR MORE INFORMATION SEE: Chicago Sunday Tribune, March 4, 1951; *Library Journal,* December 15, 1971.

BRYAN, Ashley F. 1923-

PERSONAL: Born July 13, 1923, in New York, N.Y. *Education:* Attended Cooper Union and Columbia University.

CAREER: Author and illustrator of books for children; also held the position of a professor of art at Dartmouth College, Hanover, N.H.

WRITINGS—For children; all self-illustrated; all published by Atheneum: *The Ox of the Wonderful Horns, and Other African Folktales,* 1971; *Walk Together Children: Black American Spirituals,* 1974, Volume II: *I'm Going to Sing,* 1982; *The Adventures of Aku,* 1976; *The Dancing Granny,* 1977; (editor and author of introduction) Paul Laurence Dunbar, *I Greet the Dawn: Poems,* 1978; *Beat the Story-Drum, Pum-Pum,* 1980.

Illustrator: Sir Rabindranath Tagore, *Moon, for What Do You Wait?,* Atheneum, 1967; Susan Cooper, *Jethro and the Jumbie,* Atheneum, 1979; Marie Evans, *Jim Flying High,* Doubleday, 1979.

SIDELIGHTS: ''I grew up in tough New York City neighborhoods. I learned from kindergarten that drawing and painting were the toughest assets I had to offer to my community, and I have developed them ever since. My book work is a natural outgrowth of my love of drawing and painting. I make no distinction between the fine arts and fine illustration since, through the ages, artists have used themes from tales or books as a basic resource for expression.

''In retelling the African folktales, I try to approach the spirit of the Black oral tradition. I play with sounds and I encourage others to read my stories aloud for best effect. I take the skeletal story motifs from the scholarly collections and use every resource of my background and experience to flesh them out and bring them alive. Despite extensive research, when necessary, I forgo literal authenticity to achieve this. This means that my story-telling and my illustration combine my African heritage with all the world cultural influences to which any contemporary artist falls heir. I acknowledge my extended family and believe that my sisters and brothers will have no trouble in recognizing me in the crowd.'' [Lee Kingman and others, compilers, *Illustrators of Children's Books, 1967-1976,* Horn Book, 1978.¹]

''Poetry, like music, is rooted in the oral tradition of a people. Still, most of our experience with poetry and, alas, that of most critics as well comes through seeing the poem on the page. Such an experience is limiting, just as it would be if one's knowledge of music were gained only through sight-reading, or one's conception of painting only through discussion. Hearing is so integral to poetry that it is as unlikely for one born deaf to become a poet as for one born blind to become a painter. The poem's sound must ultimately be experienced. . . . Wherever I go I read aloud from poetry to share with my listeners an experience of the living poem—and to share the work of the Black American poets whose fine contributions to American literature are generally overlooked.

''English, the language of the Black American poets whose ancestors crossed this ocean generations ago, in chains. The poets have taken this 'un-Negro tongue' and created the sounds and rhythms by which each one is uniquely identified. They have used the forms of poetry in the Western tradition, introduced variations of their own, and have sought to charge these forms with poetic meaning. This search, common to poets in all languages, encourages a freedom of experimentation and of expression that has made poetry a popular art form among Blacks.

''For my oral readings I choose from Paul Laurence Dunbar's poems in standard English. It is helpful to hear how Dunbar moves a line, the way he can vary slightly the cadence and then fall back onto the beat. I read something from his dialect poetry as well so that the listener may appreciate and acknowledge his extraordinary range. In this way a more balanced evaluation of Dunbar's poetry may be initiated. This was the purpose behind my selection of his poetry, *I Greet the Dawn.*

''A poem may indicate a Black speaker or theme, but the poem as felt poetry is open to any voice. This stimulating freedom of poetry should be exploited in order that the work of the Black American poets may reach the widest possible audience. The non-Black reader should not hesitate to cross the color line in pursuit of a poem. The specific reference to color, age, and sex in a poem is subordinate to one's identification with the poem and with the practice that makes it one's own. This is what the great Black singer Marian Anderson meant when she wrote, 'A song must belong to one before it can be given to others.'

Off they went capering and cartwheeling away!
Pom-pa-lom!
Pom-pa-lom!

(From *The Dancing Granny,* retold and illustrated by Ashley Bryan.)

ASHLEY F. BRYAN

". . . Black American poets . . . [have] been a vital source of inspiration for my own work in retelling African folktales, since we have common roots in the Black oral tradition. These poets offer some of the finest experiences of poetry in the English language. Their contribution form an integral part of American literature, which should be sought out in the poet's selected or complete works as well as in the fine anthologies of Black poetry. . . .

"There is poetry for every level of growth and a thematic range to satisfy any hunger. Poetry's 'raving' transforms not only the mother, the young lover, and the child but also the imaginary world of the phoenix, the unicorn, and the Leviathan. . . .

"The absorbing spell of poetry crosses irrelevant barriers, and the Black poet seeks an audience which includes all people for whatever can be humanly shared." [Ashley Bryan, "On Poetry and Black American Poets," *Horn Book,* February, 1979.²]

FOR MORE INFORMATION SEE: Lee Kingman and others, compilers, *Illustrators of Children's Books, 1967-1976,* Horn Book, 1978; *Horn Book,* February, 1979.

BUSHMILLER, Ernie   1905-1982

OBITUARY NOTICE: Born August 23, 1905, in New York, N.Y.; died of a heart attack, August 15, 1982, in Stamford, Conn. A cartoonist and comedy writer, Bushmiller is best known for the comic strip "Nancy" which he drew for over fifty years. Bushmiller began cartooning in 1925 when he took over the *New York Evening World* comic "Fritzi Ritz" which was begun by Larry Whittington who was leaving to start another strip. The character of Nancy was introduced into the strip after Bushmiller began working for United Features Syndicate which picked up the comic strip after the *Evening World* went out of business. Soon after, Nancy became the central character and, eventually, the strip was renamed. In 1978 Bushmiller was honored as Cartoonist of the Year by the National Cartoonists Society for his work on "Nancy" which is presently carried by over 600 newspapers around the world. *For More Information See: Authors in the News,* Volume 1, Gale, 1976; *Contemporary Authors,* Volumes 29-32, revised, Gale, 1978; *Who's Who in America,* 41st edition, Marquis, 1980; *Who's Who in American Art, 1980,* Bowker, 1980. *Obituaries: Chicago Tribune,* August 17, 1982; *New York Times,* August 17, 1982; *Newsweek,* August 30, 1982; *Time,* August 30, 1982.

Nothing is worth reading that does not require an alert mind.

    —Charles Dudley Warn

His studies were pursued but never effectually overtaken.

    —H.G. Wells

CAMP, Charles Lewis 1893-1975

OBITUARY NOTICE: Born March 12, 1893, in Jamestown, N.D.; died of cancer, August 14, 1975. Paleontologist, educator, author, and editor. Camp graduated from the University of California in 1915 and received his Ph.D. from Columbia University in 1923. He began his career as a zoological assistant at various locations, including the American Museum of Natural History. In 1923, he became a research associate at the University of California, Berkeley, where he eventually held the position of professor and chairman of the department of paleontology. From 1931 to 1949, he was also director of the Museum of Paleontology, and in 1935 received a Guggenheim fellowship which led to expeditions in Europe, South Africa, and China. Throughout his career, Camp directed several excavations which uncovered invaluable paleontological information, including the site at Sterkfontein, near Johannesburg, South Africa, where he studied the fossil remains of the "man-apes" Pleisanthropus. In 1960, he became professor emeritus at California State University, continuing his excavating activities and establishing exhibitions. Camp wrote numerous scholarly works and several books on the subject of paleontology, including *Earth Song: A Prologue to History*. For children, he wrote *Stories of Fossils* in addition to books on Western American frontier history such as *Kit Carson in California* and *Desert Rats*. *Obituaries: New York Times*, August 16, 1975.

CARY, Barbara Knapp 1912(?)-1975

OBITUARY NOTICE: Born about 1912; died May 4, 1975. Editor and author. Knapp was an associate editor of *Reader's Digest*, a position she held for forty years. In 1965 she published *Meet Abraham Lincoln*, a biography for children. She also compiled biographical articles on Lincoln and Mark Twain. *Obituaries: New York Times*, May 6, 1975.

CAVANAH, Frances 1899-1982

PERSONAL: Born September 26, 1899, in Princeton, Ind.; died May 2, 1982, in Denver, Colo.; daughter of Rufus O. and Luella (Neale) Cavanah. *Education:* DePauw University, A.B., 1920. *Residence:* Denver, Colorado.

CAREER: Book review editor for *The Continent*, 1921-23; Rand McNally & Co., Chicago, Ill., member of editorial staff, later associate editor of *Child Life*, 1923-38; Row, Peterson, Inc., Evanston, Ill., contributing writer, 1939-42, director of biographies, 1948-52; Field Enterprises, Inc., Chicago, Ill., biography editor of 1947 edition of *World Book Encyclopedia*, 1944-46, anthology editor of 1949 revision of *Childcraft*, 1947-48; free-lance writer and editor, beginning 1953. *Member:* Authors League, Colorado Authors League, Women in Communications, Inc., Washington Children's Book Guild, Society of Midland Authors, Mortar Board, Delta Delta Delta, Theta Sigma Phi. *Awards, honors:* Theta Sigma Phi Headliner Award, 1941; DePauw University citation for meritorious achievement, 1952; Indiana University Writers' Conference citation for most distinguished children's book by a Hoosier author, 1960, for *Abe Lincoln Gets His Chance*.

WRITINGS: The Treasure of Belden Place, Laidlaw, 1928, Whitman, 1932; *Thanksgiving Wonders*, Eldridge Publishing, 1929; *Children of America*, Thomas Rockwell, 1930, Follett,

FRANCES CAVANAH

1935; *A Patriot in Hoops*, R.M. McBride, 1932; *Children of the White House*, Rand McNally, 1936; *Boyhood Adventures of Our Presidents*, Rand McNally, 1936; *Boyhood Paintings: A Guide to the Masters*, Whitman, 1941; *Marta Finds the Golden Door*, Grosset, 1941; *Louis of New Orleans*, McKay, 1941; (compiler) *Told under the Christmas Tree: A Collection of Christmas Stories, Poems, and Legends*, Grosset, 1941, new edition published as *Favorite Christmas Stories: A Collection of Christmas Stories, Poems and Legends*, 1949; *Pedro of Santa Fe*, McKay, 1941; *Down the Santa Fe Trail*, Row, Peterson, 1942; (compiler and editor) *I Am an American: What We All Are Fighting For, A Handbook For Every American's Pledge to Win the Final Victory and the Peace That Shall Follow*, Whitman, 1942; (compiler with Ruth Cromer Weir) *Liberty Laughs: A Collection of the Best War Jokes and Cartoons*, Dell, 1943; (with R.C. Weir) *Private Pepper of Dogs for Defense*, Whitman, 1943; *The Happy Giraffe*, Wilcox & Follett, 1944; *Our Country's Story* (Junior Literary Guild selection), Rand McNally, 1945, revised editon, 1962; (with R.C. Weir) *Private Pepper Comes Home*, Whitman, 1945; *Benjy of Boston*, McKay, 1946; *Sandy of San Francisco*, McKay, 1946; (compiler with R.C. Weir) *A Treasury of Dog Stories*, Rand McNally, 1947; *Our New Land*, Row, Peterson, 1948; *Our New Nation*, Row, Peterson, 1948.

(Compiler with R.C. Weir) *24 Horses: A Treasury of Stories*, Rand McNally, 1950; (compiler) *Prayers for Boys and Girls*, Whitman, 1950; (editor with Lucille Pannell) *Holiday Roundup*, Macrae, 1951, revised, 1968; *They Knew Abe Lincoln*, Rand McNally, 1952; (editor) *We Came to America*, Macrae, 1954; *Two Loves for Jenny Lind*, Macrae, 1956; *Pocahontas, a Little Indian Girl of Jamestown*, Rand McNally, 1957; (editor) *Family Reading Festival*, Prentice-Hall, 1958; *They Lived in the White House*, Macrae, 1959, revised, 1961; *Abe Lincoln Gets His Chance* (*Weekly Reader* Book Club selection; illustrated by Don Sibley), Rand McNally, 1959.

(Editor) _Friends to Man: The Wonderful World of Animals_, Macrae, 1961; _Adventure in Courage: The Story of Theodore Roosevelt_, Rand McNally, 1961; _Jenny Lind and Her Listening Cat_ (illustrated by Paul Frame), Vanguard, 1961; (collaborator with Elizabeth L. Crandall) _Meet the Presidents_, Macrae, 1962, revised, 1965; _Triumphant Adventure: The Story of Franklin D. Roosevelt_, Rand McNally, 1964; _The Busters: A Story of Two Canine Gentlemen_, Macrae, 1965; _The Secret of Madame Doll: A Story of American Revolution_, Vanguard, 1965; _Our Country's Freedom_, Rand McNally, 1966; (collaborator with E. L. Crandall) _Freedom Encyclopedia: American Liberties in the Making_, Rand McNally, 1968; _Jenny Lind's America_, Chilton, 1969; _When Americans Came to New Orleans_, Garrard, 1970; _We Wanted to Be Free_, Macrae, 1971; _The Truth about the Man Who Sparked the War Between the States_, Westminster, 1975; _Marta and the Nazis_, Scholastic Book Services, 1976.

Plays: _The Transfiguration of the Gifts_, Woman's Press, 1928; _Joy-Time_, Eldridge Publishing, 1929; _The Knight of the Funny Bone, and Other Plays for Children_, Baker's Plays, 1929; _Robin Hood's Enchanted Spring, and Other One-Act Plays for Children_, Banner Play Bureau, 1930; _The Pine Tree's Blossoming: A Christmas Play_, Banner Play Bureau, 1930; _Lil' Black Heliotrope: A One-Act Play for Girls_, Baker's Plays, 1932.

Editor of "Real People" series, forty-eight titles, Row, Peterson & Co., 1948-53. Contributor to _This Week, Jack and Jill, Scholastic, Christian Science Monitor, Historic Preservation, Wilson Library Journal, Publishers Weekly_, and to anthologies and school readers.

SIDELIGHTS: "My first writing to see the light of print was in the _Evansville_ (Ind.) _Press_. I won a contest, 'My Favorite Character in _Little Women_.' The prize was two box seats for the play. My chum and I wept copiously during the sad scenes in full view of the audience. Kleenex had not yet been invented and I had forgotten my handkerchief. I then wore my hair in a long thick braid down my back so I used my pigtail to dry my eyes.

"My second venture into print was a pageant, 'The Torch of Truth' for the Presbyterian Board of Education. The one hundred dollar prize was a bonanza in those days of low salaries. I then wrote a number of plays published in magazines and pamphlets.

"My first real book was _The Treasure of Belden Place_, about an old house on the Ohio River where a friend of mine lived. It had once been a station in the Underground Railroad. Though out of print, I still get letters about it from mothers and now grandmothers. One letter read, 'I want to thank you forty years later for writing that book. I was a lonely little girl and books were my refuge. This one was my favorite."

"A fourth grader from New Orleans wrote about a history I had written. 'Just think,' she said, 'if it hadn't been for you I would never have known that Balboa discovered the Pacific.' She did not realize that many other authors had written about the thrill he felt when he first beheld the blue waters stretching as far as eye could see into the distance. I was glad that I was the first to introduce Balboa to her.

"Years later I was intrigued by the idea that Harriet Beecher Stowe, author of _Uncle Tom's Cabin_ had as her chief prototype, a man named Josiah Henson. He was completely different from the stereotype 'Uncle Tom' as we think of him today. Henson was the escaped slave who, after he reached freedom in Can-

"Go it, Pa," Abe shouted from the fence. **"Don't let that old skinflint get you down."** ■(From _Abe Lincoln Gets His Chance_ by Frances Cavanah. Illustrated by Don Sibley.)

ada, founded a colony for other fugitives. He was an astute business man and started a sawmill to help them. Though he did not learn to read or write until he was in his forties, he was an eloquent preacher. He spoke often at antislavery rallies in New England. He also preached at several churches in London, where he went to solicit business for his lumber mill. On his last visit, he was a guest of Queen Victoria at Buckingham Palace.

"I found excellent material about him in the rare book room at the University of Western Ontario, and had the thrill of visiting the frame house where Henson lived for forty years. It is now called The Uncle Tom Cabin Museum. Unlike the Uncle Tom in Mrs. Stowe's story, who had died a martyr's death, the real Uncle Tom lived to be ninety-three.

"Another favorite person out of history is Jenny Lind, known as a Swedish Nightingale. I was pleased when Madam Alexander, the famous doll designer, decided to make dolls showing Jenny as a little girl in Stockholm and also as a prima donna.

She couldn't, she simply couldn't, put this bedraggled little bunch of fur back on the doorstep. ■ (From *Jenny Lind and Her Listening Cat* by Frances Cavanah. Illustrated by Paul Frame.)

"To me the most interesting subjects are persons whose ideas and accomplishments have had an impact on their own times and continue to influence those who come after them. That is why I like to write biographies, and even when I write fiction I often find some history creeping in. Whether we call such books historical stories or period pieces, it is well to remind young readers that the present must always build on the past. This does not rule out change, since the world is always changing, and the changes that lie just ahead stagger the imagination. The present so soon becomes the past. To young people ten years from now, the 1980's will probably seem 'old hat,' and to write only about the present seems to me to impose limitations on a writer. Earlier generations also had unique problems, and all of us can take heart from the way other people have met the challenge of their times with wisdom and courage."

Cavanah's book, *Our Country's Story*, was a special Korean addition for the U.S. State Department. Her works have been recorded as Talking Books for the Blind, transcribed into Braille, translated into other languages, and are included in the Kerlan Collection at the University of Minnesota.

FOR MORE INFORMATION SEE: Chicago Schools of Journal, May-June, 1951; *Wilson Library Bulletin*, February, 1954; *Washington Post*, December 6, 1959; Muriel Fuller, *More Junior Authors*, H.W. Wilson, 1963; "Current Biography," *The Denver Post*, November 5, 1975.

CHANDLER, Edna Walker   1908-1982

OBITUARY NOTICE—See sketch in *SATA* Volume 11: Born November 16, 1908, near Macksville, Kan.; died September 14, 1982, in Mission Viejo, Calif. Educator and author of more than 50 books for children. Chandler began her career in 1927, after graduating from high school, intending to finish her education later. She taught in Kansas schools for three years, interrupting her career in 1930, to be married. Attempts to resume her education were delayed further as her family grew to include five children. She returned to teaching in 1946, serving in various schools in the San Juan School District of California, until about 1959. She earned her bachelor's degree in education from Sacramento State College in 1958, and became a full-time writer in 1959. Chandler also served as a parole advisor in Sacramento from 1971 until 1973. She was awarded first prize for an unpublished novel by the National League of American Pen Women in 1955. Her initial writing was done for use in the classroom and prduced the "Cowboy Sam" series for slow readers. Other publications for children include the "American Indian" series, the "Tom Logan" series, "Tony Story Books," *Five-Cent, Five-Cent,* and *Indian Paint Brush. For More Information See: Who's Who of American Women,* 1977-78, Marquis, 1978. *Obituaries: School Library Journal,* November, 1982.

CHARLOT, Jean   1898-1979

OBITUARY NOTICE—See sketch in *SATA* Volume 8: Born February 7, 1898, in Paris, France; died March 20, 1979, in Honolulu, Hawaii. An author, artist, and playwright, Charlot combined his many talents into a multi-faceted career. Caught up in the mural movement in Mexico, Charlot lived in that country, painted murals for the Ministry of Education, and served as staff artist for the Carnegie Archeological Expedition in Yucatan. Charlot later received a Guggenheim Fellowship to write on the mural movement. In 1929 Charlot left Mexico for the U.S. where he joined the faculties of the Art Students League and Columbia University. He served as artist-in-residence at the University of Georgia for four years and taught at numerous other institutions, including the University of Hawaii, the University of Notre Dame, and Smith College. Charlot wrote numerous art books such as *Art from the Mayans to Disney* (Sheed, 1939), *Mexican Mural Renaissance, 1920-1925* (Yale University Press, 1963), and *Posada's Dance of Death* (Pratt Graphic Art Center, 1964). He also illustrated books for both children and adults. Among the children's books he illustrated are Ann Nolan Clark's *The Secret of the Andes,* Joseph Krumgold's *. . . and Now Miguel,* both of which are Newbery Medal winners, and Margaret Wise Brown's *Sneakers: Seven Stories about a Cat. For More Information See: The Writers Directory, 1980-1982,* St. Martin's, 1979; *Who's Who in America,* 41st edition, Marquis, 1980; *Contemporary Authors New Revision Series,* Gale, 1981.

Three wise men of Gotham
Went to sea in a bowl;
If the bowl had been stronger
My story had been longer.

—Mother Goose

CLYNE, Patricia Edwards

PERSONAL: Born in New York, N.Y.; daughter of Ray Augustus and Neta Helen (Bohnsack) Edwards; married Francis Gabriel Clyne; children: Stephen Paul, Christopher Jason, Francis Joseph, Ray Augustus. *Education:* Hunter College (now of the City University of New York), B.A., 1958. *Address:* %Dodd, Mead and Co., 79 Madison Ave., New York, N.Y. 10016.

CAREER: Has worked as newspaper reporter and editor of books and magazines; currently free-lance writer. *Member:* National Speleological Society.

WRITINGS—For children, except as noted: *The Corduroy Road,* Dodd, 1973; *Tunnels of Terror* (illustrated by Frank Aloise), Dodd, 1975; *Patriots in Petticoats* (illustrated by Richard Lebenson), Dodd, 1976; *Ghostly Animals of America* (illustrated by Ted Lewin), Dodd, 1977; *Strange and Supernatural Animals* (illustrated by T. Lewin), Dodd, 1979; *Caves for Kids in Historic New York,* Library Research Associates, 1980; *The*

Frozen by fear, she could only watch as the dark form reached out an arm—no, it was a paw! The bedclothes were clawed from the cowering housekeeper, but other than that no harm was done. ■ (From *Ghostly Animals of America* by Patricia Edwards Clyne. Illustrated by Ted Lewin.)

PATRICIA EDWARDS CLYNE

Curse of Camp Gray Owl, Dodd, 1981; *Thomas Ollive Mabbott as Teacher* (adult), University of Iowa, 1981. Contributor of articles and stories to adult and children's magazines.

SIDELIGHTS: "A childhood visit to a Missouri cave resulted in a lifelong interest that is reflected in much of my writing. A member of the National Speleological Society, I enjoy exploring caves as well as such outdoor pursuits as mineral collecting and wilderness hiking.

"Another lifelong interest has been the 19th-century author Edgar Allan Poe. This interest was encouraged by the Poe scholar Thomas Ollive Mabbott, who was teaching at Hunter College when I was a student there, and I later assisted in Mabbott's edition of *The Collected Works of Edgar Allan Poe.* My brief biographical memoir, *Thomas Ollive Mabbott as Teacher,* was published by the University of Iowa in 1981.

"History and folklore also have figured prominently in my work, and I am especially concerned with imparting my own love of the past to young readers. A lot of children don't like history, and neither did I when I was in school because it was taught in such a dead and dry manner—just a lot of dates and names to be memorized. But history can be an exciting subject, and I have tried to give it a 'heartbeat' in my books and articles."

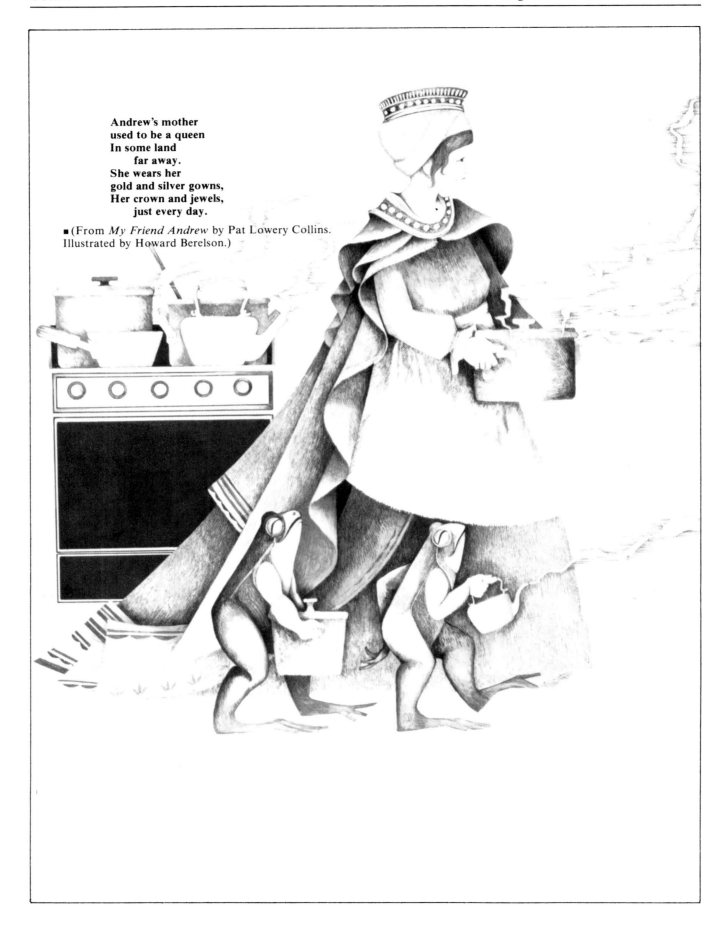

Andrew's mother
used to be a queen
In some land
        far away.
She wears her
gold and silver gowns,
Her crown and jewels,
        just every day.

■ (From *My Friend Andrew* by Pat Lowery Collins.
Illustrated by Howard Berelson.)

COLLINS, Pat Lowery 1932-

PERSONAL: Born October 6, 1932, in Los Angeles, Calif.; daughter of Joseph Michael (an accountant) and Margaret (a radio scriptwriter; maiden name, Meyer) Lowery; married Wallace Collins (an engineering manager), April 18, 1953; children: Christopher, Kimberly (Mrs. David Jermain), Colleen, Cathlin, Mathias. *Education:* Attended the University of California, Los Angeles, 1949, and Immaculate Heart College, 1950; University of Southern California, B.A., 1953; further study at Choinard Art Institute, Los Angeles, Calif., and De Cordova Museum, Lincoln, Mass. *Politics:* Republican. *Religion:* Roman Catholic. *Home and office:* 15 Reservoir St., Nashua, N.H. 03060; and 3 Wauketa Rd., W., Gloucester, Mass. 01930 (summer).

CAREER: Writer, artist. Art gallery in her summer home at Gloucester, Mass., 1980-82; Somerset Art Association, Far Hills, N.J., teacher of pastels, 1981—; is presently affiliated with the Botolph Gallery, Magnolia, Mass. President, Waterman Property Owners Association, 1980-81. *Member:* Allied Artists of America, Society of Children's Book Writers, Audubon Society, Boston Visual Arts Union.

EXHIBITIONS: 29th New England Exhibition of Painting and Sculpture, The Silvermine Guild, New Canaan, Conn., 1978; (one-person) Bernardsville, N.J., 1978; (three-person) Gloucester Lyceum and Sawyer Free Library, 1978; Spectrum '79, Fairleigh Dickenson University, Madison, N.J., 1979; Art '80, The New Jersey State Show, N.J., 1980; Allied Arts of America 67th Annual, New York, N.Y., 1980; (one-person) Ortho Pharmaceutical National Headquarters, Raritan, N.J., 1982; 28th Annual Hunterdon Art Center Juried exhibition, Clinton, N.J., 1981; Fire/Wood/Stone/Plastic, Summit Art Center, Summit, N.J., 1981; (one-person) Basking Ridge, N.J., 1981; Carrier Foundation National Competition, Carrier Foundation, Belle Mead, N.J., 1982.

WRITINGS: My Friend Andrew (juvenile; illustrated by Howard Berelson), Prentice-Hall, 1981; *The River Shares Its Secret* (textbook), Houghton, 1981; *Tumble Tumble Tumbleweed* (illustrated by Charles Robinson), A. Whitman, 1982. Poem appears in *Anthology of Writing by Women* (University of Chicago Press, 1980). Contributor to such publications as *Northshore, Primavera, Sackbut Review, Small Pond Review, WIND/Literary Journal,* and *Snippits: Pin Prick Press.*

WORK IN PROGRESS: Children's concept books; poetry; adult and middle grade nonfiction.

SIDELIGHTS: "My childhood seemed to revolve around fantasy in one form or another. My earliest memories are of playacting with my retired grandfather, who would stop everything for our games and to read to me. Our family had a puppet show that we took to various children's hospitals, schools, and orphanages. I became a radio actress at about the age of eight, and I felt very much a part of the theatrical world of Hollywood where we lived. We were neighbors to Deanna Durbin, W. C. Fields, and Cecil B. DeMille. My mother wrote radio plays, and my sister, Joan Lowery Nixon, has written many children's stories. She entertained us all as children.

"I majored in English with a view towards writing for publication. But, with an early marriage and five children coming over a seventeen-year span, my expression was limited to storytelling and poetry. During this time I continued to study fine art, which I pursue concurrently as a profession today.

PAT LOWERY COLLINS

"I began thinking seriously of publication when my youngest child entered first grade. My first book, *My Friend Andrew,* was published in January, 1981, and while progressing in the writing field, I have developed as a serious artist, exhibiting throughout New England, New Jersey and in New York City. A slide of my work, 'Chamber,' is in the permanent archives of the Smithsonian and is part of a traveling exhibition available to schools, museums, and libraries throughout the nation.

"Our family spends winters in New Hampshire and summers, for the past fourteen years, in Gloucester, where I operate a gallery by appointment. The sea figures into much of my work and has influenced our children's avocational choices. I swim and play tennis year-round, read a great deal, and enjoy early music and playing the recorder. We are presently restoring a Victorian farmhouse that's well over 100 years old."

As I was going to St. Ives,
I met a man with seven wives,
Each wife had seven sacks,
Each sack had seven cats,
Each cat had seven kits:
Kits, cats, sacks, and wives,
How many were there going to St. Ives?
—Nursery rhyme

CONOVER, Chris   1950-

PERSONAL: Born February 12, 1950, in New York, N.Y.; daughter of Robert (an artist) and Ruth (an artist; maiden name, Hageman) Conover; married Barry Lippman (a publisher), October 17, 1980; *Education:* Attended State University of New York at Buffalo, 1969-71. *Home:* 145 Arlington, Boston, Mass. 02116.

CAREER: Free-lance artist and book illustrator. *Member:* Graphic Artists Guild. *Awards, honors:* Recipient of Boston Globe-Horn Book honor award from the Boston Globe Newspaper Co., 1976, for *Six Little Ducks;* the American Institute of Graphic Arts Book Show cited *Where Did My Mother Go?* for

excellence in design and manufacture, 1979, *The Bear and the Kingbird,* 1979, *The Beast in the Bed,* 1981.

WRITINGS—For children: (Adaptor) *Six Little Ducks* (self-illustrated; *Horn Book* honor list), Crowell, 1976.

Illustrator; for children: Clyde R. Bulla, *The Wish at the Top,* Crowell, 1974; Roberta Silman, *Somebody Else's Child,* Warne, 1976; Dorothy J. Harris, *The School Mouse,* Warne, 1977; *The Gingerbread Boy,* Platt, 1977; Marilyn Ratner, *Plenty of Patches: An Introduction to Patchwork, Quilting, and Applique,* Crowell, 1978; Edna M. Preston, *Where Did My Mother Go?,* Four Winds Press, 1978; Brothers Grimm, *The Bear and the Kingbird,* translated by Lore Segal, Farrar, Straus, 1979; Margaret

His mother said, "I will never forget again." And she never did. ■(From *Where Did My Mother Go?* by Edna Mitchell Preston. Illustrated by Chris Conover.)

CHRIS CONOVER

Hodges, adaptor, *The Little Humpbacked Horse: A Russian Tale*, Farrar, Straus, 1980; Barbara Dillon, *The Beast in the Bed*, Morrow, 1981; Barbara Dillon, *What's Happened to Harry?*, Morrow, 1982.

SIDELIGHTS: "I grew up in New York City. Both my parents were artists, so my interest in drawing and painting developed early. Growing up in the city presents less opportunity to play outdoors, so books were a big part of my childhood. I think the strong impressions my books made on me was very important in my later decision to illustrate children's books. I work specifically for the child I was, and try actually to create a little world that is believable within its own context. I went on to study art in the High School of Music and Art and the State University of Buffalo.

"It wasn't until I left school and went out to live in Missoula, Montana, that I began to develop my ideas for children's books. While I was there, I wrote and illustrated *Six Little Ducks*. I brought it back to New York with me. Finally it was published. Since that time I have been a full-time freelance artist." [Lee Kingman and others, compilers, *Illustrators of Children's Books: 1967-1976*, Horn Book, 1978.]

COX, William R(obert) 1901-
(Joel Reeve)

BRIEF ENTRY: Born 1901, in Peapack, N.J. Professional writer. In addition to writing books for both adults and young adults, he has contributed more than one thousand stories to magazines, including *Saturday Evening Post, Collier's, This Week, Argosy, American Pic,* and *Blue Book.* He has also written several motion picture screenplays and scripts for more than one hundred television shows for the network programs "Fireside Theater," "Broken Arrow," "Bonanza," "Zane Grey Theater," "Route 66," and others. Cox is a member of the Western Writers of America, Academy of Magical Arts, Kansas Historical Society and Writers Guild of America, West. His books for young readers include *Five Were Chosen: A Basket Ball Story,* (under pseudonym Joel Reeve) *Goal Ahead, The Backyard Five, The Unbeatable Five, The Running Back, Game, Set, and Match, Battery Mates, Home Court Is Where You Find It,* and *The Fourth of July Kid. FOR MORE INFORMATION SEE:* Martha E. Ward and Dorothy A. Marquardt, editors, *Authors of Books for Young People,* second edition, Scarecrow Press, 1971; *Contemporary Authors,* Volumes 9-12, revised, Gale, 1974.

CRAFT, Ruth

BRIEF ENTRY: Born in Christchurch, New Zealand. Craft is an author of books for children. She began her career in 1968 as a television writer and has been employed by the British Broadcasting Corp. (BBC) as writer, advisor, and consultant to the children's television show, "Playschool." Her work with the BBC resulted in the publication of *Play School, Play Ideas* in 1971. Many of Craft's fictional books for children are written in rhymed verse, including her first picture book, *A Winter Bear,* which was a Junior Literary Guild selection. Her other books include *Peter Brueghel's "The Fair"*, 1975, *The King's Collection,* 1978, and *Carrie Hepple's Garden,* 1979.

CRANE, Barbara J. 1934-

PERSONAL: Born June 2, 1934, in Trenton, N.J.; daughter of Herman (a surgeon) and Elizabeth (a teacher; maiden name, Stein) Cohen; married Stuart G. Crane (a partner in Fahnestock and Co.), August 27, 1956; children: Susan Jill, Patricia Lynne. *Education:* Vassar College, B.A., 1956. *Residence:* Bucks County, Pa. *Office:* Crane Publishing Co., Trenton, N.J.

CAREER: Publisher and author. Trenton Public Schools, Trenton, N.J., teacher, 1956-58; Little People's Reading School, Yardley, Pa., principal, 1964-66; Newtown Friends School, Newton, Pa., reading consultant, 1966-67; Crane Publishing Co., Trenton N.J., founder and president, 1968—. Demonstration School for center city five-year-olds, Trenton State College, director, 1969. International lecturer in the teaching of reading, bilingual education, linguistics, English, and child psychology at colleges and universities, conferences, and public and private schools, 1968—. *Member:* International Reading Association, National Association for Bilingual Education, Vassar College Club. *Awards, honors:* Received grants from Vassar College, 1967-68, and Trenton State College, 1968-69.

WRITINGS—Series of comprehensive, basic reading programs; all published by Crane Publishing, except where noted: *Cat-*

BARBARA J. CRANE

egorical Sound System, Motivational Learning Program (now Crane Publishing), 1964, 1972; *Trenton State Kindergarten Study of Categorical Sound System,* Trenton State College, 1969; *Crane Reading System in Spanish,* 1975, 1978; *Crane Oral Dominance Test,* 1976, 1978; *Crane Reading System,* 1977; *Crane Reading System: PACER Program,* 1981; *Spanish Crane Reading System,* 1981.

Contributor to *Vassar Alumnae Magazine, The Reading Instruction Journal, Today's Catholic Teacher, Educational Leadership,* and *Perspectives.*

WORK IN PROGRESS: A fourth through six grade basic reading/literature program.

SIDELIGHTS: Crane began her teaching career in 1956 in Trenton, New Jersey. The majority of her students were Hispanic and Black ranging in age from six to ten. Crane tried to reach these students with traditional materials and teaching methods but failed. By the end of her first year as a teacher, she was creating her own materials. The Crane philosophy was to simplify the learning-to-read process by reducing the memory load, reducing the timeline to reach independent reading level, and therefore increasing success.

In 1968 she received a grant from the State of New Jersey to field test her materials in a study involving 2,000 pupils from four segments of the population: center city, semi-rural, sub-

urban, and private school. The result was that the experimental population of each segment significantly out-performed the control population. Young five-year-olds learned to read; ten-year-olds, with a past history of failure, learned to read. The program that was developed to teach the hard-to-reach proved to have merit with average and bright students who reached the independent reading level earlier than what was traditionally expected. When the field testing grant expired, the demand for Crane's materials increased. Subsequently she was instrumental in founding a publishing company to make these materials available.

When bilingual education became a reality in the 1970s, Crane became a major influence in the avant-garde movement of bilingual education in the United States. Crane designed the first basic, bilingual materials to be published by an American publishing company. (Programs were being imported that were not meeting the needs of students in the United States.)

Crane has continued to write materials that represent the latest trends in education and the insights of a master teacher. She has received much praise for creating child-oriented, self-motivational, logically-sequenced, success-oriented educational materials.

Crane enjoys public speaking and has taken part in talk shows on national radio and television from coast to coast. She has been the luncheon speaker and keynote speaker at many conferences and gives mini-courses at the college level as well as teacher-training at the elementary school level. Although much of her time is devoted to the running of Crane Publishing Company, public speaking and writing are very much a part of Crane's life.

FOR MORE INFORMATION SEE: Vassar Quarterly, Spring, 1973, Spring, 1977; *Instructor,* September, 1973, August, 1980, August, 1981, August, 1982; *Early Years,* October, 1973; *The Reading Teacher,* November, 1973, October, 1976; *Reading News Report,* February, 1973; *The Modern Language Journal,* April, 1977.

DANK, Milton   1920-

PERSONAL: Born September 12, 1920, in Philadelphia, Pa.; son of Charles (a barber) and Olga (Olessker) Dank; married Naomi Rand (a hospital administrator), March 18, 1954; children: Gloria, Joan. *Education:* University of Pennsylvania, B.A., 1947, Ph.D., 1953. *Politics:* "Unenthusiastic Democrat." *Religion:* "Diabolist (lapsed)." *Home:* 1022 Serpentine Ln., Wyncote, Pa. 19095.

CAREER: Owens-Illinois Glass, Toledo, Ohio, research physicist, 1953-56; General Electric (Aerospace), King of Prussia, Pa., research manager, 1958-72; research consultant in thermonuclear fusion power, laser applications, and space vehicle vulnerability, 1972—. *Military service:* U.S. Air Force, 1940-45; became first lieutenant. *Member:* American Physical Society, National World War II Glider Pilots, Authors Guild.

WRITINGS: The French Against the French, Lippincott, 1974; *The Glider Gang,* Lippincott, 1977; *The Dangerous Game,* Lippincott, 1977; *Games End,* Lippincott, 1979; *Khaki Wings,* Delacorte, 1980; *Red Flight Two,* Delacorte, 1981; *The Computer Caper,* Delacorte, 1983; *A UFO Has Landed,* Delacorte, 1983; *Albert Einstein,* Watts, 1983.

WORK IN PROGRESS: The further adventures of the Galaxy Gang.

SIDELIGHTS: "My books are all derived from my wartime experiences. *The French Against the French, The Dangerous Game,* and *Game's End* were based on my study of the behavior of the French under the German occupation.

"*The Glider Gang* is a tribute to the Allied glider pilots, my comrades-in-arm. They flew in fragile canvas and wood motorless craft at low altitudes over enemy guns, and brought in jeeps, howitzers and antitank guns to the paratroopers. Their casualties were high, as much from poor planning and faulty intelligence as from enemy resistance. They wore no parachutes because their passengers wore none. I thought it was wrong that their story should go untold.

"I wrote two books on flying in the first World War because of the similarity to glider combat in the second World War. These were novels about young men in the cauldron of war.

"*The Computer Caper* and *A UFO Has Landed* are the first two books in the Galaxy series. These tell of the adventures of a group of teenagers living in Philadelphia, some of whom are interested in the sciences and some in the arts.

Turning left on the roof, one came to the parapet and could look down on the balcony that ran around three sides of Number 93. ▪ (From *The Dangerous Game* by Milton Dank. Jacket illustration by Paul Bacon.)

MILTON DANK

"*Albert Einstein* is an attempt to explain the man and his work to teenagers. The importance of relativity theory to our view of the universe is stressed."

DAVIS, Hubert J(ackson) 1904-

PERSONAL: Born April 30, 1904, in Richlands, Va.; son of Harvey P. (a farmer) and Sarah (Horton) Davis; married Beulah Lily (a nurse), May 10, 1911 (died June 5, 1962); married Ruby Spicer (a librarian); children: (second marriage) Hubert Jackson. *Education:* Emory and Henry College, A.B., 1926; attended University of Virginia, 1932, 1936, Cornell University, 1962, and University of Colorado, 1963, George Peabody College, M.A., 1940. *Home:* 403 Leavell Rd., Portsmouth, Va. 23701.

CAREER: Coeburn High School, Coeburn, Va., head of science department, 1926-29; Cedar Bluff Junior High School, Cedar Bluff, Va., principal, 1929-32; Pocahontas Fuel Company, Amonate, Va., assistant store manager, 1932-33; Pocahontas High School, Pocahontas, Va., head of science department and assistant principal, 1933-40; Matthew Whaley High School, Williamsburg, Va., head of science department, 1940-42; College of William and Mary, Williamsburg, director of Marine Biology Educational Program and assistant professor of biology, 1942-45; Norfolk County public schools, Norfolk, Va., science supervisor and director of audio-visual program, 1945-49; Mississippi State College (now Mississippi State University), State College, Miss., assistant professor of education, 1949-52; Fredericksburg public schools, Fredericksburg, Va., director of instruction and assistant superintendant of schools, 1952-56; Portsmouth public schools, Portsmouth, Va., science and general supervisor, 1956-66; WHRO-TV, Norfolk, Va., science consultant, 1966-68. Consultant, Virginia Academy of Science, 1938-48; audio-visual consultant to U.S. State Department, 1952, and to Virginia State Board of Education; visiting professor, summers, at University of Virginia, 1942, 1944, University of Florida, 1945, 1951, Florida State University, 1946, University of New Hampshire, 1947, East Carolina Teachers College, 1948, and Mary Washington College, 1949; teacher of extension classes in education and audio-visual activities, 1956-66.

MEMBER: Portsmouth Torch Club (director, beginning 1970; president, beginning 1981), Portsmouth Friends of the Library (president, 1978), Portsmouth Reading Council, Common Cause, Rotary Club, Kiwanis Club, Lions Club, Portsmouth Family Life Service (consultant), Portsmouth Library Board (chairman). *Awards, honors:* Distinguished alumnus award from Emory and Henry College, 1976; distinguished service award from Virginia Academy of Science, 1981.

WRITINGS: The Great Dismal Swamp: Its History, Folklore and Science (illustrated by Donald L. Allen), Cavalier Press (Richmond, Va.), 1962, revised edition, Johnson Publishing Co. (Murfreesboro, N.C.), 1971; *Christmas in the Mountains: Southwest Virginia Christmas Customs and Their Origins* (il-

But when the wind is out of the west,
It sends every man the very best.

(From *A January Fog Will Freeze a Hog and Other Weather Folklore,* compiled and edited by Hubert Davis. Illustrated by John Wallner.)

HUBERT J. DAVIS

lustrated by Carolee Jackson), Johnson Publishing Co., 1972; *'Pon My Honor Hit's the Truth: Tall Tales from the Mountains* (illustrated by Jackson), Johnson Publishing Co., 1973; (editor) *The Silver Bullet, and Other American Witch Stories,* Jonathan Davis, 1975; (compiler and editor) *A January Fog Will Freeze a Hog, and Other Weather Folklore* (illustrated by John Wallner), Crown, 1977. Contributor of many articles to such periodicals as *National Education Association Journal, Science,* and *Virginia Journal of Education.*

WORK IN PROGRESS: Myths and Legends of Dismal Swamp; Animal Ditties; Folklore Ditties; Food Facts and Folklore; Ghost Stories of Virginia.

De GROAT, DIANE   1947-

PERSONAL: Born May 24, 1947, in Newton, N.J.; married Daniel Markham, 1975; children: Amanda Lee. *Education:* Attended Phoenix School of Design, New York, N.Y., 1964; Pratt Institute, B.F.A., 1969. *Address:* 44 Crawford St., Yonkers, N.Y. 10705. *Agent:* c/o Crown Publishers, One Park Ave., New York, N.Y. 10016.

CAREER: Holt, Rinehart & Winston (book publishers), Basic Reading Program project, New York City, 1969-72, began as book designer, became art director; free-lance illustrator of books for children, 1971—. Work has been exhibited in shows, including those at the Society of Illustrators Annual National Exhibition, New York City, 1973, 1975, American Institute of Graphic Arts Annual Book Show, New York, N.Y., 1978, and the Art Directors Club, New York, N.Y., 1974.

WRITINGS: Alligator's Toothache (juvenile; self-illustrated; Junior Literary Guild selection), Crown, 1977.

Illustrator; all for children: Eleanor L. Clymer, *Luke Was There,* Holt, 1973; Elinor Parker, *Four Seasons, Five Senses,* Scribner, 1974; Marcia Newfield, *A Book for Jodan,* Atheneum, 1975; Lucy Bate, *Little Rabbit's Loose Tooth,* Crown, 1975; Mamie Hegwood, *My Friend Fish,* Holt, 1975; Anne Snyder, *Nobody's Family,* Holt, 1975; Miriam B. Young, *Truth and Consequences,* Four Winds Press, 1975; Sylvia Sunderlin, *Antrim's Orange,* Scribner, 1976; Maria Polushkin, *Bubba and Babba: Based on a Russian Folktale,* Crown, 1976; Harriett M. Luger, *Chasing Trouble,* Viking, 1976; Kathryn F. Ernst, *Mr. Tamarin's Trees,* Crown, 1976; Anne Eve Bunting, *One More Flight,* Warne, 1976; K.F. Ernst, *Owl's New Cards,* Crown, 1977; Ann Tompert, *Badger on His Own,* Crown, 1978; Tobi Tobias, *How Your Mother and Father Met, and What Happened After,* McGraw, 1978; Lois Lowry, *Anastasia Krupnik,* Houghton, 1979; Seymour Simon, *Animal Fact/Animal Fable,* Crown, 1979; Elizabeth T. Billington, *Part-Time Boy,* Warne, 1980; Valerie Flournoy, *The Twins Strike Back,* Dial, 1980; L. Lowry, *Anastasia Again!,* Houghton, 1981; Christine McDonnell, *Don't Be Mad, Ivy,* Dial, 1981; Barbara Dillon, *Who Needs a Bear?,* Morrow, 1981; Lynn Luderer, *The Toad Intruder,* Houghton, 1982; C. McDonnell, *Toad Food and Measle Soup,* Dial, 1982; Jo Anna Hurwitz, *Tough Luck Karen,* Morrow, 1981; Susan Shreve, *Bad Dreams of a Good Girl,* Knopf, 1982; L. Lowry, *Anastasia At Your Service,* Houghton, 1982.

SIDELIGHTS: De Groat grew up in a small New Jersey town. She began taking painting lessons at the age of seven. As a junior in high school, she won a six-week summer scholarship to the New York Phoenix School of Design. "I was excited

DIANE de GROAT

by the professionalism of the school. We took trips to the Metropolitan Museum, which became my second home for years afterward. I won another scholarship in my senior year—this time to attend college at Pratt Institute.''

''Though always interested in art as a child, my arrival at Pratt, via a Dean's Scholarship, opened new doors and cast a new perspective on the dimensions of the field. Most of my freshman year was spent with a sketchbook as I explored the city. Courses such as photography, illustration and life drawing were pursued intensely and were to be the foundation for the work that I do today.'' [Lee Kingman and others, compilers, *Illustrators of Children's Books: 1967-1976,* Horn Book, 1978.[1]]

After graduation from Pratt Institute, De Groat worked as a book designer at Holt, Rinehart & Winston. ''Now comes the Cinderella part. I was broke and staying with friends in a one-room apartment while trying to peddle my talent. This included selling all the drawings I had done in school for one dollar each. My paintings were hung in the home of a friend of a friend. This friend had another friend who happened to be the head of a basic reading program that was about to start at Holt,

Rinehart & Winston. He asked that I bring my portfolio to the art director as they were looking for designers.''

''. . . I began work as a book designer. . . . On weekends I tried my hand at illustrating for the reading program and found a warm reception for my work. This led to my first published work. By the time I left in 1971 to become a freelance illustrator, I had a portfolio of published art work, and began eventually to receive work from other publishers.

''My work has developed along several lines. My picture books enable me to explore the world of fantasy, while the novels I've illustrated are very realistic in style. For these books, I have found that the use of live models enables me to create a greater sense of realism. . . . Today my work in fine art is an infusion of these two styles''[1]

Working with her editor at Crown Publishers, De Groat wrote her first book in 1977. ''*Alligator's Toothache* in its rough form was a dream I had around that time. Ms. Sawicki [editor] was undergoing extensive dental work, so I guess I associated Crown with teeth. Together we worked to bring Alligator's story to its final form.''

When Antrim came into the schoolroom the next morning he was afraid to look, but there was the orange still on Miss Pemberton's desk. ■ (From *Antrim's Orange* by Sylvia Sunderlin. Illustrated by Diane de Groat.)

(From *Alligator's Toothache* by Diane de Groat. Illustrated by the author.)

DE ROUSSAN, Jacques 1929-

BRIEF ENTRY: Born in 1929, in Paris, France. Author, journalist, and art critic. De Roussan graduated from the Sorbonne with a master's degree in history and geography. Following graduation, he eventually located a position at a printing plant in Canada, where he stayed for two years. He then went to work as a proofreader on a weekly newspaper, *Le Petit Journal,* and six months later, was named editor of the magazine section. In 1959 he and a group of his co-workers founded *Perspectives,* a bi-weekly magazine, of which De Roussan is managing editor. He is also founder and editor of *Vient de Paraitre,* a quarterly publication about books in French Canada, and former editor of *Vie des Arts,* a magazine of art criticism and appreciation published in Montreal. De Roussan received the Amelia Frances Howard-Gibbon Medal in 1973 from the Canadian Library Association for his children's book *Au dela du soleil/Beyond the Sun.* He wrote another book for children, *If I Came from Mars: Si J'etais Martien. For More Information See:* Irma McDonough, editor, *Profiles,* Canadian Library Association, 1975.

DIRKS, Rudolph   1877-1968

BRIEF ENTRY: Born February 26, 1877, in Heide, Germany; died April 20, 1968, in New York. Dirks, a cartoonist, came to the United States at the age of seven; by the time he was seventeen, he had published works in both *Judge* and *Life.* In 1897 while working at the *New York Journal,* he originated one of the most influential and popular comic strips in American history, the "Katzenjammer Kids." Dirks created the characters of Hans and Fritz amidst a war for circulation power between Joseph Pulitzer, owner of the *New York World,* and William Randolph Hearst, owner of the *Journal.* Following his service in the Spanish-American War, he took his artwork to the *World,* thereby setting into motion a struggle over publication rights between himself and Hearst. After a celebrated court battle, Hearst retained rights to the comic strip under the original title while Dirks was allowed to continue his work under another title. Thus, the "Katzenjammer Kids" became "Hans and Fritz," later to be changed to "Captain and the Kids" due to anti-German sentiments during World War I.

Dirks's style and innovative use of balloons and consecutive panels had a profound effect on the development of the comic strip. He was also involved in several artists' movements, including the "Ash Can School," and was co-founder of the artists' colony at Ogunquit, Maine. In his later years, much of the work on his strip was done by his son, John, who became the official artist following his father's death in 1968. The antics of the Katzenjammer Kids were presented in book form in several publications, including *The Cruise of the Katzenjammer Kids* and *Komical Katzenjammers. For More Information See: The Art of the Comic Strip,* University of Maryland, 1971; *World Encyclopedia of Comics,* Volume 1, Chelsea House, 1976. *Obituaries: New York Times,* April 22, 1968; *Time,* May 3, 1968; *Newsweek,* May 6, 1968.

DIXON, Jeanne   1936-
(Mary Wood Harper, Josephine Rector Stone)

PERSONAL: Born July 18, 1936, in Two Medicine, Mont.; daughter of Phil E. (a rancher) and Mary (a baker; maiden name, Whipple) Parker; children: Andrea, James. *Education:* Attended University of Denver and University of Montana. *Religion:* Protestant. *Address:* Box 5542, Missoula, Mont. 59806. *Agent:* Wendy Weil, Julian Bach Literary Agency, Inc., 747 Third Ave., New York, N.Y. 10017.

CAREER: Has worked as a teacher in Visalia, Ky., and Terminous, Calif. Has also worked as a cemetery salesman, a city directory interviewer, a janitor and a cook for the National Park Service.

WRITINGS—For young people; all published by Atheneum: (With Bradford Angier) *Ghost of Spirit River,* 1968; (under pseudonym Josephine Rector Stone) *Those Who Fall from the Sun* (fantasy; illustrated by Mal Luber), 1978; (under pseudonym J. R. Stone) *Praise All the Moons of Morning* (fantasy), 1979; (under pseudonym J. R. Stone) *Green Is for Galanx* (fantasy), 1980; (under pseudonym J. R. Stone) *The Mudhead* (fantasy), 1980; *Lady Cat Lost* (illustrated by Troy Howell), 1981.

WORK IN PROGRESS: Three contemporary romances for Ballantine under pseudonym Mary Wood Harper; a book about bicycle motocross racing for Atheneum.

SIDELIGHTS: "I was born in North Central Montana at the edge of the Blackfeet Reservation. My father was a trapper, a herder, an old-time mountain man, wise, humorous, tender-hearted. He became foreman of a large sheep ranch and my earliest years were spent in the company of animals. We had so much land we could not see to the end of it, so much land we could not cover it in two days on horseback. Such space was always a glory to me, and I think to my father, but it was a great trial to my mother who loved parties and conversation. I will always think of her there in our two-room house teaching me to conjugate Latin verbs and how to dance the Big Apple. This was at the end of the Depression, and there were no libraries, no bookstores. Just the same, my mother managed to find me the complete works of Dickens, and she read aloud to me every night from Dickens and from the Bible. At that time I had very few real people in my life. Apart from my parents and a baby brother, I had a sheepherder for a friend. His name was Old Sam.

"Nobody knew where Old Sam came from. He blew in on a blast of wind one day and asked my father for a job. He looked to me like Santa Claus, except that he wore bib overalls in place of the red and white suit. He had a long white beard, long white hair tumbling from his head, and a felt fedora that must have seen thirty years of weather. Old Sam was in charge of the 'hospital band,' sheep that were kept close in to the ranch. This meant that I could go out and talk to him. In those days, I rode a big sorrel gelding, named Scorpion, or sometimes a black mare, one of a work team. My dog always went with me, and five or six bum lambs (orphaned lambs) and my black cat, Boots, who usually had any number of kittens. Together we would make our way across the prairie to where Old Sam sat guarding the sheep.

"Old Sam was a most unusual man. He told me about foreign countries, taught me about other languages, other customs. He gave me some books about Baffin Bay, about the Congo, about Siam, and Tibet. My mother told me he had once been a professor at a university. And maybe he was. Every winter he disappeared and then I would have imaginary friends to visit with. These friends were always people from the far-off countries that Old Sam had told me about.

"Our lives were fairly simple then. We had no electricity, no indoor plumbing, no roads, no neighbors for thirty miles. Old Lady Flat Tail was our nearest neighbor, and she looked after me when my parents went away on business, buying sheep, or selling wool, or looking at tractors. Old Lady Flat Tail was a lady witch doctor and always had strange things bubbling in pots. She taught me cures for diseases and taught me charms to make me strong. She was a good person, I'm sure, but I was always very glad when my parents came along to pick me up.

"In addition to these two people, I had a friend named Charlie. Charlie was a year-around hand. Charlie liked to have good times. He took me fishing along the river, he took me riding back into the badlands, and in the winter he liked to go sledding. I loved these activities, most of all I liked to go into the badlands because they were always an adventure. There were strange rock formations that looked like castles, forts, and bridges. There were miles and miles of low hills made of sparkling quartz, mica, and sandstone. There were miles of low plain where we could pick up ancient dinosaur eggs and dinosaur bones. There were also a great many rattlesnakes, and coyotes. Once we found a nest of outlaws hiding out.

"When it was time for me to enter the first grade, I had to leave the ranch and go into town. This was terrible for me, because not only did I have to leave my animals and friends behind, but I did not understand about streets, or streetlights, or other children. My teacher warned me I must never jaywalk or I would go to jail. I thought this meant I was not supposed to walk like a bird, and I was very, very careful never to hop on the sidewalk—at least not in the sight of a policeman. I hated towns, I hated the school, and I was glad when my father moved us to the western slope of the Rockies.

"On the western slope, my father bought a very large farm, for very little money. In those days land was dirt-cheap. I went to a wonderful school in the country. It had only one room for eight grades, but we had a genius of a teacher. She believed that children would want to learn if they were given the opportunity, so she filled eight boxes with the books and materials for all eight grades and we could progress through the grades at our own speed. If we ran into trouble she would help us out. If a second grader was interested in what the seventh or sixth grade was doing, that person could go and sit with that grade. We were never forbidden to learn, rather we were encouraged to learn. In the mornings we did our homework and in the afternoons we prepared scenery, costumes, etc. for plays that we would put on for the local farming community. While we worked at the plays, our teacher, Mrs. Grace Hansen would read the most wonderful books to us: *King of the Golden River, Uncle Tom's Cabin, Tom Sawyer*. She was a wonderful reader and it was so cozy to sit by the fire in the old Ben Franklin and listen to her read while blizzards raged outside. Sometimes too, she would go into the teacherage, where she lived, and bake cookies or make popcorn for us. If there was any farm dog out in the storm, cold and lonely, she would let him in to sit by the fire with us while we ate popcorn and cookies and worked on properties for the play. In that one year I progressed through all eight grades in every subject except math, at which I was always very poor.

"Eventually my father sold the farm and we moved closer to town. This was a terrible catastrophe for me because I went from an environment of freedom and learning to the stifling atmosphere of a city school where we were praised for conformity and scorned for any show of individuality. In art classes, for instance, we had to make exactly the same picture, exactly the same color, at the exact same moment that the teacher made hers. I was so bored I was sick. My only escape was through my imagination. When the teacher thought that I was a good girl for following her instructions to the letter, I was actually off in a world of my own making, a world peopled with strange creatures: giant lizards, psychic dogs, and mud heads. It was at this time that I began to write. I wrote to escape the unbearable boredom of those city schools. The only good thing was that we lived close enough to town that my mother allowed me to take out a library card and the librarian allowed me four books every two weeks. This was the first time that I had ever had books to read, except the few we had at home and the few that we had had in our school.

"Years later, I took writing courses in college. I got to see nearly all the countries that Old Sam used to tell me about, and I studied many languages. I still think about Old Sam, and Old Lady Flat Tail, and Charlie, and of course I have a good many animals of my own. I have two children, and sometimes it strikes me how very different their childhood is from my

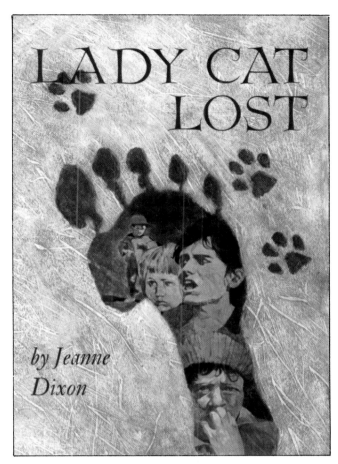

(From *Lady Cat Lost* by Jeanne Dixon. Jacket illustration by Troy Howell.)

own. Although we still live in Montana, Montana has changed, and that makes all the difference."

HOBBIES AND OTHER INTERESTS: Volunteer work, gardening, photography, reading, travel, teaching classes in writing, supporting bicycle motocross.

DOLAN, Edward F(rancis), Jr. 1924-

BRIEF ENTRY: Born February 10, 1924, in Oakland, Calif. Dolan is an author of books for children covering a wide variety of topics from historical and sports biographies to "how to" and "beginner" books. Throughout his career, he has been employed as a free-lance radio and television writer, teacher of communications, reporter, and director of publications. Dolan began writing at an early age, publishing his first story at sixteen. He has since written over twenty books for children, among them *Pasteur and the Invisible Giants, Jenner and the Miracle of Vaccine, The Complete Beginner's Guide to Ice Skating, Amnesty: The American Puzzle, Janet Guthrie: First Woman Driver at Indianapolis*, and *Adolf Hitler: A Portrait in Tyranny. Disaster 1906: The San Francisco Earthquake and Fire* was a Junior Literary Guild selection, 1967. *Agent:* Barthold Fles Literary Agency, 507 Fifth Ave., New York, N.Y. 10017. *For More Information See: Contemporary Authors*, Volumes 33-36, revised, Gale, 1978; *Authors of Books for Young People*, 2nd edition, supplement, Scarecrow, 1979.

EDWARDS, Audrey 1947-

BRIEF ENTRY: Born April 21, 1947, in Tacoma, Wash. Magazine editor and author of children's books. Edwards began her career in New York City in 1970 as an associate editor on the staff of *Redbook* magazine. She went to Columbia University in 1972 as editor for the Urban Center, remaining in that post until 1973. From 1974 to 1977 she worked as promotion editor for Fairchild Publications. She was hired by *Black Enterprise* magazine in 1977, where she served as a senior editor, leaving in 1978. Since that time Edwards has been the senior editor at *Family Circle* magazine. She was awarded the Coretta Scott King Fellowship in 1969, from the American Association of University Women. Edwards has also been a member of the National Association of Black Journalists, holding the post of program chairman for its New York chapter as well. Her books for children are *The Picture Life of Muhammad Ali*, *The Picture Life of Bobby Orr*, *The Picture Life of Stevie Wonder*, and *Muhammad Ali, the People's Champ*. *Home:* 195 Claremont Ave., New York, N.Y. 10027. *For More Information See: Black Enterprise*, December, 1978; *Contemporary Authors*, Volumes 81-84, Gale, 1979.

EDWARDS, Dorothy 1914-1982

OBITUARY NOTICE—See sketch in *SATA* Volume 4: Born November 6, 1914, in Teddington, Middlesex, England; died August 9, 1982, in Reigate, Surrey, England. A children's author and scriptwriter, Edwards wrote the "Naughty Little Sister" book series. Among the books in that series are *My Naughty Little Sister*, *My Naughty Little Sister's Friends*, *My Naughty Little Sister Goes Fishing*, and *My Naughty Little Sister and Bad Harry's Rabbit*. Edwards also wrote scripts for the British Broadcasting Corporation series "Listen to Mother," radio plays, including "The Girl Who Wanted to Eat Boys" and "The Old Woman Who Lived in a Vinegar Bottle," and books for young adults. At one time, Edwards was an editor and producer for the BBC radio station in London. In 1975, she received the Children's Rights Workship Other Award. Edwards lectured widely in England to promote her ideas about encouraging children to read. *For More Information See: Contemporary Authors*, Volumes 25-28, revised Gale, 1977; *International Authors and Writers Who's Who*, 8th edition, International Biographical Centre, 1977; *Twentieth-Century Children's Writers*, St. Martin's, 1978; *The Writer's Directory, 1982-1984*, Gale, 1981. *Obituaries: London Times*, August 12, 1982.

EISNER, Will(iam Erwin) 1917-
(Will Erwin, Willis Rensie)

PERSONAL: Born March 6, 1917, in New York, N.Y.; son of Samuel (a furrier) and Fannie (Ingber) Eisner; married Ann Louise Weingarten, June 15, 1950; children: John David, Alice Carol (deceased). *Education:* Attended Art Students League, 1935. *Home and office:* Will Eisner Studios, Inc., 51 Winslow Rd., White Plains, N.Y. 10606.

CAREER: Author, cartoonist, publisher. *New York American*, New York, N.Y., staff artist, 1936; Eisner and Iger, New York, N.Y. president, partner, founder, 1937; Eisner-Arnold Comic Group, New York, N.Y., founder, partner, 1940-46; author and cartoonist, syndicated newspaper feature, "The Spirit,"

1940-52; American Visual Corp., founder, president, and publisher, 1949; founder and producer of *P.S. Magazine*, 1950-71; creator of "Job Scene," a series of career guidance comic booklets, 1967; creator of comic strips, under name Will Eisner and pseudonyms Will Erwin and Willis Rensie, "Muss 'em Up Donovan," "The Three Brothers," "K-51," "Hawk of the Seas," "Sheena," "Blackhawk," and "Uncle Sam," and author of newspaper feature, "Odd Facts." President, Bell McClure North American Newspaper Alliance, 1962-64; executive vice-president, Koster-Dana Corp., 1962-64; president, Educational Supplements Corp., 1965-72; chairman of the board, Croft Educational Services Corp, 1972-73; president, IPD Publishing Co., Inc.; member of the faculty of School of Visual Arts, 1973—; member of the board of directors, Westchester Philharmonic. *Military service:* U.S. Army Ordnance, 1942-45. *Member:* Princeton Club (New York City). *Awards, honors:* The National Cartoonist Society named Eisner comic book artist of the year, 1967, 1968, and 1969; recipient of annual award for quality of art in comic books from the Society of Comic Art Research, 1968; International Cartoonist Award, 1974; named to Hall of Fame of the Comic Book Academy.

WRITINGS—Of interest to young people; all self-illustrated: *Dating and Hanging Out*, Baronet, 1979; *Funny Jokes and Foxy Riddles*, Baronet, 1979; *One Hundred and One Half Wild and Crazy Jokes*. Baronet, 1979; *Spaced-Out Jokes*, Baronet, 1979.

Other: *A Pictorial Arsenal of America's Combat Weapons*, Sterling, 1960; *America's Space Vehicles: A Pictorial Review*, edited by Charles Kramer, Sterling, 1962; *A Contract with God, and Other Tenement Stories*, Baronet, 1978; (with P. R. Garriock and others) *Masters of Comic Book Art*, Images Graphiques, 1978; *Odd Facts*, Ace Books, 1978; *"The City": A Narrative Portfolio*, Holy Graphic Press, 1981; *Life on Another Planet*, Kitchen Sink, 1981.

For U.S. Department of Defense, creator of comic strip instructional aid, *P.S. Magazine*, 1950, and for U.S. Department of Labor, creator of career guidance series of comic booklets, "Job Scene," 1967.

WORK IN PROGRESS: A textbook, *Comics and Sequential Art; Big City Portrait*.

SIDELIGHTS: Eisner, who is well known today as a pioneer in the educational applications of comics and cartoon strips, originally wanted to become a stage designer. While attending the Art Students League in New York City, however, he studied under George Bridgeman, which led to a staff job on the *New York American*.

"Early in 1937, a little over a year out of high school I heard about a magazine called *WOW*. It was publishing an assortment of cartoon features and was using unknown artists and cartoonists. I went down to see them and sold my first comic feature, an adventure story called 'Scott Dalton.'

"The magazine's format was rather loose and they did not seem to care that it had a continuing story. Within three issues *WOW* collapsed. But this brief affair was, for me, the doorway into the world of comics. Not only did it afford me my first publishing opportunity, but it gave me my first glimpse of the phenomenon of an emerging genre. I was standing at the confluence of the forces of 'lack of material' and the 'felt need' of a public hungry for visual literature. They were converging and I was there . . . a witness to a birth if you will.

"It was clear that there soon would be a need for complete stories. The magazines were all monthlies and would not sustain serialization as had the daily or weekly periodicals of the past. And the need for new features was, it appeared, unlimited. All the newspaper strips were committed and the pulp publishers were coming into this new market with no real experience in comics. So the receptivity for innovation was enormous. At Eisner & Iger, a company I quickly formed with the former editor of the now defunct *WOW* we began to devise comics on these frames. Its features were a compound of the pulp or short story mode in the language of comic strips.''

Since 1938 Eisner has produced a host of comic book characters to guide young people in a career choice, to instruct military personnel, and simply to entertain children. Eisner has also produced a series of comic book training booklets for developing nations. These booklets, which teach modern farming, techniques and the maintenance of military equipment, are now being used by the Agency for International Development, the United Nations, and the U.S. Department of Defense.

In 1950 Eisner founded *P.S. Magazine,* which produced instructional comics for industry, and in 1967 he created a series of guidance books used in schools and government employment agencies called ''Job Scene.'' ''The use of comic books for instructional purposes was expanded after 1950. Industry utilized this communication form, as did church groups, political parties, and social agencies. This coincided with extensive buying of entertainment comics—millions were sold on the newsstands and billions more were printed.

''In 1967, yet another breakthrough occurred. The U.S. Department of Labor, in its search for reading devices to attract school dropouts, commissioned a comic book. In its support of behavioral sciences, the department provided a grant which resulted in a series called 'Job Scene,' designed to introduce vocations to young people, particularly the disadvantaged. This series is now widely used in schools, state employment centers, and job counseling agencies.

''Comics are presently undergoing changes. Serial strips devoted to adventure are disappearing from newspapers. Today's newspaper strip encourages quick reading and instant humor without the need for reading yesterday's installment. Adventure stories are mainly found on newsstands. The-over-the-counter comics are reaching new readers with social and 'adult' themes. Elsewhere, underground comics are feeding our subcultures.

''The significance of comics as a training device is perhaps not so much the use of time-honored sequential art as the language accompanying the pictures. For example, *P.S. Magazine,* composed largely of information existing in the formal texts of the *Technical Manuals (TMS),* employed the soldier's argot, rendering militarese into common language. The magazine said, 'Clean away the crud from the flywheel,' instead of 'All foreign matter should be removed from the surface of the flywheel and rubber belt which it supports. . . .'

''*P.S. Magazine* survived early resistance by traditionalists and became a respected instrument. . . . With a monthly printing of 200,000 copies and circulation from military unit libraries (at least five readers per copy), *P.S. Magazine* has been invaluable in training some ten million soldiers. This impact on a generation's reading habits cannot be ignored.

''The series widely used in counseling youth, 'Job Scene,' has proven so successful that several publishers now produce similar material. This further underscores the excellent record

WILL EISNER

achieved when sequential-picture technique is combined with vocabulary which speaks in *the reader's terms!*

''Critics of comics have complained that while educators are trying to teach the proper use of language, comic books and strips are violating every rule. This is an understandable criticism, but it is based on the assumption that cartoons are designed primarily to teach language. *Comics are a message in themselves!*

''Characters' words spoken in overhead balloons are precise. They promote imagery and realism and have the economy of a telegram. The balloon language of comics is a soundtrack rather than a documentation. Word expressions emerging from the changing patterns of our lives are quickly assimilated and recycled.

''New words and phonetic mutants enliven and broaden our lexicon. *'Pow! Zap! Bam!'* enrich articulation in a real world that sometimes confounds standard usage. 'Good English' out of the mouth of a comic character caught in a cataclysmic situation would be unbelievable to the reader. To readers living in the ghetto and playing in the street and the school yard, comic books with their inventive language, argot, and slang serve as no other literature does.

''Comic books have appeared in school systems since 1948. Emanating from industry or special interests, they have been used as supplemental or enrichment material. The traditional resistance by educators to the use of comics as a formal teaching tool is now changing.

"Indeed, it is remarkable that reading teachers have been slow in adopting this inviting material. Armed with sophisticated diagnostic techniques and working under the demands of accountability, teachers now seem ready to employ the existing unorthodox comic book for instruction purposes.

"In schools, comic strip reprints are reaching reluctant readers who are either unresponsive or hostile to traditional books. . . .

"Certain qualities distinctive to comic books support their educational importance. Perhaps their most singular characteristic is *timeliness*. Comics appeal to readers when they deal with 'now' situations or treat them in a 'now' manner.

"A good comic story must have an exciting layout and novel characterization. The plot is secondary to visual impact, but ideas are important." [Will Eisner, "Comic Books in the Library," *Library Journal*, October 15, 1974.]

"My current interest, as it has been throughout my career, is devoted to the exploration of the potential of sequential art ('comics'). It is a valid literary form in which the artist (writer) writes the visuals. It is a unique form that employs commonly understood imagery and words in a special mix and is capable of dealing with themes far more sophisticated than we have seen. I hope to be able to continue this effort . . . contribute to and be part of the growing recognition of this literary/art form by the arbiters of our culture in the coming years."

FOR MORE INFORMATION SEE: Library Journal, October 15, 1974.

EPSTEIN, Beryl (Williams) 1910-
(Beryl Williams; joint pseudonyms with
Samuel Epstein: Adam Allen, Douglas
Coe, Martin Colt, Charles Strong)

PERSONAL: Born November 15, 1910, in Columbus, Ohio; daughter of Oswald Oliver and Iona (Frankenberg) Williams; married Samuel Epstein (a writer) April 26, 1938. *Education:* Douglass College, Rutgers University, Litt.B., 1932. *Address:* P.O. Box 1042, Southold, N.Y. 11971. *Agent:* McIntosh & Otis, Inc., 18 East 41st St., New York, N.Y. 10017.

CAREER: Daily Home News and Sunday Times, New Brunswick, N.J., reporter, editor, 1933-37; Federal Writers Project of New Jersey, editor, 1937-38; *American Scholar*, associate editor, 1938-42; free-lance writer of youth books, mainly in collaboration with husband, 1942—.

WRITINGS—With husband, Samuel Epstein; under joint pseudonym Adam Allen: *Tin Lizzie*, Stackpole, 1937; *Printer's Devil*, Macmillan, 1939; *Dynamo Farm*, Lippincott, 1942; *Water to Burn*, Lippincott, 1943; *Dollar a Share*, Random House, 1943; *New Broome Experiment*, Lippincott, 1944.

With S. Epstein; under joint pseudonym Douglas Coe: *Marconi: Pioneer of Radio*, Messner, 1943; *Road to Alaska*, Messner, 1943; *Burma Road*, Messner, 1946.

Under name Beryl Williams, except as noted: *Fashion Is Our Business*, Lippincott, 1945; *People Are Our Business*, Lippincott, 1947; *Lillian Wald: Angel of Henry Street*, Messner, 1948; *No Pattern for Love*, Messner, 1951; *Young Faces in Fashion*, Lippincott, 1956; (under name Beryl Epstein) *Lucky, Lucky*

White Horse, Harper, 1965; (with Dorritt Davis, under name Beryl Epstein) *Two Sisters and Some Hornets*, Holiday House, 1971.

With S. Epstein; under joint pseudonym Charles Strong: *Stranger at the Inlet*, Messner, 1946.

With S. Epstein; under joint pseudonym Martin Colt: *Secret of Baldhead Mountain*, Messner, 1946; *The Riddle of the Hidden Pesos*, Messner, 1948.

With S. Epstein; under name Beryl Epstein, except as noted: (Under name Beryl Williams) *Miracles from Microbes: The Road to Streptomycin*, Rutgers University Press, 1946; (under name B. Williams) *The Great Houdini*, Messner, 1950; (under name B. Williams) *The Rocket Pioneers*, Messner, 1955; (with S. Epstein and John Gunther) *Meet North Africa*, Harper, 1956; *Prehistoric Animals*, Watts, 1956; (under name B. Williams) *Francis Marion, Swamp Fox of the Revolution*, Messner, 1956; *The Andrews Raid*, Coward, 1956; (with S. Epstein and J. Gunther) *Meet South Africa*, Harper 1958; *Jackknife for a Penny*, Coward, 1958; *Change for a Penny*, Coward, 1959.

George Washington Carver (illustrated by William Moyers), Garrard, 1960; (under name B. Williams) *Plant Explorer: David Fairchild*, Messner, 1961; *Grandpa's Wonderful Glass*, Wonder Books, 1962; *Junior Science Book of Seashells*, Garrard, 1963; (under name B. Williams) *Pioneer Oceanographer: Alexander Agassiz*, Messner, 1963; *The Story of the International Red Cross*, T. Nelson, 1963; *Spring Holidays*, Garrard, 1964; *Hurricane Guest*, Random House, 1964; (under name B. Williams) *Medicine from Microbes* (Junior Literary Guild selection), Messner, 1965; *The Game of Baseball*, Garrard, 1965; *Stories of Champions*, Garrard, 1965; *Young Paul Revere's Boston*, Garrard, 1966; *The Sacramento: Golden River of California*, Garrard 1968; *Harriet Tubman: Guide to Freedom*, Garrard, 1968; *European Folk Festivals: A Holiday Book*, Garrard, 1968; *The Picture Book of F.D.R.*, Watts, 1969; *Take This Hammer*, Hawthorn, 1969; *Who Says You Can't?*, Coward, 1969; *Who Needs Holes?*, Hawthorn, 1969.

Enrico Fermi: Father of Atomic Power, Garrard, 1970; *Michael Faraday: Apprentice to Science*, Garrard, 1971; *Winston Churchill: Lion of Britain*, Garrard, 1971; *Pick It Up* (illustrated by Tomie de Paola), Holiday House, 1971; *Look in the Mirror*, Holiday House, 1971; *Hold Everything*, Holiday House, 1973; *Charles de Gaulle: Defender of France*, Garrard, 1973; *More Stories of Baseball Champions: In the Hall of Fame*, Garrard, 1973; *A Year of Japanese Festivals* (illustrated by Gordon Laite), Garrard, 1974; *Jackie Robinson: Baseball's Gallant Fighter*, Garrard, 1974; *Willie Mays: Baseball's Superstar* (illustrated by Victor Mays), Garrard, 1975; *Henry Aaron: Home-Run King*, Garrard, 1975; *Saving Electricity*, Garrard, 1977; *Mr. Peale's Mammoth* (Junior Literary Guild selection; illustrated by Martim Abillez), Coward, 1977; *Dr. Beaumont and the Man with the Hole in His Stomach* (illustrated by Joseph Serotani), Coward, 1978; *Secret in a Sealed Bottle* (illustrated by Jane Sterrett), Coward, 1979; *She Never Looked Back: Margaret Mead in Samoa* (Junior Literary Guild selection; illustrated by Victor Juhasz), Coward, 1980; *Kids in Court: The ACLU Defends Their Rights*, Four Winds, 1982.

"The Real Book of" series; all with S. Epstein; all published by Garden City Books: *The Real Book of Inventions*, 1951; *. . . Benjamin Franklin*, 1952; *. . . Pirates*, 1952; *. . . Alaska*, 1952; *. . . Spies*, 1953; *. . . the Sea*, 1954; *. . . Submarines*, 1954.

Then he laid a cloth dressing over the whole wound, pressing it firmly against the lung and the hole in the stomach. There was little more he could do, he thought. ■ (From *Dr. Beaumont and the Man with the Hole in His Stomach* by Sam and Beryl Epstein. Illustrated by Joseph Scrofani.)

"The First Book of" series all with S. Epstein; all published by Watts: *The First Book of Electricity*, 1953, revised, 1966 and 1977; . . . *Words*, 1954; . . . *Hawaii*, 1954; . . . *Printing*, 1955, revised, 1974; . . . *Glass*, 1955; . . . *Mexico*, 1955, revised, 1967 and 1982; . . . *Codes and Ciphers*, 1956; . . . *Italy*, 1958; revised, 1972; . . . *Maps and Globes*, 1959; . . . *Measurement*, 1960; . . . *the Ocean*, 1961; . . . *Washington, D.C.*, 1961, revised, 1981; . . .*Teaching Machines*, 1961; . . .

The World Health Organizaton, 1964; . . . *Switzerland*, 1964; . . . *News*, 1965.

"All About" series; all with S. Epstein; all published by Random House: *All About the Desert*, 1957; . . . *Prehistoric Cave Men*, 1959; . . . *Engines and Power*, 1962.

SIDELIGHTS: "I have been writing books for children and

young people, usually in collaboration with my husband since before we were married.

"We are both interested in facts—in what makes things work, in why things happen—and therefore most of what we write is nonfiction. But we enjoy trying our hands at a story once in a while. We especially enjoyed writing *Jackknife for a Penny* and *Change for a Penny*, two novels for young people laid in our part of Long Island during the Revolution. And I found great pleasure in drawing on an experience of my own childhood for *Lucky, Lucky White Horse*.

"Writing the kind of books we do gives us the chance to travel, which we both love, to meet people we would not otherwise have the chance to meet—for example, those anti-establishment fighters we described in *Who Says You Can't?*—and to explore subjects and ideas that are new to us."

About their method of collaboration, the Epsteins commented: "We both do research, argue over the general plan and then divide up the actual work. Each of us usually writes about one-half of the chapters of any given book. Our individual writing styles are dissimilar, but we edit each other's chapters and try to smooth out the differences. A year or so after a book has been published we're usually unable to remember which of us wrote any particular chapter, although there are always special sections that we remember with strong personal affection, or horror. We welcome assignments that involve research in the field." [Taken from the book jacket of *The Great Houdini* by Beryl Williams and Samuel Epstein, Messner, 1950.]

FOR MORE INFORMATION SEE: Muriel Fuller, editor, *More Junior Authors*, H. W. Wilson, 1963; *Contemporary Authors*, Volumes 5-8 revised, Gale, 1963; Martha E. Ward and Dorothy A. Marquardt, *Authors of Books for Young People*, Scarecrow Press, 1971.

EPSTEIN, Samuel 1909-
(Bruce Campbell; joint pseudonyms with Beryl [Williams] Epstein: Adam Allen, Douglas Coe, Martin Colt, Charles Strong)

PERSONAL: Born November 22, 1909, in Boston, Mass.; son of Joseph David and Sarah (Gershofsky) Epstein; married Beryl M. Williams (an author), April 26, 1938. *Education:* Rutgers University, Litt.B., 1932. *Address:* P.O. Box 1042, Southold, N.Y. 11971. *Agent:* McIntosh & Otis, Inc., 18 East 41st St., New York, N.Y. 10017.

CAREER: Author, 1936—. Federal Writers Project of New Jersey, assistant state director, 1936-42; New Jersey Agricultural Experiment Station, editor, 1942-44; Department of Microbiology, 1946-51. *Military service:* U.S. Army, 1944-46. *Member:* Authors League.

WRITINGS—With wife, Beryl Williams Epstein; under joint pseudonym Adam Allen: *Tin Lizzie*, Stackpole, 1937; *Printer's Devil*, Macmillan, 1939; *Dynamo Farm*, Lippincott, 1942; *Water to Burn*, Lippincott, 1943; *Dollar a Share*, Random House, 1943; *New Broome Experiment*, Lippincott, 1944.

With B. W. Epstein; under joint pseudonym Douglas Coe: *Marconi: Pioneer of Radio*, Messner, 1943; *Road to Alaska*, Messner, 1943; *Burma Road*, Messner, 1946.

With B. W. Epstein; under joint pseudonym Charles Strong: *Stranger at the Inlet*, Messner, 1946.

With B. W. Epstein; under joint pseudonym Martin Colt: *Secret of Baldhead Mountain*, Messner, 1946; *The Riddle of the Hidden Pesos*, Messner, 1948.

With B. W. Epstein: *Miracles from Microbes: The Road to Streptomycin*, Rutgers University Press, 1946; *The Great Houdini*, Messner, 1950; *William Crawford Gorgas*, Messner, 1953; *The Rocket Pioneers*, Messner, 1955; (with B. W. Epstein and John Gunther) *Meet North Africa*, Harper, 1956; *Prehistoric Animals*, Watts, 1956; *Francis Marion, Swamp Fox of the Revolution*, Messner, 1956; *The Andrews Raid*, Coward, 1956; (with B. W. Epstein and J. Gunther) *Meet South Africa*, Harper, 1958; *Jackknife for a Penny*, Coward, 1958; *Change for a Penny*, Coward, 1959.

George Washington Carver (illustrated by William Moyers), Garrard, 1960; *Plant Explorer: David Fairchild*, Messner, 1961; *Grandpa's Wonderful Glass*, Wonder Books, 1962; *Junior Science Book of Seashells*, Garrard, 1963; *Pioneer Oceanographer: Alexander Agassiz*, Messner, 1963; *The Story of the International Red Cross*, T. Nelson, 1963; *Spring Holidays*, Garrard, 1964; *Hurricane Guest*, Random House, 1964; *Medicine from Microbes* (Junior Literary Guild selection), Messner, 1965; *The Game of Baseball*, Garrard, 1965; *Stories of Champions*, Garrard, 1965; *Young Paul Revere's Boston*, Garrard, 1966; *The Sacramento: Golden River of California*, Garrard, 1968; *Harriet Tubman: Guide to Freedom*, Garrard, 1968; *European Folk Festivals: A Holiday Book*, Garrard, 1968; *The Picture Book of F.D.R.*, Watts, 1969; *Take This Hammer*, Hawthorn, 1969; *Who Says You Can't?*, Coward, 1969; *Who Needs Holes?*, Hawthorn, 1969.

Enrico Fermi: Father of Atomic Power, Garrard, 1970; *Michael Faraday: Apprentice to Science*, Garrard, 1971; *Winston Churchill: Lion of Britain*, Garrard, 1971; *Pick It Up* (illustrated by Tomie de Paola), Holiday House, 1971; *Look in the Mirror*, Holiday House, 1971; *Hold Everything*, Holiday House, 1973; *More Stories of Baseball Champions: In the Hall of Fame*, Garrard, 1973; *Charles de Gaulle: Defender of France*, Garrard, 1973; *A Year of Japanese Festivals* (illustrated by Gordon Laite), Garrard, 1974; *Jackie Robinson: Baseball's Gallant Fighter*, Garrard, 1974; *Willie Mays: Baseball's Superstar* (illustrated by Victor Mays), Garrard, 1975; *Henry Aaron: Home-Run King*, Garrard, 1975; *Saving Electricity*, Garrard, 1977; *Mr. Peale's Mammoth* (Junior Literary Guild selection; illustrated by Martim Abillez), Coward, 1977; *Dr. Beaumont and the Man with the Hole in His Stomach* (illustrated by Joseph Serotani), Coward, 1978; *Secret in a Sealed Bottle* (illustrated by Jane Sterrett), Coward, 1979; *She Never Looked Back: Margaret Mead in Samoa* (Junior Literary Guild selection; illustrated by Victor Juhasz), Coward, 1980; *Kids in Court: The ACLU Defends Their Rights*, Four Winds Press, 1982.

The "Ken Holt Mystery" series; under pseudonym Bruce Campbell; all published by Grosset: *The Secret of Skeleton Island*, 1949; *The Riddle of the Stone Elephant*, 1949; *The Black Thumb Mystery*, 1950; *The Clue of the Marked Claw*, 1950; *The Clue of the Coiled Cobra*, 1951; *The Secret of Hangman's Inn*, 1951; *The Mystery of the Iron Box*, 1952; *The Clue of the Phantom Car*, 1953; *The Mystery of the Galloping Horse*, 1954; *The Mystery of the Green Flame*, 1955; *The Mystery of the Grinning Tiger*, 1956; *The Mystery of the Vanishing Magician*, 1956; *The Mystery of the Shattered Glass*, 1958; *The Mystery of the Invisible Enemy*, 1959; *The Mystery*

... If she could convince young girls to talk with her, she felt sure her field work would go well. One advantage she knew she possessed was her height—only a few inches over five feet. She was no taller than most Samoan girls in their teens. ■ (From *She Never Looked Back: Margaret Mead in Samoa* by Sam and Beryl Epstein. Illustrated by Victor Juhasz.)

of Gallows Cliff, 1960; *The Clue of the Silver Scorpion,* 1961; *The Mystery of the Plumed Serpent,* 1962; *The Mystery of the Sultan's Scimitar,* 1963.

"The Real Book of" series; all with B. W. Epstein; all published by Garden City Books: *The Real Book of Inventions,* 1951; . . . *Benjamin Franklin,* 1952; . . . *Pirates,* 1952; . . . *Alaska,* 1952; . . . *Spies,* 1953; . . . *the Sea,* 1954; . . . *Submarines,* 1954.

"The First Book of" series all with B. W. Epstein; all published by Watts: *The First Book of Electricity,* 1953, revised, 1966 and 1977; . . . *Words,* 1954; . . . *Hawaii,* 1954; . . . *Printing,* 1955, revised, 1974; . . . *Glass,* 1955; . . . *Mexico,* 1955, revised, 1967 and 1982; . . . *Codes and Ciphers,* 1956; . . . *Italy,* 1958, revised, 1972; . . . *Maps and Globes,* 1959; . . . *Measurement,* 1960; . . . *the Ocean,* 1961; . . . *Washington, D.C.,* 1961, revised, 1981; . . .*Teaching Machines,* 1961; . . . *The World Health Organization,* 1964; . . . *Switzerland,* 1964; . . . *News,* 1965.

"All About" series; all with B. W. Epstein; all published by Random House: *All About the Desert,* 1957; . . . *Prehistoric Cave Men,* 1959; . . . *Engines and Power,* 1962.

SIDELIGHTS: "My wife and I wrote our first book for young people before we were married. We liked writing it so much that we just went on writing books.

"Most of the books we write, either in collaboration or individually, are nonfiction, probably because we are endlessly curious about people, and things, and events. Sometimes we get a book idea from reading about something or someone in a newspaper. We wrote *Who Says You Can't?* after reading reports of a number of determined individuals who decided that it was possible to fight—and defeat—such overpowering adversaries as the automobile industry, the drug industry, powerful government agencies and intrenched political machines.

"Collecting material for books gives us the opportunity to travel a great deal, which we not only enjoy, but which gives us endless opportunities to unearth new book ideas. Frequently publishers suggest subjects to us, based on their knowledge of the kind of books teachers would welcome.

"We work as a team most of the time, although we also write individually. We start by reading all the research material we have assembled. Then we collaborate on an outline. After that we divide the work, each taking about half of the book and writing it without collaboration. Then we swap the finished sections, editing each other's work. We often argue about the outline, but seldom about editorial comments. When the book finally appears, it is difficult for us to tell which of us wrote what.

"Whenever possible we like to see at firsthand what it is we're writing about. The whole world of microbes and antibiotics means more to us because I was once an editor in the Department of Microbiology of the New Jersey College of Agriculture at Rutgers University. Heading that department was Dr. Selman A. Waksman, winner of the Nobel Prize for his work in the development of streptomycin. When, in 1945, the Rutgers University Press asked us to write a book about the medical and scientific development that led to streptomycin, we had all the expert guidance and research material we needed.

"That book was published in 1946—a time when the word antibiotic was new in the public's vocabulary. But the word, and the idea of using microbes to fight microbes, has since become commonplace. New antibiotics are taken for granted, and the drama of their discovery is unknown to most young people. Because we regretted this, we decided to write a new history of antibiotics, tracing the long road from ancient medicines compounded out of spiders and snakes and the eyes of newts to medicines made for man by microbes.

"We hope that *Medicine from Microbes* served as a small tribute to a few of the many scientists who traveled down this long road. And we hope it prompted some young people to consider microbiology as a career. It is a fascinating science with an unlimited future."

Among the many biographies by the Epsteins is *Mister Peale's Mammoth,* the story of Charles Willson Peale, the man responsible for launching the first scientific expedition in America and displaying an American mammoth's skeleton in Peale's natural history museum. "We had known only that Peale had painted portraits of most of the heroes of the American Revolution—the portraits that tell us what so many of these men looked like. And we had known that he taught some of his children how to paint and that he named them after famous painters. But when we started to do research, we discovered that he was saddle-maker, artist, inventor, taxidermist, spectacle-maker, farmer, paleontologist, showman—there was practically no trade or profession this man couldn't set himself to learn. And after having learned it, he couldn't wait to teach it to someone else. Among the more than one hundred books we've written there are a number of biographies. But with the exception of Benjamin Franklin, we can't think of anyone we've written about whose interests and hobbies range as widely as Peale's. Of course this made researching the book a pleasure. But it also made writing this book particularly difficult because we were constantly having to decide what must be left out in order to have space to tell the story of his Mammoth. We hope that *Mister Peale's Mammoth* led its readers to learn more about this remarkable man."

HOBBIES AND OTHER INTERESTS: Traveling, fishing, gardening.

SAMUEL AND BERYL EPSTEIN

Again they pulled. Peter brought the rear roller forward, and once more they pulled. ■ (From *Hurricane Guest* by Sam and Beryl Epstein. Illustrated by Marilyn Miller.)

FOR MORE INFORMATION SEE: Muriel Fuller, editor, *More Junior Authors*, H. W. Wilson, 1963; *Contemporary Authors*, Volumes 5-8 revised, Gale, 1963; Martha E. Ward and Dorothy A. Marquardt, *Authors of Books for Young People*, Scarecrow Press, 1971.

ERIKSON, Mel 1937-

PERSONAL: Born March 3, 1937, in Brooklyn, N.Y.; son of Jack (a house painter) and Astrid (Magnuson) Erikson; married Diana Consiglio (a telephone company consultant), August 24, 1958; children: Robin, Tracy. *Education:* Long Island University, 1957-59. *Home:* 7 Dedham Pl., Kings Park, N.Y. 11754. *Office:* 200 13th Ave., Ronkonkoma, N.Y. 11779.

CAREER: Illustrator; designer. Mel Erikson/Art Service, Ronkonkoma, N.Y., owner, 1969—. *Military service:* U.S. Army, 1955-57. *Member:* Antique Automobile Club of America.

ILLUSTRATOR: Alvin and Virginia B. Silverstein, *The Digestive System: How Living Creatures Use Food*, Prentice-Hall, 1970; A. and V. B. Silverstein, *The Endocrine System: Hormones in the Living World*, Prentice-Hall, 1971; A. and V. B. Silverstein, *The Nervous System: The Inner Networks*, Pren-

tice-Hall, 1971; A. and V. B. Silverstein, *The Sense Organs: Our Link with the World*, Prentice-Hall, 1971; Walter Thurber, Robert Kilburn, and Peter Howell, *Action Biology Reproduction*, Allyn, 1974; W. Thurber, R. Kilburn, and P. Howell, *Exploring Earth Science*, Allyn, 1974; Herbert S. Zim and James R. Skelly, *Pipes and Plumbing Systems*, Morrow, 1974; J. Keogh Rash, *Protecting Your Health*, Globe, 1975; J. K. Rash, *Safety and First Aid*, Globe, 1975; J. K. Rash, *Consumer Education*, Globe, 1975; J. K. Rash, *Mental Health*, Globe, 1975; J. K. Rash, *The Pollution Problem*, Globe, 1975; J. K. Rash, *Drugs, Alcohol and Tobacco*, Globe, 1975; Malvins Dolmatz, and Harry K. Wong, *Ideas and Investigations in Science*, Prentice-Hall, 1976; McClenaghan, *Magruder's American Government*, Allyn, 1978. Contributor of illustrations to *Peoples and Our Country*, Holt, 1978; and *World Geography Today*, Holt, 1980.

WORK IN PROGRESS: Illustrations and maps for *Exploring World History*, to be published by Globe; illustrations for several books for Macmillan.

SIDELIGHTS: "I will do portrait commissions as a relaxation and as a diversion from my more exacting pen and ink work. I also like to restore antique furniture and automobiles when time permits."

FOR MORE INFORMATION SEE: Martha E. Ward and Dorothy A. Marquardt, *Illustrators of Books for Young People*, Scarecrow, 1975.

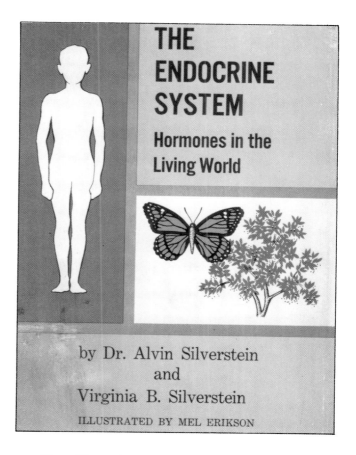

(From *The Endocrine System* by Alvin and Virginia B. Silverstein. Jacket illustration by Mel Erikson.)

MEL ERIKSON

FLEUR, Anne 1901-
(Sari)

BRIEF ENTRY: Born in Lancaster, Pa., in 1901. Fleur has written and illustrated several books for children under the pseudonym Sari. She attended the Lancaster Business School and initially studied art privately at home, later moving to New York where she attended the Art Students League. Fleur spent several years in the advertising field before discovering an interest in drawing children, which eventually led her to her career as an author and illustrator of children's books. Among her written and illustrated works are *The White Goat: A Story of Switzerland,* 1938, and *Ten Little Servants: The Story of a Little Prince,* 1939. She illustrated Rita Kissin's *Gramp's Desert Chick,* 1946, Bessie F. White's *A Bear Named Grumms,* 1953, Jean Corcoran's *Elias Howe, Inventive Boy,* 1962, and others. In addition to children's books, Fleur has also illustrated a number of textbooks. *For More Information See: Illustrators of Children's Books: 1946-1956,* Horn Book, 1958.

FLOYD, Gareth 1940-

BRIEF ENTRY: Born December 11, 1940, in Whiston, Lancashire, England. An illustrator of over a hundred children's books, Floyd has also done magazine illustrations and has been the regular artist on the "Jackanory" television show in London. A former teacher at the Leicester College of Art, Floyd is a self-employed illustrator who has been active in local politics, serving as both town and country councillor. Among the many children's books Floyd has illustrated are Sheena Porter's *The Knockers* (Oxford University Press, 1965), Christobel Mattingley's *The Battle of the Galah Trees* (Brockhampton Press, 1973), Ann Turnbull's *The Wolf King* (Kestrel Books, 1975), and Eileen Molony's *Giant, Spriggan, and Buccaboo* (Kaye & Ward, 1981). Floyd has also illustrated Margaret Greave's *Nothing Ever Happens on Sundays* (British Broadcasting Corp., 1976) which was adapted from the television program "Jackanory." In addition, Floyd illustrated the "Sparks" reading series, Stage Two, Three, and Four, which

were written by R. M. Fisher and all published by Blackie & Son. He has contributed illustrations to periodicals, including *Cricket. For More Information See: Illustrators of Children's Books: 1967-1976,* Horn Book, 1978.

FORD, George (Jr.)

PERSONAL: Born in Brooklyn, N.Y.; *Education:* Attended Art Students League, Pratt Institute, Cooper Union, School of Visual Arts, and College of the City of New York (now of the City University of New York). *Residence:* Harlem, New York, N.Y.

CAREER: Free-lance writer and artist. Has also worked as an art director for Eden Advertising and as a design director for Black Theatre, New York, N.Y. Work has appeared in shows at Atlanta University, Atlanta, Ga., 1951, Brooklyn Museum, Brooklyn, N.Y., and in the traveling exhibit, "Black Artists in Graphic Communication," 1971. *Member:* Council on Interracial Books for children, president, 1972. *Awards, honors:* Coretta Scott King Award from the American Library Asso-

The palace guards, awakened with a start, rushed to the stables and hastily jumped astride their horses. But to no avail, for Queen Cora was already far ahead. ■ (From "Queen Cora," in *The Singing Turtle and Other Tales from Haiti* by Philippe Thoby-Marcelin and Pierre Marcelin. Illustrated by George Ford.)

GEORGE FORD

ciation, 1974, for illustrations for *Ray Charles;* Jane Addams Peace Award, 1976, for illustrations for *Paul Robeson.*

WRITINGS—All for young people: (With Mel Williamson) *Walk On!* (self-illustrated), Third Press, 1972; *Baby's First Picture Book* (self-illustrated), Random House, 1979; *Gator,* Charter Books, 1980.

Illustrator; all for young people: Olivia Vlahos, *African Beginnings,* Viking, 1967; Humphrey Harman, *Tales Told Near a Crocodile: Stories from Nyanza,* Viking, 1967; O. Vlahos, *Battle-Ax People: Beginnings of Western Culture,* Viking, 1968; Alice James Napjus, *Freddie Found a Frog,* Van Nostrand, 1969; O. Vlahos, *New World Beginnings: Indian Cultures in the Americas,* Viking, 1970; Bambote, *Daba's Travels,* Pantheon, 1971; Alfred W. Wilkes, *Little Boy Black,* Scribner, 1971; Philippe Thoby-Marcelin and Pierre Marcelin, *The Singing Turtle, and Other Tales from Haiti* (translated by Eva Thoby-Marcelin), Farrar, Straus, 1971; Osmond Molarsky, *Song of the Smoggy Stars,* Walck, 1971; Nikki Giovanni, *Ego-Tripping, and Other Poems for Young People,* Lawrence Hill, 1973; Sharon Bell Mathis, *Ray Charles,* Crowell, 1973; Eloise Greenfield, *Paul Robeson,* Crowell, 1975; O. Vlahos, *Far Eastern Beginnings,* Viking, 1976; Kenneth Rudeen, *Muhammad Ali,* Crowell, 1976; Valerie Flournoy, *The Best Time of Day,* Random House, 1978; E. Greenfield, *Darlene,* Methuen, 1980.

Contributor of illustrations to periodicals, including *Harper's.*

SIDELIGHTS: Ford was born and reared in Brooklyn. He spent some of his early years in Barbados, West Indies, with his grandmother. "She was a lean, strong, religious, compassionate woman whom everyone called Old Lou. I remember two main things about her; she made everyone's problems her own, and she could draw like an angel. She loved to sit on the front steps and draw people's faces on my school slate with an ordinary piece of chalk. Of course I imitated her—and she always praised my drawings to the skies. Her interest in social concerns and in portraying human character rubbed off on me. Expressing real feeling in my drawing is always more important to me than employing new techniques for their own sake." [Lee Kingman and others, compilers, *Illustrators of Children's Books: 1967-1976,* Horn Books, 1978.]

Ford has illustrated for magazines as well as his children's books, and has designed trademarks for theaters and corporations in the Black community. As an illustrator, Ford feels it is necessary for the artist to work with both the art director and the editor to obtain the most effective total book.

Ford lives and works in Harlem where he is active with various cultural groups in the Black community.

FOR MORE INFORMATION SEE: Lee Kingman and others, compilers, *Illustrators of Children's Books: 1967-1976,* Horn Book, 1978.

FOSTER, Harold Rudolf 1892-1982
(Hal Foster)

OBITUARY NOTICE: Born August 16, 1892, in Halifax, Nova Scotia, Canada; died of a heart attack, July 27, 1982, in Spring Hill, Fla. An illustrator and cartoonist, Foster is best known for his comic strip ''Prince Valiant.'' Foster's career as a cartoonist began with a Tarzan strip he drew for United Features Syndicate in 1931. In 1937 the artist was asked by William Randolph Hearst to create a new strip for King Features, and ''Prince Valiant'' emerged. Through the years the ''Prince Valiant'' strip, which is based on the medieval period and the King Arthur legends, has been praised for its scholarly accuracy, rich color, and skillful drawing. Foster drew ''Prince Valiant'' from its conception until he retired in 1979, a total of forty-two years. The strip is presently carried in over 350 newspapers. Foster also published ''Prince Valiant'' in a series of books which includes the titles *Prince Valiant and the Golden Princess* (Hastings, 1968), *Prince Valiant in the New World* (Hastings, 1968), *Prince Valiant in the Days of King Arthur* (Hastings, 1969), and others. *For More Information See: Artists of a Certain Line: A Selection of Illustrators for Children's Books,* Bodley Head, 1960; *Authors in the News,* Volume 2, Gale, 1976; *Who's Who in American Art, 1980,* Bowker, 1980. *Obituaries: New York Times,* July 27, 1982; *Chicago Tribune,* July 28, 1982; *Newsweek,* August 9, 1982; *Time,* August 9, 1982.

FRASER, Elizabeth Marr 1928-
(Betty Fraser)

PERSONAL: Born February 25, 1928, in Boston, Mass.; daughter of William (a lawyer) and Helen (Sanford) Fraser; married John Cholakis (a television commercial producer), December 30, 1974; children: Elia (step-son). *Education:* Attended Rhode Island School of Design, 1945-49. *Home and office:* 240 Central Park South, New York, N.Y. 10019.

CAREER: Free-lance book illustrator, 1962—. Early in career worked as an assistant teacher, art director, layout artist and advertising artist. *Awards, honors:* Children's Books of the Year Award from the Child Study Association of America, 1971, for *Chemistry in the Kitchen* and 1976, for *Giraffe: The Silent Giant;* numerous books were selected for the American Institute of Graphic Arts Book Show, including, *The Tropical Forest,* 1973-74, *Giraffe: The Silent Giant,* 1975, and *A House Is A House for Me,* 1979; *Giraffe: The Silent Giant* won the certificate for outstanding science book for children from the National Science Teachers' Association and was a Children's Book Showcase selection, 1977.

ILLUSTRATOR—All under name Betty Fraser; for children, unless noted: Louisa May Alcott, *Little Women,* Macmillan, 1962; Madeleine Polland, *Queen's Blessing* (*Horn Book* honor list), Holt, 1964; Crockett Johnson, *Castles in the Sand,* Holt, 1965; Jeanne Loisy, *Sierra Summer,* translated by Irene Salem, Follett, 1965; Edith Nesbit, *Enchanted Castle,* Platt, 1966; Irene Turnblow, *Through the Years with Henrietta,* Follett, 1966; Margaret Self, *Shaggy Little Burro of San Miguel,* Hawthorn, 1967; Rowena Bennett, *Songs from Around a Toadstool Table,* Follett, 1967; Elfreida Read, *Spell of Chuchuchan,* World Publishing, 1967; Alex Rider, *We Say Happy Birthday,* Funk, 1967; Joan Aiken, *Armitage, Armitage, Fly Away Home,* Doubleday, 1968; (with Don Bolognese, Kelly Oechsli, and Walter Brooks) *Favorite Stories: A Collection of the Best-Loved Tales*

of Childhood, Western Publishing, 1968; Marjorie Holmes, *I've Got to Talk to Somebody, God: A Woman's Conversations with God* (adult prayer book), large print edition, Abingdon, 1968, revised edition, Bantam, 1974; Florence P. Heide, *Sebastian,* Funk, 1968; Marion N. Uhl, *The Spiral Horn,* Doubleday, 1968.

Marjory Sanger, *Checkerback's Journey: The Migration of the Ruddy Turnstone,* World Publishing, 1969; Margaret Hillert, *Farther than Far: Poems,* Follett, 1969; Lawrence F. Lowery, *How Does the Wind Blow?,* Holt, 1969; Lowery, *Clouds, Rain, Clouds Again,* Western Publishing, 1970; Julian May, *Dodos and Dinosaurs Are Extinct,* Creative Educational Society, 1970; Anne Kouts, *Kenny's Rat,* Viking, 1970; William B. Morris, *The Longest Journey in the World,* Holt, 1970; Myra Brown, *Sandy Signs His Name,* Hale, 1970; Bil Gilbert, *The Weasels: A Sensible Look at a Family of Predators,* Pantheon, 1970; Seymour Simon, *Chemistry in the Kitchen,* Viking, 1971; Holmes, *Who Am I, God?* (adult), Doubleday, 1971; Sigmund Kalina, *The House That Nature Built,* Lothrop, 1972; Bernice Kohn, *The Organic Living Book,* Viking, 1972; Frances Carpenter, *People from the Sky: Ainu Tales from Northern Japan,* Doubleday, 1972.

When the baby is born, it drops to the ground. But it doesn't get hurt. The mother giraffe nuzzles it and licks it clean. In about 20 minutes the baby can stand on its legs. ■ (From *Giraffe: The Silent Giant* by Miriam Schlein. Illustrated by Betty Fraser.)

A box is a house for a teabag.
A teapot's a house for some tea.
If you pour me a cup and I drink it all up,
Then the teahouse will turn into me!

(From *A House Is a House for Me* by Mary Ann Hoberman. Illustrated by Betty Fraser.)

S. Carl Hirsch, *Stilts,* Viking, 1972; Solveig P. Russell, *Through a Magic Glass,* Ginn, 1972; Aileen L. Fisher, *Filling the Bill,* Bowmar/Noble, 1973; Robert N. Peck, *Path of Hunters: Animal Struggle in a Meadow,* Knopf, 1973; Simon, *A Tree on Your Street,* Holiday House, 1973; Mary Batten, *The Tropical Forest: Ants, Ants, Animals, and Plants,* Crowell, 1973; Simon, *Pets in a Jar: Collecting and Caring for Small Wild Animals,* Viking, 1975; Miriam Schlein, *Giraffe: The Silent Giant,* Four Winds Press, 1976; Jane H. Yolen, *Simple Gifts: The Story of the Shakers,* Viking, 1976; Mary Ann Hoberman, *A House Is a House for Me* (Junior Literary Guild selection) Viking, 1978. Contributor to *Family Circle.*

SIDELIGHTS: Fraser's first achievement in art was a two dollar prize in an Easter egg coloring contest at the age of seven. She attended schools in Wellesley and Cambridge, Massachusetts, and attended the Rhode Island School of Design, graduating with a Bachelor of Fine Arts degree in 1949. "I went to art school because it was easier than college. Drawing an electric light bulb on top of books on top of a table was the exam and fortunately in high school I had an old-fashioned teacher who stressed proportion, perspective, etc. After art school I worked twelve years in advertising. The loveliest thing that ever happened to me was to settle down on my own and to be rewarded (paid) for what I do. So since 1962 I have been a full-time illustrator. I like pen and ink the best and find I am going from intricate line to very intricate. Because of working in line so much I do a lot of color separation which is tedious but the

reproduction is better." [Lee Kingman and others, compilers, *Illustrators of Children's Books: 1957-1966,* Horn Book, 1968.]

"To illustrate a picture book of 48 pages and sustain a high level of quality and consistency is impossible for me. One spread looks OK, another exciting, the next blah.

"I like to draw posters, editorial art, cards, and book jackets."

FOR MORE INFORMATION SEE: Diana Klemin, *The Illustrated Book,* Clarkson Potter, 1970; Lee Kingman and others, compilers, *Illustrators of Children's Books: 1967-1976,* Horn Book, 1978.

I know a funny little man,
As quiet as a mouse,
Who does the mischief that is done
　In everybody's house!
There's no one ever sees his face,
　And yet we all agree
That every plate we break was cracked
　By Mr. Nobody.

　　　　　　　　—Anonymous

FRIMMER, Steven 1928-

PERSONAL: Born June 29, 1928, in New York, N.Y.; son of Isidore (a psychiatrist) and Grace (Lipsky) Frimmer; married Barbara Meyers (a speech therapist), June 29, 1952; children: Erica, Andrea, Eliza. *Education:* New York University, B.A., 1950, M.A., 1951. *Home:* 255 Overpeck Ave., Ridgefield Park, N.J. 07660. *Agent:* Joan Korman Raines, 475 Fifth Ave., New York, N.Y. 10017. *Office:* Reader's Digest Press, 200 Park Ave., New York, N.Y. 10017.

CAREER: Marboro Book Club, New York, N.Y., editor, 1959-63; Mid-Century Book Society, New York, N.Y., editor 1963; G. P. Putnam's Sons, New York, N.Y., managing editor, 1963-1969; McCall Books, New York, N.Y., managing editor, 1969-71; Saturday Review Book Club, New York, N.Y., editor, 1971-72; Reader's Digest Press, New York, N.Y., editor-publisher, 1973—.

WRITINGS: The Stone That Spoke (Junior Literary Guild selection), Putnam, 1969; *Finding the Forgotten,* Putnam, 1971; *Neverland: Fabled Places and Fabulous Voyages of History and Legend,* Viking, 1975; *Dead Matter,* Holt, 1982.

GARBUTT, Bernard 1900-

BRIEF ENTRY: Born August 25, 1900, in Ontario, Calif. An author and illustrator of children's books, Garbutt worked as an animator for Disney Studios during the animation boom of the 1930s and 40s. Garbutt studied art at Chouinard and Otis Art Institutes. He has also worked as an illustrator for the *Los Angeles Times.* The children's books Garbutt has written and illustrated include *Roger, the Rosin Back* (Hastings, 1961), *The Day of the Horse* (Northland, 1976), and *Hodie* (Aladdin, 1949), with Katharine Kendig Garbutt. Garbutt is also the illustrator of a number of books. Among them are Rosalie Davidson's *Dinosaurs: The Terrible Lizards* (Children's Press, 1969) and *When the Dinosaurs Disappeared: Mammals of Long Ago* (Children's Press, 1973), Judy Van Der Veer's *Gray Mare's Colts* (Children's Press, 1971), and Alvin and Virginia Silverstein's *Mammals of the Sea.* Garbutt was the recipient of a Southern California Council on Literature for Children and Young People Award for his significant contribution in the field of illustration for Lucille N. and William D. Stratton's *Wild Wings Over the Marshes* (Golden Gate, 1963). Many of Garbutt's illustrations are of animals and reflect his desire to be a zoologist. *Residence:* Los Angeles, Calif. *For More Information See: Illustrators of Children's Books, 1946-1956,* Horn Book, 1958; *American Artist,* February 1963, January, 1977.

Cock crows in the morn,
    To tell us to rise,
And he who lies late
    Will never be wise.
For early to bed,
    And early to rise,
Is the way to be healthy
    And wealthy and wise.

                  —Nursery rhyme

GARDNER, John Champlin, Jr. 1933-1982

OBITUARY NOTICE: Born July 21, 1933, in Batavia, N.Y.; died in a motorcyle accident, September 14, 1982, in Susquehanna, Pa. Educator, translator, critic, poet, and novelist. Gardner began his academic career in 1958 as an instructor at Oberlin College. He later became professor of English at Southern Illinois University, and at the time of his death was director of the creative writing program at the State University of New York at Binghamton. He was also founder and editor of *MSS,* a small literary magazine. An innovative and highly respected writer best known for his adult novels, Gardner was the 1976 recipient of the National Book Critics Award for fiction for his *October Light.* In 1975 he published his first book for children entitled *Dragon, Dragon, and Other Timeless Tales.* It was soon followed by several others, including *Gudgekin, the Thistle Girl,* a Junior Literary Guild selection, *The Revenge of Moriarty, A Child's Bestiary,* and *King of the Hummingbirds, and Other Tales.* In addition to his many critical works, Gardner was translator of a number of Old and Middle English texts. For young readers, he wrote *The Life and Times of Chaucer. For More Information See: Contemporary Authors,* Volumes 65-68, Gale, 1977; *Authors of Books for Young People,* supplement, Scarecrow, 1979. *Obituaries: New York Times,* September 15. 1982; *Chicago Tribune,* September 16, 1982; *London Times,* September 18, 1982; *Newsweek,* September 27, 1982; *Time,* September 27, 1982; *Publishers Weekly,* October 1, 1982; *School Library Journal,* November, 1982.

GLASER, Dianne E(lizabeth) 1937-

BRIEF ENTRY: Born August 29, 1937, in Bronx, N.Y. Since 1971 Glaser has been a full-time writer of books for children. She attended the University of Alabama and lives with her husband, a creative director, and their seven children in Tennessee. In 1977 *The Diary of Trilby Frost* was named book of the year by the American Library Association. Her other books for children include *Amber Wellington, Daredevil,* 1975, *Amber Wellington, Witchwater,* 1976, *Summer Secrets,* 1977, and *The Case of the Missing Six,* 1977.

GREISMAN, Joan Ruth 1937-

PERSONAL: Born May 4, 1937, in New York, N.Y.; daughter of Jack and Pearl Greisman. *Education:* Hunter College of the City University of New York, B.A., M.S. *Religion:* Jewish. *Home and office:* 185 East 85th St., New York, N.Y. 10028. *Agent:* Curtis Brown Ltd., 575 Madison Ave., New York, N.Y. 10028.

CAREER: Associated with Board of Education of New York City, 1958—; teacher and reading specialist at elementary schools in New York City, until 1966; assistant principal at elementary school in East Harlem, N.Y.; instructor at Long Island University, 1966-75; writer, 1971—.

WRITINGS—All with Harriet Jean Wittels; all for children: *The Clear and Simple Thesaurus-Dictionary,* Grosset, 1971, published as *The Clear and Simple Thesaurus Dictionary,* Grosset, 1976; *The Perfect Speller,* Grosset, 1973; *Things I Hate,* Behavioral Publications, 1973.

**But it's nice meeting friends and getting together.
They'll be there in school, whatever the weather.**

■(From *Things I Hate!* by Harriet Wittels and Joan Greisman. Illustrated by Jerry McConnel.)

WORK IN PROGRESS: Jeff Fights for Justice, a teenage novel, with H. J. Wittels; *The Budding Business Bureau,* a teenage novel, with H. J. Wittels; *Preparing Your Child for Success with Reading,* a reference book for parents, with H. J. Wittels.

GRIDER, Dorothy   1915-
(Dottig, Patti Fenwick)

PERSONAL: Born January 19, 1915, in Bowling Green, Ky.; daughter of Rufus DuBose and Patricia (Fenwick) Grider. *Education:* Western Kentucky University, Bowling Green, Ky., B.A, 1936; attended Phoenix Art Institute, New York, N.Y., 1936-39, and Grand Chaumiere Art School, Paris, France, 1950. *Home:* 96 N. Main St., New Hope, Pa. 18938.

CAREER: Writer, illustrator, artist, and photographer. Clinton Elementary School, Clinton, Tenn., art teacher, 1939; U.S. Playing Card Co., New York, N.Y, designer, 1939-41; Norcross Greeting Cards, New York, N.Y., designer, 1941-45; free-lance artist, 1945—. *Exhibitions*—One-man shows: Three Arts Club, New York, N.Y., 1940; Barbizon Hotel, New York, N.Y., 1945; National Arts Club, New York, N.Y., 1947; Western Kentucky University, Bowling Green, Ky., 1950; Contemporary Galleries, New York, N.Y., 1952; Phillips Mill Show, New Hope, Pa., 1953; Coryell Gallery, Lambertville, N.J.; Rodman House, Doylestown, Pa. 1980. Traveling "Water Color Foursome," all over U.S., 1951. *Awards, honors:* Scholarship, 1936, Phoenix Art Institute.

WRITINGS—All self-illustrated: *Breezy: The Airminded Pigeon,* Whitman, 1945; *Peppermint,* Whitman, 1950; *Pet for Peter,* Whitman, 1951; *Back and Forth,* Lippincott, 1955; *Little Ballerina,* Rand McNally, 1959; *Little Majorette,* Rand McNally, 1959.

Illustrator: Carolyn Sherwin Bailey, *The Little Rabbit Who Wanted Red Wings,* Platt & Munk, 1945; Louise Lawrence Devine, *Mumpsy Goes to Kindergarten,* Rand McNally, 1946; Edith Pope, *The Biggety Chameleon,* Scribner, 1946; Florence Medon, *Mother's Helpers,* Garden City, 1946; Sally R. Francis, *Puppy That Found a Home,* Rand McNally, 1947; Flora L. Carpenter, *Animal Stories,* Rand McNally, 1947; *My First Picture Dictionary,* Wilcox & Follett, 1947; Carleton A. Scheinert, *DoDo the Little Wild Duck,* Whitman, 1948; Alf Evers, *A Day on the Farm,* Rand McNally, 1948; E. C. Reichert, *My Truck Book,* Rand McNally, 1948; Catherine Stahlmann, *Peter Pat and the Policeman,* Rand McNally, 1948; *Baby's Mother Goose,* Grosset, 1949; *Song Book,* Ginn, 1949; Lewis and Corchia, *Kerry the Fire Engine Dog,* Rand McNally, 1949; Marion Edey, *Open the Door,* Scribner, 1949.

Laura Mengert Hugley, *Everyone Wants a Home,* Rand McNally, 1950; Jane Shearer Moore, *Story of Toby,* Rand McNally, 1950; Joyce Glasscock, *Cowboy Eddie,* Rand McNally, 1950; Marion Edsoll, *Our Auto Trip,* Rand McNally, 1951; Jessica Potter Broderick, *Hideaway Puppy,* Rand McNally, 1952; James Browning, *Busy Bulldozer,* Rand McNally, 1952; Mary Alice Jones, *Ten Commandments,* Rand McNally, 1952; Barbara Bates, *Trudy Phillips: New Girl,* Whitman, 1953; B. Bates,

DOROTHY GRIDER

Trudy Phillips: Headline Year, Whitman, 1954; Rebecca K. Sprinkle, *Parakeet Peter,* Rand McNally, 1954; Georgiana, *That Donkey,* Whitman, 1954; Susan Bromley Dowd, *Peter and His Prayers,* Rand McNally, 1954; Mabel Watts, *Daniel the Cocker Spaniel,* Rand McNally, 1955; Miss Frances, *We Love Grandpa,* Rand McNally, 1956; Helen Drummond, *A Child's Thoughts of God,* Rand McNally, 1957; Mildred Comfort, *Moving Day,* Rand McNally, 1958; Marjorie Barrows, *Funny Hat,* Rand McNally, 1959; Diane Sherman, *Little Skater,* Rand McNally, 1959.

Virginia Hunter, *Little Swimmers,* Rand McNally, 1960; M. Watts, *Little Horseman,* Rand McNally, 1961; M. Watts, *Little Campers,* Rand McNally, 1961; M. A. Jones, *God Speaks to Me,* Rand McNally, 1961; M. A. Jones, *The Lord's Prayer,* Rand McNally, 1964; Florence Parry Heide, *Alice Gets a New Look,* Saalfield, 1964; M.A. Jones, *Tell Me God's Plan,* Rand McNally, 1965; Leroy Jackson, *Pink Lemonade and Other Stories,* Rand McNally, 1965; L. Jackson, *The Animal Show,* Rand McNally, 1965; D. Sherman, *Nancy Plays Nurse,* Rand McNally, 1965; M. A. Jones, *Me, Myself and God,* Rand McNally, 1965; Ruth Dixon, *Little Red Boot,* Rand McNally, 1966; M. A. Jones, *Tell Me about God,* Rand McNally, 1967; M. A. Jones, *Tell Me about Jesus,* Rand McNally, 1967; Helen Frances Stanley, *Backyard Circus,* Rand McNally, 1967; M. A. Jones, *Friends Are for Loving,* Rand McNally, 1968; Dorothy Aldis, *Looking In,* Rand McNally, 1968; *Mulberry Bush,* Rand McNally, 1969.

Mary Phraner Warren, *Hoppity-Skip,* Rand McNally, 1970; Malinda R. Miller, *Picnic in the Park,* Rand McNally, 1971; Dorothea J. Snow, *Billy's Treasure,* Rand McNally, 1972; Marion Michener, *From Tadpoles to Frogs,* Rand McNally, 1973; H. F. Stanley, *Magician Counting Book,* Rand McNally, 1973; Renée Bartkowski, *Dolls from Many Lands,* Rand McNally, 1975.

Illustrator under pseudonym Patti Fenwick: Phyllis Ochocki, *Beth's Happy Day,* Rand McNally, 1956; Solveig Paulson Russell, *Tommy's Tooth,* Rand McNally, 1957.

Illustrator under pseudonym Dottig: Herbert B. Walker, *A Moth Is Born,* Rand McNally, 1957.

Also illustrator of the following: Six arithmetic books by Upton and Uhlinger, American Books Co., 1950-51; paper dolls, coloring books and games for Saalfield Publishing Co.; series of filmstrips for "Family Films of Hollywood." Contributor of illustrations to *Children's Activities.*

SIDELIGHTS: Since Grider was eight years old, living in Bowling Green, Kentucky, she knew that she wanted to paint. After she graduated from Western Kentucky State College, she went to New York, and later Paris, to study art. She won a scholarship to the Phoenix Art Institute for her painting "Ol' Pete" which she did at the age of nineteen. There she studied under the tutelage of Norman Rockwell and Franklin Booth. Grider made her home in New York City until her move to New Hope in 1953 about which she admits: "I never regretted for a minute my move from New York to New Hope." [Taken from an article by Betty Karsch in *New Hope Gazette,* April 24, 1980.[1]]

Grider has designed games and their boxes, and has illustrated cocktail napkins. Before she became a free-lance artist, Grider worked for Norcross Greeting Cards, and for the United States Playing Card Company designing the backs of playing cards. Working as a free-lance commercial photographer, Grider prepared the layouts for a local lamp company's catalog.

Grider also illustrated the Betsy McCall paper doll cut-outs, plus many other paper doll cut-outs for Saalfield Publishing, designed the paper dolls for Ross Hunter's production of "Lost Horizon," and illustrated a series of religious filmstrips used in church schools.

Since the 1940s Grider has been involved in writing and illustrating children's books. She has illustrated over one hundred children's books, including five of her own. "Then I went free-lance. . . . I've done as many as twelve books in a year."

"You've got to do research on all these books, because you can't fool a child. A lot of children are smarter than adults about things . . . you don't make them too real. There's no use making it photographic." [Judy Wildman, "Illustrated: Dorothy Grider Drew on Her Abilities to Fashion an Art Career," Park City *Daily News,* May 12, 1980.[2]]

Grider uses many mediums but is presently using oils, "to get back into painting. For the last couple of years I have been painting portraits and scenes for exhibits and for my pleasure." She plans to get back into writing and illustrating children's books. "That's what I want to get into—as soon as I get painting out of my system."[2]

HOBBIES AND OTHER INTERESTS: Photography, gardening, travel, woodwork.

FOR MORE INFORMATION SEE: Bertha M. Miller and others, compilers, *Illustrators of Children's Books: 1946-1956,* Horn Book, 1958; *New Hope Gazette* (Pa.) April 24, 1980; *Park City Daily News* (Bowling Green, Ky.), May 12, 1980.

HALE, Nancy 1908-

PERSONAL: Born May 6, 1908, in Boston, Mass.; daughter of Philip L. (a painter) and Lillian (also painter; maiden name, Westcott) Hale; married (previously) Taylor Scott Hardin, Charles Wertenbaker; married Fredson Thayer Bowers (professor of English literature), 1942; children: Mark Hardin, William Wertenbaker. *Education:* Winsor School, Boston, Mass., graduate, 1926; studied art at school of the Boston Museum of Fine Arts, 1927, 1928, and in father's studio. *Home:* Woodburn, Route 11, Charlottesville, Va. 22901. *Agent:* Harold Ober Associates, Inc., 40 East 49th St., New York, N.Y. 10017.

CAREER: Vogue, New York, N.Y., assistant editor, 1928-32; *Vanity Fair,* New York, N.Y., assistant editor, 1932-33; *New York Times,* New York, N.Y., first woman reporter, 1934. Lecturer on short story, Bread Loaf Writers' conference, 1957-65. *Member:* Authors League, P.E.N., Cosmopolitan Club (New York). *Awards, honors:* O. Henry Prize for short story, 1933; Benjamin Franklin Magazine Award, special citation for short story, 1958.

WRITINGS—Juvenile: *The Night of the Hurricane,* Coward, 1978.

Other: *The Young Die Good* (novel), Scribner, 1932; *Never Any More* (novel), Scribner, 1934; *The Earliest Dreams* (short

NANCY HALE

stories), Scribner, 1936; *The Prodigal Women* (novel), Scribner, 1942; *Between the Dark and Daylight* (short stories), Scribner, 1943; *The Sign of Jonah* (novel), Scribner, 1950; *The Empress' Ring* (short stories), Scribner, 1955; *Heaven and Hardpan Farm* (novel), Scribner, 1957; *A New England Girlhood* (autobiography), Little, 1958; *Dear Beast* (novel), Little, 1959; *The Pattern of Perfection* (short stories), Little, 1960; *The Realities of Fiction: A Book about Writing,* Little, 1962; *Black Summer* (novel), Little, 1963; (editor) *New England Discovery* (anthology), Coward-McCann, 1963; *Mary Cassatt,* Doubleday, 1975.

Plays include ''Somewhere She Dances,'' and ''The Best of Everything,'' both produced at University of Virginia. Short stories in more than thirty anthologies, including O. Henry and O'Brien annual collections, many of the stories first published in *New Yorker, Harper's, Scribner's, American Mercury, Saturday Evening Post, Redbook, Ladies' Home Journal,* and *University of Virginia Quarterly.*

HOBBIES AND OTHER INTERESTS: Cooking, walking, reading.

FOR MORE INFORMATION SEE: Library Bulletin, January, 1943; *New York Herald Tribune Book Review,* November 19, 1950.

(From *Dear Beast* by Nancy Hale. Jacket illustration by Doris Reynolds.)

An' all us other children, when the supper things
   is done,
We set around the kitchen fire an' has the mostest fun
A list'nin' to the witch tales 'at Annie tells about
An' the gobble-uns 'at gits you
   Ef you
     Don't
      Watch
       Out!

          —James Whitcomb Riley

BRIAN P. HALL

HALL, Brian P(atrick)   1935-

PERSONAL: Born December 29, 1935, in London, England; son of Leonard (a clerk) and Elsie (Ross) Hall; married Diane Ellis Jones (a physical therapist and value conference facilitator), May 6, 1961; children: Martin, Christine. *Education:* University of London, certificate in chemistry and mathematics, 1958; University of British Columbia, B.A., 1962; University of Western Ontario, M.Div., 1965; Centro de Investigaciones Culturales, further graduate study, 1966; Clermont Graduate School, Dr.Rel., 1969. *Home:* 5155 Plantation Dr., Indianapolis, Ind. 46250. *Office:* Graduate Division of Counseling Psychology, University of Santa Clara, Santa Clara, Calif. 95053.

CAREER: Rogers Sugar Refinery, Vancouver, British Columbia research chemist, 1959-60; part-time chemist, 1960-63; Anglican World Mission, Canadian Mission Board, Overseas Mission, researcher on the possibilities of social services in Venezuela, 1963-66, 1966-68; ordained Episcopal priest, 1966; priest in charge of mission parish in Barrio Cuba, San Jose, Costa Rica, 1966-68; Salvation Army Family Service, Los Angeles, Calif., director of family service, 1968-69; Catholic Family Service, Gary, Ind., director of family and community programs, 1969-71; Center for Exploration of Values and Meaning, Indianapolis, Ind., co-founder and member of board of directors, 1971-73, executive director and president, 1973-1979, chairman of board of directors, 1973-75; graduate division of counseling psychology, University of Santa Clara, Santa Clara, Calif., 1979—. Licensed psychologist in State of Indiana. Adjunct professor at St. Louis University. Fund raiser for Family Institute (Costa Rica); chairman of board of Indianapolis Omega Project, 1975. *Member:* American Association

of Pastoral Counselors (diplomat), American Association of Family Counselors (clinical member).

WRITINGS: Learning to Live with Change, two volumes, with tape recording, Argus Communications, 1969; *Values: Exploration and Discovery,* with kit, Argus Communications, 1971; *Value Clarification as Learning Process,* Volume I: *A Sourcebook,* Volume II: *A Guidebook,* Volume III (with Maury Smith): *A Handbook for Christian Educators,* Paulist/Newman, 1973; (with Joseph Osburn) *Nog's Vision,* Paulist/Newman, 1973; *The Development of Consciousness: A Confluent Theory of Values,* Paulist/Newman, 1975; *The Chrysalis Child,* Paulist/Newman, 1975; *The Wizard of Maldoone,* Paulist/Newman, 1975; *The Personal Discernment Inventory,* Paulist/Newman, 1980; *Leadership Through Values,* Paulist/Newman, 1981; *God's Plan for Us,* Paulist/Newman, 1981; *Shepards and Lovers,* Paulist/Newman, 1982. Also author, with Hendrix and Smith, of five volumes in the "Wonder" series for Paulist/Newman, 1974.

Author of tape scripts on teaching. Contributor to church publications. Consultant to Dendron Publishing.

SIDELIGHTS: Several years in Latin America helped Hall to focus interest in the development of consciousness. "Questions such as how do institutions reinforce certain values in individuals, creating or limiting their freedom. The fairy tales in particular look at life styles, values and consciousness raising for alternative futures and life styles of peoples and societies."

HOBBIES AND OTHER INTERESTS: Sailing, fencing with foils, chess, painting, art history, hiking.

FOR MORE INFORMATION SEE: U.S. News and World Report, March 17, 1975.

HANCOCK, Mary A.   1923-

PERSONAL: Born March 21, 1923, in Berlin, Wis.; daughter of Gaylord and Alice (Van Fossen) Hancock. *Education:* Mitchell College, Statesville, N.C., A.A., 1943. *Home:* 5 Golf St., Apt. A, Asheville, N.C. 28801.

WRITINGS—Juveniles: Menace on the Mountain (illustrated by H. Tom Hall), Macrae, 1968; *The Thundering Prairie,* Macrae, 1969.

SIDELIGHTS: Menace on the Mountain was dramatized and produced on NBC-TV by "World of Disney," August, 1970.

HARDING, Lee   1937-
(Harold G. Nye)

BRIEF ENTRY: Born February 19, 1937, in Colac, Victoria, Australia. A writer of science fiction for adults and young people, Harding is a multiple winner of the Ditman Trophy for best Australian science fiction story of the year. In 1970 he received the award for "Dancing Gerontius" and in 1972 for his story "The Fallen Spaceman." Harding's books for young people include *The Children of Atlantis* (Cassell, 1977), *Return to Tomorrow* (Cassell, 1977), and *Misplaced Person* (Harper, 1979). He is an editor of the juvenile science fiction anthology *The Altered I: An Encounter with Science Fiction*

(Berkley Publishing, 1978) and an adult collection, *Beyond Tomorrow: An Anthology of Modern Science Fiction* (Wren, 1976), which includes an introduction by Isaac Asimov. Harding also contributes stories to periodicals, including *If* and *New Writings in Science Fiction,* sometimes writing under the pseudonym Harold G. Nye. Besides editing adult anthologies, Harding also writes adult novels. Among his titles are *A World of Shadows* (R. Hale, 1975) and *The Weeping Sky* (Cassell, 1977). Harding is a member of the Fellowship of Australian Writers and the Science Fiction Writers of America. *Address:* 17 Burwash Rd., Plustead SE18 7QY, London, England. *For More Information See: The International Authors and Writers Who's Who,* 7th edition, International Biographical Centre, 1977; *The Encyclopedia of Science Fiction: An Illustrated A to Z,* Grenada Publishing, 1979.

HAUTZIG, Deborah 1956-

PERSONAL: Born October 1, 1956, in New York, N.Y.; daughter of Walter (a musician) and Esther (a writer; maiden name, Rudomin) Hautzig. *Education:* Attended Carnegie-Mellon University, 1974-75; Sarah Lawrence College, B.A., 1978. *Politics:* "Anything reasonable." *Religion:* Jewish. *Residence:* New York, N.Y. *Office:* Random House, Inc., 201 East 50th St., New York, N.Y. 10022.

CAREER: Random House, Inc., New York, N.Y., promotion assistant in library marketing for Random House, Knopf, and Pantheon Books, 1978-80; assistant editor and staff writer for

DEBORAH HAUTZIG

Random House books, 1980—. *Awards, honors: Hey, Dollface* was named best book for young adults by American Library Association, 1978; *Second Star to the Right* was nominated for the American Book Award in children's fiction category, 1982.

WRITINGS—Children's books: *Hey, Dollface,* Greenwillow, 1978; *The Handsomest Father* (illustrated by Muriel Batherman), Greenwillow, 1979; *Rumpelstiltskin,* Random House, 1979; *Second Star to the Right,* Greenwillow, 1981.

SIDELIGHTS: "I was born in New York City in 1956, and I was born to write. I love to write more than anything else in the world. I feel unified when I write—sort of like being married to myself. Technical ability means nothing without emotional validity, and emotional outpouring without craftsmanship and discipline is ultimately powerless—and usually pretty boring. So I try to make them work together, as best I can.

"I graduated from the Chapin School, spent one year as a Fine Arts major at Carnegie-Mellon University, then transferred to Sarah Lawrence College. In my free time, I love to write (I've kept journals for eleven years and am in #28), read, paint, talk on the phone, and eavesdrop on buses. I love to travel and I love to laugh. I love honest people and I love kids—very compatible objects of affection.

"Books are kind of like children. You have a child and raise that child and think 'Oh! Now I know how to raise a child.' But then you have another child and you can't do it the same way because it's a *different child!* That's how it is with novels. The 'next book' is always a brand new challenge. Ulcer-inducing. But also thrilling.

Then Marsha showed her father the mural she had made. ■ (From *The Handsomest Father* by Deborah Hautzig. Illustrated by Muriel Batherman.)

"The one vital thing I tell myself about writing is: 'You're not out to teach; you're not out to preach. You're out to tell a story about real people, and anything else anyone derives from it is a fringe benefit.' I hope always to avoid didacticism. It's too easy to want to sound eloquent, wise, and witty, and use a book as a podium, rather than being true to its characters. You then dissipate and weaken your own book.

"When I write a book, I want to tell a good story, and tell it as well as I can. That's a given. If I can't grab a reader's attention and sustain interest, it doesn't matter a whit whether what I have to say is worth listening to! The other thing that's really important to me is honesty. Not factual honesty, or chronological honesty—but emotional honesty. Making things up is what fiction is all about. What matters is to tell the emotional truth. It's often painful, but it's worth it.

"I don't ever want to stop getting better as a writer. The minute you stop reaching you're finished. I feel very good about books I've written, and I look forward to the books I'm going to write."

HEFTER, Richard   1942-

PERSONAL: Born March 20, 1942, in New York, N.Y.; son of Joseph (a translator) and Pauline (a bookkeeper; maiden name, Cohen) Hefter; married Olivia McLaren (president of Optimum Resource, Inc.), October 23, 1967; children: Christopher, Nicholas, Gillian, Johnathan. *Education:* Pratt Institute, B.F.A., 1964. *Home:* Greenwoods East, Norfolk, Conn. 06058.

CAREER: Painter, printmaker, graphic designer, publisher, author. One Strawberry, Inc. (juvenile publishing company), New York, N.Y., president, 1975—; Euphrosyne, Inc. (licensing and publishing firm), Norfolk, Conn., vice president, 1977—; Hefter, Johnson & Associates (*WOW* magazine), Princeton, N.J., partner, 1977—; Optimum Resource, Inc. (computer software), Norfolk, Conn., vice president, 1980—. Co-creator (with Jacquelyn Reinach and Ruth Lerner Perle) of the "Sweet Pickles" characters, 1977-82. *Member:* Authors Guild. *Awards, honors:* Fulbright fellowship, 1965; American Institute of Graphic Arts Children's Book Show selection, 1971-72, for excellence in graphic design in *Everything.*

WRITINGS—All self-illustrated, except as noted: (With Martin Moskof) *Everything: An Alphabet, Number, Reading, Counting and Color Identification Book,* Parents Magazine Press, 1971; (with M. Moskof) *Christopher's Parade,* Parents Magazine Press, 1972; (with M. Moskof) *The Great Big Alphabet Picture Book with Lots of Words,* Grosset, 1972; *ABC Coloring Book,* Dover, 1973; (editor with M. Moskof) *Speedy Delivery: A Story from Mister Rogers' Neighborhood,* Small World Enterprises, 1973.

"Shufflebook" series; all with M. Moskof; all self-illustrated: *A Shufflebook* (story in phrases on cards), Western, 1970; *An Animal Shufflebook* (story in phrases on cards), Western, 1971.

"Strawberry book" series; all self-illustrated; all published by One Strawberry; except as noted: *An Animal Alphabet,* 1974; *A Noise in the Closet,* 1974; *Noses and Toes,* 1974; *One White Crocodile Smile,* 1974; *The Strawberry Picture Dictionary,* 1974; *The Strawberry Word Book,* 1974; *The Strawberry Book of Colors,* 1975; *Things That Go,* 1975; *Yes and No: A Book of Opposites,* 1975; (editor) *The Strawberry Mother Goose* (verse; illustrated by Lawrence DiFiori), 1975; *The Strawberry*

RICHARD HEFTER

Book of Shapes 1976; *One Bear Two Bears: The Strawberry Number Book,* Strawberry/McGraw, 1980; *The Strawberry Look Book,* Strawberry/McGraw, 1980.

"Sweet Pickles" series; all self-illustrated; all published by Holt, except as noted: *Hippo Jogs for Health,* 1977; *Lion Is Down in the Dumps,* 1977; *Moody Moose Buttons,* 1977; *Stork Spills the Beans,* 1977; *Very Worried Walrus,* 1977; *Yakety Yak Yak Yak,* 1977; *Zip Goes Zebra,* 1977; *Kiss Me—I'm Vulture,* 1978; *No Kicks for Dog,* 1978; *Pig Thinks Pink,* 1978; *Turtle Throws a Tantrum,* 1978; *Who Can Trust You—Kangaroo?,* 1978; *Xerus Won't Allow It,* 1978; *The Great Race,* Euphrosyne, 1981; *Quick Lunch Munch,* Euphrosyne, 1981; *Robot S.P.3,* Euphrosyne, 1981; *Wet All Over,* Euphrosyne, 1981; *The Secret Club,* Euphrosyne, 1981; *Some Friend,* Euphrosyne, 1981.

"Wow" series; all with Philip Johnson; all self-illustrated; all published by Scholastic: *The Great Wow Toy Book,* 1982; *The Great Wow Game Book,* Scholastic, 1983.

Illustrator—"Sweet Pickles" series; all written by J. Reinach, except as noted; all published by Holt, except as noted: *Elephant Eats the Profits,* 1977; *Fish and Flips,* 1977; *Fixed by Camel,* 1977; *Goose Goofs Off,* 1977; *Me Too Iguana,* 1977; *Quail Can't Decide,* 1977; *Rest Rabbit Rest,* 1977; *Who Stole Alligator's Shoe,* 1977; *Happy Birthday Unicorn,* 1978; *Jackal Wants Everything,* 1978; *Nuts to Nightingale,* 1978; *Octopus Protests,* 1978; *Scaredy Bear,* 1978; *A Bad Break,* Euphrosyne, 1980; *Rainy Day Parade,* Euphrosyne, 1980; *Wait Wait Wait,* Euphrosyne, 1980; *What a Mess,* Euphrosyne, 1980; *What's So Great About Nice?,* Euphrosyne, 1981; *Ice Cream Dreams,*

Euphrosyne, 1981; *Wet Paint,* Euphrosyne, 1981; Ruth Lerner Perle, *The Grand Prize,* Euphrosyne, 1981; Elaine P. Wonsavage, *Preschool Program,* Volumes 1-8, Weekly Reader books, 1981; E. P. Wonsavage, *Preschool Program,* Volumes 9-16, Weekly Reader Books, 1982; E. P. Wonsavage, *Preschool Program,* Volumes 17-36, Weekly Reader Books, 1982; J. Reinach and R. L. Perle (editors) *Sweet Pickles Dictionary* (16 Volumes), Time-Life Books, 1982; *Goof-Off Goose's Dinner Party,* Random House, 1982; Edith Adams, *The Scaredy Books,* Random House, 1983; E. Adams, *The Noisy Book,* Random House, 1983; Ellen Weiss, *The Angry Book,* Random House, 1983; E. Weiss, *The Messy Book,* Random House, 1983.

Other: Fred M. Rogers, adaptor, *The Elves, the Shoemaker, and the Shoemaker's Wife: A Retold Tale,* Small World Enterprises, 1973; Kathleen N. Daly, editor, *Bruno Bear's Bedtime Book* (poems), One Strawberry, 1976; Judy Freudberg, *Some More Most,* One Strawberry, 1976; Joan Lamport, *The Wordship Activity Book,* Arista, 1976.

Editor, art director and creator of *WOW* magazine through Scholastic Magazines, Inc.

ADAPTATIONS—Movies and filmstrips: "Colors" (filmstrip with guide and records or cassettes; based on *The Strawberry Book of Colors*), Miller-Brody Productions, 1976; "Noses and Toes" (filmstrip with guide and records or cassettes), Miller-Brody Productions, 1976; "One White Crocodile Smile" (filmstrip with guide and records or cassettes), Miller-Brody Productions, 1976; "Yes and No" (filmstrip with guide and records or cassettes), Miller Brody, 1976.

Computer software diskettes: "The Stickybear ABC," programmed by Steve and Janie Worthington and Spencer K. Howe, Optimum Resource, 1982; "Stickybear Numbers," programmed by S. and J. Worthington, Optimum Resource, 1982; "Stickybear Bop," programmed by Jack Rice, Optimum Resource, 1982; "Old Ironsides," programmed by J. Rice, Optimum Resource, 1982.

WORK IN PROGRESS: Ten titles featuring "Stickybear" for inclusion in the Strawberry Library of First Learning; forty Sweet Pickles books under contract to Random House.

SIDELIGHTS: "Dealing with children, my own and other people's in a simple and direct way and keeping busy are two things which have always been important to me. The first of those things seems to be providing me with an ample measure of the second.

"The single most important ingredient in any work for children is fun. If the work is fun to do and fun to read and see, kids will almost certainly respond. The underlying messages are always there and real value can be achieved without sacrificing any of the joy in a story. My books and the characters in them move in a world that allows children to laugh.

"I enjoy the spread and growth of the new technology and see micro-computers as an important part of publishing in the future. After much long, expensive and painful research, we have been able to create a standard of quality in graphics for computers which is the equal to the graphics in my books. At Optimum Resource, we work towards the blending of artist and programmer that we know will be the future of computing.

(From *One Bear Two Bears* by Richard Hefter. Illustrated by the author.)

"Well," thought Goose, "as long as I'm up, maybe I'll have some breakfast." And she went downstairs.

The kitchen floor was all gooey and slippery and wet.

"It seems I forgot to put the ice cream back in the freezer last night," said Goose. "I guess I'll have to mop the floor. But not today. I'm taking it easy today. I'll do it tomorrow."

(From *Goose Goofs Off* by Jacquelyn Reinach. Illustrated by Richard Hefter.)

''I look forward to the continuing development and growth of my characters and their world. The 'Sweet Pickles,' 'Stickybear,' and the 'Strawberry Book' gang are growing all the time. So am I.''

The twenty-six sassy animal characters who live in the Town of Sweet Pickles have good reason to sing their song these days. In less than five years, their ''mess of pickles'' is being sung to the tune $63 million dollars of gross sales in books, records, licensed merchandise and forthcoming animated television specials. Every day, more and more children between the ages of three and ten (and their parents) are laughing—and learning something about life—from the antics of such characters as Goof-Off Goose, Accusing Alligator, and Worried Walrus.

The Sweet Pickles Book Club, operated by Xerox Corporation, has distributed 20 million books. Xerox's Weekly Reader Book Services Division, the umbrella for five more major book clubs, reports that Sweet Pickles is now one of the largest children's book clubs in the world, with a membership in the United States of almost a million children.

In addition to its books, the Sweet Pickles property includes twenty-seven songs, five multi-media educational programs and designs which, so far, appear on stuffed toys, T-shirts, night wear, track shorts, pins, pendants, barrettes, belt buckles, mugs, banks, boxes and collectible figures. The Parsons School

of Design has elected to include Sweet Pickles in its '81-'82 curriculum with the goal of designing a line of clothes for boys and girls. Foreign rights have been acquired in eight languages, with international merchandising in development.

The running theme behind Sweet Pickles is the chronicled adventures of the twenty-six animal characters—thirteen boys and thirteen girls—who live in the Town of Sweet Pickles. Each has an exaggerated personality trait—procrastination, optimism, nervousness or the like—that gets him or her into, and out of, life's ''pickles.''

In the Town of Sweet Pickles, where each character has a home and a job, no one suddenly sees the light or reforms. Life goes on, problems get solved, and new problems come along. The animals manage to tolerate each other's quirks, even when they don't like what's happening. And they help each other out with surprising softness and sensitivity.

Children not only see Goof-Off Goose stalling for time at every chore, they also see her help Worried Walrus deal with nightmares. Responsible Rabbit goes berserk waiting in lines and children learn something about being patient at the same time they are laughing. Both negative situations and negative qualities are shown to have their silver linings, thus, the name, *Sweet Pickles*. Children learn that few people are entirely bad or entirely good.

HEINEMANN, George Alfred   1918-

BRIEF ENTRY: Born December 9, 1918, in Chicago, Ill. Television executive and creator of children's television programs. As program manager of television station WNBQ (now WMAQ-TV), in Chicago, Heinemann developed the program "Ding Dong School" in 1952. In 1956 he went to WRCA-TV (now WNBC-TV) in New York City. He was director of public affairs there from 1967 to 1970. In 1970 he was named vice-president of children's programming, becoming the first person to receive a vice-presidency in that field. In 1973 he became vice-president of special children's programming. Since 1978 Heinemann has been vice-president and general program executive at WNBC-TV. He has been the recipient of numerous awards, including the Peabody award in 1953, 1966 to 1968, 1972, 1974, and 1978, an Emmy nomination or award in 1952, 1962, 1964, 1968, and 1976 to 1979, and Best Children's Program in the World award at the Prix Jeunesse Internationale in 1966. Heinemann is a member of the International Radio and TV society, and of the National Academy of TV Arts and Sciences, in which he also serves as a trustee. He is the creator of the television programs "Go," "Go-USA," "Take a Giant Step," "NBC Children's Theatre," and "An Evening at Tanglewood." *Home:* 11 West 81st St., New York, N.Y. 10020.

HERMES, Patricia   1936-

PERSONAL: Born February 21, 1936, in Brooklyn, N.Y.; daughter of Frederick Joseph (a bank's trust officer) and Jessie (Gould) Martin; married Matthew E. Hermes (a research and development director for a chemical company), August 24, 1957; children: Paul, Mark, Timothy, Matthew, Jr., Jennifer. *Education:* St. John's University, Jamaica, N.Y., B.A., 1957. *Home and office:* 3036 Princess Anne Cres., Chesapeake, Va. 23321. *Agent:* Dorothy Markinko (juvenile books) and Julie Fallowfield (adult books), McIntosh & Otis, Inc., 475 Fifth Ave., New York, N.Y. 10017.

CAREER: Writer, 1977—. Rollingcrest Junior High School, Takoma Park, Md., teacher of English and social studies, 1957-58; Delcastle Technical High School, Delcastle, Del., teacher of home-bound children, 1972-73; Norfolk Public School System, Norfolk, Va., writer-in-residence, 1981—. *Member:* Authors Guild, Society of Children's Book Writers.

WRITINGS—All juveniles; all published by Harcourt: *What If They Knew,* 1980; *Nobody's Fault?,* 1981; *You Shouldn't Have to Say Goodbye* (novel), 1982; *Who Will Take Care of Me?,* 1983. Contributor to magazines, including *Women's Day, Life*

The men lifted up the stretcher, slid it into the ambulance, and then one of them climbed in back with Monse. The other closed the two big doors . . . . ■ (From *Nobody's Fault?* by Patricia Hermes. Jacket illustration by Bonnie Dann.)

PATRICIA HERMES

and Health, Connecticut, County, American Baby, Mother's Day, and newspapers.

WORK IN PROGRESS: A children's book about friendship, values, and of difficulties in being one's own person; *Interruptions,* nonfiction for adults.

SIDELIGHTS: "Although I have done many nonfiction articles and essays for adults, I write primarily for children and young adults. I think I have chosen writing for young people because I remember what it was like to be a child, remember how it felt, and remember more than anything how painful it was. As adults, we often try to deceive ourselves that childhood is a safe, pleasant place to be. It isn't—at least, not much of the time. For me, it is important to say this to young people, to let them know they are not alone and that others share their feelings, their dreams and fears and hopes. It is important for them to know that things aren't so great in other children's lives either, because I have long believed that anything is bearable when we know that we are not alone. This does not mean that my books must be sad—not at all. What it means is that I need to tell young people that there are tough times going on in their lives but other kids share those problems, and that there is HOPE. Hope is the most important thing I can hold out to them. The pleasure and joy that I find in writing is in expressing how I feel in a way with which young readers can identify. My greatest joy comes when I receive a letter from a young reader, when someone writes and says, 'You know exactly how I feel!'

"Most of the subjects of my books come, in some small way at least, from my own background. Jeremy, in my first book, has epilepsy. When I was a child, I too had epilepsy, and it was a very painful thing emotionally. I wanted to write about it to tell kids today what it's like, to help young people who might have the disease, or children who might know someone who has it. But that is not all. One does not have to have epilepsy to have the feelings that Jeremy had, to feel lonely, frightened, rejected. All children feel that way at times, so in writing about those feelings, I hope I can help them cope with

their feelings. It is up to my readers to decide if I achieve that goal.

"In *Nobody's Fault?,* a young child dies in an accident. That accident did not really happen, not to my children nor to anyone I know. But many years ago, one of my children did die from a disease when she was just an infant. In some ways then, I am talking about my own feelings in that book, my feelings about losing a child in death. These are feelings I believe a child can identify with, because children have strong feelings. They know about death and separation and loneliness.

"My nonfiction book for adults is also a result of my own feelings. I am writing about what it is like to be a woman today, brought up for roles that no longer exist, in a society that bears little resemblance to the one for which we were traditionally prepared. I write about this because I believe not enough writers are addressing the issue today and women, as well as children (and men), need to be told that they are not alone."

HILL, Robert W(hite)   1919-1982

OBITUARY NOTICE—See sketch in *SATA* Volume 12: Born September 12, 1919, in Richmond Va.; died of cancer, September 25, 1982, in Norfolk, Conn. Publisher, editor, and author of books for children. Hill began his career in publishing as a sales representative and editorial reader with Harcourt, Brace & Co. In 1955, he began an eleven-year association with John Day Co., Inc., where he served first as associate editor and later as managing editor and vice-president. At the time of his death, he was editor-in-chief of New Century Publishers. Two of Hill's books for children, *What Colonel Glenn Did All Day* and *What the Moon Astronauts Will Do All Day: The Official Plan of Project Apollo,* center around the space program, an interest which was the result of his boyhood fascination for aviation. He also wrote *The Chesapeake Bay Bridge Tunnel. For More Information See: Contemporary Authors,* Volumes 9-12, revised, Gale, 1974. *Obituaries: Publishers Weekly,* October 8, 1982.

HOUSELANDER, (Frances) Caryll   1900-1954

BRIEF ENTRY: Born in 1901, in Bath, England; died October 12, 1954, in London, England. Hollander was an author and illustrator of religious books for children and adults. She was educated in convent schools in Warwickshire and Sussex, and worked in an advertising office during 1945. Her spare time was spent in sculpture and occupational therapy for victims of World War II, both children and soldiers. She was also a contributor to *Children's Messenger.* Her writing career began with the publication of children's books, including *Inside the Ark, and Other Stories* and *Terrible Farmer Timson, and Other Stories.* She provided illustrations for a number of children's books, including Rev. Geoffrey Bliss's *A Retreat with St. Ignatius in Pictures for Children.* Among her adult titles are *The Reed of God, The Flowering Tree,* and *Guilt. The Letters of Caryll Houselander: Her Spiritual Legacy* was published posthumously in 1965, as was *The Mother of Christ,* in 1978. *For More Information See: Catholic Authors,* St. Martin's Abbey, 1948; Maisie Ward, *Caryll Houselander: That Divine Eccentric,* Sheed, 1962; Ward, editor, *The Letters of Caryll Houselander: Her Spiritual Legacy,* Sheed, 1965. *Obituaries: New York Times,* October 14, 1954; *Wilson Library Bulletin,* December, 1954.

HUGHES, Thomas 1822-1896
(Old Boy, Vacuus Viator)

PERSONAL: Born October 20, 1822 (some sources cite October 23), in Uffington, Berkshire, England; died March 22, 1896, in Brighton, England; son of John (a Berkshire squire, writer, artist, and editor); and Margaret (Wilkinson) Hughes; married Anne Frances Ford, August 17, 1847; children: Maurice, and a daughter that died at an early age. *Education:* Rugby School, 1833-42; Oriel College, Oxford, B.A., 1845; Lincoln Inn, 1845.

CAREER: Author and lecturer. Called to the Bar, 1848; member of the British House of Commons, 1865-74; appointed Queen's Council, 1869; judge of county courts, 1882. Founder, "Rugby Colony" in Tennessee, 1880; established Working Men's College, London, and served as its head, 1872-83; worked with "Christian Socialism" movement with Charles Kingsley and F. D. Maurice. *Member:* Society of Antiquaries (fellow, 1849-54).

WRITINGS—Novels for young people: (Originally published under the pseudonymn Old Boy) *Tom Brown's School Days,* Macmillan, 1857 [other editions include those illustrated by Arthur Hughes and Sydney P. Hall, Macmillan, 1869, reprinted, Godfrey Cave Assoc., 1979; Edmund J. Sullivan, Macmillan, 1902, reissued, St. Martin's, 1974; E. M. Ashe, P. F. Collier, 1903; H. M. Brock, Oxford University Press, 1907; Louis Rhead, Harper, 1911; Jeannette S. Van Abbé, Dent, 1951, reissued, 1976; Will Nickless, Collins, 1953; Ernest Shepard, Ginn, 1959], also published as *School Days at Rugby,* Ticknor & Fields, 1857; *The Scouring of the White Horse; or, The Long Vacation Ramble of a London Clerk* (illustrated by Richard Doyle), Macmillan, 1859, reprinted P.P.B. Minet, 1972; *Tom Brown at Oxford,* Ticknor & Fields, 1861, reissued, Crowell, 1961 [another edition illustrated by Sydney P. Hall, Macmillan, 1879].

Other principal writings: *Alfred the Great,* Macmillan, 1869; *Memoir of a Brother,* J. R. Osgood, 1873; *The Acolyte; or, The Christian Scholar,* Cunningham, 1876; *Working Classes in Europe, and Other Essays,* Barnes, 1877; *Old Church: What Shall We Do with It?,* Macmillan, 1878; *The Manliness of Christ,* Macmillan, 1879; (under the pseudonym Vacuus Viator) *Flying South: Recollections of France and Its Littoral,* Kegan Paul, 1881; *Rugby, Tennessee,* Macmillan, 1881, reprinted, Porcupine Press, 1975; *Memoir of Daniel Macmillan,* Macmillan, 1882; *Life and Times of Peter Cooper,* Macmillan, 1886; *James Fraser, Second Bishop of Manchester; A Memoir, 1818-1885,* Macmillan, 1887; *David Livingstone,* Macmillan, 1889; *Vacation Rambles,* Macmillan, 1895; *Early Memories for the Children* [London], 1899.

Contributor of short stories and articles to periodicals, including *Good Works, Spectator,* and *Review of Reviews.*

ADAPTATIONS—Motion pictures: "Tom Brown's Schooldays," Windsor Film Co., 1916, RKO Radio Pictures, 1940, United Artists Corp., 1951, Time-Life Multimedia, starring Anthony Murphy, 1976.

SIDELIGHTS: **October 20, 1822.** Born in Uffington, Berkshire, England, to John (a "scholarly dilettante") and Margaret (Wilkinson) Hughes; the second of eight children.

Of the frequent visits to his grandmother's he could ". . . recall the pleasing thrill of excitement which ran through us when we caught the first faint clink of hoof and roll of wheels, which

THOMAS HUGHES

told of the approach of the coach before the leaders had appeared over the brow of the gentle slope some two hundred yards from the cross-roads where, recently deposited from the phaeton (dog carts not having been yet invented) we had been waiting with our trunk beside us in joyful expectation. Thrice happy if, as the coach pulled up to take us on board, we heard the inspiring words 'room in front,' and proceeded to scramble up and take our seats behind the box, waving a cheerful adieu to the sober family servant as he turned his horse's head slowly homeward, his mission discharged.

"[Grandmother] used to take me and my brother out shopping in the early morning, and our excursions extended as far as Billingsgate fish market, then at the height of the career which has secured for it an unenviable place in our English vocabulary. It was certainly a strange place for a lady and small boys, and is connected with the most vivid of my childish memories. Toddling after my grandmother to the stall where she made her purchases, we came one morning on the end of a quarrel between a stalwart fish-hag and her fancy man. She struck him on the head with a pewter pot which flattened with the blow. He fell like a log, the first blood I had ever seen, gushing from his temples, and the scene is as fresh as ever in my memory at the end of half a century. The narrow courts in that neighbourhood are still my favourite haunts in London." [Edward C. Mack and W. G. Armytage, *Thomas Hughes: The Life of the Author of "Tom Brown's Schooldays,"* Ernest Benn, 1952.[1]]

1830-1833. Sent with brother George to Twyford School. "We had scarcely been there a week when the first crisis occurred. . . . My form had a lesson in early Greek History to get up, in which a part of the information communicated was, that Cadmus was the first man who 'carried letters from Asia

. . .And at last, having exhausted all other places, finished up with inscribing H. East, T. Brown, on the minute-hand of the great clock. . . . ■ (From *Tom Brown's School Days* by Thomas Hughes. Illustrated by Edmund J. Sullivan.)

to Greece.' When we came to be examined, the master asked us, 'What was Cadmus?' This way of putting it puzzled us all for a moment or two, when suddenly the words 'carried letters' came into my head, and, remembering the man with the leather bag who used to bring my father's papers and letters, and our marbles and whipcord, from Farringdon, I shouted, 'A postman, Sir.' The master looked very angry for a moment, but, seeing my perfect good faith, and that I had jumped up expecting to go to the head of the form, he burst out laughing. Of course all the boys joined in, and when school was over I was christened Cadmus. That I probably would not have minded, but it soon shortened into 'Cad,' at which all the blood in my eight-year-old veins was on fire." [Thomas Hughes, *Memoir of a Brother*, James R. Osgood & Co., 1873.[2]]

"We were allowed (within limits) to choose our own poets, and I always chose Scott from family tradition, and in this way learned the whole of the 'Lady of the Lake,' and most of the 'Lay of the Last Minstrel' and 'Marmion' by heart, and can repeat much of them to this day."[1]

"Though never very ambitious myself, I was more so than [George] was, and had the greatest wish to do every exercise and game as well as I possibly could. . . . But I never could get nearer to his secret than this, that it lay in a sort of unconsciousness, which I believe to be natural courage. Now, with all the thinking in the world about it, I never could have acquired this natural gift; but, by having an example of it constantly before my eyes, I got the next best thing, which was a scorn of myself for feeling fear, [and by] . . . degrees hardened into the habit of doing what I saw him do, and so I managed to pass through school and college without betraying the timidity of which I was ashamed."[2]

"Looking back over all those years, I can call to mind no single unkind, or unworthy, or untruthful, act or word of his; and amongst all the good influences for which I have to be thankful, I reckon the constant presence and example of his brave, generous, and manly life is one of the most powerful and ennobling."[1]

1833-1842. School at Rugby. "In my first three days, before the upper school came back, [I] imbibed dreadful notions of the life of slavery which lay before us. Study fagging [serving upper school boys] and night fagging in the House, and all manner of outside fagging, would soon make me a sadder as well as wiser lower-school boy. I noticed that my informants showed few symptoms of the crushing tyranny of which they spoke, but nevertheless awaited with some misgivings the arrival of our taskmasters. Well, they came; and though House fagging was not pleasant, it was endurable, and as for outside fagging, I certainly enjoyed it for the first seven or eight weeks.

"You may well believe what a power Rugby has been in my life. The years from ten to eighteen are the most important in a boy's life, and I passed all those years under the spell of this place and Arnold [the headmaster], and for half a century have never ceased to thank God for it."[1]

1842. Studied at Oxford. Met Anne Frances Ford ("Fanny"), but her father ". . . very properly said we were silly young people and must not see one another for years, or correspond that we might see whether we really knew our minds. This pulled me up short, [it was] the most important event of my life. [But] I was never very desponding, and always looked on the bright side of things. I went back to Oxford a new man.

"My engagement was a constant stimulus to work and economy, and made me indifferent as to society."[1]

August 17, 1847. Married Anne Frances Ford.

January 28, 1848. Admitted to the bar. Hughes wrote to a friend: "I don't think I am quite so sure as you that one oughtn't to change, and often feel strongly tempted to turn parson. . . . I think Fanny would make a great parsoness. . . . Meantime you and I will most likely grind on to our graves making and administering feeble and flabby laws. . . .

"We are making a famous beginning to our vacation, interrupted only by a miserable client of mine, for whom I am preparing the elaborate will of a rich gent whose brain is softening; I wish you would bring in a Bill to make it unlawful for parties to let their brains soften in the long vacation."[1]

1848-1853. Joined the Christian Socialist Movement, working for co-operatives and striving to help the working man. Hughes believed that Christian socialism ". . . is the crusade of the twentieth century."[1]

1854. Continued his law work while teaching boxing at the "working man's college." "After some four years' experience of the work of Christian socialism amongst the working people of London, it became clear to Mr. Maurice [a preacher] that something more was needed than the mere setting-up of workshops.

"So when the classes were organised the only one which I felt competent to take was the legal one. The law of partnership and association, as it affected the working classes, was familiar to me, as I had lately been helping in the promotion and passing of the first Industrial and Provident Societies Act. So the class was started, and some eight or ten pupils entered; but the subject was soon exhausted, and their interest in it, and at the end of the second term the class collapsed.

"I was anxious still to do some work, but what? All the regular classes were fully manned with teachers, and no new ones were needed. There was one opening, however, which I thought I had discovered, and, after some hesitation, named it to our principal. I had been much struck, and told him so, by the awkward gait and unhealthy look of almost all of our pupils. Round shoulders, narrow chests, stiff limbs, were, I submitted, as bad as defective grammar and arithmetic, quite as easily cured, and as much our business if we were to educate the whole man. I put up the necessary notice, brought out my old well-used gloves, had the bag room cleared and the gas lit, and awaited pupils in trowsers and flannel shirt, the sleeves rolled up above my elbows. They were shy at first, but, the ice once broken, they came by dozens, so that I had all my work cut out. And good hard work it was for some time, as I made it a rule that every pupil must spar with me only, until I had tested his temper, strength, and skill, and knew how far he could be trusted. Boxing, I impressed on them, was a science, in which no real progress was possible except according to rules and principles, which had to be mastered patiently. Nothing but loss of temper and bloody noses would come of mere pummelling matches.

"I had a right to speak confidently, as I had served a thorough apprenticeship myself. It began at school many years before, where in my early days the big boys used to set us smaller ones to pummel each other in the hall for their amusement, and the more we lost our temper and damaged each other the better they were pleased. In due course, my generation succeeded to the command, and we certainly were an improvement on our forerunners. Boxing was not stopped, but the scene of action was transferred from the hall to the sixth-form room, and compulsion ceased. Any fags who liked to come were welcome, but no boy need come who did not relish the amusement. In my last school year, I had a sort of presidentship of the room on boxing nights, and was considered an authority on the subject; and, indeed, in my own opinion, had very little to learn in the art of self-defence.

"This conceit was well taken out of me in my first term at Oxford. An ex-member of the prize ring, which was in those days an institution much in vogue with young England, was in the habit of coming down every term from London, to take orders in his trade and give lessons in boxing. He was known in the ring as 'the Flying Tailor.'. . . Now, I weighed eleven stone two pounds, and was some inches taller, and was, moreover, in good training, whereas he was puffy, and already running to stomach; so I thought his extra weight of about two stones was rather a disadvantage, and put on the gloves with no misgiving as to holding my own. In two minutes I found out my mistake. Do all I knew I couldn't get near him, while he seemed to hit me in counter and rally just as he pleased.

Lodbroc the Dane. ■ (From *The Scouring of the White Horse; or, The Long Vacation Ramble of a London Clerk* by Thomas Hughes. Illustrated by Richard Doyle.)

The only consolation I had was to notice how he winced in parrying my furious attacks, as his right forearm was a mass of bruises. However, I had found out that I must go to school again, and forget all I thought I knew, if I wanted to be a good boxer, and so swallowed my pride and all economic scruples, and took lessons of 'the Flying Tailor.'. . .

". . . The social life of the college developed naturally and vigorously, and on the whole I think has proved the most successful and healthy social work I have ever taken part in. . . ." [Thomas Hughes, "Fragments of Autobiography, Early Memories," edited by Henry C. Shelley, *The Cornhill Magazine,* January-June, 1925.[3]]

1855. Vacation by the sea, where Hughes wrote most of *Tom Brown's Schooldays.* "We are in the most ridiculously small house here you ever saw. There is no room for Maurice [his son] and me to wash, so we turn out to the beach every morning at 7 to bathe, a source of danger just now as it is very rough with a great under-tow, delicious swimming, but as you come ashore the waves cut you over and mingle you with the pebbles in a surprising manner, and as I am obliged to spend most my time among them (i.e. the breakers) holding on to Maurice who can't swim, I am having rare practice in picking myself up; I am delighted to find how plucky he is, and if not carried out to sea in the next few mornings he will make a rare young water dog."[1]

1856. Daughter Evie died. "I have got myself into the habit of looking on all visible things and all accidents which can affect (except insofar as right and wrong are involved therein) as not of the slightest importance. . . . It does not seem the least strange to me, but inexpressibly real and joyful and soothing, to have a little golden-haired angel daughter whom I cannot see, but who is far more with us all than ever she was on earth,

It was another affair altogether, a dark ride at the top of the Tally-Ho, I can tell you, in a tight Petersham Coat, and your feet dangling six inches from the floor. Then you knew what cold was . . . . ■ (From *Tom Brown's School Days* by Thomas Hughes. Frontispiece by Frank Schoonover.)

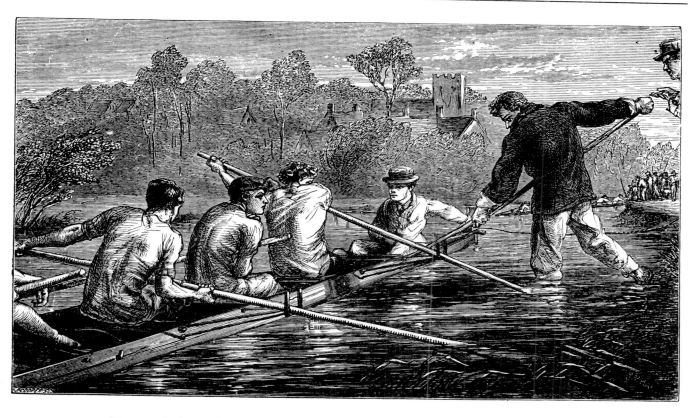

There was just room for stroke oars to dip, and that was all. The starting rope was as taut as a harp-string; will Miller's left hand hold out? ■(From *Tom Brown at Oxford* by Thomas Hughes. Illustrated by Sydney P. Hall.)

and whom I shall never have to look sternly at for not learning her lessons."[1]

April 24, 1857. *Tom Brown's Schooldays* published. Hughes wrote to Alexander Macmillan, the publisher: "My whole object in writing at all was to get the chance of preaching. When a man comes to my time of life and has his bread to make and very little time to spare, is it likely that he will spend almost the whole of his yearly vacation in writing a story just to amuse people."[1]

Tom Brown's Schooldays was originally published anonymously, but ". . . it made such a hit that the publishers soon betrayed the secret, and I became famous. . . . It is certainly very odd how it suits so many different folk."[1]

1859. Son, Maurice, died.

July, 1861. *Tom Brown at Oxford,* a sequel to *Tom Brown's Schooldays,* published. It began in serial form in *Macmillan's Magazine,* 1859.

1863. During the American Civil War, Hughes participated in a campaign in England to rally support for the North. "You may judge of the difficulty of getting our public men of note to take active sides with the North [or to go] to public meetings and speak against secession and slavery by the fact that I was about the most prominent speaker at the first great public meeting which was held in London [and] was (unwillingly) pushed a good deal to the front."[1]

1865. Elected to Parliament to represent working class. ". . . My side of the movement goes right everywhere whether we make our fortunes by trying to do justice or not. Really with a little wisdom and care poor old England may yet be made a good place for poor folk to live in."[1]

Became chairman of first congress of co-operative movement. "Every man must have some way of spending his spare cash. Some men like moors in Scotland, some like keeping hounds and horses, and for many years I have had a taste for co-operation."[1]

1866. Special London correspondent for Horace Greeley's *New York Tribune* for four months.

June, 1870. The much dreamed of trip to the United States materialized, with as its highlights a visit to the American poet, essayist and diplomat, James Russell Lowell, whose work he had admired for years. Hughes worried "whether a most precious illusion might not be about to vanish. I almost trembled as I drove up . . . in the Boston hack through Cambridge.

". . . Though we had not dined, we were too eager to get to talk, and to give no trouble, to accept any of his hospitable offers except a glass of Sherry and a biscuit. These he brought out triumphantly after a short search, excusing the slight delay as Mrs. Lowell was out. The Sherry was in a large stone jar, and looked rather light in colour as he poured us out bumpers. The first mouthful was trying to thirsty souls after a hot fourteen hours journey. It was fine old whiskey, and he hurried off to

. . .The two stand to one another like men; rally follows rally in quick succession, each fighting as if he thought to finish the whole thing out of hand. ■ (From *Tom Brown's School Days* by Thomas Hughes. Illustrated by S. Van Abbé.)

change the jar, explaining that the only alcohol in the house was in these jars, and he used it so seldom that he did not well know them apart. And so we sat on in the moonlight, falling through the 'English elms' of which he was so proud, till late into the night, when I went to bed as happy as the Queen of Sheba when she found that the realized Solomon was far better and bigger than all the accounts she had heard of him in her own land.''[1]

''I parted with Lowell and his home, feeling that the meeting had been more than successful. For these 18 or 19 years I have reveled in his books. Indeed, have got so much from them and learned to love the parent so well, as I imagined him, that I almost feared to meet him, lest pleasant illusions should be broken. I found him much better than his books.'' [Dan Goodwin, ''A Speech,'' in *Chicago Literary Club,* Smith Rogers Publisher, June 8, 1896.[4]]

Hughes was very popular in the United States and enjoyed warm welcomes during his extensive travels around the country. ''Robert Lincoln (Abe's son) and a lot of his friends are our entertainers [and] . . . I have never had a more hearty greeting or kinder words. . . .''[4]

''Certainly I never saw, heard of, or could imagine anything like the hospitality . . . it is no doubt in some degree and in

individual cases, owing to the part I took during the war in England, but Democrats as well as Republicans have been amongst our warmest hosts; in fact, I am fairly puzzled, and allow the tide at least to carry me along, floating down it and enjoying everything as well as I can.''[1]

Upon leaving, Hughes wrote: ''Almost glad to get away, for I feel awestricken and humiliated beyond expression at the sort of greeting I get from all people in this country—one ought to get in one's shell and think it all over with God—that's the real fact—and I shall hope to be able to do this on shipboard.''[1]

''. . . I was positively ashamed and scarcely knew how to meet it all, or what to say to them, but it was less embarrassing than it would have been with any other young men, for this kind of young Americans . . . is so transparently sincere that you can come out quite square with him before you have known him an hour.''[4]

1872. President of the Working Man's College.

1880-1892. Founded Rugby, Tennessee, in the hopes of creating an ideal colony for English Youth. Because of land swindles, mismanagement, and the inadaptability of the colonists, Hughes' utopia failed. ''The place has received a blow from which it will take years to recover if it ever does . . . which makes me a really poor man again at a time when it is hard to recover. . . . As to the future—I have given up of course the idea of getting back into Parliament. . . . Meantime I shall be writing again, chiefly the long abandoned pot-boiler! Fiction, which would be the most profitable, I have long felt an aversion for which I doubt if anything can overcome—besides I am too old for it now. All unpaid work . . . I give up except Co-operation, which I can't leave just now, the time being too critical. Our Union . . . is at the parting of the ways, and no one who wants it to take the right turn can take off his hand— I must remain too at the Working Men's College until they can find a suitable successor.

''It was a rash undertaking at my age, but . . . I am hot-headed more or less and the thing seized on me mightily. . . . I have risked in it more than I should have done (but that again is my temper) and have sorely repented it, though my dear brave wife like herself, though the whole thing was against her wish, has entirely pardoned it.''[1]

1882. Resigned from co-operative union and became judge in a county court. ''Politics and all public action connected with them are of course over with me now I have accepted the county court—I never thought that I should have borne the change so tranquilly, but I am really inclined to rejoice in it.''[1]

1895. ''I am well past seventy, the psalmist's age of man: I have rather lost touch with the Union. So it is quite on the cards that I may not be named as a delegate by any of the associations in Union. But 'save as aforesaid' (as we used to say in equity pleading) i.e. *if* I am still alive, *and* elected to go to Congress, I shall have great pleasure in being your guest. Nothing makes my last years so hopeful and cheery as seeing how many persons are coming out fair and square for Christian Socialism. I have been sure for these last fifty years or thereabouts that in no other way can our country (or indeed any other) be saved, and by this way she may and will be.''[1]

"He turns his cob's head and rides quietly after us just out of shot. How that'ere cob did step! We never shook him off not a dozen yards in the six mile...." ■ (From *Tom Brown's School Days* by an "Old Boy." Illustrated by Louis Rhead.)

In his old age Hughes became more at peace with himself, as he noticed in his dream patterns. "I have always been a great dreamer (at which confession I am aware that my wife and family will break into a merry laugh), but I don't mean in my waking hours, but at night, in the sleep which is common—I wish it were more common—to all men and women. . . . Dreamland was to me a most provoking country. Whatever I had to do in it, as a rule, came to grief, or perhaps I should say wouldn't come to anything. If I had to make a speech I couldn't say what I wanted to say, and often could say nothing at all; if I had to fight I could never hit out; if riding, I could never get my horse to go at a fence; and when I committed horrible crimes, was powerless either to escape or confess. But all this is reversed in the last few years. My life in dreamland has altogether changed, and, in all respects but one, in an entirely pleasant manner. I now make speeches, especially replies, in some of the many controversies of my life, which come up again and again in my dreams, of the most convincing kind; all my bodily powers have come back, and I ride, box, play cricket, and fish, as well as I could do forty years ago. Moreover, my morals have so improved that I am now almost always on the right side, and have not committed a felony for I don't know how long."[3]

March 22, 1896. Died in Brighton, England.

FOR MORE INFORMATION SEE: Thomas Hughes, *Memoir of a Brother*, James R. Osgood & Co., 1873; Dan Goodwin, "A Speech," in *Chicago Literary Club*, Smith Rogers, June 8, 1896; Thomas Hughes, "Fragments of Autobiography, Early Memories," edited by H. C. Shelly, *Cornhill Magazine*, 1925; *Junior Book of Authors*, H. W. Wilson, 1934; *British Authors of the Nineteenth Century*, H. W. Wilson, 1936; *Time*, December 25, 1939; *Queen's Quarterly*, Fall, 1943; Edward C. Mack and Walter H. G. Armytage, *Thomas Hughes: The Life of the Author of "Tom Brown's Schooldays,"* Benn, 1952; Asa Briggs, *Victorian People*, University of Chicago Press, 1955; *Who's Who of Children's Literature*, Schocken, 1968; John E. Little, *Thomas Hughes 1822-1896*, Uffington, 1972; *Travel*, August, 1974.

Obituaries: *Athenaeum*, March 28, 1896; *Critic*, March 28, 1896, April 4, 1896; *Spectator*, March 28, 1896; *Living Age*, May 9, 1896.

HUNT, Joyce   1927-

PERSONAL: Born October 31, 1927, in New York, N.Y.; daughter of Victor and Ann Wiscotch; married Irwin Hunt, June 25, 1950; children: Gregory, Ethan. *Education:* Brooklyn College (now of the City University of New York), B.A., 1949; Hunter College (now of the City University of New York), M.A., 1958. *Home:* 131 Riverside Dr., New York, N.Y. 10024.

CAREER: New York City public schools, teacher of children with learning and behavioral problems, 1968—.

WRITINGS—For children; "A First Look At" series; published by Walker & Co.; all with Millicent Ellis Selsam and illustrated by Harriet Springer: *A First Look at Fish*, 1972; . . . *Leaves*, 1972; . . . *Birds*, 1973; . . . *Mammals*, 1973; . . . *Insects*, 1974; . . . *Snakes, Lizards, and Other Reptiles*, 1975; . . . *Animals without Backbones*, 1976; . . . *Flowers*, 1976; . . . *Frogs, Toads, and Salamanders*, 1976; . . . *Animals with Backbone*, 1978; . . . *the World of Plants*, 1978; . . . *Monkeys and Apes*, 1979; . . . *Sharks*, 1979; . . . *Whales*, 1980; . . . *Cats*, 1981; . . . *Dogs*, 1981; . . . *Horses*, 1982, . . . *Dinosaurs*, 1982; . . . *Spiders*, 1983; . . . *Shells*, 1983.

SIDELIGHTS: Hunt's publications "are designed to encourage the child's powers of observation." She said she is particularly interested in developing in the child "the art of looking for differences among living things.

"I am disgustingly enthusiastic about all aspects of life. Somehow, in this world of impending doom, threatening destruction and crumbling civilization, I manage to remain sanguine and optimistic . . . the results of a happy childhood and volatile marriage.

"I love kids, nature, travel and my *Roget's Thesaurus*. I hope to indulge all to the hilt while working on a new series of science-adventure books for young children. This time my co-author is my husband!"

Alligators look like giant lizards. ■(From *A First Look at Animals with Backbones* by Millicent E. Selsam and Joyce Hunt. Illustrated by Harriet Springer.)

EDITH FISHER HUNTER

HUNTER, Edith Fisher 1919-

PERSONAL: Born December 3, 1919, in Boston, Mass.; daughter of Andrew (a chemist) and Frances (a teacher; maiden name, Way) Fisher; married (William) Armstrong Hunter III (a publisher and editor), December 19, 1943; children: Elizabeth, Graham Chambers, William Armstrong IV, Charles Way. *Education:* Wellesley College, A.B., 1941; Union Theological Seminary, B.D., M.A., 1944, Master of Divinity. *Home:* R.D. #2, Springfield, Weathersfield, Vt. 05156.

CAREER: Worked as a curriculum editor for the Unitarian Universalist Church, Boston, Mass. *The Weathersfield Weekly,* Weathersfield, Vt., writer, reporter, photographer, 1971-81, editor, 1981—. Has held civic positions such as member of Weathersfield School Board, coordinator of the Fresh Air fund, and host of Fresh Air Children.

But instead of Sue Ellen doing the kicking, the burro's side gave Sue Ellen a kick! A very surprised little girl grabbed hold of the burro's long hair with two hands again. ∎ (From *Sue Ellen* by Edith Fisher Hunter. Illustrated by Bea Holmes.)

WRITINGS—All juvenile, except as noted: *The Family Finds Out* (illustrated by Charlotte Ware), Beacon Press, 1951; *The Questioning Child and Religion* (adult), Starr King Press, 1956; *Conversations with Children* (textbook for children), Beacon Press, 1961, revised edition, 1979; *Child of the Silent Night: The Story of Laura Bridgman* (illustrated by Bea Holmes), Houghton, 1963; *Sophia Lyon Fahs: A Biography* (adult), Beacon Press, 1966; *Sue Ellen* (illustrated by B. Holmes), Houghton, 1969; *A Brief History of the Public Schools of Milford, New Hampshire, 1738-1972* (adult), Hunter Press, 1973.

Contributor of articles to periodicals, including *Parent's, Redbook, Ladies' Home Journal, Reader's Digest,* and professional religious journals.

SIDELIGHTS: Hunter, whose work consists primarily of religious education books and local histories for children and adults, holds a Master of Divinity degree from Union Theological Seminary. The mother of four children, Hunter worked in her home, writing books and articles, and serving as curriculum editor for the Unitarian Universalist Church. "I raised my four children while writing at home. Then, in 1971, when my husband and my son William started a weekly newspaper, *The Weathersfield Weekly,* I started writing articles and anything else I was needed for. When my youngest child left for boarding school in 1973 I became more actively involved in the newspaper and spend most of my time on that now, taking pictures, writing features, etc.

"Probably my most consuming interest is education. I took my youngest son out of public school and taught him myself in grades seven and eight. Until parents take on the education of their children again, formal education will continue to be expensive and often ineffective."

HÜRLIMANN, Ruth 1939-

BRIEF ENTRY: Born September 22, 1939, in Zug, Switzerland. Hürlimann is an author and illustrator of books for children. About 1960 she graduated from Kunstgewerbeschule in Lucerne, Switzerland, and began working as a designer for an advertising agency in Zurich, Switzerland. From 1963 to 1968 she continued her work as an advertising designer in Paris, France. She began illustrating books for children in 1968 and has since been employed as a free-lance illustrator and artist, returning to Switzerland in 1969. Hürlimann's work has been exhibited both in Switzerland and abroad. In 1971 she was the recipient of the Gold Medal at the Biennale of Illustrations Bratislava Exhibition in Czechoslovakia; in 1972 she was awarded the major prize for design at the International Children's Book Fair in Bologna, Italy. Her translated books for children, all self-illustrated, include *The Mouse with the Daisy Hat,* 1971, *The Fox and the Raven,* 1972, and *The Proud Cat,* 1977. In 1976, she was the recipient of the Mildred L. Batchelder Award and an award from the Association of Jewish Libraries for *The Cat and the Mouse Who Shared a House. For More Information See: Illustrators of Children's Books: 1967-1976,* Horn Book, 1978.

To acquire the habit of reading is to construct for yourself a refuge from almost all the miseries of life.
—W. Somerset Maugham

HUTCHENS, Paul   1902-1977

PERSONAL: Born April 7, 1902, in Thorntown, Ind., died in Colorado Springs, Colo., January 23, 1977; son of Ira and Eva (Bishop) Hutchens; married Jane Carolyn Freerks, December 24, 1924; children: Pauline (Mrs. Kyle Wilson). *Education:* Attended Earlham College, 1919-20, and Moody Bible Institute, 1921-23, 1927. *Politics:* Republican. *Home and office:* 120 East Winters Dr., Colorado Springs, Colo. 80907.

CAREER: Ordained Baptist minister, 1925. Teacher in a rural school, 1920-21; writer.

WRITINGS: Juveniles; all published by Eerdmans, except as indicated: *The Sugar Creek Gang,* 1939, published as *The Sugar Creek Gang and the Swamp Robber,* Moody; *Further Adventures of the Sugar Creek Gang,* 1940, published as *The Sugar Creek Gang and the Winter Rescue,* Moody, 1970; *We Killed a Bear: A Sugar Creek Gang Story,* 1940, published as *The Sugar Creek Gang and the Killer Bear,* Moody; *The Sugar Creek Gang Goes Camping,* 1941, published as *The Lost Campers,* Moody, 1968; *The Sugar Creek Gang in Chicago,* 1941, published as *The Sugar Creek Gang and the Chicago Adventure,* Moody, 1968; *The Sugar Creek Gang in School,* 1942, published as *The Secret Hideout,* Moody, 1968; *Mystery at Sugar Creek,* 1943, published as *The Sugar Creek Gang and The Mystery Cave,* Moody, 1966; *The Sugar Creek Gang Flies to Cuba,* 1944, published as *The Sugar Creek Gang and The Palm Tree Mystery,* Moody; *A New Sugar Creek Mystery,* 1946, published as *The Sugar Creek Gang and the Mystery Thief,* Moody; *One Stormy Day at Sugar Creek,* 1946; *Shenanigans at Sugar Creek,* 1947, published as *The Sugar Creek Gang and the Teacher Trouble,* Moody, 1970.

All published by Van Kampen Press, except as indicated: *The Sugar Creek Gang Goes North,* 1947, published as *The Sugar Creek Gang and Screams in the Night,* Moody, 1967; *Adventure in an Indian Cemetery: A Sugar Creek Gang Story,* 1947, published as *Indian Cemetery,* Moody, 1970; *The Sugar Creek Gang Digs for Treasure,* 1948, published as *The Sugar Creek Gang and the Treasure Hunt,* Moody, 1967; *North Woods Manhunt: A Sugar Creek Gang Story,* 1948, published as *The Sugar Creek Gang and the Thousand Dollar Fish,* Moody, 1966; *The Haunted House at Sugar Creek,* 1949, published as *The Sugar Creek and the Haunted House,* Moody, 1967; *The Sugar Creek Gang on the Mexican Border,* 1950; *Lost in a Sugar Creek Blizzard,* 1950, published as *The Sugar Creek Gang Lost in the Blizzard,* Moody, 1970; *The Green Tent Mystery at Sugar Creek,* 1950, published as *The Sugar Creek Gang and the Green Tent Mystery,* Moody; (compiler) *Trails of Yesteryear: Ye Olde Sugar Creek Scrapbook,* 1951; *10,000 Minutes at Sugar Creek,* 1952, published as *The Sugar Creek Gang and the Bull Fighter,* Moody; *Blue Cow at Sugar Creek,* 1953, published as *Sugar Creek Gang and the Blue Cow,* Moody, 1971; *The Trap Line Thief at Sugar Creek,* 1953, published as *Sugar Creek Gang and the Trapline Thief,* Moody, 1971; *The Watermelon Mystery at Sugar Creek,* 1955, published as *Sugar Creek Gang and the Watermelon Mystery,* Moody, 1971.

All published by Scripture Press, except as indicated: *Sugar Creek Gang at Snow Goose Lodge,* 1957, published as *The Sugar Creek Gang and the Timber Wolf,* Moody, 1965; *Sugar Creek Gang Goes Western,* 1957, published as *The Sugar Creek Gang and the Western Adventure,* Moody, 1966; *The Old Stranger's Secret,* 1957, published as *The Sugar Creek Gang and the Tree House Mystery,* Moody, 1972.

All published by Moody: *The Sugar Creek Gang and the Killer Cat* (originally published as *We Killed a Wildcat at Sugar Creek*), 1966; *The Sugar Creek Gang and the Ghost Dog* (originally published as *Howling Dog in the Sugar Creek Swamp*), 1968; *The Sugar Creek Gang and the Brown Box Mystery* (originally published as *Brown Box Mystery at Sugar Creek*), 1970; *The Sugar Creek Gang and the Colorado Kidnapping* (originally published as *Wild Horse Canyon Mystery*), 1970; *The Sugar Creek Gang and the White Boat Rescue* (originally published as *White Boat Rescue at Sugar Creek*), 1970; *The Sugar Creek Gang and the Battle of the Bees* (originally published as *Sleeping Beauty at Sugar Creek*), 1972; *The Sugar Creek Gang and the Cemetery Vandals* (originally published as *The Worm Turns at Sugar Creek*), 1972; *The Sugar Creek Gang and the Runaway Rescue,* (originally published as *Runaway Mystery at Sugar Creek*), 1973; *The Sugar Creek Gang: Locked in the Attic* (originally published as *Down in Sugar Creek Chimney),* 1973.

All novels, except as indicated; all published by Eerdmans, except as indicated: *Romance of Fire,* 1934; *This Way Out,* 1935; *A Song Forever,* 1936; *The Last First,* 1936; *The Voice,* 1937; *This Is Life,* 1937; *Mastering Marcus,* 1938; *Yesterday's Rain,* 1938; *Blaze Star,* 1939; *Shafted Sunlight,* 1939; *Windblown,* 1939; *The Vision,* 1940; *Cup of Cold Water,* 1941; *Eclipse,* 1942; *When God Says "No"* (lectures), 1943; *Morning Light,* 1944; (compiler) *How to Meet Your Troubles: True Adventures with Adversity* (stories), 1945; *Uninterrupted Sky,* Van Kampen Press, 1949; *The Mystery of the Marsh,* Van Kampen Press, 1952; *Yours for Four Years,* Van Kampen Press, 1954; *My Life and I* (autobiography), Sugar Creek Press, 1962; *East of the Shadows,* Moody, 1972.

Also author of *The Know-So Christian,* a nonfiction book published in the Kituba language; and author of music and lyrics for hymns.

SIDELIGHTS: **April 7, 1902.** Born in Thorntown, Indiana. As a young boy Hutchens played with his six brothers in many of the places and swam in the swimming hole he later wrote about in his popular "Sugar Creek Gang" series. "As a boy I wanted . . . the love and respect of my teachers, my friends, my parents. Also, there was a desire to be seen in God's sight as a better boy. To attain such a state, I must have forgiveness for what I did wrong—and help to do better. I wanted even God in those days to think I was worth something in His sight. . . .

"Wise was Grandmother Buck, my maternal grandmother, who realized that a boy's mind should be sown with wholesome thoughts. The Hutchens library was well supplied with Horatio Alger books which interwove with their wholesome adventures, strong principles of courage, honesty, courtesy, and thrift. The Hutchens boys could recite from memory some of the adventure passages. Especially did I admire the courage and keen thinking of Mark Mason and Andy Gordon; and even in those early days, I began to be polite, to tip my hat to the ladies and to be ambitious to be like the strong, clean young men of those books.

"On Sundays when I went to Sunday School, Mamie McBane, our boys' class teacher, sowed in our minds as much truth as she could—midst restlessness, whispers, wriggling and inattention.

"With neighbor boys I turned imagination loose, killed hundreds of Indians with hand-made wooden guns—and with word guns, also—with an ash club flailed away at the British Red Coats, cutting and slashing and leaving the dead and wounded all over our truck patch. I was George Washington, the first president and the leader in our war of Independence!

"I swam and fished in Sugar Creek, and climbed to the top of elm saplings where sometimes when I was alone I would shout at the top of my lungs, spelling out some word I had just learned. One word especially charmed me as a smaller boy as I sent it charging out across the creek and the bayou: 'O-P-P-O-R-T-U-N-I-T-Y!'

"Lincoln's Gettysburg address was heard by frogs and robins and by the trees and shrubs of our own particular section of Sugar Creek territory. In the Sugar Creek books, Bill Collins himself delights in orating the 'Four Score and Seven Years Ago' address.

"A boy feels these things tremendously. He enjoys not so much the speech, but the way it makes him feel when he is shouting it to the huge crowds that always listen spellbound to him!

"Other good seed was sown in my mind in those earlier days. The 'common' school readers carried wholesome, character-building fables, stories, proverbs which—I fear—are missing in many of today's text books." [Paul Hutchens, *My Life and I,* Sugar Creek Press, 1962.[1]]

1915. Entered high school at the age of thirteen. "I began almost abruptly to watch the mirror for signs of fuzz on my upper lip and found instead a touch of acne on my nose and chin which I treated with Jack Frost cream, secretly borrowed (?) from Grandmother Buck's supply.

"Also, because in those days *white* hands without callouses were in vogue for young men, I began to hoe potatoes, weed strawberries and plow corn with pigskin gloves to keep the hot sun from giving those hands a telltale tan.

"Biceps had been on the horizon for years, and so had my admiration of any man with muscles that bulged or rippled. Now my own were swelling. I discovered that drops of perspiration would cling to a boy's face in small beads if cold cream were put on first. Then, the hotter the sun the more profuse the sweating, the more noticeable the drops that clung—and the more important I felt.

"My brother, Haven, ahead of me in the teens by two years, was taller by six or more inches, and I begged him to tell me his 'scheme' for growing. How did he get so tall!

"He demonstrated how by climbing one of the two cherry trees that grew by the fence at the east side of the orchard, hanging by his knees with his head down. If I would do that every day my body would stretch and I would grow tall fast!

"I hung by my knees but could not add one-fourth cubit to my stature.

"My imagination, however, was developing fast.

"I was as yet only in the vestibule of adolescence. My body was changing, also my mind, and deep within there was an embryonic ambition, churning, struggling, expanding and moving toward eventual birth."[1]

Wrote his first poem. "Exerting a different and most interesting influence on my sub-teen days, was a person named Nellie, nebulous, invisible, perfumed perfection, angelic. I had never

PAUL HUTCHENS

seen her, never read of her, never known of her existence. She emerged suddenly in my world of dreams. She was of my own creation—the heroine of my first literary production. I rubbed meditatively on the Aladdin's lamp of imagination and—presto—there she was, a genie to do my bidding.

"Was it Wordsworth's delightful poem, 'Daffadils' that had introduced me to the secret of the bliss of solitude? I do not know, but there was something about the creative muse that enamored me—and still does. There *has* to be a muse or the writing, the preaching, the living even, is vain. And creative moods have to be refueled and fed as a fire is fed, or the blaze may flicker and die away to burnt-out ashes,—the attempted work of creation be no more than a lazy wind passing across a grassless desert.

"I found myself one pre-adolescent day sitting under an oak tree in the woods and writing:

> "'Old Oak, can you tell me where Nellie may be?
> Will she ever, ever come back to me?
>
> "'Old Oak, I have tried to be happy and glad
> But somehow, instead, I am gloomy and sad.
> If I meet her again on that beautiful shore,
> Will she love me the same as she did before?

"The poem completed, and the creative mood flown, I studied my creation, marked it mentally with grade 'A' and thought

I never saw a dog run so fast. In a second, it seemed, his sharp teeth were nipping at the heels of the bull, and he was barking and yelping, and dashing in and biting, and jumping back. ■ (Cover illustration from *The Sugar Creek Gang and the Bull Fighter* by Paul Hutchens.)

of *The Farmer's Guide,* a magazine that was dropped weekly into the Hutchens mailbox by the big walnut tree.

"The dreamer was also practical, 'Old Oak' which asked if Nellie would ever come back to him, might be worth money, cash with which to buy things a boy needed. It might also buy something else he needed—a sense of value, a *superlative* value, as I understand it now—recognition by others of my personal worth.

"My letter to the *Farmer's Guide,* which carried with it my first-born brain child, had in it one word designed to impress the editors—a new word recently learned that had to do with money. To my present-day sense of humor, the letter was pathetic, but I think it should be included here, unretouched, because it may help us all to understand our youngsters better:

"'Dear Sirs:

"'I am sending you my poem, "Old Oak," which I hope you will keep and print in the *Farmer's Guide.* My *pecuniary* situation is not very good. . . .'

"That was the word that would impress the editors. They would want to help a boy better his *pecuniary* situation—if he had one.

"The letter and 'Old Oak' traveled via two-cent stamp to *Farmer's Guide,* and the waiting days began to drag by; days of hope and misery and misgiving,—and fear.

"Mornings I watched within fast-running distance of the mailbox when Mr. Loveless' motorcycle would come storming down the dusty gravelled road to our house. Came the fateful morning and I ran like a hound-chased cottontail to the walnut tree to get the mail before another Hutchens could get it first.

"The return address on the long, official-looking envelope said, *Farmer's Guide.*

"What happened to the rest of the mail—perhaps only the Indianapolis *Star*—I do not now recall—and I did not care then. Like a secret with wings, I flew past the house and down into the orchard where in a place of seclusion, my heart pounding high, I tore open the long envelope, unfolded the brief letter and read, 'Thank you. . . . We do not publish any poetry, so we are. . . .'

"And there, before my tear-blurred vision was 'Old Oak,' fallen as from a mighty storm that had destroyed also the whole world. *My Nellie had come back to me.*"[1]

1916. "There were many mouths to feed in the Hutchens family, and boys with muscles could not be parasites. We must help with the grocery bills. And so, it came to pass that the first summer after my first year in high school, I was hired out to Uncle Dan Kincaid who lived in Tippecanoe County in what was called the prairie of Indiana. Twenty dollars a month and room and board, was the price paid for a fourteen-year-old boy—and I loved it. Following the spike-toothed harrow all day, *walking* all day in the dust may not have been good for my respiratory system—though others could do it without any seeming trouble."[1]

1919. After graduation from high school, entered Friends College (Earlham) at Richmond, Indiana. "As yet, I had not heard the call to preach the gospel. In fact, I hardly knew the meaning of the word, but I had felt the strong, irresistible urge to go to college. That urge had been given impetus through the counsel of one of my grade school teachers, Ebon McGreggor. 'Don't you dare stop with high school, Paul. You *must* go on!'

"But how could I when my pecuniary situation was in such a situation!

"How *could I?*. . . McGreggor told me how one Sunday during the intermission between Sunday School and church hours at Sugar Plain. The school was across the road from the church, a distance of probably one hundred yards, and we were alone at the time. 'If I could do it, *you* can do it,' he challenged me.

"'But the money—where do we get the money!'

"'You work for it,' he told me. 'I scrubbed floors, mowed lawns, raked leaves—anything I could find to do. *You can do it if you really want to!*'

"McGreggor was right—and McGreggor was wrong. Though I worked an hour a day in the home of President Edwards as payment for my room there, and on Saturdays mowed lawns, raked leaves, pushed brooms, scrubbed floors, vacuumed rugs and emptied waste-baskets, tuition and board and room at the dorm cost far more than I could earn. Brother Haven, working on a farm near the old Hutchens home, sent occasional checks. . . .

"One thing I wish I had understood more clearly. I might have avoided sacrificing breakfasts at the dormitory and thus depleting my energies. But no one told me that the breakfasts were to be paid for whether I ate them or not. How could a fellow know, if no one had told him!

"Many a day until I learned better, my first meal was at noon,—though on occasion I would walk all the way downtown to an eating place where I could get a frankfurter sandwich for only a few cents.

"Imagine my consternation then, when the statements were made out, and the one in my mailbox had me charged for three meals a day!

"One extracurricular activity was membership in the Ionian Literary Society, where members gained practical experience in conducting business meetings, learning to make the second motions, etc."[1]

1920-1921. Taught in a one-room schoolhouse in La Porte, Indiana. "As a teacher, I was also a pupil. I most certainly did not know how to sew a fine seam—only buttons and socks were in my repertoire. But I did have to *grade* the finished work of a number of amateur seamstresses.

"When I discovered there was no Bible in the one-room school, I bought a red-letter edition and read from it at the period of the day know as 'Opening Exercises.'

"There was love in my heart for these nearly-forty students from the first grade to the eighth—and in memory, they are often before me. During the year, as many as seven of these precious youngsters came to trust in Christ as their very own personal Saviour.

"Because there was a ruling that no 'religious' teachings be given during school hours, we made the brief Bible studies an entirely voluntary thing, explaining the way of salvation only *after* dismissal.

"I rode the four-mile daily trip to and from school on a then-popular Johnson motorbike. I still enjoy the memory of the wind in my face, and the feeling of 'speed' as my two-wheeled racer burned up the streets and roads at a probable twenty miles per hour!"[1]

1921. Entered Moody Bible Institute. "My decision to enter Moody Bible Institute for further education—for what could almost be called my initial training in the Bible—was made and kept, contrary to what may be considered the best educational counsel.

"To go back to the liberal arts college where I felt so little stirring in my soul to go deeper with God, was unthinkable. I had no inclination to spend time that was running out, translating from the Latin the exploits of Cicero. Trigonometry had lost its luster, so had Biblical Literature as such. I was hungry for the Word of God,—and my spirit was being satisfied in the Chicago school."[1]

. . . I saw, outside, not more than fifteen feet from the shanty, a pair of fiery eyes. But only for a fleeting flash, then a blur of grayish snow-covered fur faded away like a ghost into a swirling snow. ■ (Cover illustration from *The Sugar Creek Gang and the Timber Wolf* by Paul Hutchens.)

December 24, 1924. Married another evangelical student, Jane Freerks.

September 19, 1925. Ordained a Baptist minister. "When I knelt on the church platform and many hands were laid upon me and while Arthur Hedley prayed, I promised God complete loyalty to His Word to preach 'nothing beyond that which was written.'

"After my ordination, I felt no more spiritual power than formerly, and there was no greater influx of people to our meetings and no increase in the number of converts, but my heart was at rest that I was obeying the Lord in an important matter."[1]

1927. Graduated from the Moody Bible Institute.

1928. Suffered poor health following influenza and a serious chest cold, which led to tuberculosis. "The bent-rod-shaped dye-red bacilli had been at work a long time in the preacher's

(Cover illustration from *The Sugar Creek Gang: The Runaway Rescue* by Paul Hutchens.)

right lung, long enough to have fought back hard enough to have built a calcium ring around the area to protect the rest of the lung from inroads.''[1]

May, 1929. "Came the merry month of May—and the latter part was not so merry for Lady Jane [his wife]. Hers was a long hard thirty-six hour travail to bring our awaited Little Paul into the world. And then, on the last day, came crying Pauline Adele Hutchens. Twenty-seven years previous, in the month of April, her Father had come crying for the same personal reason.''[1]

1931. Entered a California sanitarium for treatment of tuberculosis. Began writing. "During the first week of my rest, Lady Jane brought me an unusual book from the public library. It was written by Jack London. Later I learned it was thought by those who knew him, to be his own autobiography in the form of a novel. The hero of the story was a young writer who, feeling his vocabulary was too limited, began to increase it by daily adding new words.

"That, I thought, was a good idea. I, too, would increase my vocabulary—but with no thought in view of becoming a writer. Rather, it was that when I recovered and returned to the pulpit, I would be able to express my thoughts in more colorful language. Also, it gave me a sense of well-being, that in resting, I was not wasting time.

Hutchens was released after fifteen months, although not entirely without exception every story painfully written and hopefully mailed to various magazines, came back as 'not in line' with their present needs.

"I continued trying and continued getting rejection slips. 'My pecuniary situation was not very good' and getting worse. I spent long fascinating hours making Bible crossword puzzles and sold them for one dollar each to an eastern publication. Four or five hours work for $1.00!''[1]

1934. First novel published. In the decade of the thirties Hutchens spent seven out of ten years sick in bed writing many novels and the "Sugar Creek Gang" series. ". . . *Romance of Fire* in a striking fiery-red dust jacket came off the press in the early fall and I held a first copy in my hand, and looked up at it—yes, UP, for I was in bed in our George, Iowa, apartment— and stand-by Jane and I rejoiced together.

"To climax the victory, Moody Press gave Eerdmans an order for one thousand copies on which they were to have their own imprint! The triumph was complete, and I was the acknowledged champion—yet I was on the mat and down for the count again.

"Thank God this time the count was only seven (months) rather than a year and I was up again. But it was good that I was down, for during those seven months, a second novel *This Way Out* was born.

"Someone has said that nothing is more sure of success than an idea whose time has come. The time of the Christian novel had arrived in America. *Romance of Fire* sold fast, and was reprinted many times.

"While still in bed, I had a serious relapse with high fevers of near 104 degrees. 'A serious secondary infection' of some kind, the two doctors decided. But while I rested and slept, a Friend moved over the field and sowed the word through *Romance of Fire* and *The Know-So Christian* which also was selling well.

"The 'pecuniary situation' still not being very good, Jane taught piano lessons to help—and for a brief period was pianist in the Luke Rader tabernacle in Minneapolis.

"Writing continued: *This Way Out* was soon off the press, then *A Song Forever* and we began work on *The Last First*. Sometime during these years, we moved into a new ministry, that of song-writing.''[1]

1939. First juvenile, *The Sugar Creek Gang* was published. "I had no premonition at the beginning of the book that it was to be the first in a series that would grow to more than thirty titles and be read by actual millions of youngsters throughout the world. There was, however, some evidence of the way I felt in the words in the diary under that same date: 'I believe God is giving me wisdom and guidance to write a boy's story that will reach thousands for Christ.'

"The cautious first edition was limited to 2,000 published in the fall of 1939; it was followed almost abruptly by another 2,000, and the orders were pouring in so rapidly that edition number three was increased to 6,000, all in only a few months. Bill Collins, my red-haired, fiery-tempered narrator and his

Sugar Creek Gang, including the questioned title, was accepted.''[1]

1940s. Hutchens continued to write inspirational novels and to preach for the next thirty years.

1955. Moved to Colorado for his health. ''The late summer and fall of 1954 found me in a most desperate struggle to live through the nights. On September 18, the journal records:

'''Spent one whole week in air-conditioned office, not going outdoors day nor night. . . . Jane brought my meals, and otherwise we kept in touch by phone. . . .'

''My struggle was a most terrible heartache for her, as she—when I was at home—would agonize for me and sometimes I would find her sobbing because there was nothing she could do to help.

''It was not a question now of myself alone. Hers was a wounded heart that would not heal as long as I myself fought in vain to live the life I needed to live to be able to do the work that lay ahead.

''We set out before the beginning of the ragweed season, located first in a motel in West Colorado Springs, then in Manitou Springs. Morning after morning in the early hours, I went to Soda Springs Park to write—and to my amazement and joy there was scarcely a sneeze and nary a wheeze. It was too good to be true but not too good to be accepted.

''Sugar Creek House stands high on Pyramid Mesa. The winds blow here, the snows of spring—and sometimes of winter—are clean and almost super-white; the sunshine is as the sunshine where you live. This now is our Green House. We shall try to be good stewards, though our youthful days are gone and old age is stealing on—no, not *old* age, just age that is a little older; and at that, only one day at a time.''[1]

1960s. ''Healthwise, life is good again so that I am speaking the Word once more as doors are opened. Engagements I have been privileged to fill are within the limits of my strength.

''The very latest guidance has been to activate the SUGAR CREEK PRESS, with the purpose in view of publishing henceforth, as manuscripts move through the typewriter, all our NEW works. It is a challenge indeed. . . .''[1]

January 23, 1977. Died. ''This observation, please. . . . If a good story can be a power for good—what devasting vandalism can be done to a boy's heart—or to the heart of anybody—when he is given a diet of licentious literature in book and/or magazine!

''I was a better boy because of what was planted in my mind—and because my mind was my personality in process of development, I was eventually a better man because of good books.''[1]

The ''Sugar Creek Gang'' books have been translated into French, German, Korean, and Norwegian.

HOBBIES AND OTHER INTERESTS: ''Horseshoe was one of my favorite outdoor games—and I worked at it until I at least thought I was proficient. . . . Fishing [was] a favorite sport . . . there were northwoods trips in later years, far into northern Minnesota and even into Canada—and from those settings have come the background for several of the Sugar Creek stories.''[1]

FOR MORE INFORMATION SEE: Paul Hutchens, *My Life and I,* Sugar Creek Press, 1962.

ISHMAEL, Woodi 1914-

PERSONAL: Born February 1, 1914, in Lewis County, Ky.; married Gwen Williams in 1939; children: Candace. *Education:* Attended Cleveland School of Art.

CAREER: Free-lance illustrator of books, and art director for an advertising agency in New York, beginning 1939. Other experiences include jobs in engraving and on newspapers, and as art editor of a small farm magazine.

ILLUSTRATOR—All for children: John Cournos, *A Boy Named John,* Scribner, 1941; Jeanette Eaton, *Narcissa Whitman, Pioneer of Oregon,* Harcourt, 1941; Gertrude Robinson, *Sons of Liberty,* Dutton, 1941; Bernard Robb, *Welcum Hinges,* Dutton, 1942; Gregor Felsen, *Struggle Is Our Brother,* Dutton, 1943; J. Eaton, *Lone Journey: The Life of Roger Williams* (biography; ALA Notable Book), Harcourt, 1944, reprinted, 1966; Hildegarde Hawthorne, *Give Me Liberty,* Appleton-Century, 1945; Antoni Gronowicz, *Sergei Rachmaninoff,* Dutton, 1946; G. Felsen, *Flying Correspondent,* Dutton, 1947; Jane Stuart, *White Barn,* Whippoorwill Press, 1973.

Also illustrator of Margaret Fox's *They Sailed and Sailed,* 1940.

(From *Lone Journey: The Life of Roger Williams* by Jeanette Eaton. Illustrated by Woodi Ishmael.)

SIDELIGHTS: Ishmael grew up in Kentucky and Ohio. ''The most lasting impressions on my childhood are of Kentucky, its folklore and its history. As a child my imagination was highly stimulated with tales from the land of Simon Kenton and Daniel Boone.'' [Bertha E. Miller and others, compilers, *Illustrators of Children's Books: 1946-1956,* Horn Book, 1958.[1]]

He began drawing at an early age and found that it is ''a very pleasant and satisfactory way of making a living.''[1]

FOR MORE INFORMATION SEE: Bertha E. Mahony, and others, compilers, *Illustrators of Children's Books: 1744-1945,* Horn Book, 1947; Bertha E. Miller, and others, compilers, *Illustrators of Children's Books: 1946-1956,* Horn Book, 1958.

JANSON, Dora Jane   1916-

PERSONAL: Born in 1916; married Horst Woldemar Janson (an author and educator), 1941; children: Anthony, Peter, Josephine, Charles. *Education:* Graduate of Radcliffe College; attended the Institute of Fine Art at New York University for graduate study.

CAREER: Author, lecturer. Janson has lectured at the St. Louis City Museum and the Metropolitan Museum; author of several books on the arts.

WRITINGS—All with Horst Woldemar Janson: (For children) *The Story of Painting for Young People, from Cave Painting to Modern Times,* Abrams, 1952, textbook edition, 1962, reissued as *The Story of Painting, from Cave Painting to Modern Times,* 1966, reissued, 1977; (for children) *The Picture History*

(Cover illustration from *The Story of Painting for Young People* by H. W. and Dora Jane Janson.)

of Painting, from Cave Painting to Modern Times, Abrams, 1957; *Key Monuments of the History of Art: A Visual Survey,* Prentice-Hall, 1959; *Standard Treasury of the World's Greatest Paintings,* Abrams, 1960; *History of Art: A Survey of the Major Visual Arts from the Dawn of History to the Present Day,* Prentice-Hall, 1962, revised and enlarged edition, 1969, reissued, 1977; *A History of Art and Music,* Prentice-Hall, 1968.

SIDELIGHTS: Janson and her husband, Horst Woldemar Janson, have written and edited numerous books on art and art history. Their *Story of Painting for Young People* has been highly praised for its comprehensive and entertaining account of the history of art. ''People all dream, whether they want to or not. Even animals dream. A cat's ears and tail sometimes twitch in his sleep, while dogs whine and growl and paw the air, just as if they were having a fight. Even when they are awake, animals 'see things,' so that a cat's fur will rise on his back, for no apparent reason, as he peers into a dark cupboard. And we, too, have goose pimples when we feel frightened.

''That is imagination at work. People are not only animals who have imagination, but we are the only ones who can tell each other about it. If we tell each other in words, we have made a story out of it, and if we take a pencil and draw it, we have made a picture. To imagine means to 'make an image' or a picture, in our minds.'' [Dora and Horst Woldemar Janson, *The Story of Painting for Young People,* Abrams, 1962.]

FOR MORE INFORMATION SEE: New York Times, November 16, 1952; *Christian Science Monitor,* November 29, 1962.

DORA JANE JANSON

JOHNSON, James William   1871-1938
(James Weldon Johnson)

PERSONAL: Born June 17, 1871, in Jacksonville, Fla.; died following an automobile accident, June 26, 1938, in Wiscasset, Me.; buried in Brooklyn, N.Y.; son of James (a restaurant headwaiter) and Helen Louise (a musician and school teacher; maiden name, Dillette) Johnson; married Grace Nail, February 3, 1910. *Education:* Atlanta University, A.B., 1894, A.M., 1904; graduate study at Columbia, for three years. *Politics:* Republican. *Home:* Nashville, Tenn.

CAREER: Poet, author, editor, and international diplomat. Began career as a teacher at Stanton Central Grammar School for Negroes, Jacksonville, Fla., 1891; later became principal; founder and co-editor of the *Daily American,* the first Negro daily newspaper in the United States; became the first Negro to pass the Florida bar examination since Reconstruction, 1898; practiced law for three years; moved to New York with his brother, J. Rosamond, about 1901, where, along with Bob Cole, they produced a number of songs for the theater under the name "Cole and Johnson Bros."; served as U.S. Consul to Puerto Cabello, Venezuela, 1906, and Corinto, Nicaragua, 1909-1913; editor of *The New York Age,* 1914; National Association for Advancement of Colored People (NAACP), field secretary, 1916-20, executive secretary, 1920-30; Fisk University, professor of creative literature and chairman of department, 1931-38. Visiting professor of creative literature, New York University, 1934-38. Director, The American Fund for Public Service; trustee, Atlanta University.

MEMBER: American Society of Composers, Authors, and Publishers (charter member), Academy of Political Science, Ethical Society, Civic Club (New York City). *Awards, honors:* Spingarn Medal, from the NAACP, 1925, for outstanding achievement by an American Negro; Harmon Gold Award for *God's Trombones;* received Rosenwald Grant, 1929; W.E.B. DuBois Prize for Negro literature, 1933 (another source, 1934); New York Times named *Lift Every Voice and Sing* one of the Ten Best Illustrated Children's Books of the Year, 1970; Lewis Carroll Shelf Award, from the University of Wisconsin, 1971, for *Lift Every Voice and Sing;* Litt.D., Talladega College, 1917 and Howard University, 1923.

WRITINGS—Of interest to young readers: (With brother, J. Rosamond Johnson) *Lift Every Voice and Sing,* Edward B. Marks Music Corp., 1921, new edition (illustrated by Mozelle Thompson), Hawthorn, 1970; (editor) *The Book of American Negro Poetry,* Harcourt, 1922, revised edition, (publisher unknown) 1969, (editor) *The Book of American Negro Spirituals,* Viking, 1925; (editor) *The Second Book of Negro Spirituals,* Viking, 1926; (editor) *The Books of American Negro Spirituals* (contains *The Book of American Negro Spirituals* and *The Second Book of Negro Spirituals*), Viking, 1940, reprinted, 1964; *God's Trombones: Seven Negro Sermons in Verse* (illustrated by Aaron Douglas, lettering by C. B. Falls; also see below), Viking, 1927, reprinted, Penguin, 1976; *Along This Way: The Autobiography of James Weldon Johnson,* Viking, 1933, reprinted, Da Capo Press, 1973; *Saint Peter Relates an Incident: Selected Poems,* Viking, 1935, reprinted, AMS Press, 1974; *"I'll Make a World": James Weldon Johnson's Story of the Creation* (designed by Jay Johnson; contains "The Creation" from *God's Trombones: Seven Negro Sermons in Verse,*) Hallmark, 1972.

Other writings: *The Autobiography of an Ex-Colored Man* (novel), Sherman, French, 1912, reprinted, Arden Library, 1978; (translator) Fernando Periquet, *Goyescas: or, The Rival*

James Weldon Johnson. ■ (From *Along This Way: The Autobiography of James Weldon Johnson.*)

Lovers (opera), G. Schirmer, 1915; *Fifty Years and Other Poems* (with an introduction by Brander Matthews), Cornhill, 1917, reprinted, AMS Press, 1975; (with Horace M. Kallen) *Africa in the World Democracy,* NAACP, 1919; *Self-Determining Haiti,* The Nation, 1920; *Lynching, America's National Disgrace,* NAACP, 1924; *The Race Problem and Peace* (speech), NAACP, 1924; *Fundamentalism versus Modernism: A Layman's Viewpoint,* Century, 1925; *Native African Races and Culture* (pamphlet), [Charlottesville, Va.], 1927; *Black Manhattan,* Knopf, 1930, reprinted, Arno, 1968; *Negro Americans, What Now?,* Viking, 1934, reprinted, Da Capo Press, 1973; *Selected Poems,* 1936; *The Great Awakening,* Revell, 1938.

Also contributor of poetry and articles to various periodicals, including *Century, Crisis, The Independent, Harper's, The Bookman, Forum,* and *Scholastic.*

ADAPTATIONS—Movies and filmstrips: "Reading Poetry: The Creation" (motion picture; with study guide), read by Raymond St. Jacques and Margaret O'Brien, Oxford Films, 1971; "James Weldon Johnson" (motion picture), includes an adaptation of "The Creation," read by Raymond St. Jacques, Oxford Films, 1972.

Recordings: "God's Trombones" (recording; with biographical notes by Walter White, and texts of the poems), read by Bryce Bond, music by William Martin, Folkways Records, 1965.

SIDELIGHTS: **June 17, 1871.** Born in Jacksonville, Florida. "When I was born, my mother was very ill, too ill to nurse me. Then she found a friend and neighbor in an unexpected

Moneta Barnett's drawing of Johnson. ■(From *James Weldon Johnson* by Ophelia Settle Egypt. Illustrated by Moneta Barnett.)

quarter. Mrs. McCleary, her white neighbor who lived a block away . . . hearing of my mother's plight, took me and nursed me at her breast until my mother had recovered sufficiently to give me her own milk. So it appears that in the land of black mammies I had a white one. . . .

"My mother . . . was my first teacher and began my lessons in reading before ever I went to school. She was, in fact, the first colored woman public school teacher in Florida. . . .

"No boy can make a fair estimate of his father. I was thirty years old before I was able to do it. . . . Up to ten a boy thinks his father knows everything; at twenty he indulgently looks upon the 'old man' as a back number or, maybe, something less complimentary; at thirty, if the boy himself has any sense, he recognizes all of his father's qualities pretty fairly." [James Weldon Johnson, *Along This Way: The Autobiography of James Weldon Johnson,* Viking, 1933.[1]]

1880. "I was only about nine years old but younger souls had been consecrated to God; and I was led to the mourners' bench. I knelt down at the alter. I was so wedged in that I could hardly breathe. I tried to pray. I tried to feel a conviction of sin. I, finally, fell asleep. . . . The meeting was about to close; somebody shook me by the shoulder. . . . I woke up but did not open my eyes or stir. . . . Whence sprang the whim, as cunning as could have occurred to one of the devil's own imps? The shaking continued, but I neither opened my eyes nor stirred. They gathered round me. I heard, 'Glory to God, the child's

gone off!' But I did not open my eyes or stir. My grandmother got a big, strong fellow who took me on his back and toted me that long mile home. . . . The situation stirred my sense of humor, and a chuckle ran round and round inside of me, because I did not dare to let it get out. The sensation was a delicious one, but it was suddenly chilled by the appalling thought that I could not postpone my awakening indefinitely. Each step homeward, I knew, brought the moment of reckoning nearer. I needed to think and think fast; and I did. I evolved a plan that I thought was good; when I reached home and 'awoke' I recounted a vision. The vision was based on a remembered illustration in *Home Life in the Bible* that purported to be the artist's conception of a scene in heaven. To that conception I added some original embellishments. Apparently my plan worked out to the satisfaction of everybody concerned. Indeed, for me, it worked out almost too satisfactorily, for I was called upon to repeat the vision many times thereafter—to my inward shame.

"At fourteen I was skeptical. By the time I reached my Freshman year at Atlanta University I had avowed myself an agnostic."[1]

May, 1887. Completed eighth grade at Stanton School where his mother taught. "Before I left Stanton I had begun to scribble. I had written a story about my first plug (derby) hat. Mr. Artrell [teacher] thought it was fine, and it made a hit when I read it before the school. Now an impulse set me at writing poetry, and I filled several notebooks with verses. I . . . noted the first of my poems opened with these three lines:

> "Miserable, miserable, weary of life,
> Worn with its turmoil, its din and its strife,
> And with its burden of grief.

"I did not follow this vein. Perhaps even then I sensed that there was already an over-supply of poetry by people who mistake a torpid liver for a broken heart, and frustrated sex desires for yearnings of the soul. I wrote a lot of verses lampooning certain students and teachers and conditions on the campus. However, the greater part of my output consisted of rather ardent love poems.

"I worked at the *Times-Union* until I went away to school. I worked in several capacities. For a while I was office boy to the editor. . . . Occasionally I held copy for proofreaders in the job office. When I left I was assistant in the mailing room. . . . The world of the newspaper fascinated me, and I formed a new ambition.

"My grandmother cherished the ambition for me to become a preacher. My father and mother never expressed a fixed ambition for me. The question of the child's future is a serious dilemma for Negro parents. Awaiting each colored boy and girl are cramping limitations and buttressed obstacles, in addition to those that must be met by youth in general."[1]

Fall, 1887. Entered Atlanta University preparatory class. "I was at the University only a short time before I began to get an insight into the ramifications of race prejudice and an understanding of the American race problem. . . . It was simply in the spirit of the institution; the atmosphere of the place was charged with it. Students talked 'race.' It was the subject of essays, orations, and debates."[1]

1888-1889. Because of a yellow fever epidemic, Johnson left school for a year, during which time he assisted a Jacksonville doctor.

1891. Spent summer student-teaching in a rural schoolroom. "[Summer teaching] marked the beginning of my psychological change from boyhood to manhood." [Eugene Levy, *James Weldon Johnson: Black Leader, Black Voice,* University of Chicago Press, 1973.[2]]

"I enjoyed this rustic life. It was new, in some ways exciting, and I was interested in my school. I was getting a taste of the never-failing satisfaction of telling others important things they do not know. . . .

"To get mail I had to go to Hampton; and the most convenient and dependable way I found of getting there was by walking. I used to set out on Friday afternoons after I had closed school and walk the seven or eight miles to town. . . . I always tried to reach Hampton before night, because I knew enough to know that a strange Negro on a backcountry road in Georgia was not entirely secure, not even in daylight. But I was never in any way molested.

"I was graduated in **1894.** The Atlanta University commencement program indicated no distinctions, but it was unwritten opinion that the first and last places on the program were the honor points; I was given last place. . . .

"On the morning after commencement I left Atlanta for Jacksonville. . . . The train carried a car for Negro passengers, but Georgia had not yet passed its 'Jim Crow Car' law, and, as we had first-class tickets, we got into the first-class car. When the conductor took up our tickets, he suggested very strongly that we go into the car ahead. Our little party looked to me; and I . . . told him that we were comfortable and preferred to stay where we were. The conductor said no more; but, when it was seen that we were not going to move, a murmur started in the car, and grew until it became a hubbub. . . . Threats began to reach our ears. I affected nonchalance by scanning and turning the leaves of a book I held in my hand; I might just as well have held it upside-down. Soon a white man came to me and said in tones of one who had only a deep, friendly interest in us, 'I advise you people to get into the next car; they have sent a telegram down to Baxley to have a mob come on and put you out when the train gets there. . . .'

". . . His warnings raised my fright to the point where it broke my determination to hold my ground; I went back to my friends and told them what the porter had said, and on my decision we gathered up our luggage and packages and went into the car ahead. This was my first experience with the 'Jim Crow Car.' "[1]

1895. Became principal of Stanton School. "Among my youthful ambitions, teaching had never had a place. Not until I was about to finish at Atlanta University had I given it any thought as a vocation. But I liked the work, and I was intensely interested in my plan to develop Stanton into a high school. Toward the end of my first year of principalship, however, my thoughts began to rotate around one of my early ambitions; I thought again about publishing and editing a newpaper. I finally decided to undertake it."[1]

May, 1895. Printed first issue of *The Daily American,* the second Black newspaper in Jacksonville. "The initial success of *The Daily American* astonished its founders. I was oversanguine. We kept the paper going for eight months, then were forced to suspend. As I watched the press turn for the last time I was a sadly discouraged young man."[1]

(From "The Judgment Day," in *God's Trombones* by James Weldon Johnson. Illustrated by Aaron Douglas.)

1898. Admitted to the bar. Formed a law practice with his friend, J. D. Wetmore. ". . . Immediately he and I formed a partnership. . . . We planned a division of work: he was to give the main attention to the office and the work in court, while I was to give as much time at the office as my school duties would allow, and draw the papers. The new firm began to pick up business from the start. We got cases of many kinds. It took me a while to rid myself of the state of depression resulting from the fact that our client in our first murder case was hanged."[1]

As an artistic outlet, Johnson wrote songs with his brother J. Rosamond. "A group of young men decided to hold on February 12 a celebration of Lincoln's birthday. I was put down for an address, which I began preparing; but I wanted to do something else also. My thoughts began buzzing round a central idea of writing a poem on Lincoln, but I couldn't net them. So I gave up the project as beyond me; at any rate, beyond me to carry out in so short a time; and my poem on Lincoln is still to be written. My central idea, however, took on another form. I talked over with my brother the thought I had in mind, and we planned to write a song to be sung as a part of the exercises. We planned, better still, to have it sung by schoolchildren—a chorus of five hundred voices.

"I got my first line:—Lift ev'ry voice and sing. Not a startling line; but I worked along grinding out the next five. When, near the end of the first stanza, there came to me the lines:

Sing a song full of the faith that the dark past has
taught us.
Sing a song full of the hope that the present has
brought us.

the spirit of the poem had taken hold of me. I finished the
stanza and turned it over to Rosamond.

"In composing the two other stanzas I did not use pen and
paper. While my brother worked at his musical setting I paced
back and forth on the front porch, repeating the lines over and
over to myself, going through all of the agony and ecstasy of
creating. As I worked through the opening and middle lines
of the last stanza:

God of our weary years,
God of our silent tears,
Thou who hast brought us thus far on our way,
Thou who hast by Thy might
Let us into the light,
Keep us forever in the path, we pray;
Lest our feet stray from the places, our God, where we
met Thee,
Lest, our hearts drunk with the wine of the world, we
forget Thee . . .

I could not keep back the tears, and made no effort to do so.
I was experiencing the transports of the poet's ecstasy. Feverish
ecstasy was followed by that contentment—that sense of serene
joy—which makes artistic creation the most complete of all
human experiences.

". . . Within twenty years the song was being sung in schools
and churches and on special occasions throughout the South
and in some other parts of the country. Within that time the
publishers had recopyrighted it and issued it in several arrangements. Later it was adopted by the National Association for
the Advancement of Colored People, and is now quite generally
used throughout the country as the "Negro National Hymn.'"[1]

1901. Dissolved his law practice. ". . . I saw that our partnership could not last much longer. . . . A short while after
we reached New York I went into another partnership, a curious
partnership. My brother, Bob Cole, and I formed a partnership
to produce songs and plays.

"The partnership lasted seven years, in which time we wrote
some two hundred songs that were sung in various musical
shows on Broadway and on 'the road.'

". . . I continued writing poems, most of them in dialect, and
after the style of Dunbar.

"But just at this time I came across Whitman's *Leaves of
Grass*. I was engulfed and submerged by the book, and set
floundering again. I felt that nothing I had written, with the
exception of the hymn for the Lincoln celebration, rose above
puerility. I got a sudden realization of the artificiality of con-
ventionalized Negro dialect poetry; of its exaggerated geniality,
childish optimism, forced comicality, and mawkish sentiment;
of its limitation as an instrument of expression to but two
emotions, pathos and humor, thereby making every poem either
only sad or only funny. I saw that not even Dunbar had been
able to break the mold in which dialect poetry had, long before
him, been set by representations made of the Negro on the
minstrel stage. I saw that he had cut away much of what was
coarse and 'niggerish,' and added a deeper tenderness, a higher
polish, a more delicate finish; but also I saw that, nevertheless,
practically all of his work in dialect fitted into the traditional
mold. Not even he had been able to discard those stereotyped

properties of minstrel-stage dialect: The watermelon and the
possum. He did, however, disdain to use that other ancient
'prop,' the razor.''[1]

1902. Resigned as principal of Stanton.

1904. Awarded honorary A.M. from Atlanta University. Met
W.E.B. DuBois.

1905. Left for a successful European tour. "From the day I
set foot in France, I became aware of the working of a miracle
within me. I became aware of a quick readjustment of life and
to environment. I recaptured for the first time since childhod
the sense of being just a human being. I need not try to analyze
this change for my colored readers; they will understand in a
flash what took place. For my white readers . . . I am afraid
that any analysis will be inadequate, perhaps futile. . . . I was
suddenly free; free from a sense of impending discomfort,
insecurity, danger; free from the conflict within the Man-Negro
dualism and the innumerable maneuvers in thought and behavior that it compels; free from the problem of the many
obvious of subtle adjustments to a multitude of bans and taboos;
free from special scorn, special tolerance, special condescen-
sion, special commiseration; free to be merely a man.''[1]

1906. "While we were working on the play ['Shoe Fly Reg-
iment'], Mr. Anderson [a friend] spoke to me . . . about going
into the Consular Service. I asked him to let me think it over
a little while. When I saw him next I said, 'Charlie, if the
President will appoint me, I'll go.'. . . I went to Washington
and took my examination. My appointment was United States
Consul at Puerto Cabello, Venezuela. . . .

"Spring came to an end. Bob and Rosamond [his partners]
sailed to fill their return engagement in London; I sailed for
my post in Venezuela; and the trio was dissolved.

"I fell easily into the tropical mode of life; even into the quite
sensible habit of taking a siesta. In the better house to which
I moved the Consulate, my manner of living was semi-luxu-
rious. In the tropics, 'Do not do today what *can* be put off till
tomorrow,' is a maxim that contains many grains of wisdom. . . . I strove while taking life easily not to take it too
easily. . . . When I had no official duties to perform, I made
it my business to use that period in getting ahead with my
writing. . . .

"It was while I was in Venezuela that I had my one and only
experience in line with a tradition about poetic inspiration, the
tradition of the poet seizing his pen and in 'fine frenzy' taking
dictation from a spirit hovering about his head. I had come
home from the club, and with no conscious thought of poetry
in my mind I undressed for bed. When I had finished undressing
I turned out my light and threw open the shutters to my bedroom
windows. The open windows admitted enough light from the
electric light opposite in the park to enable me to see my way
about the room. I got into bed and immediately went to sleep.
Later in the night, I woke suddenly, completely. For some
reason, the light in the park had gone out and the room was
in impenetrable darkness. I felt startled; then the darkness and
silence combined, brought down on me a feeling of uttermost
peace. I lay thinking for a long while; then I got up and fumbled
for the light, took pen and paper, and almost without hesitation
wrote a sonnet which I called *Mother Night*. Hardly bothering
to read it over, I got back into bed and at once went off to
sleep. The next day I made one or two slight revisions in the
poem, typed it, and sent it to *The Century*. Promptly I got a

(From the animated short film "The Creation," based on a poem by James Weldon Johnson. Its boldness and color are achieved by a special clay painting technique. This movie, narrated by James Earl Jones and produced by Billy Budd Films, was nominated for an Academy Award in 1982.)

letter from Mr. Gilder [editor] in which he said, 'We are overwhelmed with poetry but we must take *Mother Night*.'

"After I had served two years at Puerto Cabello, my thoughts turned more and more to the matter of a promotion. It was not that I was dissatisfied with Puerto Cabello; I was simply anxious to go up in the Service, and I knew that a consul who stayed too long a time in one post was likely to become regarded as a fixture there. . . .

"When the matter of a promotion was uppermost in my mind, I awoke to find that I was trapped in Venezuela. An epidemic of bubonic plague broke out, and every American representative got out of the country, except me. Certainly, I did not stay on because I wished to; but there I was, the only one left. . . .

"In the spring of **1909,** a cable from the State Department came advising me that I had been appointed Consul at Corinto, Nicaragua, and that I should proceed to my post by way of Washington. My new post carried a promotion to the next grade above and an increase in salary of a thousand dollars a year. . . .

"After I reached New York, I went directly to Washington and made in person as full a report as I could on the political situation in Nicaragua. Then I returned to New York on what was to me a more important and delicate mission. I went back to New York to ask Grace Nail to be my wife."[1]

February 10, 1910. "Grace Nail and I were married, and with the good wishes of many friends sailed for Corinto. . . ."[1]

1912. *The Autobiography of an Ex-Colored Man* published.

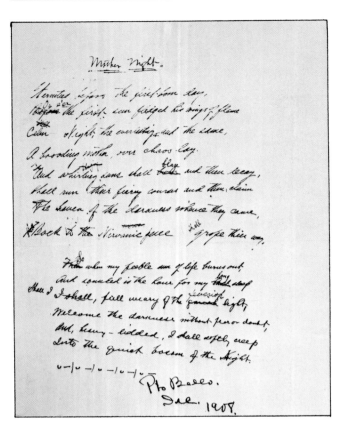

A copy of Johnson's manuscript for the poem "Mother Night." ■ (From *Along This Way: The Autobiography of James Weldon Johnson.*)

September 1, 1913. With Woodrow Wilson now in office, the future was unsure for Johnson. "I was up against politics plus race prejudice; I might be allowed to remain at my present post; if so, I should be there for another four years at least, perhaps for another eight. I came to the definite conclusion that life was too short for me to spend eight years more of it in Corinto. I wrote out my resignation."[1]

Spent several months in Jacksonville after his father's death because of problems with the estate.

1914. "I had been in New York only a few weeks when Fred R. Moore, the owner and publisher of *The New York Age*, the oldest of the New York Negro newspapers, offered me the position of editor of the paper. . . . I wrote *The Age* editorials for ten years. . . . But writing the editorials for *The New York Age* neither took all my time nor paid me as much as I needed to earn. I tried again for Broadway. . . . But I found that I had lost the touch for Broadway. I simply couldn't turn the trick again. . . ."[1]

1916. Joined the National Association for the Advancement of Colored People (NAACP). ". . . When I received Mr. Spingarn's [board chairman, later president] letter, it at once seemed to me that every bit of experience I had had, from the principalship of Stanton School to editorship on *The New York Age*, was preparation for the work I was being asked to undertake. The Board of Directors created the position of Field Secretary, and in that capacity I began work with the Association. . . .

"I got immense satisfaction out of the work which was the main purpose of the . . . [NAACP], at the same time, I struggled constantly not to permit that part of me which was artist to become entirely submerged. I had little time and less energy for creative writing, but in 1921 I began work on an anthology of poetry by American Negroes [published in 1922]."[1]

1920-1924. As part of his duties for the NAACP, Johnson was sent to Haiti to examine conditions during the American occupation there. He also lobbied strongly for the passing of the Dyer anti-lynching bill, which was voted down.

1929. Spent three weeks in Kyoto, Japan, lecturing for the NAACP. "Before I finished with my luggage, three reporters came into my stateroom; three of the same who had been interviewing and photographing me. One of them asked, 'Mr. Johnson, did you see Fujiyama this morning?' I answered that I had. 'Mr. Johnson,' he continued, 'the people of Japan would be greatly honored to have from you a poem on Fujiyama.' With that, he planked a pad down in front of me and offered me a pencil. I was never so taken unawares in my life. I lamely explained that with so inspiring a subject together with the Japanese language, a fitting poem would come spontaneously, but such a thing was impossible to a poet working in the barbarous English tongue. They went away quite disappointed."[1]

December 17, 1930. Tired by the demands of his job, and wanting more time to write, Johnson left his post with the NAACP.

1931. ". . . Dr. Thomas Elsa Jones, President of Fisk University [Tennessee] came to see me . . . and said that he wanted me on the faculty. The place he wanted me to fill was, in a general way, like that of Robert Frost at Amherst. I was to be guide and mentor of students who had the ambition and gave some evidence of talent to be writers. I was to have entire freedom to organize and carry on this work as I felt was best. The idea and plan were fascinating. The trustees of the University created the Adam K. Spence Chair of Creative Literature, and I was elected as the first occupant."[1]

While at Fisk, a racial incident involving a white colleague from another school enraged Johnson to the point of saying: "The south as an institution, can sink through the bottom of the pit of hell."[1]

June 26, 1938. Killed in an automobile collision with a train in Wiscasset, Maine. Buried in Brooklyn, New York. Funeral attended by more than two thousand.

In a pamphlet printed by the NAACP he wrote: "I will not allow one prejudiced person or one million or one hundred million to blight my life. I will not let prejudice or any of its attendant humiliations and injustices bear me down to spiritual defeat. My inner life is mine, and I shall defend and maintain its integrity against all the powers of hell."[2]

FOR MORE INFORMATION SEE: Mary W. Ovington, *Portraits in Color*, Harper, 1927, reprinted, Books for Libraries Press, 1971; James Weldon Johnson, *Black Manhattan*, Knopf, 1930, reprinted, Arno, 1968; Johnson, *Along This Way: The Autobiography of James Weldon Johnson*, Viking, 1933, reprinted, Da Capo Press, 1973; Sterling Brown, "Dunbar and the Romantic Tradition," *The Negro in American Fiction*, Associates in Negro Folk Education, 1937, reprinted in *Negro Poetry and Drama and the Negro in American Fiction*, Atheneum, 1972; J. Saunders Redding, "Emergence of the New Negro," *To Make a Poet Black*, University of North Carolina Press, 1939, reprinted, McGrath, 1968; Ovington, *Walls Came Tumbling Down*, Harcourt, 1947, reprinted, Schocken, 1970; Hugh M. Gloster, "Negro Fiction to World War I," *Negro Voices in American Fiction*, University of North Carolina Press, 1948, reprinted, Russell & Russell, 1965; Langston Hughes, *Fight for Freedom: The Story of the NAACP*, Norton, 1962; Jean Wagner, *Les Poetes Negres des Etats Unis*, Libraire Istra, 1962, translation by Kenneth Doublas published as *Black Poets of the United States: From Paul Laurence Dunbar to Langston Hughes*, University of Illinois Press, 1973; (for children) Ellen Tarry, *Young Jim: The Early Years of James Weldon Johnson*, Dodd, 1967; *Journal of Popular Culture*, spring, 1968.

Negro American Literature Forum, winter, 1970; (for children) Harold W. Felton, *James Weldon Johnson*, Dodd, 1971; Edgar A. Toppin, *Biographical History of Blacks in America since 1528*, McKay, 1971; *Crisis*, June, 1971; *New York Times*, October 12, 1971; *Phylon*, winter, 1971; Anna Wendell Bontemps, *The Harlem Renaissance Remembered*, Dodd, 1972; Eugene Levy, *James Weldon Johnson: Black Leader, Black Voice*, University of Chicago Press, 1973; James O. Young, *Black Writers of the Thirties*, Louisiana State University Press, 1973; *Virginia Quarterly*, summer, 1973; *Black World*, March, 1973; Arthur P. Davis, *From the Dark Tower*, Howard University Press, 1974; (for children) Ophelia Settle Egypt, *James Weldon Johnson* (illustrated by Moneta Barnett), Crowell, 1974; *CLA Journal*, December, 1974; Blyden Jackson and Louis D. Rubin, Jr., *Black Poetry in America: Two Essays in Historical Interpretation*, Louisiana State University Press, 1974.

Ben Richardson and W. A. Fahey, *Great Black Americans*, Crowell, 1976; Robert E. Fleming, editor, *James Weldon Johnson and Arna Wendell Bontemps*, G. K. Hall, 1978; *CLA Journal*, September, 1979; Robert B. Steptoe, "Lost in a Quest: James Weldon Johnson's *The Autobiography of an Ex-Colored Man*," in *From Behind the Veil: A Study of Afro-American Narrative*, University of Illinois Press, 1979.

Obituaries: *Survey*, July, 1938; *Nation*, July 2, 1938; *Publishers Weekly*, July 2, 1938; *Newsweek*, July 4, 1938; *Time*, July 4, 1938; *Wilson Bulletin*, September, 1938; *Etude*, October, 1938.

Movies and filmstrips: "James Weldon Johnson" (motion picture), Oxford Films, 1972.

(From *The Black Pearl* by Scott O'Dell. Illustrated by Milton Johnson.)

JOHNSON, Milton 1932-

PERSONAL: Born August 16, 1932, in Milwaukee, Wis. *Education:* Attended Milwaukee Layton School of Art, Minneapolis Institute of Art, and Boston Museum School of Fine Arts; studied with George Demetrios.

CAREER: Artist and illustrator. Work has appeared in exhibits at such places as Brandeis University, 1969, Boston Museum of Fine Arts, 1970, and Atlanta University. Work represented in the collections of the Oakland Museum and the Boston Public Library. Has taught at Boston Museum School of Fine Arts. *Awards, honors:* Travelling fellowship to Japan from the Boston Museum School of Fine Arts, 1961.

ILLUSTRATOR—For young people: Olivia E. Coolidge, *Men of Athens* (*Horn Book* honor book; ALA Notable Book), Houghton, 1962; Margaret L. Coit, *Andrew Jackson* (ALA Notable Book), Houghton, 1965; O. E. Coolidge, *Lives of Famous Romans*, Houghton, 1965; Erik C. Haugaard, *Orphans of the Wind* (*Horn Book* honor book), Houghton, 1966; Scott O'Dell, *The Black Pearl* (*Horn Book* honor book), Houghton, 1967; E. C. Haugaard, *The Little Fishes* (*Horn Book* honor book; ALA Notable Book), Houghton, 1967; *The Dark Canoe*, Houghton, 1968; O. E. Coolidge, *Come By Here* (*Horn Book* honor book; ALA Notable Book), Houghton, 1970; Nancy Veglahn, *Follow the Golden Goose*, Addison-Wesley, 1970.

SIDELIGHTS: Johnson was born in Milwaukee where he later attended the Layton School of Art. After studying at the Minneapolis Institute of Art and the Boston Museum of Fine Arts, he spent four years in Japan on a Travelling Fellowship where he studied Eastern concepts.

His paintings and prints have brought him numerous awards. When illustrating books he prefers pen and ink. He credits instructor George Demetrios as being very influential in his development in drawing and design.

FOR MORE INFORMATION SEE: *Newsweek,* June 22, 1970;
Lee Kingman and others, compilers, *Illustrators of Children's
Books: 1957-1966,* Horn Book, 1968.

JONES, Penelope 1938-

PERSONAL: Born February 17, 1938, in Rochester, N.Y.;
daughter of Gikas (in business) and Metaxia (Jebeles) Critikos;
married Graham Starr Jones II (a patent attorney), July 5, 1959;
children: Candida Starr, Kimberley Jebeles. *Education:* Smith
College, B.A., 1959. *Home:* 8 Jeffrey Lane, Chappaqua, N.Y.
10514.

CAREER: Writer, 1976—; Country Day Nursery, Chappaqua,
N.Y., teacher, 1977-82; Bedford Christian School, teacher,
1982—. Actress with Southbury Playhouse, summer, 1974;
member of Dobbs Ferry Village Players; member of board of
directors, past president, and casting director and producer of
Chappaqua Drama Group. Volunteer remedial reading teacher
at Children's Village, 1963-65; volunteer reader for Chappaqua
Library. *Member:* Chappaqua Garden Club.

*WRITINGS—*Juveniles: *I Didn't Want to Be Nice* (illustrated
by Rosalie Orlando), Bradbury, 1977; *I'm Not Moving* (illustrated by Amy Aitken), Bradbury, 1979; *Holding Together,*
Bradbury, 1981; *The Stealing Thing,* Bradbury, 1983.

SIDELIGHTS: "I feel very strongly about the importance of
children learning to love books at the preschool level. In addition to the boundless possibilities for developing the imagination, being read to gives the young child an enormous amount
of assurance, understanding, and sheer pleasure, which will
have positive effects throughout his life. Having this conviction, I am particularly interested in helping young children to
understand that their feelings of hostility, jealousy, and fear
are legitimate—everyone has them. This knowledge, I believe,
helps the child to deal with negative feelings.

"The writing of my first novel, *Holding Together,* was a marvelous adventure for me. An adventure it was because of the

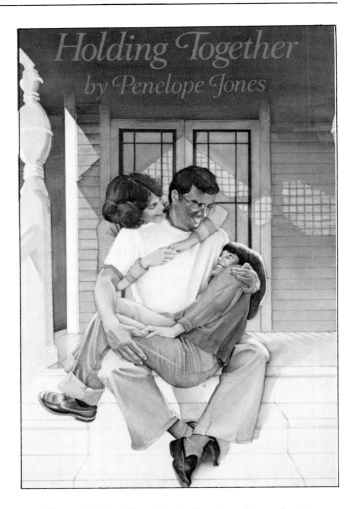

(From *Holding Together* by Penelope Jones. Jacket
illustration by Larry Raymond.)

PENELOPE JONES

obvious reason that I had never done it before. What was most
curious about the experience was the discovery that writing the
book in little installments was not unlike reading a book in
little installments. I was continually drawn to writing almost
as though I couldn't wait to find out just what was going to
happen next and how it was going to happen.

"For whom was *Holding Together* intended? All children. The
same is true of *The Stealing Thing. Holding Together* deals
with the death of a mother and the relationship between two
sisters and their father. Death is a subject which has been
largely kept away from American children. They are shielded
from it at every turn, however, they are very curious about it
and should be allowed to know and understand what they can
about the subject. *The Stealing Thing,* of course, deals with
petty thievery. It is my conviction that even if the eight to ten
year old has not actually stolen anything, often he has had the
urge to do so at one time or another. Gaining an insight into
one's urges to take something, to steal, can improve the child's
understanding of himself. The children of working parents have
been on my mind very much these past few years. When both
parents must continuously place the needs of the child in a
subordinate position to the demands of their careers, the child
is often left isolated and unhappy. My sympathies reach out
to this child in *The Stealing Thing.*"

JORDAN, E(mil) L(eopold) 1900-

BRIEF ENTRY: Born October 2, 1900, in Russ, Germany; a naturalized U.S. citizen. A professor and author, Jordan taught German at Rutgers University for over thirty-five years. Since 1967 he has been emeritus professor of the school. Jordan is popular for his work on Hammond guidebooks, atlases, and encyclopedias. Among the titles he has written are *Hammond's Nature Book of Trees, Wildflowers, Reptiles, Fishes* (1956), *Hammond's Pictorial Library of Pets, Plants, and Animals* (illustrated by Elizabeth Hammell and Barbara Amlick, 1958), and *Hammond's Nature Atlas of America* (illustrated by Walter Ferguson and John Cody, 1952). Jordan is also the author of German language books. He has also written *Americans: A New History of the Peoples Who Settled the Americas* (Norton, 1939) for young adults and *Animal Atlas of the World* (Hammond, 1969) for children. Besides writing, Jordan has worked as a translator. He is a member of the American Association of Teachers of German and the Modern Language Association of America. *Address:* Route 1, Box 333C, Blowing Rock, N.C. 28605. *For More Information See: Directory of American Scholars,* 7th edition, Bowker, 1978.

KADESCH, Robert R(udstone) 1922-

PERSONAL: Surname is pronounced *Kay*-desh; born May 14, 1922, in Cedar Falls, Iowa; son of William H. (a professor) and Mary (a teacher; maiden name, Barnum) Kadesh; married Arlene Tow, August 15, 1943; children: Joan Lea (Mrs. Steven Heinz), Ann Marie (Mrs. Thomas Carter), Thomas Robert. *Education:* University of Northern Iowa, B.S., 1943; University of Rochester, M.S., 1949; University of Wisconsin, Ph.D., 1955. *Home:* 3050 South Grace St., Salt Lake City, Utah 84109. *Office:* Department of Physics, University of Utah, Salt Lake City, Utah 84112.

CAREER: University of Utah, Salt Lake City, assistant professor, 1956-61, associate professor, 1961-65, professor of physics, 1965—, associate dean for science, 1966-68. Visiting professor at University of Minnesota, 1963-64; visiting research physicist at University of California, Berkeley, 1973-74. Writer for School Mathematics Study Group, Stanford University, summer, 1963; program manager for National Science Foundation, 1968-69; member of board of directors of Utah Common Cause, 1973, 1975-76. *Military serivce:* U.S. Naval Reserve, 1943-46; became lieutenant junior grade. *Member:* Sigma Xi, Phi Kappa Phi. *Awards, honors:* Notable book of the year award from U.S. Library Association, 1970, for *Math Menagerie.*

WRITINGS: The Crazy Cantilever and Other Science Experiments, Harper, 1961; *Math Menagerie* (illustrated by Mark A. Binn; ALA Notable book), Harper, 1970. Contributor to *Salt Lake Tribune.*

WORK IN PROGRESS: A monograph on mathematical foundations of plausible reasoning; a complete video-computer course in elementary physics.

KELLEAM, Joseph E(veridge) 1913-1975

PERSONAL: Surname rhymes with "tell 'em"; born February 11, 1913, in Boswell, Okla.; died June 15, 1975; son of Edwin Ayres (a physician) and Ophelia (Everidge) Kelleam; married Alta Tolle, October 6, 1934; children: Aljo K. Gregg, Edwina (Mrs. Covington). *Education:* Attended Oklahoma University, 1930-32, and Southwestern Technical College, 1932-34; Central State College, Edmond, Okla., B.S., 1936, graduate study, 1936. *Home:* Hugo, Okla.

CAREER: Civil servant and author. Employed in various government agencies, 1934-60, including U.S. Treasury Department, Indian Service, U.S. Army Corp of Engineers, Army Air Forces, and with private contractors throughout the United States; also employed as contract specialist with U.S. Air Force at Boeing Airplane Co., Wichita, Kan. *Member:* Science Fiction Writers of America, Oklahoma Poetry Writers, Pi Kappa Phi, Sigma Tau Delta. *Awards, honors:* Was decorated for service with U.S. Army Corp of Engineers, and for civilian contributions to Army Air Forces.

WRITINGS: Blackjack, W. Sloane, 1948; *Overload from Space* (science fiction; for young adults), Ace Books, 1956; *The Little Men* (science fiction; for young adults), Bouregy, 1960; *Hunters of Space* (science fiction; for young adults), Bouregy, 1960; *When the Red King Woke* (for young adults), Bouregy, 1966; *Days Beyond Number* (poems), Dorrance, 1971; *Good-Bye to Babylon* (poems), Naylor, 1974; *Their Tributes Were Tears,* Vantage, 1979. Also author of *Okie Jim and Queen of the Night;* contributor of short stories to magazines, including *Astounding Fiction* and *Esquire.*

SIDELIGHTS: "My family was one of the first five or six to settle in southeast Oklahoma. They were chased out of Mississippi for talking up for the Five Civilized Tribes who were also being chased out at that time.

"I went to three colleges. My father opened up quite a number of hospitals and clinics for the government and Indian Service during the Depression, and we moved around quite a bit. I went to Oklahoma University, Southwestern Tech at Weatherford, Oklahoma, and Central State College at Edmond, Oklahoma. I received a B.S. degree in English from the latter in 1936. Then another half-year toward a Master's but by then the Depression was just too rough, and I had to leave the halls of ivy.

"The name Kelleam came from the Scotch Irish border; and I have been told it is Gaelic for 'church-man,' though I'm not much of a church man. A friend of mine who once introduced me on radio and TV (later), prefaced his remarks by saying the name rhymed with 'tell 'em' and 'sell 'em'—but I *shore* haven't been able to tell 'em or sell 'em very much!" [Robert Reginald, *Science Fiction Fantasy Literature: A Checklist,* Gale, 1979.]

KELLEY, Leo P(atrick) 1928-

BRIEF ENTRY: Born September 10, 1928, in Wilkes Barre, Pa. A graduate of the New School for Social Research, Kelley is the editor and author of numerous science fiction books for young people. Kelley's career began at the McGraw-Hill Book Co. as a copywriter. He was later promoted to advertising manager, but has been a free-lance writer since 1969. Kelley's sci-fi titles for young people include *Goodbye to Earth* (1979), *King of the Stars* (1979), *Vacation in Space* (1979), *Where No Sun Shines* (1979), and *Worlds Apart* (1979), all published by Fearon. He has also written a number of science fiction books for adults, including *The Coins of Murph* (Berkley Publishing, 1971), *Deadlocked* (Fawcett, 1973), and *The Earth Tripper*

(Fawcett, 1973). Kelley is a member of Science Fiction Writers of America, Mystery Writers of America, National Fantasy Fan Federation, and Mensa. He is a contributor of stories and poetry to periodicals, including *Worlds of If* and *Commonweal*. *For More Information See: Contemporary Science Fiction Authors*, Arno, 1975; *The Encyclopedia of Science Fiction: An Illustrated A to Z*, Grenada Publishing, 1979; *Science Fiction and Fantasy Literature*, Volume 2: *Contemporary Science Fiction Authors II*, Gale, 1979.

KLAPERMAN, Libby Mindlin   1921-1982

OBITUARY NOTICE: Born December 28, 1921, in Petrikow, Russia (now U.S.S.R.); died June 18, 1982, in Lawrence, Long Island, N.Y. Administrator, educator, and author. Klaperman began her career in 1950 as the education director of the Women's Branch of the Union of the Orthodox Jewish Congregations of America, an organization which she eventually served as vice-president. She taught humanities at Far Rockaway High School in New York City before becoming a professor of religious studies at Stern College for Women. Klaperman was the author of many books for children, including *The Dreidel Who Wouldn't Spin, Jeremy and Torah, Jeremy's ABC Book,* and *Five Brothers Macabee: A Novel for Young Readers Based on the Story of Chanukah*. She and her husband also wrote the four-volume *Story of the Jewish People* for adults. *For More Information See: Contemporary Authors,* Volumes 9-12, revised, Gale, 1974. *Obituaries: New York Times*, June 23, 1982.

RON KLUG

X is for Xylophone
We can play Christmas songs on our xylophone.

(From *My Christmas ABC Book* by Ron and Lyn Klug. Illustrated by Jim Roberts.)

KLUG, Ron(ald)   1939-

PERSONAL: Surname is pronounced "Kloog"; born June 26, 1939, in Milwaukee, Wis.; son of Harold A. (a factory worker) and Linda (Kavemeier) Klug; married Lynda Rae Hosler (an author), February 20, 1971; children: Rebecca, Paul, Hans. *Education:* Dr. Martin Luther College (New Ulm, Minn), B.S., 1962; graduate study at University of Wisconsin, Milwaukee, 1965-68. *Religion:* Lutheran. *Home:* 1115 S. Division St., Northfield, Minn. 55057.

CAREER: St. Matthew Lutheran School, Oconomowoc, Wis., teacher, 1962-65; University of Wisconsin, Milwaukee, teaching assistant, 1965-68; Concordia Publishing House, St. Louis, Mo., copywriter, 1968-69; Augsburg Publishing House, Minneapolis, Minn., book editor, 1970-76; American School, Fort Dauphin, Madagascar, missionary teacher, 1976-80; free-lance writer and editor, 1980—. *Member:* Minnesota Christian Writers' Guild (president, 1982-83).

WRITINGS: Strange Young Man in the Desert: John the Baptist (juvenile; illustrated by Betty Wind), Concordia, 1971; *Lord, I've Been Thinking: Prayer Thoughts for High School Boys,* Augsburg, 1978; *Psalms: A Guide to Prayer and Praise,* Harold Shaw, 1979; *Following Christ: Prayers from the "Imitation of Christ" in the Language of Today,* Concordia, 1981; *Philippians: God's Guide to Joy,* Harold Shaw, 1981; *Job: God's Answer to Suffering,* Harold Shaw, 1982; *How to Keep a Spiritual Journal,* T. Nelson, 1982; *My Prayer Journal,* Concordia, 1982; *Growing in Joy,* Augsburg, 1982.

With wife, Lyn Klug: *Family Prayers*, Augsburg, 1979; *Please, God*, Augsburg, 1980; *Thank You, God* (juvenile; illustrated by Sally Matthews), Augsburg, 1980; *I'm a Good Helper* (juvenile; illustrated by S. Matthews), Augsburg, 1981; *My Christmas ABC Book* (juvenile; illustrated by Jim Roberts), Augsburg, 1981; *Bible Readings for Parents*, Augsburg, 1982; *The Christian Family Bedtime Reading Book* (juvenile; illustrated by Koechel/Peterson Design), Augsburg, 1982; *Jesus Lives!* (juvenile; illustrated by Paul Konsterlie), Augsburg.

HOBBIES AND OTHER INTERESTS: Prayer and religious studies family life, children's books.

KRAHN, Fernando 1935-

BRIEF ENTRY: Born January 4, 1935, in Santiago, Chile. An author and illustrator, Krahn began his career as a cartoonist for such magazines as *Esquire, New Yorker, Horizon, Show, Evergreen, Atlantic Monthly,* and *Reporter.* Most of his work, however, is concentrated in the field of children's literature. Among the books he has written and illustrated for young people are *Journeys of Sebastian* (Delacorte, 1968), *Robot-Bot-Bot* (Dutton, 1979), *Here Comes Alex Pumpernickel* (Little, Brown, 1981), and *The First Peko-Neko Bird* (Simon & Schuster, 1969), co-authored with his wife Maria de la Luz Uribe. Krahn has also illustrated the books of other authors, including Jan Wahl's *Abe Lincoln's Beard* (Delacorte, 1972), William J. Smith's *Laughing Time: Nonsense Poems* (Delacorte, 1980), and Sonia Levitin's *Nobody Stole the Pie* (Harcourt, 1980).

Krahn's books have received numerous awards and recognitions, *Uncle Timothy's Traviata* (Delacorte, 1967), written by Alastair Reid, and *Hildegarde and Maximilian* (Delacorte, 1969) have been included in the Children's Book Shows of the American Institute of Graphic Arts. *The Life of Numbers* (Simon & Schuster, 1970), written with his wife, was chosen by the *New York Times* as one of the outstanding children's books of 1970, and *April Fools* (Dutton, 1974) was included in the Children's Book Showcase in 1975. In 1973 Krahn received a Guggenheim fellowship to continue his work in the field of film animation. His first film, "The Perfect Crime," was presented at the Oberhausen Film Festival in Germany. *Address:* San Guadencio 23, Sitges, Spain. *For More Information See: Contemporary Authors,* Volumes 65-68, Gale, 1977; *Illustrators of Children's Books, 1967-1976,* Horn Book, 1978; *Fourth Book of Junior Authors and Illustrators,* H.W. Wilson, 1978; *Graphis 34,* 1978-79.

LAFFIN, John (Alfred Charles) 1922-
(Carl Dekker, Mark Napier, Dirk Sabre)

PERSONAL: Born September 21, 1922, in Sydney, Australia; son of Charles George and Nellie (a nursing sister; maiden name, Pike) Laffin; married Hazelle Gloria Stonham (now her husband's assistant), October 6, 1943; children: Bronwen Diane, Craig Antony, Pirenne Debra. *Education:* University of London, M.A., 1961. *Politics:* "Completely uncommitted." *Religion:* Christian humanist. *Home:* Oxford House, Church St., Knighton, Powys, Wales.

CAREER: Associated Newspapers, Sydney, Australia, associate editor, 1945-51; York Editing Service, Sydney, managing director, 1951-56; International Corresponding Schools, Syd-

JOHN LAFFIN

ney, chief instructor and examiner in creative journalism and short story writing, 1951-56; Mayfield College, Sussex, England, head of the departments of English, geography, and sociology, 1959-69; full-time writer, 1969—. Chairman of Sussex branch of British Legion, 1967-69. *Military service:* Australian Army, Infantry, 1940-45; served in New Guinea. *Member:* Royal Geographical Society (fellow), Royal Historical Society (fellow), Society for Army Historical Research, Society of Authors, Military History Society of Ireland, Society for Nautical Research, Society of Antiquaries of Scotland, Royal United Service Institution. *Awards, honors:* Brantridge College, Sussex, D.Litt., 1972.

WRITINGS—Of interest to young people: *Codes and Ciphers: Secret Writing Through the Ages* (illustrated by C. De La Nougarede, Junior Literary Guild selection), Abelard, 1964; *Boys in Battle,* Abelard, 1967. Also author of adult fiction and nonfiction under the pseudonyms Carl Dekker, Mark Napier, and Dirk Sabre. For a complete bibliographical listing see *Contemporary Authors,* Volumes 53-56.

WORK IN PROGRESS: A history of jihad (holy war); a play about God; a novel set in Vietnam; an autobiography.

SIDELIGHTS: When Laffin was only 15 his first adult short story was published and his work was included in an Australian national anthology (*Tales by Australians,* British Authors Press, 1937). Although much of his work since then has been in the field of war and military history, Laffin stated that he "refuses to glorify war but recognises that men 'find themselves' in war." His military interests include problems of leadership and command, the psychology of combat, and the development of war, as well as visiting battlefields with his wife as companion and assistant. He wrote that he has "explored thousands of years of fields of combat and is a pioneer in battlefield archaeology.

"As a person I am interested in everything so as a writer I have several different fields. My main reputation seems to be in war and in the problems of the Middle East, but writing serious novels and poetry means more to me. I lecture quite often on a wide variety of subjects, from body language to the Islamic religion." He continues to write on war, "only because I am trapped by my reputation." He wants to write to warn people of great dangers—their own apathy, refusal to think for themselves, willingness to follow the loudest voice or the brightest flag. He is "appalled by the physical and intellectual flabbiness of modern man. I like them physically hard but mentally flexible—like the blade of a foil.

"I am hungry for more and more existence; I want to meet and talk with people—really to talk, not just chat. Discovering new places is important for me and I like to have my emotions and intellect and perception stretched and challenged. My family says that if I did not have a problem I would create one—and they are probably right. Mastering a difficulty or problem is satisfying and stimulating.

"I hope that I never feel too old for adventure, which was always part of me. Some of my experiences might be better described as foolhardy rather than adventurous. Without any previous experience I did a freefall parachute jump and came close to killing myself; I helped some East Germans escape into West Germany; I have talked my way into terrorist strongholds; and, metaphorically, I have put my head into the tiger's mouth many times.

"All this has made me a better writer and, I think, a more understanding person. I have never experienced boredom and I feel deeply sorry for young people who are bored. Perhaps they have never been introduced to the adventure of reading. As a boy I had a voracious appetite for books; when I could not afford to buy a coveted book I would read it at the shop's shelves. In this way I learned to read quickly—a lifelong advantage. Too many people go through life wanting to be 'safe' and 'secure.' Security lies in your own self-confidence, not in pension plans.

"Whenever I am asked to sign an autograph book or a prize book, I write 'Always ask "Why?"' I do this because I consider it life's most important question. From the answers you receive you soon learn to make judgments.

"I have only one fear and it is not of death—just that I might die before I finish what I came to do. Not that I shall ever know when I am finished. As for what I value most, well, nothing ranks higher than close friendship and the inspiration which comes from it."

Angry about the treatment of authors in Britain, Laffin contends that "free public libraries rob all but a handful of writers of the opportunity to earn a living by their typewriter. It is the price we are forced to pay for being nonconformists. We are the last independents."

LAITE, Gordon   1925-

PERSONAL: Born July 11, 1925, in New York, N.Y.; foster son of Charles (an actor) and Blanche (an illustrator; maiden name, Fisher) Laite; married his wife, Jeanne in 1948; children: three. *Education:* Attended Beloit College and Chicago Art Institute. *Religion:* Baha'i. *Residence:* Gallup, New Mexico.

CAREER: Illustrator of books for children.

ILLUSTRATOR—All for children: R. C. Mackay, *They Sang a New Song*, Abingdon, 1959; Mildred C. Luckhardt, *The Story of St. Nicholas*, Abingdon, 1960; Natalia M. Belting, *Elves and Ellefolk: Tales of the Little People*, Holt, 1961; Alice I. Hazeltine, editor, *Hero Tales from Many Lands*, Abingdon, 1961; E. Dolch, *Stories from India*, Garrard, 1961; M. C. Luckhardt, *Good King Wenceslas*, Abingdon, 1964; *The Book of the Covenant People* (religious text), Covenant Life Curriculum Press, 1966; Ralph W. Sockman, *The Easter Story for Children*, Abingdon, 1966; Elizabeth Seeger, *The Five Sons of King Pandu: The Story of the Mahabhárata* (adapted from the translation of Kisari Mohan Ganguli), W. R. Scott, 1967; Leonard Wolcott and Carolyn Wolcott, *Religions around the World*, Abingdon, 1967; Michael Daves, *Young Readers Book of Christian Symbolism*, Abingdon, 1967; Alice Kelsey, *The Thirty Gilt Pennies*, Abingdon, 1968; Virginia F. Voight, *The Adventures of Hiawatha*, Garrard, 1969; Harold W. Felton, *Big Mose, Hero Fireman*, Garrard, 1969; Willis Lindquist, *Folktales from Many Lands*, L. W. Singer, 1969; E. Seeger, *The Ramayana* (adapted from the translation of Hari Prasad Shastri; ALA Notable Book), W. R. Scott, 1969.

Lawrence F. Lowery, *Up, Up in a Balloon*, new edition, Western Publishing, 1970; Polly Curren, *The World Builds the Bridge* (nonfiction), Harvey House, 1970; Clyde R. Bulla, *Joseph, the Dreamer*, Crowell, 1971; Sara S. Beattie, *School on a Raft*, Ginn, 1971; Peter Seymour, *Snow White*, Hallmark, 1971; V. F. Voight, *Close to the Rising Sun: Algonquian Indian Legends*, Garrard, 1972; Daphne D. Hogstrom, *One Silver Second: A Fable for All Ages*, Rand McNally, 1972; David L. Harrison, *Children Everywhere*, Rand McNally, 1973; Aileen Fisher, *Now That Days Are Colder*, Bowmar, 1973; Carol Mullan, *Bible Picture Stories from the Old and New Testaments*, Golden Press, 1974; Samuel Epstein and Beryl Epstein, *A Year of Japanese Festivals*, Garrard, 1974; Lee Wyndham, *Holidays in Scandinavia*, Garrard, 1975; Alma Gilleo, editor, *The Elves and the Shoemaker* (with cassette), Society for Visual Education, 1977; Matt H. Newman, editor, *Goldilocks and the Three Bears* (with cassette), Society for Visual Education, 1980; M. H. Newman, editor, *Rumpelstiltskin* (with cassette), Society for Visual Education, 1980; M. H. Newman, editor, *The Selfish Giant* (with cassette), Society for Visual Education, 1980.

SIDELIGHTS: Laite was born in New York City of Polish immigrant parents. Reared by foster parents, Charles Laite, an actor on the Broadway stage, and his wife Blanche Fisher Laite, who illustrated the *Real Mother Goose* in 1916, Laite's childhood was spent in Yonkers, Mt. Vernon and on a farm in North Gage Corners, New York. "I have drawn, colored and painted since the age of six. The work of Howard Pyle, the illustrations for *Wind in the Willows*, even Pogany and Maxwell Parrish all affected my early impressions. A course in Art History made the progress of man's artistic endeavor vivid and so alive. From this dates my inability to pin myself to one style." [Lee Kingman and others, compilers, *Illustrators of Children's Books: 1957-1966*, Horn Book, 1968.[1]]

As Indians count the years, Hiawatha was eight summers old. ■ (From *The Adventures of Hiawatha* by Virginia Frances Voight. Illustrated by Gordon Laite.)

Laite illustrates predominantly with ink in line, line and wash, or line in several colors with color laid over. He and his wife Jeanne "embraced the teachings of the Baha'i faith. Out of this has grown a supreme delight in doing illustrations depicting natural inter-racial association as well as showing people of the other lands."[1]

The Laites have three children and live in Gallup, New Mexico. "We have discovered the beauty and integrity of the American Indian. Their painting and weaving have had their influence, too."[1]

FOR MORE INFORMATION SEE: Lee Kingman and others, compilers, *Illustrators of Children's Books: 1957-1966,* Horn Book, 1968.

LAMB, Elizabeth Searle 1917-

PERSONAL: Born January 22, 1917, in Topeka, Kan.; daughter of Howard Sanford (in insurance) and Helen (a musician; maiden name, Shaver) Searle; married F. Bruce Lamb (a forester and writer), December 11, 1941; children: Carolyn. *Education:* University of Kansas, B.A., 1939, B.M., 1940. *Religion:* Protestant. *Home:* 970 Acequia Madre, Santa Fe, N.M. 87501. *Agent:* Bertha Klausner International Literary Agency, Inc., 71 Park Ave., New York, N.Y. 10016.

CAREER: Professional harpist and composer in earlier years; Canon City correspondent for *Pueblo Chieftain,* Pueblo, Colo., 1957-59. Has given poetry readings and led poetry and haiku workshops; also judge for various haiku contests. *Member:* National League of American Pen Women, American Harp Society, Haiku Society of America (charter member; president,

1971), Women Poets of New York, Society of Children's Book Writers, Rio Grand Writers Association, Phi Beta Kappa, Pi Kappa Lambda, Mu Phi Epsilon. *Awards, honors:* Awards from National League of American Pen Women for writings, annually, 1965-69, 1971-72, 1974-80; second prize in Ruben Darin International Memorial Poetry Contest sponsored by Organization of American States, 1967; Harold G. Henderson Haiku Award, 1978, 1981, 1982; Dellbrook Poetry Award, 1979; Haiku Award from the Museum of Haiku Literature, Tokyo, Japan, 1981; Sakuma Award from Yuki Teiki Haiku Society, 1981; Audio-Visual Poetry Foundation Award for individually read poem on tape, Edition No. 2, 1981; other awards for poetry, including haiku and concrete poetry.

WRITINGS: (With Jean Bailey and Patricia Maloney Markun) *The Pelican Tree and Other Panama Adventures,* North River Press, 1953; *Today and Every Day,* Unity Books, 1970; *Inside Me, Outside Me,* Unity Books, 1974; *in this blaze of sun* (haiku), From Here Press, 1975; (with husband, F. Bruce Lamb) *Picasso's "Bust of Sylvette"* (haiku), Garlinghouse Printers, 1977; *39 Blossoms* (haiku), High/Coo Press, 1982.

Contributor of articles to music magazines, of poetry and prose to religious magazines, of music and dance entries to *Young Students Encyclopedia,* 1973, and *My Weekly Reader,* 1974, and of juvenile material to *Children's Activities, Jack and Jill, Highlights for Children,* and *Wee Wisdom;* contributor of poetry to anthologies and to *New York Herald Tribune, Christian Science Monitor, Poetry Digest, Lyric, Haiku* (Toronto), *American Haiku, Haiku Highlights, Tweed, Bonsai, Cicada, Studia Mystica, Hai* (Japan), *Frogpond, Wind Chimes, Blue Unicorn, Poets On,* and other publications. Wrote lyrics for six songs in "New Dimensions in Music" series, American Book Co., 1970.

ELIZABETH SEARLE LAMB

WORK IN PROGRESS: Three books of poetry, *Readings from a Double Compass, Let All the Banners Fly,* and *All Night Singing* (haiku); *Western Haiku: A Brief History.*

SIDELIGHTS: "My earliest memories are of books and being read to when I was very small and lying on the floor on my stomach with a page of newspaper and underlining in red the words I recognized. They were *the, and, I, you*—as I learned to read, somehow, quite a while before I started school. *A Child's Garden of Verses* by Robert Louis Stevenson given me on my third Christmas remains one of my most cherished possessions, and reading and the gathering of books to have and to hold have remained a joy in all the years since.

"When I was in about the sixth grade I saw a marionette show and between acts a harpist played. It was love at first sight! Shortly thereafter there was a chance to buy a small used harp and my beloved grandmother, who made her home with us, bought it for me. Music became the main focus of my life and all through high school and then college I played as soloist, in chamber groups, with high school and the University of Kansas symphony. Even before I graduated from college I spent one summer in Tulsa, Oklahoma as harpist with their Starlight Symphony. After graduation I went to Kansas City as second harpist with the Kansas City Symphony and harp teacher at the Kansas City Conservatory. During this time I was writing occasional music articles and brief personal inspirational features . . . but I was sure my life was to be spent as a professional harpist.

"Before my second year in Kansas City was finished though, I packed up the harp, a trunk full of books and music and clothes and gifts of sterling silver and went off to Port of Spain, Trinidad in the British West Indies. There Bruce Lamb and I were married just a few days after the attack on Pearl Harbor which brought the United States into World War II. Bruce was on his first job after graduating as a forester from the University

of Michigan . . . working with the U.S. Engineers to build a 'lend-lease' air base on the island. But we had met years before at the University of Kansas where he was majoring in music and playing the flute (which has remained a love).

"The second assignment for him was up the Amazon River in Brazil, and there my harp could not go! It made it safely back to Kansas through submarine-infested waters, while I traveled with only a typewriter to play on after we settled down (in a manner of speaking) in the little town of Santarem, five hundred miles up the Amazon. Bruce traveled much of the time further inland, and often no one else in the little town spoke English, so I began to do more writing. And from that time on writing of all kinds has been an important part of my life.

"To music and inspirational material was added travel stories. Many more moves checkered our pattern of life, and with the arrival of a daughter I began to write children's stories and articles. Still later, came poetry. And always the sights and sounds and smells and experiences we were living amidst became the rough ore from which I attempted to fashion the gold of the written word. Panama, Colombia, Central America, Puerto Rico—and then fourteen years in Greenwich Village, New York City—and through it all the typewriter has accepted my thoughts and made them accessible to editors, publishers, and finally to readers.

"Now Bruce is a retired forester and spends hours every day with his flute; my harp is with us but is played seldom. It is the typewriter that continues to make its music for hours every day. Here in Santa Fe I am adding with joy the knowledge of the three cultures—Native American, Hispanic, Anglo—which have made the Southwest into a unique place. And my haiku and other poetry already show this influence. Soon there will be stories and, I hope, books set in this exciting and wonderful land."

HOBBIES AND OTHER INTERESTS: Music, including amateur chamber music, collecting materials pertaining to haiku.

FOR MORE INFORMATION SEE: Haiku Highlights, July-August, 1971; *The Village Voice,* May 3, 1976; *Modern Haiku,* August, 1976, August, 1979; *High/Coo,* February, 1979.

LAVINE, David   1928-

PERSONAL: Born November 11, 1928, in New York, N.Y.; son of Abraham Lincoln and Joan (Bragman) Lavine; married Gladys Bozyan, April 28, 1963; children: Rachel, Adam, Rebecca. *Education:* DePauw University, B.A., 1948; further study at New York University, 1949-50. *Politics:* Democrat. *Home:* Dead Hill Rd., Durham, Conn. 06422.

CAREER: New York State Civil Service Commission, N.Y., administrative intern, 1953-54; New York State Department of Welfare, N.Y., 1953-54; New York City public schools, teacher, 1954-61; Connecticut General Assembly, Hartford, Conn., state representative, 1971—. Educational consultant, Community Participation in Education Program, 1966-71; director, Connecticut Inland Wetlands Project, 1973-75; citizens' advisory group, New England River Basins Commission, 1975—; advisory board, Connecticut Valley Hospital, 1975—; executive director, Temporary Nuclear Power Evaluation Council, 1976. *Awards, honors:* Environmental Legislator of the Year, Fourteen-State Environmental Organization in Co-

Proposed laws go to committees for thorough study. ■ (From *What Does a Senator Do?* by David Lavine. Photographs by Ira Mandelbaum.)

alition, 1973; Conservationist of the Year, Middlesex County Soil and Water Service, 1973; citation for outstanding service, Sierra Club, Connecticut chapter, 1973.

WRITINGS—All for young people: (With Ira Mandelbaum) *What Does a Peace Corps Volunteer Do?*, introduction by Sargent Shriver, Dodd, 1964; *What Does a Congressman Do?* (photographs by I. Mandelbaum), introduction by John V. Lindsay, Dodd, 1965; *The Mayor and the Changing City* (photographs by I. Mandelbaum), Random House, 1966; *Outposts of Adventure: The Story of the Foreign Service,* introduction by Dean Rusk, Doubleday, 1966; *Under the City* (photographs by I. Mandelbaum), Doubleday, 1967; *What Does a Senator Do?* (photographs by I. Mandelbaum), introduction by Robert F. Kennedy, Dodd, 1967.

LEVY, Elizabeth 1942-

PERSONAL: Born April 4, 1942, in Buffalo, N.Y.; daughter of Elmer Irving and Mildred (Kirschenbaum) Levy; married Dr. George R. Vickers, January 26, 1979. *Education:* Brown University, B.A. (cum laude), 1964; Columbia University, M.A.T., 1968. *Home:* New York, N.Y. *Agent:* Elaine Markson Literary Agency, Inc., 44 Greenwich Ave., New York, N.Y. 10011.

CAREER: American Broadcasting Co., New York City, editor and researcher in news department, 1964-66; Macmillan Co., New York City, assistant editor, 1967-69; New York Public Library, New York City, writer in public relations, 1969; JPM Associates (urban affairs consultants), New York City, staff writer, 1970-71; free-lance writer, 1971—. *Member:* Authors Guild of Authors League of America, Mystery Writers of America. *Awards, honors: Struggle and Lose, Struggle and Win* was named outstanding book of the year by the *New York Times,* 1977.

WRITINGS—Of interest to young people: *The People Lobby: The SST Story,* Delacorte, 1973; *Something Queer Is Going On* (*Weekly Reader* Book Club selection), Delacorte, 1973; *Nice Little Girls* (illustrated by Mordicai Gerstein), Delacorte, 1974; *Lawyers for the People: A New Breed of Defenders and Their Work,* Knopf, 1974; *By-Lines: Profiles in Investigative Journalism,* Four Winds, 1975; *Something Queer at the Ballpark* (Junior Literary Guild selection), Delacorte, 1975; *Lizzie Lies A Lot* (illustrated by John Wallner), Dell, 1976; *Something Queer at the Library,* Delacorte, 1977; (with cousin, Robie H. Harris) *Before You Were Three: How You Began to Walk, Talk, Explore, and Have Feelings* (alternate selection of Book-of-the-Month Club), Delacorte, 1977; (with Mara Miller) *Doctors for Today: Profiles of Six Who Serve,* Knopf, 1977; (with Tad Richards) *Struggle and Lose, Struggle and Win: The United Mineworkers Story,* Four Winds, 1977; (with Earl and Liz

ELIZABETH LEVY

Hammond) *Our Animal Kingdom*, Delacorte, 1977; *Nice Little Girls*, Delacorte, 1978; *The Tryouts*, Four Winds, 1979; *Frankenstein Moved in on the Fourth Floor*, Harper, 1979; *Politicians for the People*, Dell, 1979; *Something Queer on Vacation*, Delacorte, 1980; *Running Out of Time*, Knopf, 1980; *Come Out Smiling: A Novel*, Delacorte, 1981; *Running Out of Magic with Houdini*, Knopf, 1981; *Something Queer at the Haunted School*, Delacorte, 1982; *Something Queer at the Lemonade Stand*, Delacorte, 1982.

"Jody and Jake Mystery" series; all published by Archway: *The Case of the Counterfeit Racehorse*, 1980; *The Case of the Dark Horse*, 1980; *The Case of the Frightened Rock Star*, 1980; *The Case of the Fired-Up Gang*, 1981; *The Case of the Wild River Ride*, 1981.

"Fat Albert" Books (novelizations of the TV show); all published by Dell: *Mr. Big Time*, 1981; *The Runt*, 1981; *The Shuttered Window*, 1981; *Take Two, They're Small*, 1981; *Spare the Rod*, 1981; *Mom or Pop*, 1981.

Plays: (Co-author) "Croon" (one-act), first produced in New York City at Performing Garage, March 28, 1976; (co-author) "Never Waste a Virgin" (two-act), first produced in New York City at Wonderhorse Theatre, December 3, 1977.

ADAPTATIONS: (Play) "Lizzie Lies A Lot," produced by the Cutting Edge, 1978.

WORK IN PROGRESS: A novel about a boy who steals a chess computer and a teen-age novel about close friends who are kinder to each other than they are to their boyfriends.

SIDELIGHTS: "It is a strange sensation to be asked to list all my books. Looking at the titles of my books is like going through a scrap book and trying to recall the impulse that made you want to save something.

"In real life I have very little trouble throwing out old papers and old clothes. I am not a pack rat, although my husband is.

But when I look at my titles, I realize that I am an imaginary pack rat, insisting on hoarding and putting into form almost anything and everything.

"For example, *Something Queer at the Ballpark* reminds me that I wrote that book when the New York Mets made it to the World Series, and then lost. *The Case of the Wild River Ride* reminds me that I took a raft trip down the Colorado right after I recovered from an operation. I wanted to prove to myself that I was whole and healthy again. In fact, bits and pieces of my life are in all my books. I feel that I can no longer brag that I travel light.

"Sometimes years will go by between the time that I experience something and then decide to write about it, but when I look at my long list of books, I realize that I seem to have some kind of compulsion to get it all in. As a child I read all the time and omniverously. I read everything from *Nancy Drew* to *War and Peace*. My mother recalls coming into my room when I was twelve years old and finding *Winnie-the-Pooh*, *War and Peace, Peyton Place*, and a *Nancy Drew* mystery scattered on my bed. My eclectic reading habits haven't changed much since then, which accounts in part for the variety of books I write.

"Working alone on fiction I act like a person whose chair was bought at an auction from a fun house, one that pinches you whenever you sit down. In reading about authors, I'm always impressed when they talk about losing themselves in their work, shutting off the phone, and closing the door to family and friends. I lose myself in everything *but* my writing. My kitchen cabinets are never as neat as when I'm trying to work. Since I actually do enjoy writing fiction and laughing at my own jokes, I'm hard put to explain why it is so difficult to stay in my chair. I only know it is.

"Collaborating with another author is one solution to the anxiety of writing alone. I wrote *Before You Were Three* with my friend and cousin Robie Harris. When Robie had her first child, we were both fascinated by his development. There is a cliché that only parents want to hear anecdotes about babies, but Robie and I talked for hours about her children because we couldn't get over the fact that we ourselves had been that little, had learned to talk, and had once showed our emotions so transparently.

"In talks with her nephews, Robie found they asked questions like: 'Why can't he walk yet?' 'When did I start to walk?' 'How do you know what he's feeling?' 'Does he mind that we're talking about him?' Gradually we evolved the idea of writing a book for children on the first three years of life. Robie and I wrote in the same room, passing pieces of paper back and forth and occasionally feeling like we were acting out scenes from a musical comedy. The book took several years to write, and it's a tribute both to family ties and our friendship that we are exploring the possibility of working together again.

"From 1977-78 I became involved with an experimental theater group called the Cutting Edge, co-writing plays based on improvisations by the actors. I received a grant from the New York State Council on the Arts to write a play version of *Lizzie Lies a Lot*. It was a strange experience to go back to characters I thought I was finished with, especially when those characters happened to be me, my parents, and my grandmother. *Lizzie Lies a Lot* is the most autobiographical of my books. I did lie a lot as a child, and I can distinctly remember what it felt like when I knew I was lying and no one else did. Like Lizzie in

"Are you going to be a nice little girl from now on?" asked Mrs. James.

"I **am** a girl!" said Jackie. "And I think it would be nice if you let me build a box."

Jackie went into a corner and started hammering.

(From *Nice Little Girls* by Elizabeth Levy. Illustrated by Mordicai Gerstein.)

"Oh my God!" shrieked Nana as she opened the door. Lizzie sat on the chair, ropes around her chest and feet. Sara stood behind her, the sharp scissors pointed at Lizzie's back. ■ (From *Lizzie Lies a Lot* by Elizabeth Levy. Illustrated by John Wallner.)

my novel, I told my mother I had been asked to perform in a school assembly and I kept up that lie for months.

"Oddly enough, my first published work was a lie. When I was in third grade, a newspaper published my poem 'When I Grow Up I Want to be a Nurse All Dressed in White.' I didn't want to be a nurse. If I wanted to be anything, I wanted to be a writer, but the idea of being a writer seemed a fantasy. I grew up without any concrete ambitions, but with an entire card catalog of fantasies. Even though I enjoyed schoolwork and took great pleasure in writing short stories, it literally never occurred to me to write for a living.

"I grew up at a time when little girls were not asked what they wanted to be because it was assumed they would be wives and mothers and that work would not be important. I would like to think of myself as a feminist before her time, a little rebel like Jackie in *Nice Little Girls*. I wasn't. But my characters can be. I hate to confess that in the first draft of the mystery *Something Queer Is Going On* the lead character was male.

Then I said to myself, 'Just because it's an inquisitive, active character, why should it be a boy?' and 'Gwen' started to tap her braces.

"When I write for children, I am really writing about things that seem funny or interesting to me now. I don't think writing a good book for children is very different from writing one for teenagers or adults. The emotions we have as children are in many ways as complex as those we have as adults. The best children's writers know this and are not tempted to oversimplify.

"I think about my own childhood a lot, and when I write about a certain age I have very vivid memories of what it felt like then. I think that memories from childhood are like dreams. It's not important to remember all of them, but what you do remember is important.

"Lately I have been dividing my time between writing mysteries and novels for children and teen-agers. I find writing mysteries very different from writing novels. The great pleasure of writing a mystery is that I know how the book will end. Before I begin a mystery, I have to have figured out who did it and why. I know that by the end of the book my detectives will expose this character. Usually I do not know the path my detectives will take to make this discovery. I have to go back and on the second and third drafts I must change significant parts of the book to lay clues that develop towards the end of the book.

"However, the end is always in place. I think that is why we like mysteries. People who don't read mysteries can never understand how I can read them at night before I go to sleep. 'Don't they keep you up?' friends ask. I find mysteries comforting. I read them when I'm tired or upset. Unless the writer is a cheat, I know the book will have a satisfactory ending. The bad will be punished and the characters I like will survive to live in another book. I only like mystery 'series.'

"Novels are completely different. Usually I write a novel about a conflict that I remember from my own childhood or something that I have experienced recently but believe that I also experienced when I was younger. I believe that the gift of a novel is to let others know that they are not alone, and that our secrets are usually far more shameful if kept hidden than if allowed out in the open. In most of my books, friendship is important. My friends are a huge part of my life, without them I would be bereft, and in my books I try to celebrate the healing power of friendship.''

We are now at the point where we must educate people in what nobody knew yesterday, and prepare in our schools for what no one knows yet but what some people must know tomorrow.

—Margaret Mead

A wise system of education will at least teach us how little man yet knows, how much he has still to learn.

—Sir John Lubbock

I read forever and am determined to sacrifice my eyes like John Milton rather than give up the amusement without which I should despair.

—John Adams

When a cargo ship docks in the harbor, its big booms and cranes quickly unload everything onto the docks—wild animals, ripe bananas, crates filled with goods from foreign lands. ■ (From *Busy Boats* by Peter Lippman. Illustrated by the author.)

LIPPMAN, Peter J. 1936-

PERSONAL: Born May 19, 1936, in Flushing, N.Y. *Education:* Columbia University, B.A., 1957, B.Arch., 1960, M.Arch., 1976; further study at Art Students League. *Home:* Montgomery Hollow, Roxbury, N.Y. 12474.

CAREER: Author and illustrator of books for children. *Military service:* U.S. Army. *Member:* Sierra Club, Audubon Society, National Wildlife Federation. *Awards, honors: Plunkety Plunk* was chosen by the *New York Times* as one of the ten best illustrated children's books of the year, 1963; Child Study Association of America children's books of the year award for *Science Experiments You Can Eat,* 1972, and *Supersuits,* 1975.

WRITINGS—All self-illustrated; all for children: *Plunkety Plunk,* Ariel Books, 1963; *New at the Zoo,* Harper, 1969; *The Little Riddle Book,* Harper, 1972; *Busy Wheels,* Random House, 1973; *The Great Escape; or, The Sewer Story,* Golden Press, 1973; *Ingrid Our Turtle,* Golden Press, 1973; *The Mix or Match Storybook: 2,097,152 Silly Stories,* Random House, 1974; *Archibald; or, I Was Very Shy,* Windmill Books, 1975; *From Here to There,* Bookstore Press, 1975; *Animals! Animals!,* Golden Press, 1976; *Busy Boats,* Random House, 1977; *Peter Lippman's One and Only Wacky Wordbook,* Golden Press, 1979; *Peter Lippman's Great Mix or Match Book,* Random House, 1980; *Busy Trains,* Random House, 1981; *Mix or Match Mystery Book* (tentative title), Random House, 1983.

Illustrator; all for children: George Selden (pseudonym of George Selden Thompson), *Sparrow Socks,* Harper, 1965; G. Selden, *Oscar Lobster's Fair Exchange,* Harper, 1966; G. Selden, *The Dunkard,* Harper, 1968; Bill Martin, Jr., *The Haunted House,* Holt, 1970; Vicki Cobb, *Science Experiments You Can Eat,* Lippincott, 1972; V. Cobb, *Arts and Crafts You Can Eat,*

Lippincott, 1974; V. Cobb, *Supersuits,* Lippincott, 1975; *Noodles, This Little Thing,* Holt, 1979; Jovial Bob Stine, *The Pigs' Book of World Records,* Random House, 1980; J. B. Stine, *Gnasty Gnomes,* Random House, 1981.

"The Know-It-Alls" series; all published by Doubleday, 1982: *The Know-It-Alls Go to Sea; . . . Help Out; . . . Mind the Store; . . . Take a Winter Vacation.*

Contributor of articles on the history of architecture to periodicals, and of illustrations to *Holiday, New York Times, Town & Country, National Wildlife,* and *Bananas.*

WORK IN PROGRESS: The Know-It-All's Truck Book for Doubleday.

SIDELIGHTS: "As a child, I drew and painted intermittently. In college, I took courses in the School of Painting and Sculpture at Columbia University and also spent a considerable part of my time working on the college literary magazine, *The Columbia Review,* as its art editor. After a tour of duty in the Army, I worked very briefly for an architect and decided that I preferred graphics. I turned to children's books as I considered it one of the most promising areas in which to do artistically worthwhile commercial work."

In 1965 Lippman spent a year "mostly in Spain and Portugal where I divided my time between children's books, magazine satire, and sculpting in bronze. My hobby is collecting 19th century illustrated books and children's books." [Lee Kingman and others, compilers, *Illustrators of Children's Books: 1957-1966,* Horn Book, 1968.]

Lippman owns a 185-acre farm where he writes and illustrates his children's books, and maintains a studio in New York City

To Construct a Pigsty

Pull on jeans and work boots.

Make nice, round snowballs.

Place on a workbench.

Bake in a hot oven.

Decorate with icing and candles.

You've built a fine pigsty!

Now take a big bite.

(From *Peter Lippman's Great Mix or Match Book* by Peter Lippman. Illustrated by the author.)

where he concentrates on his magazine and advertising projects. He has also taught courses in illustration and design of children's books at the University of Montana.

Lippman is an "avid supporter of environmental causes especially interested in preserving what is left of wilderness land."

HOBBIES AND OTHER INTERESTS: Hiking, backpacking, ice skating, cross-country skiing, downhill skiing, stone wall building, gardening and maintenance of a 185-acre farm, collecting nineteenth-century illustrated books and children's books.

FOR MORE INFORMATION SEE: Lee Kingman and others, compilers, *Illustrators of Children's Books: 1957-1966,* Horn Book, 1968; *New York Times Book Review,* November 9, 1969.

LISOWSKI, Gabriel 1946-

BRIEF ENTRY: Born January 20, 1946, in Jerusalem. Lisowski is an author and illustrator of books for children. He attended the Academy of Fine Arts in Vienna, Austria, where he lives with his wife, a psychologist. From 1965 to 1970 Lisowski was a member of "Movin' Part," a Viennese rock and roll band. Beginning in 1970, he has been employed as a freelance advertising designer. He has written and illustrated several books for children, among them *Two Stories about Foolish People,* 1974, *On the Little Hearth,* 1978, and *The Invitation,* 1980. *Witch of Four Street,* by Myson Levoy, was included in the Children's Book Showcase, 1974. Additional illustrated works include Eugene Schwart's *Two Brothers,* Stefan Hegin's *Cymbelinchen,* and Sonia Levitin's *A Sound to Remember. For More Information See: Contemporary Authors,* Volumes 97-100, Gale, 1981.

MacKENZIE, Garry 1921-

BRIEF ENTRY: Born September 7, 1921, in Portage La Prairie, Manitoba. A free-lance illustrator since 1945, MacKenzie stud-

ied at the Chouinard Art Institute in Los Angeles, Calif. After spending much of his childhood in southern England, MacKenzie returned with his parents to the U.S. and settled in Hollywood, California. In 1945 he went to New York to pursue a career in illustrating and worked in Cambridge, England, between 1949 and 1952. MacKenzie illustrated Alice E. Goudey's "Here Come the . . ." series, which includes *Here Come the Bears!* (Scribner, 1954), *Here Come the Bees!* (Scribner, 1960), and *Here Come the Cottontails!* (Scribner, 1965). MacKenzie also illustrated Carolyn Sherwin Bailey's *Flickertail* (Walck, 1962) and Eve Merriam's *Small Fry* (Knopf, 1965). *For More Information See: Illustrators of Children's Books, 1957-1966,* Horn Book, 1968; *Illustrators of Books for Young People,* Scarecrow, 1975.

MANNICHE, Lise 1943-

PERSONAL: Last syllable of surname is pronounced "kay"; born May 9, 1943, in Copenhagen, Denmark; daughter of Henry William (a civil servant) and Aase (Östrup) Manniche; children: Julie Aisha. *Education:* Attended the Sorbonne, 1967; University of Copenhagen, M.A., 1971. *Address:* c/o Christ's College, Cambridge, England. *Agent:* ICBS, Skindergade 3B, 1159 Copenhagen K, Denmark.

CAREER: Egyptologist. University of Copenhagen, Copenhagen, Denmark, researcher, 1971-79; ICBS (publishers and agents), Gentofte, Denmark, production manager, 1974-75.

WRITINGS—All juvenile; all self-illustrated: Translator, *How Djadja-Em-Ankh Saved the Day: A Tale from Ancient Egypt,* Crowell, 1976; *The Prince Who Knew His Fate,* Philomel Books, 1981.

Author of monographs on Egypt, including *Ancient Egyptian Musical Instruments,* [Munich], 1975; *Musical Instruments from the Tomb of Tutankhamun,* Griffith Institute, 1976; *Ægyptisk Kunst* (title means "Egyptian Art"), Berlingske Forlag (Copenhagen), 1981; *Calcite Vessels from the Tomb of Tutank-*

hamun, Griffith Institute, in press. Contributor of articles and reviews to professional journals, including *Acta Orientalia, Göttinger Miszellen, Bibliotheca Orientalis, Chronique d'Égypte,* and *Kristeligt Dagblad.*

WORK IN PROGRESS: Hieroglyphs for Fun, The Lion and the Mouse, and a book on arts and crafts in ancient Egypt.

SIDELIGHTS: ''My vocation is Egyptology. It may sound terribly stuffy and prehistoric, but it is a subject which can be made interesting to everyone. I have lived for three years in Egypt, and in the sixties I studied Egyptology at the Sorbonne, Paris. My main activities are at the university level; I have begun a period of study and research at the University of Cambridge where I am preparing a Ph.D. thesis concerning the private tombs at Thebes, which were visited by the early travelers to Egypt (pre-1850) but whose whereabouts are no longer known. I am attempting to reconstruct these tombs on paper from the drawings and descriptions made 150 years ago and trying to connect them with fragments of wall-paintings in museums. The results up till now seem promising. Within my field I am particularly interested in artistic and archaeological subjects (musical instruments, symbolism, color application, interpretation of aspects of Egyptian art).

''My interest in writing books for young readers coincided with my having a child of my own and my finding temporary employment with an acquaintance of mine, who later became my literary agent. One day I brought to the office a photocopied version of *Djadja,* intended as a Christmas card for some young friends of mine. My employer became immediately interested, and after a year of collaboration, *How Djadja-Em-Ankh Saved the Day* was born in six countries. By then I had already produced a dramatized puppet theater version of *The Prince Who Knew His Fate,* which later came out as a filmstrip in Danish and Swedish.

''I have had the chance to write about my subject at all levels. Some of my children's books contain new ideas which I have not yet had the time to work out in scientific papers. It is extremely useful in my scientific writing to have the experience of expressing myself clearly for young readers. Yet, I think that virtually any topic can be described and explained to young readers, and I expect my book on hieroglyphs to be proof of this.

''I usually illustrate my books myself by carefully copying ancient reliefs and paintings. The setting of *The Prince Who Knew His Fate,* for instance, is in the so-called Amarna period of Egyptian civilization. This choice is not arbitrary, but based on serious research. I think that there is a tendency among my colleagues to take children's books seriously, and if you include some interesting ideas, it may become even less disreputable to write to such a large and varied group of readers.''

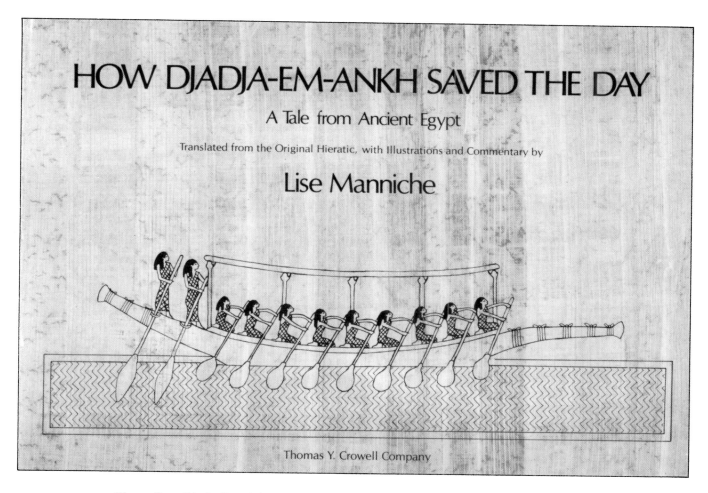

(From *How Djadja-Em-Ankh Saved the Day: A Tale from Ancient Egypt,* translated and illustrated by Lise Manniche.)

LISE MANNICHE

Manniche speaks Danish, English and French fluently, and has a good knowledge of German, Italian, Arabic, modern Greek, and a number of ancient languages. She writes in both Danish and English. Besides Egypt, she has traveled in Greece, Italy, France, Iceland, India, Nepal, the United States and Canada.

MAROKVIA, Artur   1909-

PERSONAL: Born July 21, 1909, in Stuttgart, Germany; came to United States in 1949; son of Valentine and Anna Maria (Koppenhofer) Marokvia; married Mireille (an author), 1918. *Education:* Attended Akademie, Stuttgart, Germany, and Académie de la Grande Chaumière, Paris, France; School of Music, Dresden, Germany, received diploma. *Home:* New Mexico.

CAREER: Artist, illustrator, and author. Worked as an engineer, painter and pianist in Germany; painted in France, Greece, Austria, Mexico, Yugoslavia, Finland, Italy, Russia, and Spain.

EXHIBITIONS: Gallery Billiet-Worms, Paris, France, 1936; Gallery Carmine, Paris, France, 1937, 1938; Kunsthalle, Stuttgart, Germany, 1946; Kunsthalle, Baden-Baden, Germany, 1946; Kunsthalle, Freiburg, Germany, 1947; Gallery Les Mages, Vence, France, 1948; Gallery Vergel, Nice, France, 1948; Gallery Lambert, Cannes, France, 1948; Society of Illustrators, New York, 1961; Gallery Calmecac, Cuernavaca, Mexico, 1971; Gallery La Palomita Blanca, Cuernavaca, Mexico, 1973; Institute of Fine Arts, Cuernavaca, Mexico, 1973, 1974; Mexican American Cultural Institute, Mexico City, Mexico, 1974; Blair Galleries, Santa Fe, New Mexico, 1975; Austin Gallery, Scottsdale, Arizona, 1975.

ILLUSTRATOR—All for children: Nicholas Kalashnikoff, *Toyon, a Dog of the North and His People,* Harper, 1950; Isabelle Lawrence, *Niko,* Viking, 1956; Robert Shaffer, *Lost Ones,* Holt, 1956; Marjorie G. Fribourg, *Ching-Ting and the Ducks,* Sterling, 1957; Anne Molloy, *The Christmas Rocket,* Hastings House, 1958; A. Molloy, *The Tower Treasure,* Hastings House, 1958; Mireille Marokvia, *Jannot, a French Rabbit,* Lippincott, 1959; Kimyong Ik, *The Happy Days,* Little, Brown, 1960; M. Marokvia, *Nanette, a French Goat,* Lippincott, 1960; Virginia Haviland, *Favorite Fairy Tales Told in Ireland,* Little, Brown, 1961; M. Marokvia, *Grococo, a French Crow,* Lippincott, 1961; Maxine W. Kumin, *Follow the Fall,* Putnam, 1961; M. W. Kumin, *Spring Things,* Putnam, 1961; M. W. Kumin, *Summer Story,* Putnam, 1961; M. W. Kumin, *A Winter Friend,* Putnam, 1961; Gladys Conklin, *We Like Bugs,* Holiday House, 1962; M. Marokvia, *Belle Arabelle,* Lippincott, 1962; M. Marokvia, *A French School for Paul,* Lippincott, 1963; K. IK, *Blue in the Seed,* Little, Brown, 1964; Dorothy Aldis, *Is Anybody Hungry?,* Putnam, 1964; G. Conklin, *If I Were a Bird,* Holiday House, 1965; G. Conklin, *I Caught a Lizard,* Holiday House, 1967; G. Conklin, *When Insects Are Babies* (Junior Literary Guild selection), Holiday House, 1969. Contributor of twelve self-illustrated articles to *Motor and Sport* magazine (Berlin, Germany).

Marokvia's works are included in the Kerlan Collection at the University of Minnesota.

WORK IN PROGRESS: Murals and other paintings.

Every day I'll feed him a live grasshopper or a small worm or a fat spider. ■ (From *I Caught a Lizard* by Gladys Conklin. Illustrated by Artur Marokvia.)

MARRIOTT, Alice Lee   1910-

PERSONAL: Born January 8, 1910, in Wilmette, Ill.; daughter of Richard Goulding and Sydney (Cunningham) Marriott. *Education:* Oklahoma City University, B.A., 1930; University of Oklahoma, B.A. (anthropology), 1935. *Religion:* Episcopalian. *Office:* Southwest Research Associates, 1836 Northwest 56th St., Oklahoma City, Okla. 73118.

CAREER: Field representative with U.S. Department of Interior Indian Arts and Craft Board, 1938-42, and with American Red Cross in southwest United States, 1942-45; University of Oklahoma, Norman, associate professor of anthropology, 1964-66; Central State University, Edmond, Okla., artist-in-residence, 1968—. Associate director, Southwest Research Associates, 1960—; consultant to Oklahoma Indian Council, 1962—. *Member:* American Anthropological Association (fellow), Writers Guild, Oklahoma Museum Association, Phi Beta Kappa, Sigma Xi. *Awards, honors:* University of Oklahoma Achievement Award, 1952; member of Oklahoma Hall of Fame, 1958; Oklahoma City University Achievement Award, 1968; Key Award from Theta Sigma Pi, 1969; Oklahoma Literary Hall of Fame, 1972.

WRITINGS: The Ten Grandmothers, University of Oklahoma Press, 1945; *Winter-telling Stories* (also see below), Crowell, 1947, reprinted, 1968; *Indians on Horseback* (also see below), Crowell, 1948; *Maria, the Potter of San Halefonso,* University of Oklahoma Press, 1948; *Valley Below,* University of Oklahoma Press, 1949; *These Are the People,* Laboratory of Anthropology (Santa Fe), 1951; *Indians of the Four Corners,* Crowell, 1952; *Greener Fields: Experiences Among the American Indians,* Crowell, 1952; *Hell on Horses and Women,* University of Oklahoma Press, 1953; *Sequoyah: Leader of the Cherokees,* Random House, 1956; *Black Stone Knife,* Crowell, 1957.

First Comers: Indians of America's Dawn, Longmans, Green, 1960; (with Edwin C. McReynolds and Estelle Faulconer) *Oklahoma: Its Past and Its Present,* University of Oklahoma Press, 1961; *Saynday's People* (includes *Winter-telling Stories* and *Indians on Horseback*), University of Nebraska Press, 1963; *Indian Anne: Kiowa Captive,* McKay, 1965; *Kiowa Years: A Study in Culture Impact,* Macmillan, 1968; *American Indian Mythology,* Crowell, 1968; (with Carol K. Rachlin) *American Epic: The Story of the American Indian,* Putnam, 1969; (with C. K. Rachlin) *Peyote,* Putnam, 1971; (with C. K. Rachlin) *Oklahoma: The Forty-sixth Star,* Doubleday, 1972; (with C. K. Rachlin) *Plains Indian Mythology,* Crowell, 1975; (with C. K. Rachlin) *Dance Around the Sun: The Life of Mary Little Bear Inkanish,* Crowell, 1977. Contributor to magazines.

WORK IN PROGRESS: Editing field notes; working on a review of *The Arts and Crafts Board: 1936-1942* with C. K. Rachlin.

SIDELIGHTS: "An early influence was my grandfather Marriott, who used to visit a friend, curator of Egyptology, at what was then the Field Museum of Natural History in Chicago. A five-year-old cannot be held immobile by a conversation about dynasties, no matter how much she loves one of the elderly gentlemen involved. So I wandered off—the Egyptology office was in the basement—and discovered the totem poles which had been put there, because there was nowhere else with a ceiling high enough to take them. In 1965, the last time I went to the Chicago Museum of Natural History, they were still there.

"I took my first college degree in library science, and worked for a few years in libraries. 'You always meet nice people there, and she can't get into trouble,' to quote my father. I didn't get into any more trouble than anyone else trying to support herself in the early thirties, but I did find out that the people you meet outside the library reading rooms are not particularly nice. They're too busy playing politics.

"One year the library where I was working ran out of buying money, so I put in my time and the taxpayer's money indexing books on local history, including Henry Rowe Schoolcraft's monumental *Indian Tribes of the United States.* Since Oklahoma then had fifty-seven tribes which were formally recognized by the United States Government, I decided to find out more.

"At the University of Oklahoma in 1935, I received the first degree in anthropology awarded to a woman, and the third degree in the subject given to anybody. During this time I made my first long field trip. I went to Oregon to study with a group of other graduate students. We lived in tents, interviewed elderly Modoc Indians, and I fell completely and permanently in love with the desert country in general and with Oregon in particular.

"The job with the Indian Arts and Crafts Board came about six months after my second graduation. I had spent intervening University vacations, and the waiting time, with the Kiowa Indians in southwestern Oklahoma, and accumulated stacks of field notes. I was one of the lucky few who worked with Plains Indians while the last of the old buffalo hunters were still around. I'm still writing up those notes.

"With the Indian Arts and Crafts Board and the American Red Cross I traveled border to border and coast to coast, learned to speak kitchen Spanish, to make tortillas, to drive roads that are now paved out of recognition, and to work with all kinds of people, from Supreme Court Justices to the remnants of Rommel's North African Desert Rats. I spent time at the White Sands site, and had almost forgotten that particular desert until

ALICE LEE MARRIOTT

Columbia III landed there. I worked at Los Alamos while it was still a 'closed town,' and saw it opened to general occupation.

"Always back to the Plains. The Kiowa, the Cheyenne, the Arapaho, the Comanche and the neighboring southern Apache. My last field work was in 1955, with the Hopi, and I am still working over that material.

"I have never married, I've been too busy. My brothers both did, so I have nephews and nieces and now great-nephews and great-nieces, to keep me in touch with the world. Two standard poodles help in that endeavour, too.

"I regard myself as a perfectly ordinary middle class citizen of the United States, who happens to be female, and, like Georgia O'Keefe, I can say, 'I am not interesting. It is what I have done with where I have been that is.'"

MARSTON, Hope Irvin 1935-

PERSONAL: Born January 31, 1935, in Fishing Creek (now Mill Hall), Pa.; daughter of Charles James (a farmer) and Orpha (Harber) Irvin; married Arthur Wakefield Marston, Jr. (an artificial inseminator), August 28, 1961. *Education:* Milligan College, B.A., 1956; State University of New York College at Geneseo, M.A., 1972. *Politics:* Republican. *Religion:* Christian and Missionary Alliance. *Home and office address:* R.F.D. 1, Box 362, Black River, N.Y. 13612.

CAREER: Junior and senior high school teacher of science, English, and social studies in Aberdeen, Md., 1956-61; high school teacher of English and Spanish in Buckfield, Maine,

Hope Irvin Marston with Morgan.

1962-67; Case Junior High School, Watertown, N.Y., teacher of English, 1967-70, librarian, 1970—. *Member:* American Federation of Teachers, American Library Association, New York State United Teachers, New York Library Association, Black River Valley Writers Club, Adirondack Mountain Club, Delta Kappa Gamma.

*WRITINGS—*Juvenile: *Trucks, Trucking, and You,* Dodd, 1978; *Big Rigs* (Junior Literary Guild selection), Dodd, 1979; *Machines on the Farm,* Dodd, 1982. Contributor to *Yankee, Grit,* and religious journals.

WORK IN PROGRESS: A juvenile book on fire engines, an adult devotional book for dog lovers, and an adult novel.

SIDELIGHTS: "When I was nine years old, my sister Shirley gave me a copy of *Heidi* for Christmas. This was probably not the first book I ever owned, but it's the one I remember most. How I loved that cheerful little Heidi, her rather eccentric grandfather, and her somewhat surly friend Peter. I tasted the warm goats' milk and the delicious cheese that was toasted on the hearth. Since I am a dreamer by nature, it was easy for me to lose myself amidst the delicate little flowers, the fragrant mountain breezes, and Heidi's ever-widening circle of friends. Forgotten were my parents, my eight brothers and sisters, and the hired man who made up our busy farm home as I trooped up the mountain with Peter, Heidi, and the frisky goats.

"Recently I re-read my Christmas book and found it still a delight . . . perhaps because Johanna Spyri's story is a celebration of the values I have chosen as important in my life. I want my readers to love God and to appreciate and respect all of His creation. It's hard for me to get that message across in my non-fiction books. That's why I am considering fiction writing. It excites me to realize that I can create my own world and people it with folks I conjure up in my mind. I can control their environment and make things end as I wish.

"That is not to say I want to play God. He has already created an orderly universe and when man doesn't mess things up, there's no way anyone can improve upon it. But I want children to see there's lots of goodness in this world put there by a loving, benevolent heavenly Father.

"My relationship to God and to Jesus Christ gives purpose to my life. I gave myself to Jesus Christ when I was twelve years old. Since then I have tried, and too often failed, to live in accordance with the Bible as I understand it. I have taught Sunday School longer than I've taught in public schools. I've learned much from teaching. I've learned the importance of beginning each day as well as each writing session asking the Lord, through His Holy Spirit, to make my efforts count for eternity.

"I am convinced that books have the power to mold their readers' minds. I want to write of loving families and the everyday events that bring them peace and contentment in their lives. There's a lot of good in the world. I want children to know that and to be encouraged even when they are momentarily in a hard place.

"Having grown up in a large family that was long on love though sometimes a bit short on cash gives me a perspective that I need to share with my young readers who may be hurting.

"I am positive that God loves me and has a plan for my life. That plan is perfect for me. My personal goal is to find and fit into it. God has given me some writing ability. I want to

What is a big rig?

A big rig is the biggest kind of truck you will see on the highway. It is a truck with two parts—a tractor and a trailer. ■ (From *Big Rigs* by Hope Irvin Marston. Jacket photograph courtesy of Mack Trucks, Inc.)

develop that talent so that it will reflect honor to the Giver. The way my first books were received shows me God is blessing my efforts. It also encourages me to continue writing, but I never write without first taking time to pray for wisdom to say what I want to say in a manner that the Lord will ultimately receive the credit for any talent that my work might demonstrate.''

HOBBIES AND OTHER INTERESTS: Walking, hiking and mountain-climbing. ''I am very fond of boxer dogs. Sewing, quilts and crafts also interest me, but I cannot fit them into my busy schedule.''

MARTIN, Rupert (Claude) 1905-

PERSONAL: Born July 2, 1905; son of Col. C. B. Martin; married Ellen Guernsey, 1931 (died, 1966); children: one son, two daughters. *Education:* Attended Shrewsbury School; Queen's College, Oxford (second class honors), 1927. *Home:* Quantocks, Burnham-on-Sea, Somersetshire, England.

CAREER: St. Paul's School, London, England, assistant master, 1927-37, house master, 1930-37; King's School, Bruton, Somersetshire, headmaster, 1937-46, governor, 1949—; St. Dunstan's School, Burnham-on-Sea, Somersetshire, headmaster, 1948-66. Representative, British Council in Switzerland, 1946-48. *Member:* Incorporated Association of Preparatory Schools (vice-chairman, 1957), I Zingari Club, Alpine Club, Authentics Club (Oxford), Free Foresters Club, Vincent's Club, Marylebone Cricket Club.

WRITINGS—All for young people: *Aspects of Roman Life,* Mills & Boon, 1928; *Aspects of Greek Life,* Mills & Boon, 1929; (with Anthony Noel Gurney Richards) *H.A.P. Sawyer, St. Bees and Shrewsbury: A Memoir,* Walding & Son, 1948; *Switzerland,* A. & C. Black, 1951, 3rd revised edition, Macmillan, 1961; *Italy,* Macmillan, 1953; *Your Ski Holiday* (illustrated by Haro), Laurie, 1954; *Spain,* A. & C. Black, 1955,

Fishing boats at Tarifa, the southernmost point of Spain. The mountains of North Africa can be seen in the distance. ■ (From *Looking at Spain* by Rupert Martin. Photograph by Jonathan Rutland.)

published as *The Land and People of Spain,* 1958; *The Land and People of Morocco,* Macmillan, 1967; *Looking at Italy,* Lippincott, 1967; *Looking at Spain,* Lippincott, 1969.

SIDELIGHTS: Martin, a former headmaster at schools in Somersetshire, England, wrote books of the "Lands and Peoples" series. A reviewer of the *Times Literary Supplement* commented on *Looking at Italy* of the series: "The emphasis is on 'looking,' and the younger children for whom this book is intended will form a fair impression of what Italy looks like from the very good photographs. . . . The accompanying text, clear and uncluttered by too much detail, gives an equally good picture. . . ."

HOBBIES AND OTHER INTERESTS: Mountaineering and travel.

MAZER, Harry 1925-

PERSONAL: Born May 31, 1925, in New York, N.Y.; son of Sam (a dressmaker) and Rose (a dressmaker; maiden name, Lazernick) Mazer; married Norma Fox (an author), February 12, 1950; children: Anne, Joseph, Susan, Gina. *Education:* Union College, B.A., 1948; Syracuse University, M.A., 1960. *Home and office:* Brown Gulf Rd., Jamesville, N.Y. 13078.

Agent: Curtis Brown Ltd., 575 Madison Ave., New York, N.Y. 10022.

CAREER: New York Construction, Syracuse, N.Y., sheet metal worker, 1957-59; Central Square School, Central Square, N.Y., teacher of English, 1959-60; Aerofin Corp., Syracuse, welder, 1960-63; full-time writer, 1963—. *Military service:* U.S. Army Air Forces, 1943-45; became sergeant; received Purple Heart and Air Medal. *Member:* Writers Guild, Civil Liberties Union. *Awards, honors:* Kirkus Choice award, 1974, for *The Dollar Man;* award for best book for young adults from American Library Association, 1978, for *The War on Villa Street,* 1979, for *The Last Mission,* and 1981, for *I Love You, Stupid!;* best books of the year award from *New York Times,* 1979, for *The Last Mission.*

WRITINGS—Of interest to young people; all published by Delacorte, except as noted: *Guy Lenny,* 1971; *Snow Bound: A Story of Raw Survival,* 1973; *The Dollar Man,* 1974; (with wife, Norma Fox Mazer) *The Solid Gold Kid,* 1977; *The War on Villa Street* (novel), 1978; *The Last Mission,* 1979; *The Island Keeper* (Junior Literary Guild selection), 1981; *I Love You, Stupid!,* Crowell, 1981.

ADAPTATIONS: "Snow Bound," produced by Learning Corp., an NBC-TV Special, 1978.

WORK IN PROGRESS: When the Phone Rang for Scholastic.

SIDELIGHTS: "I feel—I've always felt—that I write and speak with difficulty. I am a writer not because this is something I do well—an inborn talent—but perhaps for the opposite reason, because I do it so poorly. Whatever I've done as a writer I've done despite the feeling that I have no natural talent. I've never felt articulate or fluent, rarely felt that flow of language that marks the writer.

"When I was growing up I knew no writers. My parents didn't write. My father read, but there were few books in the house. I think we got them through a newspaper promotion: the complete set of Dickens and a complete set of Mark Twain, a set of Jack London. One book used to come every month or so and it would be a big moment.

"There were no writers or professionals anywhere in my family among my cousins, aunts and uncles. They were immigrants, Polish and Russian Jews, first generation Americans. One uncle was a housepainter, another peddled candy and cigarettes, another had a clothing store. My father worked in a factory making dresses. On my mother's side one aunt ran a chicken

HARRY MAZER

farm, another was a secretary, and my mother, like my father, worked in a dress factory.

"A writer in our family? I could hardly dream of it. I was a reader. Reading was my great pleasure. I was very interested in every library I ever entered, and I remember it was like a rite of passage for me to go from the juvenile section to the adult section of a library. . . . I was really hungry for these books in the library. I know that at one point or another when I was young I was out to read every book. I never got very far with it.

"As a boy my plan was to read my way through the library, starting with the letter A. My father thought I was ruining my eyes reading so much. As for my friends, they were mostly interested in science. One was going to be an electrical engineer, another a chemist, a third a dentist. I said I'd be a scientist and I applied to the Bronx High School of Science.

"I made attempts at writing, but they were sporadic and not really satisfactory, and I didn't publish things in high school. I really didn't think I could write; my standards were too high and anything that I attempted just looked so awful to me that I couldn't carry on with it. . . . I didn't know what the world of writing was like. All I had were the classics, and they just told me I was hopeless. So it took me many years before I began to write.

"I dreamed of making the world a better place. I met Norma Fox. She loved books, she was beautiful, and she wrote. Did I know then that she would help me turn to writing? For a

Her mother had died nine years ago . . . . And now her sister in another stupid freak accident. How could they both be dead? ■ (From *The Island Keeper* by Harry Mazer. Jacket illustration by Peter Caras.)

time, our interest in each other, the family, children, and work filled our lives. I was a husband, a father, a provider. Life was interesting. I worked as a longshoreman, a railroad worker, a welder, an iron worker. But more and more I was dissatisfied with the work I did.

"I didn't seriously begin writing until I was in my mid-thirties, after I'd gone through a number of different kinds of jobs I didn't like and wasn't satisfied with.

"'What do you really want to do?' Norma asked me one day. 'If you could do exactly what you wanted?'

"'Be a writer?' I smiled because the idea was so absurd. Write? What had I ever written? What did I have to write about? And who was going to support us and our three kids, while I learned?

"But something changed that day. We talked late into the night, earnestly, practically. It wasn't just me. Norma wanted to write, too. If we didn't let ourselves get discouraged, didn't set ourselves impossible goals, if we wrote a little each day, then in time, maybe we would be writers.

"When we first began to write, our desks were jammed into a converted back porch bedroom next to the kitchen. While the kids were growing up, Norma insulated me from them. (I've only gradually become liberated in my thinking.) I remember very well, at times she'd be writing in the dining room, with all of them right around her. So I said, 'You have these great powers of concentration.' I'd be working in another room with the door closed. The same way I couldn't hear the kids at night when they woke up; she never had any trouble. We tend to keep the same working hours. When we were just beginning to write and I was doing other kinds of work, Norma, the year when she was pregnant with our fourth child, was waking up at 3:30 in the morning, and she thought it was a great idea for both of us to get up and write. So we started getting up at 3:30 and writing until about 6:00 or 6:30, when I'd have to go off to work. And that worked well. I have enjoyed the discipline of having someone else keeping the same schedule.

"For several years we followed that routine, losing it often, but getting back to it, till we'd learned enough so that we could risk giving up the factory paycheck, and we began to write full time.

"Though we have collaborated on one book, *The Solid Gold Kid,* most of our literary work is separate. However, we talk about everything. We discuss every stage of the writing, read the other's work, encourage and support each other, make editorial suggestions, celebrate each other's successes, comfort the other in times of doubt and adversity.

"But then we get into ego things. Norma's second book, *Figure of Speech,* received a National Book Award nomination, and I wasn't getting any special awards. That was hard to take. Then she had a book called *Dear Bill, Remember Me?,* a collection of short stories, which got a lot of rave reviews, and I was having trouble finishing *The War on Villa Street.* Well, we talked. You really have to say those awful things you're feeling, things that you're ashamed to say out loud: you're angry, you're jealous. Once you are able to voice what you feel, it tends to dissipate. This is what we've had to do at every turn in our writing lives, a lot of talking. It's brought us much closer than we were before I came home and started writing."

About his writing for young people, Mazer commented: "It was partially a conscious decision. I had an agent at the time and she encouraged me to write in this area. The readers were there with a great hunger for books. But I don't think that would have been enough if I didn't feel attracted to writing for young people. It's such an alive period of life. People have a lot of hope, wanting, desire for love, desire for discovery; and I find that in spite of my age I remain very interested in beginnings: how people get started, all the freshness and hope you feel when you're young. So I continue to enjoy writing in this area. I keep telling people that I'm going to do a grown-up book someday, but so far all my books have been for young people. There's a lot of freedom. I can do just about anything I want. My books are welcome; there's an interest in them. Once you are successful in a particular area, in a sense it becomes difficult to break out.''

"From time to time when I meet people I get the feeling that they're eyeing the gray in my chin and wondering, what's that middle aged man doing writing for the young? How does he know what's going on? They come right out with it sometimes: 'How do you keep in touch with what's happening, the changes in language, dress, and manner, I mean, man, what gives you the right?'

"And not only strangers. My own kids, too, have let me know plenty of times. 'Dad, you don't know . . . you don't know what it's like.'

"'It's like liquor,' I suggest. This on the subject of dope.

"'No,' my son says. 'You don't know.'

"'You don't understand,' one of my daughters says when we discuss the proprieties of visiting a boy in his room. 'Why can't we close the door? What's wrong with that?'

"It wasn't so bad when I was a welder. Ironworkers aren't expected to understand kids. But writers are. The way kids talk, and act. They have their own language, their own dress, their own rituals. It is as if the world were newly created with them. And of course they're right.

"But how many books are there written by writers under 20, or 25, for that matter? A handful maybe. There's a rightness in the old—I mean, of course, the mature—writing for the young. The young, after all, are young, they're impatient, they've got ants in their pants. I wonder if they can sit still long enough to give form to their own thoughts and feelings. (At that age I couldn't.) Maybe the trappings of dress and manner have changed, but the emotions of the young are not a foreign country. We've all been there. We recognize our ties to the young, even when they don't recognize their ties to us. . . .

"The inner life joins us all: girl, boy, middle-aged woman and old man. We all live two lives simultaneously. The visible life in which we grow up, marry, take jobs, acquire homes and cars. And the other life—the secret life—of our fantasies, longings.

"As a writer, I'm primarily interested in my characters' inner life. Not the trappings of character but their feelings, their dreams and fantasies, the way they distort reality, their hopes and disappointments.

(From the movie "Snowbound." Produced by Learning Corporation of America, 1978.)

"That kind of insight into people is not often revealed. Not many volunteer the information. The writer has to do it himself. To get in touch with his characters he must get in touch with himself.

"The things I never knew I knew or felt or thought of till I started writing. I don't mean know yourself the way, say, an analyst does, with all his preconceptions, theories, categories. I mean 'know' only in the sense of 'being aware,' turning a ready ear to that sometimes dimly heard inner voice. A voice persistent nonetheless, demanding, often outrageous—a voice that won't be stilled.

"When I first started writing . . . I naively believed that if I sat in front of that blank paper long enough I'd sure write something.

"And finally it happened. I wrote a line, and then another. I don't know why I wrote them or what I had in my mind.

"I wrote: 'Isabel, you'll never know what you did to me. How could you? I never spoke to you.'

"Isabel was a girl in my sixth-grade class in PS 96 in the Bronx, a tall, skinny girl with long hair. I followed her slavishly around for weeks. My sixth-grade picture shows me a big fat kid, in need of a haircut, the only one wearing a dark shirt in a field of white shirts and blouses.

"I never spoke to Isabel. I never talked to anyone about her. Not my friends, certainly not my parents. I followed her around everywhere. She lived on the third floor of an apartment house on Bronx Park East. In the evening after supper, I used to stand across the street from her house and look longingly up at the lighted windows and wonder which one was hers.

"Once I boldly crossed the street, and went up the stairs, and stood outside her door. What was I doing there? What did I want? What would I have done if she had opened the door? What if it was her father? The moment I heard a noise at the door I fled.

"She noticed me only once. I was across the street one day. She was with a girl friend. When they saw me they threw their arms around each other and started laughing and jeering at me.

"That was the story I started writing when I finally sat down to write, more than twenty years after the event. 'Isabel, you'll never know what you did to me.' How I loved that line. The poet Auden wrote, 'A sentence uttered makes a world appear / where all things happen as it says they do.' As I wrote, I spoke to Isabel as I could never have spoken to her then. 'You'll never know what you did to me.' I wrote of desire, longing, frustration, bewilderment. I made everything more intense— the building taller, the steps steeper and darker; Isabel cooler and more inaccessible. The light blazed from her window. I made things happen with an intensity of detail and emotion that they'd never truly had. In a word, I made a story of it.

"Here it is forty years later and that puppy-love incident I call Isabel still works itself into my books. . . . In _The Dollar Man_ . . . Marcus stands on the street looking longingly up at Vivian's windows, alternately dreaming of rescuing her, and creating fantasies about a father he has never known.

"It's the inner life that makes the connection possible between the middle-aged writer and his young reader. The inner life that connects us all. I address myself to the reader at 13, at 30, at 72, to the reader in myself. As a writer for the young, the limitations I accept are not limitations of language or of subject matter, but only those imposed by the necessarily narrowed experience and outlook of my young protagonists. Not looking down on that young person, but looking out at the world through his eyes.

"I share the writer's conceit that what interests me will interest you, that what arouses emotion in me will arouse emotion in you. With good fortune, I'll touch the reader, leave him or her with a sense that what he's read is perhaps something that he's always known but hasn't quite expressed.

"The inner life is timeless. It connects us all. It connects the 13-year-old boy with the 50-year-old man. We wrinkle on the outside but the inner self is ageless. We half close our eyes to the lies the mirror tells us and the child appears. We don't forget." [_Notes from Delacorte Press: Books for Young Readers,_ Delacorte, Summer-Fall, 1975.[1]]

"The problems in my books have more to do with the problems of constructing a novel: the need for conflict, the need for something important to be at stake, something that's not easily resolved. You can't do a book that deals with superficial questions. So I really don't think that I'm specifically answering questions about alcoholism and brutality; what I'm very much concerned with is survival, in one form or another. If I have a message, it's that you, too, can cope; you can get through this period in your life. You have the strength in yourself. Very often in my books the character becomes disillusioned, particularly with the father, and realizes that he must and can face the world on his own strength.

"It's true that the problems change, but I think the underlying emotions remain the same. My generation knew about alcohol, but we didn't know about drugs. But that's what your imagination is for. If I have to, I'll research and I'll interview. There are so many things you don't know that you have to learn about. The other side of it is that you really don't want to be too much in the mode when you're writing. You can't hope to keep up with trends, because a book takes a year to write. Trends change sometimes faster than that. You can just write yourself out of style if you try to keep in style. Growing up may change in form, but there are constants: the future is unknown, there is uncertainty, the need for love and recognition—all those things don't change."

Mazer remarked about the adaptation of his book, _Snow Bound,_ for television. "I had mixed feelings about it. I was glad that it was done. A television production will tend to bring readers to the book. In the book _Snow Bound_ the protagonist is about thirteen or fourteen years old, and in the movie they turned him into a kind of Robert Redford eighteen-year-old. They gave him a girl friend, which he certainly didn't have in the book. The book is about a relationship of Tony and Cindy, and they frame the movie with this other relationship. They bring the girl friend in at the beginning and again at the end. Then they added scenes: they had a fire, which I didn't write; they had a helicopter—things that probably were useful in scripting the movie. But what kids—and adults—who read the book and saw the movie said was that they liked the book more than the movie. And I suppose that's my feeling as well. But in general my reaction was positive.

"I think that if another of my books were taken for a television or movie production, I would try to get involved. I would hope it would give me a little more control over what happens.

"Before I got into the writing that I'm doing now, I did write some television scripts that were directed at various shows that were popular at the time but are gone now. I know the form. It's just a very difficult area to get into. At the time I was told that if I would come to California, which is where most of these movies are made, it would be possible to write for television. But where I was in New York State, I really couldn't get started."

Mazer gave the following advice to aspiring writers. "For a beginning writer, I think it's wise to read widely in the area of children's books being done today. Get a feeling what's being done and how it's being done. And then I'd say, write the book that is in _you,_ that hasn't been done, the one you feel you can do better. Read what's being written and see the range and scope of it; but most important, see what's lacking. Write the book that you wanted written when you were young.

"Beyond that, a beginning writer should recognize that writing requires a long apprenticeship. This is something that I didn't know when I was young, which is what kept me from writing. Desire makes up a great part of being a writer, and then there's work: writing, writing—and writing badly, of course, before you write well. I would write a lot and pay close attention to any professional advice or criticism received along the way, and then revise and revise. Nothing is right the first time. That's another thing I didn't recognize in the beginning. Revision, attention to detail, is going to make your book. That's what I think is the hardest."

About his book, _The War on Villa Street,_ which was named best book for young adults in 1978 by the American Library Association, Mazer commented: "_The War on Villa Street_ took me longer to write than any of my other books. With hindsight, I think this was because the book deals with two strong ideas: The relationship of Willis Pierce, a lonely, tense boy, and his father, who's an alcoholic; and that between Willis and Richard Hayfoot, a retarded boy, who in some ways is more fortunate than Willis.

"The strange thing is that Willis came to light in a previous book of mine, _The Dollar Man._ In that book Willis plays a minor role, and not a sympathetic one. Willis is a skinny little spider of a kid who clings to the fence of the Prescott Street playground, tormenting Marcus Rosenbloom. 'Jump on those bars again, Rosen Balloon, I want to see you bend them.'

"Marcus hates Willis, and for good reason. In school 'whenever the teacher left the room, the other students would practically fall off their seats laughing as Willis waddled around imitating Marcus . . . "Clump, clump, clump, this is the way you look, Rosen Balloon," Willis would huff, slapping his feet down heavily on the floor. "Everyone head for the hills! Here comes Marcus the Elephant!"' In _The Dollar Man_ there's nothing likeable about Willis Pierce. I didn't like him, myself.

"Toward the end of *The Dollar Man* there's a scene where Marcus, standing on the roof of an apartment house, looks down into the lighted windows of another building. Marcus, who hungers for the love of the father he's never known sees Willis and his father sitting at a table across from each other. When I began to think about the story that became *The War on Villa Street,* that rooftop scene came back to me. I kept thinking about it, coming back to it. Maybe it was what Marcus thought that interested me. 'He was seeing Willis in a secret way, a way he wasn't supposed to, but one that was more truthful than all the other ways.' As a writer this is what intrigues me. As much as telling a good story, I want to show my readers that behind the facade that we all throw up to protect ourselves, there exists a human heart.

"Once I began to think about the real Willis Pierce, my attitude toward him changed. I had been looking at him through Marcus's eyes, seeing him as a nasty, little, dried-up punk, without an ounce of goodness in his body. Then I began to understand him as a very lonely, deprived, and suffering kid, whose real, good core was hidden behind a tough guy exterior.

"What Marcus saw when he stood on the roof in *The Dollar Man* became the final scene of *The War on Villa Street.* I was no longer outside looking in, but in the Pierce's apartment, in Willis's mind and heart, seeing all the love and hate he felt for his father.

"That scene between Willis and his father, for me was at the heart of *The War on Villa Street.* I wrote it before I wrote anything else. In fact, although the book was written and rewritten several times before I got it right, that last reconciliation scene survived all the rewrites with little change."

Some of Mazer's books have been translated into German, French, Danish and Finnish.

FOR MORE INFORMATION SEE: New York Times Book Review, August 12, 1974, November 17, 1974; *Notes from Delacorte Press: Books for Young Readers,* Delacorte, Summer-Fall, 1975; *Washington Post Book World,* July 10, 1977; *New York Times,* December 4, 1979.

McCLURE, Gillian Mary 1948-

PERSONAL: Born October 29, 1948, in Bradford, England; daughter of Paul Curtis (a poet) and Jean Mary (a music teacher;

Gillian Mary McClure and students.

A little further on Rory Wolf saw a fisherman. Rory Wolf loved fish; he would have liked to have been a fisherman himself but was far too fidgety to catch fish.

(From *What's the Time, Rory Wolf?* by Gillian McClure. Illustrated by the author.)

maiden name, Parker) Coltman; married Ian Patrick McClure (a picture restorer), September 26, 1970; children: Calum Hugh, Brendan Paul, and Aidan John. *Education:* Received degree with honors from University of Bristol, 1970. *Home and office:* South Cottage, South Street, Great Chesterford, Essex, England. *Agent:* Curtis Brown Ltd., 1 Craven Hill, London W2 3EP, England.

CAREER: Writer and illustrator of children's books, 1970—. Infant and nursery teacher at schools in Midlothian, Scotland and Glasgow, Scotland, 1971-74.

WRITINGS—Self-illustrated children's books: *The Emperor's Singing Bird*, Deutsch, 1974; *Prickly Pig*, Deutsch, 1976, Dutton, 1980; *Fly Home McDoo*, Dutton, 1979; *What's the Time Rory Wolf?*, Deutsch, 1982.

WORK IN PROGRESS: Teddy Bear's Picnic and *Norrie the Knee-Creeper, the Deep Freezer Thief*, both for children.

SIDELIGHTS: "Eldest of four daughters, I lived all my childhood in Sussex, right under the South Downs. The countryside I explored with my sisters has had a lasting influence on my illustrations; we made dens among the exposed roots of the big beech trees in the woods, we scoured the hedgerows for nests, sailed a raft on the pond and got into trouble with the farmer when we romped in his hay barns.

"My best friend was my dog, Agrippa, who got into trouble with us when he chased pheasants and rabbits. When I was eleven I wrote and illustrated Agrippa's biography. This was

not my first book; I had written and illustrated stories and magazines for my younger sisters ever since I could write, though I never could spell.

"My father wrote poetry about the Sussex weald and downland and I illustrated some of this. I am still working on the illustrations of one of his poems that won a prize in a national poetry competition; we hope to publish it as a children's book.

"When I married I moved to Scotland where I wrote books for the infant and nursery children I taught. I spent a lot of time drawing the derelict tenement areas in Glasgow.

"Now, back in England again, I write and illustrate for my own three sons. It is very exciting to be able to do this while they are still exactly at the right age for my books. The time they take away from me because they are all still very young is so worthwhile when I see their delight at a new book published.

"I find many children's picture books on the market today too sophisticated; they are books for adults posing as children's books. When I am writing and illustrating a book I like to try it out on children, either my own or groups of children in libraries and schools. Very often they contribute ideas. I have also made puppets and masks of all the characters in my books for the children to use.

"Being a writer and illustrator, it is hard to distinguish whether my books start from a visual or a literary idea, for the text and illustrations tend to be closely integrated. Although I am not short of new ideas for books, I take a long time to execute them and do a lot of reworking. I have been working on my current books on and off for two years.''

FOR MORE INFORMATION SEE: Scottish Field, September, 1974; *Stirling Observer,* October 12, 1979; *Glasgow Evening Times,* Scotland, October 26, 1979.

McFARLANE, Leslie 1902-1977
(Franklin W. Dixon, James Cody Ferris, Carolyn Keene, Roy Rockwood)

PERSONAL: Born October 25, 1902, in Carleton Place, Ontario, Canada; died September 6, 1977, in Whitby, Ontario; son of John Henry (an elementary school principal) and Rebecca (Barnett) McFarlane; married Amy Arnold (died, 1955); married Beatrice Greenaway Kenney; children: (first marriage) Patricia, Brian, Norah. *Education:* Attended schools in Haileybury, Ontario, Canada. *Home:* Whitby, Ontario; and Sarasota, Fla.

CAREER: Reporter for various newspapers, Ontario, Canada and Springfield, Mass., 1919-26; Stratemeyer Syndicate, East Orange, N.J., ghost writer, 1926-46; free-lance writer, 1926—; National Film Board of Canada, Ontario, documentary film director, 1943-55; Canadian Broadcasting Corp., chief editor of television drama, 1959-60. Author of the first book in the ''Hardy Boys'' series, *The Tower Treasure. Awards, honors:* British Film Academy Award, 1951, for ''Royal Journey''; Academy Award nominee, 1953, for ''Herring Hunt''; *Liberty* magazine award, 196(?), for best television playwright of the year.

WRITINGS—All of interest to young readers, except as noted: *Streets of Shadow* (adult fiction), Dutton, 1930; *The Murder Tree* (adult fiction), 1931; *The Last of the Great Picnics* (illustrated by Lewis Parker), McClelland & Stewart, 1965; *McGonigle Scores!*, McClelland & Stewart, 1966; *The Dynamite Flynns*, Methuen, 1975; *Agent of the Falcon*, Methuen, 1975; *The Mystery of Spider Lake*, Methuen, 1975; *Squeeze Play*, Methuen, 1975; *A Kid in Haileybury* (autobiography), Highway Book Shop (Cobalt, Ont.), 1975; *The Snow Hawk*, Methuen, 1976; *Breakaway*, Methuen, 1976; *Ghost of the Hardy Boys* (adult autobiography), Two Continents Publishing, 1976.

The pseudonyms indicated below are house pseudonyms used by McFarlane and other writers employed by the Stratemeyer Syndicate. McFarlane has identified the titles listed below as his own work.

Under pseudonym Roy Rockwood; the ''Dave Fearless'' books; all published by Garden City Publishing: *Dave Fearless under the Ocean*, 1926; *. . . in the Black Jungle*, 1926; *. . . near the South Pole*, 1926; *. . . among the Malay Pirates*, 1926; *. . . on the Ship of Mystery*, 1926; *. . . on the Lost Brig*, 1926; *. . . At Whirlpool Point*, 1926.

Under pseudonym Franklin W. Dixon; the ''Hardy Boys'' series; all published by Grosset: *The Tower Treasure* (illustrated by Walter S. Rogers), c. 1927; *The House on the Cliff*, c. 1927; *The Secret of the Old Mill* (illustrated by Walter S. Rogers), 1927; *The Missing Chums* (illustrated by Rogers), 1928; *Hunting for Hidden Gold* (illustrated by Rogers), 1928; *The Shore Road Mystery* (illustrated by Rogers), 1928; *The Secret of the Caves* (illustrated by Rogers), 1929; *The Mystery of Cabin Island* (illustrated by Rogers), 1929; *The Great Airport Mystery* (illustrated by Rogers), 1930; *What Happened at Midnight*

LESLIE McFARLANE

(illustrated by Rogers), 1931; *While the Clock Ticked* (illustrated by J. Clemens Gretter), 1932; *Footprints under the Window*, 1933; *The Mark on the Door*, 1934; *The Hidden Harbor Mystery*, 1935; *The Sinister Sign Post* (illustrated by Gretter), 1936; *A Figure in Hiding* (illustrated by Paul Laune), 1937; *The Secret Warning* (illustrated by Laune), 1938; *The Flickering Torch Mystery* (illustrated by Laune), 1943; *The Short Wave Mystery*, 1945; *The Secret Panel* (illustrated by Russell H. Tandy), 1946; *The Phantom Freighter*, 1947.

Under pseudonym Carolyn Keene, author of four books in the ''Dana Girls'' series, including *In the Shadow of the Tower*, Grosset, 1934; *The Secret of Lone Tree Cottage*, Grosset, 1934; *By the Light of the Study Lamp*, Grosset, 1934; *A Three-Cornered Mystery*, Grossets, 1935.

Under pseudonym James Cody Ferris, author of one volume in the ''X Bar X Boys'' series, *The Border Patrol*, published by Grosset.

Also author of film script, ''Royal Journey'' (documentary), United Artists, 1951, ''Herring Hunt'' (documentary), RKO, 1953; author and director of numerous films including ''The Boy Who Stopped Niagra,'' 1947 and ''A Friend at the Door,'' 1950; author of over seventy plays for television, including ''The Eyeopener Man'' and ''Pilgrim, Why Do You Come?''. Contributor of short stories, novelettes, and serials in magazines.

SIDELIGHTS: **October 25, 1902.** Born in Carleton Place, Ontario, Canada, and reared in Haileybury, a northern Ontario mining town where he attended the school of which his father was principal. ''Because our father was the principal, our little comrades had a notion that my brothers and I would be specially favored and that we would get high marks no matter how dumb we were. It didn't work that way. Dad leaned over backward

"Our only chance is to make a break for it," Frank decided. "Head for the car. There'll be only one man to get past." ■ (From *The Sinister Signpost* by Franklin W. Dixon. Illustrated by J. Clemens Gretter.)

to prove that he didn't believe in nepotism. At the same time he indicated that he expected better than normal performance so that we would be a credit to him. In this I was a disappointment to him.

"He was a kind father, a good man, diligent and conscientious who read a chapter from the Bible to us at breakfast and went to church twice every Sunday. On these occasions, during the period of prayer he must have asked the Almighty to give him a hand. And when Divine help failed to materialize he must have asked God just where he had gone wrong, where he had erred, what exactly had he done to deserve me.

"The reason for this despair was that he couldn't teach me anything about arithmetic. He often said he was tempted to give up the teaching profession and go into life insurance, because he couldn't even teach his own son to multiply six times twelve. He was clearly in the wrong field and a failure by any reasonable standard.

". . . I remember my childhood as a happy time. I can recall my father's bookcase with its leather-bound one-volume edi-

tions of Longfellow, Milton, Tennyson, Wordsworth and Shakespeare. He had a deep affection for poetry, which I was unable to share, but I fell upon the *Complete Works of Charles Dickens* with absolute joy the day the set arrived in the house. Those red-bound volumes introduced me to a world of imagination and magic that can be evoked by a master. Dickens and an Empire typewriter which my father bought at about the same time resolved my future. He seldom used the typewriter himself, but neither encouraged nor discouraged its use by his boys. So I used it, learning by trial and error with two fingers.

"I realize now, of course, that by today's standards any kid brought up in a remote northern town during the second decade of this century was underprivileged. It was a good thing that we didn't know it. We didn't know the boon of organized recreation. In summer we could play ball in a lumpy vacant lot (without a certified coach to show us how and a gallery of howling parents to inspire us), go swimming in a lake frigid enough to turn us blue in five minutes. In winter we could play a scrambly kind of hockey—about twenty youngsters to a side—on a backyard rink bordered by snowbanks. In the light of the superior advantages enjoyed by young athletes of today's Little Leagues, it is clear that we grew up under such wretched conditions that I can't understand why it seemed to me that we had such a hell of a lot of fun. We just didn't know any better.

"To compensate for our dismal lack of other entertainment, there was a copious supply of reading matter—admittedly uncertified, unpasteurized and probably unhealthy—easily available to the growing boy. At Christmas every normal Canadian lad felt neglected if he failed to receive a five-pound volume of either *The Boy's Own Annual* or *Chums*. These were the collected numbers of two weekly magazines for boys, published in England and bound annually in hard covers for export to the colonies. With pen and ink illustrations, printed in 1,000 pages of eyestraining type, they were packed with fiction calculated to brighten the most monotonous juvenile existence.

". . . We had imports from the U.S.A. such as the Alger books, the Rover Boys and Frank Merriwell, a clean-living American boy who excelled at every sport devised by man, from tiddlywinks to polo. Frank was exceptionally clean. In fact, all this literature put a high premium on clean living, which confused us a lot because we were never quite sure what it meant. Clean living was never actually spelled out. Obviously it meant using your toothbrush every day and washing your feet every week, but we knew it couldn't be that simple. We had an uneasy feeling that it also meant giving up masturbation but the books didn't say.

"Clean living or not, under these literary influences the Canadian boy grew up in a state of proper humility. His reading taught him that British boys were courageous, daring, ingenious and always in the right so that they always came out on top while, incidentally, having more fun than anyone. At the same time his reading taught him that American boys were likewise courageous, daring and ingenious and, moreover, so devoted to honest toil that they always wound up rich. Canadian boys, who apparently had no history worth writing about and no forebears who ever made it as heroes of books, were clearly made of inferior stuff. This probably explains why the adult, male Canadian today is a docile, modest fellow who knows his place and is never given to throwing his weight around." [Leslie McFarlane, *Ghost of the Hardy Boys: An Autobiography,* Methuen, 1976.¹]

1919. "When I got out of high school . . . it was time to make a living. I was given a paper indicating that I had passed but the marks in algebra and geometry were deplorable. Let us say I left by a process of elimination like a tapeworm."[1]

Moved to Cobalt, Ontario, where he began his career in journalism working as a reporter for the local paper, the *Nugget*. ". . . Cobalt had a daily newspaper, called the *Nugget*. Mining-camp papers always seemed to go in for gaudy and imaginative titles, as witness the immortal *Tombstone Epitaph*. I decided to give it a try. So one morning my mother ironed a fresh shirt for me, inspected my shoes, straightened my tie, told me the world was full of disappointments which must be met with good cheer, and gave me a kiss. I thought I was merely going on a journey of five miles, but she knew how long that journey was going to be.

"I took the trolley to Cobalt and sought an interview with Mr. Browning, editor of the *Nugget*. He was a gentle man, soft of voice, kind of manner, who said yes, they could use a young reporter who was not afraid of hard work and who was willing to learn. I could begin immediately, at nine dollars a week.

"My career was under way."[1]

1920. Moved to Sudbury, Ontario. "My mother cried. My father presented me with one of the new safety razors and refrained from good advice. He had done all he could; the rest was up to Providence.

"My three brothers concealed their grief bravely. My brother, Frank, who would now have a whole bed to himself, insisted on helping me pack and carried my suitcase to the railway station a good half hour before the southbound train was due.

". . . Sudbury was a rowdy, brawling railway center and mining town in the middle of a region that produced more nickel than any other place in the world. Although the community itself rejoiced in lawns, flower gardens and even a beautiful lake, the surrounding countryside was a forbidding jungle of barren rock that resembled a Wellsian vision of the mountains of the moon. . . .

"After a few months of learning how to spell names correctly and street addresses exactly, I discovered through the 'Male Help Wanted' column of the Toronto *Globe* that experienced reporters were in demand all over Ontario. Any week you could take your pick of a dozen openings. On the principle that I had nothing whatever to lose, I answered all the ads. Consequently, to my great astonishment, I found myself engaged by the *Sudbury Star* at the glittering salary of twenty-five dollars a week.

"When I became a reporter, I had no intention of making newspaper journalism a career, no secret hope of some day becoming an editor or publisher. Instead, I wanted to become an author.

"In Canada in the Twenties such an ambition, if I had dared say it aloud, would have been regarded as imbecilic. Authors, unless they were also clergymen or professors, just didn't make any money and even then they didn't make much. This answered everything.

"Thanks to my Irish ancestry, however, I was bull-headed and stubborn about the matter. Newspaper work; especially on the *Sudbury Star*, left practically no time for after-hours ventures into literature. But by staying awake until two o'clock one morning, I did manage to write a short story, supposedly hu-

For one sickening moment Frank swung like a pendulum beneath the cliff. With all his strength, Joe jerked the belt again and a moment later helped Frank clamber to safety. ■ (From *The Missing Chums* by Franklin W. Dixon. Illustrated by Walter S. Rogers.)

morous. I sent it to the *Toronto Star Weekly,* the magazine section of a large newspaper which came out with the Saturday edition. The *Weekly* printed quite a bit of serious writing, usually by reporters who worked on the *Daily.* One of them was a bright young fellow called Ernest Hemingway and there was another by the name of Callaghan. . . ."[1]

Before the year was over McFarlane quit the *Sudbury Star* in order to devote himself full time to writing. He rented a summer cottage on nearby Lake Ramsey. "Fifty years later I might have grown a beard, forsworn baths, acquired a guitar and a girl with stringy hair and set out on the highway to find myself. I was a good deal more conservative, perhaps less adventurous. I merely bought a second-hand typewriter, rented the cabin for a season and moved in with a stock of provisions and two cases of beer. A green canoe provided transportation between the cabin and Sudbury, three miles up the lake.

"Besides, I was very serious about making a living as a writer of fiction. It would be gratifying to report that this came easily, but it didn't. The trouble was that I wanted to begin at the top, in *Harper's Magazine* or the *Atlantic Monthly*. The stories they printed seemed to have very little plot, which was convenient because I wasn't very good at making up plots. Clearly, in these great magazines it wasn't the story that counted but how you told it. Plots were for popular magazine writers, not for talented authors in embryo.''[1]

1926. Accepted a position in the newsroom of the *Springfield Republican*, Springfield, Massachusetts. "During the previous year *Adventure* had printed one of my more ambitious tales, 20,000 words long, called 'Impostor,' about a broken-down fur trader who presided over a broken-down trading post in the Hudson Bay wilderness. Because I was living in northern Ontario when this manuscript went into the mail, the editors of *Adventure* assumed that I had a profound knowledge of wilderness life—indeed, that I might even be a broken-down fur trader myself. So they published the story.

"Alan Dinehart, a popular actor of the day, read it in Chicago while touring in a comedy called 'Applesauce.' Not only did he like it but he decided that a drama of the north woods might be just what he needed for a change of pace. Not that he wanted to stumble around the stage in a role of a drink-sodden reprobate. That wasn't his bag. Mr. Dinehart, who was blessed with an ingratiating personality, liked the part of the upstanding young adventurer who arrived at the trading post posing as the factor's grandson.

"He sent off a telegram to *Adventure* offering to buy the rights for $500. When this was conveyed to me I rejected it promptly. Everyone knew that playwrights earned huge sums of money on Broadway and always ended up in Hollywood owning mansions and mistresses. I was not interested in paltry sums. I would write the play myself, so eventually we got together to discuss turning 'Impostor' into a starring vehicle for Mr. Dinehart.

"Two little matters bothered him, he confessed. First, I had never written a play. Second, the story—like most *Adventure* stories—lacked female characters. It would be necessary, he thought, to introduce an attractive young woman with whom the imposter, played by Dinehart, would fall in love. His public would expect it.

"The great thing about reaching the age of twenty-three is that nothing seems impossible. I assured Dinehart that if my lack of experience in dramaturgy disturbed him, he need have no fears. I was quite positive that I could come up with two and a half hours of lively dialogue and tense action. As for female interest I could see no reason why a luscious damsel could not become involved in the goings-on at the trading post. She could be a missionary's motherless daughter, helping her father bring the word of God to the heathen. In fact I could even supply another girl, if he liked, a fiery halfbreed of jealous disposition and explosive temperament.

"Mr. Dinehart was cheered. We shook hands and parted.

"Now, confronting my typewriter every morning in my room on Pearl Street, I tried to bring my confident promises to life. Because reporters weren't required to show up at the *Republican* office before two o'clock in the afternoon, the mornings were free for the daily tussle with the broken-down trader. It became more than a tussle. It became a battle, and a losing battle at that.

"There is a great difference, I found, between the creation of a small piece of fiction in which the characters are free to roam all over the place and the construction of a play which confines them to a one-room trading post. The problem becomes even tougher when this trading post is so far north that it has no phone service.''[1]

Looking for writing assignments in all directions, McFarlane scoured the classified ads. "In the Springtime of 1926 I found Springfield, Massachusetts, a delightful place. I was twenty-three, healthy and footloose, free to latch onto any opportunity, pick up any challenge. The ad that ran in the classified columns of the trade journal *Editor and Publisher* seemed to combine both.

Experienced Fiction Writer Wanted
to Work from
Publisher's Outlines

A box number was appended for replies. That was all. Because most of the other ads were for reporters, deskmen and copywriters this one stood out. Who ever heard of anyone actually advertising for the services of a fiction writer?

"I considered my experience, which didn't take long. . . .

"So I sat down at my typewriter in the cityroom of the *Springfield Republican*, hammered out a reply to the ad and dropped it in the mailbox. Then I went about my business, which was to cover the hotel beat for the day and work up some kind of feature piece that might give a little sparkle to the Sunday edition.''[1]

Three weeks later, McFarlane received a reply from publisher Edward Stratemeyer. McFarlane realized that Stratemeyer was the publisher and ghost writer of one of his childhood favorite writers, Roy Rockwood, author of the "Dave Fearless" series. "During adolescence Roy Rockwood had always been one of my favorite people. I pictured him seated at his desk, pen in hand, white shirt open at the throat, a bulldog pipe in his teeth. The creator of Bomba the Jungle Boy had a steady gaze, a firm mouth, a determined jaw. The walls of his study bristled with heads of leopard, grizzly and saber-tooth tiger. True, I had never actually seen a picture of the great author but I didn't have to. I just knew that's how he would look.

"Discovery of the truth about Roy Rockwood left me a little stunned.

"When you read a book you know it must have been written by somebody. You assume that the author is the somebody named on the cover. You take it for granted that this writer lives and breathes, that he eats breakfast every morning, argues occasionally with his wife, takes aspirin for his headaches, resents paying income tax and has a sour opinion of most politicians. In short, that he is a human being.

"Now I learned from an unimpeachable source that Roy Rockwood wasn't a human being at all; he didn't exist, he never had existed. He was just as fictitious as Bomba the Jungle Boy. . . .

"Mr. Stratemeyer suggested that I read the two specimen books and choose one. Informed of my choice he would then send me an outline of the opening chapters of the series volume presently in preparation, which I would be asked to expand into about 2,000 words of publishable fiction. This trial run would not, of course, involve payment. However, if the two chapters pleased Mr. Stratemeyer, he would commission me to complete the book, twenty chapters in all, for a guaranteed sum of $100, flat rate, no royalty, with the prospect of further lucrative assignments to follow.

"The letter opened a window on a very strange corner of the publishing world. It had never occurred to me that books could be written and printed in this odd fashion. But why question the methods of an established author? If Edward Stratemeyer decided that it was quicker and easier to conjure up plots in preference to writing entire books, if he thought it sound policy to hire wordsmiths to turn his plots into publishable manuscripts, who was I to criticize?

"I estimated that it probably took Nat Ridley, Jr. forty-five seconds to whip out that page of prose. Perhaps a whole minute if he typed with two fingers. On that basis he probably knocked out the whole book in less than four hours. Let's say a half day's work.

"Viewed in that light, Edward Stratemeyer's proposition began to look attractive. To write a chapter of a book without having to worry about character, action or plot would call for little more than the ability to hit the keys of a typewriter. By staying on in the office for an hour or so after the day's work, I could probably hammer out a book in a week. Four books a month at $100 a book worked out to $400 a month, more than double my salary at the *Republican*.

"Could I afford to turn it down?

"It was true that neither of the sample books had even a smidgeon of merit. They had less content than a football bladder and no more style than a drunken camel. Garbage. But then, they didn't pretend to be works of literature. They were straightforward, cheap paperbacks for a public that would neither read nor relish anything better. And besides, I would be under no obligation to *read* the stuff. I would merely have to write it, hammer out the words in some reasonable progression so that they would make sense even if the plots didn't.

"In fact it might even be fun. I talked myself into it and wrote to Edward Stratemeyer that night, telling him that I'd like to try my hand at a Dave Fearless book.

"As the defendant said, I didn't know it was loaded.

"I heaved a gusty sigh as the typewriter clattered 'The End' and I pulled the final page from the typewriter. The manuscript, unread, unrevised and uncorrected, went into a large, brown envelope which, in turn, went into the outgoing mail basket. There wasn't even a carbon copy. The postal service would have been flattered by this manifestation of utter faith; any professional writer would have been horrified.

"My first book!

"'A poor thing, but not entirely my own,' I thought ruefully; one had to admit the Stratemeyer contribution.

"When Mr. Stratemeyer handed down his verdict he allowed, with his customary restraint, that *Dave Fearless Under the Ocean* was 'a lively narrative.' He didn't say he was unable to put down the manuscript until he finished it but, after all, he was in a position to know how it came out anyway. More to the point, he sent along a check for $100.

"I somehow expected that a check from a big syndicate would be an impressively gaudy affair, in several colors perhaps, with the amount typed in capital letters and at least a couple of splashy signatures. . . . Mr. Stratemeyer's check, however, was as modest in size as it was in value and he had written it personally from date to signature in crabbed handwriting that resembled that of my grandfather. Obviously an old-fashioned man who didn't bother trying to impress people.

"Even more to the point, he sent along another three-page outline of the next book in the saga. This was to be called *Dave Fearless in the Black Jungle* (or *Lost Among the Cannibals*). He wanted to know if I would take on an assignment every month and make myself available for work on other series.

"That did it.

"By working full time for the Stratemeyer Syndicate I could easily whack out four books a month, double my income and get some sleep at night. There would even be time to spare for higher endeavors, literature in the Joseph Conrad vein, for example.

"Clearly I couldn't afford to go on working for the *Republican*."[1] Quitting his job, he moved back to Canada, dividing his time between working on the "Dave Fearless" series and his own short fiction. "By the end of summer half a dozen stories that once looked like reliable ice floes had turned into rejection slips that wouldn't support the weight of a flea. The cheerful assumption that Dave Fearless would keep me afloat while I leaped nimbly toward the solvency represented by the approval of magazine editors who paid real money had vanished in the blizzard of little printed notes that expressed regrets and assured me that no lack of merit was implied. The butcher, the grocer and the man who sold beer weren't exactly baying for my blood but they were making discouraging noises.

"In short, I was damn near broke. . . .

"It turned out that I *could* count on Edward Stratemeyer. Before the week was out a long envelope brought another outline, accompanied by a letter explaining his 'other plans.' He had observed, Stratemeyer wrote, that detective stories had become very popular in the world of adult fiction. He instanced the works of S. S. Van Dine, which were selling in prodigious numbers as I was well aware. S. S. Van Dine was neither an ocean liner nor a living man but the pseudonym of Willard Hungtington Wright, a literary craftsman who wrote sophisticated stories for Mencken's *Smart Set*.

"It had recently occurred to him, Stratemeyer continued, that the growing boys of America might welcome similar fare. Of course, he had already given them Nat Ridley, but Nat really didn't solve mysteries; he merely blundered into them and, after a given quota of hairbreadth escapes, blundered out again. What Stratemeyer had in mind was a series of detective stories on the juvenile level, involving two brothers of high-school age who would solve such mysteries as came their way. To lend credibility to their talents, they would be the sons of a professional private investigator, so big in his field that he had become a sleuth of international fame. His name—Fenton Hardy. His sons, Frank and Joe, would therefore be known as. . . .

"The Hardy Boys!

"This would be the title of the series. My pseudonym would be Franklin W. Dixon. (I never did learn what the 'W' represented. Certainly not Wealthy.)

"Stratemeyer noted that the books would be clothbound and therefore priced a little higher than paperbacks. This in turn would justify a little higher payment for the manuscript—$125 to be exact. He had attached an information sheet for guidance and the plot outline of the initial volume, which would be called *The Tower Treasure*. In closing, he promised that if the

Joe toppled over the railing into space! ■ (From *The Tower Treasure* by Franklin W. Dixon. Illustrated by Walter S. Rogers.)

manuscript came up to expectations—which were high—I would be asked to do the next two volumes of the series.

"I skimmed through the outline. It was about a robbery in a towered mansion belonging to Hurd Applegate, an eccentric stamp collector. The Hardy Boys solved it.

"What a change from Dave Fearless! No man-eating sharks. No octopi. No cannibals, polar bears or man-eating trees. Just the everyday doings of everyday lads in everyday surroundings. They didn't go wandering all over the seven seas, pursued by imbecile relatives. They stayed at home, checked in for dinner every night like other kids. They even went to school. Granted, they didn't appear to spend very much time at school; most of the outline seemed to be devoted to extracurricular activities after four and on weekends. But they went.

"I was so relieved to be free of Dave Fearless and his dreary helpers that I greeted Frank and Joe Hardy with positive rapture, and I wrote to Stratemeyer to accept the assignment. Then I rolled a sheet of paper into the typewriter and prepared to go to work.

"Then I paused and gave the project a little thought. The sensible course would have been to hammer out the thing at breakneck speed, regardless of style, spelling or grammar, and

let the Stratemeyer editors tidy it up. Bang it out, stuff the typed sheets in an envelope and put it in the mail, the quicker the better, and get going on the next book. In this sort of business, at the payment involved, time was money, output was everything.

"Writers, however, aren't always sensible. Many of them enjoy writing so much that they would go on doing it even if deprived of bylines and checks, which is why agents are born. The enjoyment implies doing the best one can with the task in hand, even if it is merely an explanatory letter to the landlord. (There is no special virtue in this. Writers just can't help it.)

"It seemed to me that the Hardy boys deserved something better than the slapdash treatment Dave Fearless had been getting. It was still hack work, no doubt, but did the new series have to be all that hack? There was, after all, the chance to contribute a little style, occasional words of more than two syllables, maybe a little sensory stimuli.

"Take food, for example. From my boyhood reading I recalled enjoying any scenes that involved eating. Boys are always hungry. Whether the outline called for it or not, I decided that the Hardy boys and their chums would eat frequently. When Laura Hardy packed a picnic lunch the provender would be described in detail, not only when she stowed it away but when the boys did. And when the boys solved the mystery of the theft, Hurd Applegate wouldn't stop at a mere cash reward. He would come up with a lavish dinner, good for at least two pages of lip smacking. Maybe even belches.

"And then there was humor. There hadn't been so much as a snicker in the whole Dave Fearless series. This stood to reason: a man-eating shark is no laughing matter. Next to food, however, boys like jokes. Why not inject a few rib ticklers into *The Tower Treasure*? Chet Morton was described as a 'fun loving lad,' and, as he was supposed to be 'chubby,' it followed that food interest might be maintained by making him a glutton. The cast of characters also gave passing mention to Chief Collig, head of the Bayport Police Department, and his associate, Detective Smuff. While the outline did not suggest that these lawmen were comical fellows, it did seem that anyone named Collig had to be a pretty stodgy cop and that Smuff would simply have to be a dunderhead.

"I could hardly wait to get at them.

"But why go to all this trouble? If *The Tower Treasure* was a little better written than the usual fifty-cent juvenile, who would get the credit? The nonexistent Franklin W. Dixon. If better writing and a little humor helped make the series a success, who would benefit financially? The Stratemeyer Syndicate and the publishers. The writer who brought the skeleton outline to life wouldn't get a penny even if the books sold a million—which, of course, seemed impossible at the time.

"So what? I decided against the course of common sense. I opted for Quality."[1]

Returned to Haileybury. "In small-town communities it is generally assumed that if a home-town boy comes back for more than a brief round of handshakes he has failed to Make Good. Somehow, he has blown it in the outside world. If he remains he is of interest only as visible evidence of the superior wisdom of the natives who stayed put.

"So it was that when I returned to Haileybury, moved back in with my parents and brothers, rented an office above a bank and set up shop as author-in-residence, no one was visibly impressed. Perhaps it was because no one had ever heard of Dave Fearless.

"In the forty-seven years since then, in fact, I have never encountered anyone who has heard of Dave Fearless. I have never seen a Dave Fearless book in a bookstore, on a paperback rack, on a library shelf or even in any of the dusty caves in obscure shops where old books go when they die. I have never come across any reference to Dave in any book or article. On a shelf in my small library the yellowing volumes I hammered out for Edward Stratemeyer stand as the solid evidence that there actually was a Dave Fearless series. Otherwise I might begin to doubt.

"I didn't even mention the Hardy Boys in Haileybury, except to my mother, because I was at an age when one is easily intimidated by any document that looks legal. I had taken very seriously that contract which enjoined me to secrecy about my labors for the Syndicate and which made me subject to unmentionable penalties if I blabbed. Unmentionable because they weren't mentioned, which made them all the more sinister. So I nursed my guilty secret and went on nursing it, in fact, for many years after anyone had stopped caring.

"I furnished my new office in Haileybury with a desk and chair bought from a politician who had just closed his campaign quarters after a disastrous election. He was glad to retrieve ten dollars from the wreckage. The desk is still in use, which works out at about twenty-one cents a year and more millions of words than anyone would believe. It was time to get going on the final book of the Hardy Boys trilogy, Volume Three, *The Secret of the Old Mill*."[1]

Married Amy Arnold. "And so, with a check for a Hardy Boys book in my pocket and an order for another, along with encouraging words of promise from a few editors, Amy Arnold and I were married in Montreal and went to live in a little village nearby. If our parents thought us insane they refrained from comment. We defined our action as merely indicating confidence in the future. After all, I had my sheet anchor to windward—two Frank-and-Joe books a year. Not a very strong anchor, to be sure, but better than none at all. . . .

"When my young wife told her friends that she had married a writer, their good wishes sounded more like condolences. Especially a Canadian writer! One good woman said, 'God help you, my dear!' with compassion. We thought it amusing at the time. Later we realized what she meant.

"Writers are not good husband material. (I am not qualified to speak for the husbands of female writers.) Not because they are worse characters than men of other occupations. They aren't. Not because they are impractical and untidy. They are. Not because their income is chancy. It is. But they are always underfoot. The unbroken presence of a mate who hammers at a typewriter and bawls for silence can become, at the very least, irksome. In fact, he turns into an intolerable nuisance. Every time she lays eyes on the pest she is provoked into considering his imperfections.

"When he summons her into his presence occasionally so that he may read aloud some particularly happy expression of his genius, she must applaud if she knows what is good for her. Otherwise the Master will be hurt and go into a fit of the sulks. When a story is going well, he withdraws into another world, gazes at her as if wondering who she is and where she came from, sits at the dinner table mumbling to himself. When a

Frank snapped on the wall switch. There a horrifying sight met the Hardys' eyes.

The farmer and his wife, bound and gagged, were tied to chairs in the middle of the room! ■ (From *The House on the Cliff* by Franklin W. Dixon.)

story goes badly, he mopes and becomes unfit for human society. The days turn on the arrival of the postman with good news or bad—or even worse, no news at all."[1]

1930. Stratemeyer died. "I had never met him, had never even spoken to him on the telephone. At the time of my marriage, he sent a check for $25 and a similar check on the birth of our first daughter. Now the letter said that in his will he bequeathed each of his writers a sum equal to one-fifth of their earnings from the Syndicate. Although he was all business when it came to dealings that involved the Syndicate, he had his kind side. I had a feeling of loss."[1]

It was announced that Stratemeyer's daughters would carry on the work of the Syndicate. One of Stratemeyer's daughters, Mrs. Harriet Adams, was the creator of the famous Nancy Drew. Mrs. Adams asked McFarlane to write the new *Dana Girl* mysteries. "I felt almighty foolish about becoming Carolyn Keene, but my wife promised she wouldn't tell anyone. . . .

"After the breeders were launched I did another volume. Then the whole thing became too much for me and I begged off. Starvation seemed preferable. The series went on, because no ghost is irreplaceable. It is still going on, in fact, but the Dana Girls have never really threatened Nancy Drew.

"I never felt comfortable as Carolyn Keene, and I was glad to don Franklin W. Dixon's cap again. . . ."[1]

1938. Wrote radio scripts for the Canadian broadcasting system.

1943. Moved to Ottawa. Soon after, he discontinued writing for the Syndicate to become a film director. "We moved to Ottawa, where I drew a regular paycheck for the first time in years doing public relations work for the Department of Munitions and Supply. About a year later John Grierson, who had come from England to establish the National Film Board of Canada, invited me to join his group of documentary film makers. They toiled in an abandoned sawmill and I thought they were all demented, with the exception of the great Grierson and a weedy disciple named Norman MacLaren.

"I never could understand why I was hired because Grierson didn't think writers belonged in documentary film work and never hesitated to express his low opinion of them. You didn't write films; you directed and edited films. Grierson didn't believe in actors, either. Or sets. Documentary film was a Movement, concerned with normal people going about their normal concerns in a normal way. The trouble was that when you brought lights and cameras into a lumber camp or an aircraft factory and aimed them at anyone at work people ceased to work naturally. Give them lines to say and they forgot the words, mumbled and stumbled, and all illusion vanished.

"So I became a director and spent the next fifteen years roaming from the coast of Gaspé to the lush valleys of the Caribou country in British Columbia with camera and sound crews. My wife, who had just become nicely adjusted to an underfoot husband, was now obliged to adjust to a husband who was seldom at home at all. She managed the one just as she had survived the other. The films I made are now forgotten, although I won a few awards in a field where it is difficult to escape getting awards. I wrote a script for a documentary short subject called 'Herring Hunt' which was nominated for a Hollywood Oscar and didn't win, and for a feature called 'Royal Journey' which was nominated for a British Film Academy Award, and did.

"As for the Hardy Boys, after *The Short Wave Mystery* (in which the boys went scientific) and *The Secret Panel,* I bowed out with *The Phantom Freighter* which was written in 1946 in motel rooms at night on a location in Nova Scotia when I was directing a film. For me, that was the end of the Hardy Boys. I didn't need them any more, and certainly they didn't need me, because they have continued to this day.

"There was no quarrel, no dramatic break with the Syndicate for which I had toiled over a period of twenty years and ground more than two million words. I merely sent in the manuscript with a note to the effect that I was too busy to take on any further assignments. The Syndicate didn't plead with me to continue. In fact, the Syndicate didn't seem to care much one way or the other. Other spooks were always available. If the parting involved any emotion at all, it was one of relief, as if a couple of relatives who came for the weekend had finally moved on after sticking around for years.

"I was pretty bored with the Hardy boys by that time anyway. Not with the books, because I never read them. Whenever a new one arrived I might skim through a few pages and then

the volume would join its predecessors on a bookcase shelf. Under glass, like a row of embalmed owls, so the dust wouldn't get at them.

"Perhaps a psychologist would have been interested in this extraordinary indifference to the physical evidence of work that had occupied so many hours over so many years (about twenty volumes in all), not counting the Dave Fearless paperbacks, the Dana Girls and assorted extras that have utterly vanished from my memory. But to me it was as if some force within my mind insisted on thrusting the books into limbo the moment the final page of a final chapter came out of the typewriter. Not revulsion. Complete indifference. Perhaps this also accounted for the fact that, although I had been in New York many times, I was never tempted to cross the river and drop into the Stratemeyer Syndicate office in East Orange. I had nothing whatever against Edward Stratemeyer or his daughters or the Syndicate people, and I am sure I would have been welcome, but somehow it just never seemed to matter. The dozens of stories I had written for magazines good and bad on both sides of the Atlantic were all carefully collected and bound, some of them occasionally reread, but I never curled up with a Hardy Boys book to spend a happy hour reading it all the way through.

"It was not until sometime in the 1940s, as a matter of fact, that I had discovered that Franklin W. Dixon and the Hardy Boys were conjurable names. One day my son had come into the workroom, which had never been exalted into a 'study,' and pointed to the bookcase with its shelf of Hardy Boys originals. 'Why do you keep these books, Dad? Did you read them when you were a kid?'

"'Read them? I wrote them.' And then, because it doesn't do to deceive any youngster, 'At least, I wrote the words.'

"He stared. I saw incredulity. Then open-mouthed respect.

"'Why didn't you tell me?'

"'I suppose it never occurred to me.'

"This was true. The Hardy Boys were never mentioned in the household. They were never mentioned to friends. Maybe it was a holdover from Edward Stratemeyer's long past injunction to secrecy. Habit. I wasn't ashamed of them. I had done them as well as I could, at the time. They had merely provided a way of making a living.

"'But they're wonderful books,' he said. 'I used to borrow them from the other kids all the time until I found them here.'

"'Other kids read them?'

"'Dad, where have you been? Everybody reads them. You can buy them in Simpson's. Shelves of them.'

"Next day I went to the department store and damned if the lad wasn't right! They *did* have shelves of them. There were *The Tower Treasure, The House on the Cliff, The Secret of the Old Mill, The Great Airport Mystery,* all the remembered titles, the whole score of them, and more I had never heard of. And over on another shelf, a dozen titles in the Dana Girls series, considerably outnumbered by a massive collection of Nancy Drew.

"I began to see the Hardy Boys books wherever I went, in small bookstores and large, even in railway depots and corner

(From the weekly television series "The Hardy Boys Mysteries," based on Franklin Dixon's characters. Starring Parker Stevenson as Frank Hardy and Shaun Cassidy as Joe Hardy. First presented on ABC-TV, January 30, 1977.)

stores. There seemed to be an epidemic. Whenever I saw a small boy on a train or plane, he was almost invariably absorbed in a bright blue volume, lost in Bayport and environs. 'They must have sold a lot of those things,' I reflected. 'Maybe a hundred thousand or so.'

"I asked a clerk if the Hardy Boys books were popular.

"'Most popular boys' books we carry,' he said. 'Matter of fact, they're supposed to be the best-selling boys' books in the world.'

"'Imagine that!' I said in downright wonderment.

"The Film Board experience ended with the death of my wife in **1955.** She had lived to make her husband happy and to see our three children grown, graduated and married. I left Ottawa, took to writing for television, and was invited to become drama editor of the Canadian Broadcasting Corporation. I met Bea Kenney, a widow, who didn't mind having a husband underfoot, married again and went back to freelancing once more."[1]

McFarlane and his wife, Bea, lived in Sarasota, Florida, during the winter, and in Whitby, Ontario for the remainder of the year. "Whenever I am interviewed, which is oftener than I wish, the interview invariably turns to the matter of money. No one seems remotely interested in the effect of the Hardy Boys on the kids who read them, or how and when the books were written, or the circumstances which brought them into being. No one is ever interested in the fact that I have written hundreds of short stories, dozens of radio plays and seventy television plays, some of which were really very good.

"The interest lies wholly in the fact that publishers and the Syndicate made a great deal of money out of books that have sold in the high millions, for which I was paid about $5,000.

"I always realize that the interviewer feels I should be regarded as an object of sympathy or contempt—sympathy as a victim of one of the great swindles of modern times, contempt as the dumbest sucker of the age. This maddens me. It also saddens me.

"I was not swindled. I accepted the terms of Edward Stratemeyer and the importance of the money was related to my needs. I was free to reject any of the assignments.

"Writing is not a profession on which one embarks under duress. No one forces anyone to become a writer. No one even asks him. He writes because he enjoys writing, and if he doesn't enjoy it he should get out of the profession. It follows, then, that if he is doing something he enjoys he should not complain if the financial rewards are less than he expected or thinks he deserves."[1]

September 6, 1977. Died in Whitby, Ontario.

FOR MORE INFORMATION SEE: A Kid in Haileybury (autobiography), Highway Book Shop, 1975; Leslie McFarlane, *Ghost of the Hardy Boys* (autobiography), Two Continents Publishing, 1976; *Rolling Stone,* October 21, 1976; *Canadian Children's Literature,* Number 11, 1978.

McLEOD, Emilie Warren   1926-1982

OBITUARY NOTICE—See sketch in *SATA* Volume 23: Born December 2, 1926, in Boston, Mass.; died October 2, 1982, following a long illness, at her home in Mass. Editor and author of children's books. After her graduation from Mt. Holyoke College in 1948, McLeod worked on such publications as the Falmouth (Mass.) *Enterprise,* the *Ladies' Home Journal,* and *Presbyterian Life* magazine. From 1950 until 1952, she was assistant editor of children's books at Houghton Mifflin before joining Atlantic Monthly Press, where she served as children's book editor from 1956 until 1977, and as associate director from 1976 until 1977. During the last five years of her life, McLeod published books under her own imprint, Unicorn Books, in association with E. P. Dutton. Titles which she has edited include *The Incredible Journey* by Sheila Burnford, *Ounce, Dice, Trice,* written by Alastair Reid and illustrated by Ben Shahn, and *A Room Made of Windows* by Eleanor Cameron. McLeod is also credited with helping to promote such authors and illustrators as Bernarda Bryson, Sid Fleischman, Richard Kennedy, and David McPhail. Her own books for children are: *The Seven Remarkable Bears, Clancy's Witch, One Snail and Me,* and *The Bear's Bicycle. For More Information See: Contemporary Authors,* Volumes 69-72, Gale, 1978. *Obituaries: Publishers Weekly,* October 15, 1982; *School Library Journal,* November, 1982.

McPHARLIN, Paul   1903-1948

BRIEF ENTRY: Born December 22, 1903, in Detroit, Mich.; died September 28, 1948, in Birmingham, Mich. A founding member of Puppeteers of America, McPharlin was also involved in many facets of the graphic arts. He was the author of numerous books on the puppetry field, including *The Puppet Theater in America: A History, 1524-1948* (Harper, 1949) which is still respected as an authoritative study on puppetry. McPharlin was a graduate of Wayne University (now Wayne State University), where he taught classes in puppetry and bookmaking in the 1930s, and the University of Michigan. He was at one time director of the Marionette Fellowship of Evanston, Ill. and travelled throughout Europe and the United States studying the art of puppetry and performing.

McPharlin's prominence in the field of graphic arts was a result of his illustrations, book designs, engravings, and active participation in publishing and industrial graphic arts. Among the many books he illustrated are Samuel Taylor Coleridge's *The Rime of the Ancient Mariner* (Peter Pauper Press, 1939), Gilbert and Sullivan's *Mikado* (Peter Pauper Press, 1940), and Benjamin Franklin's *Satires and Bagatelles* (Fine Book Circle, 1937). Between 1935 and 1938 McPharlin served as publisher in the Fine Book Circle of Detroit. He was a member of the American Institute of Graphic Arts, which often included his books in their Fifty Books of the Year exhibit. He wrote articles for numerous periodicals, including *American Artist, American Printer, Theatre Arts,* and *Magazine of Art,* and was a contributing editor to *Publishers Weekly.* McPharlin owned the largest private library on the field of puppetry in the United States, which he bequeathed, along with his extensive collection of puppets, to the Detroit Institute of Arts. *Residence:* Birmingham, Mich. *For More Information See: Current Biography Yearbook, 1945,* H. W. Wilson, 1946. *Obituaries: New York Herald Tribune,* October 1, 1948; *New York Times,* October 1, 1948; *Publishers Weekly,* October 9, 1948.

McWHIRTER, A(lan) Ross   1925-1975

OBITUARY NOTICE: Born August 12, 1925, in London, England; died of gunshot wounds suffered in an Irish Republican Army terrorist attack, November 27, 1975, in London, England. A former publisher and newspaper reporter, McWhirter, together with his brother Norris, established and compiled the popular *Guinness Book of Records.* Since the age of ten, the McWhirter twins collected reference materials as a hobby. Following their graduation from Oxford University, they began to make a career out of their hobby, and opened a fact-finding office. The brothers were approached by Guinness Brewery with the idea for the book of trivia. The book is now among the world's all-time best-selling copyrighted books with sales exceeding 85,000 copies per week. It is published in a variety of languages, including Japanese, Czech, Dutch, and Portuguese. Other compilations that McWhirter published include *The Guinness Book of Daring Deeds and Fascinating Facts, The Guinness Book of Astounding Feats and Events, The Guinness Book of Extraordinary Exploits,* and *The Guinness Book of Phenomenal Happenings. For More Information See: Publishers Weekly,* April 15, 1968; *Contemporary Authors,* Volumes 17-20, revised, Gale, 1976. *Obituaries: Washington Post,* November 28, November 29, 1975; *New York Times,* November 29, 1975; *Newsweek,* December 8, 1975; *Publishers Weekly,* December 8, 1975; *Time,* December 8, 1975; *AB Bookman's Weekly,* December 22, 1975; *Bookseller,* January 17, 1976.

MERIWETHER, Louise   1923-

BRIEF ENTRY: Born May 8, 1923, in Haverstraw, N.Y. A free-lance writer and former newspaper reporter, Meriwether is a graduate of New York University and the University of California—Los Angeles. Among her books for young readers are *The Freedom Ship of Robert Smalls* (Prentice-Hall, 1971), *Heart Man: Dr. Daniel Hale Williams* (Prentice-Hall, 1972), and *Don't Ride the Bus on Mondays: The Rosa Parks Story* (Prentice-Hall, 1973). She is also the author of the adult novel *Daddy Was a Number Runner* (Prentice-Hall, 1970). A former legal secretary, Meriwether has worked as a reporter for the *Los Angeles Sentinel* and as a story analyst for Universal Studios. She has contributed short stories and articles to numerous periodicals, including *Antioch Review, Negro Digest,* and *Essence.* Much of her work appears in various anthologies. *Address:* 1691 East 174th St., Apt. 7D, Bronx, N.Y. 10472. *For More Information See: Ebony,* September, 1966, July, 1970; *Jet,* November 12, 1970; *The Ebony Success Library,* Volume 1: *1000 Successful Blacks,* Johnson, 1973; *Contemporary Authors,* Volumes 77-80, Gale, 1979; *In Black and White,* Gale, 1980.

MILLER, Albert G(riffith)   1905-1982

OBITUARY NOTICE—See sketch in *SATA* Volume 12: Born December 28, 1905, in Philadelphia, Pa.; died after a long illness, June 25, 1982, in New York. Playwright, scriptwriter, and author of books for children. In 1928 Miller began working as a radio scriptwriter for N. W. Ayer and Son. He wrote material for major advertising accounts as well as for such celebrities as Fred Allen, Ben Bernie, and Boris Karloff. He was the author of numerous books for children, including *My Friend the Dragon, The Wishing Ring, Mark Twain in Love, Backward Beasts from A to Z,* over fifteen "Pop-up" books, and three "Talk-to-Me" books. He was also the adapter of

classics such as *The Wizard of Oz, Alice in Wonderland,* and *The Emperor's New Clothes.* As a playwright, Miller wrote two plays on the advertising industry which reflected his personal experiences in the business, "The Sellout," which opened on Broadway in 1933, and the 1950 musical "The Shaggy Dog." He also wrote several feature-length screenplays as well as a number of scripts for television. *For More Information See: Contemporary Authors,* New Revision Series, Volume 1, Gale, 1981. *Obituaries: New York Times,* June 29, 1982.

MOSER, Donald Bruce   1932-
(Don Moser)

PERSONAL: Born October 19, 1932, in Cleveland, Ohio; son of Donald Lyman and Kathryn (McHugh) Moser; married Penny Lee Ward (a journalist), December 20, 1975. *Education:* Ohio University, B.A., 1957; graduate study at Stanford University, 1957-58, and University of Sydney, 1959-60. *Agent:* Curtis Brown Ltd., 575 Madison Ave., New York, N.Y. 10022. *Office:* Smithsonian Magazine, 900 Jefferson Dr., Washington, D.C. 20007.

CAREER: Life, New York, N.Y., writer and reporter, 1961-64, West Coast bureau chief, 1964-65, Far East bureau chief, 1966-69, assistant managing editor, 1970-72; *Smithsonian,* Washington, D.C., managing editor, 1978-80, editor, 1980—. *Military service:* U.S. Army, 1953-55. *Member:* Phi Beta Kappa. *Awards, honors:* Stegner fellowship, 1957; Fulbright scholarship, 1959; *A Heart to the Hawks* was named to the Hans Christian Andersen honor list, 1979.

WRITINGS—All under name Don Moser: *The Peninsula: A Story of the Olympic Country in Words and Photographs,* Sierra Books, 1962; (with Jerry Cohen) *The Pied Piper of Tucson,* New American Library, 1968; (with the editors of Time-Life Books) *The Snake River Country* (juvenile), Time-Life, 1974; (with the editors of Time-Life Books) *Central American Jungles* (juvenile; photographs by C. Rentmeester), Time-Life, 1975; *A Heart to the Hawks* (juvenile novel), Atheneum, 1975; *China-Burma-India Theater,* Time-Life, 1977.

Contributor of articles to periodicals such as *Life, National Geographic, Smithsonian, Audubon, Harper's, Sports Illustrated,* and *American Heritage.*

WORK IN PROGRESS: A novel for young adults.

SIDELIGHTS: Moser's interest in our natural environment began in Ohio, where he spent his youth. An avowed bird watcher, Moser used to collect birds' eggs from his neighborhood woods as a young teenager.

His interest in nature continued through his college days. He worked as a forest service fire lookout in northern Idaho, and as a seasonal ranger and naturalist in Grand Teton National Park. "When I went west . . . to work as a lookout and smoke-chaser in the St. Joe National Forest in Idaho, it was the glamour of fighting fire that drew me like a magnet, as it has drawn thousands of young men and women before and since. We practiced the skills we learned at the district's fire school, and we listened reverently to tales of derring-do of the elite smoke-jumpers and hotshot crews. As the midsummer forest grew bone-dry and the lightning-filled anvilheads drifted over the mountains like battleships, we got edgy with anticipation. We built trails, piled slash, and pulled maintenance details around the station, but that was just filling in time. We were waiting for the moment when the bull cook would clang the bell and the ranger alternate, who had a flair for the dramatic, would come out and say, 'Let's go boys—there's fire on the mountain.'" [Don Moser, "New Fire on the Mountain," *Audubon* magazine, September, 1974.]

After receiving his B.A. at Ohio University, Moser did graduate work at Stanford and later at the University of Sydney (Australia) on a Fulbright scholarship. For twelve years he worked as a writer, reporter, and managing editor of *Life* magazine. On leave from *Life* in the early '60s, he served as special assistant to the U.S. Secretary of Interior, Stewart Udall. Presently, he is executive editor of *Smithsonian* magazine and the author of several books about the environment as well as a fiction book for children about conservation of our natural resources, *A Heart to the Hawks*.

FOR MORE INFORMATION SEE: Life, November 8, 1963, January 22, 1971; *Audubon*, September, 1974.

MOSS, Elaine Dora   1924-

BRIEF ENTRY: Born in London, England, in 1924. Moss is an author, editor, and critic of books for children. She has been employed as a director of children's books reviews for *Spectator* and as a writer for several publications, including *The Times "Saturday Review"* and *Children's Book News.* Her books for children include *Twirly*, 1963, *The Wait and See Book*, 1964, and *Polar*, 1975. From 1970 to 1979 she was the editor of the National Book League and British Council's *Children's Books of the Year.* Throughout her career, she has edited several books on reading material for children, among them *Reading for Enjoyment: Two to Five Year Olds*, 1970, *From Morn to Midnight*, a collection of children's verse, 1977, and *Picture Books for Young People: Nine to Thirteen*, 1981, as well as a 1961 edition of *Gulliver's Travels.* Her reviews on children's books have appeared in *Sunday Times, Times Educational Supplement, Times Literary Supplement, Signal,* and others.

POWERS, Bill   1931-

BRIEF ENTRY: Born February 3, 1931, in Brooklyn, N.Y. A free-lance writer and photographer, Powers attended Pratt Institute and Mexico City College. He has written many books for children and young adult readers, including *The Weekend* (F. Watts, 1978), *Love Lost, and Found* (F. Watts, 1979), and *A Test of Love* (F. Watts, 1979). Also an illustrator of children's books, Powers has illustrated Donald Honig's *Breaking In* (F. Watts, 1974), *Playing for Keeps* (F. Watts, 1974), *Going the Distance* (F. Watts, 1976), among others. Powers has worked as a free-lance commercial artist in New York City and was at one time theatrical director of the Second City Players. While with Second City he was the recipient of an Obie Award, given by the *Village Voice* for excellence in off-Broadway and off off-Broadway productions. Powers is a member of the American Society of Magazine Photographers and was a sergeant in the U.S. Air Force in the 1950s. *Address:* 72 Barrow St., New York, N.Y. 10014. *For More Information See: Contemporary Authors*, Volumes 77-80, Gale, 1979.

ROBINSON, Nancy K(onheim)   1942-

BRIEF ENTRY: Born August 12, 1942, in New York, N.Y. Robinson is a free-lance writer and researcher, and an author of children's books. She is a member of several professional organizations, including Authors Guild, Authors League of America, PEN American Center, and American Society of Picture Professionals. In 1981 she received the Four-Leaf Clover Award from Scholastic Book Services "in recognition of her contribution to the reading pleasure of seven and eight year olds." Her books, all for children, include *Jungle Laboratory: The Story of Ray Carpenter and the Howling Monkeys* (nonfiction), *Wendy and the Bullies, Just Plain Cat, Mom, You're Fired,* and *Veronica the Show-Off.* Robinson is also the author of a PBS-TV documentary, "Men of Bronze." *Residence:* New York, N.Y.

ROSE, Carl   1903-1971
(Earl Cros)

BRIEF ENTRY: Born in 1903; died June 20, 1971, in Rowayton, Conn. Rose, a native New Yorker, was a cartoonist and illustrator whose career spanned more than forty-five years. He began working professionally in 1925 when one of his cartoons was published in the *New Yorker.* The magazine published over six hundred of his cartoons throughout his career. His work appeared in numerous periodicals, including *Collier's Weekly, Saturday Evening Post,* and *Cosmopolitan.* For twenty years, he was the illustrator and, at times, writer for the *Atlantic Monthly's* section on humor, "Accent on Living." Rose's most famous cartoon, published in the *New Yorker* in 1928, depicts a small child refusing to eat spinach with a gag line that quickly made "spinach" synonymous with "distasteful" for his many followers.

From 1927 to 1929 he contributed Sunday features and editorial cartoons to the *New York World*, and from 1929 to 1932 he was a political cartoonist for the *Boston Herald.* Under the pseudonym Earl Cros, he illustrated "Our New Age," a syndicated Sunday newspaper feature on the advancements of science. In 1946 Rose published *One Dozen Roses*, a collection of his cartoons previously seen in various periodicals. For children he wrote and illustrated *The Crazy Zoo that Dudley Drew*, 1963. He also illustrated Margaret Embry's *Blue-Nosed Witch*, 1956, and Maxine W. Kamin's *The Wonderful Babies of 1809 and Other Years*, 1968. In all, he illustrated over fifty books for children and adults, including George Jessel's *Hello Momma*, Richard Grossman's *A New Leash on Life*, and Bennett A. Cerf's *Book of Laughs.*

FOR MORE INFORMATION SEE: The World Encyclopedia of Cartoons, Volume 2, Gale, 1980. Obituaries: *New York Times*, June 22, 1971; *New Yorker*, July 3, 1971; *Newsweek*, July 5, 1971.

We can never know that a piece of writing is bad unless we have begun by trying to read it as if it was very good and ended by discovering that we were paying the author an undeserved compliment.

—C.S. Lewis

ROWLAND-ENTWISTLE, (Arthur) Theodore (Henry) 1925- (John Briquebec, Anyon Ellis, James Hall-Clarke, T. E. Henry, J. T. Lawrence)

PERSONAL: Born July 30, 1925, in Clayton-le-Moors, Lancashire, England; son of Arthur (an author and journalist) and Sylvia Morton (a teacher; maiden name, Clarke) Rowland-Entwistle; married Jean Isobel Esther Cooke (a writer and editor), March 18, 1968. *Education:* Downsend School, Leatherhead; Open University, B.A., 1977. *Religion:* Church of England. *Home:* West Dene, Stonestile Lane, Hastings, East Sussex TN35 4PE, England. *Agent:* Rupert Crew Ltd., King's Mews, Gray's Inn Rd., London WC1N 2JA, England.

CAREER: Daily Mail, Manchester and London, England, sub-editor, 1944-55; *TV Times,* London, chief sub-editor, 1955-56, production editor, 1956-61, assistant editor, 1961; *World Book Encyclopedia,* London, senior editor, 1961-67; Leander Associates Ltd. (an editorial agency), director, 1967-69; First Features Ltd. (a newspaper features agency), director, 1972-79. *Member:* Royal Geographical Society (fellow), Zoological Society of London (fellow).

WRITINGS—All of interest to young people: *Teach Yourself the Violin,* English Universities Press, 1967, published as *Violin,* McKay, 1974; (editor) Paddy Hopkirk, *The Longest Drive of All: Paddy Hopkirk's Story of the London-Sydney Motor Rally* (illustrated by John C. Smith), Geoffrey Chapman, 1969; (under name John Briquebec) *Winston Churchill,* McGraw, 1972; *Napoleon,* Hart-Davis, 1973; *Facts and Records Book*

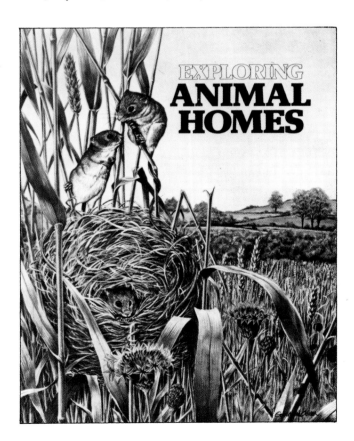

(From *Animal Homes* by Theodore Rowland-Entwistle. Cover illustrated by Graham Allen.)

THEODORE ROWLAND-ENTWISTLE

of Animals, Purnell, 1975; *The World You Never See: Insect Life,* Rand McNally, 1976; *Our Earth,* World Distributor, 1977; *The Restless Earth,* Purnell, 1977; *Exploring Animal Homes* (illustrated by Graham Allen and others), Watts, 1978; *Exploring Animal Journeys* (illustrated by G. Allen and others), Watts, 1978; *Let's Look at Wild Animals,* Jennifer Justice, editor (illustrated by Mike Atkinson), Ward Lock, 1978; *Habits and Habitats: Insects,* World Distributor, 1979; *Natural Wonders of the World,* Octopus, 1980; *The Illustrated Atlas of the Bible Lands,* Longman, 1981; *Ancient World,* Galley Press, 1981; (under name John Briquebec) *Animals and Man,* Purnell, 1982; (under name Anyon Ellis) *Wild Animals,* Granada, 1982; (under name John Briquebec) *Trees,* Granada, 1982; (under name J. T. Lawrence) *Fossils,* Granada, 1982; *Insects,* Granada, 1983; (under name T. E. Henry) *The Seashore,* Granada, 1983; (under name James Hall-Clarke) *Fishes,* Granada, 1983.

With wife, Jean Cooke: *Animal Worlds* (illustrated by Bernard Robinson and others), Sampson Low, 1974, Watts, 1976; *Famous Composers,* David & Charles, 1974; *Famous Explorers,* David & Charles, 1974; *Famous Kings and Emperors,* David & Charles, 1976; (with Ann Kramer) *World of History,* Hamlyn, 1977; (editors) *The Junior General Knowledge Encyclopedia,* foreword by Magnus Magnusson, Octopus, 1978; (editors) *Purnell's Concise Encyclopedia of the Arts,* Purnell, 1979; (editors) *Purnell's Pictorial Encyclopedia,* Purnell, 1979; (editors) *Purnell's Pictorial Encyclopedia of Nature*, Purnell, 1980; (with A. Kramer) *History Factfinder*, Ward Lock, 1981.

Contributor of articles and consultant to encyclopedias, including *New Junior World Encyclopedia, Encyclopedia of Wild Life, Apollo Encyclopedia, Modern Century Illustrated Encyclopedia, Encyclopedia of Africa, Encyclopedia of Inventions, Concise Encyclopedia of Geography, Concise Encyclopedia of History, Rainbow Encyclopedia,* and *Pictorial Encyclopedia of History.* Contributor of articles and consultant to atlases, including *St. Michael Atlas of World Geography* and *My First Picture Atlas.*

Editor, *Hastings Talking Newspaper for the Blind*, 1981—. Contributor of articles to periodicals, including *Mind Alive* and *The Woodworker.* Contributor of crossword puzzles to periodicals. Contributor of questions to television programs, including "It's Your Word," BBC, 1971 and "Brainchild," BBC, 1972.

WORK IN PROGRESS: The Sub-Editor's Craft, completion expected in 1985; *Selected Poems*, completion expected in 1986.

SIDELIGHTS: "Apart from my unpublished poetry, I am a non-creative writer. I produce reference material for young people and non-specialist adults. Consequently, my main objectives are accuracy and clarity.

"I would recommend the discipline of sub-editing for a national newspaper as training for any writer—but don't stick at it too long.

"I am fortunate to be able to collaborate with my wife on most of my work.

"It's an added bonus to be able to use my training as a journalist in the service of the blind. I enjoy this voluntary work enormously. As with my career work, I do this in collaboration with my wife, whose years as a studio manager with the BBC complement my own experience for making tapes."

SAVILLE, (Leonard) Malcolm   1901-1982

OBITUARY NOTICE—See sketch in *SATA* Volume 23: Born February 21, 1901, in Hastings, Sussex, England; died June 30, 1982, in Hastings. Publicist, editor, and author of more than eighty books for children. Saville worked in the publicity departments of several British publishers, including Oxford University Press, from the 1920s until 1936. While serving in World War II he wrote his first children's story, *Mystery at Witchend.* The novel introduced the Lone Piners, a group of youngsters whose adventures became the subject of twenty subsequent books, the last of which was *Home to Witchend* in 1978. More than two million volumes of the "Witchend" series have been sold since 1943. During the 1960s Saville issued the "Marston Baines" series about a secret agent fighting to halt drug traffic. The seven-book series of thrillers was aimed at an eleven-to-twelve-year-old audience, and was intended to provide the excitement of adult novels without explicit sex and violence. In addition to his novels for children, Saville published several nonfiction books about gardening and a biography of Jesus Christ entitled *King of Kings. For More Information See:* Brian Doyle, *The Who's Who of Children's Literature*, Schocken Books, 1968; *Who Was Who among English and European Authors, 1921-1939*, Gale, 1976; *Twen-*

tieth Century Children's Writers, St. Martin's, 1978; *Sussex Life*, September, 1978; *The Writers Directory, 1982-84*, Gale, 1981. *Obituaries: London Times*, July 3, 1982.

SCHATZKI, Walter   1899-

BRIEF ENTRY: Born August 26, 1899, in Klafeld, Westphalia, Germany; became a U.S. citizen, 1943. A book dealer and collector, Schatzki is the compiler of *Old and Rare Children's Books* (1941, reprinted, Gale, 1974), a catalogue that is an important tool in the antiquarian book field. Schatzki became interested in books at an early age. Inspired by an aunt who often received materials from bookstores in neighboring Cologne, Schatzki took a job with one of the booksellers in that city while still a high school student. In 1919 he became involved with the group Wanderbuchhandlung, whose members traveled to small towns and villages to sell books. Schatzki, who was also a fiddle player, traveled into the remote areas of central Germany, playing his fiddle at the country fairs and selling his books. At the age of twenty, and with an inheritance from his aunt, Schatzki opened his first bookstore in Frankfurt. There he began to assemble an extensive collection of old and rare children's books, many of which he bought at auctions for a fraction of their value. The collection has been exhibited in the United States and was eventually purchased by the New York Public Library. A recognized expert in his field, Schatzki has lectured widely and served as a consultant for many book collectors. *Residence:* New York, N.Y. *For More Information See: Who's Who in the East*, 16th edition, Marquis, 1977.

JOEL SCHICK

They was two great big Black Things
a-standin' by her side.

(From *The Gobble-uns'll Git You Ef You Don't Watch Out!* by James Whitcomb Riley.
Illustrated by Joel Schick.)

SCHICK, Joel 1945-

PERSONAL: Born May 27, 1945, in Chicago, Ill.; son of
Henry (a printer) and Muriel (Peterson) Schick; married Alice
Raffer (a children's author), June 22, 1967; children: Morgan.
Education: Attended Northwestern University, 1963-64 and
Augustana College, 1964-65; Roosevelt University, B.A., 1968.
Home: P.O. Box 101, Monterey, Mass. 01245.

CAREER: Author and illustrator of books for young people.
Has worked as an art director and book designer.

WRITINGS—All for children, except as noted; all self-illus-
trated: *Undertoe at Dawn* (adult), privately printed, 1968; *El-
bow Thumdowdy* (poetry; adult), privately printed, 1972; *Joel
Schick's Christmas Present* (poetry), Lippincott, 1977; (with
wife, Alice Schick) *Viola Hates Music,* Lippincott, 1977; (with
A. Schick) *Just This Once,* Lippincott, 1978; (with A. Schick)
Santaberry and the Snard, Lippincott, 1979; (reteller with A.
Schick) *Frankenstein,* Dell, 1980; (reteller with A. Schick)
Dracula, Delacorte, 1980.

Illustrator; all for children, except as noted: Rozanne R. Knud-
son, *Jesus Song,* Delacorte, 1973; Malcolm Hall, *Derek Koo-
gar Was a Star,* Coward, 1975; M. Hall, *The Electric Book,*
Coward, 1975; Tillie S. Pine and Joseph Levine, *Energy All
Around,* McGraw, 1975; James W. Riley, *The Gobble-Uns'll
Git You Ef You Don't Watch Out!,* Lippincott, 1975; Alfred
Slote, *My Robot Buddy,* Lippincott, 1975; Marjorie N. and

Carl Allen, *Farley, Are You for Real?,* Coward, 1976; William
H. Hooks, *The Seventeen Gerbils of Class 4A,* Coward, 1976;
T. Pine and J. Levine, *The Arabs Knew,* McGraw, 1976; A.
Schick and M. Allen, *The Remarkable Ride of Israel Bissel,
as Related by Molly the Crow,* Lippincott, 1976; A. Schick,
The Siamang Gibbons: An Ape Family, Follett, 1976; Wilma
Shore, *Who in the Zoo?,* Lippincott, 1976; David C. Knight,
Dinosaur Days, McGraw, 1977; A. Schick, *Serengeti Cats,*
Lippincott, 1977; Seymour Reit and Alvin Cooperman, *The
Fourth King,* Marble Arch, 1977.

Elizabeth James and Carol Barkin, *How to Keep a Secret:
Writing and Talking in Code,* Lothrop, 1978; E. James and C.
Barkin, *What Do You Mean by "Average"?: Means, Medians,
and Modes,* Lothrop, 1978; T. Pine and J. Levine, *Scientists
and Their Discoveries,* McGraw, 1978; A. Schick and Sara
Ann Friedman, *Zoo Year,* Lippincott, 1978; Victoria Gomez,
Scream Cheese and Jelly: Jokes, Riddles, and Puns, Lothrop,
1979; E. James and C. Barkin, *How to Grow a Hundred Dollars,* Lothrop, 1979; Terry Wolfe Phelan, *The Week Mom Un-
plugged the TVs,* Four Winds Press, 1979; Jane Thayer (pseudonym of Catherine Wooley), *Try Your Hand,* Morrow, 1979;
V. Gomez, *Wags to Witches: More Jokes, Riddles, and Puns,*
Morrow, 1980; Thomas Rockwell, *How to Eat Fried Worms,
and Other Plays,* Delacorte, 1980; Beverly Conrad, *Kitty Tales*
(adult), Delta, 1980; B. Conrad, *Doggy Tales* (adult), Delta,
1980; Phyllis Green, *Bagdad Ate It,* Watts, 1980; Anita Gustafson, *Burrowing Birds,* Morrow, 1981; Patricia Elmore, *Su-
sannah and the Poison-Green Halloween,* Dutton, 1982. Art

Santa was so pleased that he made the Snard an honorary reindeer. ■ (From *Santaberry and the Snard* by Alice and Joel Schick. Illustrated by Joel Schick.)

director and principal illustrator of *3 To Get Ready* (Sunday newspaper supplement), 1980-81.

WORK IN PROGRESS: Doggy Dramas, a comic strip and *The Mummy*, both with A. Schick.

SIDELIGHTS: Schick grew up in Maywood, Illinois, spending much time in his father's print shop. At age eleven he published a humor magazine, *Angry*. He enjoyed television movies, especially his heroes, Hitchcock and Ford, who were great visual story-tellers.

While in college he published his first book, *Undertoe at Dawn*, which he printed at night in his father's shop. Before starting his career as an illustrator he worked as a book designer and art director.

Schick and his wife, Alice, a children's author, have collaborated in their work. ''We both love animals, and some of my favorite work is illustrating Alice's nature books. We also enjoy working together to create unified picture books for all ages, books in which neither words nor pictures can stand alone, but which communicate as a whole.

''Illustration is storytelling by someone who can draw. *Good* illustration is storytelling by someone who respects and loves children and can draw. Media, economics, scheduling—all

these are secondary. A good illustrator will produce good illustration even if he has to carve it out of a potato and print it with a stamp pad. Telling a good story to a good audience is the prime concern.'' [Lee Kingman and others, compilers, *Illustrators of Children's Books: 1967-1976*, Horn Book, 1978.]

FOR MORE INFORMATION SEE: Lee Kingman and others, compilers, *Illustrators of Children's Books: 1967-1976*, Horn Book, 1978.

Read not to contradict and confute, nor yet to believe and take for granted, nor to find talk and discourse, but to weigh and consider.

—Francis Bacon
(From *Of Studies*)

Reading furnishes our mind only with materials of knowledge; it is thinking makes what we read ours.

—John Locke
(From *An Essay Concerning Human Understanding*)

SCHILLER, Justin G.   1943-

BRIEF ENTRY: Born in 1943. Bookseller, reviewer, critic, and specialist in historical children's books. Schiller began his career as a bookseller and collector at a very early age. When he was only ten years old, he began collecting the books of L. Frank Baum, author of *The Wizard of Oz.* At the age of twelve he lent the Columbia University Library several books from his personal collection for its Baum exhibition. He founded the International Wizard of Oz Club when he was fourteen. In the early 1960s Schiller was invited by Howard S. Mott, then the chief dealer in Baum's works, to assist him and his wife Phyllis, at the annual antiquarian book fairs held in New York. Now a bookseller in New York City, Schiller served as one of three judges in selecting the 1973 *New York Times* Choice of Best Illustrated Children's Books of the Year. He is co-editor, with Alison Lurie, of the series "Classics of Children's Literature,. 1621-1932," which includes Robert Ballantyne's *The Coral Island,* Martha Finley's *Elsie Dinsmore, The History of Tom Thumb,* Charles Perrault's *Histories; or, Tales of Past Times,* and Oscar Wilde's *The Happy Prince and Other Tales.* Schiller also wrote the text for *The Doll House,* a reproduction of Lothar Meggendorfer's pop-up book *Das Puppenhaus. For More Information See: Hobbies,* September, 1957; *Horn Book,* October, 1973.

SCOTT, Jack Denton   1915-

PERSONAL: Born in 1915; married Maria Luisa Scott. *Residence:* Washington, Connecticut.

CAREER: Writer. Former syndicated columnist on outdoor life and dog editor for *Field and Stream. Awards, honors:* American Institute of Graphic Arts Book Show award, 1976, for *Discovering the American Stork.*

WRITINGS—For children; all illustrated by Ozzie Sweet, except where noted: *Loggerhead Turtle: Survivor from the Sea,* Putnam, 1974; *The Survivors: Enduring Animals of North America* (illustrated by Daphne Gillen), Harcourt, 1975; *That Wonderful Pelican,* Putnam, 1975; *Canada Geese* (Junior Literary Guild selection), Putnam, 1976; *Discovering the American Stork,* Harcourt, 1976; *Return of the Buffalo,* Putnam, 1976; *The Gulls of Smuttynose Island* (Junior Literary Guild selection), Putnam, 1977; *Little Dogs of the Prairie,* Putnam, 1977; *City of Birds and Beasts: Behind the Scenes at the Bronx Zoo,* Putnam, 1978; *Discovering the Mysterious Egret* (illustrated by Pamela S. Distler), Harcourt, 1978; *Island of Wild Horses* (Junior Literary Guild selection), Putnam, 1978; *The Book of the Goat* (Junior Literary Guild selection), Putnam, 1979; *The Submarine Bird* (Junior Literary Guild selection), Putnam, 1979; *The Book of The Pig,* Putnam, 1981; *The Sea File,* McGraw, 1981; *Moose,* Putnam, 1981; *Orphans from the Sea,* Putnam, 1982.

Other: (With Anne Damer) *Too Lively to Live,* Doubleday, 1943; *The Weimaraner,* Fawcett-Dearing Printing, 1953; *All Outdoors: Hunting and Fishing with the Author of America's Largest Outdoor Column,* Stackpole, 1956; (editor) *Your Dog's Health Book,* Macmillan, 1956; *Forests of the Night* (photographs by wife, Maria Luisa Scott), Rinehart, 1959; *How to Write and Sell for the Out-of-Doors,* Macmillan, 1962; *The Duluth Mongoose* (illustrated by Lydia Fruhauf), Morrow, 1965; *Passport to Adventure* (photographs by M. L. Scott), Random House, 1966; *Speaking Wildly* (illustrated by Lydia Rosier), Morrow, 1966; *Elephant Grass,* Harcourt, 1969; *Spargo: A*

For the most part, during the first ten days there is no association between other mares and foals, although they may be within yards of one another. ■ (From *Island of Wild Horses* by Jack Denton Scott. Photograph by Ozzie Sweet.)

Novel of Espionage, World Publishing, 1971; *Journey into Silence,* Reader's Digest Press, 1976.

Cookbooks: *The Complete Book of Pasta: An Italian Cookbook* (illustrated by Melvin Klapholz; photographs by Samuel Chamberlain), Morrow, 1968; (with Antoine Gilly) *Antoine Gilly's Feast of France: A Cookbook of Masterpieces in French Cuisine* (illustrated by William Teodecki), Crowell, 1971; (with M. L. Scott) *Informal Dinners for Easy Entertaining: Over 150 Easy but Elegant Meals You Can Eat with a Fork,* Simon & Schuster, 1975; (with M. L. Scott) *Cook Like a Peasant, Eat Like a King,* Follett, 1976; (with M. L. Scott) *Mastering Microwave Cooking,* Bantam, 1976; (with M. L. Scott) *A World of Pasta: Unique Pasta Recipes from Around the World,* McGraw, 1978; (with M. L. Scott) *The Great Potato Cookbook,* Bantam, 1980; (with M. L. Scott) *The Chicken and Egg Cookbook,* Bantam, 1981; (with M. L. Scott) *The Complete Convection Oven Cookbook,* Bantam, 1981.

Contributor of articles to periodicals, including *Colliers, Saturday Evening Post, Cosmopolitan, Audubon, Redbook, Coronet, Reader's Digest, Holiday, Outdoor Life, National Wildlife, International Wildlife,* and *Smithsonian.*

SIDELIGHTS: Scott wrote his first short story when he was sixteen. Three years later he had his first article published in a national magazine and has been a professional writer ever since. "I have what you might call a wide range, novels, natural history, travel, essays, cookbooks, adventure, and children's books. I have been a war correspondent in World War II—in Europe, Egypt, and Africa—traveling with soldiers and fliers.

I was shot down over England and landed, unharmed, in the ocean near Land's End. My wife and I have been around the world more than a dozen times, particularly liking the off-the-beaten-track places. From 1959 to 1964 we traveled over 600,000 miles.''

''Although I have written [several] books . . . ranging from a travel book, *Passport to Adventure* [written in 1966], that took me five years and more than 500,000 miles of foreign travel to complete, to *The Complete Book of Pasta,* an Italian cookbook, which (and, which, incidentally, I wrote because I consider cooking an art and it is an ardent hobby) also took five years to put together and is a first in the cookbook world, what I always wanted to be since age twelve was a novelist. And the more I wrote (for most of the major magazines, also a syndicated newspaper column) the more I knew that what I really wanted from my art, my craft, my profession, was to be a story teller. I wanted the freedom of the novelist, the ability to get behind the eyes, the facade of the people, and tell what they were really like. I wanted to shine the bright novelist's light into the dark places to show what they were really like.

''You might say that travel—and the hundreds of thousands of nonfiction words I have published—made me a novelist. Just as a doctor, a lawyer, a musician, must study and prepare and practice and work in his field before he attains sure skill and eventual success, so did I feel the need to work with words to prepare myself for my chosen field of novelist. Thus, I wrote (among others) a juvenile, an animal book, a book of essays of the natural world, a travel book, a cookbook, all nationally reviewed well, even enthusiastically. Naturally, this brought some confidence—and . . . I felt I was ready and went to the south of Spain and did the first draft of my first novel *Elephant Grass* [1969].

''It took four more drafts and another year (I am fortunate in having as literary agent a man who has a keen, even brilliant insight into what a novel needs, and also one of the top editors in the publishing field) and expert help before the novel was ready and I was bleeding inside with what I had torn out of myself to make my book and its people alive. I discovered that writing a novel was much tougher than writing a book of nonfiction. In nonfiction, polish, solid research and letting the facts speak for themselves go a long way toward success. In a novel, well, vast research is also necessary, but so also is the ability to *think.* If you cannot concentrate completely and lose yourself in your created world, if you cannot truly think, you cannot write a novel. . . .

''Travel, getting to intimately know places and people you write about, is important. In my case, in *Elephant Grass,* I wrote about the foothills of the Himalayas, an extremely wild region that to my knowledge had never been the background of a novel. So I lived there for a time with the aboriginal people, even went tiger hunting with parties to get the feel and knowledge of that 'sport.' Out of it came the novel, wherein I believe that my heart lies with the wounded tiger and my enmity with the careless killers who call big game hunting a sport. Basically that is the book. But also I wanted to have Indians and Americans meet, get to know one another, fall in love, I wanted to 'get behind the eyes' of these people, for me that is the singular art of the novelist. I hope that I have done this, gotten into their secret lives, made them live—and above all, I hope that I have made them interesting.

''For without a reader there is no writer. Thus my aim is to entertain—and inform. But first to entertain, make my work,

my people, my plots, my scenes, MOVE—give my writing thrust that will carry a reader along, MAKE him want to read on and finish my books. Too seldom is this done today. Done honestly and with talent. This so-called Black Humor that is upon us uses filth and shallowness and a spitting upon beliefs to try to achieve this. I think talent and having a story to tell and telling it well have been with us for a long time and will outlast the freaks who call their work writing. I call it typing. Examples of books I believe will sweep the bad out of existence are *Red Sky at Morning* and *True Grit.*

''Reading has influenced me. I read constantly. But I can think of no writer who has had any great influence upon me. Perhaps Graham Greene. He writes with great clarity, with deep insight. He researches beautifully. His people live. He makes you think.

''[I now] live in Washington, Connecticut. [I was] brought up in Elmira, New York . . . [I] am married (Maria Luisa); we both are owned by two Siamese cats, Shan and Thai-Shan, the color of a natural mink we brought with us from Bangkok.'' [*Library Journal,* February 1, 1969.[1]]

Besides writing, Scott is a naturalist whose children's books reflect this interest. About *Canada Geese,* a natural photo-essay illustrated by Ozzie Sweet, he said: ''The Canada goose is my favorite bird, embodying all that is mysterious, romantic, and exciting about the wilderness. I began concentrating on the goose seriously in 1957, when I was writing my three-times-a-week column, 'Adventure Unlimited,' for the New York Herald Tribune Syndicate. I followed the flights of Canadas from Hudson Bay in the far north, to a mesa in Mexico. They were the subject of my first column in that series.''

Scott gave credit to Ozzie Sweet's wife, Diane, for inspiring another of his nature books, *The Submarine Bird.* ''Like everyone else, she had seen cormorants in many places and wondered what they were. Once at Nag's Head on the Outer Banks, I stood on the beach watching a flock of cormorants fishing in concert. Others beside me were referring to them as black ducks or funny geese. Very few ever seem able to identify them, even though they are probably our oldest bird. But while there at Nag's Head I did meet a fisherman who told me he had caught a cormorant in his net over 200 feet below the surface, 'where he had gone chasin' my fish!'

''I have seen one species of cormorant or another in many places: Japan, the Arctic, Long Island, North Carolina, Virginia, but not until Diane Sweet suggested it did Ozzie and I zero in on them. One of those zeroing-ins was dramatic. The Sweets, my wife, and I went to the Isles of Shoals, a group of islands ten miles straight out in the Atlantic from the coast of Maine. We were heading to visit a 'cormorant rock' noted along that coast as a breeding place. We stayed at Appledore Island, where Cornell University has a marine lab, and took a boat from there, courtesy of Cornell, to the cormorant rock. It was aptly named; a barren, rocky island towering out of the sea, nothing on it, little vegetation, the only objects cormorants and their constant tormentors, gulls.

''Ozzie used his cameras, even though it was raining hard; and we studied the birds, nests, young, attitude of gulls, etc., until a fierce storm began. Then we huddled under a rock, waiting for the boat to come. It didn't come; the sea was wild, great waves breaking over the island, the wind increasing. It was hours later that we finally saw a boat riding the top of the waves. The officials on Appledore had asked for volunteers to come get us. It was one brave guy, a Norwegian who had learned his seamanship in the rough waters off his own rocky

With their thick coats and hardiness, the buffalo have lived through blizzards that froze lesser animals. ▪ (From *Return of the Buffalo* by Jack Denton Scott. Photograph by Ozzie Sweet.)

Pigs are superb mothers. ■(From *The Book of the Pig* by Jack Denton Scott. Photograph by Ozzie Sweet.)

country. We'll never forget that ride back. Rough! Skipping and bouncing from wave to wave. Norway may be my favorite country."

One of his latest children's books, also illustrated by Sweet, is *The Book of the Goat.* "In the Canary Islands I have bought goat milk from a man who led his goat to my door and milked her into a bowl I gave him. In India, a Sarat goat was the friend of a trained hunting elephant, Kali. So close were elephant and goat that the elephant wouldn't go afield unless the goat was on her back. I have watched goats climb trees in Morocco, carry packs in the Himalayas, and over the years I have come to respect them very much. They are highly intelligent and appealing—and maligned. All of the old views of the goat are prejudiced: they are unruly, like to butt people, are dirty and love to scrabble in the local dump, etc.

"So I researched the goat and found that there never had been a complete book on them, that they were probably man's oldest

friend, that their history was impressive, and their appeal and value almost universal. In *The Book of the Goat* I attempted to right some old wrongs, give the goat its due, tell the reader some facts about the goat that would make him regard this unique animal in a new light and with respect. My teammate, Ozzie Sweet, tackled this assignment with enthusiasm, as he, too, had always liked the goat. As a result he has brought the animal alive in the pages of its own book. Ozzie Sweet and I continue our collaboration with enthusiasm and dedication. We work closely. It is teamwork of the highest order, as is our friendship, which goes back many years."

FOR MORE INFORMATION SEE: Best Sellers, July 15, 1965, December 15, 1966; *New York Times Book Review,* May 15, 1966; *New York Review of Books,* December 19, 1968; *Library Journal,* February 1, 1969; *Scientific American,* December, 1978.

SEAMAN, Augusta Huiell   1879-1950

PERSONAL: Born April 3, 1879, in New York, N.Y.; died June 4, 1950, in Seaside Park, N.J.; daughter of John Valentine and Augusta Chesseman (Curtis) Huiell; married Robert Reece Seaman, October 3, 1906 (died March, 1927); married Francis Parkman Freeman, March, 1928 (deceased); children: (first marriage) Helen Roberta. *Education:* Hunter College, A.B., 1900. *Politics:* Independent Democrat. *Religion:* Presbyterian. *Residence:* Seaside Park, N.J.

CAREER: Author of mysteries and adventure stories for young people. Began career as contributor of stories to magazines, 1907; later became regular contributor of juvenile mystery serials to periodicals, including *St. Nicholas, Youth's Companion,* and *American Girl,* which were later published in book form. *Member:* Pen and Brush Club.

WRITINGS—All for children: *Jacqueline of the Carrier-Pigeons* (illustrated by George W. Edwards), Sturgis & Walton, 1910; *When a Cobbler Ruled the King* (illustrated by Edwards), Sturgis & Walton, 1911; *Little Mamselle of the Wilderness: A Story of La Salle and His Pioneers* (illustrated by Edwards), Sturgis & Walton, 1913; *The Boarded-Up House* (illustrated by C. Clyde Squires), Century, 1915; *The Sapphire Signet* (illustrated by C. M. Relyea), Century, 1916; *The Girl Next Door* (illustrated by Relyea), Century, 1917; *Melissa Across-the-Fence* (illustrated by Relyea), Century, 1918; *Three Sides of Paradise Green* (illustrated by Relyea), Century, 1918; *Americans All: Stories to Tell Boys and Girls of Ten to Twelve,* Everyland Press, 1919; *The Slipper Point Mystery* (illustrated by Relyea), Century, 1919; *The Crimson Patch* (illustrated by Relyea), Century, 1920; *The Dragon's Secret* (illustrated by Relyea), Century, 1921; *The Mystery at Number Six* (illustrated by W. P. Couse), Century, 1922; *Tranquility House* (illustrated by Couse), Century, 1923; *The Edge of Raven Pool* (illustrated by Harold Sichel), Century, 1924; *Sally Simms Adventures It* (illustrated by Ethel C. Taylor), Century, 1924.

Bluebonnet Bend (illustrated by Relyea), Century, 1925; *The Adventure of the Seven Keyholes,* Century, 1926; *The Secret of Tate's Beach* (illustrated by Relyea), Century, 1926; *The Shadow on the Dial,* Century, 1927; *The Disappearance of Anne Shaw,* Doubleday, Doran, 1928, reprinted, Doubleday, 1946; *A Book of Mysteries: Three Baffling Tales* (illustrated by Kurt Wiese), Doubleday, Doran, 1929; *The Charlemonte Crest* (illustrated by Manning de V. Lee), Doubleday, Doran, 1930; *The Brass Keys of Kenwick* (illustrated by Lee), Doubleday, Doran, 1931; *The House in Hidden Lane: Two Mysteries for Younger Girls* (illustrated by Ann Brockman), Doubleday, Doran, 1931; *The Stars of Sabra* (illustrated by Lee), Doubleday, Doran, 1932; *The Mystery of the Empty Room* (illustrated by Irving Nurick), Doubleday, Doran, 1933; *Bitsy Finds the Clue: A Mystery of Williamsburg, Old and New* (illustrated by Nurick), Doubleday, Doran, 1934; *The Riddle at Live Oaks: Two Mysteries for Youngest Enthusiasts, Both Boys and Girls* (illustrated by Genevieve Foster; contains *The Riddle at Live Oaks* and *The Inn of the Twin Anchors;* also see below), Doubleday, Doran, 1934, reprinted, Doubleday, 1949.

The Figurehead of the "Folly" (illustrated by Elizabeth C. Tazelaar), Doubleday, Doran, 1935; *The River Acres Riddle: A Book of Mysteries,* Doubleday, Doran, 1936; *The Strange Pettingill Puzzle: Two Mysteries for Boys and Girls* (illustrated by Foster), Doubleday, Doran, 1936; *The Pine Barrens Mystery* (illustrated by Carolyn Haywood), Doubleday, Doran, 1937; *Voice in the Dark* (illustrated by Lee), Appleton-Century, 1937; *The Vanderlyn Silhouette* (illustrated by Lee), Appleton-Cen-

"I had the *worst* time puzzling this out!" she said. ■
(From *The Sapphire Signet* by Augusta Huiell Seaman. Illustrated by C.M. Relyea.)

tury, 1938; *The Mystery at Linden Hall* (illustrated by Lee), Appleton-Century, 1939; *The Curious Affair at Heron Shoals* (illustrated by Lee), Appleton-Century, 1940; *The Missing Half* (illustrated by Lee), Appleton-Century, 1941; *The Case of the Calico Crab* (illustrated by Lee), Appleton-Century, 1942; *Mystery of the Folding Key* (illustrated by Lee), Appleton-Century, 1943; *The Half-Penny Adventure* (illustrated by Sylvia Haggander), Appleton-Century, 1945; *The Mystery of the Other House,* Doubleday, 1947; *The Vanishing Octant Mystery* (illustrated by Ursula Koering), Doubleday, 1949; *The Mystery of the Old Violin* (illustrated by William Hutchinson; originally published as *The Inn of the Twin Anchors* in *The Riddle at Live Oaks*), TAB Books, 1960.

SIDELIGHTS: "'How do you write a mystery story?' is a question that is often asked me. And it is usually followed by the remark, 'I suppose you always make a very careful scenario first and have the whole thing plotted out before you really start in.' And then I always have to confess, apologetically, that I work in a most unorthodox way. I *never* have a plot all nicely diagramed, and I haven't the slightest idea how a story is going to turn out when I begin it.

"After I have selected a location for the story, generally chosen because of some historic or traditional interest connected with the spot, I think out a certain group of persons and some intriguing or mysterious situation or happening connected with the spot and these persons. And then, somehow, I seem to turn

Augusta Huiell Seaman with Girl Scouts about 1923.

them loose in my brain and let them work out their own story from day to day, often never knowing the night before how they are going to conduct themselves the next day, or what new clue or twist of the mystery they are going to unearth. So the story gets itself written after a while and, as a friend once aptly commented, I 'keep myself in the dark all through, and surprise myself at the end just as much as the reader is surprised.'

"When the story also involves certain definite historical associations, I do a great deal of reading and research work in the field besides, and it becomes an actual adventure to dig out of dusty histories and memoirs some obscure but interesting incidents to link up with my plot.

"Such was the case with the mystery of *The Charlemonte Crest*. The writing of it grew out of several happenings. First, because my own family history is linked with a baby refugee of the long-ago French massacre, I have always been interested in Haiti. Then came a delightful visit there with the family of the commanding office of the Marines at Cape Haitien.

(From *Little Mamselle of the Wilderness: A Story of La Salle and His Pioneers* by Augusta Huiell Seaman. Illustrated by George Wharton Edwards.)

"One of this family was the charming little daughter, Molly, who later became the heroine of the book. While there, I was fortunate enough to be able to read a priceless and deeply interesting collection of letters once written to Aaron Burr by a friend who was living in Cape Haitien at the very time of the revolt of the slaves against their French masters. And this gave me the idea for the letters used in my own plot. We also had the adventure of the wonderful 'Citadel' trip and the exploring of many an ancient ruin. And after all that, the story just about wrote itself.

"Wherever I go, I always find something that suggests a story. Perhaps an old house such as the queer, gabled one on our Jersey beach which provided the setting for *The Disappearance of Anne Shaw;* perhaps a deserted garden such as I found in North Carolina and used in *The Shadow on the Dial;* and once, a winter on a Texas ranch gave me the idea for *Bluebonnet Bend*. Somehow, wherever I go, stories are always around me, waiting to be written."

FOR MORE INFORMATION SEE: New York Times, April 27, 1924; *Boston Transcript,* May 7, 1924; *New York Herald Tribune Books,* September 16, 1934; *Junior Book of Authors,* 2nd edition, revised, H. W. Wilson, 1951; *Authors of Books for Young People,* Scarecrow, 1964.

OBITUARIES: New York Times, June 5, 1950; *Publishers Weekly,* June 24, 1950; *Wilson Library Bulletin,* September, 1950.

SITOMER, Harry   1903-

PERSONAL: Born December 31, 1903, in Russia (now U.S.S.R.); son of Benjamin (a butcher) and Rose (Pontach) Sitomer; married Mindel Miller, August 31, 1923; children: Alice Sitomer Ross, Daniel. *Education:* New York University, B.A. (summa cum laude), 1926; Columbia University, M.A., 1927. *Residence:* Huntington, N.Y.

CAREER: High school teacher, 1927-61; Long Island University, C. W. Post College, Brookville, N.Y., associate professor, 1967-73; writer, 1973—. *Member:* American Mathematical Society, Association of Teachers of Mathematics (chairman).

WRITINGS—Children's books; with wife, Mindel Sitomer; "Young Math Book" series; all published by Crowell: *What Is Symmetry?* (illustrated by Ed Emberly), 1970; *Circles* (illustrated by George Giusti), 1971; *Lines, Segments, Polygons* (illustrated by Robert Quackenbush), 1972; *Spirals* (illustrated by Pam Makie), 1974; *How Did Numbers Begin?* (illustrated by Richard Cuffari), 1976; *Zero Is Not Nothing* (illustrated by R. Cuffari), 1978.

Other: (Co-author) *The City Junior Mathematics*, C. E. Merrill, 1941, revised edition, 1942; (with Myron Frederick Rosskopf) *Modern Mathematics: Geometry*, Silver Burdett, 1966; (with M. F. Rosskopf and others) *Geometry*, Silver Burdett, 1971; (with Allan Gewirtz and others) *Constructive Linear Algebra*, Prentice-Hall, 1974. Contributor to mathematics journals.

SIDELIGHTS: "I have been a composer of contest problems for Nassau County for twenty-four years and New York City for about fifteen years. My major interest in my retirement is playing the cello in amateur chamber music groups."

**Before a race, runners are told "Get on your mark!"
The race starts at this mark, and this is sometimes
called the zero point of the race.** ■ (From *Zero Is Not
Nothing* by Mindel and Harry Sitomer. Illustrated by
Richard Cuffari.)

On a Celsius thermometer, zero is the separation point between freezing and melting of water.

Zero can be a separation point. ■ (From *Zero Is Not Nothing* by Mindel and Harry Sitomer.
Illustrated by Richard Cuffari.)

SITOMER, Mindel 1903-

PERSONAL: Born May 5, 1903, in New York, N.Y.; daughter of Morris (a machinist) and Lena (Gogolick) Miller; married Harry Sitomer (a professor and writer), August 31, 1923; children: Alice Sitomer Ross, Daniel. *Education:* New York University, B.S. (cum laude), 1931. *Residence:* Huntington, N.Y.

CAREER: Department of Welfare, New York, N.Y., investigator, 1939; school clerk in Brooklyn, N.Y., 1947-53; writer, 1970—. *Member:* Phi Beta Kappa.

WRITINGS—Children's books; all with husband, Harry Sitomer; "Young Math Book" series; all published by Crowell: *What Is Symmetry?* (illustrated by Ed Emberly), 1970; *Circles* (illustrated by George Giusti), 1971; *Lines, Segments, Polygons* (illustrated by Robert Quackenbush), 1972; *Spirals* (illustrated by Pam Makie), 1974; *How Did Numbers Begin?* (illustrated by Richard Cuffari), 1976; *Zero Is Not Nothing* (illustrated by R. Cuffari), 1978.

SMITH, Elva S(ophronia) 1871-1965

BRIEF ENTRY: Born April 28, 1871, in Burke Hollow, Vt.; died October 26, 1965, in Concord, N.H.; buried at Lyndon Cemetery, Lyndon Center, Vt. Educator, librarian, and author. In 1891 Smith moved from her Vermont home to California, where she taught in public schools from 1892 until 1898, studied librarianship in 1899, and tutored a family of children from 1900 until 1901. Then she moved to Pittsburgh, Pennsylvania, to attend the Training School for Children's Librarians in the Carnegie Library. Two years later she became an instructor in the school and an assistant cataloger in the library. From 1904 until 1944, she taught the history of children's literature, book selection for children, the cataloging of children's books, and other areas of librarianship for children. Her professional publications include *The History of Children's Literature* and *Subject Headings for Children's Books.* Smith is credited, with Frances Jenkins Olcott, with developing a collection of historical children's books that eventually became a part of the University of Pittsburgh's Graduate School of Library and Information Science. She was a prolific writer of stories, poems, history and legends for children, articles for journals, and guides for librarians. Her publications for children include *A Book of Lullabies* and *The Year Around: Poems for Children.* For More Information See: *Who Was Who in America, with World Notables,* Volume V: *1969-73,* Marquis, 1973; *Who Was Who among North American Authors, 1921-1939,* Gale, 1976; *Dictionary of American Library Biography,* Libraries Unlimited, 1978.

SOBOL, Donald J. 1924-

PERSONAL: Born October 4, 1924, in New York, N.Y.; son of Ira J. and Ida (Gelula) Sobol; married Rose Tiplitz, 1955; children: Diane, Glenn, Eric, John. *Education:* Oberlin College, B.A., 1948. *Residence:* Miami, Fla. *Agent:* McIntosh & Otis, 475 Fifth Ave., New York, N.Y. 10017.

CAREER: New York Sun, New York, N.Y., editorial staff, 1948; *Long Island Daily Press,* New York, N.Y., editorial staff, 1949-51; R. H. Macy, New York, N.Y., merchandising, 1953-54; free-lance writer, beginning 1954. *Military service:* U.S. Army, Combat Engineers, World War II; served in Pacific Theater. *Member:* Authors Guild. *Awards, honors:* Young

DONALD J. SOBOL

Readers Choice Award from the Pacific Northwest Library Association, 1972, for *Encyclopedia Brown Keeps the Peace;* Edgar award from the Mystery Writers of America, 1976, for entire body of work; Garden State Children's Book Award, 1977, for *Encyclopedia Brown Lends a Hand;* Aiken County Children's Book Award, 1977, for *Encyclopedia Brown Takes the Case.*

WRITINGS—Juvenile: *The Double Quest* (illustrated by Lili Rethi), Watts, 1957; *The Lost Dispatch* (illustrated by Anthony Palombo), Watts, 1958; *First Book of Medieval Man* (illustrated by L. Rethi), Watts, 1959 (revised edition published in England as *The First Book of Medieval Britain,* Mayflower, 1960); *Two Flags Flying* (illustrated by Jerry Robinson), Platt, 1960; *The Wright Brothers at Kitty Hawk* (illustrated by Stuart Mackenzie), T. Nelson, 1961; (editor) *A Civil War Sampler* (illustrated by Henry S. Gillette), Watts, 1961; *The First Book of the Barbarian Invaders, A.D. 375-511* (illustrated by W. Kirtman Plummer), Watts, 1962; (with wife, Rose Sobol) *Stocks and Bonds,* Watts, 1963; (editor) *An American Revolutionary War Reader,* Watts, 1964; *Lock, Stock, and Barrel* (illustrated by Edward J. Smith), Westminster, 1965; *The Strongest Man in the World* (illustrated by Cliff Schule), Westminster, 1967; *Secret Agents Four* (illustrated by Leonard Shortall), Four Winds, 1967; *Two-Minute Mysteries,* Dutton, 1967.

Milton the Model A (illustrated by J. Drescher), Harvey House, 1970; *Greta the Strong* (illustrated by Trina Schart Hyman), Follett, 1970; *More Two-Minute Mysteries,* Dutton, 1971; *The Amazons of Greek Mythology,* A. S. Barnes, 1972; *Still More Two-Minute Mysteries,* Dutton, 1975; *True Sea Adventures,* T. Nelson, 1975; *Great Sea Stories,* Dutton, 1977; *Disaster,*

"I'd planned to work today in the basement with my number one yo-yo. It glows in the dark," said Elmo. "But I made the best of things. I went outside and put a blanket over my head." ■ (From *Encyclopedia Brown and the Case of the Midnight Visitor* by Donald J. Sobol. Illustrated by Lillian Brandi.)

Archway, 1979; (editor) *The Best Animal Stories of Science Fiction and Fantasy,* Warne, 1979; *Angie's First Case* (illustrated by Gail Owens), Four Winds, 1981.

"Encyclopedia Brown" series; all published by T. Nelson, except as noted; all illustrated by Leonard Shortall, except as noted: *Encyclopedia Brown: Boy Detective,* 1963; *. . . and the Case of the Secret Pitch,* 1965; *. . . Finds the Clues,* 1966; *. . . Gets His Man,* 1967; *. . . Solves Them All,* 1968; *. . . Keeps the Peace,* 1969; *. . . Saves the Day,* 1970; *. . . Tracks Them Down,* 1971; *. . . Shows the Way,* 1972; *. . . Takes the Case,* 1973; *. . . Lends a Hand,* 1974; *. . . and the Case of the Dead Eagles* (Junior Literary Guild selection), 1975; *. . . and the Eleven: Case of the Exploding Plumbing and Other Mysteries,* Dutton, 1976; *. . . and the Case of the Midnight Visitor* (illustrated by Lillian Brandi), 1977; *Encyclopedia Brown's Record Book of Weird and Wonderful Facts* (illustrated by Sal Murdocca), Delacorte, 1979; *. . . Carries On* (illustrated by Ib Ohlsson), Four Winds, 1980; *Encyclopedia Brown's Second Record Book of Weird Facts,* Delacorte, 1981; *. . . Sets the Pace,* Dutton, 1981; *Encyclopedia Brown's Book of Wacky Crimes,* Dutton, 1982.

Contributor of more than one hundred stories and articles to national magazines under a variety of pen names; author of syndicated column, "Two Minute-Mystery Series."

ADAPTATIONS—Filmstrip: "The Best of Encyclopedia Brown" (includes "The Case of Natty Nut," "The Case of the Scattered Cards," "The Case of the Hungry Hitchhiker," "The Case of the Whistling Ghost"), filmstrip with cassette, color, Miller-Brody, 1977.

SIDELIGHTS: Sobol was born in 1924 in New York City where he attended the Ethnical Cultural Schools. During World War II, he served with the engineer corps in the Pacific, and after his discharge he earned a B.A. degree from Oberlin College. While at Oberlin he first thought of becoming a writer when he took a short-story writing course, but it was years before he made writing his profession.

His first job was as a copyboy for the New York *Sun.* After that he was a journalist for the *Sun* and for the Long Island *Daily News.* "At the age of thirty I quit job-holding for good, married Rose Tiplitz, an engineer, and began to write full time. . . . I have turned out more than fifty books, forty-five of them under my own name."

"My first book about the boy detective, Encyclopedia Brown, was rejected by twenty-six publishers before being accepted by Thomas Nelson. The series has reached nineteen books, and chapters from them have appeared in twenty-one elementary school texts.

"Readers constantly ask me if Encyclopedia Brown is a real boy. The answer is no. He is, perhaps, the boy I wanted to be—doing the things I wanted to read about but could not find in any book when I was ten."

Ten-year-old Leroy Brown, the hero of Sobol's famous series, is called "Encyclopedia" because he carries so many facts in his head and is so adept at finding clues that he helps his father, the Chief of Police, solve criminal cases.

The series has been translated into thirteen languages and adapted into various media forms, including filmstrips by Miller-Brody. In 1977 Esquire Film Productions bought the television and motion picture rights to the series. These rights were transferred to Howard David Deutsch Productions and Warner Brothers in 1979, with the intention of placing a full-length theatrical feature before the camera.

Sobol has also written an internationally syndicated newspaper feature, "Two Minute-Mystery Series," hundreds of articles and stories for adult magazines, historical books, and biographies. He is the editor of two history collections, *A Civil War Sampler* and *An American Revolutionary War Reader* and the author of a book on stocks and bonds. He prefers writing fiction for young people. "As to my own writing, I prefer the plotted story to one which arises out of character."

Sobol lives with his wife and four children in Florida, "a paradise for raising children." Besides travel, Sobol enjoys restoring antique cars, boating, fishing, and scuba diving.

FOR MORE INFORMATION SEE: Christian Science Monitor, October 5, 1967; *Young Readers' Review,* November, 1967, November, 1968; *New York Times Book Review,* November 5, 1967; *Christian Century,* December 13, 1967; D. L. Kilpatrick, editor, *Twentieth Century Children's Authors,* St. Martin's Press, 1978; Doris de Montreville and Elizabeth D. Crawford, editors, *Fourth Book of Junior Authors,* H. W. Wilson, 1978; *Contemporary Authors, New Revision Series,* Volume 1, Gale, 1981.

STEIN, R(ichard) Conrad 1937-

PERSONAL: Born April 22, 1937, in Chicago, Ill.; son of Konrad G. (a truckdriver) and Mary (Kariolich) Stein. *Education:* University of Illinois, B.A., 1964; University of Guanajuato, Mexico, M.A., M.F.A., 1976. *Politics:* "Varies, but mainly Democratic." *Religion:* Roman Catholic. *Home:* San Miguel de Allende, Guanajuato, Mexico and 4221 N. Hamlin St., Chicago, Ill.

CAREER: Has worked at a variety of jobs, including social worker, truckdriver, merchant seaman, chauffeur, machinist, and salesman; teacher of writing at Instituto Allende, San Miguel de Allende, Mexico; free-lance writer of children's books. *Military service:* U.S. Marine Corps, 1955-58; became sergeant.

WRITINGS—For children; all published by Childrens Press, except as noted: *The Big Abzul-Raider Game*, Science Research Association, 1967; *Steel Driving Man: The Legend of John Henry*, 1969; *My Tribe*, 1970; *No Hablo Ingles*, 1970; *Hey, Taxie!*, 1970; *Look to the Light Side*, 1970; *A World of Books*, 1970; *People Are My Profession*, 1970; *Benjamin Franklin: Inventor, Statesman, and Patriot*, Rand McNally, 1972; *The Story of the USS Arizona*, 1976; *The Battle of D-Day*, 1977; *The Story of the Battle of Iwo Jima*, 1977; *The Story of the Battle of the Bulge*, 1977; *The Story of the Homestead Act*, 1978; *The Story of the Lewis and Clark Expedition*, 1978; *The Story of the Golden Spike*, 1978; *The Story of Arlington National Cemetery*, 1979; *The Story of Ellis Island*, 1979; *The Story of the Smithsonian Institution*, 1979; *The Story of the Underground Railroad*, 1981; *The Story of the Pony Express*, 1981; *The Story of the Flight at Kitty Hawk*, 1981; *The Story of the Clipper Ships*, 1981; *The Story of Marquette and Jolliet*, 1981; *Me and Dirty Arnie*, Harcourt, 1982; *The Story of the Panama Canal*, 1982; *The Story of the 19th Amendment*, 1982; *The Story of the Barbary Pirates*, 1982; *The Fall of Singapore*, 1982; *Hiroshima*, 1982; *Resistance Movements*, 1982; *The Evacuation of Dunkirk*, 1982.

SIDELIGHTS: "I am now self-employed as an author of children's books. My most recent regular job was as a college teacher at the Instituto Allende, a small, English-language college in San Miguel de Allende, Mexico. I taught a course in creative writing, the writing of non-fiction, and writing for children and young people. Before that I have worked as a social worker, merchant seaman, truckdriver, machinist, and salesman.

"I enjoy writing fiction, far out fantasy, and humor, but this does not always sell. So I make my living writing history and biography. I see no conflict in this. History is fun to write, and it should be fun to read. History is far more than just dry dates, places, and passages of time. It is a rich and exciting study, and I try to bring the richness into each one of my history books. Right now I write strictly for children and young people. Some day soon, however, I hope to try to write for movies and television.

"In Mexico I enjoy reading and hiking in the mountains near my home. In Chicago I like walking, riding my bicycle, and going to Cub games to cheer for a team that has not won a pennant since 1945."

The Chinese worked hard and did not strike. They also seemed to be genuinely happy working for two dollars a day. ▪ (From *The Story of the Golden Spike* by R. Conrad Stein. Illustrated by Tom Dunnington.)

STINE, Robert Lawrence 1943-
(Jovial Bob Stine)

PERSONAL: Born October 8, 1943, in Columbus, Ohio; son of Lewis (a shipping clerk) and Anne (Feinstein) Stine; married Jane Waldhorn (an editorial director of children's magazines and books), June 22, 1969; children: Matthew Daniel. *Education:* Ohio State University, B.A., 1965; graduate study at New York University, 1966-67. *Religion:* Jewish. *Home:* 225 West 71st St., New York, N.Y. 10023. *Office:* Scholastic Magazines, 50 West 44th St., New York, N.Y. 10036.

CAREER: Columbus, Ohio, public schools, junior high school social studies teacher, 1967-68; *Junior Scholastic* (magazine), New York City, associate editor, 1969-71; *Search* (magazine), New York City, editor, 1972-75; *Bananas* (magazine), New York City, editor, 1975—.

WRITINGS—All for young people; all under name Jovial Bob Stine: *The Absurdly Silly Encyclopedia and Flyswatter* (illustrated by Bob K. Taylor), Scholastic Book Services, 1978; *How to Be Funny: An Extremely Silly Guidebook* (illustrated by Carol Nicklaus), Dutton, 1978; *The Complete Book of Nerds* (illustrated by Sam Viviano), Scholastic Book Services, 1979; *The Dynamite Do-It-Yourself Pen Pal Kit* (illustrated by Jared Lee), Scholastic Book Services, 1980; *Dynamite's Funny Book of the Sad Facts of Life* (illustrated by J. Lee), Scholastic Book Services, 1980; *Going Out! Going Steady! Going Bananas!* (photos by Dan Nelken), Scholastic Book Services, 1980; *The Pigs' Book of World Records* (illustrated by Peter Lippman), Random House, 1980; (with wife, Jane Stine) *The Sick of Being Sick Book* (edited by Ann Durrell; illustrated by C. Nicklaus), Dutton, 1980; *Bananas Looks at TV* (illustrated by S. Viviano), Scholastic Book Services, 1981; *The Beast Handbook* (illustrated by B. K. Taylor), Scholastic Book Services, 1981; (with J. Stine) *The Bored with Being Bored Book* (illustrated by Jerry Zimmerman), Four Winds Press, 1981; (with J. Stine) *The Cool Kids' Guide to Summer Camp* (illustrated by J. Zimmerman), Scholastic Book Services, 1981; *Gnasty Gnomes* (illustrated by P. Lippman), Random House, 1981; *Don't Stand in the Soup* (illustrated by C. Nicklaus), Bantam Books, 1982.

WORK IN PROGRESS: Four volumes (with wife) entitled, *The Stines' Super Survival Kits* for Random House.

ROBERT LAWRENCE STINE

SIDELIGHTS: "I believe that kids as well as adults are entitled to books of no socially redeeming value. I try to write children's books that are only funny and not helpful in any way. Although my wife and I are not known to that many adults, we most likely have more readers under the age of sixteen than anyone!"

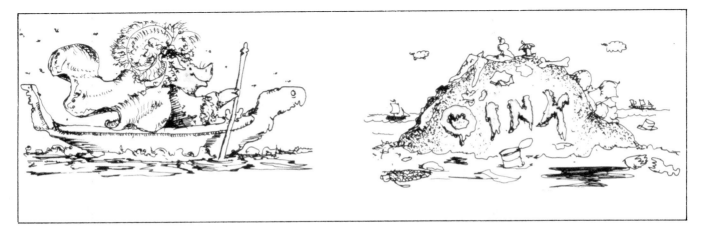

1620
Pigs sail on *Mayflower*. Are first to deface Plymouth Rock. ■ (From *The Pigs' Book of World Records* by Bob Stine. Illustrated by Peter Lippman.)

Expedition landing in a storm on the Arctic coast of Canada, August 23, 1821. ■(From *Journey into Ice: Sir John Franklin and the Northwest Passage* by Ann and Myron Sutton. Engraving from a drawing by George Back.)

SUTTON, Ann (Livesay)   1923-

PERSONAL: Born September 5, 1923, in Ashley, Ill.; daughter of George M. (a dentist) and Jennie (Smith) Livesay; married Myron Daniel Sutton (an international park specialist and author) September 19, 1953; children: Michael, Larry. *Education:* University of Illinois, B.A., 1944, M.S., 1945; University of Colorado, further graduate study, 1946-48. *Religion:* Protestant. *Home:* 3318 Sundance Dr., Bozeman, Mont. 59715.

CAREER: Illinois State Museum, Springfield, curator of geology, 1947-49; University of Kentucky, Lexington, geology instructor, 1950-53; U.S. Geological Survey, Washington, D.C., geologist, 1954-57. *Member:* Phi Beta Kappa, Phi Kappa Phi. *Awards, honors:* Science Book of the Year award from Chautauqua Literary and Scientific Institution, 1962, for *Nature on the Rampage; Exploring with the Bartrams* was selected as one of *New York Times* Hundred Best Books of 1963; Notable Book Award from American Library Association, 1967, for *Among the Maya Ruins;* 22nd Annual Chicago Book Clinic Award, 1971, for *The Secret Places;* Special Award from New York Academy of Sciences, 1980, for *Wildlife of the Forests.*

WRITINGS—Of interest to young people; all with husband, Myron Sutton: *Exploring with the Bartrams* (biography; illustrated by Paula A. Hutchinson), Rand McNally, 1963; *Animals on the Move* (illustrated by P. A. Hutchinson), Rand McNally, 1965; *Guarding the Treasured Lands: The Story of the National Park Service,* Lippincott, 1965; *The Life of the Desert,* McGraw, 1966; *Among the Maya Ruins: The Adventures of John Lloyd Stephens and Frederick Catherwood* (biography), Rand McNally, 1967; *New Worlds for Wildlife,* Rand McNally, 1970.

Other—All with husband, M. D. Sutton: *Steller of the North* (biography; illustrated by Leonard E. Fisher), Rand McNally, 1961; *Nature on the Rampage: A Natural History of the Elements,* Lippincott, 1962; *Journey into Ice: Sir John Franklin and the Northwest Passage* (biography), Rand McNally, 1965 (published in England as *The Endless Quest: The Life of John Franklin, Explorer,* Constable, 1966); *The Appalachian Trail: Wilderness on the Doorstep* (foreword by Stewart L. Udall), Lippincott, 1967; *The American West: A Natural History* (illustrated with photographs by Ansel Adams and others), Random House, 1969.

The Secret Places: Wonders of Scenic America (illustrated with photographs by the authors), Rand McNally, 1970; *The Wilderness World of the Grand Canyon: "Leave It as It Is"* (illustrated with photographs by Philip Hyde), Lippincott, 1970; *Yellowstone: A Century of the Wilderness Idea* (illustrated with photographs by Charles Steinhacker and others), Macmillan, 1972; *The Wild Places: A Photographic Celebration of Unspoiled America* (photographs by Tom Algire and others; collected and edited by Milton Rugoff and Ann Guilfoyle), Harper, 1973; *Wilderness Areas of North America* (illustrated with photographs by the authors), Funk, 1974; *The Pacific Crest Trail: Escape to the Wilderness* (illustrated with photographs by the authors), Lippincott, 1975; *The Wild Shores of North America,* Knopf, 1977; *Wildlife of the Forests,* Abrams, 1979; *The Audubon Society Book of Trees,* Abrams, 1981.

Contributor, John Kieran's *A Treasury of Great Nature Writing.* Has contributed approximately sixty articles to popular magazines, including *Arizona Highways, Popular Science;* also a contributor to encyclopedias. Book reviewer, *GeoTimes,* for American Geological Institute.

WORK IN PROGRESS: Four books, on history, natural history, philosophy, and travel.

SIDELIGHTS: Speaks French and Spanish. Hobbies are gardening. stamp collecting, photography, hiking, and music.

FOR MORE INFORMATION SEE: Philadelphia Sunday Bulletin, August 5, 1962.

SUTTON, Felix   1910(?)-

PERSONAL: Born about 1910, in West Virginia. *Education:* Graduated from West Virginia University. *Residence:* Wilton, Conn.

CAREER: Author of books for young people. Has worked as a sports reporter and as a copy writer for an advertising agency.

WRITINGS: The Big Book of Dogs (illustrated by Percy Leason), Grosset, 1952; *Mighty Mouse* (illustrated by Chad), Treasure Books, 1953; *Mighty Mouse: Dinky Learns to Fly* (illustrated by Chad), Treasure Books, 1953; *The Big Treasure Book of Wheels: 70 Things That Move on Wheels* (illustrated by Art Seiden), Grosset, 1953, a later edition published as *The Big Book of Wheels: 70 Things That Move on Wheels,* Grosset, 1965; *The Big Treasure Book of Clowns* (illustrated by James Schucker), Grosset, 1953, a later edition published as *The Book of Clowns,* Grosset, 1966; *Mighty Mouse and the Sacred Scarecrow* (illustrated by Chad), Treasure Books, 1954; *The Big Book of Cars* (illustrated by Tom Hill), Grosset, 1954; *The Magic Clown* (illustrated by J. Schucker), Treasure Books, 1954; *Let's Take a Trip in Our Car* (illustrated by J. Schucker), Treasure Books, 1954; *The Big Book of Wild Animals* (illustrated by Bob Kuhn), Grosset, 1954; *The Nine Friendly Dogs* (illustrated by June Goldsborough), Wonder Books, 1954; (with Gladys E. Cook) *The Big Book of Cats,* Grosset, 1954.

Adventures of the Range Rider (illustrated by Louis Glanzman), Wonder Books, 1955; *The Terry Bears Win the Cub Scout Badge* (illustrated by J. Robert Moore), Treasure Books, 1955; *Mighty Mouse, Santa's Helper* (illustrated by Chad), Treasure Books, 1955; *The Picture Story of Davy Crockett* (illustrated by H. B. Vestal), Wonder Books, 1955; *Daniel Boone* (illustrated by De Witt Whistler Jayne), Grosset, 1956; *Wild Bill Hickok* (illustrated by Jon Nielsen), Wonder Books, 1956; *We Were There at Pearl Harbor* (illustrated by Frank Vaughn), Grosset, 1957; (with Leon A. Hausman) *The Illustrated Book of the Sea* (illustrated by Art Renshaw and Herman Bischoff), Grosset, 1957; *Skin Diving for Sunken Treasure,* Young America Books, 1957; *We Were There at the Battle of Lexington and Concord* (illustrated by H. B. Vestal), Grosset, 1958; *Dangerous Safari: Big Game Hunting in Africa,* Young Amer-

FELIX SUTTON

ica Books, 1958; (with Leon Jason) *The Terrytoons Playhouse* (illustrated by Chad), Grosset, 1958; *Hot Rock of Hondo: Prospecting for Uranium in the Western Badlands,* Young America Books, 1958; *The Illustrated Book about Africa* (illustrated by H. B. Vestal), Grosset, 1959.

Big Game Hunter: Carl Akeley, Messner, 1960; *The How and Why Wonder Book of Our Earth* (illustrated by John Hull), Grosset, 1960; *The Planet We Live On* (illustrated by J. Hull), Grosset, 1960; *We Were There at the First Airplane Flight* (illustrated by Laszlo Matulay), Grosset, 1960; *The City under the Sea,* Duell, Sloan, 1961; *The Valiant Virginian: Stonewall Jackson,* Messner, 1961; *The How and Why Wonder Book of World War II* (illustrated by Darrell Sweet), Grosset, 1962; (with Charles F. Gieg) *The Last Voyage of the Albatross,* Duell, Sloan, 1962; *The Illustrated Book about Europe* (illustrated by J. Hull), Grosset, 1962; *The How and Why Wonder Book of Winning of the West* (illustrated by Leonard Vosburgh), Grosset, 1963; *The How and Why Wonder Book of the Moon* (illustrated by Raul Mina Mora), Grosset, 1963; *The How and Why Wonder Book of the American Revolution* (illustrated by Leonard Vosburgh), Grosset, 1963; *Horses of America* (illustrated by Walter J. Wilwerding), Putnam, 1964; *The How and Why Wonder Book of the First World War* (illustrated by Robert Doremus), Grosset, 1964; *The How and Why Wonder Book of North American Indians* (illustrated by L. Vosburgh), Grosset, 1965; (with Earl S. Miers) *America during Four Wars* (illustrated by L. Vosburgh), Grosset, 1965; (with V. Phillips Weaver) *Discoverers of America: Primitive Man to Spanish Conquerors* (illustrated by L. Vosburgh), Grosset, 1965.

The circus gives them their own dressing room with a separate entrance to the Big Top. This is called Clown Alley. ■ (From *The Book of Clowns* by Felix Sutton. Illustrated by James Schucker.)

Logging camp, 1902. ■ (From *West Virginia* by Felix Sutton. Photograph courtesy of Mc Clain Printing Company, Parsons, West Virginia.)

The How and Why Wonder Book of Deserts, Grosset, 1966; *West Virginia,* Coward-McCann, 1968; *Master of Ballyhoo: The Story of P. T. Barnum,* Putnam, 1968; *The How and Why Wonder Book of Our Earth* (illustrated by J. Hull), Grosset, 1969; *Getting to Know Virginia* (illustrated by Paul Frame), Coward-McCann, 1969; (with Alvin Maurer) *Conquest of the Moon* (illustrated by R. M. Mora), Grosset, 1969; *Sons of Liberty* (illustrated by Bill Barss), Messner, 1969; *Indian Chiefs of the West* (illustrated by Russell Hoover), Messner, 1970; *The Big Show: A History of the Circus,* Doubleday, 1971.

Adaptor of books for children, including, Eric M. Knight, *Lassie Come-Home;* Johanna Spyri, *Heidi: Child of the Mountains;* Mark Twain, *Adventures of Tom Sawyer;* Herman Melville, *Moby Dick;* Albert P. Terhune, *Lad, a Dog;* Johann D. Wyss, *The Swiss Family Robinson;* Robert Louis Stevenson, *Kidnapped.*

SIDELIGHTS: "I was born . . . in the hills of West Virginia. During the winter months I went to school in Clarksburg, but summers were spent on our family farm just outside the little town of Sutton, which an ancestor had settled about the time of the Revolutionary War. There I learned the lore of the woods and the habits of the wild 'critters' that live in them. I fished the crystal mountain streams and, as soon as my father felt I was old enough to handle a gun, hunted squirrels and deer and wild turkeys in the woods and quail in the broad upland meadows. It was a wonderful life for a boy.

"Since I had always wanted to write, I entered the School of Journalism at West Virginia University, where I graduated in 1935. After a stint on several newspapers, I came to New York determined to earn my living with my typewriter. However, while in college I had married a charming girl from North Carolina, and soon we discovered that the occasional check I received for a short story or an article fell far short of what was required to pay the grocer and landlord. So in search of a steady income, I went to work for an advertising agency. During the fifteen years that followed, I wrote countless thousands of magazine ads, radio and television commercials. But every year I managed to get away for a week or two to go hunting in Canada or northern New England or the western mountains.

"Then I wrote an adventure book for boys, which was published. And then another and another—and soon I realized that I was going to have to choose between writing books or television commercials. The choice was not a difficult one to make. In the past . . . years I have written a good number of books for young people, mostly about sports, outdoor life, adventure, animals and biography. . . ." [Taken from the book jacket of *Big Game Hunter: Carl Akeley,* Messner, 1960.]

FOR MORE INFORMATION SEE: Kirkus, July 1, 1959; *Saturday Review,* May 7, 1960.

SUTTON, Myron Daniel 1925-

PERSONAL: Born October 9, 1925, in Prescott, Ariz.; son of A. T. (a postman) and Goldie (a musician; maiden name, Womack) Sutton; married Ann Livesay (an author and conservationist), September 19, 1953; children: Michael, Larry. *Education:* Northern Arizona University, B.S., 1950, D.Sc., 1971. *Home and office:* 3318 Sundance Dr., Bozeman, Mont. 59715.

CAREER: Writer. National Park Service, ranger, naturalist, planner, international affairs specialist, 1947-79; University of Wyoming, Laramie, Wyo., professor of parks, tourism, and recreation, 1975-79. *Military service:* U.S. Army Signal Corps, 1944-46, 1950-51. *Member:* Appalachian Trail Conference, Wilderness Society, Montana Wilderness Association, Authors Guild. *Awards, honors:* Recipient of Ohio Valley Reading Circle Award, 1962; Science Book of the Year award from Chautauqua Literary and Scientific Institution, 1962, for *Nature on the Rampage; Exploring with the Bartrams* was selected as one of *New York Times* Hundred Best Books of 1963; Notable Book Award from American Library Association, 1967, for *Among the Maya Ruins;* 22nd Annual Chicago Book Clinic Award, 1971, for *The Secret Places;* Special Award from New York Academy of Sciences, 1980, for *Wildlife of the Forests;* honorary Doctor of Sciences degree from Northern Arizona University.

WRITINGS—Of interest to young people; all with wife, Ann Livesay Sutton: *Exploring with the Bartrams* (biography; illustrated by Paula A. Hutchinson), Rand McNally, 1963; *Animals on the Move* (illustrated by P. A. Hutchinson), Rand McNally, 1965; *Guarding the Treasured Lands: The Story of the National Park Service,* Lippincott, 1965; *The Life of the Desert,* McGraw, 1966; *Among the Maya Ruins: The Adventures of John Lloyd Stephens and Frederick Catherwood* (biography), Rand McNally, 1967; *New Worlds for Wildlife,* Rand McNally, 1970.

Other, all with wife, A. L. Sutton: *Steller of the North* (biography; illustrated by Leonard E. Fisher), Rand McNally, 1961; *Nature on the Rampage: A Natural History of the Elements,* Lippincott, 1962; *Journey into Ice: Sir John Franklin and the Northwest Passage* (biography), Rand McNally, 1965 (published in England as *The Endless Quest: The Life of John Franklin, Explorer,* Constable, 1966); *The Appalachian Trail: Wilderness on the Doorstep* (foreword by Stewart L. Udall), Lippincott, 1967; *The American West: A Natural History* (illustrated with photographs by Ansel Adams and others), Random House, 1969.

The Secret Places: Wonders of Scenic America (illustrated with photographs by the authors), Rand McNally, 1970; *The Wilderness World of the Grand Canyon: "Leave It as It Is"* (illustrated with photographs by Philip Hyde), Lippincott, 1970;

MYRON AND ANN SUTTON

Yellowstone: A Century of the Wilderness Idea (illustrated with photographs by Charles Steinhacker and others), Macmillan, 1972; *The Wild Places: A Photographic Celebration of Unspoiled America* (photographs by Tom Algire and others; collected and edited by Milton Rugoff and Ann Guilfoyle), Harper, 1973; *Wilderness Areas of North America* (illustrated with photographs by the authors), Funk, 1974; *The Pacific Crest Trail: Escape to the Wilderness* (illustrated with photographs by the authors), Lippincott, 1975; *The Wild Shores of North America,* Knopf, 1977; *Wildlife of the Forests,* Abrams, 1979; *The Audubon Society Book of Trees,* Abrams, 1981.

Contributor of about seventy articles to anthologies, scientific papers, and booklets, and of articles to periodicals, including *American Forests, Science Digest, Nature Magazine, Popular Science Monthly, American Mercury, Natural History, Arizona Highways,* and *Audubon Magazine.*

WORK IN PROGRESS: The Kodak Guide to World Travel Photography.

SIDELIGHTS: Sutton and his wife, Ann, are fluent in French and Spanish. They have travelled to over fifty countries and to the fifty states of the U.S.A. "to gather research, photographs, present lectures, and assist governments in planning for national park and conservation reserves."

In their work, Sutton said, he and his wife have "organized seminars on tourism, natural areas, and conservation, and conducted expeditions into American and world wilderness areas." They have specialized, Sutton commented, "in the preparation and presentation of spectacular panoramic three-screen programs on great national parks of the world, wilderness areas of North America, and tourism and outdoor education."

FOR MORE INFORMATION SEE: New York Herald Tribune Books, May 6, 1962; *New York Times Book Review,* April 9, 1967, June 18, 1967; *Natural History,* May, 1967, January, 1974.

TEAGUE, Robert 1929-
(Bob Teague)

BRIEF ENTRY: Born in 1929, in Milwaukee, Wis. A journalist and author, Teague has worked as a reporter for the *Milwaukee Journal* and the *New York Times.* A newscaster for the National Broadcasting Co., Teague was the first Black newsman ever hired by that television network. Teague is the author of several children's books, among them *Adam in Blunderland* (Doubleday, 1971), *Agent K-Thirteen the Super Spy* (Doubleday, 1974), and *Super-Spy K-Thirteen in Outer Space* (Doubleday, 1980). Teague has also written an adult novel, *Climate of Candor,* and has contributed articles to such periodicals as *Look, Reader's Digest,* and *Redbook.* A graduate of the University of Wisconsin, Teague was a star halfback on the university's Big Ten football team. He is a recipient of the Amistad Award from the American Missionary Association for "his dignity and journalistic skill." *For More Information See: Ebony,* November, 1955; *Selected Black American Authors: An Illustrated Bio-Bibliography,* G. K. Hall, 1977.

THOMSON, Peggy 1922-

PERSONAL: Born November 6, 1922, in St. Louis, Mo.; daughter of Jules (a chemical engineer) and Helen (Gilli) Bebie; married John Seabury Thomson (a government employee), May

11, 1945; children: Christopher, Hilary, David. *Education:* Swarthmore College, B.A. (with high honors), 1943. *Politics:* Democrat. *Religion:* Unitarian-Universalist. *Home and office:* 23 Grafton St., Chevy Chase, MD. 20815.

CAREER: Life, New York, N.Y., researcher, 1943-47; *Washington Post,* Washington, D.C., writer for magazine section, 1964-67; free-lance writer. *Member:* Washington Independent Writers (member of board of directors, 1976, 1978), Children's Book Guild of Washington, D.C. (program chairman, 1981-82).

WRITINGS—Of interest to young people; all published by Prentice-Hall: *On Reading Palms* (illustrated by Dale Payson), 1974; *Museum People, Collectors and Keepers at the Smithsonian* (illustrated by Joseph Low), 1977. Contributor of articles and reviews to magazines and newspapers, including *Smithsonian, American Education, Living Wilderness,* and *Washington Post.*

WORK IN PROGRESS: Research on museum and natural history subjects, including more about the Smithsonian.

SIDELIGHTS: "My writing as a career began right after college with a job as researcher for four years (1943-47) with *Life* magazine. I held lights for photographers and interviewed tea partying DAR ladies, homecoming Marines, unlucky giant sea turtles awaiting turns in the soup pot. It was more than a decade

The Smithsonian's Zoo provides the best opportunities for eavesdropping and snooping. ■(From *Museum People, Collectors and Keepers at the Smithsonian* by Peggy Thomson. Illustrated by Joseph Low.)

Peggy Thomson (right) interviewing folklorist Arie Carpenter.

later that I began free-lance writing, having edited in the years we lived in Wisconsin and, while the children were small, attended writing classes at which we discussed protecting movie rights for our not-yet-written works. In the 60s, living in Washington, D.C., I found that the *Washington Post* magazine *Potomac* welcomed cottage-industry articles stitched up at home. I became a regular part-time writer with a desktop and typewriter at the *Post* and a photographer with whom to work. I miss that. Stories come out differently when writer and photographer do them together. Today most magazines assign photographers after the text is accepted. When I tried branching out, I began stock-piling rejected stories. I'd also been inspired—by one of my own stories—to volunteer as a counselor-aide in the D.C. schools, working one-to-one with falling-behind students. Many of the projects at Harrison School had to do with children's writing—based on neighborhood walks or a day's prowl at the railroad station or interviews with an admired gym teacher. That experience led to my giving a series of classes to a fifth grade on interviewing—the pleasurable business of getting people to talk about themselves.

"Many of my stories (which have appeared in *Washington Post, Star, New York Times, Smithsonian, Ms., Progressive,* as well as education, outdoors and U.S. information service magazines, etc.) deal with young people—learning through filmmaking, bookmaking, hands-on science, outdoor programs, the arts, environmental living programs at historic sites, learning through 'Foxfire' or bilingually or in migrant daycare situations. Or they deal with such a problem as the high incidence of lead poisoning in inner-city children. The Appalachian Trail also. And beach plums. And horseshoe crabs."

"I like doing heavy research and writing with as light a touch as possible. When I'd done one book for a children's book editor, a skeptic's look at reading palms, she let me do the book I wanted to do, a look behind the scenes at the Smithsonian Institution. *Museum People* consists of interviews with the animal freeze-drier, a hanger of airplanes, a designer of monkey furniture, collectors of First Lady dresses, neon signs and Presidential memorabilia, the special-effects technician, curators of volcanology, postal history, and the zoo lizards keeper. It also has chapters on collecting, keeping track of things, conserving and exhibiting. What a treat for someone who loves to eavesdrop and watch and talk to people who love their work! Writing that book was a lovely excuse to snoop and to communicate the marvelous things people do and say in an ordinary workaday way.

"I'm continuing my prowls through museum cupboards and attics and exhibits for more museum books. And meanwhile, through a small writers' group within the Children's Book Guild of Washington, I'm trying a non-fiction writer's hand at fiction—without yet creating a silk purse or a children's story book."

TICHY, William 1924-

PERSONAL: Born January 17, 1924, in Timisoura, Rumania; son of Martin (an engineer) and Elizabeth (Bartolff) Tichy; married Dorothy Figgemeier (in public relations), September 8, 1952; children: Allen, Sandra (Mrs. Gary Gray), Deanna (Mrs. Steve Gunning). *Education:* Washington University, St. Louis, Mo., 1949. *Home:* 1118 Gum, Broken Arrow, Okla. 74012.

CAREER: Emerson Electric Co., St. Louis, Mo., spectroscopist, 1949-55; General Electric Co., chemist, Cincinnati, Ohio, 1955-61, San Jose, Calif., 1961-68, Livermore, Calif., 1973-75; Varian Associates, Walnut Park, Calif., engineering writer, 1975-77; self-employed, beginning in 1977. *Military service:* U.S. Army, 1943-46; became technical sergeant; received Bronze Star and Presidential Unit Citation. *Member:* American Chemical Society, Society for Applied Spectroscopy, Technical Writers Association.

WRITINGS: Poisons: Antidotes and Anecdotes (juvenile; self-illustrated), Sterling, 1977. Contributor of book reviews to *Applied Spectroscopy,* of abstracts to *Chemical Abstracts,* and of a feature article to *Chemistry.*

WORK IN PROGRESS: "The Poison Mystique: The Natural Poisons in History," dealing with human attitudes toward poison, completion expected in 1984; a book, *Metatime,* which explores the question, "What is time, really?"

SIDELIGHTS: "On more than one occasion, the place of my birth has led to the strange notion that it had something to do with my interest in poisons and the other shadowy things of nature. Timisoura is just a stone's throw away from the infamous castle of the Transylvanian vampire, Count Dracula. Actually, there was more than such remote ancestry behind the book *Poisons: Antidotes and Anecdotes.* Years ago, I was exposed to Rudyard Kipling's book about a cobra and its archenemy, a mongoose Kipling called Rikki-Tikki-Tavi. I was inclined to wonder about the deadly potion possessed by the cobra. The question of deadliness quite naturally flowed over to the venom of the black widow spider, then to other creatures. My exposure to poisons and poisonings spawned one supreme lingering question: Why is it that so tiny a dose of poison—perhaps a smidgen on the tip of an arrow or the fine droplet on the fangs of an insect—could do [such damage] in beast or man? The book represents my way of explaining away much of the mystery which surrounds the powerful poisons."

WILLIAM TICHY

"My childhood on a farm provided an opportunity to observe nature directly. From the plants and animals close at hand, it was easily obvious that each had a personality of sorts. Cobras and the other more exotic beasts, not at hand, required a modest imagination for filling in the gaps and completing the picture. For even cobras have personalities—it all depends on the point of view.

"The perpetual student category would apply to me, for I have completed almost every science course—astronomy, geology, and so on—offered by the evening divisions of the local colleges or junior colleges. I have also taken business courses, philosophy, history, and pencil drawing. I have accumulated a respectable home library, including works on the classics, mythology, and the newest of the metasciences."

HOBBIES AND OTHER INTERESTS: Hiking and camping in mountainous areas, deserts and seashores; historical and biographical reading; the various metasciences.

FOR MORE INFORMATION SEE: Appraisal, Spring, 1978.

WALLACE TRIPP

TRIPP, Wallace (Whitney)   1940-

PERSONAL: Born June 26, 1940, in Boston, Mass.; son of Kenneth and Frances Whitney Tripp; married Marcia Bixby (president of Pawprints, Inc.) in 1965; children: two sons, one daughter. *Education:* Graduated from Boston Museum School; received B.Ed. from Keene State College; graduate study at University of New Hampshire. *Residence:* New Hampshire. *Office:* Sparhawk Books, Inc., Box 446, Jaffrey, N.H. 03452.

CAREER: Has worked as an English teacher. Free-lance illustrator and author, 1965—; Pawprints Greeting Cards, illustrator, 1972—; Sparhawk Books, Jaffrey, N.H., president and creative director, 1981—. *Member:* Authors Guild. *Awards, honors:* Recipient of Boston Globe-Horn Book Award, 1977, for *Granfa' Grig Had a Pig.*

WRITINGS—Self-illustrated; all for children: (Adaptor) *The Tale of a Pig: A Caucasian Folktale,* McGraw, 1968; (compiler) *A Great Big Ugly Man Came Up and Tied His Horse to Me* (verse; ALA Notable Book), Little, Brown, 1973; *My Uncle Podger: A Picture Book* (based on a passage from *Three Men in a Boat* by Jerome K. Jerome), Little, Brown, 1975; (compiler) *Granfa' Grig Had a Pig and Other Rhymes Without Reason from Mother Goose* (verse), Little, Brown, 1976; *Sir Toby Jingle's Beastly Journey* (Junior Literary Guild selection), Coward, 1976; (compiler) *Rhymes without Reason from Mother Goose,* World's Work, 1980.

Other: *Wallace Tripp's Wurst Seller* (humor for adults), Sparhawk Books, 1981.

Illustrator—all children's fiction, except as indicated: Reginald B. Hegarty, *Rope's End,* Houghton, 1965; Lisa Tsarelka, *Stay Away from My Lawnmower,* Houghton, 1965; Ruth C. Carlsen, *Henrietta Goes West,* Houghton, 1966; R. C. Carlsen, *Hildy and the Cuckoo Clock,* Houghton, 1966; Ilse Kleberger, *Grandmother Oma,* Atheneum, 1967; Andrew Lang, editor, *Read Me Another Fairy Tale,* Grosset, 1967; Katherine E. Miller, *Saint George: A Christmas Mummers' Play,* Houghton, 1967; Gerald Dumas, *Rabbits Rafferty,* Houghton, 1968; R. C. Carlsen, *Sam Bottleby,* Houghton, 1968; Felice Holman, *The Holiday Rat, and The Utmost Mouse* (short stories), Norton, 1969; John Erwin, *Mrs. Fox,* Simon & Schuster, 1969;

Scott Corbett, *The Baseball Bargain,* Little, Brown, 1970; Tom Paxton, *Jennifer's Rabbit,* Putnam, 1970; René Guillot, *Little Dog Lost,* translated by Joan Selby-Lowndes, Lothrop, 1970; Betty Brock, *No Flying in the House,* Harper, 1970; Ferdinand N. Monjo, *Pirates in Panama,* Simon & Schuster, 1970; Robert S. Bigelow, *Stubborn Bear,* Little, Brown, 1970.

Julian Bagley, *Candle-Lighting Time in Bodidalee* (folktales), American Heritage Publishing Co., 1971; Peggy Parish, *Come Back, Amelia Bedelia,* Harper, 1971; Victor Sharoff, *The Heart of the Wood,* Coward, 1971; Marguerita Rudolph, adaptor, *The Magic Egg, and Other Folk Stories of Rumania,* Little, Brown, 1971; Peter Hallard, *Puppy Lost in Lapland,* F. Watts, 1971; Patricia Thomas, *"Stand Back," said the Elephant, "I'm Going to Sneeze!",* Lothrop, 1971; Miriam A. Bourne, *Tigers in the Woods,* Coward, 1971; Tony Johnston, *The Adventures of Mole and Troll,* Putnam, 1972; Cynthia Jameson, adaptor, *Catofy the Clever* (folktale), Coward, 1972; Liesel M. Skorpen, *Old Arthur,* Harper, 1972; P. Parish, *Play Ball, Amelia Bedelia,* Harper, 1972; Carolyn Lane, *The Voices of Greenwillow Pond,* Houghton, 1972.

Boris Zakhoder, *The Crocodile's Toothbrush,* translated by Marguerita Rudolph, McGraw, 1973; Malcolm Hall, *Headlines* (Junior Literary Guild selection), Coward, 1973; T. Johnston, *Mole and Troll Trim the Tree* (Junior Literary Guild selection), Putnam, 1974, revised edition, 1980; Jan Wahl, *Pleasant Fieldmouse's Halloween Party,* Putnam, 1974; Robert Fremlin, *Three Friends,* Little, Brown, 1975; Ernest L. Thayer, *Casey at the Bat: A Ballad of the Republic, Sung in the Year 1888* (verse), Coward, 1978; Hilaire Belloc, *The Bad Child's Book of Beasts,* revised edition, Sparhawk Books, 1982.

An epicure, dining at Crewe,
Found quite a large mouse in his stew.
    Said the waiter, "Don't shout,
    And wave it about,
Or the rest will be wanting one, too!"

(From *A Great Big Ugly Man Came Up and Tied His Horse to Me*, compiled and illustrated by Wallace Tripp.)

ADAPTATIONS—Filmstrips: "Come Back, Amelia, Bedelia" and "Play Ball, Amelia, Bedelia," both Miller-Brody Productions.

*SIDELIGHTS:*Tripp was born in Boston, Massachusetts and grew up in New Hampshire and New York. After graduating from high school, he earned a diploma in graphic arts from the Boston Museum School of Fine Arts and a B.Ed. in English from Keene State College. Before beginning his career in illustrating and writing, Tripp taught English.

As a child Tripp always enjoyed drawing pictures and reading books. "My grandfather gave me *The Boy's King Arthur* when I was too young to read it, but the N.C. Wyeth pictures made a strong impression and still do. Later Ernest Shepard and Garth Williams made their mark."

Tripp remembered the two-room school he attended "in darkest New Hampshire. Some children came by horse; I had a long walk, often in cold and deep snow. Wildlife has always been a special interest, something I hope is conveyed in my books."

One of his grammar school teachers ". . . for two years impressed on us her favorite subject, art.

"My parents encouraged my art and, as both have a sense of humor, tended to foster whatever of the risible was in me. Boyhood interests were the American Indian, knights and chivalry, airplanes and animals. Luckily these all involved plenty of reading, researching, examining pictures and often interpretive drawing—sound early training for an illustrator. It is heresy to admit, perhaps, but the better-drawn comic books were a great source of instruction. Today I maintain my interest in all these areas, adding music and travel. . . .

". . . In children's books I look for artist (not necessarily the best draftsmen, either) with vitality, integrity, humor and a powerful story-telling bent. There is too much arty, pretentious, self-indulgent illustration (often not a considered accurate reflection of what the story says) looking as if intended as a portfolio presentation or a contest entry. Give me N. C. Wyeth, Ernest Shepard, Garth Williams, Bill Peet, Raymond Briggs, Richard Scarry and Graham Oakley and [forget] those [who perpetrate] lovely curlicues and fabulous puce washes." [Lee Kingman and others, *Illustrators of Children's Books: 1967-1976,* Horn Book, 1978.[1]]

"Since boyhood I've enjoyed mythology, knights, chivalry, and castles, not to mention animals and old people. *Sir Toby Jingle's Beastly Journey* was a natural combination of those things. The idea had been running through my mind for quite a few years and evolved through several written versions. The style changed from quasi-archaic (fake old-fashioned!) to the present combination of prose and balloon captions. Perhaps living in England for a year and traveling in Europe with visits to dozens of castles and places associated with legendary figures—animal and human—helped to make the story come alive.

He set his alarm for Christmas. ■(From *Pleasant Fieldmouse's Halloween Party* by Jan Wahl. Illustrated by Wallace Tripp.)

Originally I use animal characters, so having a human hero seemed almost odd to me (though i am in fact human). Part of the fun of doing *Sir Toby Jingle's Beastly Journey* was in pitting the wit and wisdom of ancient Sir Toby against the brute strength of the beasts. Probably it is evident that, even though Sir Toby is the hero, my sympathies were almost as much with the animals, who after all were being true to their own natures when they were being 'bad.'''

Tripp's wife, Marcia writes: ''Wallace researches constantly, feeling he has a duty to his audience to be correct. His strong drafting skills, knowledge of anatomy and sense of humor combine to make his art 'right' somehow. He is a master of expression and vitality, drawing from experience and imagination.

"He is a very private person, does not grant interviews, but has his gift of humor and art to offer to his public instead."

HOBBIES AND OTHER INTERESTS: Classical music, traveling, aviation, English humor.

FOR MORE INFORMATION SEE: New York Times Book Review, March 5, 1968, May 27, 1973, September 12, 1976; *Times Literary Supplement,* December 5, 1968, December 6, 1974; *Publishers Weekly,* February 23, 1976; Lee Kingman and others, *Illustrators of Children's Books: 1967-1976,* Horn Book, 1978.

TURSKA, Krystyna (Zofia)   1933-

PERSONAL: Born August 28, 1933, in Poland; emigrated to England in 1948; married K. Voelpel. *Education:* Graduated from Hammersmith School of Arts and Crafts. *Residence:* London, England.

CAREER: Illustrator of children's books and adaptor of children's tales, folklore, and mythology. *Awards, honors:* Commended for the Kate Greenaway Medal, 1970, for *Pegasus;* Kate Greenaway Medal, 1972, for *Woodcutter's Duck.*

WRITINGS—All for children; all retold by Turska: *Pegasus* (Greek mythology), Watts, 1970; *Tamara and the Sea Witch* (folklore), Hamish Hamilton, 1971, Parents Magazine Press, 1972; *The Woodcutter's Duck* (fairy tale; *Horn Book* honor list), Macmillan, 1972; *The Magician of Cracow* (folklore; *Horn Book* honor list), Greenwillow, 1975.

Illustrator: William Mayne, *Book of Heroes,* Dutton, 1966; Jacynth Hope-Simpson, *The Hamish Hamilton Book of Witches* (fiction), Hamish Hamilton, 1966, published as *A Cavalcade of Witches,* Walck, 1967; James Reeves, *The Trojan Horse* (fiction), Hamish Hamilton, 1968, Watts, 1969; Alan Garner, *A Cavalcade of Goblins,* Walck, 1969; Gillian Avery and others, *Authors' Choice: Stories* (fiction), Hamish Hamilton, 1970, Crowell, 1971; Roger L. Green, *A Cavalcade of Dragons* (stories), Walck, 1970, published as *Hamish Hamilton Book of Dragons,* Hamish Hamilton, 1970; Geoffrey Trease, *A Masque for the Queen* (fiction), Hamish Hamilton, 1970; G. Avery, *Ellen and the Queen* (fiction), Hamish Hamilton, 1971, Elsevier-Nelson, 1974; Michael Brown, *The Hamish Hamilton Book of Sea Legends* (folklore), Hamish Hamilton, 1971, pub-

lished as *A Cavalcade of Sea Legends,* Walck, 1972; G. Avery, *Red Letter Days,* Hamish Hamilton, 1971; J. Reeves, *The Path of Gold,* Hamish Hamilton, 1972; Joan Aiken and others, *Authors' Choice 2: Stories* (fiction), Hamish Hamilton, 1973, Crowell, 1974; Francis Eagar, *The Dolphin of the Two Seas,* Hamish Hamilton, 1973; Janet McNeill, *The Snow-Clean Pinny,* Hamish Hamilton, 1973; Barbara Willard, compiler, *Happy Families* (prose), Macmillan, 1974.

Elizabeth Jane Coatsworth, *Marra's World* (fiction), Greenwillow, 1975; Kathleen Killip, *Saint Bridget's Night: Stories from the Isle of Man,* Hamish Hamilton, 1975; James Riordan, *Russian Tales* (folklore), Viking Press, 1976; Honor Arundel, *The High House,* Hamish Hamilton, circa 1977; John Ruskin, *The King of the Golden River* (fairy tales), Greenwillow, 1978; Charles Causley, *The Last King of Cornwall,* Hodder and Stoughton, 1978; Helen Cooper, *Great Grandmother Goose,* Greenwillow, 1979; W. Mayne, *The Mouse and the Egg,* Greenwillow, 1981; Ruzena Wood, *The Palace of the Moon and Other Tales from Czechoslovakia,* Deutsch, 1981.

SIDELIGHTS: ''I was born in Poland to a family who had, particularly on my mother's side, a number of artists. I do not remember a lot from the early days of my childhood in Poland because I was only six when the war broke out. After a brief period of what I recall as air-raids, bomb explosions and some heavy fighting, Russia [overran this part] of Poland. One early morning of February, 1940, my family and I were arrested and taken to a concentration camp near Archangel in northern Russia, where we spent the next two years. Very luckily for all of us, the creation of new Polish Armed Forces in Russian territory gave us the opportunity to get away. After a very long and extremely tiring journey through Russia, we were allowed to enter Persia and were immediately placed in the care of the Allied Forces.

''After going through Iraq, Palestine and Egypt our wandering finally came to a stop when we arrived in the United Kingdom in 1948. Here we have found a new home, and, gradually, a new country which has given me freedom, education, art training, and a chance to practice my profession. This is something I shall always value very much and be grateful for.

''During my studies, and even after getting my diploma in illustration, I never imagined that, one day, I would illustrate children's books. Maybe it was because I wanted so much to do it that it seemed absolutely impossible for me to enter this 'charmed' field. And now, every book that I illustrate presents a new challenge, new problems, and makes me seek new ways of approach.

''I love my work enormously in spite of self-doubts, uncertainties and many frustrations, but life would seem a lot happier if only I could open one of my books without thinking, 'You could have done that a lot better!''' [Lee Kingman and others, compilers, *Illustrators of Children's Books: 1967-1976,* Horn Book, 1978.]

FOR MORE INFORMATION SEE: New York Times Book Review, November 16, 1975; *Times Literary Supplement,* December 5, 1975; *Horn Book,* February, 1976, August, 1979; Lee Kingman and others, compilers, *Illustrators of Children's Books: 1967-1976,* Horn Book, 1978.

"Why don't you sell your feather?" said Hans, sneeringly. "Out with you."

"A little bit," said the old gentleman.

"Be off!" said Schwartz.

"Pray, gentlemen."

(From *The King of the Golden River* by John Ruskin. Illustrated by Krystyna Turska.)

The magician got into the sleigh and they drove through the snow for many hours. At last, through the darkness, in the distance, they suddenly saw the light of an inn.

"Shall we stop at this inn to get warm and rest the horses?'' asked the false messenger.

The magician was feeling cold and tired. He agreed and they stopped at the inn.

(From *The Magician of Cracow* by Krystyna Turska. Illustrated by the author.)

TWORKOV, Jack 1900-1982

OBITUARY NOTICE: Born August 15, 1900, in Biala, Poland; died September 4, 1982, in Provincetown, Mass. A painter and author, Tworkov was a leader of the abstract expressionist school of painting. After coming to the United States at the age of thirteen and attending New York public schools, Tworkov went on to study art at the National Academy of Design, the Art Students League, and with Ross E. Moffett and Karl Knaths in Provincetown, where Tworkov began showing his work. During the 1930s Tworkov worked as a puppeteer and with government public art projects. Tworkov's work has been shown around the world. In 1974 he received the painter-of-the-year award from the Skowhegan School of Art. Tworkov has taught art at numerous art schools and universities, including Yale University, Cooper Union, Dartmouth College, American Academy in Rome, and Black Mountain College. For children he has written *The Camel Who Took a Walk* and *Tigers Don't Bite,* both illustrated by Roger Duvoisin. *For More Information See: Art News,* May, 1953; *Who's Who in American Art, 1980,* Bowker, 1980; *Who's Who in America, 1980-1981,* Marquis, 1980. *Obituaries: New York Times,* September 6, 1982; *Newsweek,* September 20, 1982; *Time,* September 20, 1982.

VASS, George 1927-

BRIEF ENTRY: Born March 27, 1927, in Leipzig, Germany. A graduate of Northwestern and Washington Universities, Vass has been a sports reporter for the *Chicago Daily News* since 1958. He is also the author of juvenile books on sports figures and teams. Among the juvenile titles he has written are *Champions of Sports* (Reilly & Lee, 1970), *Reggie Jackson: From Superstar to Candy Bar* (Children's Press, 1979), and *Steve Garvey: The Bat Boy Who Became a Star* (Children's Press, 1979). Vass is also the author of books that appeal to adult readers. They include *The Chicago Black Hawks Story* (Follett, 1970), *George Halas and the Chicago Bears* (Regnery, 1971), and *Like Nobody Else: The Fergie Jenkins Story* (Regnery, 1973). Vass has contributed stories to *Baseball Digest* and *Hockey Digest.* In 1968, 1970, and 1971, he was the recipient of the Illinois Associated Press prize for stories on sports. Vass is a member of the Authors Guild, the Baseball Writers Association of America, and the National Hockey League Writers Association. *Address:* 9039 Major Ave., Morton Grove, Ill. 60053. *For More Information See: Contemporary Authors,* Volumes 37-40, revised, Gale, 1979.

VLAHOS, Olivia 1924-

PERSONAL: Surname is pronounced *Vlay*-hose; born January 8, 1924, in Houston, Tex.; daughter of Robert (a salesman) and Sophia (Riesner) Lockart; married John Vlahos (a playwright), June 25, 1947; children: Michael, Melissa, Stephanie. *Education:* Sullins College, student, 1941; University of Texas, B.F.A., 1945; Sarah Lawrence College, M.A., 1965. *Home:* 18 Crawford Rd., Westport, Conn. 06880.

CAREER: Giezendanner Advertising Agency, Houston, Tex., copywriter, 1942; actress with Interstate Players, professional touring company based in Austin, Tex., 1946; Glenn Advertising Agency, Hollywood, Calif., secretary, 1948-49; Hughes Aircraft Co., Culver City, Calif., administrative secretary, 1949-51; Norwalk Community College, Norwalk, Conn., began as lecturer, now professor of social sciences, 1967—. *Awards, honors:* Recipient of a National Endowment for the Humanities grant, 1975, and a Connecticut Humanities Council grant, 1978.

WRITINGS—Of interest to young people: *Human Beginnings,* Viking, 1966; *African Beginnings,* Viking, 1967; *Battle-Ax People: Beginnings of Western Culture,* Viking, 1968; *New World Beginnings,* Viking, 1970; *Far Eastern Beginnings,* Viking, 1976.

Adult: *Body, the Ultimate Symbol,* Lippincott, 1980.

SIDELIGHTS: Vlahos's books reflect her interest in archaeology. A professor of anthropology at Norwalk Community College for many years, she has received grants from the National Endowment for the Humanities and from the Connecticut Humanities Council for two unique college programs: "Archaeology as an Avocation" and "Archaeology in the Community."

About her latest young-adult book, *Far Eastern Beginnings,* Vlahos commented: "Of all earth's regions, none is so rich in history and prehistory, in diverse life ways, languages, and lore as the Far East. It is possible to devote a lifetime to the study of one small portion of this intellectual immensity—to one of the Chinese dynasties, one cave excavated in Southeast Asia, one aspect of Buddhism, one of the Confucian Classics. Legions of scholars have done just that. Should any of them

OLIVIA VLAHOS

(From *Far Eastern Beginnings* by Olivia Vlahos. Illustrated by George Ford.)

open . . . pages of [my book], he or she may well object to the foreshortened record of events, to the simplification of beliefs and ideas so rich and so complex. But I am taking a bird's-eye view of the area: a view of the forest in which individual trees tend to merge into a general green blur. If such a view provides a framework for further study, if it stimulates the reader's curiosity, makes him long to read more, then the book will have served its purpose, and I shall be content." [Olivia Vlahos, "Author's Note," *Far Eastern Beginnings,* Viking, 1976.¹]

WALKER, Alice 1944-

PERSONAL: Born February 9, 1944, in Eatonton, Ga.; daughter of Willie Lee and Minnie Tallulah (Grant) Walker; married Melvyn Rosenman Leventhal (a civil rights lawyer), March 17, 1967 (marriage ended); children: Rebecca Grant. *Education:* Attended Spelman College, 1961-63; Sarah Lawrence College, B.A., 1965. *Agent:* Wendy Weil, Julian Bach Literary Agency, 3 East 48th St., New York, N.Y.

CAREER: Teacher of writing and Black literature at Jackson State College and Tougaloo College, Miss., 1968-70; Wellesley College, Wellesley, Mass., lecturer in writing and literature, 1972—; University of Massachusetts, Boston, lecturer in

literature, 1972—. *Awards, honors:* Breadloaf Writer's Conference, scholar, 1966; Merrill Writing fellowship, 1967; McDowell Colony Fellowship, 1967; National Endowment for the Arts grant, 1969; Radcliffe Institute fellowship, 1971-73; Rosenthal Award of the National Institute of Arts and Letters for *In Love and Trouble: Stories of Black Women,* 1973; Lillian Smith Award for *Revolutionary Petunias,* 1973.

WRITINGS—Of interest to young readers: *Langston Hughes, American Poet,* Crowell, 1973.

Other: *Once* (poems), Harcourt, 1968; *The Third Life of Grange Copeland* (novel), Harcourt, 1970; *Revolutionary Petunias* (poems), Harcourt, 1973; *In Love and Trouble: Stories of Black Women* (short stories), Harcourt, 1973; *I Love Myself When I Am Laughing: A Zora Neale Hurston Reader,* Feminist Press, 1979; *Goodnight Willie Lee, I'll See You in the Morning* (poems), Dial, 1979; *You Can't Keep a Good Woman Down,* Harcourt, 1980; *The Color Purple,* Harcourt, 1982; *Meridian,* Washington Square Press, 1982.

WORK IN PROGRESS: A collection of essays entitled, *In Search of Our Mothers' Gardens.*

SIDELIGHTS: Born on **February 9, 1944** in Eatonton, Georgia, the youngest of eight children into a share-cropping family. "Sometimes I thought I'd gotten into the family by mistake. I always seemed to need more peace and quiet than anybody else. That's very difficult when you're living with ten people in three or four rooms. So I found what privacy I had by walking in the fields. We had to get our water from a spring, so that was a time to be alone, too. I spent so much time out of doors that when I started writing—and I found myself writing my first book of poems, *Once,* under a tree in Kenya—it seemed quite normal.

"I also had terrific teachers. When I was four and my mother had to go work in the fields, my first-grade teacher let me start in her class. Right on through grammar school and high school and college, there was one—sometimes even two—teachers who saved me from feeling alone; from worrying that the world I was stretching to find might not even exist.

"Of course, the schools were all-black and that gave us a feeling that they really belonged to us. If they needed desks or a stage, the men in the community built them. My parents gave what they called get-togethers to raise money for the grammar school when I was there. There was a lot of self-help and community.

"My teachers lent me books: *Jane Eyre* was my friend for a long time. Books became my world because the world I was in was very hard. My mother was working as a maid, so she was away from six-thirty in the morning until after dark. Because one sister was living up North and the other one had become a beautician, I was supposed to take care of the house and do the cooking. I was twelve, coming home to an empty house and cleaning and fixing dinner—for people who didn't really appreciate the struggle it was to fix it. I missed my mother very much.

"From the time I was eight, I kept a notebook. I found it lately and I was surprised—they were horrible poems, but they were poems. There's even a preface that thanks all the people who were forced to hear this material—my mother, my teacher, my blind Uncle Frank." [Gloria Steinem, "Do You Know This Woman? She Knows You: A Profile of Alice Walker," *Ms.,* June, 1982.¹]

ALICE WALKER

". . . I could go into my room and shut the door and lie on the bed and read, knowing I would never be interrupted. No matter what was needed, there was no word about making me leave a book. It was not just the 'permission' to read. My mother trusted me implicitly and completely. She never questioned me about any relationships with boys. She trusted my ability to go out into the world and learn about the world. I suppose because I was the last child there was a special rapport between us and I was permitted a lot more freedom. Once when I was eight or nine she was about to whip my brothers and me for something and when she finished whipping the others and got to me, she turned around and dropped the switch and said, 'You know, Alice, I don't have to whip you; I can talk to you.'" [Mary Helen Washington, "Her Mother's Gift," *Ms.*, June, 1982.[2]]

1952. While playing with her older brothers, Walker was blinded in her right eye by a shot from one of their BB guns. Scar tissue covered the eye like a large cataract. "I used to pray every night that I would wake up and somehow it would be gone. I couldn't look at people directly because I thought I was ugly. Flannery O'Connor says that a writer has to be able to stare, to see everything that's going on. I never looked up.

"Then when I was fourteen, I visited my brother Bill to take care of his children in the summer. He took me to a hospital where they removed most of the scar tissue—and I was a *changed person.* I promptly went home, scooped up the best-looking guy, and by the time I graduated from high school, I was Valedictorian, voted 'Most Popular,' and crowned Queen!"[1]

Walker's mother gave her three gifts, which later came to take on an important symbolic value for her. When Walker was fifteen or sixteen, her mother gave her a sewing machine for her birthday so she could learn to make her own clothes. "I even made my own prom dress, such as it was, something chartreuse net, I think. But the message about independence and self-sufficiency was clear."[2]

The second gift was a suitcase, a high school graduation gift, "as nice a one as anyone in Eatonton had ever had. That suitcase gave me permission to travel and part of the joy in going very far from home was the message of that suitcase. Just a year later I was in Russia and Eastern Europe."[2]

The third gift was a typewriter. "Oh yes, she bought me a typewriter when I was in high school. How did my mama ever get that typewriter? She must have ordered it from Sears. A typewriter and a little typewriter table. She did all this on less than twenty dollars a week."[2]

March 17, 1967. Married Mel Leventhal, a white civil rights lawyer. "Mel and I had been living together perfectly happily for almost a year, but we could see that, given the history, we couldn't go off into the world and do political work unless we were married. We could challenge the laws against intermarriage at the same time—in addition to which, we really loved each other. Love, politics, work—it was a mighty coming together.

"He was also the first person who consistently supported me in my struggle to write. Whenever we moved, the first thing he did was fix a place for me to work. He might be astonished and sometimes horrified at what came out, but he was always right there."[1] The union lasted for ten years.

Of her writing, Walker explained: "If you're silent for a long time, people just arrive in your mind. It makes you believe the world was created in silence.

On the ranch in Mexico there was an Indian boy who took care of the horses. His name was Maximiliano . . . and Maximiliano taught him to ride a horse bareback. They became good friends. ■(From *Langston Hughes, American Poet* by Alice Walker. Illustrated by Don Miller.)

''Writing *The Color Purple* was writing in my first language. I had to do a lot of living to get the knowledge, but the writing itself was really easy. There was a moment when I remember feeling real rage that black people or other people of color who have different patterns of speech can't just routinely write in this natural, flowing way.

''Books are by-products of our lives. Deliver me from writers who say the way they live doesn't matter. I'm not sure a bad person can write a good book. If art doesn't make us better, then what on earth is it for?''[1]

FOR MORE INFORMATION SEE: Book World, November 3, 1968; *Library Journal,* June 15, 1970; *Poetry,* February, 1971; *New Leader,* January 25, 1971; *Ms.,* June, 1982.

WALTHER, Thomas A.   1950-
(Tom Walther)

PERSONAL: Born February 20, 1950, in Elko, Nev.; son of Paul (co-owner of an appliance business) and Marjory (co-owner of an appliance business; maiden name, Sutcliffe) Walther; married Geraldine Lamboley (a violist), June 12, 1977. *Education:* California College of Arts and Crafts, B.F.A., 1973; attended Burklyn Business School, 1980. *Home:* 4323 Montgomery St., Oakland, Calif. 94611.

(From *Make Mine Music: How to Make and Play Instruments and Why They Work* by Tom Walther. Cover illustration by the author.)

CAREER: Free-lance teacher at schools including California College of Arts and Crafts, Oakland, Calif., Northern Nevada Community College, Elko, Nev., and others, 1973—; free-lance writer and illustrator, 1973—; owner of company that manufactures wood products and musical instruments, Emeryville, Calif. *Member:* Authors Guild.

WRITINGS—For children; under name Tom Walther; self-illustrated: *A Spider Might,* Scribner, 1978; *Make Mine Music: How to Make and Play Instruments and Why They Work,* Little, Brown, 1981.

SIDELIGHTS: Walther believes freedom in life comes from understanding. ''I am particularly interested in the magic unveiled by clearing away the mystery that separates people from understanding and feeling a part of our magical world. I like to see how simple things are—to find out the principles. When we understand how things work, how to create, how wonderful we and the world are, we are then in a powerful place to create magical lives, a beautiful environment, and freedom in our lives.''

WEISSENBORN, Hellmuth   1898-1982

OBITUARY NOTICE: Born December 29, 1898, in Leipzig, East Germany; died September 2, 1982, in Kensington, England. Graphic artist, painter, teacher, publisher, and author. Weissenborn and his wife, Lesley Macdonald, founded Acorn Press, publishers of children's books and signed limited editions. His major work, written in collaboration with his wife, was a translation of Gimmelshausen's autobiographical novel of the Thirty Years War, *Simplicius Simplicissimus.* Weissenborn's art work has been published in more than fifty books and is displayed in several museums, including the Imperial War Museum and the Victoria and Albert Museum. *Obituaries: London Times,* September 11, 1982.

WELLER, George (Anthony)   1907-
(Michael Wharf)

PERSONAL: Born July 13, 1907, in Boston, Mass.; son of George Joseph (a lawyer) and Matilda B. (a social worker; maiden name, McAleer) Weller; married Katherine Deupree, 1932 (divorced, 1944); married Charlotte Ebener, January 23, 1948; children: Ann Weller Tagge, Anthony. *Education:* Harvard University, B.A., 1929; graduate study at University of Vienna and Max Reinhardt School of Theatre, 1930-31. *Home:* Annisquam, Mass.; and Via Vasca Moresca 20, San Felice di Circeo, Italy. *Agent:* Harold Ober Associates, Inc., 40 East 49th St., New York, N.Y. 10017. *Office:* Stampa Estera, Via della Mercede 55, Rome, Italy.

CAREER: Teacher in Tucson, Ariz., 1929-30; *New York Times,* New York, N.Y., correspondent for Greece and the Balkans, 1932-35; Homeland Foundation, New York, N.Y., director, 1937-40; *Chicago Daily News,* Chicago, Ill., correspondent, 1940-72 (covered news events in all parts of the world except western Africa). *Member:* Foreign Press Club of Rome, Stampa Estera (president, 1954-55; vice-president, 1973-74), Overseas Press Club, Dutch Treat Club, Explorers Club, Drama League, Phi Beta Kappa. *Awards, honors:* Pulitzer Prize, for description of appendectomy aboard a submarine, 1943; Nieman fellow at Harvard University, 1947-48; George Polk prize, 1955; British drama contest awards, 1960, for ''Second Saint of Cyprus'';

U.S. Navy public service citation, for volunteer work with U.S. Mediterranean Fleet, 1948-1970.

WRITINGS—Of interest to young people: *The Story of Paratroops* (history), Random House, 1958; *Story of Submarines* (history), Random House, 1962.

Other: *Not to Eat, Not for Love* (novel), Smith & Haas, 1933; (translator under pseudonym Michael Wharf) Ignazio Silone, *Fontamara,* Random House, 1935; *Clutch and Differential* (novel), Random House, 1936; *Singapore Is Silent* (history), Harcourt, 1943; *Bases Overseas* (geopolitics), Harcourt, 1944; *The Crack in the Column* (novel), Random House, 1949. Author of plays: "Second Saint of Cyprus," 1960, and "Walking Time," 1965. Contributor of stories and articles to national magazines.

WORK IN PROGRESS: A geopolitical history; historic study of foreign correspondents; biography on Borodin, the Soviet revolutionist in China.

SIDELIGHTS: "After a brief experience teaching, I began as a novelist and playwright, and then went into foreign correspondence in order to see the world and obtain a realistic education. I have served as a foreign correspondent everywhere in the world except West Africa, and was the first war correspondent in the Pacific to qualify as a trained paratrooper (seven jumps). My area of most intense and longest commitment has been the Middle East.

"My retirement in 1972 allows me to renew broken pledges to more subjective forms: the novel, the theatre, the new geopolitics. The mantraps of over-diversification remain.

"I live in the Mediterranean because my tastes are historical as well as artistic. I speak Italian, French, and German and have a working use of modern Greek and Spanish."

A paratroop officer tells his men they will be the first American troops to land on Sicily. ■(From *The Story of the Paratroops* by George Weller. Illustrated by W.T. Mars.)

GEORGE WELLER

WHITLOCK, Pamela   1921(?)-1982

OBITUARY NOTICE: Born about 1921; died June 3, 1982. Author of children's books. Whitlock and co-author Katharine Hull were still in their teens when they wrote their first novels, a trilogy describing the freedom young people experience during summer holidays. The books, *The Far Distant Oxus, Escape to Persia,* and *Oxus in Summer,* were popular with children for many years. She is also co-author with Hull of *Crowns,* and editor of *An Anthology of Poetry for Children: All Day Long. Obituaries: London Times,* June 15, 1982.

WILKIE, Katharine E(lliott)   1904-1980

PERSONAL: Born February 6, 1904, in Lexington, Ky.; died April 5, 1980; daughter of J. Milward and Katharine (Crockett) Elliott; married Raymond Abell Wilkie (a hardware salesman), 1925; children: Raymond Abell, Jr., Milward Elliott. *Education:* University of Kentucky, B.A., 1924, M.A., 1939. *Religion:* Methodist. *Home:* 312 Irvine Rd., Lexington, Ky. 40502.

CAREER: Teacher in Kentucky schools, 1925-26, 1951-69, and for three years in private schools; author of children's books. Teacher of course in writing children's literature in the Over 57 Writer's Workshop, conducted by University of Kentucky, summers, 1968 and 1970. *Member:* National League of American Pen Women, National Education Association, Kentucky Educational Association, Central Kentucky Educational Association, Mortar Board, Theta Sigma Phi, Chi Delta Phi, Kappa Delta Pi.

WRITINGS: Zack Taylor: Young Rough and Ready, Bobbs-Merrill, 1952; *Will Clark: Boy in Buckskins,* Bobbs-Merrill, 1953; *Mary Todd Lincoln: Girl of the Bluegrass,* Bobbs-Merrill, 1954; *George Rogers Clark: Boy of the Old Northwest,* Bobbs-Merrill, 1958; *John Sevier: Son of Tennessee,* Messner, 1958; *Simon Kenton: Young Trail Blazer,* Bobbs-Merrill, 1960; *Daniel Boone: Taming the Wilds,* Garrard, 1960; *Robert Louis Stevenson: Storyteller and Adventurer,* Houghton, 1961; *The Man Who Wouldn't Give Up: Henry Clay,* Messner, 1961; *William Fargo: Boy Mail Carrier,* Bobbs-Merrill, 1962; (with Elizabeth R. Moseley) *Father of the Constitution: James Madison,* Messner, 1963; *Ferdinand Magellan: Noble Captain,* Houghton, 1963; *William Penn: Friend to All,* Garrard, 1964; *Kentucky Government* (published in connection with Ralph W. Steen's *Government by the People*), Steck, 1964, revised edition, 1975; (with Moseley) *Teacher of the Blind: Samuel Gridley Howe,* Messner, 1965; *Maria Mitchell: Stargazer,* Garrard, 1966; (with Moseley) *Kentucky Heritage,* Steck, 1966; *Clyde Beatty: Young Animal Trainer,* Bobbs-Merrill, 1968; *Pocahontas, Indian Princess,* Garrard, 1969; (with Moseley) *Frontier Nurse: Mary Breckenridge,* Messner, 1969; *Helen Keller: Handicapped Girl,* Bobbs-Merrill, 1969; *Charles Dickens: An Inimitable Boz,* Abelard, 1970; *Atlantis,* Messner, 1978.

SIDELIGHTS: ''I was born in Lexington, Kentucky, and have lived here ever since, and—

By now Daniel had forgotten the cattle. He had forgotten everything but the wonderful bow, his new friend, and the wide, wild woods. ■ (From *Daniel Boone: Taming the Wilds* by Katharine E. Wilkie. Illustrated by E. Harper Johnson.)

KATHARINE E. WILKIE

"East, west—
home's best.

"I have loved books a long time, and growing up an only child I learned to read early. And writing? I can't remember when I didn't have 'writer's itch.'

"However, I didn't write my first book until 1952. Perhaps, just *perhaps,* my favorite is *Mary Todd Lincoln,* although *Robert Louis Stevenson* and *Charles Dickens,* both men being great heroes of mine, are close seconds.

"But Mary Todd was born in my home town. Recently her girlhood home was restored and opened to the public. When you go there and see the very rooms in which she lived and later visited with her husband, Abraham Lincoln, and their two small sons, Robert and Eddie, you step back into history.

"Then I am interested in her and another house where she lived when she was a small child for another reason. Now torn down, it was next door to that of her Grandmother Parker—the widow Parker. Mary must have crossed the wide lawn to her grandmother's house every day.

"By some quirk of fate my maternal grandmother, also a widow, owned that house from 1890 to 1900 and reared her children there. When I was a child, it was a home for orphans and my mother took me there more than once to see her old home.

"I have loved history almost as long as I have loved books. Much of that I owe to my father who loved both.

"When I was a young married woman, I belonged to a club whose favorite speaker was Mrs. W. T. Lafferty, a well-known Kentucky historian of the time. Once a year she would charter a Greyhound bus and we would all ride merrily over the Blue-

grass to spots of interest where we would unload and listen to her as she told about the houses and the people who had lived there. Those days linger in my memory as enchanted ones.

"But I have other interests besides books and history. We have four grandchildren and watched them all grow up. Now all are married to wonderful people, and we had our first great-grandchild on Christmas Day, 1977, another . . . in . . . 1978. Aren't we lucky?

"And dogs. Don't forget the dogs. There are two, a . . . beagle named Snoopy and a . . . cocker spaniel named Lanny. . . . The dogs own our house, but they are kind enough to let us live here."

Father of the Constitution: James Madison has been translated into Spanish and Portuguese.

HOBBIES AND OTHER INTERESTS: "Mixing and mingling with people, reading, collecting books and antiques."

FOR MORE INFORMATION SEE: Horn Book, October, 1965.

WILKOŃ, Józef   1930-

PERSONAL: Born February 12, 1930, in Bogucice, Poland; son of Piotr and Karolina (Olech) Wilkoń; married Malgorzata Jagoszewska, December 22, 1955; children: Piotr. *Education:* Jagiellonian University, Cracow, Poland, diploma, 1954; Academy of Fine Arts, Cracow, Poland, diploma, 1955. *Religion:* Roman Catholic, *Home:* Hoza 39, Apt. 79, 00-681 Warsaw, Poland. *Agent:* Agencja Autorska-ZAIKS, Hipoteczna 2, 00-950 Warsaw, Poland.

CAREER: Illustrator. Arkady Publishers, Warsaw, Poland, art director, 1979—. *Exhibitions*—One-man shows: Warsaw, 1959, 1960, 1970; Cracow, 1961; Vienna, 1963; Lublin, Chelm, Toruń, 1967-68; Manchester, 1969; West Berlin, 1971; Cologne, 1973, 1980; Polish Museum of America, Chicago, 1976; MAG Gallery, Zurich, 1980.

Group shows: Rzeszów, 1955; London, 1960, 1967; Moscow, 1964, 1974; Riga, Berlin, Warsaw, 1964; Tokyo, 1966, 1968, 1970, 1982; Brussels, Gandava, Mexico, 1968; Hannover, 1969. *Member:* Union of Polish Artists and Designers, Society of Authors (ZAIKS).

AWARDS, HONORS: Prize from Polish Publishers Association for "The Most Beautiful Book of the Year" was awarded to: *Iv i Finetta,* 1959, *Pawie wiersze,* 1960, *Zaczarowana jagoda,* 1964, *Maciupinka,* 1970, *Grajmy,* 1973, *Kraina Sto Piatej Tajemnicy,* 1974, *Od gór do morza,* 1974; Gold Medal, International Book Exhibition, Leipzig, 1959; Deutscher Jugendbuchpreis für Graphische Gestaltung, Düsseldorf, 1966, for *Herr Minkepatt und seine Freunde;* State's Award for achievements in the field of book illustrations, Warsaw, 1967; Gold Medal, Bratislava Biennale of Book Illustration, 1969, for *W Nieparyzu i Gdzieindziej;* "Srebrne Koziolki," Biennale of Arts for Children, Poznań, 1973, for *Siedem księzyców;* Medal of National Education Committee for artistic activity for children, 1973; distinction award, Bratislava Biennale, 1974, for *List do Warszawy;* Premio Grafico, 1974; Prime Minister's Prize for the production of children's books, 1974; Gold Medal, International Book Exhibition (Moscow), 1975, for illustrations for *Pan Tadeusz;* "Zlote Koziolki," Biennale of Arts for Children, Poznań, 1977; diploma of "Loisirs Jeunes," Paris, 1980. Recipient of many other awards for illustration.

WRITINGS—Self-illustrated: *Little Tom and the Big Cats*, Dent, 1978; *Minka*, Parabel Verlag, 1978.

Illustrator: Natalia Galczyńska, *Iv i Finetta* (title means "Iv and Finetta"), Ruch, 1959; Tadeusz Kubiak, *Pawie wiersze* (title means "Peacock's Poems"), Nasza Ksiegarnia, 1960; *Beowulf*, Nasza Ksiegarnia, 1962; Mieczyslawa Buczkówna, *Zaczarowana jagoda* (title means "Magic Berry"), Czytelnik, 1964; *Marcin spod Dzikiej Jabloni* [original American edition, Eleanor Farjeon, *Martin Pippin in the Apple Orchard*, Stokes, 1922], Nasza Ksiegarnia, 1964; Paul Schaaf, *The Crane with One Leg*, Warne, 1965; Ursula Valentin, *Herr Minkepatt und seine Freunde*, Middelhauve Verlag, 1965, published in America as *Herr Minkepatt and His Friends*, Dobson, 1965; Anna Kamieńska, *W Nieparyzu i Gdzieindziej* (title means "Not in Paris and Elsewhere"), Nasza Ksiegarnia, 1967; Robert W. Schnell, *Bonko*, Middelhauve Verlag, 1969; Wanda Chotomska, *Siedem ksiezyców* (title means "Seven Moons"), Ruch, 1970; Jerzy Ficowski, *Maciupinka*, Ruch, 1970; Uwe Friesel, *Herr Timm und seine Zauberflöte*, Middelhauve Verlag, 1970, published in America as *Tim, the Peacemaker* by Scroll; Robert Louis Stevenson, *Die Schatzinsel* (title means "Treasure Is-

(From *Treasure Island* by Robert Louis Stevenson. Illustrated by Józef Wilkoń.)

land"), Loewes Verlag, 1971; Hanna Januszewska, *Grajmy* (title means "Let's Play"), Ruch, 1973; Daniel Defoe, *Robinson Crusoe*, Loewes Verlag, 1973; Günter Spang, *Kossik*, Parabel Verlag, 1974; Tadeusz Kubiak, *List do Warszawy* (title means "Letter to Warsaw"), Nasza Ksiegarnia, 1974; Zbigniew Zakiewicz, *Kraina Sto Piatej Tajemnicy* (title means "Country of 105 Mysteries"), Czytelnik, 1974; Marta Tomaszewska, *Wyprawa Tapatików* (title means "The Tapatikos Expedition"), Krajowa Agencja Wydawnicza, 1974; Jerzy Kierst, *Od gór do morza* (title means "From Mountains to the Sea"), Krajowa Agencja Wydawnicza, 1974; G. Spang, *Wolfskinder* (title means "Children of Wolf"), Parabel Verlag, 1975; Ludwik Jerzy Kern, *Nasze podwórko* (title means "Our Playard"), Nasza Ksiegarnia, 1975; Wladimir Majakowskij, *Ein Löwe ist Kein Elefant*, Middelhauve Verlag, 1975, published in England as *Lions Are Not Elephants*, Hodder & Stoughton, 1979; Mark Twain, *Tom Sawyer*, Loewes Verlag, 1979; Mateusz Siuchniński, *The Illustrated History of Poland*, Interpess, 1979; Irina Korschunow, *Jussuf will ein Tiger sein*, Parabel Verlag, 1978, published in England as *Timothy an Extraordinary Tiger*, Dent, 1979; Kurt Baumann, *Waldkonzert*, Bohem Press, 1980, published in England as *The Concert of the Birds*, Hutchinson, 1980; Max Bollinger, *Der Bärenberg* (title means "The Bear's Mountain"), Bohem Press, 1982; Peter Nickl, *Die Geschichte vom Guten Wolf*, Nord-Süd Verlag, 1982, translation published as *The Story of the Kind Wolf*, Faber, 1982; Fredrik Vahle, *Wem gibt der Elefant die Hand* (title means "With whom the Elephant Shakes Hands"), Middelhauve Verlag, 1982.

(From *Tom Sawyer* by Mark Twain. Illustrated by Józef Wilkoń.)

He picked up the little rabbit and carried it back to his home. He tucked it up in his own warm bed and made a strong brew of hot camomile tea and honey. ■ (From *The Story of the Kind Wolf* by Peter Nickl. Illustrated by Józef Wilkoń.)

WORK IN PROGRESS: Illustrations for the Anthology of Russian Poetry, *W zakletym dworze* (title means "The Magic Forest") for Nasza Ksiegarnia; Józef Czechowicz, *Zloty Kogucik* (title means "The Golden Cock") for Wydawnictwo Lubelskie; *Weihnachten* (title means "Christmas") for Nord-Süd Verlag.

SIDELIGHTS: "An equal partnership of text and art in literature has become a fact—both in the field of styling and presentation of a book, and in freedom of stimulating a reader's imagination.

"Many great artists have been involved in the art of illustrating literary works.

"I am expanding my own emotions just as much when I paint and when I do illustration. Were it not so, I would have long ago ceased illustrating books."

When asked for whom his art was intended, Wilkoń responded: "For everybody. Even when I do things that are obviously for children, I do not lose sight of adults.

"Children are perhaps less restrained and biased. But an adult who is sensitive and familiarized with art, responds more completely, more consciously, and hence more keenly. However, bad taste or a lack of contact with art renders adults more helpless than children when it comes to the perception of a picture.

". . . Half of the blame [for the decrease in the intensity of the imagination when a child reaches adulthood] lies in nature itself. Don't animals behave similarly? The gait of an adult horse, however beautiful, lacks the spontaneity and the enchanting frenzy of a colt's gallop. A natural need to play, to experience intense feelings, naturally disinterested reactions and a strong imagination thrown in, all that vanishes when childhood is over. Who manages to retain it and to what extent? Perhaps only those few adults who are bold enough to remain something of a child till the end of life." [*Projekt,* (Poland), January 1, 1979.[1]]

When asked what we know about a child's response to a book and if a child's needs and reactions can be examined, Wilkoń acknowledged that "we are not yet able precisely to record the child's response to art. Observations are usually carried out too late when his mental life has become the resultant of various pressures and images suggested to, or imposed on him by adults. Questions and tests are drawn up by adults and children's answers are often very cunning, flattering the adult taste. We think that we can understand children by way of the 'bank of memory' of our own childhood, which is very deceitful. This 'bank of memory' is distorted by a mature person's different rhythm of life. That is why we cannot identify the heartbeat of a child with our own adult pulse when we compare the scale and the quality of emotions experienced by children and by adults. However, some teachers 'travel' to childhood more successfully than others. It happens when the subject of their exploration is not art and the child's response to it but the child's existence in general. I think that in this sense Janusz Korczak knew a good deal about children.

"When the child passes the threshold of childhood, he becomes more fascinated with the real world than with that of the imagination. In Polish book illustrations, the bizarre and the fantastic prevail both quantitatively and qualitatively over matter-of-fact and realistic represention. One must say that in this field we have not too many artists whose talent and work-

JÓZEF WILKOŃ

manship could fully satisfy the needs of the market. A number of reasons are responsible for it but the most important is probably the fact that both the curricula of art schools and Polish art in general have unduly evaded realism for the last few decades. Attempts at subject representation were usually sneered at as naturalistic, which was equivalent to bad taste and bad traditions. This accounts for the fact than an important section of illustrative work has been deprived on the foundation of good craftsmanship. I think that a number of opinions on that matter have been straightened out and that we will live to see better textbooks for young people, provided the quality of print and paper improve. A satisfactory primer is the result of both the talent and the skill of the designer, the initiative of the publishing house and the work of the printers. I think that we tend to overlook the psychological factor—a beautifully edited textbook could release in a child more emotion and contribute to the effectiveness of the educational process. This is particularly important in the case of a primer that affects children's overall attitude to books."[1]

In responding to the link between illustrations and the most important things going on in art today, Wilkoń admitted: ". . . All over the world, galleries and private collections of illustrations are springing up like mushrooms. As yet, there is no gallery or museum of illustrations in Poland to be reckoned with, but we must remember that poster design had gone through a bad time before the establishment of the poster gallery of Wilanów. There are a multitude of Biennales and exhibitions. Books illustration is growing in popularity and importance and has attracted prominent graphic arts. Mass editions in thousands of copies are rather tempting. I am not trying to say what is paramount in art. Personally, I think that in painting one gets closest to the idea of freedom. I do not believe that painting is on the decline.''[1]

When executing an illustration, ''I really have the child at heart and I often think of him but, to be quite frank, I do my illustrations for myself. Having worked on children's books as long as I have I see no other possibility. Artists have to choose either to trust themselves or to flatter imaginary tastes, thus joining the dignified body of the world's infantilists.''[1]

Wilkoń has illustrated over 100 books, most of them for children.

FOR MORE INFORMATION SEE: Polska ilustracja ksiazkowa, Wydawnictwa Artystyczne i Filmowe, 1964; Jerzy Stajuda, ''Milioner,'' *Polska,* 3/1965; Danuta Wróblewska, ''Józef Wilkoń,'' *Projekt,* 1/1968, ''Józef Wilkoń Talks with the Editor,'' *Projekt,* 1/1979; Lee Kingman and others, compilers, *Illustrators of Children's Books: 1957-1966,* Horn Book, 1968; *Biennale of Illustrations Bratislava '67 '69,* Mlade leta, 1971; *Graphis 155,* Volume 27, Graphis Press, 1971-72; *Ilustracje W ksiazkach Naszej Ksiegarni,* Nasza Ksiegarnia, 1972; Martha E. Ward and Dorothy A. Marquardt, *Illustrators of Books for Young People,* Scarecrow, 1975; *Children's Book Illustration* [3], Graphis Press, 1975; *Under the Star of Fantasy,* Krajowa Agencja Wydawnicza, 1977; *Modern European Children's Book Illustrators,* Bohem's Artists (Zurich), 1982.

WILSON, Dagmar 1916-

BRIEF ENTRY: Born January 25, 1916, in New York, N.Y. An illustrator of books for children, Wilson is a graduate of Slade School, University College. She has taught art at Burgess Hill School, London, England, and Teachers College, New York City. She has also worked as a coordinator of international-American affairs for the United States government. Since 1946 she has been a free-lance artist and illustrator. Wilson has illustrated a number of books for children, including Barbee O. Carleton's *Benny and the Bear,* Nicholas P. Georgiady's *Gertie the Duck,* Josette Frank's *More Poems to Read to the Very Young,* Anita Feagles's *Casey, the Utterly Impossible Horse,* Eileen Daly's *Somebody Hides,* and H. B. Locke's *Energy Users Databook.* She has also illustrated a series of fairy tale books, in French, German, and Italian, for the Berlitz Schools of Languages.

Wilson's illustrating career has been accompanied by a turbulent political involvement which began in 1961 when she founded Women Strike for Peace (WSP), an organization against nuclear armament. The following year, she was summoned to testify before the House Un-American Activities Committee (HUAC) on charges of alleged Communist infiltration of the organization, which she denied. In 1965 she was convicted on charges of contempt of Congress after refusing to testify before a closed session of HUAC. Her conviction was later overturned on a technicality. In 1967 she was arrested during an anti-Vietnam war demonstration, and subsequently withdrew as leader of WSP. *For More Information See: Political Profiles: The Kennedy Years,* Facts on File, 1976.

WILSON, Lionel 1924-
(Peter Blackton, Herbert Ellis, L. E. Salzer)

BRIEF ENTRY: Born March 22, 1924, in New York, N.Y. An actor since 1942, Wilson has appeared on Broadway, on television, and in winter and summer stock productions throughout the United States. He is the author of numerous children's books, including *The Cat Who Never Enjoyed Himself* (Guidance Associates, 1975), *The First Stunt Stars of Hollywood* (C.P.I., 1978), *The Mystery of Dracula: Fact or Fiction?* (C.P.I., 1979), and *Attack of the Killer Grizzly* (Raintree Publishers, 1980). Wilson also writes under the pseudonyms Peter Blackton, Herbert Ellis, and L. E. Salzer. He is the author of the play ''Come and Be Killed'' which was first produced at Berkshire Drama Festival in Massachusetts, 1976. He has also contributed to the television serial ''Secret Storm'' (CBS-TV). Wilson is working on his first adult novel as well as additional audiovisual programs for Guidance Associates, Walt Disney Educational Media, C.P.I., and the Board of Jewish Education. *Address:* 308 East 79th St., New York, N.Y. 10021. *For More Information See: Contemporary Authors,* Volume 105, Gale, 1982.

WISEMAN, Ann (Sayre) 1926-
(Ann Wiseman Denzer)

PERSONAL: Born July 20, 1926, in New York, N.Y.; daughter of Mark Huntington (a writer) and Eve Sayre (Norton) Wiseman; married Weyer Vermeer (a physician); married Peter W. Denzer; children: (first marriage) Piet; (second marriage) Erik. *Education:* Attended Art Students League, New York City and Grande Chaumiere, Paris, France, between 1944 and 1949. Lesley College, Cambridge, Mass., M.A. *Residence:* Huron Ave., Cambridge, Mass. 02138.

CAREER: Artist and writer. Lord & Taylor, New York City, display artist, 1946; Museum of Modern Art, New York City, teacher of art classes for children, 1948-50; Stuart Country Day School, Princeton, N.J., chairman of art department, 1966-70; Boston Children's Museum, Boston, Mass., program director, 1970-71; Lesley College, Cambridge, Mass., teacher of methods, materials, and art therapy at Graduate School, 1977-82. Conductor of Metropolitan Museum children's tapestry program, 1967-68, and Boston Bicentennial senior citizens' tapestry program, 1976. Participated in twenty-five intensive workshops for 1,250 elementary school teachers of southern New Hampshire, New Hampshire Commission on the Arts, New Hampshire State Department, 1971-72. Her own tapestry, painting, and kinetic sand-fountains have been exhibited in group shows at museums and galleries and are in private collections.

MEMBER: Society of Women Geographers, American Association of Artists Therapists, Boston Visual Artists Union. *Awards, honors:* Karolyi Foundation fellowship in France, 1970.

WRITINGS: (Under name Ann Wiseman Denzer) *Tony's Flower* (children's book), Vanguard, 1959; *Rags, Rugs, and Wool Pictures,* Scribner, 1969; *Rag Tapestries and Wool Mosaics,* Van Nostrand, 1969; *Making Things: Hand Book of Creative Discovery,* Little, Brown, Book I, 1973, Book II, 1975; *Bread Sculpture: The Edible Art,* 101 Productions, 1975; *Cuts of Cloth,* Little, Brown, 1978; *Making Musical Things,* Scribner, 1979; *Welcome to the World: How Mary Has Kittens,* Addison-

(From *Making Things* by Ann Wiseman. Illustrated by the author.)

Wesley, 1980; *Finger Paints and Pudding Prints*, Addison-Wesley, 1981.

Film: "Rag Tapestry of New York City," International Film Foundation, 1968.

WORK IN PROGRESS: Hand Logic: Children's Tapestries; illustrated travel journals; *Garment Cores: Primitive Crafts; Dream Journals; Find the Image and Satisfy It; The Nightmares of Childhood.*

SIDELIGHTS: "After teaching for twenty years without any degrees, I returned to school and got an M.A. in education and psycho-imagery therapy to enhance my workshops in dreams imagery and art therapy which I conduct around the country and at Lesley College.

"I've been spending my summers painting in Provincetown and have decided to try my second winter on the Provincetown bay.

"My children's nightmare book has not yet found a publisher, but I'm hoping the importance of dreams will get off the 'couch' and reach teachers and parents in early education."

Wiseman has traveled in France, Italy, Greece, Portugal, Mexico, the Netherlands, England, and India.

WITTELS, Harriet Joan 1938-

PERSONAL: Born April 6, 1938, in New York, N.Y.; daughter of Rudolph Edward (a salesman) and Evelyn (an office manager) Wittels. *Education:* Hunter College. *Home and office:* 185 East 85th St., New York, N.Y. 10028. *Agent:* Curtis Brown Ltd., 575 Madison Ave., New York, N.Y. 10022.

But then there are times shopping sure can be fun.
When we're late for the bus, and we've both got to run.

■(From *Things I Hate!* by Harriet Wittels and Joan Greisman. Illustrated by Jerry McConnel.)

CAREER: Elementary school assistant principal, New York, N.Y. "Sweet Shop" owner and manager in Manhattan.

WRITINGS—All with Joan Ruth Greisman; all for children: *The Young People's Thesaurus Dictionary*, edited and with an introduction by William Morris, Grosset, 1971, published as *The Clear and Simple Thesaurus Dictionary*, Grosset, 1976; *The Perfect Speller*, Grosset, 1973; *Things I Hate!*, Human Sciences Press, 1973.

WORK IN PROGRESS: Novels for young adults, *Jeff Fights for Justice* and *The Budding Business Bureau;* a reference book for parents, *Preparing Your Child for Success with Reading.*

SIDELIGHTS: Wittels and Joan Greisman have not only collaborated together in their literary efforts but have both worked for several years in the New York City school system as assistant principals. "Our vocational backgrounds . . . provide the natural motivation for the writing of 'word' books, as well as story books for and about children."

WOLITZER, Hilma   1930-

PERSONAL: Born January 25, 1930, in Brooklyn, N.Y.; daughter of Abraham V. and Rose (Goldberg) Liebman; married Morton Wolitzer (a psychologist), September 7, 1952; children: Nancy, Margaret. *Education:* Attended Brooklyn Museum Art School, Brooklyn College of the City University of New York, and New School for Social Research. *Home:*

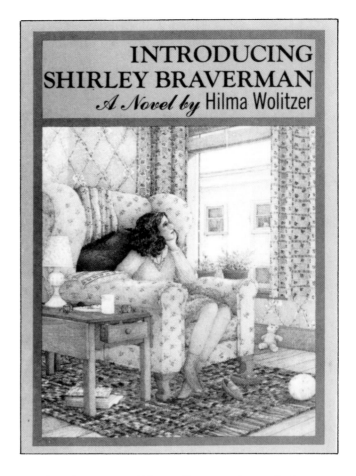

The sirens went off just as I was coming to the best part of the book, the chapter where the heroine discovers that her new friend is really her long-lost sister. ■ (From *Introducing Shirley Braverman* by Hilma Wolitzer. Jacket illustration by Ruth Bowen.)

11 Ann Dr., Syosset, N.Y. 11791. *Agent:* McIntosh & Otis, Inc., 475 Fifth Ave., New York, N.Y.

CAREER: Writer and teacher of writing workshops. Has also worked as nursery school teacher and portrait artist at a resort. Bread Loaf Writers Conference, staff assistant, 1975 and 1976, staff member, 1977, 1978, 1980, 1981, and 1982. *Member:* International P.E.N., Authors Guild of Authors League of America. *Awards, honors:* Bread Loaf Writers Conference scholarship, 1970, fellowship, 1974; award from Great Lakes College Association, 1974-75, for *Ending;* Guggenheim fellowship, 1976-77; National Endowment for the Arts Fellowship, 1978; New York State English Council Excellence in Letters Award, 1980; American Academy and Institute of Arts and Letters Award in Literature, 1981.

WRITINGS: Ending (adult), Morrow, 1974; *Introducing Shirley Braverman* (juvenile), Farrar, Straus, 1975; *Out of Love* (juvenile), Farrar, Straus, 1976; *In the Flesh* (adult), Morrow, 1977; *Toby Lived Here* (juvenile), Farrar, Straus, 1978; *Hearts* (adult), Farrar, Straus, 1980; *In the Palomar Arms* (adult), Farrar, Straus, 1983.

Work represented in anthologies, including *The Secret Life of Our Times*, edited by Gordon Lish, Doubleday, 1973; *Bitches*

HILMA WOLITZER

and Sad Ladies, edited by Pat Rotter, Harper Magazine Press, 1975; *All Our Secrets Are the Same*, edited by Gordon Lish, Norton, 1976. Contributor of stories to *Saturday Evening Post, Esquire, New American Review,* and *Ms.* magazine.

SIDELIGHTS: "The first thing I ever had published was a poem about winter, in *The Junior Inspectors' Club Journal,* sponsored by the New York City Department of Sanitation. I was ten years old. My mother took me downtown to get a certificate and I remember that the streets were lined with garbage trucks. They made the occasion seem official, and I was thrilled. Despite this early success, and the fact that I was the kind of kid who read *everything*—the dictionary, my mother's home medical advisor, cereal boxes at breakfast, shampoo bottles in the bathtub—I was really a late bloomer. Aside from some adolescent poetry, the next thing I published was a short story in the old *Saturday Evening Post,* and I was thirty-five by then. This time I was hooked, and I've been writing ever since."

"I got a late start and I didn't have the background for writing. No college, for example. I really regret that, not so much for what I could have learned but for the *time* college offers—time to read the great literary classics when you should, when you aren't distracted by other responsibilities. But when I got out of high school, the prospect of earning $28 a week was more attractive than a degree."[1] [Jean F. Mercier, "Hilma Wolitzer," *Publishers Weekly,* July 17, 1978.[1]]

"I don't know why I started writing when I did, but I'm very glad. It's brought many pleasures: travel for readings and teaching, wonderful new friends, and the joy of work itself. I still read a great deal—whenever I can. In my own writing I care most about the characters and about the use of language. Characters I care about seem to find their own plots, wake me in the middle of the night to tell their stories."

Wolitzer feels that she has not had the exciting adventures many authors use for the basis of their writing. Her stories are not based directly on personal experience, but the "small details are familiar ones in my life" and her writing contains "my view and response to the world."

"The only glamour I can claim is going to the same high school as Maurice Sendak!"

"I know that authorities insist one should follow the cardinal rule, to write about what you know. But I agree only so far. There were times when I had to fight the famous writer's block, considering my years as 'just a housewife.' I realized, though, that a person leading an 'ordinary' life isn't necessarily blind and deaf to happenings in the lives of others. And fiction is, after all, a mixture of imagination and reality. Besides imagination, you get help from dreams, fantasies—all kinds of ideas surface when you concentrate on inventing."[1]

"In between books, I have written a script for the television show 'Family' and done some screenplays. I try to be working on something all the time, even if it's only in my head."

"I've taught at the Bread Loaf Writers' Conference at Middlebury College in Vermont and at the writing programs at the University of Iowa and Columbia University."

"These sessions are terrific learning experiences; the company of other writers is stimulating . . . the chance to exchange ideas and philosophies with people of similar aims and interests."[1]

"I'm married to a psychologist and we have two daughters. Nancy is a visual artist and Meg is a writer."

FOR MORE INFORMATION SEE: Jean F. Mercier, "Hilma Wolitzer," *Publishers Weekly,* July 17, 1978.

WYNANTS, Miche   1934-

BRIEF ENTRY: Born March 12, 1934, in Louvain, Belgium. A children's author and illustrator, Wynants studied decorative art and illustration in Belgium at Ecole Nationale Superieure D'Architecture et Des Arts and at Decoratifs de L'Abbaye de la Cambre. Among the children's books which Wynants has written and illustrated are *Noah's Ark* and *The Giraffe of King Charles X,* as well as the French language books *Je connais ma famille* and *Je connais mes amis.* The *New York Times* included *The Giraffe of King Charles X* on its list of best illustrated children's books of 1964. Besides illustrating her own books, Wynants also illustrates the works of other authors, including Antoine De Virck's *Wim of the Wind* (Doubleday, 1974). Wynants is married to the Belgian potter Pierre Culot. *Residence:* Incourt, Belgium. *For More Information See: Illustrators of Children's Books, 1957-66,* Horn Book, 1968.

YATES, Raymond F(rancis)   1895-1966 (Borden Hall, Pioneer)

PERSONAL: Born September 1, 1895, in Lockport, N.Y.; died September 23, 1966; buried at St. Peter's Cemetery, Lockport, N.Y.; son of Charles Henry and Barbara (Leadmeyer) Yates; married Marion Jane Rew, January 2, 1919 (died June 29, 1929); married Marguerite Louise Wendel (a writer), June 27, 1932; children: Brock Wendel. *Education:* Attended Columbia University. *Residence:* Carlisle Gardens, Lockport, N.Y.

CAREER: Editor, *Everyday Mechanics,* 1916-19; editor, *Everyday Engineering,* 1919-20; managing editor, *Popular Science Monthly,* 1920-21; columnist and radio editor, *New York Evening Mail,* 1922-24; radio editor and critic (under pseudonym Pioneer), *New York Herald Tribune,* 1924-26; editor, *Popular Radio,* 1926-29. Also served as vice-president of New Fiction Publishing Company; director and president of Krome Alume, Inc.; contributing editor to *Science and Mechanics* and *Modern Mechanics and Inventions;* member of Hoover Radio Conference, 1925; special lecturer, American Museum of Natural History, New York Board of Education, and others. *Member:* American Institute for the Advancement of Radio (former secretary), American Institute of Electrical Engineers, American Physical Society, American Society of Mechanical Engineers, Institute of Radio Engineers, Authors' League, Niagara County Historical Society (former president), Clinton Club.

WRITINGS—Juvenile: Boys' Book of Model Boats, Century Co., 1920, revised edition, Appleton-Century, 1943; *The Boys' Playbook of Chemistry* (self-illustrated), Century Co., 1923; *The Boys' Book of Magnetism,* Harper & Brothers, 1941, revised edition, Harper, 1959; *Science Calls to Youth: A Guide to Career-Planning in the Sciences,* Appleton-Century, 1941; *A Boy and a Battery* (self-illustrated), Harper & Brothers, 1942; *The Boys' Book of Communications,* Harper & Brothers, 1942; *A Boy and a Motor* (self-illustrated), Harper & Brothers, 1944; *The Boys' Book of Rockets* (self-illustrated), Harper, 1947; *The Boys' Book of Model Railroading* (self-illustrated), Harper,

RAYMOND F. YATES

1951; *Atomic Experiments for Boys* (self-illustrated), Harper, 1952; *Model Jets and Rockets for Boys* (illustrated by son, Brock W. Yates), Harper, 1952; *Faster and Faster: The Story of Speed*, Harper, 1956; *The Boys' Book of Tools*, Harper, 1957; *Under Three Flags: Western New York State from the Ice Age to the Atomic Age*, Henry Stewart, 1958; *The Young Inventors' Guide*, Harper, 1959.

Other: (Editor) *Model Making, Including Workshop Practice, Design and Construction of Models*, Norman W. Henley Publishing, 1919, revised and enlarged edition, 1925; *How to Make and Use a Small Chemical Laboratory*, Norman W. Henley Publishing, 1920, revised and enlarged by S. A. Pellerano, 1939; *Shop Practice for Home Mechanics: Use of Tools, Shop Processes, Construction of Small Machines*, Norman W. Henley Publishing, 1920; *Soldering and Brazing*, Norman W. Henley Publishing, 1920; (with Louis G. Pacent) *The Complete Radio Book*, Century Co., 1922; *Lathe Work for Beginners*, Norman W. Henley Publishing, 1922; (with Samuel L. Rothafel) *Broadcasting, Its New Day*, Century Co., 1925, reprinted, Arno, 1971; *A Thousand Needed Inventions*, Bureau of Inventive Science, 1925; (editor) *Everyman's Guide to Radio: A Practical Course of Common-Sense Instruction in the World's Most Fascinating Science*, Popular Radio, 1927; *ABC of Television; or, Seeing by Radio*, Norman W. Henley Publishing, 1929.

Exploring with the Microscope, Appleton-Century, 1934; *Inventors' Selling Guide*, Donley Publishing, 1934; *The Art of Inventing and What to Invent*, Appleton-Century, 1935; *Take Out Your Own Patents*, Donley Publishing, 1935; *1,500 Needed Inventions*, Donley Publishing, 1936; *How to Make Electric Toys*, Appleton-Century, 1937; *These Amazing Electrons*, Macmillan, 1937; *Making and Operating Model Railroads*, Appleton-Century, 1938; *Machines Over Men*, Frederick A. Stokes, 1939.

Science with Simple Things (self-illustrated), Appleton-Century, 1940; *Model Gasoline Engines: Their Operation and Use*, Appleton-Century, 1941; *Super-Electricity: What You Can Do in Electronics*, Appleton-Century, 1942; *2,100 Needed Inventions*, W. Funk, 1942, published as *3,100 Needed Inventions*, W. Funk, 1951; *Fun with Your Microscope*, Appleton-Century, 1943; *Young Men and Machines: Career Guidance for the Machine Tool and Mass Production Industries*, Dodd, 1944; *Atom Smashers: A Story of Discovery*, Didier, 1945; *Fun with Electrons*, Appleton-Century, 1945; *The Weather for a Hobby: A Guide to the Construction and Use of Weather Instruments Intended for Amateurs* (self-illustrated), Dodd, 1946; *The Working Electron: An Introduction to Electronics*, Harper & Brothers, 1946; *The Niagara Story*, Foster & Stewart Publishing, 1947, reprinted, 1980; *How to Restore Antiques*, Harper, 1948; *How to Restore Furniture*, W. Funk, 1948, published as *How to Repair Furniture*, N. Kaye, 1950; *New Television, the Magic Screen*, Didier, 1948; *Guide to Successful Inventing*, W. Funk, 1949; (with wife, Marguerite W. Yates) *A Guide to Victorian Antiques: With Notes on the Early Nineteenth Century* (self-illustrated), Harper, 1949.

Antique Fakes and Their Detection (self-illustrated), Harper, 1950; *Antique Reproductions for the Home Craftsman* (self-illustrated), Whittlesey House, 1950; *The Hobby Book of Stenciling and Brush-Stroke Painting* (self-illustrated), McGraw, 1951; *New Furniture from Old* (self-illustrated with B. W. Yates), W. Funk, 1951; (under pseudonym Borden Hall) *The Amateur Finisher's Guidebook*, Harper, 1952; (compiler) *The Antique Collector's Manual: A Price Guide and Data Book*, Harper, 1952; (with M. Yates) *How to Make Beautiful Gifts at Home*, W. Funk, 1952; *How to Improve Your Model Railroad* (self-illustrated), Harper, 1953; *How to Restore China, Bric-a-Brac, and Small Antiques* (self-illustrated), Harper, 1953; (with M. Yates) *Early American Crafts and Hobbies: A Treasury of Skills, Avocations, Handicrafts, and Forgotten Pastimes and Pursuits from the Golden Age of the American Home*, edited by Mary Lyon, W. Funk, 1954, reprinted, Funk, 1974; *Sport and Racing Cars* (self-illustrated with B. W. Yates; introduction by Wilbur Shaw), Harper, 1954; (under pseudonym Borden Hall) *Living in the Back Yard*, Harper, 1955; *New Methods for Home Repair and Improvement*, Longmans, Green (New York), 1955; (with M. E. Russell) *Space Rockets and Missiles*, Harper, 1960.

Contributor of over 2,000 articles to periodicals, including *Scientific American, Illustrated World, Current History Magazine* of the *New York Times, Outlook, North American Review, Parents' Magazine, Science Digest, Nature Magazine, Better Homes and Gardens, Aviation,* and *Popular Mechanics.*

FOR MORE INFORMATION SEE: Muriel Fuller, editor, *More Junior Authors*, H. W. Wilson, 1963.

Grown-ups never understand anything for themselves, and it is tiresome for children to be always and forever explaining things to them.

—Antoine de Saint-Exupéry

All that mankind has done, thought, gained or been: it is lying as in magic preservation in the pages of books.

—Thomas Carlyle

YOUNG, Dorothea Bennett 1924-
(Dorothea Bennett)

PERSONAL: Born January 28, 1924, in Burma; married Terrence Young (a film director). *Home:* Ferme des Roses, Huemoz sur Ollon, Vaud, Switzerland. *Agent:* Curtis Brown Ltd., 1 Craven Hill, London W2 3EW, England.

WRITINGS—Under name Dorothea Bennett: *Dry Taste of Fear,* Barker, 1960; *Under the Skin,* Barker, 1961, Mill, 1962; *The Jigsaw Man,* Coward, 1976. Writer of screen scripts.

HOBBIES AND OTHER INTERESTS: Skiing, sailing, gardening.

YOUNG, Percy M(arshall) 1912-
(Percy Marshall)

PERSONAL: Born May 17, 1912, in Northwich, England; son of William Joseph (a clerk) and Annie (a nurse; maiden name, Marshall) Young; married Anna Letitia Carson, August 7, 1937 (deceased); married Renee Morris, February 10, 1969. *Education:* Selwyn College, Cambridge, B.A. and Mus. B., 1933, M.A., 1937; Trinity College, Dublin, Mus. D., 1937. *Politics:* Labour. *Religion:* Church of England. *Home:* 72 Clark Rd., Wolverhampton WV3 9PA, England. *Agent:* A. P. Watt & Son, 26 Bedford Row, London W.C. 1R 4HL, England.

CAREER: Stranmillis Teacher's Training College, Belfast, Northern Ireland, director of music, 1934-37; Stoke-on-Trent, England, musical adviser to city schools, 1937-44; College of Technology, Wolverhampton, Staffordshire, England, director of music, 1944-66. Writer, lecturer, conductor, and composer, 1966—. Visiting scholar, University Center, Georgia, 1971; visiting lecturer, Bucknell University, 1972.

MEMBER: Wolverhampton Borough Council, Dolmetsch Foundation, International Society of Musicology, Royal Musical Association (associate member), Royal College of Organists, Incorporated Society of Musicians, Performing Rights Society, Gesellschaft fuer Musik-forshung, Society of Authors, National Book League, Royal Commonwealth Society, British-Caribbean Association, Hungarian Friendship Society, Hallische Haendel-Gesellschaft, Goettinger Haendel-Gesellschaft, Ernst Thaelmann Brigade (honorary member), Selwyn College Association, Grand Theatre Club, Old Blues, Wolverhampton Council for Community Relations, Midland Federation of Community Relations Councils, National Association of Community Relations Councils, Wolverhampton Community Health Council, Wolverhampton Cricket Club, Wine Society. *Awards, honors:* Handel Prize, Halle, Germany, 1961.

WRITINGS—Of interest to young people: *Music Is for You: A Guide to Music for Young People,* Lutterworth, 1948; *Music Makers,* Dobson, 1951, Roy, 1953; (compiler) *Carols for the Twelve Days of Christmas,* Dobson, 1952, Roy, 1954; *More Music Makers,* Roy, 1955; *Instrumental Music,* Methuen, 1955, Roy, 1958; *The Story of Song,* Methuen, 1956, Roy, 1958; *In Search of Music,* Lutterworth, 1956; (with Edward Ardizzone) *Ding Dong Bell,* Dobson, 1957, Dover, 1969; *Read and Sing,* two books, Allen & Unwin, 1958; *Music Makers of Today* (illustrated by Milein Cosman), Roy, 1958, 2nd edition, 1966.

Music and Its Story, Lutterworth, 1960, Roy, 1962, revised edition, 1970; *The Young Musician,* T. Nelson, 1961; (under pseudonym Percy Marshall) *Masters of the English Novel,* Dobson, 1962; *Music,* T. Nelson, 1963; *Handel,* Benn, 1965, David White, 1966, revised edition, Dent, 1975; *Mozart,* Benn, 1965, David White, 1966; *Music for Children,* Record Books, 1965; *Beethoven,* David White, 1966; *World Composers,* Abelard, 1966; (under pseudonym Percy Marshall) *Masters of English Poetry,* Dobson, 1966; *Britten* (illustrated by Richard Shirley-Smith), David White, 1966; *Keyboard Musicians of the World,* Abelard, 1967; *Debussy* (illustrated by R. Shirley-Smith), David White, 1968; *Tchaikovsky* (illustrated by R. Shirley-Smith), David White, 1968; *Haydn,* David White, 1969; *Stravinsky* (illustrated by R. Shirley-Smith), David White, 1969; *Dvořák* (illustrated by Paul Newland), David White, 1970; *Schubert* (illustrated by P. Newland), David White, 1970; *A Concise History of Music,* David White, 1974.

Other: *Pageant of England's Music,* Heffer, 1939; *Handel,* Dutton, 1947, revised edition, Collier, 1963; *Introduction to the Music of Mendelssohn,* Dobson, 1949; *The Oratorios of Handel,* Dobson, 1949, Roy, 1950.

Messiah: Study in Interpretation, Dobson, 1951; *Vaughan Williams,* Dobson, 1953; *A Handbook of Choral Technique,* Dobson, 1953; *Biographical Dictionary of Composers, with Classified List of Music for Performance and Study,* Crowell, 1954 (published in England as *A Critical Dictionary of Composers and Their Music,* Dobson, 1954); *Elgar, O.M.: A Study of a Musician,* Collins, 1955, Greenwood Press, 1980; (editor and annotator) Edward Elgar, *Letters and Other Writings,* Bles, 1956; *Tragic Muse: The Life and Works of Robert Schumann,* Hutchinson, 1957, enlarged edition, Dobson, 1961; *Symphony,* Phoenix House, 1957, Crescendo, 1968; *Music and the Young Child,* McDougall's Educational Co., 1957; *Concerto,* Phoenix House, 1957.

Johann Sebastian Bach: The Story of His Life and Work, Boosey & Hawkes, 1960; *Musical Composition for Pleasure,* Hutchinson, 1961; *The Choral Tradition: An Historical and Analytical Survey from the Sixteenth Century to the Present Day,* Norton, 1962; *Zoltan Kodaly: A Hungarian Musician,* Benn, 1964, Greenwood Press, 1976; *The Concert Tradition,* Roy, 1965; (editor) Edward Elgar, *Letters to Nimrod,* Dobson, 1965; *World Conductors,* Abelard, 1966; *A History of British Music,* Norton, 1967; *Great Ideas in Music* (edited by Patrick Pringle), Maxwell, 1967, David White, 1968; (editor) Edward Elgar, *A Future for English Music,* Dobson, 1968; *The Enjoyment of Music,* E.M.I. Records (London), 1968; *Choral Music of the World,* Abelard, 1969.

The Bachs, 1500-1850, Crowell, 1970; *Sir Arthur Sullivan,* Dent, 1971, Norton, 1972; *Beethoven: A Victorian Tribute,* Dobson, 1976; *Alice Elgar: Portrait of a Victorian Lady,* Dobson, 1978; (with Renee Morris) *Castles in Wales,* Dobson, 1978; *George Grove, 1820-1900,* Macmillan, 1980.

Sports books: *Football: Facts and Fancies: or The Art of Spectatorship* (juvenile), Dobson, 1950; *Appreciation of Football* (juvenile), Dobson, 1951; *Football Year* (juvenile), Phoenix House, 1956; *Football through the Ages* (juvenile), Methuen, 1957; *The Wolves: The First Eighty Years,* Stanley Paul, 1959; *Manchester United,* Heinemann, 1960; *Bolton Wanderers,* Stanley Paul, 1961; *Football in Sheffield,* Stanley Paul, 1962; *Football on Merseyside,* Stanley Paul, 1963; *A History of British Football,* Stanley Paul, 1968; (with Derek Dougan) *On the Spot: Football as a Profession,* Stanley Paul, 1974; *Centenary Wolves,* Wolverhampton Wanderers Football Club, 1976.

(From *Ding Dong Bell* by Percy Young and Edward Ardizzone. Illustrated by Edward Ardizzone.)

(From *Ding Dong Bell* by Percy Young and Edward Ardizzone. Illustrated by Edward Ardizzone.)

Editor, ''Student's Music Library'' series, Dobson, 1951—. Contributor to *Grove's Dictionary of Music and Musicians, Book of Association Football,* and *Football Yearbook;* also contributor to *Encyclopaedia Britannica, Collier's Encyclopedia, World Book Encyclopedia, Children's Encyclopaedia,* and other publications in Germany and the United States.

Has written more than twenty published musical compositions and more than thirty published arrangements and/or editions of music. He has had more than ten musical commissions which are unpublished. Also has edited various musical compositions.

WORK IN PROGRESS: Editing two collections, for Broude, *The Madrigal in the Romantic Era,* and *Music of the Great Churches;* a book on the life of Charles Hubert Hastings Parry; a book on Elgar's ''friends pictured within,'' the persons who were the subjects for his ''Enigma'' *Variations.*

SIDELIGHTS: While at Cambridge, Young was an organ scholar of Selwyn College, a university scholar in Sacred Music and holder of the Barclay Squire Prize for Musical Palaeography. He holds degrees in English, history and music and is a world-renowned conductor, lecturer, composer and author.

''I have traveled and lectured in Britain, America, Germany, Switzerland and Africa. My books and musical editions have been published in Britain, America, Germany and Japan, and I have contributed to journals in Britain, America, Germany and Hungary. Of more than fifty published books, more than twenty are especially for children and of more than twenty published musical compositions, more than fifteen are especially for children, including *A Pageant of Carols,* written for Northicote School in Wolverhampton, which has been performed abroad since. I have had broadcasts on radio and television from time to time which included regular children's music programs on BBC radio in the 1940s.''

In addition to his scholarly works on several composers of the eighteenth century, textbooks, and contributions to scholarly journals, Young has written many books for younger readers including *Music Is for You, Music and its Story, Keyboard Musicians of the World,* and *Music Makers of Today.* ''I must confess that it alarms me to discover how the general knowledge of the arts stops short somewhere about the year 1900; with the result that the young music-lover assumes that the best books, the best poetry have all been made by people long since dead. While all the time there are around us composers, painters, architects, poets, who are proving that art is without end; that the present is as stimulating as the past; and that all of us are engaged in the making of history.

''Every now and then we have the good fortune, perhaps, to meet a notable contemporary composer. Is he, we ask, to be numbered one day among the immortals? The final answer in any one case is not, of course, for us to give. But we are, I suspect, deterred from even thinking this way for the silliest of reasons: the outstanding composer of our acquaintance appears to dress as other men, to behave without the eccentricities formerly thought exclusive to musicians, and to be a normal member of the community.

''Some of the 'stories' of the great of other days have a strong, romantic appeal. Do you not think that sometimes the 'romantic' element in biography may not have been warmed up a bit in later times? Handel, Bach, Mozart, Haydn—they are picturesque characters to us, not because they were more picturesque than their contemporaries but because the whole of the eighteenth century seems a more highly coloured age than our own.

''One day no doubt the present age will be looked back on in a similar way. Then the composers . . . [today] will seem picturesque, eccentric, what you will, to a degree that would surprise them.

''This is by way of prelude; for the treatment of modern composers' biographies is inevitably rather different from that of the 'classics.' Different in two ways especially. We must see how musicians of our own time are related to us by reason of belonging to the same community, or the same culture. In answering problems that in greater or lesser degree perplex every member of society some show a remarkable fortitude, even heroism. Secondly there is the music itself. As we live amidst change (and any writer of any age writing about his own period feels this) some aspects of new style and technique must be noted.

''At the beginning of this century there was a revolution in music as extensive as that which occurred at the beginning of the seventeenth century. Among the principal revolutionaries were the figures with whom we deal. And theirs, for the most part, are the influences that affect every young composer who must for the present content himself with such antics with time as place him, in our scheme, among the Music Makers of Tomorrow.

''I am, as I say, appalled at the way in which teachers and examiners assume that the present doesn't exist. On the other hand I am amazed at the amount of readily attractive modern music that lies ready for the hand of the young player or singer. Try some of the piano pieces of Nielsen, or Prokofiev, or Ravel, or Walton; the songs of Copland or Falla; the choral arrangements of Bartók or Hindemith. Begin to know as much music as you can from the inside. That will instruct you that the springs of music did not suddenly dry up with Brahms or Tchaikovsky.'' [Taken from the preface of *Music Makers of Today* by Percy M. Young, Roy, 1966.]

''Besides my interests that are reflected in my various associations and memberships, my favorite recreations are traveling with my wife, spending time with her and our cats working in the garden at home, and supporting Wolverhampton Wanderers Football Club and soccer—and the sport scene—in general.'' Young's interest in sports has led to several books on football, including four for juveniles.

HOBBIES AND OTHER INTERESTS: Traveling, gardening, sports.

FOR MORE INFORMATION SEE: Martha E. Ward and Dorothy A. Marquardt, *Authors of Books for Young People,* second edition, Scarecrow, 1971; *Contemporary Authors,* Volumes 13-16, revised, Gale, 1975.

CUMULATIVE INDEX TO ILLUSTRATIONS AND AUTHORS

Illustrations Index

(In the following index, the number of the volume in which an illustrator's work appears is given *before* the colon, and the page on which it appears is given *after* the colon. For example, a drawing by Adams, Adrienne appears in Volume 2 on page 6, another drawing by her appears in Volume 3 on page 80, another drawing in Volume 8 on page 1, and another drawing in Volume 15 on page 107.)

YABC

Index citations including this abbreviation refer to listings appearing in *Yesterday's Authors of Books for Children*, also published by the Gale Research Company, which covers authors who died prior to 1960.

Aas, Ulf, *5:* 174
Abbé, S. van. *See* van Abbé, S.
Abel, Raymond, *6:* 122; *7:* 195; *12:* 3; *21:* 86; *25:* 119
Abrahams, Hilary, *26:* 205; *29:* 24-25
Accorsi, William, *11:* 198
Acs, Laszlo, *14:* 156
Adams, Adrienne, *2:* 6; *3:* 80; *8:* 1; *15:* 107; *16:* 180; *20:* 65; *22:* 134-135
Adams, John Wolcott, *17:* 162
Adamson, George, *30:* 23, 24
Adkins, Alta, *22:* 250
Adkins, Jan, *8:* 3
Adler, Peggy, *22:* 6; *29:* 31
Adler, Ruth, *29:* 29
Agard, Nadema, *18:* 1
Aichinger, Helga, *4:* 5, 45
Aitken, Amy, *31:* 34
Akasaka, Miyoshi, *YABC 2:* 261
Akino, Fuku, *6:* 144
Alajalov, *2:* 226
Albright, Donn, *1:* 91
Alcorn, John, *3:* 159; *7:* 165; *31:* 22
Alden, Albert, *11:* 103
Aldridge, Andy, *27:* 131
Alexander, Martha, *3:* 206; *11:* 103; *13:* 109; *25:* 100
Alexeieff, Alexander, *14:* 6; *26:* 199
Aliki. *See* Brandenberg, Aliki
Allamand, Pascale, *12:* 9
Alland, Alexander, *16:* 255
Alland, Alexandra, *16:* 255
Allen, Gertrude, *9:* 6
Allen, Graham, *31:* 145
Almquist, Don, *11:* 8; *12:* 128; *17:* 46; *22:* 110
Aloise, Frank, *5:* 38; *10:* 133; *30:* 92
Althea. *See* Braithwaite, Althea
Altschuler, Franz, *11:* 185; *23:* 141

Ambrus, Victor G., *1:* 6-7, 194; *3:* 69; *5:* 15; *6:* 44; *7:* 36; *8:* 210; *12:* 227; *14:* 213; *15:* 213; *22:* 209; *24:* 36; *28:* 179; *30:* 178
Ames, Lee J., *3:* 12; *9:* 130; *10:* 69; *17:* 214; *22:* 124
Amon, Aline, *9:* 9
Amoss, Berthe, *5:* 5
Amundsen, Dick, *7:* 77
Amundsen, Richard E., *5:* 10; *24:* 122
Ancona, George, *12:* 11
Anderson, Alasdair, *18:* 122
Anderson, C. W. , *11:* 10
Anderson, Carl, *7:* 4
Anderson, Erica, *23:* 65
Anderson, Laurie, *12:* 153, 155
Anderson, Wayne, *23:* 119
Andrew, John, *22:* 4
Andrews, Benny, *14:* 251; *31:* 24
Angelo, Valenti, *14:* 8; *18:* 100; *20:* 232
Anglund, Joan Walsh, *2:* 7, 250-251
Anno, Mitsumasa, *5:* 7
Antal, Andrew, *1:* 124; *30:* 145
Appleyard, Dev, *2:* 192
Archer, Janet, *16:* 69
Ardizzone, Edward, *1:* 11, 12; *2:* 105; *3:* 258; *4:* 78; *7:* 79; *10:* 100; *15:* 232; *20:* 69, 178; *23:* 223; *24:* 125; *28:* 25, 26, 27, 28, 29, 30, 31, 33, 34, 35, 36, 37; *31:* 192, 193; *YABC 2:* 25
Arenella, Roy, *14:* 9
Armer, Austin, *13:* 3
Armer, Laura Adams, *13:* 3
Armer, Sidney, *13:* 3
Armitage, Eileen, *4:* 16
Armstrong, George, *10:* 6; *21:* 72
Arno, Enrico, *1:* 217; *2:* 22, 210; *4:* 9; *5:* 43; *6:* 52; *29:* 217, 219

Arnosky, Jim, *22:* 20
Arrowood, Clinton, *12:* 193; *19:* 11
Artzybasheff, Boris, *13:* 143; *14:* 15
Aruego, Ariane, *6:* 4
See also Dewey, Ariane
Aruego, Jose, *4:* 140; *6:* 4; *7:* 64
Asch, Frank, *5:* 9
Ashby, Gail, *11:* 135
Ashley, C. W., *19:* 197
Ashmead, Hal, *8:* 70
Atene, Ann, *12:* 18
Atkinson, J. Priestman, *17:* 275
Atwood, Ann, *7:* 9
Augarde, Steve, *25:* 22
Austerman, Miriam, *23:* 107
Austin, Margot, *11:* 16
Austin, Robert, *3:* 44
Averill, Esther, *1:* 17; *28:* 39, 40, 41
Axeman, Lois, *2:* 32; *11:* 84; *13:* 165; *22:* 8; *23:* 49
Ayer, Jacqueline, *13:* 7
Ayer, Margaret, *15:* 12

B.T.B. *See* Blackwell, Basil T., *YABC 1:* 68, 69
Babbitt, Natalie, *6:* 6; *8:* 220
Back, George, *31:* 161
Bacon, Bruce, *4:* 74
Bacon, Paul, *7:* 155; *8:* 121; *31:* 55
Bacon, Peggy, *2:* 11, 228
Baker, Alan, *22:* 22
Baker, Charlotte, *2:* 12
Baker, Jeannie, *23:* 4
Baker, Jim, *22:* 24
Baldridge, C. LeRoy, *19:* 69
Balet, Jan, *11:* 22
Balian, Lorna, *9:* 16
Ballantyne, R. M., *24:* 34
Ballis, George, *14:* 199
Bang, Molly Garrett, *24:* 37, 38

Banik, Yvette Santiago, *21:* 136
Banner, Angela. *See* Maddison,
    Angela Mary
Bannerman, Helen, *19:* 13, 14
Bannon, Laura, *6:* 10; *23:* 8
Bare, Arnold Edwin, *16:* 31
Bargery, Geoffrey, *14:* 258
Barker, Carol, *31:* 27
Barkley, James, *4:* 13; *6:* 11;
    13: 112
Barling, Tom, *9:* 23
Barlowe, Dot, *30:* 223
Barner, Bob, *29:* 37
Barnes, Hiram P., *20:* 28
Barnett, Moneta, *16:* 89; *19:* 142;
    31: 102
Barney, Maginel Wright,
    YABC 2: 306
Barnum, Jay Hyde, *11:* 224; *20:* 5
Barrer-Russell, Gertrude, *9:* 65;
    27: 31
Barrett, Ron, *14:* 24; *26:* 35
Barron, John N., *3:* 261; *5:* 101;
    14: 220
Barrows, Walter, *14:* 268
Barry, Ethelred B., *YABC 1:* 229
Barry, James, *14:* 25
Barry, Katharina, *2:* 159; *4:* 22
Barry, Robert E., *6:* 12
Barth, Ernest Kurt, *2:* 172; *3:* 160;
    8: 26; *10:* 31
Barton, Byron, *8:* 207; *9:* 18;
    23: 66
Barton, Harriett, *30:* 71
Bartram, Robert, *10:* 42
Bartsch, Jochen, *8:* 105
Baskin, Leonard, *30:* 42, 43, 46, 47
Batchelor, Joy, *29:* 41, 47, 48
Bate, Norman, *5:* 16
Bates, Leo, *24:* 35
Batherman, Muriel, *31:* 79
Batten, John D., *25:* 161, 162
Bauernschmidt, Marjorie, *15:* 15
Baum, Allyn, *20:* 10
Baum, Willi, *4:* 24-25; *7:* 173
Baumhauer, Hans, *11:* 218;
    15: 163, 165, 167
Baynes, Pauline, *2:* 244; *3:* 149;
    13: 133, 135, 137-141; *19:* 18,
    19, 20
Beame, Rona, *12:* 40
Beard, Dan, *22:* 31, 32
Beard, J. H., *YABC 1:* 158
Bearden, Romare, *9:* 7; *22:* 35
Beardsley, Aubrey, *17:* 14; *23:* 181
Bearman, Jane, *29:* 38
Beaton, Cecil, *24:* 208
Beaucé, J. A., *18:* 103
Beck, Charles, *11:* 169
Beck, Ruth, *13:* 11
Becker, Harriet, *12:* 211
Beckett, Sheilah, *25:* 195
Beckhoff, Harry, *1:* 78; *5:* 163
Bedford, F. D., *20:* 118, 122
Bee, Joyce, *19:* 62
Beeby, Betty, *25:* 36

Beech, Carol, *9:* 149
Beek, *25:* 51, 55, 59
Beerbohm, Max, *24:* 208
Behr, Joyce, *15:* 15; *21:* 132;
    23: 161
Behrens, Hans, *5:* 97
Belden, Charles J., *12:* 182
Bell, Corydon, *3:* 20
Bemelmans, Ludwig, *15:* 19, 21
Benda, W. T., *15:* 256; *30:* 76, 77
Bendick, Jeanne, *2:* 24
Bennett, F. I., *YABC 1:* 134
Bennett, Jill, *26:* 61
Bennett, Rainey, *15:* 26; *23:* 53
Bennett, Richard, *15:* 45; *21:* 11,
    12, 13; *25:* 175
Bennett, Susan, *5:* 55
Bentley, Roy, *30:* 162
Benton, Thomas Hart, *2:* 99
Berelson, Howard, *5:* 20; *16:* 58;
    31: 50
Berenstain, Jan, *12:* 47
Berenstain, Stan, *12:* 47
Berg, Joan, *1:* 115; *3:* 156; *6:* 26,
    58
Berger, William M., *14:* 143;
    YABC 1: 204
Bering, Claus, *13:* 14
Berkowitz, Jeanette, *3:* 249
Bernadette. *See* Watts, Bernadette
Bernstein, Zena, *23:* 46
Berrill, Jacquelyn, *12:* 50
Berry, Erick. *See* Best, Allena.
Berry, William A., *6:* 219
Berry, William D., *14:* 29; *19:* 48
Berson, Harold, *2:* 17-18; *4:* 28-29,
    220; *9:* 10; *12:* 19; *17:* 45;
    18: 193; *22:* 85
Bertschmann, Harry, *16:* 1
Beskow, Elsa, *20:* 13, 14, 15
Best, Allena, *2:* 26
Bethers, Ray, *6:* 22
Bettina. *See* Ehrlich, Bettina
Betts, Ethel Franklin, *17:* 161,
    164-165; *YABC 2:* 47
Bewick, Thomas, *16:* 40-41, 43-45,
    47; *YABC 1:* 107
Bianco, Pamela, *15:* 31; *28:* 44, 45,
    46
Bible, Charles, *13:* 15
Bice, Clare, *22:* 40
Biggers, John, *2:* 123
Bileck, Marvin, *3:* 102
Bimen, Levent, *5:* 179
Binks, Robert, *25:* 150
Binzen, Bill, *24:* 47
Birch, Reginald, *15:* 150; *19:* 33,
    34, 35, 36; *YABC 1:* 84;
    YABC 2: 34, 39
Bird, Esther Brock, *1:* 36; *25:* 66
Birmingham, Lloyd, *12:* 51
Biro, Val, *1:* 26
Bjorklund, Lorence, *3:* 188, 252;
    7: 100; *9:* 113; *10:* 66;
    19: 178; *YABC 1:* 242

Blackwell, Basil T., *YABC 1:* 68,
    69
Blades, Ann, *16:* 52
Blaisdell, Elinore, *1:* 121; *3:* 134
Blake, Quentin, *3:* 170; *9:* 21;
    10: 48; *13:* 38; *21:* 180;
    26: 60; *28:* 228; *30:* 29, 31
Blake, William, *30:* 54, 56, 57, 58,
    59, 60
Blass, Jacqueline, *8:* 215
Blegvad, Erik, *2:* 59; *3:* 98; *5:* 117;
    7: 131; *11:* 149; *14:* 34, 35;
    18: 237; *YABC 1:* 201
Bloch, Lucienne, *10:* 12
Blumenschein, E. L., *YABC 1:* 113,
    115
Blumer, Patt, *29:* 214
Blundell, Kim, *29:* 36
Boardman, Gwenn, *12:* 60
Bobri, *30:* 138
Bock, Vera, *1:* 187; *21:* 41
Bock, William Sauts, *8:* 7; *14:* 37;
    16: 120; *21:* 141
Bodecker, N. M., *8:* 13; *14:* 2;
    17: 55-57
Bohdal, Susi, *22:* 44
Bolian, Polly, *3:* 270; *4:* 30; *13:* 77;
    29: 197
Bolognese, Don, *2:* 147, 231;
    4: 176; *7:* 146; *17:* 43;
    23: 192; *24:* 50
Bond, Arnold, *18:* 116
Bond, Barbara Higgins, *21:* 102
Bonsall, Crosby, *23:* 6
Booth, Franklin, *YABC 2:* 76
Bordier, Georgette, *16:* 54
Boren, Tinka, *27:* 128
Borja, Robert, *22:* 48
Bornstein, Ruth, *14:* 44
Borten, Helen, *3:* 54; *5:* 24
Boston, Peter, *19:* 42
Bottner, Barbara, *14:* 46
Bourke-White, Margaret,
    15: 286-287
Boutet de Monvel, M., *30:* 61, 62,
    63, 65
Bowen, Ruth, *31:* 188
Bower, Ron, *29:* 33
Bowser, Carolyn Ewing, *22:* 253
Boyle, Eleanor Vere, *28:* 50, 51
Bozzo, Frank, *4:* 154
Bradford, Ron, *7:* 157
Bradley, Richard D., *26:* 182
Bradley, William, *5:* 164
Brady, Irene, *4:* 31
Braithwaite, Althea, *23:* 12-13
Bram, Elizabeth, *30:* 67
Bramley, Peter, *4:* 3
Brandenberg, Aliki, *2:* 36-37;
    24: 222
Brandi, Lillian, *31:* 158
Brandon, Brumsic, Jr., *9:* 25
Bransom, Paul, *17:* 121
Brenner, Fred, *22:* 85
Brett, Bernard, *22:* 54
Brett, Harold M., *26:* 98, 99, 100

Brett, Jan, *30:* 135
Brick, John, *10:* 15
Bridwell, Norman, *4:* 37
Briggs, Raymond, *10:* 168; *23:* 20, 21
Bright, Robert, *24:* 55
Brinckloe, Julie, *13:* 18; *24:* 79, 115; *29:* 35
Brisley, Joyce L., *22:* 57
Brock, C. E., *15:* 97; *19:* 247, 249; *23:* 224, 225; *YABC 1:* 194, 196, 203
Brock, Emma, *7:* 21
Brock, Henry Matthew, *15:* 81; *16:* 141; *19:* 71
Bromhall, Winifred, *5:* 11; *26:* 38
Brooke, L. Leslie, *16:* 181-183, 186; *17:* 15-17; *18:* 194
Brooker, Christopher, *15:* 251
Brotman, Adolph E., *5:* 21
Brown, David, *7:* 47
Brown, Denise, *11:* 213
Brown, Judith Gwyn, *1:* 45; *7:* 5; *8:* 167; *9:* 182, 190; *20:* 16, 17, 18; *23:* 142; *29:* 117
Brown, Marc Tolon, *10:* 17, 197; *14:* 263
Brown, Marcia, *7:* 30; *25:* 203; *YABC 1:* 27
Brown, Margery W., *5:* 32-33; *10:* 3
Brown, Paul, *25:* 26; *26:* 107
Browne, Dik, *8:* 212
Browne, Gordon, *16:* 97
Browne, Hablot K., *15:* 80; *21:* 14, 15, 16, 17, 18, 19, 20; *24:* 25
Browning, Coleen, *4:* 132
Browning, Mary Eleanor, *24:* 84
Bruce, Robert, *23:* 23
Brule, Al, *3:* 135
Brundage, Frances, *19:* 244
Brunhoff, Jean de, *24:* 57, 58
Brunhoff, Laurent de, *24:* 60
Bryan, Ashley, *31:* 44
Brychta, Alex, *21:* 21
Bryson, Bernarda, *3:* 88, 146
Buba, Joy, *12:* 83; *30:* 226
Buchanan, Lilian, *13:* 16
Buck, Margaret Waring, *3:* 30
Buehr, Walter, *3:* 31
Buff, Conrad, *19:* 52, 53, 54
Buff, Mary, *19:* 52, 53
Bull, Charles Livingston, *18:* 207
Bullen, Anne, *3:* 166, 167
Burchard, Peter, *3:* 197; *5:* 35; *6:* 158, 218
Burger, Carl, *3:* 33
Burgeson, Marjorie, *19:* 31
Burkert, Nancy Ekholm, *18:* 186; *22:* 140; *24:* 62, 63, 64, 65; *26:* 53; *29:* 60, 61; *YABC 1:* 46
Burn, Doris, *6:* 172
Burningham, John, *9:* 68; *16:* 60-61
Burns, Howard M., *12:* 173
Burns, M. F., *26:* 69
Burns, Raymond, *9:* 29

Burns, Robert, *24:* 106
Burr, Dane, *12:* 2
Burra, Edward, *YABC 2:* 68
Burridge, Marge Opitz, *14:* 42
Burris, Burmah, *4:* 81
Burton, Virginia Lee, *2:* 43; *YABC 1:* 24
Busoni, Rafaello, *1:* 186; *3:* 224; *6:* 126; *14:* 5; *16:* 62-63
Butterfield, Ned, *1:* 153; *27:* 128
Buzonas, Gail, *29:* 88
Buzzell, Russ W., *12:* 177
Byfield, Barbara Ninde, *8:* 18
Byrd, Robert, *13:* 218

Caddy, Alice, *6:* 41
Cady, Harrison, *17:* 21, 23; *19:* 57, 58
Caldecott, Randolph, *16:* 98, 103; *17:* 32-33, 36, 38-39; *26:* 90; *YABC 2:* 172
Calder, Alexander, *18:* 168
Calderon, W. Frank, *25:* 160
Caldwell, Doreen, *23:* 77
Callahan, Kevin, *22:* 42
Callahan, Philip S., *25:* 77
Cameron, Julia Margaret, *19:* 203
Campbell, Ann, *11:* 43
Campbell, Walter M., *YABC 2:* 158
Camps, Luis, *28:* 120-121
Caras, Peter, *31:* 127
Caraway, James, *3:* 200-201
Carbe, Nino, *29:* 183
Carigiet, Alois, *24:* 67
Carle, Eric, *4:* 42; *11:* 121; *12:* 29
Carrick, Donald, *5:* 194
Carrick, Malcolm, *28:* 59, 60
Carrick, Valery, *21:* 47
Carroll, Lewis. *See* Dodgson, Charles L., *20:* 148; *YABC 2:* 98
Carroll, Ruth, *7:* 41; *10:* 68
Carter, Harry, *22:* 179
Carter, Helene, *15:* 38; *22:* 202, 203; *YABC 2:* 220-221
Carty, Leo, *4:* 196; *7:* 163
Cary, *4:* 133; *9:* 32; *20:* 2; *21:* 143
Cary, Page, *12:* 41
Case, Sandra E., *16:* 2
Cassel, Lili. *See* Wronker, Lili Cassel, *3:* 247; *10:* 204; *21:* 10
Cassels, Jean, *8:* 50
Cassel-Wronker, Lili. *See also* Wronker, Lili Cassel
Castle, Jane, *4:* 80
Cather, Carolyn, *3:* 83; *15:* 203
Cellini, Joseph, *2:* 73; *3:* 35; *16:* 116
Chalmers, Mary, *3:* 145; *13:* 148
Chambers, C. E., *17:* 230
Chambers, Dave, *12:* 151
Chambers, Mary, *4:* 188
Chandler, David P., *28:* 62
Chapman, C. H., *13:* 83, 85, 87
Chapman, Frederick T., *6:* 27

Chappell, Warren, *3:* 172; *21:* 56; *27:* 125
Charles, Donald, *30:* 154, 155
Charlip, Remy, *4:* 48
Charlot, Jean, *1:* 137, 138; *8:* 23; *14:* 31
Charmatz, Bill, *7:* 45
Chartier, Normand, *9:* 36
Chase, Lynwood M., *14:* 4
Chastain, Madye Lee, *4:* 50
Chauncy, Francis, *24:* 158
Chen, Tony, *6:* 45; *19:* 131; *29:* 126
Cheney, T. A., *11:* 47
Chess, Victoria, *12:* 6
Chesterton, G. K., *27:* 43, 44, 45, 47
Chew, Ruth, *7:* 46
Chin, Alex, *28:* 54
Cho, Shinta, *8:* 126
Chollick, Jay, *25:* 175
Chorao, Kay, *7:* 200-201; *8:* 25; *11:* 234
Christensen, Gardell Dano, *1:* 57
Christy, Howard Chandler, *17:* 163-165, 168-169; *19:* 186, 187; *21:* 22, 23, 24, 25
Chronister, Robert, *23:* 138
Church, Frederick, *YABC 1:* 155
Chute, Marchette, *1:* 59
Chwast, Jacqueline, *1:* 63; *2:* 275; *6:* 46-47; *11:* 125; *12:* 202; *14:* 235
Chwast, Seymour, *3:* 128-129; *18:* 43; *27:* 152
Cirlin, Edgard, *2:* 168
Clarke, Harry, *23:* 172, 173
Clayton, Robert, *9:* 181
Cleaver, Elizabeth, *8:* 204; *23:* 36
Cleland, T. M., *26:* 92
Clement, Charles, *20:* 38
Clevin, Jörgen, *7:* 50
Coalson, Glo, *9:* 72, 85; *25:* 155; *26:* 42
Cober, Alan, *17:* 158
Cochran, Bobbye, *11:* 52
CoConis, Ted, *4:* 41
Coerr, Eleanor, *1:* 64
Coggins, Jack, *2:* 69
Cohen, Alix, *7:* 53
Cohen, Vincent O., *19:* 243
Cohen, Vivien, *11:* 112
Colbert, Anthony, *15:* 41; *20:* 193
Colby, C. B., *3:* 47
Cole, Herbert, *28:* 104
Cole, Olivia H. H., *1:* 134; *3:* 223; *9:* 111
Collier, David, *13:* 127
Collier, John, *27:* 179
Colonna, Bernard, *21:* 50; *28:* 103
Connolly, Jerome P., *4:* 128; *28:* 52
Conover, Chris, *31:* 52
Cook, G. R., *29:* 165
Cookburn, W. V., *29:* 204
Cooke, Donald E., *2:* 77

Coombs, Patricia, *2:* 82; *3:* 52;
 22: 119
Cooney, Barbara, *6:* 16-17, 50;
 12: 42; *13:* 92; *15:* 145;
 16: 74, 111; *18:* 189; *23:* 38,
 89, 93; *YABC 2:* 10
Cooper, Mario, *24:* 107
Cooper, Marjorie, *7:* 112
Copelman, Evelyn, *8:* 61; *18:* 25
Copley, Heather, *30:* 86
Corbett, Grahame, *30:* 114
Corbino, John, *19:* 248
Corcos, Lucille, *2:* 223; *10:* 27
Corey, Robert, *9:* 34
Corlass, Heather, *10:* 7
Cornell, James, *27:* 60
Cornell, Jeff, *11:* 58
Corrigan, Barbara, *8:* 37
Corwin, Judith Hoffman, *10:* 28
Cory, Fanny Y., *20:* 113
Cosgrove, Margaret, *3:* 100
Costello, David F., *23:* 55
Cox, Charles, *8:* 20
Cox, Palmer, *24:* 76, 77
Craft, Kinuko, *22:* 182
Crane, Alan H., *1:* 217
Crane, H. M., *13:* 111
Crane, Walter, *18:* 46-49, 53-54,
 56-57, 59-61; *22:* 128; *24:* 210,
 217
Credle, Ellis *1:* 69
Crofut, Susan, *23:* 61
Crowell, Pers, *3:* 125
Cruikshank, George, *15:* 76, 83;
 22: 74, 75, 76, 77, 78, 79, 80,
 81, 82, 84, 137; *24:* 22, 23
Crump, Fred H., *11:* 62
Cruz, Ray, *6:* 55
Cuffari, Richard, *4:* 75; *5:* 98;
 6: 56; *7:* 13, 84, 153; *8:* 148,
 155; *9:* 89; *11:* 19; *12:* 55, 96,
 114; *15:* 51, 202; *18:* 5;
 20: 139; *21:* 197; *22:* 14, 192;
 23: 15, 106; *25:* 97; *27:* 133;
 28: 196; *29:* 54; *30:* 85; *31:* 35
Cugat, Xavier, *19:* 120
Cummings, Chris, *29:* 167
Cummings, Richard, *24:* 119
Cunette, Lou, *20:* 93; *22:* 125
Cunningham, Aline, *25:* 180
Cunningham, David, *11:* 13
Cunningham, Imogene, *16:* 122,
 127
Curry, John Steuart, *2:* 5; *19:* 84
Curtis, Bruce, *23:* 96; *30:* 88

Dabcovich, Lydia, *25:* 105
D'Amato, Alex, *9:* 48; *20:* 25
D'Amato, Janet, *9:* 48; *20:* 25;
 26: 118
Daniel, Alan, *23:* 59; *29:* 110
Daniel, Lewis C., *20:* 216
Daniels, Steve, *22:* 16
Dann, Bonnie, *31:* 83

Danska, Herbert, *24:* 219
Danyell, Alice, *20:* 27
Darley, F.O.C., *16:* 145; *19:* 79,
 86, 88, 185; *21:* 28, 36;
 YABC 2: 175
Darling, Lois, *3:* 59; *23:* 30, 31
Darling, Louis, *1:* 40-41; *2:* 63;
 3: 59; *23:* 30, 31
Darrow, Whitney, Jr., *13:* 25
Darwin, Len, *24:* 82
Dauber, Liz, *1:* 22; *3:* 266; *30:* 49
Daugherty, James, *3:* 66; *8:* 178;
 13: 27-28, 161; *18:* 101;
 19: 72; *29:* 108; *YABC 1:* 256;
 YABC 2: 174
d'Aulaire, Edgar, *5:* 51
d'Aulaire, Ingri, *5:* 51
David, Jonathan, *19:* 37
Davidson, Kevin, *28:* 154
Davis, Allen, *20:* 11; *22:* 45;
 27: 222; *29:* 157
Davis, Bette J., *15:* 53; *23:* 95
Davis, Marguerite, *31:* 38;
 YABC 1: 126, 230
Dawson, Diane, *24:* 127
Dean, Bob, *19:* 211
de Angeli, Marguerite, *1:* 77;
 27: 62, 65, 66, 67, 69, 70, 72;
 YABC 1: 166
Deas, Michael, *27:* 219, 221;
 30: 156
de Bosschère, Jean, *19:* 252; *21:* 4
De Bruyn, M(onica) G., *13:* 30-31
De Cuir, John F., *1:* 28-29
De Grazia, *14:* 59
de Groat, Diane, *9:* 39; *18:* 7;
 23: 123; *28:* 200-201; *31:* 58,
 59
de Groot, Lee, *6:* 21
Delaney, A., *21:* 78
Delaney, Ned, *28:* 68
de Larrea, Victoria, *6:* 119, 204;
 29: 103
Delessert, Etienne, *7:* 140;
 YABC 2: 209
Delulio, John, *15:* 54
Denetsosie, Hoke, *13:* 126
Dennis, Morgan, *18:* 68-69
Dennis, Wesley, *2:* 87; *3:* 111;
 11: 132; *18:* 71-74; *22:* 9;
 24: 196, 200
Denslow, W. W., *16:* 84-87;
 18: 19-20, 24; *29:* 211
de Paola, Tomie, *8:* 95; *9:* 93;
 11: 69; *25:* 103; *28:* 157;
 29: 80
Detmold, Edward J., *22:* 104, 105,
 106, 107; *YABC 2:* 203
Detrich, Susan, *20:* 133
DeVelasco, Joseph E., *21:* 51
de Veyrac, Robert, *YABC 2:* 19
DeVille, Edward A., *4:* 235
Devito, Bert, *12:* 164
Devlin, Harry, *11:* 74
Dewey, Ariane, *7:* 64
 See also Aruego, Ariane

de Zanger, Arie, *30:* 40
Diamond, Donna, *21:* 200; *23:* 63;
 26: 142
Dick, John Henry, *8:* 181
Dickey, Robert L., *15:* 279
DiFiori, Lawrence, *10:* 51; *12:* 190;
 27: 97
Dillard, Annie, *10:* 32
Dillon, Corinne B., *1:* 139
Dillon, Diane, *4:* 104, 167; *6:* 23;
 13: 29; *15:* 99; *26:* 148;
 27: 136, 201
Dillon, Leo, *4:* 104, 167; *6:* 23;
 13: 29; *15:* 99; *26:* 148;
 27: 136, 201
Dinan, Carol, *25:* 169
Dines, Glen, *7:* 66-67
Dinsdale, Mary, *10:* 65; *11:* 171
Disney, Walt, *28:* 71, 72, 73, 76,
 77, 78, 79, 80, 81, 87, 88, 89,
 90, 91, 94
Dixon, Maynard, *20:* 165
Doares, Robert G., *20:* 39
Dobias, Frank, *22:* 162
Dobrin, Arnold, *4:* 68
Dodd, Ed, *4:* 69
Dodgson, Charles L., *20:* 148;
 YABC 2: 98
Dodson, Bert, *9:* 138; *14:* 195
Dohanos, Stevan, *16:* 10
Dolson, Hildegarde, *5:* 57
Domanska, Janina, *6:* 66-67;
 YABC 1: 166
Domjan, Joseph, *25:* 93
Donahue, Vic, *2:* 93; *3:* 190; *9:* 44
Donald, Elizabeth, *4:* 18
Donna, Natalie, *9:* 52
Doré, Gustave, *18:* 169, 172, 175;
 19: 93, 94, 95, 96, 97, 98, 99,
 100, 101, 102, 103, 104, 105;
 23: 188; *25:* 197, 199
Doremus, Robert, *6:* 62; *13:* 90;
 30: 95, 96, 97
Dorfman, Ronald, *11:* 128
Doty, Roy, *28:* 98; *31:* 32
Dougherty, Charles, *16:* 204; *18:* 74
Douglas, Aaron, *31:* 103
Douglas, Goray, *13:* 151
Dowd, Vic, *3:* 244; *10:* 97
Dowden, Anne Ophelia, *7:* 70-71;
 13: 120
Dowdy, Mrs. Regera, *29:* 100.
 See also Gorey, Edward
Doyle, Richard, *21:* 31, 32, 33;
 23: 231; *24:* 177; *31:* 87
Drath, Bill, *26:* 34
Drawson, Blair, *17:* 53
Drescher, Joan, *30:* 100, 101
Drew, Patricia, *15:* 100
Drummond, V. H., *6:* 70
du Bois, William Pene, *4:* 70;
 10: 122; *26:* 61; *27:* 145, 211
Duchesne, Janet, *6:* 162
Duffy, Pat, *28:* 153
Duke, Chris, *8:* 195

Dulac, Edmund, *19:* 108, 109, 110, 111, 112, 113, 114, 115, 117; *23:* 187; *25:* 152; *YABC 1:* 37; *YABC 2:* 147
Dulac, Jean, *13:* 64
Dunn, Phoebe, *5:* 175
Dunn, Tris, *5:* 175
Dunnington, Tom, *3:* 36; *18:* 281; *25:* 61; *31:* 159
Dutz, *6:* 59
Duvoisin, Roger, *2:* 95; *6:* 76-77; *7:* 197; *28:* 125; *30:* 101, 102, 103, 104, 105, 107
Dypold, Pat, *15:* 37

E.V.B. *See* Boyle, Eleanor Vere (Gordon)
Eachus, Jennifer, *29:* 74
Eagle, Michael, *11:* 86; *20:* 9; *23:* 18; *27:* 122; *28:* 57
Earle, Olive L., *7:* 75
Earle, Vana, *27:* 99
Easton, Reginald, *29:* 181
Eaton, Tom, *4:* 62; *6:* 64; *22:* 99; *24:* 124
Ebel, Alex, *11:* 89
Ebert, Len, *9:* 191
Edrien, *11:* 53
Edwards, George Wharton, *31:* 155
Edwards, Gunvor, *2:* 71; *25:* 47
Edwards, Jeanne, *29:* 257
Edwards, Linda Strauss, *21:* 134
Eggenhofer, Nicholas, *2:* 81
Egielski, Richard, *11:* 90; *16:* 208
Ehrlich, Bettina, *1:* 83
Eichenberg, Fritz, *1:* 79; *9:* 54; *19:* 248; *23:* 170; *24:* 200; *26:* 208; *YABC 1:* 104-105; *YABC 2:* 213
Einsel, Naiad, *10:* 35; *29:* 136
Einsel, Walter, *10:* 37
Einzig, Susan, *3:* 77
Eitzen, Allan, *9:* 56; *12:* 212; *14:* 226; *21:* 194
Elgaard, Greta, *19:* 241
Elgin, Kathleen, *9:* 188
Ellacott, S. E., *19:* 118
Elliott, Sarah M., *14:* 58
Emberley, Ed, *8:* 53
Englebert, Victor, *8:* 54
Enos, Randall, *20:* 183
Enright, Maginel Wright, *19:* 240, 243
Erhard, Walter, *1:* 152
Erickson, Phoebe, *11:* 83
Erikson, Mel, *31:* 69
Escourido, Joseph, *4:* 81
Estrada, Ric, *5:* 52, 146; *13:* 174
Ets, Marie Hall, *2:* 102
Eulalie, *YABC 2:* 315
Evans, Katherine, *5:* 64
Ewing, Juliana Horatia, *16:* 92

Falls, C. B., *1:* 19

Farmer, Peter, *24:* 108
Fatigati, Evelyn, *24:* 112
Faul-Jansen, Regina, *22:* 117
Faulkner, Jack, *6:* 169
Fava, Rita, *2:* 29
Fax, Elton C., *1:* 101; *4:* 2; *12:* 77; *25:* 107
Feelings, Tom, *5:* 22; *8:* 56; *12:* 153; *16:* 105; *30:* 196
Fehr, Terrence, *21:* 87
Feiffer, Jules, *3:* 91; *8:* 58
Fellows, Muriel H., *10:* 42
Fenton, Carroll Lane, *5:* 66; *21:* 39
Fenton, Mildred Adams, *5:* 66; *21:* 39
Fetz, Ingrid, *11:* 67; *12:* 52; *16:* 205; *17:* 59; *29:* 105; *30:* 108, 109
Fiammenghi, Gioia, *9:* 66; *11:* 44; *12:* 206; *13:* 57, 59
Field, Rachel, *15:* 113
Fink, Sam, *18:* 119
Finlay, Winifred, *23:* 72
Fiorentino, Al, *3:* 240
Firmin, Charlotte, *29:* 75
Fischer, Hans, *25:* 202
Fisher, Leonard Everett, *3:* 6; *4:* 72, 86; *6:* 197; *9:* 59; *16:* 151, 153; *23:* 44; *27:* 134; *29:* 26; *YABC 2:* 169
Fisher, Lois, *20:* 62; *21:* 7
Fisk, Nicholas, *25:* 112
Fitschen, Marilyn, *2:* 20-21; *20:* 48
Fitzgerald, F. A., *15:* 116; *25:* 86-87
Fitzhugh, Louise, *1:* 94; *9:* 163
Fitzhugh, Susie, *11:* 117
Fitzsimmons, Arthur, *14:* 128
Fix, Philippe, *26:* 102
Flack, Marjorie, *21:* 67; *YABC 2:* 122
Flagg, James Montgomery, *17:* 227
Flax, Zeona, *2:* 245
Fleishman, Seymour, *14:* 232; *24:* 87
Fleming, Guy, *18:* 41
Floethe, Richard, *3:* 131; *4:* 90
Floherty, John J., Jr., *5:* 68
Flora, James, *1:* 96; *30:* 111, 112
Florian, Douglas, *19:* 122
Flory, Jane, *22:* 111
Floyd, Gareth, *1:* 74; *17:* 245
Flynn, Barbara, *7:* 31; *9:* 70
Fogarty, Thomas, *15:* 89
Folger, Joseph, *9:* 100
Folkard, Charles, *22:* 132; *29:* 128, 257-258
Forberg, Ati, *12:* 71, 205; *14:* 1; *22:* 113; *26:* 22
Ford, George, *24:* 120; *31:* 70, 177
Ford, H. J., *16:* 185-186
Ford, Pamela Baldwin, *27:* 104
Foreman, Michael, *2:* 110-111
Fortnum, Peggy, *6:* 29; *20:* 179; *24:* 211; *26:* 76, 77, 78; *YABC 1:* 148

Foster, Genevieve, *2:* 112
Foster, Gerald, *7:* 78
Foster, Laura Louise, *6:* 79
Foster, Marian Curtis, *23:* 74
Fox, Charles Phillip, *12:* 84
Fox, Jim, *6:* 187
Fracé, Charles, *15:* 118
Frame, Paul, *2:* 45, 145; *9:* 153; *10:* 124; *21:* 71; *23:* 62; *24:* 123; *27:* 106; *31:* 48
Francois, André, *25:* 117
Francoise. *See* Seignobosc, Francoise, *21:* 145, 146
Frank, Lola Edick, *2:* 199
Frank, Mary, *4:* 54
Frankenberg, Robert, *22:* 116; *30:* 50
Franklin, John, *24:* 22
Frascino, Edward, *9:* 133; *29:* 229
Frasconi, Antonio, *6:* 80; *27:* 208
Fraser, Betty, *2:* 212; *6:* 185; *8:* 103; *31:* 72, 73
Fraser, F. A., *22:* 234
Freas, John, *25:* 207
Freeman, Don, *2:* 15; *13:* 249; *17:* 62-63, 65, 67-68; *18:* 243; *20:* 195; *23:* 213, 217
Fregosi, Claudia, *24:* 117
French, Fiona, *6:* 82-83
Friedman, Marvin, *19:* 59
Frith, Michael K., *15:* 138; *18:* 120
Fromm, Lilo, *29:* 85
Frost, A. B., *17:* 6-7; *19:* 123, 124, 125, 126, 127, 128, 129, 130; *YABC 1:* 156-157, 160; *YABC 2:* 107
Fry, Guy, *2:* 224
Fry, Rosalie, *3:* 72; *YABC 2:* 180-181
Fry, Rosalind, *21:* 153, 168
Fuchs, Erich, *6:* 84
Fulford, Deborah, *23:* 159
Fuller, Margaret, *25:* 189
Funk, Tom, *7:* 17, 99
Furchgott, Terry, *29:* 86
Furukawa, Mel, *25:* 42

Gaberell, J., *19:* 236
Gackenbach, Dick, *19:* 168
Gaetano, Nicholas, *23:* 209
Gag, Flavia, *17:* 49, 52
Gág, Wanda, *YABC 1:* 135, 137-138, 141, 143
Gagnon, Cécile, *11:* 77
Gal, Laszlo, *14:* 127
Galdone, Paul, *1:* 156, 181, 206; *2:* 40, 241; *3:* 42, 144; *4:* 141; *10:* 109, 158; *11:* 21; *12:* 118, 210; *14:* 12; *16:* 36-37; *17:* 70-74; *18:* 111, 230; *19:* 183; *21:* 154; *22:* 150, 245
Gallagher, Sears, *20:* 112
Galster, Robert, *1:* 66

Gammell, Stephen, 7: 48; 13: 149;
    29: 82
Gannett, Ruth Chrisman, 3: 74;
    18: 254
Garbutt, Bernard, 23: 68
Gardner, Richard. See Cummings,
    Richard, 24: 119
Garnett, Eve, 3: 75
Garraty, Gail, 4: 142
Garrett, Edmund H., 20: 29
Garrison, Barbara, 19: 133
Gates, Frieda, 26: 80
Gaughan, Jack, 26: 79
Gaver, Becky, 20: 61
Gay, Zhenya, 19: 135, 136
Geary, Clifford N., 1: 122; 9: 104
Geer, Charles, 1: 91; 3: 179;
    4: 201; 6: 168; 7: 96; 9: 58;
    10: 72; 12: 127
Geisel, Theodor Seuss, 1: 104-105,
    106; 28: 108, 109, 110, 111,
    112, 113
Geldart, William, 15: 121; 21: 202
Genia, 4: 84
Gentry, Cyrille R., 12: 66
George, Jean, 2: 113
Gérard, Rolf, 27: 147, 150
Geritz, Franz, 17: 135
Gerstein, Mordicai, 31: 117
Gervase, 12: 27
Gibbons, Gail, 23: 78
Giguère, George, 20: 111
Gilbert, John, 19: 184;
    YABC 2: 287
Gill, Margery, 4: 57; 7: 7; 22: 122;
    25: 166; 26: 146, 147
Gillen, Denver, 28: 216
Gillette, Henry J., 23: 237
Gilman, Esther, 15: 124
Giovanopoulos, Paul, 7: 104
Githens, Elizabeth M., 5: 47
Gladstone, Gary, 12: 89; 13: 190
Gladstone, Lise, 15: 273
Glanzman, Louis S., 2: 177; 3: 182
Glaser, Milton, 3: 5; 5: 156;
    11: 107; 30: 26
Glass, Marvin, 9: 174
Glattauer, Ned, 5: 84; 13: 224;
    14: 26
Glauber, Uta, 17: 76
Gleeson, J. M., YABC 2: 207
Gliewe, Unada, 3: 78-79; 21: 73
Glovach, Linda, 7: 105
Gobbato, Imero, 3: 180-181;
    6: 213; 7: 58; 9: 150; 18: 39;
    21: 167
Goble, Paul, 25: 121; 26: 86
Godfrey, Michael, 17: 279
Goffstein, M. B., 8: 71
Golbin, Andrée, 15: 125
Goldfeder, Cheryl, 11: 191
Goldsborough, June, 5: 154-155;
    8: 92, 14: 226; 19: 139
Goldstein, Leslie, 5: 8; 6: 60;
    10: 106

Goldstein, Nathan, 1: 175; 2: 79;
    11: 41, 232; 16: 55
Goodall, John S., 4: 92-93;
    10: 132; YABC 1: 198
Goode, Diane, 15: 126
Goodwin, Harold, 13: 74
Goodwin, Philip R., 18: 206
Gordon, Gwen, 12: 151
Gordon, Margaret, 4: 147; 5: 48-49;
    9: 79
Gorecka-Egan, Erica, 18: 35
Gorey, Edward, 1: 60-61; 13: 169;
    18: 192; 20: 201; 29: 90, 91,
    92-93, 94, 95, 96, 97, 98, 99,
    100; 30: 129.
    See also Dowdy, Mrs. Regera
Gorsline, Douglas, 1: 98; 6: 13;
    11: 113; 13: 104; 15: 14;
    28: 117, 118; YABC 1: 15
Gosner, Kenneth, 5: 135
Gotlieb, Jules, 6: 127
Gough, Philip, 23: 47
Govern, Elaine R., 26: 94
Grabianski, 20: 144
Graham, A. B., 11: 61
Graham, L., 7: 108
Graham, Margaret Bloy, 11: 120;
    18: 305, 307
Grahame-Johnstone, Anne, 13: 61
Grahame-Johnstone, Janet, 13: 61
Gramatky, Hardie, 1: 107; 30: 116,
    119, 120, 122, 123
Grant, Gordon, 17: 230, 234;
    25: 123, 124, 125, 126;
    YABC 1: 164
Grant, (Alice) Leigh, 10: 52;
    15: 131; 20: 20; 26: 119
Gray, Reginald, 6: 69
Green, Eileen, 6: 97
Greenaway, Kate, 17: 275; 24: 180;
    26: 107; YABC 1: 88-89;
    YABC 2: 131, 133, 136,
    138-139, 141
Greenwald, Sheila, 1: 34; 3: 99;
    8: 72
Gregorian, Joyce Ballou, 30: 125
Gregory, Frank M., 29: 107
Greiffenhagen, Maurice, 16: 137;
    27: 57; YABC 2: 288
Greiner, Robert, 6: 86
Gretter, J. Clemens, 31: 134
Gretz, Susanna, 7: 114
Gretzer, John, 1: 54; 3: 26; 4: 162;
    7: 125; 16: 247; 18: 117;
    28: 66; 30: 85, 211
Grey Owl, 24: 41
Gri, 25: 90
Grieder, Walter, 9: 84
Grifalconi, Ann, 2: 126; 3: 248;
    11: 18; 13: 182
Griffin, Gillett Good, 26: 96
Griffin, James, 30: 166
Griffiths, Dave, 29: 76
Gringhuis, Dirk, 6: 98; 9: 196
Gripe, Harald, 2: 127
Grisha, 3: 71

Gropper, William, 27: 93
Grose, Helen Mason, YABC 1: 260;
    YABC 2: 150
Grossman, Nancy, 24: 130; 29: 101
Grossman, Robert, 11: 124
Groth, John, 15: 79; 21: 53, 54
Gschwind, William, 11: 72
Guggenheim, Hans, 2: 10; 3: 37;
    8: 136
Guilbeau, Honoré, 22: 69
Guthrie, Robin, 20: 122

Haas, Irene, 17: 77
Hader, Berta H., 16: 126
Hader, Elmer S., 16: 126
Hafner, Marylin, 22: 196, 216;
    24: 44; 30: 51
Halas, John, 29: 41, 47, 48
Haldane, Roger, 13: 76; 14: 202
Hale, Irina, 26: 97
Hale, Kathleen, 17: 79
Hall, Chuck, 30: 189
Hall, Douglas, 15: 184
Hall, H. Tom, 1: 227; 30: 210
Hall, Sydney P., 31: 89
Hall, Vicki, 20: 24
Halpern, Joan, 10: 25
Hamberger, John, 6: 8; 8: 32;
    14: 79
Hamil, Tom, 14: 80
Hamilton, Bill and Associates,
    26: 215
Hamilton, Helen S., 2: 238
Hamilton, J., 19: 83, 85, 87
Hammond, Chris, 21: 37
Hammond, Elizabeth, 5: 36, 203
Hampshire, Michael, 5: 187;
    7: 110-111
Hampson, Denman, 10: 155;
    15: 130
Handville, Robert, 1: 89
Hane, Roger, 17: 239
Hanley, Catherine, 8: 161
Hann, Jacquie, 19: 144
Hanson, Joan, 8: 76; 11: 139
Hardy, David A., 9: 96
Hardy, Paul, YABC 2: 245
Harlan, Jerry, 3: 96
Harnischfeger, 18: 121
Harper, Arthur, YABC 2: 121
Harrington, Richard, 5: 81
Harrison, Florence, 20: 150, 152
Harrison, Harry, 4: 103
Harrison, Jack, 28: 149
Hart, William, 13: 72
Hartelius, Margaret, 10: 24
Hartshorn, Ruth, 5: 115; 11: 129
Harvey, Gerry, 7: 180
Hassell, Hilton, YABC 1: 187
Hasselriis, Else, 18: 87;
    YABC 1: 96
Hauman, Doris, 2: 184; 29: 58, 59
Hauman, George, 2: 184; 29: 58,
    59

Hausherr, Rosmarie, *15:* 29
Hawkinson, John, *4:* 109; *7:* 83; *21:* 64
Hawkinson, Lucy, *21:* 64
Haxton, Elaine, *28:* 131
Haydock, Robert, *4:* 95
Hayes, Geoffrey, *26:* 111
Haywood, Carolyn, *1:* 112; *29:* 104
Healy, Daty, *12:* 143
Hechtkopf, H., *11:* 110
Hedderwick, Mairi, *30:* 127
Hefter, Richard, *28:* 170; *31:* 81, 82
Heigh, James, *22:* 98
Heighway, Richard, *25:* 160
Hellebrand, Nancy, *26:* 57
Henneberger, Robert, *1:* 42; *2:* 237; *25:* 83
Henry, Everett, *29:* 191
Henry, Thomas, *5:* 102
Hensel, *27:* 119
Henstra, Friso, *8:* 80
Hepple, Norman, *28:* 198
Herbert, Wally, *23:* 101
Herbster, Mary Lee, *9:* 33
Hergé. *See* Remi, Georges
Hermanson, Dennis, *10:* 55
Herrington, Roger, *3:* 161
Heustis, Louise L., *20:* 28
Heyduck-Huth, Hilde, *8:* 82
Heyer, Hermann, *20:* 114, 115
Heyman, Ken, *8:* 33
Higginbottom, J. Winslow, *8:* 170; *29:* 105, 106
Hildebrandt, Greg, *8:* 191
Hildebrandt, Tim, *8:* 191
Hilder, Rowland, *19:* 207
Himler, Ronald, *6:* 114; *7:* 162; *8:* 17, 84, 125; *14:* 76; *19:* 145; *26:* 160; *31:* 43
Hiroshige, *25:* 71
Hirsh, Marilyn, *7:* 126
Hitz, Demi, *11:* 135; *15:* 245
Ho, Kwoncjan, *15:* 132
Hoban, Lillian, *1:* 114; *22:* 157; *26:* 72; *29:* 53
Hoban, Tana, *22:* 159
Hoberman, Norman, *5:* 82
Hodges, C. Walter, *2:* 139; *11:* 15; *12:* 25; *23:* 34; *25:* 96; *YABC 2:* 62-63
Hodges, David, *9:* 98
Hofbauer, Imre, *2:* 162
Hoff, Syd, *9:* 107; *10:* 128
Hoffman, Rosekrans, *15:* 133
Hoffmann, Felix, *9:* 109
Hofsinde, Robert, *21:* 70
Hogan, Inez, *2:* 141
Hogarth, Paul, *YABC 1:* 16
Hogenbyl, Jan, *1:* 35
Hogner, Nils, *4:* 122; *25:* 144
Hogrogian, Nonny, *3:* 221; *4:* 106-107; *5:* 166; *7:* 129; *15:* 2; *16:* 176; *20:* 154; *22:* 146; *25:* 217; *27:* 206; *YABC 2:* 84, 94

Hokusai, *25:* 71
Holberg, Richard, *2:* 51
Holiday, Henry, *YABC 2:* 107
Holland, Janice, *18:* 118
Holland, Marion, *6:* 116
Holldobler, Turid, *26:* 120
Holling, Holling C., *15:* 136-137
Hollinger, Deanne, *12:* 116
Holmes, B., *3:* 82
Holmes, Bea, *7:* 74; *24:* 156; *31:* 93
Holz, Loretta, *17:* 81
Homar, Lorenzo, *6:* 2
Homer, Winslow, *YABC 2:* 87
Honigman, Marian, *3:* 2
Hood, Susan, *12:* 43
Hook, Frances, *26:* 188; *27:* 127
Hook, Jeff, *14:* 137
Hook, Richard, *26:* 188
Hoover, Carol A., *21:* 77
Hoover, Russell, *12:* 95; *17:* 2
Horder, Margaret, *2:* 108
Horvat, Laurel, *12:* 201
Horvath, Ferdinand Kusati, *24:* 176
Hotchkiss, De Wolfe, *20:* 49
Hough, Charlotte, *9:* 112; *13:* 98; *17:* 83; *24:* 195
Houlihan, Ray, *11:* 214
Housman, Laurence, *25:* 146, 147
Houston, James, *13:* 107
How, W. E., *20:* 47
Howard, Alan, *16:* 80
Howard, J. N., *15:* 234
Howe, Stephen, *1:* 232
Howell, Pat, *15:* 139
Howell, Troy, *23:* 24; *31:* 61
Howes, Charles, *22:* 17
Hudnut, Robin, *14:* 62
Huffaker, Sandy, *10:* 56
Huffman, Joan, *13:* 33
Huffman, Tom, *13:* 180; *17:* 212; *21:* 116; *24:* 132
Hughes, Arthur, *20:* 148, 149, 150
Hughes, Shirley, *1:* 20, 21; *7:* 3; *12:* 217; *16:* 163; *29:* 154
Hülsmann, Eva, *16:* 166
Hummel, Lisl, *29:* 109; *YABC 2:* 333-334
Humphrey, Henry, *16:* 167
Humphreys, Graham, *25:* 168
Hunt, James, *2:* 143
Hurd, Clement, *2:* 148, 149
Hurd, Peter, *24:* 30, 31, *YABC 2:* 56
Hustler, Tom, *6:* 105
Hutchins, Pat, *15:* 142
Hutchinson, William M., *6:* 3, 138
Hutchison, Paula, *23:* 10
Hutton, Clarke, *YABC 2:* 335
Hutton, Warwick, *20:* 91
Huyette, Marcia, *29:* 188
Hyman, Trina Schart, *1:* 204; *2:* 194; *5:* 153; *6:* 106; *7:* 138, 145; *8:* 22; *10:* 196; *13:* 96; *14:* 114; *15:* 204; *16:* 234; *20:* 82; *22:* 133; *24:* 151;

25: 79, 82; *26:* 82; *29:* 83; *31:* 37, 39

Ichikawa, Satomi, *29:* 152
Ide, Jacqueline, *YABC 1:* 39
Ilsley, Velma, *3:* 1; *7:* 55; *12:* 109
Inga, *1:* 142
Ingraham, Erick, *21:* 177
Innocenti, Roberto, *21:* 123
Inoue, Yosuke, *24:* 118
Ipcar, Dahlov, *1:* 124-125
Irvin, Fred, *13:* 166; *15:* 143-144; *27:* 175
Irving, Laurence, *27:* 50
Isaac, Joanne, *21:* 76
Ishmael, Woodi, *24:* 111; *31:* 99
Ives, Ruth, *15:* 257

Jacobs, Barbara, *9:* 136
Jacobs, Lou, Jr., *9:* 136; *15:* 128
Jacques, Robin, *1:* 70; *2:* 1; *8:* 46; *9:* 20; *15:* 187; *19:* 253; *YABC 1:* 42
Jagr, Miloslav, *13:* 197
Jakubowski, Charles, *14:* 192
Jambor, Louis, *YABC 1:* 11
James, Gilbert, *YABC 1:* 43
James, Harold, *2:* 151; *3:* 62; *8:* 79; *29:* 113
James, Will, *19:* 150, 152, 153, 155, 163
Janosch. *See* Eckert, Horst
Jansson, Tove, *3:* 90
Jaques, Faith, *7:* 11, 132-33; *21:* 83, 84
Jaques, Frances Lee, *29:* 224
Jauss, Anne Marie, *1:* 139; *3:* 34; *10:* 57, 119; *11:* 205; *23:* 194
Jeffers, Susan, *17:* 86-87; *25:* 164-165; *26:* 112
Jefferson, Louise E., *4:* 160
Jeruchim, Simon, *6:* 173; *15:* 250
Jeschke, Susan, *20:* 89
Jessel, Camilla, *29:* 115
John, Diana, *12:* 209
John, Helen, *1:* 215; *28:* 204
Johns, Jeanne, *24:* 114
Johnson, Bruce, *9:* 47
Johnson, Crockett. *See* Leisk, David
Johnson, D. William, *23:* 104
Johnson, Harper, *1:* 27; *2:* 33; *18:* 302; *19:* 61; *31:* 181
Johnson, James David, *12:* 195
Johnson, James Ralph, *1:* 23, 127
Johnson, Milton, *1:* 67; *2:* 71; *26:* 45; *31:* 107
Johnson, Pamela, *16:* 174
Johnstone, Anne, *8:* 120
Johnstone, Janet Grahame, *8:* 120
Jones, Carol, *5:* 131
Jones, Elizabeth Orton, *18:* 124, 126, 128-129

Jones, Harold, *14:* 88
Jones, Laurian, *25:* 24, 27
Jones, Robert, *25:* 67
Jones, Wilfred, *YABC 1:* 163
Jucker, Sita, *5:* 93
Juhasz, Victor, *31:* 67
Jullian, Philippe, *24:* 206; *25:* 203
Jupo, Frank, *7:* 148-149

Kakimoo, Kozo, *11:* 148
Kalmenoff, Matthew, *22:* 191
Kamen, Gloria, *1:* 41; *9:* 119;
    10: 178
Kane, Henry B., *14:* 90;
    18: 219-220
Kane, Robert, *18:* 131
Kappes, Alfred, *28:* 104
Karlin, Eugene, *10:* 63; *20:* 131
Katona, Robert, *21:* 85; *24:* 126
Kaufman, Angelika, *15:* 156
Kaufman, John, *13:* 158
Kaufmann, John, *1:* 174; *4:* 159;
    8: 43, 192; *10:* 102;
    18: 133-134; *22:* 251
Kaye, Graham, *1:* 9
Keane, Bil, *4:* 135
Keats, Ezra Jack, *3:* 18, 105, 257;
    14: 101, 102
Keegan, Marcia, *9:* 122
Keely, John, *26:* 104
Keen, Eliot, *25:* 213
Keeping, Charles, *9:* 124, 185;
    15: 28, 134; *18:* 115
Keith, Eros, *4:* 98; *5:* 138; *31:* 29
Kelen, Emery, *13:* 115
Keller, Arthur I., *26:* 106
Kellogg, Steven, *8:* 96; *11:* 207;
    14: 130; *20:* 58; *29:* 140-141;
    30: 35; *YABC 1:* 65, 73
Kelly, Walt, *18:* 136-141, 144-146,
    148-149
Kemble, E. W., *YABC 2:* 54, 59
Kemp-Welsh, Lucy, *24:* 197
Kennedy, Paul Edward, *6:* 190;
    8: 132
Kennedy, Richard, *3:* 93; *12:* 179;
    YABC 1: 57
Kent, Jack, *24:* 136
Kent, Rockwell, *5:* 166; *6:* 129;
    20: 225, 226, 227, 229
Kepes, Juliet, *13:* 119
Kerr, Judity, *24:* 137
Kessler, Leonard, *1:* 108; *7:* 139;
    14: 107, 227; *22:* 101
Ketcham, Hank, *28:* 140, 141, 142
Kettelkamp, Larry, *2:* 164
Key, Alexander, *8:* 99
Kiakshuk, *8:* 59
Kiddell-Monroe, Joan, *19:* 201
Kidder, Harvey, *9:* 105
Kimball, Yeffe, *23:* 116
Kindred, Wendy, *7:* 151
King, Robin, *10:* 164-165
Kingman, Dong, *16:* 287

Kingsley, Charles, *YABC 2:* 182
Kipling, John Lockwood,
    YABC 2: 198
Kipling, Rudyard, *YABC 2:* 196
Kipniss, Robert, *29:* 59
Kirchhoff, Art, *28:* 136
Kirk, Ruth, *5:* 96
Kirmse, Marguerite, *15:* 283;
    18: 153
Kirschner, Ruth, *22:* 154
Klapholz, Mel, *13:* 35
Kleinman, Zalman, *28:* 143
Knight, Christopher, *13:* 125
Knight, Hilary, *1:* 233; *3:* 21;
    15: 92, 158-159; *16:* 258-260;
    18: 235; *19:* 169;
    YABC 1: 168-169, 172
Knotts, Howard, *20:* 4; *25:* 170
Kocsis, J. C. *See* Paul, James
Koering, Ursula, *3:* 28; *4:* 14
Koerner, Henry. *See* Koerner,
    W.H.D.
Koerner, W. H. D., *14:* 216;
    21: 88, 89, 90, 91; *23:* 211
Komoda, Kiyo *9:* 128; *13:* 214
Konashevicha, V., *YABC 1:* 26
Konigsburg, E. L., *4:* 138
Korach, Mimi, *1:* 128-129; *2:* 52;
    4: 39; *5:* 159; *9:* 129; *10:* 21;
    24: 69
Koren, Edward, *5:* 100
Kossin, Sandy, *10:* 71; *23:* 105
Kostin, Andrej, *26:* 204
Kovacević, Zivojin, *13:* 247
Krahn, Fernando, *2:* 257
Kramer, Frank, *6:* 121
Kraus, Robert, *13:* 217
Kredel, Fritz, *6:* 35; *17:* 93-96;
    22: 147; *24:* 175; *29:* 130;
    YABC 2: 166, 300
Krementz, Jill, *17:* 98
Kresin, Robert, *23:* 19
Krush, Beth, *1:* 51, 85; *2:* 233;
    4: 115; *9:* 61; *10:* 191;
    11: 196; *18:* 164-165
Krush, Joe, *2:* 233; *4:* 115; *9:* 61;
    10: 191; *11:* 196; *18:* 164-165
Kubinyi, Laszlo, *4:* 116; *6:* 113;
    16: 118; *17:* 100; *28:* 227;
    30: 172
Kuhn, Bob, *17:* 91
Künstler, Mort, *10:* 73
Kurelek, William, *8:* 107
Kuriloff, Ron, *13:* 19
Kuskin, Karla, *2:* 170
Kutzer, Ernst, *19:* 249

LaBlanc, André, *24:* 146
Laboccetta, Mario, *27:* 120
La Croix, *YABC 2:* 4
Laimgruber, Monika, *11:* 153
Laite, Gordon, *1:* 130-131; *8:* 209;
    31: 113
Lamb, Jim, *10:* 117

Lambert, Saul, *23:* 112
Lambo, Don, *6:* 156
Landa, Peter, *11:* 95; *13:* 177
Landshoff, Ursula, *13:* 124
Lane, John, *15:* 176-177; *30:* 146
Lane, John R., *8:* 145
Lang, Jerry, *18:* 295
Langler, Nola, *8:* 110
Lantz, Paul, *1:* 82, 102; *27:* 88
Larsen, Suzanne, *1:* 13
Larsson, Karl, *19:* 177
La Rue, Michael D., *13:* 215
Lasker, Joe, *7:* 186-187; *14:* 55
Latham, Barbara, *16:* 188-189
Lathrop, Dorothy, *14:* 117,
    118-119; *15:* 109; *16:* 78-79,
    81; *YABC 2:* 301
Lattimore, Eleanor Frances, *7:* 156
Lauden, Claire, *16:* 173
Lauden, George, Jr., *16:* 173
Laune, Paul, *2:* 235
Lawrence, John, *25:* 131; *30:* 141
Lawrence, Stephen, *20:* 195
Lawson, Carol, *6:* 38
Lawson, George, *17:* 280
Lawson, Robert, *5:* 26; *6:* 94;
    13: 39; *16:* 11; *20:* 100, 102,
    103; *YABC 2:* 222,
    224-225, 227-235, 237-241
Lazarevich, Mila, *17:* 118
Lazarus, Keo Felker, *21:* 94
Lazzaro, Victor, *11:* 126
Leacroft, Richard, *6:* 140
Leaf, Munro, *20:* 99
Leander, Patricia, *23:* 27
Lear, Edward, *18:* 183-185
Lebenson, Richard, *6:* 209; *7:* 76;
    23: 145
Le Cain, Errol, *6:* 141; *9:* 3;
    22: 142; *25:* 198; *28:* 173
Lee, Doris, *13:* 246
Lee, Manning de V., *2:* 200;
    17: 12; *27:* 87; *YABC 2:* 304
Lee, Robert J., *3:* 97
Leech, John, *15:* 59
Lees, Harry, *6:* 112
Legrand, Edy, *18:* 89, 93
Lehrman, Rosalie, *2:* 180
Leichman, Seymour, *5:* 107
Leighton, Clare, *25:* 130
Leisk, David, *1:* 140-141; *11:* 54;
    30: 137, 142, 143, 144
Leloir, Maurice, *18:* 77, 80, 83, 99
Lemke, Horst, *14:* 98
Lemon, David Gwynne, *9:* 1
Lenski, Lois, *1:* 144; *26:* 135, 137,
    139, 141
Lent, Blair, *1:* 116-117; *2:* 174;
    3: 206-207; *7:* 168-169
Lerner, Sharon, *11:* 157; *22:* 56
Leslie, Cecil, *19:* 244
Levin, Ted, *12:* 148
Levit, Herschel, *24:* 223
Levy, Jessica Ann, *19:* 225

Lewin, Ted, 4: 77; 8: 168; 20: 110;
   21: 99, 100; 27: 110; 28: 96,
   97; 31: 49
Lewis, Allen, 15: 112
Leydon, Rita Flodén, 21: 101
Lieblich, Irene, 22: 173; 27: 209,
   214
Liese, Charles, 4: 222
Lilly, Charles, 8: 73; 20: 127
Lincoln, Patricia Henderson, 27: 27
Lindberg, Howard, 10: 123;
   16: 190
Linden, Seymour, 18: 200-201
Linder, Richard, 27: 119
Line, Les, 27: 143
Linell. See Smith, Linell
Lionni, Leo, 8: 115
Lipinsky, Lino, 2: 156; 22: 175
Lippman, Peter, 8: 31; 31: 119,
   120, 160
Lisker, Sonia O., 16: 274; 31: 31
Lissim, Simon, 17: 138
Little, Harold, 16: 72
Little, Mary E., 28: 146
Livesly, Lorna, 19: 216
Llerena, Carlos Antonio, 19: 181
Lloyd, Errol, 11: 39; 22: 178
Lo, Koon-chiu, 7: 134
Lobel, Anita, 6: 87; 9: 141; 18: 248
Lobel, Arnold, 1: 188-189; 5: 12;
   6: 147; 7: 167, 209;
   18: 190-191; 25: 39, 43;
   27: 40; 29: 174
Loefgren, Ulf, 3: 108
Loescher, Ann, 20: 108
Loescher, Gil, 20: 108
Lofting, Hugh, 15: 182-183
Lonette, Reisie, 11: 211; 12: 168;
   13: 56
Longtemps, Ken, 17: 123; 29: 221
Looser, Heinz, YABC 2: 208
Lopshire, Robert, 6: 149; 21: 117
Lord, John Vernon, 21: 104; 23: 25
Lorraine, Walter H., 3: 110; 4: 123;
   16: 192
Loss, Joan, 11: 163
Louderback, Walt, YABC 1: 164
Low, Joseph, 14: 124, 125; 18: 68;
   19: 194; 31: 166
Lowenheim, Alfred, 13: 65-66
Lowitz, Anson, 17: 124; 18: 215
Lowrey, Jo, 8: 133
Lubell, Winifred, 1: 207; 3: 15;
   6: 151
Lubin, Leonard B., 19: 224;
   YABC 2: 96
Luhrs, Henry, 7: 123; 11: 120
Lupo, Dom, 4: 204
Lustig, Loretta, 30: 186
Lydecker, Laura, 21: 113
Lynch, Charles, 16: 33
Lynch, Marietta, 29: 137; 30: 171
Lyon, Elinor, 6: 154
Lyon, Fred, 14: 16
Lyons, Oren, 8: 193
Lyster, Michael, 26: 41

Maas, Dorothy, 6: 175
Macdonald, Alister, 21: 55
MacDonald, Norman, 13: 99
MacDonald, Roberta, 19: 237
Macguire, Robert Reid, 18: 67
MacIntyre, Elisabeth, 17: 127-128
Mack, Stan, 17: 129
Mackay, Donald, 17: 60
Mackinlay, Miguel, 27: 22
Mackinstry, Elizabeth, 15: 110
Maclise, Daniel, YABC 2: 257
Madden, Don, 3: 112-113; 4: 33,
   108, 155; 7: 193; YABC 2: 211
Maddison, Angela Mary, 10: 83
Maestro, Giulio, 8: 124; 12: 17;
   13: 108; 25: 182
Magnuson, Diana, 28: 102
Mahood, Kenneth, 24: 141
Maik, Henri, 9: 102
Maisto, Carol, 29: 87
Maitland, Antony, 1: 100, 176;
   8: 41; 17: 246; 24: 46;
   25: 177, 178
Malvern, Corrine, 2: 13
Mandelbaum, Ira, 31: 115
Manet, Edouard, 23: 170
Mangurian, David, 14: 133
Manniche, Lise, 31: 121
Manning, Samuel F., 5: 75
Maraja, 15: 86; YABC 1: 28;
   YABC 2: 115
Marcellino, Fred, 20: 125
Marchiori, Carlos, 14: 60
Margules, Gabriele, 21: 120
Mariana. See Foster, Marian Curtis
Marino, Dorothy, 6: 37; 14: 135
Markham, R. L., 17: 240
Marokvia, Artur, 31: 122
Marriott, Pat, 30: 30
Mars, W. T., 1: 161; 3: 115;
   4: 208, 225; 5: 92, 105, 186;
   8: 214; 9: 12; 13: 121;
   27: 151; 31: 180
Marsh, Christine, 3: 164
Marsh, Reginald, 17: 5; 19: 89;
   22: 90, 96
Marshall, Anthony D., 18: 216
Marshall, James, 6: 160
Martin, David Stone, 23: 232
Martin, Fletcher, 18: 213; 23: 151
Martin, Rene, 7: 144
Martin, Stefan, 8: 68
Martinez, John, 6: 113
Marx, Robert F., 24: 143
Masefield, Judith, 19: 208, 209
Mason, George F., 14: 139
Massie, Diane Redfield, 16: 194
Massie, Kim, 31: 43
Matsubara, Naoko, 12: 121
Matsuda, Shizu, 13: 167
Matte, L'Enc, 22: 183
Matthews, F. Leslie, 4: 216
Matthieu, Joseph, 14: 33
Matulay, Laszlo, 5: 18
Matus, Greta, 12: 142
Mauldin, Bill, 27: 23

Mawicke, Tran, 9: 137; 15: 191
Maxwell, John Alan, 1: 148
Mayan, Earl, 7: 193
Mayer, Mercer, 11: 192;
   16: 195-196; 20: 55, 57
Mayhew, Richard, 3: 106
Mays, Victor, 5: 127; 8: 45, 153;
   14: 245; 23: 50
Mazza, Adriana Saviozzi, 19: 215
McBride, Angus, 28: 49
McBride, Will, 30: 110
McCann, Gerald, 3: 50; 4: 94;
   7: 54
McClary, Nelson, 1: 111
McClintock, Theodore, 14: 141
McCloskey, Robert, 1: 184-185;
   2: 186-187; 17: 209
McClung, Robert, 2: 189
McClure, Gillian, 31: 132
McConnel, Jerry, 31: 75, 187
McCormick, Dell J., 19: 216
McCrady, Lady, 16: 198
McCrea, James, 3: 122
McCrea, Ruth, 3: 122; 27: 102
McCully, Emily, 2: 89; 4: 120-121,
   146, 197; 5: 2, 129; 7: 191;
   11: 122; 15: 210
McCurdy, Michael, 13: 153; 24: 85
McDermott, Beverly Brodsky,
   11: 180
McDermott, Gerald, 16: 201
McDonald, Jill, 13: 155; 26: 128
McDonald, Ralph J., 5: 123, 195
McDonough, Don, 10: 163
McFall, Christie, 12: 144
McGee, Barbara, 6: 165
McGregor, Malcolm, 23: 27
McHugh, Tom, 23: 64
McKay, Donald, 2: 118
McKee, David, 10: 48; 21: 9
McKie, Roy, 7: 44
McKillip, Kathy, 30: 153
McKinney, Ena, 26: 39
McLachlan, Edward, 5: 89
McMillan, Bruce, 22: 184
McNaught, Harry, 12: 80
McPhail, David, 14: 105; 23: 135
McQueen, Lucinda, 28: 149
McVay, Tracy, 11: 68
Meddaugh, Susan, 20: 42; 29: 143
Melo, John, 16: 285
Mendelssohn, Felix, 19: 170
Meng, Heinz, 13: 158
Merrill, Frank T., 16: 147; 19: 71;
   YABC 1: 226, 229, 273
Meryman, Hope, 27: 41
Meryweather, Jack, 10: 179
Meth, Harold, 24: 203
Meyer, Herbert, 19: 189
Meyer, Renate, 6: 170
Meyers, Bob, 11: 136
Micale, Albert, 2: 65; 22: 185
Middleton-Sandford, Betty, 2: 125
Mikolaycak, Charles, 9: 144;
   12: 101; 13: 212; 21: 121;
   22: 168; 30: 187

Miles, Jennifer, *17:* 278
Milhous, Katherine, *15:* 193; *17:* 51
Millais, John E., *22:* 230, 231
Millar, H. R., *YABC 1:* 194-195, 203
Millard, C. E., *28:* 186
Miller, Don, *15:* 195; *16:* 71; *20:* 106; *31:* 178
Miller, Edna, *29:* 148
Miller, Frank J., *25:* 94
Miller, Grambs, *18:* 38; *23:* 16
Miller, Jane, *15:* 196
Miller, Marcia, *13:* 233
Miller, Marilyn, *1:* 87; *31:* 69
Miller, Mitchell, *28:* 183
Miller, Shane, *5:* 140
Mizumura Kazue, *10:* 143; *18:* 223
Mochi, Ugo, *8:* 122
Mohr, Nicholasa, *8:* 139
Montresor, Beni, *2:* 91; *3:* 138
Moon, Carl, *25:* 183, 184, 185
Moon, Eliza, *14:* 40
Moon, Ivan, *22:* 39
Mora, Raul Mina, *20:* 41
Mordvinoff, Nicolas, *15:* 179
Moore, Mary, *29:* 160
Morrill, Leslie, *18:* 218; *29:* 177
Morrow, Gray, *2:* 64; *5:* 200; *10:* 103, 114; *14:* 175
Morton, Marian, *3:* 185
Moses, Grandma, *18:* 228
Moskof, Martin Stephen, *27:* 152
Moss, Donald, *11:* 184
Moyers, William, *21:* 65
Mozley, Charles, *9:* 87; *20:* 176, 192, 193; *22:* 228; *25:* 205; *YABC 2:* 89
Mueller, Hans Alexander, *26:* 64; *27:* 52, 53
Mugnaini, Joseph, *11:* 35; *27:* 52, 53
Mullins, Edward S., *10:* 101
Munari, Bruno, *15:* 200
Munowitz, Ken, *14:* 148
Munson, Russell, *13:* 9
Murphy, Bill, *5:* 138
Murr, Karl, *20:* 62
Mussino, Attilio, *29:* 131
Mutchler, Dwight, *1:* 25
Myers, Bernice, *9:* 147
Myers, Lou, *11:* 2

Nachreiner, Tom, *29:* 182
Nakai, Michael, *30:* 217
Nakatani, Chiyoko, *12:* 124
Nason, Thomas W., *14:* 68
Nast, Thomas, *21:* 29; *28:* 23
Natti, Susanna, *20:* 146
Navarra, Celeste Scala, *8:* 142
Naylor, Penelope, *10:* 104
Neebe, William, *7:* 93
Needler, Jerry, *12:* 93
Neel, Alice, *31:* 23

Negri, Rocco, *3:* 213; *5:* 67; *6:* 91, 108; *12:* 159
Neill, John R., *18:* 8, 10-11, 21, 30
Ness, Evaline, *1:* 164-165; *2:* 39; *3:* 8; *10:* 147; *12:* 53; *26:* 150, 151, 152, 153
Neville, Vera, *2:* 182
Newberry, Clare Turlay, *1:* 170
Newfeld, Frank, *14:* 121; *26:* 154
Ng, Michael, *29:* 171
Nicholson, William, *15:* 33-34; *16:* 48
Nickless, Will, *16:* 139
Nicolas, *17:* 130, 132-133; *YABC 2:* 215
Niebrugge, Jane, *6:* 118
Nielsen, Jon, *6:* 100; *24:* 202
Nielsen, Kay, *15:* 7; *16:* 211-213, 215, 217; *22:* 143; *YABC 1:* 32-33
Niland, Deborah, *25:* 191; *27:* 156
Niland, Kilmeny, *25:* 191
Ninon, *1:* 5
Nixon, K., *14:* 152
Noguchi, Yoshie, *30:* 99
Noonan, Julia, *4:* 163; *7:* 207; *25:* 151
Nordenskjold, Birgitta, *2:* 208
Norman, Michael, *12:* 117; *27:* 168
Numeroff, Laura Joffe, *28:* 161; *30:* 177
Nussbaumer, Paul, *16:* 219
Nyce, Helene, *19:* 219
Nygren, Tord, *30:* 148

Oakley, Graham, *8:* 112; *30:* 164, 165
Oakley, Thornton, *YABC 2:* 189
Obligado, Lilian, *2:* 28, 66-67; *6:* 30; *14:* 179; *15:* 103; *25:* 84
Obrant, Susan, *11:* 186
Oechsli, Kelly, *5:* 144-145; *7:* 115; *8:* 83, 183; *13:* 117; *20:* 94
Ohlsson, Ib, *4:* 152; *7:* 57; *10:* 20; *11:* 90; *19:* 217
Oliver, Jenni, *23:* 121
Olschewski, Alfred, *7:* 172
Olsen, Ib Spang, *6:* 178-179
Olugebefola, Ademola, *15:* 205
O'Neil, Dan IV, *7:* 176
O'Neill, Jean, *22:* 146
O'Neill, Steve, *21:* 118
Ono, Chiyo, *7:* 97
Orbaan, Albert, *2:* 31; *5:* 65, 171; *9:* 8; *14:* 241; *20:* 109
Orbach, Ruth, *21:* 112
Orfe, Joan, *20:* 81
Ormsby, Virginia H., *11:* 187
Orozco, José Clemente, *9:* 177
Orr, Forrest W., *23:* 9
Orr, N., *19:* 70
Osmond, Edward, *10:* 111
O'Sullivan, Tom, *3:* 176; *4:* 55
Otto, Svend, *22:* 130, 141

Oudry, J. B., *18:* 167
Oughton, Taylor, *5:* 23
Overlie, George, *11:* 156
Owens, Carl, *2:* 35; *23:* 52
Owens, Gail, *10:* 170; *12:* 157; *19:* 16; *22:* 70; *25:* 81; *28:* 203, 205
Oxenbury, Helen, *3:* 150-151; *24:* 81

Padgett, Jim, *12:* 165
Page, Homer, *14:* 145
Paget, Sidney, *24:* 90, 91, 93, 95, 97
Pak, *12:* 76
Palazzo, Tony, *3:* 152-153
Palladini, David, *4:* 113
Palmer, Heidi, *15:* 207; *29:* 102
Palmer, Juliette, *6:* 89; *15:* 208
Palmer, Lemuel, *17:* 25, 29
Panesis, Nicholas, *3:* 127
Papas, William, *11:* 223
Papin, Joseph, *26:* 113
Papish, Robin Lloyd, *10:* 80
Paraquin, Charles H., *18:* 166
Park, W. B., *22:* 189
Parker, Lewis, *2:* 179
Parker, Nancy Winslow, *10:* 113; *22:* 164; *28:* 47, 144
Parker, Robert, *4:* 161; *5:* 74; *9:* 136; *29:* 39
Parker, Robert Andrew, *11:* 81; *29:* 186
Parnall, Peter, *5:* 137; *16:* 221; *24:* 70
Parrish, Anne, *27:* 159, 160
Parrish, Dillwyn, *27:* 159
Parrish, Maxfield, *14:* 160, 161, 164, 165; *16:* 109; *18:* 12-13; *YABC 1:* 149, 152, 267; *YABC 2:* 146, 149
Parry, David, *26:* 156
Parry, Marian, *13:* 176; *19:* 179
Pascal, David, *14:* 174
Pasquier, J. A., *16:* 91
Paterson, Diane, *13:* 116
Paterson, Helen, *16:* 93
Paton, Jane, *15:* 271
Patterson, Robert, *25:* 118
Paul, James, *4:* 130; *23:* 161
Paull, Grace, *24:* 157
Payne, Joan Balfour, *1:* 118
Payson, Dale, *7:* 34; *9:* 151; *20:* 140
Payzant, Charles, *21:* 147
Peake, Mervyn, *22:* 136, 149; *23:* 162, 163, 164; *YABC 2:* 307
Peat, Fern B., *16:* 115
Peck, Anne Merriman, *18:* 241; *24:* 155
Pederson, Sharleen, *12:* 92
Pedersen, Vilhelm, *YABC 1:* 40

Peet, Bill, *2:* 203
Peltier, Leslie C., *13:* 178
Pendle, Alexy, *7:* 159; *13:* 34;
   29: 161
Pennington, Eunice, *27:* 162
Peppé, Mark, *28:* 142
Peppe, Rodney, *4:* 164-165
Perl, Susan, *2:* 98; *4:* 231;
   5: 44-45, 118; *6:* 199; *8:* 137;
   12: 88; *22:* 193; *YABC 1:* 176
Perry, Patricia, *29:* 137; *30:* 171
Perry, Roger, *27:* 163
Pesek, Ludek, *15:* 237
Petersham, Maud, *17:* 108, 147-153
Petersham, Miska, *17:* 108,
   147-153
Peterson, R. F., *7:* 101
Peterson, Russell, *7:* 130
Petie, Haris, *2:* 3; *10:* 41, 118;
   11: 227; *12:* 70
Petrides, Heidrun, *19:* 223
Peyton, K. M., *15:* 212
Pfeifer, Herman, *15:* 262
Phillips, Douglas, *1:* 19
Phillips, F. D., *6:* 202
Phillips, Thomas, *30:* 55
"Phiz." *See* Browne, Hablot K.,
   15: 65; *21:* 14, 15, 16, 17, 18,
   19, 20
Piatti, Celestino, *16:* 223
Picarella, Joseph, *13:* 147
Pickard, Charles, *12:* 38; *18:* 203
Picken, George A., *23:* 150
Pickens, David, *22:* 156
Pienkowski, Jan, *6:* 183; *30:* 32
Pimlott, John, *10:* 205
Pincus, Harriet, *4:* 186; *8:* 179;
   22: 148; *27:* 164, 165
Pinkney, Jerry, *8:* 218; *10:* 40;
   15: 276; *20:* 66; *24:* 121
Pinkwater, Manus, *8:* 156
Pinto, Ralph, *10:* 131
Pitz, Henry C., *4:* 168; *19:* 165;
   YABC 2: 95, 176
Pitzenberger, Lawrence J., *26:* 94
Pogany, Willy, *15:* 46, 49; *19:* 222,
   256; *25:* 214
Poirson, V. A., *26:* 89
Polgreen, John, *21:* 44
Politi, Leo, *1:* 178; *4:* 53; *21:* 48
Polseno, Jo, *1:* 53; *3:* 117; *5:* 114;
   17: 154; *20:* 87
Ponter, James, *5:* 204
Poortvliet, Rien, *6:* 212
Portal, Colette, *6:* 186; *11:* 203
Porter, George, *7:* 181
Potter, Beatrix, *YABC 1:* 208-210,
   212, 213
Potter, Miriam Clark, *3:* 162
Powers, Richard M., *1:* 230;
   3: 218; *7:* 194; *26:* 186
Pratt, Charles, *23:* 29
Price, Christine, *2:* 247; *3:* 163,
   253; *8:* 166
Price, Garrett, *1:* 76; *2:* 42
Price, Hattie Longstreet, *17:* 13

Price, Norman, *YABC 1:* 129
Primavera, Elise, *26:* 95
Prince, Leonora E., *7:* 170
Prittie, Edwin J., *YABC 1:* 120
Pudlo, *8:* 59
Purdy, Susan, *8:* 162
Puskas, James, *5:* 141
Pyk, Jan, *7:* 26
Pyle, Howard, *16:* 225-228,
   230-232, 235; *24:* 27

Quackenbush, Robert, *4:* 190;
   6: 166; *7:* 175, 178; *9:* 86;
   11: 65, 221
Quennell, Marjorie (Courtney),
   29: 163, 164
Quidor, John, *19:* 82
Quirk, Thomas, *12:* 81

Rackham, Arthur, *15:* 32, 78,
   214-227; *17:* 105, 115;
   18: 233; *19:* 254; *20:* 151;
   22: 129, 131, 132, 133;
   23: 175; *24:* 161, 181; *26:* 91;
   YABC 1: 25, 45, 55, 147;
   YABC 2: 103, 142, 173, 210
Rafilson, Sidney, *11:* 172
Raible, Alton, *1:* 202-203; *28:* 193
Ramsey, James, *16:* 41
Ransome, Arthur, *22:* 201
Rand, Paul, *6:* 188
Rao, Anthony, *28:* 126
Raphael, Elaine, *23:* 192
Rappaport, Eva, *6:* 190
Raskin, Ellen, *2:* 208-209; *4:* 142;
   13: 183; *22:* 68; *29:* 139
Rau, Margaret, *9:* 157
Raverat, Gwen, *YABC 1:* 152
Ravielli, Anthony, *1:* 198; *3:* 168;
   11: 143
Ray, Deborah, *8:* 164; *29:* 238
Ray, Ralph, *2:* 239; *5:* 73
Raymond, Larry, *31:* 108
Rayner, Mary, *22:* 207
Raynor, Dorka, *28:* 168
Raynor, Paul, *24:* 73
Razzi, James, *10:* 127
Read, Alexander D. "Sandy,"
   20: 45
Reid, Stephen, *19:* 213; *22:* 89
Reiss, John J., *23:* 193
Relf, Douglas, *3:* 63
Relyea, C. M., *16:* 29; *31:* 153
Remi, Georges, *13:* 184
Remington, Frederic, *19:* 188
Renlie, Frank, *11:* 200
Reschofsky, Jean, *7:* 118
Rethi, Lili, *2:* 153
Reusswig, William, *3:* 267
Rey, H. A., *1:* 182; *26:* 163, 164,
   166, 167, 169; *YABC 2:* 17
Reynolds, Doris, *5:* 71; *31:* 77

Rhead, Louis, *31:* 91
Ribbons, Ian, *3:* 10
Rice, Elizabeth, *2:* 53, 214
Rice, James, *22:* 210
Richards, Henry, *YABC 1:* 228, 231
Richardson, Ernest, *2:* 144
Richardson, Frederick, *18:* 27, 31
Richman, Hilda, *26:* 132
Richmond, George, *24:* 179
Rieniets, Judy King, *14:* 28
Riger, Bob, *2:* 166
Riley, Kenneth, *22:* 230
Ringi, Kjell, *12:* 171
Rios, Tere. *See* Versace, Marie
Ripper, Charles L., *3:* 175
Rivkin, Jay, *15:* 230
Roach, Marilynne, *9:* 158
Roberts, Cliff, *4:* 126
Roberts, Doreen, *4:* 230; *28:* 105
Roberts, Jim, *22:* 166; *23:* 69;
   31: 110
Roberts, W., *22:* 2, 3
Robinson, Charles, *3:* 53; *5:* 14;
   6: 193; *7:* 150; *7:* 183; *8:* 38;
   9: 81; *13:* 188; *14:* 248-249;
   23: 149; *26:* 115; *27:* 48;
   28: 191
Robinson, Charles [1870-1937],
   17: 157, 171-173, 175-176;
   24: 207; *25:* 204;
   YABC 2: 308-310, 331
Robinson, Jerry, *3:* 262
Robinson, Joan G., *7:* 184
Robinson, T. H., *17:* 179, 181-183;
   29: 254
Robinson, W. Heath, *17:* 185, 187,
   189, 191, 193, 195, 197, 199,
   202; *23:* 167; *25:* 194; *29:* 150;
   YABC 1: 44; *YABC 2:* 183
Rocker, Fermin, *7:* 34; *13:* 21;
   31: 40
Rockwell, Anne, *5:* 147
Rockwell, Gail, *7:* 186
Rockwell, Norman, *23:* 39, 196,
   197, 199, 200, 203, 204, 207;
   YABC 2: 60
Rodriguez, Joel, *16:* 65
Roever, J. M., *4:* 119; *26:* 170
Rogers, Carol, *2:* 262; *6:* 164;
   26: 129
Rogers, Frances, *10:* 130
Rogers, Walter S., *31:* 135, 138
Rogers, William A., *15:* 151,
   153-154
Rojankovsky, Feodor, *6:* 134, 136;
   10: 183; *21:* 128, 129, 130;
   25: 110; *28:* 42
Rose, Carl, *5:* 62
Rose, David S., *29:* 109
Rosenblum, Richard, *11:* 202;
   18: 18
Rosier, Lydia, *16:* 236; *20:* 104;
   21: 109; *22:* 125; *30:* 151, 158
Ross, Clare, *3:* 123; *21:* 45
Ross, John, *3:* 123; *21:* 45
Ross, Tony, *17:* 204

Rossetti, Dante Gabriel, *20:* 151, 153
Roth, Arnold, *4:* 238; *21:* 133
Rouille, M., *11:* 96
Rounds, Glen, *8:* 173; *9:* 171; *12:* 56; *YABC 1:* 1-3
Rowe, Gavin, *27:* 144
Roy, Jeroo, *27:* 229
Rubel, Nicole, *18:* 255; *20:* 59
Rud, Borghild, *6:* 15
Rudolph, Norman Guthrie, *17:* 13
Ruffins, Reynold, *10:* 134-135
Ruse, Margaret, *24:* 155
Russell, E. B., *18:* 177, 182
Russo, Susan, *30:* 182
Ruth, Rod, *9:* 161
Rutherford, Meg, *25:* 174
Rutland, Jonathan, *31:* 126
Ryden, Hope, *8:* 176

Sabaka, Donna R., *21:* 172
Sacker, Amy, *16:* 100
Sagsoorian, Paul, *12:* 183; *22:* 154
Saint Exupéry, Antoine de, *20:* 157
Sale, Morton, *YABC 2:* 31
Sambourne, Linley, *YABC 2:* 181
Sampson, Katherine, *9:* 197
Samson, Anne S., *2:* 216
Sandberg, Lasse, *15:* 239, 241
Sanderson, Ruth, *21:* 126; *24:* 53; *28:* 63
Sandin, Joan, *4:* 36; *6:* 194; *7:* 177; *12:* 145, 185; *20:* 43; *21:* 74; *26:* 144; *27:* 142; *28:* 224, 225
Sandoz, Edouard, *26:* 45, 47
Sapieha, Christine, *1:* 180
Sarg, Tony, *YABC 2:* 236
Sargent, Robert, *2:* 217
Saris, *1:* 33
Sarony, *YABC 2:* 170
Sasek, Miroslav, *16:* 239-242
Sassman, David, *9:* 79
Sätty, *29:* 203, 205
Savage, Steele, *10:* 203; *20:* 77
Savitt, Sam, *8:* 66, 182; *15:* 278; *20:* 96; *24:* 192; *28:* 98
Say, Allen, *28:* 178
Scabrini, Janet, *13:* 191
Scarry, Richard, *2:* 220-221; *18:* 20
Schaeffer, Mead, *18:* 81, 94; *21:* 137, 138, 139
Scharl, Josef, *20:* 132; *22:* 128
Scheel, Lita, *11:* 230
Scheib, Ida, *29:* 28
Schermer, Judith, *30:* 184
Schick, Joel, *16:* 160; *17:* 167; *22:* 12; *27:* 176; *31:* 147, 148
Schindelman, Joseph, *1:* 74; *4:* 101; *12:* 49; *26:* 51
Schindler, Edith, *7:* 22
Schlesinger, Bret, *7:* 77
Schmid, Eleanore, *12:* 188
Schmiderer, Dorothy, *19:* 224
Schmidt, Elizabeth, *15:* 242

Schneider, Rex, *29:* 64
Schoenherr, John, *1:* 146-147, 173; *3:* 39, 139; *17:* 75; *29:* 72
Schomburg, Alex, *13:* 23
Schongut, Emanuel, *4:* 102; *15:* 186
Schoonover, Frank, *17:* 107; *19:* 81, 190, 233; *22:* 88, 129; *24:* 189; *31:* 88; *YABC 2:* 282, 316
Schottland, Miriam, *22:* 172
Schramm, Ulrik, *2:* 16; *14:* 112
Schreiber, Elizabeth Anne, *13:* 193
Schreiber, Ralph W., *13:* 193
Schreiter, Rick, *14:* 97; *23:* 171
Schroeder, E. Peter, *12:* 112
Schroeder, Ted, *11:* 160; *15:* 189; *30:* 91
Schrotter, Gustav, *22:* 212; *30:* 225
Schucker, James, *31:* 163
Schulz, Charles M., *10:* 137-142
Schwartz, Charles, *8:* 184
Schwartzberg, Joan, *3:* 208
Schweitzer, Iris, *2:* 137; *6:* 207
Schweninger, Ann, *29:* 172
Scott, Anita Walker, *7:* 38
Scott, Trudy, *27:* 172
Scribner, Joanne, *14:* 236; *29:* 78
Scrofani, Joseph, *31:* 65
Searle, Ronald, *24:* 98
Sebree, Charles, *18:* 65
Sedacca, Joseph M., *11:* 25; *22:* 36
Ségur, Adrienne, *27:* 121
Seignobosc, Francoise, *21:* 145, 146
Sejima, Yoshimasa, *8:* 187
Selig, Sylvie, *13:* 199
Seltzer, Isadore, *6:* 18
Seltzer, Meyer, *17:* 214
Sempé, *YABC 2:* 109
Sendak, Maurice, *1:* 135, 190; *3:* 204; *7:* 142; *15:* 199; *17:* 210; *27:* 181, 182, 183, 185, 186, 187, 189, 190-191, 192, 193, 194, 195, 197, 198, 199, 203; *28:* 181, 182; *YABC 1:* 167
Sengler, Johanna, *18:* 256
Seredy, Kate, *1:* 192; *14:* 20-21; *17:* 210
Sergeant, John, *6:* 74
Servello, Joe, *10:* 144; *24:* 139
Seton, Ernest Thompson, *18:* 260-269, 271
Seuss, Dr. *See* Geisel, Theodor
Severin, John Powers, *7:* 62
Sewall, Marcia, *15:* 8; *22:* 170
Seward, Prudence, *16:* 243
Sewell, Helen, *3:* 186; *15:* 308
Shanks, Anne Zane, *10:* 149
Sharp, William, *6:* 131; *19:* 241; *20:* 112; *25:* 141
Shaw, Charles G., *13:* 200; *21:* 135
Shecter, Ben, *16:* 244; *25:* 109
Shekerjian, Haig, *16:* 245
Shekerjian, Regina, *16:* 245; *25:* 73

Shenton, Edward, *YABC 1:* 218-219, 221
Shepard, Ernest H., *3:* 193; *4:* 74; *16:* 101; *17:* 109; *25:* 148; *YABC 1:* 148, 153, 174, 176, 180-181
Shepard, Mary, *4:* 210; *22:* 205; *30:* 132, 133
Sherman, Theresa, *27:* 167
Sherwan, Earl, *3:* 196
Shields, Charles, *10:* 150
Shields, Leonard, *13:* 83, 85, 87
Shimin, Symeon, *1:* 93; *2:* 128-129; *3:* 202; *7:* 85; *11:* 177; *12:* 139; *13:* 202-203; *27:* 138; *28:* 65
Shinn, Everett, *16:* 148; *18:* 229; *21:* 149, 150, 151; *24:* 218
Shore, Robert, *27:* 54; *YABC 2:* 200
Shortall, Leonard, *4:* 144; *8:* 196; *10:* 166; *19:* 227, 228-229, 230; *25:* 78; *28:* 66, 167
Shortt, T. M., *27:* 36
Shulevitz, Uri, *3:* 198-199; *17:* 85; *22:* 204; *27:* 212; *28:* 184
Siberell, Anne, *29:* 193
Sibley, Don, *1:* 39; *12:* 196; *31:* 47
Sidjakov, Nicolas, *18:* 274
Siebel, Fritz, *3:* 120; *17:* 145
Siegl, Helen, *12:* 166; *23:* 216
Sills, Joyce, *5:* 199
Silverstein, Alvin, *8:* 189
Silverstein, Virginia, *8:* 189
Simon, Eric M., *7:* 82
Simon, Hilda, *28:* 189
Simon, Howard, *2:* 175; *5:* 132; *19:* 199
Simont, Marc, *2:* 119; *4:* 213; *9:* 168; *13:* 238, 240; *14:* 262; *16:* 179; *18:* 221; *26:* 210
Singer, Edith G., *2:* 30
Singer, Julia, *28:* 190
Sivard, Robert, *26:* 124
Skardinski, Stanley, *23:* 144
Slackman, Charles B., *12:* 201
Slater, Rod, *25:* 167
Sloan, Joseph, *16:* 68
Sloane, Eric, *21:* 3
Slobodkin, Louis, *1:* 200; *3:* 232; *5:* 168; *13:* 251; *15:* 13, 88; *26:* 173, 174, 175, 176, 178, 179
Slobodkina, Esphyr, *1:* 201
Smalley, Janet, *1:* 154
Smee, David, *14:* 78
Smith, Alvin, *1:* 31, 229; *13:* 187; *27:* 216; *28:* 226
Smith, E. Boyd, *19:* 70; *22:* 89; *26:* 63; *YABC 1:* 4-5, 240, 248-249
Smith, Edward J., *4:* 224
Smith, Eunice Young, *5:* 170
Smith, Howard, *19:* 196
Smith, Jacqueline Bardner, *27:* 108
Smith, Jessie Willcox, *15:* 91; *16:* 95; *18:* 231; *19:* 57, 242;

21: 29, 156, 157, 158, 159, 160, 161; *YABC 1:* 6; *YABC 2:* 180, 185, 191, 311, 325
Smith, Lee, *29:* 32
Smith, Linell Nash, *2:* 195
Smith, Maggie Kaufman, *13:* 205
Smith, Ralph Crosby, *2:* 267
Smith, Robert D., *5:* 63
Smith, Susan Carlton, *12:* 208
Smith, Terry, *12:* 106
Smith, Virginia, *3:* 157
Smith, William A., *1:* 36; *10:* 154; *25:* 65
Smyth, M. Jane, *12:* 15
Snyder, Andrew A., *30:* 212
Snyder, Jerome, *13:* 207; *30:* 173
Snyder, Joel, *28:* 163
Sofia, *1:* 62; *5:* 90
Solbert, Ronni, *1:* 159; *2:* 232; *5:* 121; *6:* 34; *17:* 249
Solonevich, George, *15:* 246; *17:* 47
Sommer, Robert, *12:* 211
Sorel, Edward, *4:* 61
Sotomayor, Antonio, *11:* 215
Soyer, Moses, *20:* 177
Spaenkuch, August, *16:* 28
Spanfeller, James, *1:* 72, 149; *2:* 183; *19:* 230, 231, 232; *22:* 66
Sparks, Mary Walker, *15:* 247
Spence, Geraldine, *21:* 163
Spiegel, Doris, *29:* 111
Spier, Jo, *10:* 30
Spier, Peter, *3:* 155; *4:* 200; *7:* 61; *11:* 78
Spilka, Arnold, *5:* 120; *6:* 204; *8:* 131
Spivak, I. Howard, *8:* 10
Spollen, Christopher J., *12:* 214
Sprattler, Rob, *12:* 176
Spring, Bob, *5:* 60
Spring, Ira, *5:* 60
Springer, Harriet, *31:* 92
Spurrier, Steven, *28:* 198
Staffan, Alvin E., *11:* 56; *12:* 187
Stahl, Ben, *5:* 181; *12:* 91
Stamaty, Mark Alan, *12:* 215
Stanley, Diana, *3:* 45
Steichen, Edward, *30:* 79
Steig, William, *18:* 275-276
Stein, Harve, *1:* 109
Steinel, William, *23:* 146
Stephens, Charles H., *YABC 2:* 279
Stephens, William M., *21:* 165
Steptoe, John, *8:* 197
Stern, Simon, *15:* 249-250; *17:* 58
Stevens, Mary, *11:* 193; *13:* 129
Stewart, Charles, *2:* 205
Stiles, Fran, *26:* 85
Stirnweis, Shannon, *10:* 164
Stobbs, William, *1:* 48-49; *3:* 68; *6:* 20; *17:* 117, 217; *24:* 150; *29:* 250
Stone, David, *9:* 173

Stone, David K., *4:* 38; *6:* 124; *9:* 180
Stone, Helen V., *6:* 209
Stratton-Porter, Gene, *15:* 254, 259, 263-264, 268-269
Streano, Vince, *20:* 173
Strong, Joseph D., Jr., *YABC 2:* 330
Ströyer, Poul, *13:* 221
Strugnell, Ann, *27:* 38
Stubis, Talivaldis, *5:* 182, 183; *10:* 45; *11:* 9; *18:* 304; *20:* 127
Stubley, Trevor, *14:* 43; *22:* 219; *23:* 37; *28:* 61
Stuecklen, Karl W., *8:* 34, 65; *23:* 103
Stull, Betty, *11:* 46
Suba, Susanne, *4:* 202-203; *14:* 261; *23:* 134; *29:* 222
Sugarman, Tracy, *3:* 76; *8:* 199
Sullivan, Edmund J., *31:* 86
Sullivan, James F., *19:* 280; *20:* 192
Sumichrast, Józef, *14:* 253; *29:* 168, 213
Summers, Leo, *1:* 177; *2:* 273; *13:* 22
Svolinsky, Karel, *17:* 104
Swain, Su Zan Noguchi, *21:* 170
Swan, Susan, *22:* 220-221
Sweat, Lynn, *25:* 206
Sweet, Darryl, *1:* 163; *4:* 136
Sweet, Ozzie, *31:* 149, 151, 152
Sweetland, Robert, *12:* 194
Sylvester, Natalie G., *22:* 222
Szafran, Gene, *24:* 144
Szasz, Susanne, *13:* 55, 226; *14:* 48
Szekeres, Cyndy, *2:* 218; *5:* 185; *8:* 85; *11:* 166; *14:* 19; *16:* 57, 159; *26:* 49, 214

Tait, Douglas, *12:* 220
Takakjian, Portia, *15:* 274
Takashima, Shizuye, *13:* 228
Talarczyk, June, *4:* 173
Tallon, Robert, *2:* 228
Tamas, Szecskó, *29:* 135
Tamburine, Jean, *12:* 222
Tandy, H. R., *13:* 69
Tanobe, Miyuki, *23:* 221
Tarkington, Booth, *17:* 224-225
Teale, Edwin Way, *7:* 196
Teason, James, *1:* 14
Tee-Van, Helen Damrosch, *10:* 176; *11:* 182
Tempest, Margaret, *3:* 237, 238
Templeton, Owen, *11:* 77
Tenggren, Gustaf, *18:* 277-279; *19:* 15; *28:* 86; *YABC 2:* 145
Tenney, Gordon, *24:* 204
Tenniel, John, *YABC 2:* 99
Thacher, Mary M., *30:* 72
Thackeray, William Makepeace, *23:* 224, 228

Thelwell, Norman, *14:* 201
Thistlethwaite, Miles, *12:* 224
Thollander, Earl, *11:* 47; *18:* 112; *22:* 224
Thomas, Allan, *22:* 13
Thomas, Eric, *28:* 49
Thomas, Harold, *20:* 98
Thomas, Martin, *14:* 255
Thompson, George, *22:* 18; *28:* 150
Thomson, Arline K., *3:* 264
Thomson, Hugh, *26:* 88
Thorne, Diana, *25:* 212
Thorvall, Kerstin, *13:* 235
Thurber, James, *13:* 239, 242-245, 248-249
Tichenor, Tom, *14:* 207
Tilney, F. C., *22:* 231
Timmins, Harry, *2:* 171
Tinkelman, Murray, *12:* 225
Tolford, Joshua, *1:* 221
Tolkien, J. R. R., *2:* 243
Tolmie, Ken, *15:* 292
Tomes, Jacqueline, *2:* 117; *12:* 139
Tomes, Margot, *1:* 224; *2:* 120-121; *16:* 207; *18:* 250; *20:* 7; *25:* 62; *27:* 78, 79; *29:* 81, 199
Toner, Raymond John, *10:* 179
Toothill, Harry, *6:* 54; *7:* 49; *25:* 219
Toothill, Ilse, *6:* 54
Torbert, Floyd James, *22:* 226
Toschik, Larry, *6:* 102
Totten, Bob, *13:* 93
Tremain, Ruthven, *17:* 238
Tresilian, Stuart, *25:* 53
Trez, Alain, *17:* 236
Trier, Walter, *14:* 96
Tripp, F. J., *24:* 167
Tripp, Wallace, *2:* 48; *7:* 28; *8:* 94; *10:* 54, 76; *11:* 92; *31:* 170, 171
Trnka, Jiri, *22:* 151; *YABC 1:* 30-31
Troyer, Johannes, *3:* 16; *7:* 18
Tsinajinie, Andy, *2:* 62
Tsugami, Kyuzo, *18:* 198-199
Tuckwell, Jennifer, *17:* 205
Tudor, Bethany, *7:* 103
Tudor, Tasha, *18:* 227; *20:* 185, 186, 187; *YABC 2:* 46, 314
Tulloch, Maurice, *24:* 79
Tunis, Edwin, *1:* 218-219; *28:* 209, 210, 211, 212
Turkle, Brinton, *1:* 211, 213; *2:* 249; *3:* 226; *11:* 3; *16:* 209; *20:* 22; *YABC 1:* 79
Turska, Krystyna, *12:* 103; *31:* 173, 174-175
Tusan, Stan, *6:* 58; *22:* 236-237
Tzimoulis, Paul, *12:* 104

Uchida, Yoshiko, *1:* 220
Ulm, Robert, *17:* 238
Unada. *See* Gliewe, Unada, *3:* 78-79; *21:* 73; *30:* 220

Ungerer, Tomi, *5:* 188; *9:* 40; *18:* 188; *29:* 175
Unwin, Nora S., *3:* 65, 234-235; *4:* 237; *YABC 1:* 59; *YABC 2:* 301
Utpatel, Frank, *18:* 114
Utz, Lois, *5:* 190

Van Abbé, S., *16:* 142; *18:* 282; *31:* 90; *YABC 2:* 157, 161
Vandivert, William, *21:* 175
Van Everen, Jay, *13:* 160; *YABC 1:* 121
Van Loon, Hendrik Willem, *18:* 285, 289, 291
Van Stockum, Hilda, *5:* 193
Van Wely, Babs, *16:* 50
Varga, Judy, *29:* 196
Vasiliu, Mircea, *2:* 166, 253; *9:* 166; *13:* 58
Vavra, Robert, *8:* 206
Vawter, Will, *17:* 163
Veeder, Larry, *18:* 4
Ver Beck, Frank, *18:* 16-17
Verney, John, *14:* 225
Verrier, Suzanne, *5:* 20; *23:* 212
Versace, Marie, *2:* 255
Vestal, H. B., *9:* 134; *11:* 101; *27:* 25
Victor, Joan Berg, *30:* 193
Viereck, Ellen, *3:* 242; *14:* 229
Vigna, Judith, *15:* 293
Vilato, Gaspar E., *5:* 41
Vimnèra, A., *23:* 154
Vo-Dinh, Mai, *16:* 272
Vogel, Ilse-Margret, *14:* 230
von Schmidt, Eric, *8:* 62
von Schmidt, Harold, *30:* 80
Vosburgh, Leonard, *1:* 161; *7:* 32; *15:* 295-296; *23:* 110; *30:* 214
Voter, Thomas W., *19:* 3, 9
Vroman, Tom, *10:* 29

Wagner, John, *8:* 200
Wagner, Ken, *2:* 59
Waide, Jan, *29:* 225
Wainwright, Jerry, *14:* 85
Waldman, Bruce, *15:* 297
Walker, Charles, *1:* 46; *4:* 59; *5:* 177; *11:* 115; *19:* 45
Walker, Dugald Stewart, *15:* 47
Walker, Gil, *8:* 49; *23:* 132
Walker, Jim, *10:* 94
Walker, Mort, *8:* 213
Walker, Stephen, *12:* 229; *21:* 174
Wallace, Beverly Dobrin, *19:* 259
Waller, S. E., *24:* 36
Wallner, Alexandra, *15:* 120
Wallner, John C., *9:* 77; *10:* 188; *11:* 28; *14:* 209; *31:* 56, 118
Wallower, Lucille, *11:* 226
Walters, Audrey, *18:* 294

Walther, Tom, *31:* 179
Walton, Tony, *11:* 164; *24:* 209
Waltrip, Lela, *9:* 195
Waltrip, Mildred, *3:* 209
Waltrip, Rufus, *9:* 195
Wan, *12:* 76
Ward, Keith, *2:* 107
Ward, Lynd, *1:* 99, 132, 133, 150; *2:* 108, 158, 196, 259; *18:* 86; *27:* 56; *29:* 79, 187, 253, 255
Warner, Peter, *14:* 87
Warren, Betsy, *2:* 101
Warren, Marion Cray, *14:* 215
Warshaw, Jerry, *30:* 197, 198
Washington, Nevin, *20:* 123
Washington, Phyllis, *20:* 123
Waterman, Stan, *11:* 76
Watkins-Pitchford, D. J., *6:* 215, 217
Watson, Aldren, *2:* 267; *5:* 94; *13:* 71; *19:* 253; *YABC 2:* 202
Watson, Gary, *19:* 147
Watson, J. D., *22:* 86
Watson, Karen, *11:* 26
Watson, Wendy, *5:* 197; *13:* 101
Watts, Bernadette, *4:* 227
Webber, Helen, *3:* 141
Webber, Irma E., *14:* 238
Weber, William J., *14:* 239
Webster, Jean, *17:* 241
Wegner, Fritz, *14:* 250; *20:* 189
Weidenear, Reynold H., *21:* 122
Weihs, Erika, *4:* 21; *15:* 299
Weil, Lisl, *7:* 203; *10:* 58; *21:* 95; *22:* 188, 217
Weiner, Sandra, *14:* 240
Weisgard, Leonard, *1:* 65; *2:* 191, 197, 204, 264-265; *5:* 108; *21:* 42; *30:* 200, 201, 203, 204; *YABC 2:* 13
Weiss, Emil, *1:* 168; *7:* 60
Weiss, Harvey, *1:* 145, 223; *27:* 224, 227
Wells, Frances, *1:* 183
Wells, H. G., *20:* 194, 200
Wells, Rosemary, *6:* 49; *18:* 297
Wells, Susan, *22:* 43
Wendelin, Rudolph, *23:* 234
Werenskiold, Erik, *15:* 6
Werner, Honi, *24:* 110
Werth, Kurt, *7:* 122; *14:* 157; *20:* 214
Westerberg, Christine, *29:* 226
Weston, Martha, *29:* 116; *30:* 213
Wetherbee, Margaret, *5:* 3
Wheatley, Arabelle, *11:* 231; *16:* 276
Wheelright, Rowland, *15:* 81; *YABC 2:* 286
Whistler, Rex, *16:* 75; *30:* 207, 208
White, David Omar, *5:* 56; *18:* 6
Whithorne, H. S., *7:* 49
Whitney, George Gillett, *3:* 24
Whittam, Geoffrey, *30:* 191

Wiese, Kurt, *3:* 255; *4:* 206; *14:* 17; *17:* 18-19; *19:* 47; *24:* 152; *25:* 212
Wiesner, William, *4:* 100; *5:* 200, 201; *14:* 262
Wiggins, George, *6:* 133
Wikland, Ilon, *5:* 113; *8:* 150
Wilbur, C. Keith, M.D., *27:* 228
Wilde, George, *7:* 139
Wildsmith, Brian, *16:* 281-282; *18:* 170-171
Wilkinson, Gerald, *3:* 40
Wilkoń, Józef, *31:* 183, 184
Williams, Ferelith Eccles, *22:* 238
Williams, Garth, *1:* 197; *2:* 49, 270; *4:* 205; *15:* 198, 302-304, 307; *16:* 34; *18:* 283, 298-301; *29:* 177, 178, 179, 232-233, 241-245, 248; *YABC 2:* 15-16, 19
Williams, Maureen, *12:* 238
Williams, Patrick, *14:* 218
Wilson, Charles Banks, *17:* 92
Wilson, Dagmar, *10:* 47
Wilson, Edward A., *6:* 24; *16:* 149; *20:* 220-221; *22:* 87; *26:* 67
Wilson, Forrest, *27:* 231
Wilson, Jack, *17:* 139
Wilson, John, *22:* 240
Wilson, Peggy, *15:* 4
Wilson, Rowland B., *30:* 170
Wilson, W. N., *22:* 26
Wilwerding, Walter J., *9:* 202
Winchester, Linda, *13:* 231
Wind, Betty, *28:* 158
Windham, Kathryn Tucker, *14:* 260
Winslow, Will, *21:* 124
Winter, Milo, *15:* 97; *19:* 221; *21:* 181, 203, 204, 205; *YABC 2:* 144
Wise, Louis, *13:* 68
Wiseman, Ann, *31:* 187
Wiseman, B., *4:* 233
Wishnefsky, Phillip, *3:* 14
Wiskur, Darrell, *5:* 72; *10:* 50; *18:* 246
Wittman, Sally, *30:* 219
Woehr, Lois, *12:* 5
Wohlberg, Meg, *12:* 100; *14:* 197
Wolf, J., *16:* 91
Wondriska, William, *6:* 220
Wonsetler, John C., *5:* 168
Wood, Grant, *19:* 198
Wood, Myron, *6:* 220
Wood, Owen, *18:* 187
Wood, Ruth, *8:* 11
Woodson, Jack, *10:* 201
Woodward, Alice, *26:* 89
Wool, David, *26:* 27
Wooten, Vernon, *23:* 70
Worboys, Evelyn, *1:* 166-167
Worth, Wendy, *4:* 133
Wosmek, Frances, *29:* 251
Wrenn, Charles L., *YABC 1:* 20, 21
Wright, Dare, *21:* 206
Wright, George, *YABC 1:* 268

Wright, Joseph, *30:* 160
Wronker, Lili Cassel, *3:* 247;
    10: 204; *21:* 10
Wyeth, Andrew, *13:* 40;
    YABC 1: 133-134
Wyeth, N. C., *13:* 41; *17:* 252-259,
    264-268; *18:* 181; *19:* 80, 191,
    200; *21:* 57, 183; *22:* 91;
    23: 152; *24:* 28, 99;
    YABC 1: 133, 223;
    YABC 2: 53, 75, 171, 187, 317

Yang, Jay, *1:* 8; *12:* 239
Yap, Weda, *6:* 176
Yashima, Taro, *14:* 84
Yohn, F. C., *23:* 128; *YABC 1:* 269
Young, Ed, *7:* 205; *10:* 206;
    YABC 2: 242

Young, Noela, *8:* 221

Zacks, Lewis, *10:* 161
Zalben, Jane Breskin, *7:* 211
Zallinger, Jean, *4:* 192; *8:* 8, 129;
    14: 273
Zallinger, Rudolph F., *3:* 245
Zelinsky, Paul O., *14:* 269
Zemach, Margot, *3:* 270; *8:* 201;
    21: 210-211; *27:* 204, 205,
    210; *28:* 185
Zemsky, Jessica, *10:* 62
Zinkeisen, Anna, *13:* 106
Zonia, Dhimitri, *20:* 234-235
Zweifel, Francis, *14:* 274; *28:* 187

Illustrations Index

Author Index

(In the following index, the number of the volume in which an author's sketch appears is given *before* the colon, and the page on which it appears is given *after* the colon. For example, the sketch of Aardema, Verna, appears in Volume 4 on page 1).

YABC

Index citations including this abbreviation refer to listings appearing in *Yesterday's Authors of Books for Children,* also published by the Gale Research Company, which covers authors who died prior to 1960.

Aardema, Verna 1911- , *4: 1*
Aaron, Chester 1923- , *9: 1*
Abbott, Alice. *See* Borland, Kathryn Kilby, *16: 54*
Abbott, Alice. *See* Speicher, Helen Ross (Smith), *8: 194*
Abbott, Jacob 1803-1879, *22: 1*
Abbott, Manager Henry. *See* Stratemeyer, Edward L., *1: 208*
Abdul, Raoul 1929- , *12: 1*
Abel, Raymond 1911- , *12: 2*
Abell, Kathleen 1938- , *9: 1*
Abercrombie, Barbara (Mattes) 1939- , *16: 1*
Abernethy, Robert G. 1935- , *5: 1*
Abisch, Roslyn Kroop 1927- , *9: 3*
Abisch, Roz. *See* Abisch, Roslyn Kroop, *9: 3*
Abodaher, David J. (Naiph) 1919- , *17: 1*
Abrahall, C. H. *See* Hoskyns-Abrahall, Clare, *13: 105*
Abrahall, Clare Hoskyns. *See* Hoskyns-Abrahall, Clare, *13: 105*
Abrahams, Hilary (Ruth) 1938- , *29: 23*
Abrahams, Robert D(avid) 1905- , *4: 3*
Abrams, Joy 1941- , *16: 2*
Ackerman, Eugene 1888-1974, *10: 1*
Adair, Margaret Weeks (?)-1971, *10: 1*
Adam, Cornel. *See* Lengyel, Cornel Adam, *27: 140*
Adams, Adrienne 1906- , *8: 1*
Adams, Andy 1859-1935, *YABC 1: 1*
Adams, Dale. *See* Quinn, Elisabeth, *22: 197*

Adams, Harriet S(tratemeyer) 1893(?)-1982, *1:* 1; *29: 26* (Obituary)
Adams, Harrison. *See* Stratemeyer, Edward L., *1: 208*
Adams, Hazard 1926- , *6: 1*
Adams, Richard 1920- , *7: 1*
Adams, Ruth Joyce, *14: 1*
Adams, William Taylor 1822-1897, *28: 21*
Adamson, Gareth 1925-1982(?), *30: 23* (Obituary)
Adamson, George Worsley 1913- , *30: 23*
Adamson, Graham. *See* Groom, Arthur William, *10: 53*
Adamson, Joy 1910-1980, *11:* 1; *22: 5* (Obituary)
Adamson, Wendy Wriston 1942- , *22: 6*
Addona, Angelo F. 1925- , *14: 1*
Addy, Ted. *See* Winterbotham, R(ussell) R(obert), *10: 198*
Adelberg, Doris. *See* Orgel, Doris, *7: 173*
Adelson, Leone 1908- , *11: 2*
Adkins, Jan 1944- , *8: 2*
Adler, C(arole) S(chwerdtfeger) 1932- , *26: 21*
Adler, David A. 1947- , *14: 2*
Adler, Irene. *See* Storr, Catherine (Cole), *9: 181*
Adler, Irving 1913- , *1:* 2; *29: 26*
Adler, Peggy, *22: 6*
Adler, Ruth 1915-1968, *1: 4*
Adoff, Arnold 1935- , *5: 1*
Adorjan, Carol 1934- , *10: 1*
Adshead, Gladys L. 1896- , *3: 1*
Aesop, Abraham. *See* Newbery, John, *20: 135*
Agapida, Fray Antonio. *See* Irving, Washington, *YABC 2: 164*
Agard, Nadema 1948- , *18: 1*
Agle, Nan Hayden 1905- , *3: 2*

Agnew, Edith J(osephine) 1897- , *11: 3*
Ahern, Margaret McCrohan 1921- , *10: 2*
Aichinger, Helga 1937- , *4: 4*
Aiken, Clarissa (Lorenz) 1899- , *12: 4*
Aiken, Conrad (Potter) 1889-1973, *3:* 3; *30: 25*
Aiken, Joan 1924- , *2:* 1; *30: 24*
Ainsworth, Norma, *9: 4*
Ainsworth, Ruth 1908- , *7: 1*
Ainsworth, William Harrison 1805-1882, *24: 21*
Aistrop, Jack 1916- , *14: 3*
Aitken, Dorothy 1916- , *10: 2*
Akers, Floyd. *See* Baum, L(yman) Frank, *18: 7*
Albert, Burton, Jr. 1936- , *22: 7*
Alberts, Frances Jacobs 1907- , *14: 4*
Albion, Lee Smith, *29: 32*
Albrecht, Lillie (Vanderveer) 1894- , *12: 5*
Alcorn, John 1935- , *30:* 33 (Brief Entry); *31: 21*
Alcott, Louisa May 1832-1888, *YABC 1: 7*
Alden, Isabella (Macdonald) 1841-1930, *YABC 2: 1*
Alderman, Clifford Lindsey 1902- , *3: 6*
Aldis, Dorothy (Keeley) 1896-1966, *2: 2*
Aldon, Adair. *See* Meigs, Cornelia, *6: 167*
Aldous, Allan (Charles) 1911- , *27: 21*
Aldrich, Ann. *See* Meaker, Marijane, *20: 124*
Aldrich, Thomas Bailey 1836-1907, *17: 2*
Aldridge, Josephine Haskell, *14: 5*
Alegria, Ricardo E. 1921- , *6: 1*

Alexander, Anna Cooke 1913- ,
  1: 4
Alexander, Frances 1888- , *4:* 6
Alexander, Jocelyn (Anne) Arundel
  1930- , *22:* 9
Alexander, Linda 1935- , *2:* 3
Alexander, Lloyd 1924- , *3:* 7
Alexander, Martha 1920- , *11:* 4
Alexander, Rae Pace. *See*
  Alexander, Raymond Pace,
  22: 10
Alexander, Raymond Pace
  1898-1974, *22:* 10
Alexander, Sue 1933- , *12:* 5
Alexander, Vincent Arthur
  1925-1980, *23:* 1 (Obituary)
Alexeieff, Alexandre A. 1901- ,
  14: 5
Alger, Horatio, Jr. 1832-1899,
  16: 3
Alger, Leclaire (Gowans)
  1898-1969, *15:* 1
Aliki. *See* Brandenberg, Aliki,
  2: 36
Alkema, Chester Jay 1932- ,
  12: 7
Allamand, Pascale 1942- , *12:* 8
Allan, Mabel Esther 1915- , *5:* 2
Allee, Marjorie Hill 1890-1945,
  17: 11
Allen, Adam [Joint pseudonym].
  See Epstein, Beryl *1:* 85;
  31: 64; Epstein, Samuel, *1:* 87;
  31: 66
Allen, Allyn. *See* Eberle,
  Irmengarde, *2:* 97; *23:* 68
  (Obituary)
Allen, Betsy. *See* Cavanna, Betty,
  1: 54; *30:* 84
Allen, Gertrude E(lizabeth)
  1888- , *9:* 5
Allen, Jack 1899- , *29:* 32 (Brief
  Entry)
Allen, Leroy 1912- , *11:* 7
Allen, Marjorie 1931- , *22:* 11
Allen, Maury 1932- , *26:* 23
Allen, Merritt Parmelee
  1892-1954, *22:* 12
Allen, Nina (Strömgren) 1935- ,
  22: 13
Allen, Rodney F. 1938- , *27:* 22
Allen, Samuel (Washington)
  1917- , *9:* 6
Allerton, Mary. *See* Govan,
  Christine Noble, *9:* 80
Alleyn, Ellen. *See* Rossetti,
  Christina (Georgina), *20:* 147
Allison, Bob, *14:* 7
Allred, Gordon T. 1930- , *10:* 3
Allsop, Kenneth 1920-1973,
  17: 13
Almedingen, E. M. 1898-1971,
  3: 9
Almedingen, Martha Edith von. *See*
  Almedingen, E. M., *3:* 9
Almquist, Don 1929- , *11:* 8

Alsop, Mary O'Hara 1885-1980,
  2: 4; *24:* 26 (Obituary)
Alter, Robert Edmond 1925-1965,
  9: 8
Althea. *See* Braithwaite, Althea,
  23: 11
Altsheler, Joseph A(lexander)
  1862-1919, *YABC 1:* 20
Alvarez, Joseph A. 1930- , *18:* 2
Ambler, C(hristopher) Gifford
  1886- , *29:* 33 (Brief Entry)
Ambrus, Victor G(tozo) 1935- ,
  1: 6
Amerman, Lockhart 1911-1969,
  3: 11
Ames, Evelyn 1908- , *13:* 1
Ames, Gerald 1906- , *11:* 9
Ames, Lee J. 1921- , *3:* 11
Ames, Mildred 1919- , *22:* 14
Amon, Aline 1928- , *9:* 8
Amoss, Berthe 1925- , *5:* 4
Anastasio, Dina 1941- , *30:* 33
  (Brief Entry)
Anckarsvard, Karin 1915-1969,
  6: 2
Ancona, George 1929- , *12:* 10
Andersen, Hans Christian
  1805-1875, *YABC 1:* 23
Andersen, Ted. *See* Boyd, Waldo
  T., *18:* 35
Andersen, Yvonne 1932- , *27:* 23
Anderson, Brad(ley Jay) 1924- ,
  31: 22 (Brief Entry)
Anderson, C(larence) W(illiam)
  1891-1971, *11:* 9
Anderson, Clifford [Joint
  pseudonym]. *See* Gardner,
  Richard, *24:* 119
Anderson, Ella. *See* MacLeod,
  Ellen Jane (Anderson), *14:* 129
Anderson, Eloise Adell 1927- ,
  9: 9
Anderson, George. *See* Groom,
  Arthur William, *10:* 53
Anderson, J(ohn) R(ichard) L(ane)
  1911-1981, *15:* 3; *27:* 24
  (Obituary)
Anderson, Joy 1928- , *1:* 8
Anderson, LaVere (Francis
  Shoenfelt) 1907- , *27:* 24
Anderson, (John) Lonzo 1905- ,
  2: 6
Anderson, Lucia (Lewis) 1922- ,
  10: 4
Anderson, Madelyn Klein, *28:* 24
Anderson, Margaret J(ean)
  1931- , *27:* 26
Anderson, Mary 1939- , *7:* 4
Anderson, Norman D(ean) 1928- ,
  22: 15
Andre, Evelyn M(arie) 1924- ,
  27: 27
Andrews, Benny 1930- , *31:* 22
Andrews, F(rank) Emerson
  1902-1978, *22:* 17

Andrews, J(ames) S(ydney)
  1934- , *4:* 7
Andrews, Julie 1935- , *7:* 6
Andrews, Roy Chapman
  1884-1960, *19:* 1
Angell, Judie 1937- , *22:* 18
Angell, Madeline 1919- , *18:* 3
Angelo, Valenti 1897- , *14:* 7
Angier, Bradford, *12:* 12
Angle, Paul M(cClelland)
  1900-1975, *20:* 1 (Obituary)
Anglund, Joan Walsh 1926- , *2:* 7
Angrist, Stanley W(olff) 1933- ,
  4: 9
Anita. *See* Daniel, Anita, *23:* 65
Annett, Cora. *See* Scott, Cora
  Annett, *11:* 207
Annixter, Jane. *See* Sturtzel, Jane
  Levington, *1:* 212
Annixter, Paul. *See* Sturtzel,
  Howard A., *1:* 210
Anno, Mitsumasa 1920- , *5:* 6
Anrooy, Frans van. *See* Van
  Anrooy, Francine, *2:* 252
Antell, Will D. 1935- , *31:* 26
Anthony, Barbara 1932- , *29:* 33
Anthony, C. L. *See* Smith, Dodie,
  4: 194
Anthony, Edward 1895-1971,
  21: 1
Anticaglia, Elizabeth 1939- ,
  12: 13
Anton, Michael (James) 1940- ,
  12: 13
Appel, Benjamin 1907-1977,
  21: 5 (Obituary)
Appiah, Peggy 1921- , *15:* 3
Appleton, Victor [Collective
  pseudonym], *1:* 9
Appleton, Victor II [Collective
  pseudonym], *1:* 9; *29:* 26
  (Obituary)
Apsler, Alfred 1907- , *10:* 4
Aquillo, Don. *See* Prince, J(ack)
  H(arvey), *17:* 155
Arbuthnot, May Hill 1884-1969,
  2: 9
Archer, Frank. *See* O'Connor,
  Richard, *21:* 111
Archer, Jules 1915- , *4:* 9
Archer, Marion Fuller 1917- ,
  11: 12
Archibald, Joseph S. 1898- ,
  3: 12
Arden, Barbie. *See* Stoutenburg,
  Adrien, *3:* 217
Ardizzone, Edward 1900-1979,
  1: 10; *21:* 5 (Obituary); *28:* 25
Arehart-Treichel, Joan 1942- ,
  22: 18
Arenella, Roy 1939- , *14:* 9
Armer, Alberta (Roller) 1904- ,
  9: 11
Armer, Laura Adams 1874-1963,
  13: 2
Armour, Richard 1906- , *14:* 10

Armstrong, George D. 1927- ,
10: 5

Armstrong, Gerry (Breen) 1929- ,
10: 6

Armstrong, Richard 1903- ,
11: 14

Armstrong, William H. 1914- ,
4: 11

Arnett, Carolyn. See Cole, Lois
Dwight, 10: 26; 26: 43
(Obituary)

Arno, Enrico 1913-1981, 28: 38
(Obituary)

Arnold, Elliott 1912-1980, 5: 7;
22: 19 (Obituary)

Arnold, Oren 1900- , 4: 13

Arnoldy, Julie. See Bischoff, Julia
Bristol, 12: 52

Arnosky, Jim 1946- , 22: 19

Arnott, Kathleen 1914- , 20: 1

Arnov, Boris, Jr. 1926- , 12: 14

Arnstein, Helene S(olomon)
1915- , 12: 15

Arntson, Herbert E(dward)
1911- , 12: 16

Aronin, Ben 1904-1980, 25: 21
(Obituary)

Arora, Shirley (Lease) 1930- ,
2: 10

Arquette, Lois S(teinmetz) 1934- ,
1: 13

Arrowood, (McKendrick Lee)
Clinton 1939- , 19: 10

Arthur, Ruth M(abel) 1905-1979,
7: 6; 26: 23 (Obituary)

Artis, Vicki Kimmel 1945- ,
12: 17

Artzybasheff, Boris (Miklailovich)
1899-1965, 14: 14

Aruego, Ariane. See Dewey,
Ariane, 7: 63

Aruego, Jose 1932- , 6: 3

Arundel, Honor (Morfydd)
1919-1973, 4: 15; 24: 26
(Obituary)

Arundel, Jocelyn. See Alexander,
Jocelyn (Anne) Arundel, 22: 9

Asbjörnsen, Peter Christen
1812-1885, 15: 5

Asch, Frank 1946- , 5: 9

Ashabranner, Brent (Kenneth)
1921- , 1: 14

Ashe, Geoffrey (Thomas) 1923- ,
17: 14

Ashey, Bella. See Breinburg,
Petronella, 11: 36

Ashford, Daisy. See Ashford,
Margaret Mary, 10: 6

Ashford, Margaret Mary
1881-1972, 10: 6

Ashley, Elizabeth. See Salmon,
Annie Elizabeth, 13: 188

Ashton, Warren T. See Adams,
William Taylor, 28: 21

Asimov, Isaac 1920- , 1: 15;
26: 23

Asinof, Eliot 1919- , 6: 5

Aston, James. See White, T(erence)
H(anbury), 12: 229

Atene, Ann. See Atene, (Rita)
Anna, 12: 18

Atene, (Rita) Anna 1922- , 12: 18

Atkinson, M. E. See Frankau, Mary
Evelyn, 4: 90

Atkinson, Margaret Fleming, 14: 15

Atticus. See Fleming, Ian
(Lancaster), 9: 67

Atwater, Florence (Hasseltine
Carroll), 16: 11

Atwater, Montgomery Meigs
1904- , 15: 10

Atwater, Richard Tupper
1892-1948, 27: 28 (Brief
Entry)

Atwood, Ann 1913- , 7: 8

Aubry, Claude B. 1914- , 29: 34

Augarde, Steve 1950- , 25: 21

Ault, Phillip H. 1914- , 23: 1

Aung, (Maung) Htin 1910- ,
21: 5

Aung, U. Htin. See Aung, (Maung)
Htin, 21: 5

Austin, Elizabeth S. 1907- , 5: 10

Austin, Margot, 11: 15

Austin, Oliver L., Jr. 1903- ,
7: 10

Austin, Tom. See Jacobs, Linda C.,
21: 78

Averill, Esther 1902- , 1: 16;
28: 39

Avery, Al. See Montgomery,
Rutherford, 3: 134

Avery, Gillian 1926- , 7: 10

Avery, Kay 1908- , 5: 11

Avery, Lynn. See Cole, Lois
Dwight, 10: 26; 26: 43
(Obituary)

Avi. See Wortis, Avi, 14: 269

Ayars, James S(terling) 1898- ,
4: 17

Ayer, Jacqueline 1930- , 13: 7

Ayer, Margaret, 15: 11

Aylesworth, Thomas G(ibbons)
1927- , 4: 18

Aymar, Brandt 1911- , 22: 21

Baastad, Babbis Friis. See Friis-
Baastad, Babbis, 7: 95

Babbis, Eleanor. See Friis-Baastad,
Babbis, 7: 95

Babbitt, Natalie 1932- , 6: 6

Babcock, Dennis Arthur 1948- ,
22: 21

Bach, Alice (Hendricks) 1942- ,
27: 29 (Brief Entry); 30: 34

Bach, Richard David 1936- ,
13: 7

Bachman, Fred 1949- , 12: 19

Bacmeister, Rhoda W(arner)
1893- , 11: 18

Bacon, Elizabeth 1914- , 3: 14

Bacon, Margaret Hope 1921- ,
6: 7

Bacon, Martha Sherman
1917-1981, 18: 4; 27: 29
(Obituary)

Bacon, Peggy 1895- 2: 11

Bacon, R(onald) L(eonard)
1924- , 26: 33

Baden-Powell, Robert (Stephenson
Smyth) 1857-1941, 16: 12

Baerg, Harry J(ohn) 1909- ,
12: 20

Bagnold, Enid 1889-1981, 1: 17;
25: 23

Bahti, Tom, 31: 26 (Brief Entry)

Bailey, Alice Cooper 1890- ,
12: 22

Bailey, Bernadine Freeman, 14: 16

Bailey, Carolyn Sherwin
1875-1961, 14: 18

Bailey, Jane H(orton) 1916- ,
12: 22

Bailey, Maralyn Collins (Harrison)
1941- , 12: 24

Bailey, Matilda. See Radford, Ruby
L., 6: 186

Bailey, Maurice Charles 1932- ,
12: 25

Bailey, Ralph Edgar 1893- ,
11: 18

Baird, Bil 1904- , 30: 36

Baity, Elizabeth Chesley 1907- ,
1: 18

Bakeless, John (Edwin) 1894- ,
9: 12

Bakeless, Katherine Little 1895- ,
9: 13

Baker, Alan 1951- , 22: 22

Baker, Augusta 1911- , 3: 16

Baker, Betty (Lou) 1928- , 5: 12

Baker, Charlotte 1910- , 2: 12

Baker, Elizabeth 1923- , 7: 12

Baker, James W. 1924- , 22: 23

Baker, Janice E(dla) 1941- ,
22: 24

Baker, Jeannie 1950- , 23: 3

Baker, Jeffrey J(ohn) W(heeler)
1931- , 5: 13

Baker, Jim. See Baker, James W.,
22: 23

Baker, Laura Nelson 1911- ,
3: 17

Baker, Margaret 1890- , 4: 19

Baker, Margaret J(oyce) 1918- ,
12: 25

Baker, Mary Gladys Steel
1892-1974, 12: 27

Baker, (Robert) Michael 1938- ,
4: 20

Baker, Nina (Brown) 1888-1957,
15: 12

Baker, Rachel 1904-1978, 2: 13;
26: 33 (Obituary)

Baker, Samm Sinclair 1909- ,
12: 27

Baker, Susan (Catherine) 1942- ,
  29: 35
Balaam. *See* Lamb, G(eoffrey)
  F(rederick), *10:* 74
Balch, Glenn 1902- , *3:* 18
Baldridge, Cyrus LeRoy 1889- ,
  29: 36 (Brief Entry)
Balducci, Carolyn Feleppa 1946- ,
  5: 13
Baldwin, Anne Norris 1938- ,
  5: 14
Baldwin, Clara, *11:* 20
Baldwin, Gordo. *See* Baldwin,
  Gordon C., *12:* 30
Baldwin, Gordon C. 1908- ,
  12: 30
Baldwin, James 1841-1925,
  24: 26
Baldwin, James (Arthur) 1924- ,
  9: 15
Baldwin, Stan(ley C.) 1929- ,
  28: 43 (Brief Entry)
Bales, Carol Ann 1940- , *29:* 36
  (Brief Entry)
Balet, Jan (Bernard) 1913- ,
  11: 21
Balian, Lorna 1929- , *9:* 16
Ball, Zachary. *See* Masters,
  Kelly R., *3:* 118
Ballantyne, R(obert) M(ichael)
  1825-1894, *24:* 32
Ballard, Lowell Clyne 1904- ,
  12: 30
Ballard, (Charles) Martin 1929- ,
  1: 19
Balogh, Penelope 1916- , *1:* 20
Balow, Tom 1931- , *12:* 31
Bamfylde, Walter. *See* Bevan,
  Tom, *YABC 2:* 8
Bamman, Henry A. 1918- ,
  12: 32
Bancroft, Griffing 1907- , *6:* 8
Bancroft, Laura. *See* Baum,
  L(yman) Frank, *18:* 7
Baner, Skulda V(anadis)
  1897-1964, *10:* 8
Bang, Garrett. *See* Bang, Molly
  Garrett, *24:* 37
Bang, Molly Garrett 1943- ,
  24: 37
Banks, Laura Stockton Voorhees
  1908(?)-1980, *23:* 5 (Obituary)
Banks, Sara (Jeanne Gordon
  Harrell) 1937- , *26:* 33
Banner, Angela. *See* Maddison,
  Angela Mary, *10:* 82
Bannerman, Helen (Brodie Cowan
  Watson) 1863(?)-1946, *19:* 12
Bannon, Laura d. 1963, *6:* 9
Barbary, James. *See* Baumann,
  Amy (Brown), *10:* 9
Barbary, James. *See* Beeching,
  Jack, *14:* 26
Barber, Antonia. *See* Anthony,
  Barbara, *29:* 33

Barbour, Ralph Henry 1870-1944,
  16: 27
Barclay, Isabel. *See* Dobell,
  I.M.B., *11:* 77
Bare, Arnold Edwin 1920- ,
  16: 31
Barish, Matthew 1907- , *12:* 32
Barker, Albert W. 1900- , *8:* 3
Barker, Carol (Minturn) 1938- ,
  31: 26
Barker, Melvern 1907- , *11:* 23
Barker, S. Omar 1894- , *10:* 8
Barker, Will 1908- , *8:* 4
Barkley, James Edward 1941- ,
  6: 12
Barnaby, Ralph S(tanton) 1893- ,
  9: 17
Barner, Bob 1947- , *29:* 37
Barnes, (Frank) Eric Wollencott
  1907-1962, *22:* 25
Barnouw, Adriaan Jacob
  1877-1968, *27:* 29 (Obituary)
Barnouw, Victor 1915- , *28:* 43
  (Brief Entry)
Barnstone, Willis 1927- , *20:* 3
Barnum, Jay Hyde 1888(?)-1962,
  20: 4
Barnum, Richard [Collective
  pseudonym], *1:* 20
Baron, Virginia Olsen 1931- ,
  28: 43 (Brief Entry)
Barr, Donald 1921- , *20:* 5
Barr, George 1907- , *2:* 14
Barr, Jene 1900- , *16:* 32
Barrer, Gertrude. *See* Barrer-
  Russell, Gertrude, *27:* 29
Barrer-Russell, Gertrude 1921- ,
  27: 29
Barrett, Judith 1941- , *26:* 34
Barrett, Ron 1937- , *14:* 23
Barrie, J(ames) M(atthew)
  1860-1937, *YABC 1:* 48
Barry, James P(otvin) 1918- ,
  14: 24
Barry, Katharina (Watjen) 1936- ,
  4: 22
Barry, Robert 1931- , *6:* 12
Barth, Edna 1914-1980, *7:* 13;
  24: 39 (Obituary)
Barthelme, Donald 1931- , *7:* 14
Bartlett, Philip A. [Collective
  pseudonym], *1:* 21
Bartlett, Robert Merrill 1899- ,
  12: 33
Barton, Byron 1930- , *9:* 17
Barton, May Hollis [Collective
  pseudonym], *1:* 21; *29:* 26
  (Obituary)
Bartos-Hoeppner, Barbara 1923- ,
  5: 15
Baruch, Dorothy W(alter)
  1899-1962, *21:* 6
Bas, Rutger. *See* Rutgers van der
  Loeff, An(na) Basenau,
  22: 211

Bashevis, Isaac. *See* Singer, Isaac
  Bashevis, *3:* 203; *27:* 202
Baskin, Leonard 1922- , *27:* 32
  (Brief Entry); *30:* 41
Bason, Lillian 1913- , *20:* 6
Bassett, John Keith. *See* Keating,
  Lawrence A, *23:* 107
Batchelor, Joy 1914- , *29:* 37
  (Brief Entry)
Bate, Lucy 1939- , *18:* 6
Bate, Norman 1916- , *5:* 15
Bates, Barbara S(nedeker) 1919- ,
  12: 34
Bates, Betty 1921- , *19:* 15
Batten, H(arry) Mortimer
  1888-1958, *25:* 34
Batten, Mary 1937- , *5:* 17
Batterberry, Ariane Ruskin
  1935- , *7:* 187; *13:* 10
Battles, Edith 1921- , *7:* 15
Baudouy, Michel-Aime 1909- ,
  7: 18
Bauer, Helen 1900- , *2:* 14
Bauer, Marion Dane 1938- , *20:* 8
Bauernschmidt, Marjorie 1926- ,
  15: 14
Baum, Allyn Z(elton) 1924- ,
  20: 9
Baum, L(yman) Frank 1856-1919,
  18: 7
Baum, Willi 1931- , *4:* 23
Baumann, Amy (Brown) 1922- ,
  10: 9
Baumann, Hans 1914- , *2:* 16
Baumann, Kurt 1935- , *21:* 8
Bawden, Nina. *See* Kark, Nina
  Mary, *4:* 132
Baylor, Byrd 1924- , *16:* 33
Baynes, Pauline (Diana) 1922- ,
  19: 17
BB. *See* Watkins-Pitchford, D. J.,
  6: 214
Beach, Charles. *See* Reid, (Thomas)
  Mayne, *24:* 170
Beach, Charles Amory [Collective
  pseudonym], *1:* 21
Beach, Edward L(atimer) 1918- ,
  12: 35
Beach, Stewart Taft 1899- , *23:* 5
Beachcroft, Nina 1931- , *18:* 31
Bealer, Alex W(inkler III)
  1921-1980, *8:* 6; *22:* 26
  (Obituary)
Beals, Carleton 1893- , *12:* 36
Beals, Frank Lee 1881-1972,
  26: 35 (Obituary)
Beame, Rona 1934- , *12:* 39
Beaney, Jan. *See* Udall, Jan
  Beaney, *10:* 182
Beard, Charles Austin 1874-1948,
  18: 32
Beard, Dan(iel Carter) 1850-1941,
  22: 26
Bearden, Romare (Howard)
  1914- , *22:* 34

Beardmore, Cedric. *See* Beardmore, George, *20:* 10

Beardmore, George 1908-1979, *20:* 10

Bearman, Jane (Ruth) 1917- , *29:* 38

Beatty, Elizabeth. *See* Holloway, Teresa (Bragunier), *26:* 122

Beatty, Hetty Burlingame 1907-1971, *5:* 18

Beatty, Jerome, Jr. 1918- , *5:* 19

Beatty, John (Louis) 1922-1975, *6:* 13; *25:* 35 (Obituary)

Beatty, Patricia (Robbins) *1:* 21; *30:* 48

Bechtel, Louise Seaman 1894- , *4:* 26

Beck, Barbara L. 1927- , *12:* 41

Becker, Beril 1901- , *11:* 23

Becker, John (Leonard) 1901- , *12:* 41

Beckman, Gunnel 1910- , *6:* 14

Bedford, A. N. *See* Watson, Jane Werner, *3:* 244

Bedford, Annie North. *See* Watson, Jane Werner, *3:* 244

Beebe, B(urdetta) F(aye) 1920- , *1:* 23

Beebe, (Charles) William 1877-1962, *19:* 21

Beeby, Betty 1923- , *25:* 37

Beech, Webb. *See* Butterworth, W. E., *5:* 40

Beeching, Jack 1922- , *14:* 26

Beeler, Nelson F(rederick) 1910- , *13:* 11

Beers, Dorothy Sands 1917- , *9:* 18

Beers, Lorna 1897- , *14:* 26

Beers, V(ictor) Gilbert 1928- , *9:* 18

Begley, Kathleen A(nne) 1948- , *21:* 9

Behn, Harry 1898- , *2:* 17

Behnke, Frances L., *8:* 7

Behr, Joyce 1929- , *15:* 15

Behrens, June York 1925- , *19:* 30

Behrman, Carol H(elen) 1925- , *14:* 27

Beiser, Arthur 1931- , *22:* 36

Beiser, Germaine 1931- , *11:* 24

Belaney, Archibald Stansfeld 1888-1938, *24:* 39

Belknap, B. H. *See* Ellis, Edward S(ylvester), *YABC 1:* 116

Bell, Corydon 1894- , *3:* 19

Bell, Emily Mary. *See* Cason, Mabel Earp, *10:* 19

Bell, Gertrude (Wood) 1911- , *12:* 42

Bell, Gina. *See* Iannone, Jeanne, *7:* 139

Bell, Janet. *See* Clymer, Eleanor, *9:* 37

Bell, Margaret E(lizabeth) 1898- , *2:* 19

Bell, Norman (Edward) 1899- , *11:* 25

Bell, Raymond Martin 1907- , *13:* 13

Bell, Robert S(tanley) W(arren) 1871-1921, *27:* 32 (Brief Entry)

Bell, Thelma Harrington 1896- , *3:* 20

Bellairs, John 1938- , *2:* 20

Belloc, (Joseph) Hilaire (Pierre) 1870-1953, *YABC 1:* 62

Bell-Zano, Gina. *See* Iannone, Jeanne, *7:* 139

Belpré, Pura 1899-1982, *16:* 35; *30:* 53 (Obituary)

Belting, Natalie Maree 1915- , *6:* 16

Belton, John Raynor 1931- , *22:* 37

Belvedere, Lee. *See* Grayland, Valerie, *7:* 111

Bemelmans, Ludwig 1898-1962, *15:* 15

Benary, Margot. *See* Benary-Isbert, Margot, *2:* 21; *21:* 9

Benary-Isbert, Margot 1889-1979, *2:* 21; *21:* 9 (Obituary)

Benasutti, Marion 1908- , *6:* 18

Benchley, Nathaniel (Goddard) 1915-1981, *3:* 21; *25:* 39; *28:* 43 (Obituary)

Benchley, Peter 1940- , *3:* 22

Bender, Lucy Ellen 1942- , *22:* 38

Bendick, Jeanne 1919- , *2:* 23

Bendick, Robert L(ouis) 1917- , *11:* 25

Benedict, Dorothy Potter 1889-1979, *11:* 26; *23:* 5 (Obituary)

Benedict, Lois Trimble 1902-1967, *12:* 44

Benedict, Rex 1920- , *8:* 8

Benedict, Stewart H(urd) 1924- , *26:* 36

Benét, Laura 1884-1979, *3:* 23; *23:* 6 (Obituary)

Benét, Stephen Vincent 1898-1943, *YABC 1:* 75

Benet, Sula 1903- , *21:* 10

Benezra, Barbara 1921- , *10:* 10

Bennett, Dorothea. *See* Young, Dorothea Bennett, *31:* 191

Bennett, Jay 1912- , *27:* 32 (Brief Entry)

Bennett, John 1865-1956, *YABC 1:* 84

Bennett, Rainey 1907- , *15:* 27

Bennett, Richard 1899- , *21:* 11

Bennett, Russell H(oradley) 1896- , *25:* 45

Benson, Sally 1900-1972, *1:* 24; *27:* 32 (Obituary)

Bently, Nicolas Clerihew 1907-1978, *24:* 43 (Obituary)

Bentley, Phyllis (Eleanor) 1894-1977, *6:* 19; *25:* 45 (Obituary)

Berelson, Howard 1940- , *5:* 20

Berenstain, Janice, *12:* 44

Berenstain, Stan(ley) 1923- , *12:* 45

Beresford, Elisabeth, *25:* 45

Berg, Dave. *See* Berg, David, *27:* 32

Berg, David 1920- , *27:* 32

Berg, Jean Horton 1913- , *6:* 21

Berg, Joan. *See* Victor, Joan Berg, *30:* 192

Bergaust, Erik 1925-1978, *20:* 12

Berger, Melvin H. 1927- , *5:* 21

Berger, Terry 1933- , *8:* 10

Berkebile, Fred D(onovan) 1900-1978, *26:* 37 (Obituary)

Berkey, Barry Robert 1935- , *24:* 44

Berkowitz, Freda Pastor 1910- , *12:* 48

Berliner, Franz 1930- , *13:* 13

Berna, Paul 1910- , *15:* 27

Bernadette. *See* Watts, Bernadette, *4:* 226

Bernard, Jacqueline (de Sieyes) 1921- , *8:* 11

Bernstein, Joanne E(ckstein) 1943- , *15:* 29

Bernstein, Theodore M(enline) 1904-1979, *12:* 49; *27:* 35 (Obituary)

Berrien, Edith Heal. *See* Heal, Edith, *7:* 123

Berrill, Jacquelyn (Batsel) 1905- , *12:* 50

Berrington, John. *See* Brownjohn, Alan, *6:* 38

Berry, B. J. *See* Berry, Barbara J., *7:* 19

Berry, Barbara J. 1937- , *7:* 19

Berry, Erick. *See* Best, Allena Champlin, *2:* 25; *25:* 48 (Obituary)

Berry, Jane Cobb 1915(?)-1979, *22:* 39 (Obituary)

Berry, William D(avid) 1926- , *14:* 28

Berson, Harold 1926- , *4:* 27

Berwick, Jean. *See* Meyer, Jean Shepherd, *11:* 181

Beskow, Elsa (Maartman) 1874-1953, *20:* 13

Best, (Evangel) Allena Champlin 1892-1974, *2:* 27; *25:* 48 (Obituary)

Best, (Oswald) Herbert 1894- , *2:* 27

Beth, Mary. *See* Miller, Mary Beth, *9:* 145

Bethancourt, T. Ernesto 1932- , *11:* 27

Bethell, Jean (Frankenberry)
1922- , *8:* 11
Bethers, Ray 1902- , *6:* 22
Bethune, J. G. *See* Ellis, Edward
S(ylvester), *YABC 1:* 116
Betteridge, Anne. *See* Potter,
Margaret (Newman), *21:* 119
Bettina. *See* Ehrlich, Bettina, *1:* 82
Betz, Eva Kelly 1897-1968,
10: 10
Bevan, Tom 1868-1930(?),
YABC 2: 8
Bewick, Thomas 1753-1828,
16: 38
Beyer, Audrey White 1916- ,
9: 19
Bialk, Elisa, *1:* 25
Bianco, Margery (Williams)
1881-1944, *15:* 29
Bianco, Pamela 1906- , *28:* 44
Bibby, Violet 1908- , *24:* 45
Bible, Charles 1937- , *13:* 14
Bice, Clare 1909-1976, *22:* 39
Bickerstaff, Isaac. *See* Swift,
Jonathan, *19:* 244
Biegel, Paul 1925- , *16:* 49
Biemiller, Carl Ludwig
1912-1979, *21:* 13 (Obituary)
Bierhorst, John 1936- , *6:* 23
Billout, Guy René 1941- , *10:* 11
Binkley, Anne. *See* Rand, Ann
(Binkley), *30:* 173
Binzen, Bill, *24:* 48
Binzen, William. *See* Binzen, Bill,
24: 48
Birch, Reginald B(athurst)
1856-1943, *19:* 31
Birmingham, Lloyd 1924- ,
12: 51
Biro, Val 1921- , *1:* 26
Bischoff, Julia Bristol 1909-1970,
12: 52
Bishop, Claire (Huchet), *14:* 30
Bishop, Curtis 1912-1967, *6:* 24
Bishop, Elizabeth 1911-1979,
24: 49 (Obituary)
Bisset, Donald 1910- , *7:* 20
Bitter, Gary G(len) 1940- , *22:* 41
Bixby, William 1920- , *6:* 24
Bjerregaard-Jensen, Vilhelm Hans.
See Hillcourt, William, *27:* 111
Black, Algernon David 1900- ,
12: 53
Black, Irma S(imonton)
1906-1972, *2:* 28; *25:* 48
(Obituary)
Black, Mansell. *See* Trevor,
Elleston, *28:* 207
Blackburn, Claire. *See* Jacobs,
Linda C., *21:* 78
Blackburn, John(ny) Brewton
1952- , *15:* 35
Blackburn, Joyce Knight 1920- ,
29: 39
Blackett, Veronica Heath 1927- ,
12: 54

Blackton, Peter. *See* Wilson,
Lionel, *31:* 186 (Brief Entry)
Blades, Ann 1947- , *16:* 51
Bladow, Suzanne Wilson 1937- ,
14: 32
Blaine, John. *See* Goodwin, Harold
Leland, *13:* 73
Blaine, John. *See* Harkins, Philip,
6: 102
Blaine, Margery Kay 1937- ,
11: 28
Blair, Eric Arthur 1903-1950,
29: 39
Blair, Helen 1910- , *29:* 49 (Brief
Entry)
Blair, Ruth Van Ness 1912- ,
12: 54
Blair, Walter 1900- , *12:* 56
Blake, Olive. *See* Supraner, Robyn,
20: 182
Blake, Quentin 1932- , *9:* 20
Blake, Walker E. *See* Butterworth,
W. E., *5:* 40
Blake, William 1757-1827, *30:* 54
Bland, Edith Nesbit. *See* Nesbit,
E(dith), *YABC 1:* 193
Bland, Fabian [Joint pseudonym].
See Nesbit, E(dith),
YABC 1: 193
Blane, Gertrude. *See* Blumenthal,
Gertrude, *27:* 35 (Obituary)
Blassingame, Wyatt (Rainey)
1909- , *1:* 27
Bleeker, Sonia 1909-1971, *2:* 30;
26: 37 (Obituary)
Blegvad, Erik 1923- , *14:* 33
Blegvad, Lenore 1926- , *14:* 34
Blishen, Edward 1920- , *8:* 12
Bliss, Reginald. *See* Wells,
H(erbert) G(eorge), *20:* 190
Bliss, Ronald G(ene) 1942- ,
12: 57
Bliven, Bruce, Jr. 1916- , *2:* 31
Bloch, Lucienne 1909- , *10:* 11
Bloch, Marie Halun 1910- , *6:* 25
Bloch, Robert 1917- , *12:* 57
Blochman, Lawrence G(oldtree)
1900-1975, *22:* 42
Block, Irvin 1917- , *12:* 59
Blood, Charles Lewis 1929- ,
28: 48
Blos, Joan W. 1929(?)- , *27:* 35
(Brief Entry)
Blough, Glenn O(rlando) 1907- ,
1: 28
Blue, Rose 1931- , *5:* 22
Blume, Judy (Sussman) 1938- ,
2: 31; *31:* 28
Blumenthal, Gertrude 1907-1971,
27: 35 (Obituary)
Blutig, Eduard. *See* Gorey, Edward
St. John, *27:* 104 (Brief Entry);
29: 89
Blyton, Carey 1932- , *9:* 22
Blyton, Enid (Mary) 1897-1968,
25: 48

Boardman, Fon Wyman, Jr.
1911- , *6:* 26
Boardman, Gwenn R. 1924- ,
12: 59
Boase, Wendy 1944- , *28:* 48
Boatner, Mark Mayo III 1921- ,
29: 49
Bobbe, Dorothie 1905-1975,
1: 30; *25:* 61 (Obituary)
Bock, Hal. *See* Bock, Harold I.,
10: 13
Bock, Harold I. 1939- , *10:* 13
Bock, William Sauts Netamux'we,
14: 36
Bodecker, N. M. 1922- , *8:* 12
Boden, Hilda. *See* Bodenham, Hilda
Esther, *13:* 16
Bodenham, Hilda Esther 1901- ,
13: 16
Bodie, Idella F(allaw) 1925- ,
12: 60
Bodker, Cecil 1927- , *14:* 39
Bodsworth, (Charles) Fred(erick)
1918- , *27:* 35
Boeckman, Charles 1920- ,
12: 61
Boesch, Mark J(oseph) 1917- ,
12: 62
Boesen, Victor 1908- , *16:* 53
Boggs, Ralph Steele 1901- , *7:* 21
Bohdal, Susi 1951- , *22:* 43
Boles, Paul Darcy 1919- , *9:* 23
Bolian, Polly 1925- , *4:* 29
Bollen, Roger 1941(?)- , *29:* 50
(Brief Entry)
Bolliger, Max 1929- , *7:* 22
Bolognese, Don(ald Alan) 1934- ,
24: 49
Bolton, Carole 1926- , *6:* 27
Bolton, Elizabeth. *See* Johnston,
Norma, *29:* 116
Bolton, Evelyn. *See* Bunting, Anne
Evelyn, *18:* 38
Bond, Gladys Baker 1912- ,
14: 41
Bond, J. Harvey. *See*
Winterbotham, R(ussell)
R(obert), *10:* 198
Bond, Michael 1926- , *6:* 28
Bond, Nancy (Barbara) 1945- ,
22: 44
Bond, Ruskin 1934- , *14:* 43
Bonehill, Captain Ralph. *See*
Stratemeyer, Edward L., *1:* 208
Bonham, Barbara 1926- , *7:* 22
Bonham, Frank 1914- , *1:* 30
Bonner, Mary Graham 1890-1974,
19: 37
Bonsall, Crosby (Barbara Newell)
1921- , *23:* 6
Bontemps, Arna 1902-1973,
2: 32; *24:* 51 (Obituary)
Bonzon, Paul-Jacques 1908- ,
22: 46
Boone, Pat 1934- , *7:* 23
Bordier, Georgette 1924- , *16:* 53

Borja, Corinne 1929- , *22:* 47
Borja, Robert 1923- , *22:* 47
Borland, Hal 1900-1978, *5:* 22;
  24: 51 (Obituary)
Borland, Harold Glen. *See* Borland,
  Hal, *5:* 22; *24:* 51 (Obituary)
Borland, Kathryn Kilby 1916- ,
  16: 54
Bornstein, Ruth 1927- , *14:* 44
Borski, Lucia Merecka, *18:* 34
Borten, Helen Jacobson 1930- ,
  5: 24
Borton, Elizabeth. *See* Treviño,
  Elizabeth B. de, *1:* 216
Bortstein, Larry 1942- , *16:* 56
Bosco, Jack. *See* Holliday, Joseph,
  11: 137
Boshell, Gordon 1908- , *15:* 36
Boshinski, Blanche 1922- , *10:* 13
Boston, Lucy Maria (Wood)
  1892- , *19:* 38
Bosworth, J. Allan 1925- , *19:* 45
Bothwell, Jean, *2:* 34
Bottner, Barbara 1943- , *14:* 45
Boulle, Pierre (Francois Marie-
  Louis) 1912- , *22:* 49
Bourne, Leslie. *See* Marshall,
  Evelyn, *11:* 172
Bourne, Miriam Anne 1931- ,
  16: 57
Boutet De Monvel, (Louis)
  M(aurice) 1850(?)-1913,
  30: 61
Bova, Ben 1932- , *6:* 29
Bowen, Betty Morgan. *See* West,
  Betty, *11:* 233
Bowen, Catherine Drinker
  1897-1973, *7:* 24
Bowen, David. *See* Bowen, Joshua
  David, *22:* 51
Bowen, Joshua David 1930- ,
  22: 51
Bowen, Robert Sidney
  1900(?)-1977, *21:* 13
  (Obituary)
Bowie, Jim. *See* Stratemeyer,
  Edward L., *1:* 208
Bowman, James Cloyd
  1880-1961, *23:* 7
Bowman, John S(tewart) 1931- ,
  16: 57
Boyce, George A(rthur) 1898- ,
  19: 46
Boyd, Waldo T. 1918- , *18:* 35
Boyer, Robert E(rnst) 1929- ,
  22: 52
Boyle, Ann (Peters) 1916- ,
  10: 13
Boyle, Eleanor Vere (Gordon)
  1825-1916, *28:* 49
Boylston, Helen (Dore) 1895- ,
  23: 8
Boz. *See* Dickens, Charles, *15:* 55
Bradbury, Bianca 1908- , *3:* 25
Bradbury, Ray (Douglas) 1920- ,
  11: 29

Bradley, Virginia 1912- , *23:* 11
Brady, Esther Wood 1905- ,
  31: 35
Brady, Irene 1943- , *4:* 30
Brady, Lillian 1902- , *28:* 51
Bragdon, Elspeth 1897- , *6:* 30
Bragdon, Lillian (Jacot), *24:* 51
Bragg, Mabel Caroline 1870-1945,
  24: 52
Braithwaite, Althea 1940- ,
  23: 11
Bram, Elizabeth 1948- , *30:* 66
Brancato, Robin F(idler) 1936- ,
  23: 14
Brandenberg, Aliki Liacouras, *2:* 36
Brandenberg, Franz 1932- , *8:* 14
Brandhorst, Carl T(heodore)
  1898- , *23:* 16
Brandon, Brumsic, Jr. 1927- ,
  9: 25
Brandon, Curt. *See* Bishop, Curtis,
  6: 24
Brandreth, Gyles 1948- , *28:* 53
Brandt, Keith. *See* Sabin, Louis,
  27: 174
Branfield, John (Charles) 1931- ,
  11: 36
Branley, Franklyn M(ansfield)
  1915- , *4:* 32
Branscum, Robbie 1937- , *23:* 17
Bratton, Helen 1899- , *4:* 34
Braude, Michael 1936- , *23:* 18
Braymer, Marjorie 1911- , *6:* 31
Brecht, Edith 1895-1975, *6:* 32;
  25: 61 (Obituary)
Breck, Vivian. *See* Breckenfeld,
  Vivian Gurney, *1:* 33
Breckenfeld, Vivian Gurney
  1895- , *1:* 33
Breda, Tjalmar. *See* DeJong, David
  C(ornel), *10:* 29
Breinburg, Petronella 1927- ,
  11: 36
Breisky, William J(ohn) 1928- ,
  22: 53
Brennan, Joseph L. 1903- , *6:* 33
Brennan, Tim. *See* Conroy, Jack
  (Wesley), *19:* 65
Brenner, Barbara (Johnes) 1925- ,
  4: 34
Brent, Stuart, *14:* 47
Brett, Bernard 1925- , *22:* 53
Brett, Grace N(eff) 1900-1975,
  23: 19
Brett, Hawksley. *See* Bell, Robert
  S(tanley) W(arren), *27:* 32
  (Brief Entry)
Brewster, Benjamin. *See* Folsom,
  Franklin, *5:* 67
Brewton, John E(dmund) 1898- ,
  5: 25
Brick, John 1922-1973, *10:* 14
Bridgers, Sue Ellen 1942- ,
  22: 56
Bridges, William (Andrew) 1901-
  5: 27

Bridwell, Norman 1928- , *4:* 36
Brier, Howard M(axwell)
  1903-1969, *8:* 15
Briggs, Katharine Mary
  1898-1980, *25:* 62 (Obituary)
Briggs, Peter 1921-1975, *31:* 36
  (Obituary)
Briggs, Raymond (Redvers)
  1934- , *23:* 19
Bright, Robert 1902- , *24:* 54
Brightwell, L(eonard) R(obert)
  1889- , *29:* 51 (Brief Entry)
Brimberg, Stanlee 1947- , *9:* 25
Brin, Ruth F(irestone) 1921- ,
  22: 56
Brinckloe, Julie (Lorraine) 1950- ,
  13: 17
Brindel, June (Rachuy) 1919- ,
  7: 25
Brindze, Ruth 1903- , *23:* 22
Brink, Carol Ryrie 1895-1981,
  1: 34; *27:* 36 (Obituary);
  31: 36
Brinsmead, H(esba) F(ay) 1922- ,
  18: 36
Briquebec, John. *See* Rowland-
  Entwistle, (Arthur) Theodore
  (Henry), *31:* 145
Brisco, Pat A. *See* Matthews,
  Patricia, *28:* 153
Brisco, Patty. *See* Matthews,
  Patricia, *28:* 153
Brisley, Joyce Lankester 1896- ,
  22: 57
Britt, Albert 1874-1969, *28:* 55
  (Obituary)
Britt, Dell, 1934- *1:* 35
Bro, Margueritte (Harmon)
  1894-1977, *19:* 46; *27:* 36
  (Obituary)
Broadhead, Helen Cross 1913- ,
  25: 62
Brock, Betty 1923- , *7:* 27
Brock, Emma L(illian) 1886-1974,
  8: 15
Brockett, Eleanor Hall 1913-1967,
  10: 15
Brockman, C(hristian) Frank
  1902- , *26:* 37
Broderick, Dorothy M. 1929- ,
  5: 28
Bröger, Achim 1944- , *31:* 42
Brokamp, Marilyn 1920- , *10:* 15
Bromhall, Winifred, *26:* 37
Brommer, Gerald F(rederick)
  1927- , *28:* 55
Brondfield, Jerome 1913- , *22:* 55
Brondfield, Jerry. *See* Brondfield,
  Jerome, *22:* 55
Bronson, Lynn. *See* Lampman,
  Evelyn Sibley, *4:* 140; *23:* 115
  (Obituary)
Brooke, L(eonard) Leslie
  1862-1940, *17:* 15
Brooke-Haven, P. *See* Wodehouse,
  P(elham) G(renville), *22:* 241

Brookins, Dana 1931- , *28:* 57
Brooks, Anita 1914- , *5:* 28
Brooks, Charlotte K., *24:* 56
Brooks, Gwendolyn 1917- , *6:* 33
Brooks, Jerome 1931- , *23:* 23
Brooks, Lester 1924- , *7:* 28
Brooks, Polly Schoyer 1912- ,
    12: 63
Brooks, Walter R(ollin)
    1886-1958, *17:* 17
Brosnan, James Patrick 1929- ,
    14: 47
Brosnan, Jim. *See* Brosnan, James
    Patrick, *14:* 47
Broun, Emily. *See* Sterne, Emma
    Gelders, *6:* 205
Brower, Millicent, *8:* 16
Brower, Pauline (York) 1929- ,
    22: 59
Browin, Frances Williams 1898- ,
    5: 30
Brown, Alexis. *See* Baumann, Amy
    (Brown), *10:* 9
Brown, Bill. *See* Brown,
    William L., *5:* 34
Brown, Billye Walker. *See*
    Cutchen, Billye Walker, *15:* 51
Brown, Bob. *See* Brown, Robert
    Joseph, *14:* 48
Brown, Conrad 1922- , *31:* 43
Brown, David. *See* Myller, Rolf,
    27: 153
Brown, Dee (Alexander) 1908- ,
    5: 30
Brown, Eleanor Frances 1908- ,
    3: 26
Brown, George Earl 1883-1964,
    11: 40
Brown, Irene Bennett 1932- ,
    3: 27
Brown, Irving. *See* Adams, William
    Taylor, *28:* 21
Brown, Ivor (John Carnegie)
    1891-1974, *5:* 31; *26:* 38
    (Obituary)
Brown, Judith Gwyn 1933- ,
    20: 15
Brown, Marc Tolon 1946- ,
    10: 17
Brown, Marcia 1918- , *7:* 29
Brown, Margaret Wise 1910-1952,
    YABC 2: 9
Brown, Margery, *5:* 31
Brown, Marion Marsh 1908- ,
    6: 35
Brown, Myra Berry 1918- , *6:* 36
Brown, Pamela 1924- , *5:* 33
Brown, Robert Joseph 1907- ,
    14: 48
Brown, Rosalie (Gertrude) Moore
    1910- , *9:* 26
Brown, Vinson 1912- , *19:* 48
Brown, Walter R(eed) 1929- ,
    19: 50
Brown, Will. *See* Ainsworth,
    William Harrison, *24:* 21

Brown, William L(ouis)
    1910-1964, *5:* 34
Browne, Hablot Knight
    1815-1882, *21:* 13
Browne, Matthew. *See* Rands,
    William Brighty, *17:* 156
Browning, Robert 1812-1889,
    YABC 1: 85
Brownjohn, Alan 1931- *6:* 38
Bruce, Dorita Fairlie 1885-1970,
    27: 36 (Obituary)
Bruce, Mary 1927- , *1:* 36
Bruna, Dick 1927- , *30:* 68 (Brief
    Entry)
Brunhoff, Jean de 1899-1937,
    24: 56
Brunhoff, Laurent de 1925- ,
    24: 59
Bryan, Ashley F. 1923- , *31:* 44
Bryant, Bernice (Morgan) 1908- ,
    11: 40
Brychta, Alex 1956- , *21:* 21
Bryson, Bernarda 1905- , *9:* 26
Buchan, John 1875-1940,
    YABC 2: 21
Buchwald, Art(hur) 1925- ,
    10: 18
Buchwald, Emilie 1935- , *7:* 31
Buck, Lewis 1925- , *18:* 37
Buck, Margaret Waring 1910- ,
    3: 29
Buck, Pearl S(ydenstricker)
    1892-1973, *1:* 36; *25:* 63
Buckeridge, Anthony 1912- ,
    6: 38
Buckley, Helen E(lizabeth)
    1918- , *2:* 38
Buckmaster, Henrietta, *6:* 39
Budd, Lillian 1897- , *7:* 33
Buehr, Walter 1897-1971, *3:* 30
Buff, Conrad 1886-1975, *19:* 51
Buff, Mary Marsh 1890-1970,
    19: 54
Bugbee, Emma 1888(?)-1981,
    29: 51 (Obituary)
Bulla, Clyde Robert 1914- , *2:* 39
Bunin, Catherine 1967- , *30:* 68
Bunin, Sherry 1925- , *30:* 68
Bunting, A. E.. *See* Bunting, Anne
    Evelyn, *18:* 38
Bunting, Anne Evelyn 1928- ,
    18: 38
Bunting, Eve. *See* Bunting, Anne
    Evelyn, *18:* 38
Bunting, Glenn (Davison) 1957- ,
    22: 60
Burch, Robert J(oseph) 1925- ,
    1: 38
Burchard, Peter D(uncan), *5:* 34
Burchard, Sue 1937- , *22:* 61
Burchardt, Nellie 1921- , *7:* 33
Burdick, Eugene (Leonard)
    1918-1965, *22:* 61
Burford, Eleanor. *See* Hibbert,
    Eleanor, *2:* 134
Burger, Carl 1888-1967, *9:* 27

Burgess, Anne Marie. *See* Gerson,
    Noel B(ertram), *22:* 118
Burgess, Em. *See* Burgess, Mary
    Wyche, *18:* 39
Burgess, (Frank) Gelett
    1866-1951, *30:* 70 (Brief
    Entry)
Burgess, Mary Wyche 1916- ,
    18: 39
Burgess, Michael. *See* Gerson, Noel
    B(ertram), *22:* 118
Burgess, Robert F(orrest) 1927- ,
    4: 38
Burgess, Thornton W(aldo)
    1874-1965, *17:* 19
Burgess, Trevor. *See* Trevor,
    Elleston, *28:* 207
Burgwyn, Mebane H. 1914- ,
    7: 34
Burke, John. *See* O'Connor,
    Richard, *21:* 111
Burkert, Nancy Ekholm 1933- ,
    24: 62
Burland, C. A. *See* Burland, Cottie
    A., *5:* 36
Burland, Cottie A. 1905- , *5:* 36
Burlingame, (William) Roger
    1889-1967, *2:* 40
Burman, Alice Caddy
    1896(?)-1977, *24:* 66
    (Obituary)
Burman, Ben Lucien 1896- ,
    6: 40
Burn, Doris 1923- , *1:* 39
Burnett, Frances (Eliza) Hodgson
    1849-1924, *YABC 2:* 32
Burnford, S. D. *See* Burnford,
    Sheila, *3:* 32
Burnford, Sheila 1918- , *3:* 32
Burningham, John (Mackintosh)
    1936- , *16:* 58
Burns, Paul C., *5:* 37
Burns, Raymond (Howard)
    1924- , *9:* 28
Burns, William A. 1909- , *5:* 38
Burroughs, Jean Mitchell 1908- ,
    28: 57
Burroughs, Polly 1925- , *2:* 41
Burroway, Janet (Gay) 1936- ,
    23: 24
Burt, Jesse Clifton 1921-1976,
    20: 18 (Obituary)
Burt, Olive Woolley 1894- , *4:* 39
Burton, Hester 1913- , *7:* 35
Burton, Maurice 1898- , *23:* 27
Burton, Robert (Wellesley)
    1941- , *22:* 62
Burton, Virginia Lee 1909-1968,
    2: 42
Burton, William H(enry)
    1890-1964, *11:* 42
Busby, Edith (?)-1964, *29:* 51
    (Obituary)
Busch, Phyllis S. 1909- , *30:* 70
Bushmiller, Ernie 1905-1982,
    31: 45 (Obituary)

Busoni, Rafaello 1900-1962, *16:* 61
Butler, Beverly 1932- , *7:* 37
Butler, Suzanne. *See* Perreard, Suzanne Louise Butler, *29:* 162 (Brief Entry)
Butters, Dorothy Gilman 1923- , *5:* 39
Butterworth, Oliver 1915- , *1:* 40
Butterworth, W(illiam) E(dmund III) 1929- , *5:* 40
Byars, Betsy 1928- , *4:* 40
Byfield, Barbara Ninde 1930- , *8:* 19

C.3.3. *See* Wilde, Oscar (Fingal O'Flahertie Wills), *24:* 205
Cable, Mary 1920- , *9:* 29
Caddy, Alice. *See* Burman, Alice Caddy, *24:* 66 (Obituary)
Cadwallader, Sharon 1936- , *7:* 38
Cady, (Walter) Harrison 1877-1970, *19:* 56
Cain, Arthur H. 1913- , *3:* 33
Cain, Christopher. *See* Fleming, Thomas J(ames), *8:* 19
Cairns, Trevor 1922- , *14:* 50
Caldecott, Moyra 1927- , *22:* 63
Caldecott, Randolph (J.) 1846-1886, *17:* 31
Caldwell, John C(ope) 1913- , *7:* 38
Calhoun, Mary (Huiskamp) 1926- , *2:* 44
Calkins, Franklin. *See* Stratemeyer, Edward L., *1:* 208
Call, Hughie Florence 1890-1969, *1:* 41
Callahan, Philip S(erna) 1923- , *25:* 77
Callen, Larry. *See* Callen, Lawrence Willard, Jr., *19:* 59
Callen, Lawrence Willard, Jr. 1927- , *19:* 59
Calvert, John. *See* Leaf, (Wilbur) Munro, *20:* 99
Cameron, Ann 1943- , *27:* 37
Cameron, Edna M. 1905- , *3:* 34
Cameron, Eleanor (Butler) 1912- , *1:* 42; *25:* 78
Cameron, Elizabeth. *See* Nowell, Elizabeth Cameron, *12:* 160
Cameron, Elizabeth Jane 1910-1976, *30:* 73 (Obituary)
Cameron, Polly 1928- , *2:* 45
Camp, Charles Lewis 1893-1975, *31:* 46 (Obituary)
Camp, Walter (Chauncey) 1859-1925, *YABC 1:* 92
Campbell, Ann R. 1925- , *11:* 43
Campbell, Bruce. *See* Epstein, Samuel, *1:* 87; *31:* 66
Campbell, Camilla 1905- , *26:* 39

Campbell, Hope, *20:* 19
Campbell, Jane. *See* Edwards, Jane Campbell, *10:* 34
Campbell, R. W. *See* Campbell, Rosemae Wells, *1:* 44
Campbell, Rosemae Wells 1909- , *1:* 44
Campion, Nardi Reeder 1917- , *22:* 64
Candell, Victor 1903-1977, *24:* 66 (Obituary)
Canfield, Dorothy. *See* Fisher, Dorothy Canfield, *YABC 1:* 122
Cannon, Cornelia (James) 1876-1969, *28:* 58 (Brief Entry)
Canusi, Jose. *See* Barker, S. Omar, *10:* 8
Caplin, Alfred Gerald 1909-1979, *21:* 22 (Obituary)
Capp, Al. *See* Caplin, Alfred Gerald, *21:* 22
Cappel, Constance 1936- , *22:* 65
Capps, Benjamin (Franklin) 1922- , *9:* 30
Carafoli, Marci. *See* Ridlon, Marci, *22:* 211
Caras, Roger A(ndrew) 1928- , *12:* 65
Carbonnier, Jeanne, *3:* 34
Carey, Bonnie 1941- , *18:* 40
Carey, Ernestine Gilbreth 1908- , *2:* 45
Carigiet, Alois 1902- , *24:* 66
Carini, Edward 1923- , *9:* 30
Carle, Eric 1929- , *4:* 41
Carleton, Captain L. C. *See* Ellis, Edward S(ylvester), *YABC 1:* 116
Carley, V(an Ness) Royal 1906-1976, *20:* 20 (Obituary)
Carlisle, Clark, Jr. *See* Holding, James, *3:* 85
Carlsen, G(eorge) Robert 1917- , *30:* 73
Carlsen, Ruth C(hristoffer), *2:* 47
Carlson, Bernice Wells 1910- , *8:* 19
Carlson, Dale Bick 1935- , *1:* 44
Carlson, Daniel 1960- , *27:* 39
Carlson, Natalie Savage, *2:* 48
Carlson, Vada F. 1897- , *16:* 64
Carmer, Carl (Lamson) 1893-1976, *30:* 74 (Obituary)
Carmer, Elizabeth Black 1904- , *24:* 68
Carol, Bill J. *See* Knott, William Cecil, Jr., *3:* 94
Carpelan, Bo (Gustaf Bertelsson) 1926- , *8:* 20
Carpenter, Allan 1917- , *3:* 35
Carpenter, Frances 1890-1972, *3:* 36; *27:* 39 (Obituary)
Carpenter, Patricia (Healy Evans) 1920- , *11:* 43

Carr, Glyn. *See* Styles, Frank Showell, *10:* 167
Carr, Harriett Helen 1899- , *3:* 37
Carr, Mary Jane, *2:* 50
Carrick, Carol 1935- , *7:* 39
Carrick, Donald 1929- , *7:* 40
Carrick, Malcolm 1945- , *28:* 58
Carrighar, Sally, *24:* 69
Carroll, Curt. *See* Bishop, Curtis, *6:* 24
Carroll, Latrobe, *7:* 40
Carroll, Laura. *See* Parr, Lucy, *10:* 115
Carroll, Lewis. *See* Dodgson, Charles Lutwidge, *YABC 2:* 297
Carse, Robert 1902-1971, *5:* 41
Carson, Captain James. *See* Stratemeyer, Edward L., *1:* 208
Carson, John F. 1920- , *1:* 46
Carson, Rachel (Louise) 1907-1964, *23:* 28
Carson, Rosalind. *See* Chittenden, Margaret, *28:* 62
Carson, S. M. *See* Gorsline, (Sally) Marie, *28:* 116
Carter, Bruce. *See* Hough, Richard (Alexander), *17:* 83
Carter, Dorothy Sharp 1921- , *8:* 21
Carter, Helene 1887-1960, *15:* 37
Carter, (William) Hodding 1907-1972, *2:* 51; *27:* 39 (Obituary)
Carter, Katharine J(ones) 1905- , *2:* 52
Carter, Phyllis Ann. *See* Eberle, Irmengarde, *2:* 97; *23:* 68 (Obituary)
Carter, William E. 1927- , *1:* 47
Cartner, William Carruthers 1910- , *11:* 44
Carver, John. *See* Gardner, Richard, *24:* 119
Cartwright, Sally 1923- , *9:* 30
Cary. *See* Cary, Louis F(avreau), *9:* 31
Cary, Barbara Knapp 1912(?)-1975, *31:* 46 (Obituary)
Cary, Louis F(avreau) 1915- , *9:* 31
Caryl, Jean. *See* Kaplan, Jean Caryl Korn, *10:* 62
Case, Marshal T(aylor) 1941- , *9:* 33
Case, Michael. *See* Howard, Robert West, *5:* 85
Casewit, Curtis 1922- , *4:* 43
Casey, Brigid 1950- , *9:* 33
Casey, Winifred Rosen. *See* Rosen, Winifred, *8:* 169
Cason, Mabel Earp 1892-1965, *10:* 19
Cass, Joan E(velyn), *1:* 47
Cassedy, Sylvia 1930- , *27:* 39

Cassel, Lili. *See* Wronker, Lili Cassell, *10:* 204

Cassel-Wronker, Lili. *See* Wronker, Lili Cassell, *10:* 204

Castellanos, Jane Mollie (Robinson) 1913- , *9:* 34

Castillo, Edmund L. 1924- , *1:* 50

Castle, Lee. [Joint pseudonym]. *See* Ogan, George F. and Margaret E. (Nettles), *13:* 171

Caswell, Helen (Rayburn) 1923- , *12:* 67

Cate, Dick. *See* Cate, Richard (Edward Nelson), *28:* 60

Cate, Richard (Edward Nelson) 1932- , *28:* 60

Cather, Willa (Sibert) 1873-1947, *30:* 75

Catherall, Arthur 1906- , *3:* 38

Cathon, Laura E(lizabeth) 1908- , *27:* 40

Catlin, Wynelle 1930- , *13:* 19

Catton, (Charles) Bruce 1899-1978, *2:* 54; *24:* 71 (Obituary)

Catz, Max. *See* Glaser, Milton, *11:* 106

Caudill, Rebecca 1899- , *1:* 50

Causley, Charles 1917- , *3:* 39

Cavallo, Diana 1931- , *7:* 43

Cavanah, Frances 1899-1982, *1:* 52; *31:* 46

Cavanna, Betty 1909- , *1:* 54; *30:* 84

Cawley, Winifred 1915- , *13:* 20

Caxton, Pisistratus. *See* Lytton, Edward G(eorge) E(arle) L(ytton) Bulwer-Lytton, Baron, *23:* 125

Cebulash, Mel 1937- , *10:* 19

Ceder, Georgiana Dorcas, *10:* 21

Cerf, Bennett 1898-1971, *7:* 43

Cerf, Christopher (Bennett) 1941- , *2:* 55

Cervon, Jacqueline. *See* Moussard, Jacqueline, *24:* 154

Cetin, Frank (Stanley) 1921- , *2:* 55

Chadwick, Lester [Collective pseudonym], *1:* 55

Chaffee, Allen, *3:* 41

Chaffin, Lillie D(orton) 1925- , *4:* 44

Chaikin, Miriam 1928- , *24:* 71

Challans, Mary 1905- , *23:* 33

Chalmers, Mary 1927- , *6:* 41

Chambers, Aidan 1934- , *1:* 55

Chambers, Catherine E. *See* Johnston, Norma, *29:* 116

Chambers, Margaret Ada Eastwood 1911- , *2:* 56

Chambers, Peggy. *See* Chambers, Margaret Ada Eastwood, *2:* 56

Chandler, Caroline A(ugusta) 1906-1979, *22:* 66; *24:* 72 (Obituary)

Chandler, David Porter 1933- , *28:* 61

Chandler, Edna Walker 1908-1982, *11:* 45; *31:* 48 (Obituary)

Chandler, Ruth Forbes 1894-1978, *2:* 56; *26:* 40 (Obituary)

Channel, A. R. *See* Catherall, Arthur, *3:* 38

Chapian, Marie 1938- , *29:* 51

Chapman, Allen [Collective pseudonym], *1:* 55

Chapman, (Constance) Elizabeth (Mann) 1919- , *10:* 21

Chapman, John Stanton Higham 1891-1972, *27:* 41 (Obituary)

Chapman, Maristan [Joint pseudonym]. *See* Chapman, John Stanton Higham, *27:* 41 (Obituary)

Chapman, Walker. *See* Silverberg, Robert, *13:* 206

Chappell, Warren 1904- , *6:* 42

Chardiet, Bernice (Kroll), *27:* 42

Charles, Donald. *See* Meighan, Donald Charles, *30:* 153

Charles, Louis. *See* Stratemeyer, Edward L., *1:* 208

Charlip, Remy 1929- , *4:* 46

Charlot, Jean 1898-1979, *8:* 22; *31:* 48 (Obituary)

Charmatz, Bill 1925- , *7:* 45

Charosh, Mannis 1906- , *5:* 42

Chase, Alice. *See* McHargue, Georgess, *4:* 152

Chase, Mary (Coyle) 1907-1981, *17:* 39; *29:* 52 (Obituary)

Chase, Mary Ellen 1887-1973, *10:* 22

Chastain, Madye Lee 1908- , *4:* 48

Chauncy, Nan 1900-1970, *6:* 43

Chaundler, Christine 1887-1972, *1:* 56; *25:* 83 (Obituary)

Chen, Tony 1929- , *6:* 44

Chenault, Nell. *See* Smith, Linell Nash, *2:* 227

Chenery, Janet (Dai) 1923- , *25:* 84

Cheney, Cora 1916- , *3:* 41

Cheney, Ted. *See* Cheney, Theodore Albert, *11:* 46

Cheney, Theodore Albert 1928- , *11:* 46

Chernoff, Goldie Taub 1909- , *10:* 23

Cherryholmes, Anne. *See* Price, Olive, *8:* 157

Chesterton, G(ilbert) K(eith) 1874-1936, *27:* 42

Chetin, Helen 1922- , *6:* 46

Chew, Ruth, *7:* 45

Chidsey, Donald Barr 1902-1981, *3:* 42; *27:* 47 (Obituary)

Childress, Alice 1920- , *7:* 46

Childs, (Halla) Fay (Cochrane) 1890-1971, *1:* 56; *25:* 84 (Obituary)

Chimaera. *See* Farjeon, Eleanor, *2:* 103

Chinery, Michael 1938- , *26:* 40

Chipperfield, Joseph E(ugene) 1912- , *2:* 57

Chittenden, Elizabeth F. 1903- , *9:* 35

Chittenden, Margaret 1933- , *28:* 62

Chittum, Ida 1918- , *7:* 47

Choate, Judith (Newkirk) 1940- , *30:* 86

Chorao, (Ann Mc)Kay (Sproat) 1936- , *8:* 24

Chrisman, Arthur Bowie 1889-1953, *YABC 1:* 94

Christensen, Gardell Dano 1907- , *1:* 57

Christgau, Alice Erickson 1902- , *13:* 21

Christian, Mary Blount 1933- , *9:* 35

Christopher, John. *See* Youd, (Christopher) Samuel, *30:* 222 (Brief Entry)

Christopher, Matt(hew F.) 1917- , *2:* 58

Christy, Howard Chandler 1873-1952, *21:* 22

Chu, Daniel 1933- , *11:* 47

Chukovsky, Kornei (Ivanovich) 1882-1969, *5:* 43

Church, Richard 1893-1972, *3:* 43

Churchill, E. Richard 1937- , *11:* 48

Chute, B(eatrice) J(oy) 1913- , *2:* 59

Chute, Marchette (Gaylord) 1909- , *1:* 58

Chwast, Jacqueline 1932- , *6:* 46

Chwast, Seymour 1931- , *18:* 42

Ciardi, John (Anthony) 1916- , *1:* 59

Clair, Andrée, *19:* 61

Clapp, Patricia 1912- , *4:* 50

Clare, Helen. *See* Hunter Blair, Pauline, *3:* 87

Clark, Ann Nolan 1898- , *4:* 51

Clark, Frank J(ames) 1922- , *18:* 43

Clark, Garel [Joint pseudonym]. *See* Garelick, May, *19:* 130

Clark, Leonard 1905-1981, *29:* 53 (Obituary); *30:* 86

Clark, Margaret Goff 1913- , *8:* 26

Clark, Mavis Thorpe, *8:* 27

Clark, Merle. *See* Gessner, Lynne, *16:* 119

Clark, Patricia (Finrow) 1929- , *11:* 48

Clark, Ronald William 1916- , *2:* 60

Clark, Van D(eusen) 1909- ,
2: 61
Clark, Virginia. *See* Gray, Patricia,
7: 110
Clark, Walter Van Tilburg
1909-1971, 8: 28
Clarke, Arthur C(harles) 1917- ,
13: 22
Clarke, Clorinda 1917- , 7: 48
Clarke, Joan B. 1921- , 27: 48
(Brief Entry)
Clarke, John. *See* Laklan, Carli,
5: 100
Clarke, Mary Stetson 1911- ,
5: 46
Clarke, Michael. *See* Newlon,
Clarke, 6: 174
Clarke, Pauline. *See* Hunter Blair,
Pauline, 3: 87
Clarkson, Ewan 1929- , 9: 36
Cleary, Beverly (Bunn) 1916- ,
2: 62
Cleaver, Bill 1920-1981, 22: 66;
27: 48 (Obituary)
Cleaver, Carole 1934- , 6: 48
Cleaver, Elizabeth (Mrazik)
1939- , 23: 34
Cleaver, Vera, 22: 67
Cleishbotham, Jebediah. *See* Scott,
Sir Walter, YABC 2: 280
Cleland, Mabel. *See* Widdemer,
Mabel Cleland, 5: 200
Clemens, Samuel Langhorne
1835-1910, YABC 2: 51
Clements, Bruce 1931- , 27: 48
Clemons, Elizabeth. *See* Nowell,
Elizabeth Cameron, 12: 160
Clerk, N. W. *See* Lewis, C. S.,
13: 129
Cleven, Cathrine. *See* Cleven,
Kathryn Seward, 2: 64
Cleven, Kathryn Seward, 2: 64
Clevin, Jörgen 1920- , 7: 49
Clewes, Dorothy (Mary) 1907- ,
1: 61
Clifford, Eth. *See* Rosenberg, Ethel,
3: 176
Clifford, Harold B. 1893- ,
10: 24
Clifford, Margaret Cort 1929- ,
1: 63
Clifford, Martin. *See* Hamilton,
Charles Harold St. John, 13: 77
Clifford, Mary Louise (Beneway)
1926- , 23: 36
Clifford, Peggy. *See* Clifford,
Margaret Cort, 1: 63
Clifton, Harry. *See* Hamilton,
Charles Harold St. John, 13: 77
Clifton, Lucille 1936- , 20: 20
Clifton, Martin. *See* Hamilton,
Charles Harold St. John, 13: 77
Clinton, Jon. *See* Prince, J(ack)
H(arvey), 17: 155
Clive, Clifford. *See* Hamilton,
Charles Harold St. John, 13: 77

Cloudsley-Thompson, J(ohn)
L(eonard) 1921- , 19: 61
Clymer, Eleanor 1906- , 9: 37
Clyne, Patricia Edwards, 31: 49
Coalson, Glo 1946- , 26: 41
Coates, Belle 1896- , 2: 64
Coates, Ruth Allison 1915- ,
11: 49
Coats, Alice M(argaret) 1905- ,
11: 50
Coatsworth, Elizabeth 1893- ,
2: 65
Cobb, Jane. *See* Berry, Jane Cobb,
22: 39 (Obituary)
Cobb, Vicki 1938- , 8: 31
Cobbett, Richard. *See* Pluckrose,
Henry (Arthur), 13: 183
Cober, Alan E. 1935- , 7: 51
Cobham, Sir Alan. *See* Hamilton,
Charles Harold St. John, 13: 77
Cocagnac, A(ugustin) M(aurice-
Jean) 1924- , 7: 52
Cochran, Bobbye A. 1949- ,
11: 51
Cockett, Mary, 3: 45
Coe, Douglas [Joint pseudonym].
See Epstein, Beryl 1: 85;
31: 64; Epstein, Samuel, 1: 87;
31: 66
Coe, Lloyd 1899-1976, 30: 88
(Obituary)
Coen, Rena Neumann 1925- ,
20: 24
Coerr, Eleanor 1922- , 1: 64
Coffin, Geoffrey. *See* Mason, F.
van Wyck, 3: 117; 26: 146
(Obituary)
Coffman, Ramon Peyton 1896- ,
4: 53
Coggins, Jack (Banham) 1911- ,
2: 68
Cohen, Barbara 1932- , 10: 24
Cohen, Daniel 1936- , 8: 31
Cohen, Joan Lebold 1932- , 4: 53
Cohen, Miriam 1926- , 29: 53
Cohen, Peter Zachary 1931- ,
4: 54
Cohen, Robert Carl 1930- , 8: 33
Cohn, Angelo 1914- , 19: 63
Coit, Margaret L(ouise), 2: 70
Colbert, Anthony 1934- , 15: 39
Colby, C. B. 1904- , 3: 46
Colby, Jean Poindexter 1909- ,
23: 37
Cole, Annette. *See* Steiner, Barbara
A(nnette), 13: 213
Cole, Davis, *See* Elting, Mary,
2: 100
Cole, Jack. *See* Stewart, John
(William), 14: 189
Cole, Jackson. *See* Schisgall, Oscar,
12: 187
Cole, Lois Dwight 1903(?)-1979,
10: 26; 26: 43 (Obituary)
Cole, Sheila R(otenberg) 1939- ,
24: 73

Cole, William (Rossa) 1919- ,
9: 40
Coles, Robert (Martin) 1929- ,
23: 38
Collier, Christopher 1930- ,
16: 66
Collier, Ethel 1903- , 22: 68
Collier, James Lincoln 1928- ,
8: 33
Collier, Jane. *See* Collier, Zena,
23: 41
Collier, Zena 1926- , 23: 41
Collins, David 1940- , 7: 52
Collins, Hunt. *See* Hunter, Evan,
25: 153
Collins, Pat Lowery 1932- ,
31: 51
Collins, Ruth Philpott 1890-1975,
30: 88 (Obituary)
Collodi, Carlo. *See* Lorenzini,
Carlo, 29: 128
Colman, Hila, 1: 65
Colman, Morris 1899(?)-1981,
25: 85 (Obituary)
Colonius, Lillian 1911- , 3: 48
Colorado (Capella), Antonio J(ulio)
1903- , 23: 42
Colt, Martin [Joint pseudonym]. *See*
Epstein, Beryl, 31: 64; Epstein,
Samuel, 1: 87; 31: 66
Colum, Padraic 1881-1972, 15: 42
Columella. *See* Moore, Clement
Clarke, 18: 224
Colver, Anne 1908- , 7: 54
Colwell, Eileen (Hilda) 1904- ,
2: 71
Comfort, Jane Levington. *See*
Sturtzel, Jane Levington,
1: 212
Comfort, Mildred Houghton
1886- , 3: 48
Comins, Ethel M(ae), 11: 53
Comins, Jeremy 1933- , 28: 64
Commager, Henry Steele 1902- ,
23: 43
Comus. *See* Ballantyne, R(obert)
M(ichael), 24: 32
Conan Doyle, Arthur. *See* Doyle,
Arthur Conan, 24: 89
Condit, Martha Olson 1913- ,
28: 64
Cone, Molly (Lamken) 1918- ,
1: 66; 28: 65
Conford, Ellen 1942- , 6: 48
Conger, Lesley. *See* Suttles, Shirley
(Smith), 21: 166
Conklin, Gladys (Plemon) 1903- ,
2: 73
Conkling, Hilda 1910- , 23: 45
Conly, Robert Leslie
1918(?)-1973, 23: 45
Connell, Kirk [Joint pseudonym].
See Chapman, John Stanton
Higham, 27: 41 (Obituary)
Connelly, Marc(us Cook)
1890-1980, 25: 85 (Obituary)

Connolly, Jerome P(atrick)
1931- , *8:* 34
Conover, Chris 1950- , *31:* 52
Conquest, Owen. *See* Hamilton,
Charles Harold St. John, *13:* 77
Conrad, Joseph 1857-1924, *27:* 49
Conroy, Jack (Wesley) 1899- ,
19: 65
Conroy, John. *See* Conroy, Jack
(Wesley), *19:* 65
Constant, Alberta Wilson
1908-1981, *22:* 70; *28:* 67
(Obituary)
Conway, Gordon. *See* Hamilton,
Charles Harold St. John, *13:* 77
Cook, Bernadine 1924- , *11:* 55
Cook, Fred J(ames) 1911- , *2:* 74
Cook, Joseph J(ay) 1924- , *8:* 35
Cook, Lyn. *See* Waddell, Evelyn
Margaret, *10:* 186
Cooke, David Coxe 1917- , *2:* 75
Cooke, Donald Ewin 1916- ,
2: 76
Cookson, Catherine (McMullen)
1906- , *9:* 42
Coolidge, Olivia E(nsor) 1908- ,
1: 67; *26:* 44
Coombs, Charles 1914- , *3:* 49
Coombs, Chick. *See* Coombs,
Charles, *3:* 49
Coombs, Patricia 1926- , *3:* 51
Cooney, Barbara 1917- , *6:* 49
Cooper, Gordon 1932- , *23:* 47
Cooper, James Fenimore
1789-1851, *19:* 68
Cooper, James R. *See* Stratemeyer,
Edward L., *1:* 208
Cooper, John R. [Collective
pseudonym], *1:* 68
Cooper, Kay 1941- , *11:* 55
Cooper, Lee (Pelham), *5:* 47
Cooper, Susan 1935- , *4:* 57
Copeland, Helen 1920- , *4:* 57
Copeland, Paul W., *23:* 48
Coppard, A(lfred) E(dgar)
1878-1957, *YABC 1:* 97
Corbett, Scott 1913- , *2:* 78
Corbin, Sabra Lee. *See* Malvern,
Gladys, *23:* 133
Corbin, William. *See* McGraw,
William Corbin, *3:* 124
Corby, Dan. *See* Catherall, Arthur,
3: 38
Corcoran, Barbara 1911- , *3:* 53
Corcos, Lucille 1908-1973, *10:* 27
Cordell, Alexander. *See* Graber,
Alexander, *7:* 106
Corey, Dorothy, *23:* 49
Corfe, Thomas Howell 1928- ,
27: 58
Corfe, Tom. *See* Corfe, Thomas
Howell, *27:* 58
Cormack, M(argaret) Grant
1913- , *11:* 56
Cormier, Robert Edmund 1925- ,
10: 28

Cornell, J. *See* Cornell, Jeffrey,
11: 57
Cornell, James (Clayton, Jr.)
1938- , *27:* 59
Cornell, Jean Gay 1920- , *23:* 50
Cornell, Jeffrey 1945- , *11:* 57
Cornish, Samuel James 1935- ,
23: 51
Correy, Lee. *See* Stine, G. Harry,
10: 161
Corrigan, (Helen) Adeline 1909- ,
23: 53
Corrigan, Barbara 1922- , *8:* 36
Cort, M. C. *See* Clifford, Margaret
Cort, *1:* 63
Corwin, Judith Hoffman 1946- ,
10: 28
Cosgrave, John O'Hara II
1908-1968, *21:* 26 (Obituary)
Coskey, Evelyn 1932- , *7:* 55
Costello, David F(rancis) 1904- ,
23: 53
Cott, Jonathan 1942- , *23:* 55
Cottam, Clarence 1899-1974,
25: 85
Cottler, Joseph 1899- , *22:* 71
Cottrell, Leonard 1913-1974,
24: 74
Courlander, Harold 1908- , *6:* 51
Courtis, Stuart Appleton
1874-1969, *29:* 54 (Obituary)
Cousins, Margaret 1905- , *2:* 79
Cowie, Leonard W(allace) 1919- ,
4: 60
Cowley, Joy 1936- , *4:* 60
Cox, Donald William 1921- ,
23: 56
Cox, Jack. *See* Cox, John Roberts,
9: 42
Cox, John Roberts 1915- , *9:* 42
Cox, Palmer 1840-1924, *24:* 75
Cox, Wally 1924-1973, *25:* 86
Cox, William R(obert) 1901- ,
31: 53 (Brief Entry)
Coy, Harold 1902- , *3:* 53
Craft, Ruth, *31:* 53 (Brief Entry)
Craig, Alisa. *See* MacLeod,
Charlotte (Matilda Hughes),
28: 147
Craig, John Eland. *See*
Chipperfield, Joseph, *2:* 57
Craig, John Ernest 1921- , *23:* 58
Craig, M. Jean, *17:* 45
Craig, Margaret Maze 1911-1964,
9: 43
Craig, Mary Francis 1923- , *6:* 52
Crane, Barbara J. 1934- , *31:* 53
Crane, Caroline 1930- , *11:* 59
Crane, Roy. *See* Crane, Royston
Campbell, *22:* 72 (Obituary)
Crane, Royston Campbell
1901-1977, *22:* 72 (Obituary)
Crane, Stephen (Townley)
1871-1900, *YABC 2:* 94
Crane, Walter 1845-1915, *18:* 44

Crane, William D(wight) 1892- ,
1: 68
Crary, Margaret (Coleman)
1906- , *9:* 43
Craven, Thomas 1889-1969,
22: 72
Crawford, Charles P. 1945- ,
28: 67
Crawford, Deborah 1922- , *6:* 53
Crawford, John E. 1904-1971,
3: 56
Crawford, Phyllis 1899- , *3:* 57
Craz, Albert G. 1926- , *24:* 78
Crayder, Dorothy 1906- , *7:* 55
Crayder, Teresa. *See* Colman, Hila,
1: 65
Crayon, Geoffrey. *See* Irving,
Washington, *YABC 2:* 164
Crecy, Jeanne. *See* Williams,
Jeanne, *5:* 202
Credle, Ellis 1902- , *1:* 68
Cresswell, Helen 1934- , *1:* 70
Cretan, Gladys (Yessayan)
1921- , *2:* 82
Crew, Helen (Cecilia) Coale
1866-1941, *YABC 2:* 95
Crews, Donald, *30:* 88 (Brief Entry)
Crichton, (J.) Michael 1942- ,
9: 44
Crofut, Bill. *See* Crofut, William E.
III, *23:* 59
Crofut, William E. III 1934- ,
23: 59
Cromie, Alice Hamilton 1914- ,
24: 78
Cromie, William J(oseph) 1930- ,
4: 62
Crompton, Anne Eliot 1930- ,
23: 61
Crompton, Richmal. *See* Lamburn,
Richmal Crompton, *5:* 101
Cronbach, Abraham 1882-1965,
11: 60
Crone, Ruth 1919- , *4:* 63
Cronin, A(rchibald) J(oseph)
1896-1981, *25:* 89 (Obituary)
Cros, Earl. *See* Rose, Carl, *31:* 144
(Brief Entry)
Crosby, Alexander L. 1906-1980,
2: 83; *23:* 62 (Obituary)
Crosher, G(eoffry) R(obins)
1911- , *14:* 51
Cross, Helen Reeder. *See*
Broadhead, Helen Cross,
25: 62
Cross, Wilbur Lucius III 1918- ,
2: 83
Crossley-Holland, Kevin, *5:* 48
Crouch, Marcus 1913- , *4:* 63
Crout, George C(lement) 1917- ,
11: 60
Crowe, Bettina Lum 1911- , *6:* 53
Crowell, Pers 1910- , *2:* 84
Crowfield, Christopher. *See* Stowe,
Harriet (Elizabeth) Beecher,
YABC 1: 250

Crownfield, Gertrude 1867-1945,
  YABC 1: 103
Crowther, James Gerald 1899- ,
  14: 52
Cruikshank, George 1792-1878,
  22: 73
Crump, Fred H., Jr. 1931- ,
  11: 62
Crump, J(ames) Irving 1887-1979,
  21: 26 (Obituary)
Cruz, Ray 1933- , *6:* 54
Ctvrtek, Vaclav 1911-1976,
  27: 60 (Obituary)
Cuffari, Richard 1925-1978,
  6: 54; *25:* 89 (Obituary)
Cullen, Countee 1903-1946,
  18: 64
Culp, Louanna McNary
  1901-1965, *2:* 85
Cumming, Primrose (Amy)
  1915- , *24:* 79
Cummings, Betty Sue 1918- ,
  15: 51
Cummings, Parke 1902- , *2:* 85
Cummings, Richard. *See* Gardner,
  Richard, *24:* 109
Cummins, Maria Susanna
  1827-1866, *YABC 1:* 103
Cunliffe, John Arthur 1933- ,
  11: 62
Cunningham, Captain Frank. *See*
  Glick, Carl (Cannon), *14:* 72
Cunningham, Cathy. *See*
  Cunningham, Chet, *23:* 63
Cunningham, Chet 1928- , *23:* 63
Cunningham, Dale S(peers) 1932-,
  11: 63
Cunningham, E. V. *See* Fast,
  Howard, *7:* 80
Cunningham, Julia W(oolfolk)
  1916- , *1:* 72; *26:* 48
Cunningham, Virginia. *See*
  Holmgren, Virginia
  C(unningham), *26:* 124
Curiae, Amicus. *See* Fuller,
  Edmund (Maybank), *21:* 45
Curie, Eve 1904- , *1:* 73
Curley, Daniel 1918- , *23:* 63
Curry, Jane L(ouise) 1932- ,
  1: 73
Curry, Peggy Simson 1911- ,
  8: 37
Curtis, Bruce (Richard) 1944- ,
  30: 89
Curtis, Patricia 1921- , *23:* 64
Curtis, Peter. *See* Lofts, Norah
  Robinson, *8:* 119
Curtis, Richard (Alan) 1937- ,
  29: 54
Curtis, Wade. *See* Pournelle, Jerry
  (Eugene), *26:* 161
Cushman, Jerome, *2:* 86
Cutchen, Billye Walker 1930- ,
  15: 51
Cutler, (May) Ebbitt 1923- , *9:* 46
Cutler, Ivor 1923- , *24:* 80

Cutler, Samuel. *See* Folsom,
  Franklin, *5:* 67
Cutt, W(illiam) Towrie 1898- ,
  16: 67
Cuyler, Stephen. *See* Bates, Barbara
  S(nedeker), *12:* 34

Dahl, Borghild 1890- , *7:* 56
Dahl, Roald 1916- , *1:* 74; *26:* 50
Dahlstedt, Marden 1921- , *8:* 38
Dale, Jack. *See* Holliday, Joseph,
  11: 137
Dalgliesh, Alice 1893-1979,
  17: 47; *21:* 26 (Obituary)
Daly, Jim. *See* Stratemeyer, Edward
  L., *1:* 208
Daly, Maureen, *2:* 87
D'Amato, Alex 1919- , *20:* 24
D'Amato, Janet 1925- , *9:* 47
Damrosch, Helen Therese. *See* Tee-
  Van, Helen Damrosch,
  10: 176; *27:* 221 (Obituary)
Dana, Barbara 1940- , *22:* 84
Dana, Richard Henry, Jr.
  1815-1882, *26:* 62
Danachair, Caoimhin O. *See*
  Danaher, Kevin, *22:* 85
Danaher, Kevin 1913- , *22:* 85
D'Andrea, Kate. *See* Steiner,
  Barbara A(nnette), *13:* 213
Dangerfield, Balfour. *See*
  McCloskey, Robert, *2:* 185
Daniel, Anita 1893(?)-1978,
  23: 65; *24:* 81 (Obituary)
Daniel, Anne. *See* Steiner, Barbara
  A(nnette), *13:* 213
Daniel, Hawthorne 1890- , *8:* 39
Daniels, Guy 1919- , *11:* 64
Dank, Milton 1920- , *31:* 54
Danziger, Paula 1944- , *30:* 90
  (Brief Entry)
Darby, J. N. *See* Govan, Christine
  Noble, *9:* 80
Darby, Patricia (Paulsen), *14:* 53
Darby, Ray K. 1912- , *7:* 59
Daringer, Helen Fern 1892- ,
  1: 75
Darke, Marjorie 1929- , *16:* 68
Darling, Kathy. *See* Darling, Mary
  Kathleen *1:* 208
Darling, Lois M. 1917- , *3:* 57
Darling, Louis, Jr. 1916-1970,
  3: 59; *23:* 66 (Obituary)
Darling, Mary Kathleen 1943- ,
  9: 48
Darrow, Whitney, Jr. 1909- ,
  13: 24
Darwin, Len. *See* Darwin, Leonard,
  24: 81
Darwin, Leonard 1916- , *24:* 81
Dasent, Sir George Webbe
  1817-1896, *29:* 55 (Brief
  Entry)
Dauer, Rosamond 1934- , *23:* 66

Daugherty, Charles Michael
  1914- , *16:* 70
Daugherty, James (Henry)
  1889-1974, *13:* 26
Daugherty, Sonia Medwedeff
  (?)-1971, *27:* 60 (Obituary)
d'Aulaire, Edgar Parin 1898- ,
  5: 49
d'Aulaire, Ingri (Maartenson Parin)
  1904-1980 *5:* 50; *24:* 82
  (Obituary)
Daveluy, Paule Cloutier 1919- ,
  11: 65
Davenport, Spencer. *See*
  Stratemeyer, Edward L., *1:* 208
David, Jonathan. *See* Ames, Lee J.,
  3: 11
Davidson, Basil 1914- , *13:* 30
Davidson, Jessica 1915- , *5:* 52
Davidson, Margaret 1936- , *5:* 53
Davidson, Marion. *See* Garis,
  Howard R(oger), *13:* 67
Davidson, Mary R. 1885-1973,
  9: 49
Davidson, Rosalie 1921- , *23:* 67
Davies, Andrew (Wynford)
  1936- , *27:* 60
Davis, Bette J. 1923- , *15:* 53
Davis, Burke 1913- , *4:* 64
Davis, Christopher 1928- , *6:* 57
Davis, Daniel S(heldon) 1936- ,
  12: 68
Davis, Hubert J(ackson) 1904- ,
  31: 55
Davis, Julia 1904- , *6:* 58
Davis, Louise Littleton 1921- ,
  25: 89
Davis, Mary L(ee) 1935- , *9:* 49
Davis, Mary Octavia 1901- , *6:* 59
Davis, Paxton 1925- , *16:* 71
Davis, Robert 1881-1949,
  YABC 1: 104
Davis, Russell G. 1922- , *3:* 60
Davis, Verne T. 1889-1973, *6:* 60
Dawson, Elmer A. [Collective
  pseudonym], *1:* 76
Dawson, Mary 1919- , *11:* 66
Day, Maurice 1892- , *30:* 90
  (Brief Entry)
Day, Thomas 1748-1789,
  YABC 1: 106
Dazey, Agnes J(ohnston), *2:* 88
Dazey, Frank M., *2:* 88
Deacon, Eileen. *See* Geipel, Eileen,
  30: 114
Deacon, Richard. *See* McCormick,
  (George) Donald (King),
  14: 141
Dean, Anabel 1915- , *12:* 69
de Angeli, Marguerite 1889- ,
  1: 76; *27:* 61
DeArmand, Frances Ullmann,
  10: 29
deBanke, Cecile 1889-1965,
  11: 67
De Bruyn, Monica 1952- , *13:* 30

de Camp, Catherine C(rook) 1907- , *12:* 70

DeCamp, L(yon) Sprague 1907- , *9:* 49

Decker, Duane 1910-1964, *5:* 53

Deedy, John 1923- , *24:* 83

Defoe, Daniel 1660(?)-1731, *22:* 86

DeGering, Etta 1898- , *7:* 60

De Groat, Diane 1947- , *31:* 57

de Grummond, Lena Young, *6:* 61

Deiss, Joseph J. 1915- , *12:* 72

DeJong, David C(ornel) 1905-1967, *10:* 29

de Jong, Dola, *7:* 61

De Jong, Meindert 1906- , *2:* 89

de Kay, Ormonde, Jr. 1923- , *7:* 62

de Kiriline, Louise. *See* Lawrence, Louise de Kirilene, *13:* 126

Dekker, Carl. *See* Laffin, John (Alfred Charles), *31:* 111

deKruif, Paul (Henry) 1890-1971 *5:* 54

De Lage, Ida 1918- , *11:* 67

de la Mare, Walter 1873-1956, *16:* 73

Delaney, Harry 1932- , *3:* 61

Delaney, Ned 1951- , *28:* 68

Delano, Hugh 1933- , *20:* 25

De La Ramée, (Marie) Louise 1839-1908, *20:* 26

Delaune, Lynne, *7:* 63

DeLaurentis, Louise Budde 1920- , *12:* 73

Delderfield, Eric R(aymond) 1909- , *14:* 53

Delderfield, R(onald) F(rederick) 1912-1972, *20:* 34

De Leeuw, Adele Louise 1899- , *1:* 77; *30:* 90

Delessert, Etienne 1941- , *27:* 73 (Brief Entry)

Delmar, Roy. *See* Wexler, Jerome (LeRoy), *14:* 243

Deloria, Vine (Victor), Jr. 1933- , *21:* 26

Del Rey, Lester 1915- , *22:* 97

Delton, Judy 1931- , *14:* 54

Delulio, John 1938- , *15:* 54

Delving, Michael. *See* Williams, Jay, *3:* 256; *24:* 221 (Obituary)

Demarest, Doug. *See* Barker, Will, *8:* 4

Demas, Vida 1927- , *9:* 51

Deming, Richard 1915- , *24:* 83

Denney, Diana 1910- , *25:* 90

Dennis, Morgan 1891(?)-1960, *18:* 68

Dennis, Wesley 1903-1966, *18:* 70

Denniston, Elinore 1900-1978, *24:* 85 (Obituary)

Denslow, W(illiam) W(allace) 1856-1915, *16:* 83

Denzer, Ann Wiseman. *See* Wiseman, Ann (Sayre), *31:* 186

de Paola, Thomas Anthony 1934- , *11:* 68

de Paola, Tomie. *See* de Paola, Thomas Anthony, *11:* 68

DePauw, Linda Grant 1940- , *24:* 85

deRegniers, Beatrice Schenk (Freedman) 1914- , *2:* 90

Derleth, August (William) 1909-1971, *5:* 54

Derman, Sarah Audrey 1915- , *11:* 71

de Roo, Anne Louise 1931- , *25:* 91

De Roussan, Jacques 1929- , *31:* 59 (Brief Entry)

Derry Down Derry. *See* Lear, Edward, *18:* 182

Derwent, Lavinia, *14:* 56

De Selincourt, Aubrey 1894-1962, *14:* 56

Desmond, Alice Curtis 1897- , *8:* 40

Detine, Padre. *See* Olsen, Ib Spang, *6:* 177

Deutsch, Babette 1895- , *1:* 79

De Valera, Sinead 1879(?)-1975, *30:* 93 (Obituary)

Devaney, John 1926- , *12:* 74

Devereux, Frederick L(eonard), Jr. 1914- , *9:* 51

Devlin, Harry 1918- , *11:* 73

Devlin, (Dorothy) Wende 1918- , *11:* 74

DeWaard, E. John 1935- , *7:* 63

Dewey, Ariane 1937- , *7:* 63

DeWit, Dorothy May Knowles 1916(?)-1980, *28:* 70 (Obituary)

Deyneka, Anita 1943- , *24:* 86

Deyrup, Astrith Johnson 1923- , *24:* 87

Diamond, Donna 1950- , *30:* 93 (Brief Entry)

Dick, Trella Lamson 1889-1974, *9:* 51

Dickens, Charles 1812-1870, *15:* 55

Dickens, Monica 1915- , *4:* 66

Dickerson, Roy Ernest 1886-1965, *26:* 67 (Obituary)

Dickinson, Emily (Elizabeth) 1830-1886, *29:* 55

Dickinson, Peter 1927- , *5:* 55

Dickinson, Susan 1931- , *8:* 41

Dickinson, William Croft 1897-1973, *13:* 32

Dickson, Helen. *See* Reynolds, Helen Mary Greenwood Campbell, *26:* 169 (Obituary)

Dickson, Naida 1916- , *8:* 41

Dietz, David H(enry) 1897- , *10:* 30

Dietz, Lew 1907- , *11:* 75

Dillard, Annie 1945- , *10:* 31

Dillard, Polly (Hargis) 1916- , *24:* 88

Dillon, Diane 1933- , *15:* 98

Dillon, Eilis 1920- , *2:* 92

Dillon, Leo 1933- , *15:* 99

Dilson, Jesse 1914- , *24:* 89

Dines, Glen 1925- , *7:* 65

Dinsdale, Tim 1924- , *11:* 76

Dirks, Rudolph 1877-1968, *31:* 60 (Brief Entry)

Disney, Walt(er Elias) 1901-1966, *27:* 73 (Brief Entry); *28:* 70

DiValentin, Maria 1911- , *7:* 68

Dixon, Franklin W. [Collective pseudonym], *1:* 80. *See also* Adams, Harriet S(tratemeyer), *1:* 1; *29:* 26 (Obituary); McFarlane, Leslie, *31:* 133; Stratemeyer, Edward L., *1:* 208; Svenson, Andrew E., *2:* 238; *26:* 185 (Obituary)

Dixon, Jeanne 1936- , *31:* 60

Dixon, Peter L. 1931- , *6:* 62

Doane, Pelagie 1906-1966, *7:* 68

Dobell, I(sabel) M(arian) B(arclay) 1909- , *11:* 77

Dobkin, Alexander 1908-1975, *30:* 94 (Obituary)

Dobler, Lavinia G. 1910- , *6:* 63

Dobrin, Arnold 1928- , *4:* 67

Dockery, Wallene T. 1941- , *27:* 74

"Dr. A." *See* Silverstein, Alvin, *8:* 188

Dodd, Ed(ward) Benton 1902- , *4:* 68

Dodge, Bertha S(anford) 1902- , *8:* 42

Dodge, Mary (Elizabeth) Mapes 1831-1905, *21:* 27

Dodgson, Charles Lutwidge 1832-1898, *YABC 2:* 97

Dodson, Kenneth M(acKenzie) 1907- , *11:* 77

Doherty, C. H. 1913- , *6:* 65

Dolan, Edward F(rancis), Jr. 1924- , *31:* 61 (Brief Entry)

Dolson, Hildegarde 1908- , *5:* 56

Domanska, Janina, *6:* 65

Domino, John. *See* Averill, Esther, *28:* 39

Domjan, Joseph 1907- , *25:* 92

Donalds, Gordon. *See* Shirreffs, Gordon D., *11:* 207

Donna, Natalie 1934- , *9:* 52

Donovan, Frank (Robert) 1906-1975, *30:* 94 (Obituary)

Donovan, John 1928- , *29:* 65 (Brief Entry)

Donovan, William. *See* Berkebile, Fred D(onovan), *26:* 37 (Obituary)

Doob, Leonard W(illiam)　1909- ,
　8: 44
Dor, Ana. See Ceder, Georgiana
　Dorcas, 10: 21
Doré, (Louis Christophe Paul)
　Gustave　1832-1883, 19: 92
Doremus, Robert　1913- , 30: 94
Dorian, Edith M(cEwen)　1900-
　5: 58
Dorian, Harry. See Hamilton,
　Charles Harold St. John, 13: 77
Dorian, Marguerite, 7: 68
Dorman, Michael　1932- , 7: 68
Dorson, Richard M(ercer)
　1916-1981, 30: 97
Doss, Helen (Grigsby)　1918- ,
　20: 37
Doss, Margot Patterson, 6: 68
Dottig. See Grider, Dorothy, 31: 75
Doty, Jean Slaughter　1929- ,
　28: 95
Doty, Roy　1922- , 28: 99
Doubtfire, Dianne (Abrams)
　1918- , 29: 65
Dougherty, Charles　1922- ,
　18: 74
Douglas, James McM. See
　Butterworth, W. E., 5: 40
Douglas, Kathryn. See Ewing,
　Kathryn, 20: 42
Douglas, Marjory Stoneman
　1890- , 10: 33
Douglass, Frederick　1817(?)-1895,
　29: 67
Douty, Esther M(orris)　1911-1978,
　8: 44; 23: 68 (Obituary)
Dow, Emily R.　1904- , 10: 33
Dowdell, Dorothy (Florence) Karns
　1910- , 12: 75
Dowden, Anne Ophelia　1907- ,
　7: 69
Dowdey, Landon Gerald　1923- ,
　11: 80
Dowdy, Mrs. Regera. See Gorey,
　Edward St. John, 27: 104
　(Brief Entry); 29: 89
Downer, Marion　1892(?)-1971,
　25: 93
Downey, Fairfax　1893- , 3: 61
Downie, Mary Alice　1934- ,
　13: 32
Doyle, Arthur Conan　1859-1930,
　24: 89
Doyle, Richard　1824-1883, 21: 31
Draco, F. See Davis, Julia, 6: 58
Dragonwagon, Crescent　1952- ,
　11: 81
Drake, Frank. See Hamilton,
　Charles Harold St. John, 13: 77
Drapier, M. B. See Swift, Jonathan,
　19: 244
Drawson, Blair　1943- , 17: 52
Dresang, Eliza (Carolyn
　Timberlake)　1941- , 19: 106
Drescher, Joan E(lizabeth)　1939- ,
　30: 99

Drew, Patricia (Mary)　1938- ,
　15: 100
Drewery, Mary　1918- , 6: 69
Drucker, Malka　1945- , 29: 71
　(Brief Entry)
Drummond, V(iolet) H.　1911- ,
　6: 71
Drummond, Walter. See Silverberg,
　Robert, 13: 206
Drury, Roger W(olcott)　1914- ,
　15: 101
Dryden, Pamela. See Johnston,
　Norma, 29: 116
du Blanc, Daphne. See Groom,
　Arthur William, 10: 53
Du Bois, Shirley Graham
　1907-1977, 24: 105
du Bois, William Pene　1916- ,
　4: 69
DuBose, LaRocque (Russ)　1926- ,
　2: 93
Du Chaillu, Paul (Belloni)
　1831(?)-1903, 26: 68
Ducornet, Erica　1943- , 7: 72
Dudley, Nancy. See Cole, Lois
　Dwight, 10: 26; 26: 43
　(Obituary)
Dudley, Robert. See Baldwin,
　James, 24: 26
Dudley, Ruth H(ubbell)　1905- ,
　11: 82
Dueland, Joy V(ivian), 27: 74
Dugan, Michael (Gray)　1947- ,
　15: 101
Duggan, Alfred Leo　1903-1964,
　25: 95
Duggan, Maurice (Noel)
　1922-1975, 30: 101 (Obituary)
du Jardin, Rosamond (Neal)
　1902-1963, 2: 94
Dulac, Edmund　1882-1953,
　19: 107
Dumas, Alexandre (the elder)
　1802-1870, 18: 74
du Maurier, Daphne　1907- ,
　27: 74
Duncan, Gregory. See McClintock,
　Marshall, 3: 119
Duncan, Jane. See Cameron,
　Elizabeth Jane, 30: 73
　(Obituary)
Duncan, Julia K. [Collective
　pseudonym], 1: 81
Duncan, Lois. See Arquette, Lois
　S., 1: 13
Duncan, Norman　1871-1916,
　YABC 1: 108
Duncombe, Frances (Riker)
　1900- , 25: 97
Dunlop, Agnes M. R., 3: 62
Dunlop, Eileen (Rhona)　1938- ,
　24: 108
Dunn, Judy. See Spangenberg,
　Judith Dunn, 5: 175
Dunn, Mary Lois　1930- , 6: 72
Dunnahoo, Terry　1927- , 7: 73

Dunne, Mary Collins　1914- ,
　11: 83
Dupuy, T(revor) N(evitt)　1916- ,
　4: 71
Durant, John　1902- , 27: 85
Durrell, Gerald (Malcolm)　1925- ,
　8: 46
Du Soe, Robert C.　1892-1958,
　YABC 2: 121
Dutz. See Davis, Mary Octavia,
　6: 59
Duvall, Evelyn Millis　1906- ,
　9: 52
Duvoisin, Roger (Antoine)
　1904-1980, 2: 95; 23: 68
　(Obituary); 30: 101
Dwiggins, Don　1913- , 4: 72
Dwight, Allan. See Cole, Lois
　Dwight, 10: 26; 26: 43
　(Obituary)
Dygard, Thomas J.　1931- ,
　24: 109

E.V.B. See Boyle, Eleanor Vere
　(Gordon), 28: 49
Eagar, Frances　1940- , 11: 85
Eager, Edward (McMaken)
　1911-1964, 17: 54
Eagle, Mike　1942- , 11: 86
Earle, Olive L., 7: 75
Earnshaw, Brian　1929- , 17: 57
Eastman, Charles A(lexander)
　1858-1939, YABC 1: 110
Eastwick, Ivy O., 3: 64
Eaton, George L. See Verral,
　Charles Spain, 11: 255
Eaton, Jeanette　1886-1968,
　24: 110
Eaton, Tom　1940-, 22: 99
Ebel, Alex　1927- , 11: 88
Eber, Dorothy (Margaret) Harley
　1930- , 27: 85
Eberle, Irmengarde　1898-1979,
　2: 97; 23: 68 (Obituary)
Eccles. See Williams, Ferelith
　Eccles, 22: 237
Eckblad, Edith Berven　1923- ,
　23: 68
Eckert, Allan W.　1931- , 27: 86
　(Brief Entry); 29: 71
Eckert, Horst　1931- , 8: 47
Edell, Celeste, 12: 77
Edelman, Lily (Judith)　1915- ,
　22: 100
Edey, Maitland A(rmstrong)
　1910- , 25: 98
Edgeworth, Maria　1767-1849,
　21: 33
Edmonds, I(vy) G(ordon)　1917- ,
　8: 48
Edmonds, Walter D(umaux)
　1903- , 1: 81; 27: 86
Edmund, Sean. See Pringle,
　Laurence, 4: 171

Edsall, Marian S(tickney) 1920- , *8:* 50

Edwards, Audrey 1947- , *31:* 62 (Brief Entry)

Edwards, Bertram. *See* Edwards, Herbert Charles, *12:* 77

Edwards, Bronwen Elizabeth. *See* Rose, Wendy, *12:* 180

Edwards, Cecile (Pepin) 1916- , *25:* 99

Edwards, Dorothy 1914-1982, *4:* 73; *31:* 62 (Obituary)

Edwards, Harvey 1929- , *5:* 59

Edwards, Herbert Charles 1912- , *12:* 77

Edwards, Jane Campbell 1932- , *10:* 34

Edwards, Julie. *See* Andrews, Julie, *7:* 6

Edwards, Julie. *See* Stratemeyer, Edward L., *1:* 208

Edwards, Monica le Doux Newton 1912- , *12:* 78

Edwards, Sally 1929- , *7:* 75

Edwards, Samuel. *See* Gerson, Noel B(ertram), *22:* 118

Eggenberger, David 1918- , *6:* 72

Eggleston, Edward 1837-1902, *27:* 93

Egielski, Richard 1952- , *11:* 89

Egypt, Ophelia Settle 1903- , *16:* 88

Ehrlich, Amy 1942- , *25:* 100

Ehrlich, Bettina (Bauer) 1903- , *1:* 82

Eichberg, James Bandman. *See* Garfield, James B., *6:* 85

Eichenberg, Fritz 1901- , *9:* 53

Eichner, James A. 1927- , *4:* 73

Eifert, Virginia S(nider) 1911-1966, *2:* 99

Einsel, Naiad, *10:* 34

Einsel, Walter 1926- , *10:* 37

Eiseman, Alberta 1925- , *15:* 102

Eisenberg, Azriel 1903- , *12:* 79

Eisner, Will(iam Erwin) 1917- , *31:* 62

Eitzen, Allan 1928- , *9:* 57

Eitzen, Ruth (Carper) 1924- , *9:* 57

Elam, Richard M(ace, Jr.) 1920- , *9:* 57

Elfman, Blossom 1925- , *8:* 51

Elia. *See* Lamb, Charles, *17:* 101

Eliot, Anne. *See* Cole, Lois Dwight, *10:* 26; *26:* 43 (Obituary)

Elisofon, Eliot 1911-1973, *21:* 38 (Obituary)

Elkin, Benjamin 1911- , *3:* 65

Elkins, Dov Peretz 1937- , *5:* 61

Ellacott, S(amuel) E(rnest) 1911- , *19:* 117

Elliott, Sarah M(cCarn) 1930- , *14:* 57

Ellis, Anyon. *See* Rowland-Entwistle, (Arthur) Theodore (Henry), *31:* 145

Ellis, Edward S(ylvester) 1840-1916, *YABC 1:* 116

Ellis, Ella Thorp 1928- , *7:* 76

Ellis, Harry Bearse 1921- , *9:* 58

Ellis, Herbert. *See* Wilson, Lionel, *31:* 186 (Brief Entry)

Ellis, Mel 1912- , *7:* 77

Ellison, Lucile Watkins 1907(?)-1979, *22:* 102 (Obituary)

Ellison, Virginia Howell 1910- , *4:* 74

Ellsberg, Edward 1891- , *7:* 78

Elspeth. *See* Bragdon, Elspeth, *6:* 30

Elting, Mary 1906- , *2:* 100

Elwart, Joan Potter 1927- , *2:* 101

Emberley, Barbara A(nne), *8:* 51

Emberley, Ed(ward Randolph) 1931- , *8:* 52

Embry, Margaret (Jacob) 1919- , *5:* 61

Emerson, Alice B. [Collective pseudonym], *1:* 84

Emerson, William K(eith) 1925- , *25:* 101

Emery, Anne (McGuigan) 1907- , *1:* 84

Emrich, Duncan (Black Macdonald) 1908- , *11:* 90

Emslie, M. L. *See* Simpson, Myrtle L(illias), *14:* 181

Engdahl, Sylvia Louise 1933- , *4:* 75

Engle, Eloise Katherine 1923- , *9:* 60

Englebert, Victor 1933- , *8:* 54

Enright, D(ennis) J(oseph) 1920- , *25:* 102

Enright, Elizabeth 1909-1968, *9:* 61

Epp, Margaret A(gnes), *20:* 38

Epple, Anne Orth 1927- , *20:* 40

Epstein, Anne Merrick 1931- , *20:* 41

Epstein, Beryl (Williams) 1910- , *1:* 85; *31:* 64

Epstein, Perle S(herry) 1938- , *27:* 95

Epstein, Samuel 1909- , *1:* 87; *31:* 66

Erdman, Loula Grace, *1:* 88

Erdoes, Richard 1912- , *28:* 100 (Brief Entry)

Erhard, Walter 1920- , *30:* 107 (Brief Entry)

Erickson, Russell E(verett) 1932- , *27:* 96

Ericson, Walter. *See* Fast, Howard, *7:* 80

Erikson, Mel 1937- , *31:* 69

Erlich, Lillian (Feldman) 1910- , *10:* 38

Ernest, William. *See* Berkebile, Fred D(onovan), *26:* 37 (Obituary)

Ernst, Kathryn (Fitzgerald) 1942- , *25:* 103

Ervin, Janet Halliday 1923- , *4:* 77

Erwin, Will. *See* Eisner, Will(iam Erwin), *31:* 62

Eshmeyer, R(einhart) E(rnst) 1898- , *29:* 73

Estep, Irene (Compton), *5:* 62

Estes, Eleanor 1906- , *7:* 79

Estoril, Jean. *See* Allan, Mabel Esther, *5:* 2

Ets, Marie Hall, *2:* 102

Eunson, Dale 1904- , *5:* 63

Evans, Eva Knox 1905- , *27:* 98

Evans, Katherine (Floyd) 1901-1964, *5:* 64

Evans, Mari, *10:* 39

Evans, Mark, *19:* 118

Evans, Patricia Healy. *See* Carpenter, Patricia, *11:* 43

Evarts, Esther. *See* Benson, Sally, *27:* 32 (Obituary)

Evarts, Hal G. (Jr.) 1915- , *6:* 72

Evernden, Margery 1916- , *5:* 65

Evslin, Bernard 1922- , *28:* 100 (Brief Entry)

Ewen, David 1907- , *4:* 78

Ewing, Juliana (Horatia Gatty) 1841-1885, *16:* 90

Ewing, Kathryn 1921- , *20:* 42

Eyerly, Jeannette Hyde 1908- , *4:* 80

Eyre, Katherine Wigmore 1901-1970, *26:* 71

Fabe, Maxene 1943- , *15:* 103

Faber, Doris 1924- , *3:* 67

Faber, Harold 1919- , *5:* 65

Fabre, Jean Henri (Casimir) 1823-1915, *22:* 102

Facklam, Margery Metz 1927- , *20:* 43

Fadiman, Clifton (Paul) 1904- , *11:* 91

Fair, Sylvia 1933- , *13:* 33

Fairfax-Lucy, Brian (Fulke Cameron-Ramsay) 1898-1974, *6:* 73; *26:* 72 (Obituary)

Fairman, Joan A(lexandra) 1935- , *10:* 41

Faithfull, Gail 1936- , *8:* 55

Falconer, James. *See* Kirkup, James, *12:* 120

Falkner, Leonard 1900- , *12:* 80

Fall, Thomas. *See* Snow, Donald Clifford, *16:* 246

Falls, C(harles) B(uckles) 1874-1960, *27:* 99 (Brief Entry)

Fanning, Leonard M(ulliken) 1888-1967, *5:* 65

Faralla, Dana 1909- , *9:* 62

Faralla, Dorothy W. *See* Faralla, Dana, *9:* 62

Farb, Peter 1929-1980, *12:* 81; *22:* 109 (Obituary)

Farber, Norma 1909- , *25:* 104

Farge, Monique. *See* Grée, Alain, *28:* 118

Farjeon, (Eve) Annabel 1919- , *11:* 93

Farjeon, Eleanor 1881-1965, *2:* 103

Farley, Carol 1936- , *4:* 81

Farley, Walter, *2:* 106

Farnham, Burt. *See* Clifford, Harold B., *10:* 24

Farquhar, Margaret C(utting) 1905- , *13:* 35

Farr, Finis (King) 1904- , *10:* 41

Farrell, Ben. *See* Cebulash, Mel, *10:* 19

Farrington, Benjamin 1891-1974, *20:* 45 (Obituary)

Farrington, Selwyn Kip, Jr. 1904- , *20:* 45

Fassler, Joan (Grace) 1931- , *11:* 94

Fast, Howard 1914- , *7:* 80

Fatchen, Max 1920- , *20:* 45

Father Xavier. *See* Hurwood, Bernhardt J., *12:* 107

Fatigati, (Frances) Evelyn de Buhr 1948- , *24:* 112

Fatio, Louise, *6:* 75

Faulhaber, Martha 1926- , *7:* 82

Faulkner, Anne Irvin 1906- , *23:* 70

Faulkner, Nancy. *See* Faulkner, Anne Irvin, *23:* 70

Fax, Elton Clay 1909- , *25:* 106

Feagles, Anita MacRae, *9:* 63

Feague, Mildred H. 1915- , *14:* 59

Fecher, Constance 1911- , *7:* 83

Feder, Paula (Kurzband) 1935- , *26:* 72

Feelings, Muriel (Grey) 1938- , *16:* 104

Feelings, Thomas 1933- , *8:* 55

Feelings, Tom. *See* Feelings, Thomas, *8:* 55

Feiffer, Jules 1929- , *8:* 57

Feikema, Feike. *See* Manfred, Frederick F(eikema), *30:* 150

Feil, Hila 1942- , *12:* 81

Feilen, John. *See* May, Julian, *11:* 175

Feldman, Anne (Rodgers) 1939- , *19:* 121

Fellows, Muriel H., *10:* 41

Felsen, Henry Gregor 1916- , *1:* 89

Felton, Harold William 1902- , *1:* 90

Felton, Ronald Oliver 1909- , *3:* 67

Fenner, Carol 1929- , *7:* 84

Fenner, Phyllis R(eid) 1899-1982, *1:* 91; *29:* 73 (Obituary)

Fenten, Barbara D(oris) 1935- , *26:* 73

Fenten, D. X. 1932- , *4:* 82

Fenton, Carroll Lane 1900-1969, *5:* 66

Fenton, Edward 1917- , *7:* 86

Fenton, Mildred Adams 1899- , *21:* 38

Fenwick, Patti. *See* Grider, Dorothy, *31:* 75

Feravolo, Rocco Vincent 1922- , *10:* 42

Ferber, Edna 1887-1968, *7:* 87

Ferguson, Bob. *See* Ferguson, Robert Bruce, *13:* 35

Ferguson, Robert Bruce 1927- , *13:* 35

Fergusson, Erna 1888-1964, *5:* 67

Fermi, Laura (Capon) 1907-1977, *6:* 78; *28:* 100 (Obituary)

Fern, Eugene A. 1919- , *10:* 43

Ferris, Helen Josephine 1890-1969, *21:* 39

Ferris, James Cody [Collective pseudonym], *1:* 92. *See also* McFarlane, Leslie, *31:* 133; Stratemeyer, Edward L., *1:* 208

Fetz, Ingrid 1915- , *30:* 107

Fiammenghi, Gioia 1929- , *9:* 64

Fiarotta, Noel 1944- , *15:* 104

Fiarotta, Phyllis 1942- , *15:* 105

Fichter, George S. 1922- , *7:* 92

Fidler, Kathleen, *3:* 68

Fiedler, Jean, *4:* 83

Field, Edward 1924- , *8:* 58

Field, Elinor Whitney 1889-1980, *28:* 100 (Obituary)

Field, Eugene 1850-1895, *16:* 105

Field, Rachel (Lyman) 1894-1942, *15:* 106

Fife, Dale (Odile) 1910- , *18:* 110

Fighter Pilot, A. *See* Johnston, H(ugh) A(nthony) S(tephen), *14:* 87

Figueroa, Pablo 1938- , *9:* 66

Fijan, Carol 1918- , *12:* 82

Fillmore, Parker H(oysted) 1878-1944, *YABC 1:* 121

Finder, Martin. *See* Salzmann, Siegmund, *25:* 207

Fine, Anne 1947- , *29:* 73

Fink, William B(ertrand) 1916- , *22:* 109

Finke, Blythe F(oote) 1922- , *26:* 73

Finkel, George (Irvine) 1909-1975, *8:* 59

Finlay, Winifred 1910- , *23:* 71

Finlayson, Ann 1925- , *8:* 61

Firmin, Charlotte 1954- , *29:* 74

Firmin, Peter 1928- , *15:* 113

Fischbach, Julius 1894- , *10:* 43

Fisher, Aileen (Lucia) 1906- , *1:* 92; *25:* 108

Fisher, Clavin C(argill) 1912- , *24:* 113

Fisher, Dorothy Canfield 1879-1958, *YABC 1:* 122

Fisher, John (Oswald Hamilton) 1909- , *15:* 115

Fisher, Laura Harrison 1934- , *5:* 67

Fisher, Leonard Everett 1924- , *4:* 84

Fisher, Margery (Turner) 1913- , *20:* 47

Fisk, Nicholas 1923- , *25:* 111

Fitch, Clarke. *See* Sinclair, Upton (Beall), *9:* 168

Fitch, John, IV. *See* Cormier, Robert Edmund, *10:* 28

Fitschen, Dale 1937- , *20:* 48

Fitzalan, Roger. *See* Trevor, Elleston, *28:* 207

Fitzgerald, Captain Hugh. *See* Baum L(yman) Frank, *18:* 7

Fitzgerald, Edward Earl 1919- , *20:* 49

Fitzgerald, F(rancis) A(nthony) 1940- , *15:* 115

Fitzgerald, John D(ennis) 1907- , *20:* 50

Fitzhardinge, Joan Margaret 1912- , *2:* 107

Fitzhugh, Louise 1928-1974, *1:* 94; *24:* 114 (Obituary)

Flack, Marjorie 1899-1958, *YABC 2:* 123

Flash Flood. *See* Robinson, Jan M., *6:* 194

Fleischer, Max 1889-1972, *30:* 109 (Brief Entry)

Fleischhauer-Hardt, Helga 1936- , *30:* 109

Fleischman, (Albert) Sid(ney) 1920- , *8:* 61

Fleming, Alice Mulcahey 1928- , *9:* 67

Fleming, Ian (Lancaster) 1908-1964, *9:* 67

Fleming, Thomas J(ames) 1927- , *8:* 64

Fletcher, Charlie May 1897- , *3:* 70

Fletcher, Colin 1922- , *28:* 100

Fletcher, Helen Jill 1911- , *13:* 36

Fleur, Anne 1901- , *31:* 70 (Brief Entry)

Flexner, James Thomas 1908- , *9:* 70

Flitner, David P. 1949- , *7:* 92

Floethe, Louise Lee 1913- , *4:* 87

Floethe, Richard 1901- , *4:* 89

Floherty, John Joseph 1882-1964, *25:* 113

Flood, Flash. *See* Robinson, Jan M., *6:* 194

Flora, James (Royer) 1914- , *1:* 95; *30:* 110

Florian, Douglas 1950- , *19:* 122

Flory, Jane Trescott 1917- , *22:* 110

Floyd, Gareth 1940- , *31:* 70 (Brief Entry)

Flynn, Barbara 1928- , *9:* 71

Flynn, Jackson. *See* Shirreffs, Gordon D., *11:* 207

Fodor, Ronald V(ictor) 1944- , *25:* 115

Foley, (Anna) Bernice Williams 1902- , *28:* 101

Foley, Rae. *See* Denniston, Elinore, *24:* 85 (Obituary)

Folkard, Charles James 1878-1963, *28:* 103 (Brief Entry)

Follett, Helen (Thomas) 1884(?)-1970, *27:* 99 (Obituary)

Folsom, Franklin (Brewster) 1907- , *5:* 67

Fooner, Michael, *22:* 112

Forberg, Ati 1925- , *22:* 113

Forbes, Cabot L. *See* Hoyt, Edwin P(almer), Jr., *28:* 132

Forbes, Esther 1891-1967, *2:* 108

Forbes, Graham B. [Collective pseudonym], *1:* 97

Forbes, Kathryn. *See* McLean, Kathryn (Anderson), *9:* 140

Ford, Albert Lee. *See* Stratemeyer, Edward L., *1:* 208

Ford, Elbur. *See* Hibbert, Eleanor, *2:* 134

Ford, George (Jr.), *31:* 70

Ford, Hilary. *See* Youd, (Christopher) Samuel, *30:* 222 (Brief Entry)

Ford, Hildegarde. *See* Morrison, Velma Ford, *21:* 110

Ford, Marcia. *See* Radford, Ruby L., *6:* 186

Ford, Nancy K(effer) 1906-1961, *29:* 75 (Obituary)

Foreman, Michael 1938- , *2:* 110

Forest, Antonia, *29:* 75

Forester, C(ecil) S(cott) 1899-1966, *13:* 38

Forman, Brenda 1936- , *4:* 90

Forman, James Douglas 1932- , *8:* 64

Forrest, Sybil. *See* Markun, Patricia M(aloney), *15:* 189

Forsee, (Frances) Aylesa, *1:* 97

Fortnum, Peggy 1919- , *26:* 75

Foster, Doris Van Liew 1899- , *10:* 44

Foster, E(lizabeth) C(onnell) 1902- , *9:* 71

Foster, Elizabeth 1905-1963, *10:* 45

Foster, Elizabeth Vincent 1902- , *12:* 82

Foster, F. Blanche 1919- , *11:* 95

Foster, G(eorge) Allen 1907-1969, *26:* 79

Foster, Genevieve (Stump) 1893-1979, *2:* 111; *23:* 73 (Obituary)

Foster, Hal. *See* Foster, Harold Rudolf, *31:* 72 (Obituary)

Foster, Harold Rudolf 1892-1982, *31:* 72 (Obituary)

Foster, John T(homas) 1925- , *8:* 65

Foster, Laura Louise 1918- , *6:* 78

Foster, Margaret Lesser 1899-1979, *21:* 43 (Obituary)

Foster, Marian Curtis 1909-1978, *23:* 73

Fourth Brother, The. *See* Aung, (Maung) Htin, *21:* 5

Fowke, Edith (Margaret) 1913- , *14:* 59

Fowles, John 1926- , *22:* 114

Fox, Charles Philip 1913- , *12:* 83

Fox, Eleanor. *See* St. John, Wylly Folk, *10:* 132

Fox, Fontaine Talbot, Jr. 1884-1964, *23:* 75 (Obituary)

Fox, Fred 1903(?)-1981, *27:* 100 (Obituary)

Fox, Freeman. *See* Hamilton, Charles Harold St. John, *13:* 77

Fox, Larry, *30:* 113

Fox, Lorraine 1922-1976, *11:* 96; *27:* 100 (Obituary)

Fox, Michael Wilson 1937- , *15:* 117

Fox, Paula 1923- , *17:* 59

Fradin, Dennis Brindel 1945- , *29:* 77

Frances, Miss. *See* Horwich, Frances R., *11:* 142

Franchere, Ruth, *18:* 111

Francis, Charles. *See* Holme, Bryan, *26:* 123

Francis, Dorothy Brenner 1926- , *10:* 46

Francis, Pamela (Mary) 1926- , *11:* 97

Francois, André 1915- , *25:* 116

Francoise. *See* Seignobosc, Francoise, *21:* 145

Frank, Josette 1893- , *10:* 47

Frank, R., Jr. *See* Ross, Frank (Xavier), Jr., *28:* 175

Frankau, Mary Evelyn 1899- , *4:* 90

Frankel, Bernice, *9:* 72

Frankenberg, Robert 1911- , *22:* 115

Franklin, Harold 1920- , *13:* 53

Franklin, Max. *See* Deming, Richard, *24:* 83

Franklin, Steve. *See* Stevens, Franklin, *6:* 206

Franzén, Nils-Olof 1916- , *10:* 47

Frasconi, Antonio 1919- , *6:* 79

Fraser, Betty. *See* Fraser, Elizabeth Marr, *31:* 72

Fraser, Elizabeth Marr 1928- , *31:* 72

Frazier, Neta Lohnes, *7:* 94

Freed, Alvyn M. 1913- , *22:* 117

Freedman, Benedict 1919- , *27:* 100

Freedman, Nancy 1920- , *27:* 101

Freedman, Russell (Bruce) 1929- , *16:* 115

Freeman, Barbara C(onstance) 1906- , *28:* 103

Freeman, Don 1908-1978, *17:* 60

Freeman, Ira M(aximilian) 1905- , *21:* 43

Freeman, Lucy (Greenbaum) 1916- , *24:* 114

Freeman, Mae (Blacker) 1907- , *25:* 117

Fregosi, Claudia (Anne Marie) 1946- , *24:* 116

French, Allen 1870-1946, *YABC 1:* 133

French, Dorothy Kayser 1926- , *5:* 69

French, Fiona 1944- , *6:* 81

French, Kathryn. *See* Mosesson, Gloria R(ubin), *24:* 153

French, Paul. *See* Asimov, Isaac, *1:* 15; *26:* 23

Freund, Rudolf 1915-1969, *28:* 104 (Brief Entry)

Frewer, Glyn 1931- , *11:* 98

Frick, C. H. *See* Irwin, Constance Frick, *6:* 119

Frick, Constance. *See* Irwin, Constance Frick, *6:* 119

Friedlander, Joanne K(ohn) 1930- , *9:* 73

Friedman, Estelle 1920- , *7:* 95

Friedlich, Dick. *See* Friedlich, Richard J., *11:* 99

Friedlich, Richard J. 1909- , *11:* 99

Friermood, Elisabeth Hamilton 1903- , *5:* 69

Friis, Babbis. *See* Friis-Baastad, Babbis, *7:* 95

Friis-Baastad, Babbis 1921-1970, *7:* 95

Frimmer, Steven 1928- , *31:* 74

Friskey, Margaret Richards 1901- , *5:* 72

Fritz, Jean (Guttery) 1915- , *1:* 98; *29:* 79

Froissart, Jean 1338(?)-1410(?), *28:* 104

Froman, Elizabeth Hull 1920-1975, *10:* 49

Froman, Robert (Winslow) 1917- , *8:* 67

Fromm, Lilo 1928- , *29:* 84
Frost, A(rthur) B(urdett) 1851-1928, *19:* 122
Frost, Erica. *See* Supraner, Robyn, *20:* 182
Frost, Lesley 1899- , *14:* 61
Frost, Robert (Lee) 1874-1963, *14:* 63
Fry, Rosalie 1911- , *3:* 71
Fuchs, Erich 1916- , *6:* 84
Fujikawa, Gyo, *30:* 113 (Brief Entry)
Fujita, Tamao 1905- , *7:* 98
Fujiwara, Michiko 1946- , *15:* 120
Fuka, Vladimir 1926-1977, *27:* 102 (Obituary)
Fuller, Catherine L(euthold) 1916- , *9:* 73
Fuller, Edmund (Maybank) 1914- , *21:* 45
Fuller, Iola. *See* McCoy, Iola Fuller, *3:* 120
Fuller, Lois Hamilton 1915- , *11:* 99
Fuller, Margaret. *See* Ossoli, Sarah Margaret (Fuller) marchesa d', *25:* 186
Funk, Thompson. *See* Funk, Tom, *7:* 98
Funk, Tom 1911- , *7:* 98
Funke, Lewis 1912- , *11:* 100
Furchgott, Terry 1948- , *29:* 86
Furukawa, Toshi 1924- , *24:* 117
Fyleman, Rose 1877-1957, *21:* 46

Gackenbach, Dick, *30:* 113 (Brief Entry)
Gaeddert, Lou Ann (Bigge) 1931- , *20:* 58
Gàg, Flavia 1907-1979, *24:* 119 (Obituary)
Gág, Wanda (Hazel) 1893-1946, *YABC 1:* 135
Gage, Wilson. *See* Steele, Mary Q., *3:* 211
Gagliardo, Ruth Garver 1895(?)-1980, *22:* 118 (Obituary)
Galdone, Paul 1914- , *17:* 69
Galinsky, Ellen 1942- , *23:* 75
Gallant, Roy (Arthur) 1924- , *4:* 91
Gallico, Paul 1897-1976, *13:* 53
Galt, Thomas Franklin, Jr. 1908- , *5:* 72
Galt, Tom. *See* Galt, Thomas Franklin, Jr., *5:* 72
Gamerman, Martha 1941- , *15:* 121
Gannett, Ruth Stiles 1923- , *3:* 73
Gannon, Robert (Haines) 1931- , *8:* 68

Gantos, Jack. *See* Gantos, John (Bryan), Jr., *20:* 59
Gantos, John (Bryan), Jr. 1951- , *20:* 59
Garbutt, Bernard 1900- , *31:* 74 (Brief Entry)
Gard, Joyce. *See* Reeves, Joyce, *17:* 158
Gard, Robert Edward 1910- , *18:* 113
Gardam, Jane 1928- , *28:* 107 (Brief Entry)
Garden, Nancy 1938- , *12:* 85
Gardner, Dic. *See* Gardner, Richard, *24:* 119
Gardner, Jeanne LeMonnier, *5:* 73
Gardner, John Champlin, Jr. 1933-1982, *31:* 74 (Obituary)
Gardner, Martin 1914- , *16:* 117
Gardner, Richard 1931- , *24:* 119
Gardner, Richard A. 1931- , *13:* 84
Garelick, May, *19:* 130
Garfield, James B. 1881- , *6:* 85
Garfield, Leon 121- , *1:* 99
Garis, Howard R(oger) 1873-1962, *13:* 67
Garner, Alan 1934- , *18:* 114
Garnett, Eve C. R., *3:* 75
Garraty, John A. 1920- , *23:* 76
Garrett, Helen 1895- , *21:* 48
Garrigue, Sheila 1931- , *21:* 49
Garrison, Barbara 1931- , *19:* 132
Garrison, Frederick. *See* Sinclair, Upton (Beall), *9:* 168
Garrison, Webb B(lack) 1919- , *25:* 119
Garst, Doris Shannon 1894- , *1:* 100
Garst, Shannon. *See* Garst, Doris Shannon, *1:* 100
Garthwaite, Marion H. 1893- , *7:* 100
Garton, Malinda D(ean) (?)-1976, *26:* 80 (Obituary)
Gates, Doris 1901- , *1:* 102
Gates, Frieda 1933- , *26:* 80
Gathorne-Hardy, Jonathan G. 1933- , *26:* 81
Gatty, Juliana Horatia. *See* Ewing, Juliana (Horatia Gatty), *16:* 90
Gatty, Margaret Scott 1809-1873, *27:* 103 (Brief Entry)
Gauch, Patricia Lee 1934- , *26:* 81
Gault, Frank 1926- , *30:* 113 (Brief Entry)
Gault, William Campbell 1910- , *8:* 69
Gaver, Becky. *See* Gaver, Rebecca, *20:* 60
Gaver, Rebecca 1952- , *20:* 60
Gay, Francis. *See* Gee, H(erbert) L(eslie), *26:* 83 (Obituary)
Gay, Kathlyn 1930- , *9:* 74

Gay, Zhenya 1906-1978, *19:* 134
Gee, H(erbert) L(eslie) 1901-1977, *26:* 83 (Obituary)
Geipel, Eileen 1932- , *30:* 114
Geis, Darlene, *7:* 101
Geisel, Helen 1898-1967, *26:* 83
Geisel, Theodor Seuss 1904- , *1:* 104; *28:* 107
Geldart, William 1936- , *15:* 121
Gelinas, Paul J. 1911- , *10:* 49
Gelman, Steve 1934- , *3:* 75
Gemming, Elizabeth 1932- , *11:* 104
Gendel, Evelyn W. 1916(?)-1977, *27:* 103 (Obituary)
Gentleman, David 1930- , *7:* 102
George, Jean Craighead 1919- , *2:* 112
George, John L(othar) 1916- , *2:* 114
George, S(idney) C(harles) 1898- , *11:* 104
George, W(illiam) Lloyd 1900(?)-1975, *30:* 115 (Obituary)
Georgiou, Constantine 1927- , *7:* 102
Geras, Adele (Daphne) 1944- , *23:* 76
Gergely, Tibor 1900-1978, *20:* 61 (Obituary)
Geringer, Laura 1948- , *29:* 87
Gerson, Noel B(ertram) 1914- , *22:* 118
Gessner, Lynne 1919- , *16:* 119
Gewe, Raddory. *See* Gorey, Edward St. John, *29:* 89
Gibbons, Gail 1944- , *23:* 77
Gibbs, Alonzo (Lawrence) 1915- , *5:* 74
Gibbs, (Cecilia) May 1877-1969, *27:* 103 (Obituary)
Gibson, Josephine. *See* Joslin, Sesyle, *2:* 158
Gidal, Sonia 1922- , *2:* 115
Gidal, Tim N(ahum) 1909- , *2:* 116
Giegling, John A(llan) 1935- , *17:* 75
Gilbert, Harriett 1948- , *30:* 115
Gilbert, (Agnes) Joan (Sewell) 1931- , *10:* 50
Gilbert, Nan. *See* Gilbertson, Mildred, *2:* 116
Gilbert, Sara (Dulaney) 1943- , *11:* 105
Gilbertson, Mildred Geiger 1908- , *2:* 116
Gilbreath, Alice (Thompson) 1921- , *12:* 87
Gilbreth, Frank B., Jr. 1911- , *2:* 117
Gilfond, Henry, *2:* 118
Gilge, Jeanette 1924- , *22:* 121
Gill, Derek L(ewis) T(heodore) 1919- , *9:* 75

Gill, Margery Jean 1925- , 22: 122

Gillett, Mary, 7: 103

Gillette, Henry Sampson 1915- , 14: 71

Gilman, Dorothy. See Butters, Dorothy Gilman, 5: 39

Gilman, Esther 1925- , 15: 123

Gilmore, Iris 1900- , 22: 123

Gilson, Barbara. See Gilson, Charles James Louis, YABC 2: 124

Gilson, Charles James Louis 1878-1943, YABC 2: 124

Ginsburg, Mirra, 6: 86

Giovanni, Nikki 1943- , 24: 120

Giovanopoulos, Paul 1939- , 7: 104

Gipson, Frederick B. 1908-1973, 2: 118; 24: 121 (Obituary)

Girion, Barbara 1937- , 26: 84

Gittings, Jo Manton 1919- , 3: 76

Gittings, Robert 1911- , 6: 88

Gladstone, Gary 1935- , 12: 88

Gladwin, William Zachary. See Zollinger, Gulielma, 27: 232 (Brief Entry)

Glaser, Dianne E(lizabeth) 1937- : 31: 74 (Brief Entry)

Glaser, Milton 1929- , 11: 106

Glaspell, Susan 1882-1948, YABC 2: 125

Glauber, Uta (Heil) 1936- , 17: 75

Glazer, Tom 1914- , 9: 76

Gleasner, Diana (Cottle) 1936- , 29: 88

Gleason, Judith 1929- , 24: 121

Glendinning, Richard 1917- , 24: 121

Glendinning, Sally. See Glendinning, Sara W(ilson), 24: 122

Glendinning, Sara W(ilson) 1913- , 24: 122

Gles, Margaret Breitmaier 1940- , 22: 124

Glick, Carl (Cannon) 1890-1971, 14: 72

Glick, Virginia Kirkus 1893-1980, 23: 78 (Obituary)

Gliewe, Unada 1927- , 3: 77

Glines, Carroll V(ane), Jr. 1920- , 19: 137

Glovach, Linda 1947- , 7: 105

Glubok, Shirley, 6: 89

Gluck, Felix 1924(?)-1981, 25: 120 (Obituary)

Glynne-Jones, William 1907- , 11: 107

Goble, Dorothy, 26: 85

Goble, Paul 1933- , 25: 120

Godden, Rumer 1907- , 3: 79

Gode, Alexander. See Gode von Aesch, Alexander (Gottfried Friedrich), 14: 74

Gode von Aesch, Alexander (Gottfried Friedrich) 1906-1970, 14: 74

Godfrey, William. See Youd, (Christopher) Samuel, 30: 222 (Obituary)

Goettel, Elinor 1930- , 12: 89

Goetz, Delia 1898- , 22: 125

Goffstein, M(arilyn) B(rooke) 1940- , 8: 70

Golann, Cecil Paige 1921- , 11: 109

Golbin, Andrée 1923- , 15: 124

Gold, Phyllis 1941- , 21: 50

Gold, Sharlya, 9: 77

Goldberg, Herbert S. 1926- , 25: 122

Goldberg, Stan J. 1939- , 26: 87

Goldfeder, Cheryl. See Pahz, Cheryl Suzanne, 11: 189

Goldfeder, Jim. See Pahz, James Alon, 11: 190

Goldfrank, Helen Colodny 1912- , 6: 89

Goldin, Augusta 1906- , 13: 72

Goldsborough, June 1923- , 19: 138

Goldsmith, Howard 1943- , 24: 123

Goldsmith, Oliver 1728-1774, 26: 87

Goldstein, Philip 1910- , 23: 79

Goldston, Robert (Conroy) 1927- , 6: 90

Goll, Reinhold W(eimar) 1897- , 26: 93

Gonzalez, Gloria 1940- , 23: 80

Goodall, John S(trickland) 1908- , 4: 92

Goode, Diane 1949- , 15: 125

Goodman, Elaine 1930- , 9: 78

Goodman, Walter 1927- , 9: 78

Goodrich, Samuel Griswold 1793-1860, 23: 82

Goodwin, Hal. See Goodwin, Harold Leland, 13: 73

Goodwin, Harold Leland 1914- , 13: 73

Goossen, Agnes. See Epp, Margaret A(gnes), 20: 38

Gordon, Bernard Ludwig 1931- , 27: 103

Gordon, Colonel H. R. See Ellis, Edward S(ylvester), YABC 1: 116

Gordon, Dorothy 1893-1970, 20: 61

Gordon, Esther S(aranga) 1935- , 10: 50

Gordon, Frederick [Collective pseudonym], 1: 106

Gordon, Hal. See Goodwin, Harold Leland, 13: 73

Gordon, John 1925- , 6: 90

Gordon, Lew. See Baldwin, Gordon C., 12: 30

Gordon, Margaret (Anna) 1939- , 9: 79

Gordon, Mildred 1912-1979, 24: 124 (Obituary)

Gordon, Selma. See Lanes, Selma G., 3: 96

Gordon, Sol 1923- , 11: 111

Gordon, Stewart. See Shirreffs, Gordon D., 11: 207

Gordons, The [Joint pseudonym]. See Gordon, Mildred, 24: 124 (Obituary)

Gorelick, Molly C. 1920- , 9: 80

Gorey, Edward St. John 1925- , 27: 104 (Brief Entry); 29: 89

Gorham, Michael. See Folsom, Franklin, 5: 67

Gorsline, Douglas (Warner) 1913- , 11: 112

Gorsline, (Sally) Marie 1928- , 28: 116

Gorsline, S. M. See Gorsline, (Sally) Marie, 28: 116

Goryan, Sirak. See Saroyan, William, 23: 210; 24: 181 (Obituary)

Gottlieb, Bill. See Gottlieb, William P(aul), 24: 124

Gottlieb, Gerald 1923- , 7: 106

Gottlieb, William P(aul), 24: 124

Goudey, Alice E. 1898- , 20: 64

Goudge, Elizabeth 1900- , 2: 119

Gough, Catherine 1931- , 24: 125

Goulart, Ron 1933- , 6: 92

Gould, Jean R(osalind) 1919- , 11: 114

Gould, Lilian 1920- , 6: 92

Gould, Marilyn 1923- , 15: 127

Govan, Christine Noble 1898- , 9: 80

Govern, Elaine 1939- , 26: 94

Graber, Alexander, 7: 106

Graber, Richard (Fredrick) 1927- , 26: 95

Grabianski, Janusz 1929-1976, 30: 115 (Obituary)

Graff, Polly Anne. See Colver, Anne, 7: 54

Graff, (S.) Stewart 1908- , 9: 82

Graham, Ada 1931- , 11: 115

Graham, Eleanor 1896- , 18: 116

Graham, Frank, Jr. 1925- , 11: 116

Graham, John 1926- , 11: 117

Grahm, Kennon. See Harrison, David Lee, 26: 101

Graham, Lorenz B(ell) 1902- , 2: 122

Graham, Margaret Bloy 1920- , 11: 119

Graham, Robin Lee 1949- , 7: 107

Graham, Shirley. See Du Bois, Shirley Graham, 24: 105

Grahame, Kenneth 1859-1932, YABC 1: 144

Gramatky, Hardie 1907-1979, *1:* 107; *23:* 89 (Obituary); *30:* 116

Grange, Peter. *See* Nicole, Christopher Robin, *5:* 141

Granger, Margaret Jane 1925(?)-1977, *27:* 105 (Obituary)

Granger, Peggy. *See* Granger, Margaret Jane, *27:* 105 (Obituary)

Granstaff, Bill 1925- , *10:* 51

Grant, Bruce 1893-1977, *5:* 75; *25:* 122 (Obituary)

Grant, Eva 1907- , *7:* 108

Grant, Evva H. 1913-1977, *27:* 105 (Obituary)

Grant, Gordon 1875-1962, *25:* 123

Grant, (Alice) Leigh 1947- , *10:* 52

Grant, Matthew C. *See* May, Julian, *11:* 175

Grant, Myrna (Lois) 1934- , *21:* 51

Grant, Neil 1938- , *14:* 75

Gravel, Fern. *See* Hall, James Norman, *21:* 54

Graves, Charles Parlin 1911-1972, *4:* 94

Gray, Elizabeth Janet 1902- , *6:* 93

Gray, Genevieve S. 1920- , *4:* 95

Gray, Jenny. *See* Gray, Genevieve S., *4:* 95

Gray, Nicholas Stuart 1922-1981, *4:* 96; *27:* 105 (Obituary)

Gray, Patricia, *7:* 110

Gray, Patsey. *See* Gray, Patricia, *7:* 110

Grayland, V. Merle. *See* Grayland, Valerie, *7:* 111

Grayland, Valerie, *7:* 111

Great Comte, The. *See* Hawkesworth, Eric, *13:* 94

Greaves, Margaret 1914- , *7:* 113

Grée, Alain 1936- , *28:* 118

Green, Adam. *See* Weisgard, Leonard, *2:* 263; *30:* 198

Green, D. *See* Casewit, Curtis, *4:* 43

Green, Hannah. *See* Greenberg, Joanne (Goldenberg), *25:* 127

Green, Jane 1937- , *9:* 82

Green, Mary Moore 1906- , *11:* 120

Green, Morton 1937- , *8:* 71

Green, Norma B(erger) 1925- , *11:* 120

Green, Phyllis 1932- , *20:* 65

Green, Roger (Gilbert) Lancelyn 1918- , *2:* 123

Green, Sheila Ellen 1934- , *8:* 72

Greenaway, Kate 1846-1901, *YABC 2:* 129

Greenberg, Harvey R. 1935- , *5:* 77

Greenberg, Joanne (Goldenberg) 1932- , *25:* 127

Greene, Bette 1934- , *8:* 73

Greene, Carla 1916- , *1:* 108

Greene, Constance C(larke) 1924- , *11:* 121

Greene, Ellin 1927- , *23:* 89

Greene, Graham 1904- , *20:* 66

Greene, Wade 1933- , *11:* 122

Greenfeld, Howard, *19:* 140

Greenfield, Eloise 1929- , *19:* 141

Greening, Hamilton. *See* Hamilton, Charles Harold St. John, *13:* 77

Greenleaf, Barbara Kaye 1942- , *6:* 95

Greenwald, Sheila. *See* Green, Sheila Ellen, *8:* 72

Gregg, Walter H(arold) 1919- , *20:* 75

Gregori, Leon 1919- , *15:* 129

Gregorian, Joyce Ballou 1946- , *30:* 124

Gregorowski, Christopher 1940- , *30:* 125

Greisman, Joan Ruth 1937- , *31:* 74

Grendon, Stephen. *See* Derleth, August (William), *5:* 54

Grenville, Pelham. *See* Wodehouse, P(elham) G(renville), *22:* 241

Gretz, Susanna 1937- , *7:* 114

Gretzer, John, *18:* 117

Grey, Jerry 1926- , *11:* 123

Grey Owl. *See* Belaney, Archibald Stansfeld, *24:* 39

Gri. *See* Denney, Diana, *25:* 90

Grice, Frederick 1910- , *6:* 96

Grider, Dorothy 1915- , *31:* 75

Gridley, Marion E(leanor) 1906-1974, *26:* 95 (Obituary)

Grieder, Walter 1924- , *9:* 83

Griese, Arnold A(lfred) 1921- , *9:* 84

Grifalconi, Ann 1929- , *2:* 125

Griffin, Gillett Good 1928- , *26:* 95

Griffith, Jeannette. *See* Eyerly, Jeanette, *4:* 80

Griffiths, G(ordon) D(ouglas) 1910-1973, *20:* 75 (Obituary)

Griffiths, Helen 1939- , *5:* 77

Grimm, Jacob Ludwig Karl 1785-1863, *22:* 126

Grimm, Wilhelm Karl 1786-1859, *22:* 126

Grimm, William C(arey) 1907- , *14:* 75

Grimshaw, Nigel (Gilroy) 1925- , *23:* 91

Grimsley, Gordon. *See* Groom, Arthur William, *10:* 53

Gringhuis, Dirk. *See* Gringhuis, Richard H. *6:* 97; *25:* 128 (Obituary)

Gringhuis, Richard H. 1918-1974, *6:* 97; *25:* 128 (Obituary)

Grinnell, George Bird 1849-1938, *16:* 121

Gripe, Maria (Kristina) 1923- , *2:* 126

Groch, Judith (Goldstein) 1929- , *25:* 128

Grode, Redway. *See* Gorey, Edward St. John, *27:* 104 (Brief Entry)

Grohskopf, Bernice, *7:* 114

Grol, Lini Richards 1913- , *9:* 85

Grollman, Earl A. 1925- , *22:* 152

Groom, Arthur William 1898-1964, *10:* 53

Gross, Sarah Chokla 1906-1976, *9:* 86; *26:* 96 (Obituary)

Grossman, Nancy 1940- , *29:* 101

Grossman, Robert 1940- , *11:* 124

Groth, John 1908- , *21:* 53

Gruenberg, Sidonie M(atsner) 1881-1974, *2:* 127; *27:* 105 (Obituary)

Guck, Dorothy 1913- , *27:* 105

Gugliotta, Bobette 1918- , *7:* 116

Guillaume, Jeanette G. (Flierl) 1899- , *8:* 74

Guillot, Rene 1900-1969, *7:* 117

Gundrey, Elizabeth 1924- , *23:* 91

Gunston, Bill. *See* Gunston, William Tudor, *9:* 88

Gunston, William Tudor 1927- , *9:* 88

Gunterman, Bertha Lisette 1886(?)-1975, *27:* 106 (Obituary)

Gunther, John 1901-1970, *2:* 129

Gurko, Leo 1914- , *9:* 88

Gurko, Miriam, *9:* 89

Gustafson, Sarah R. *See* Riedman, Sarah R., *1:* 183

Guthrie, Anne 1890-1979, *28:* 123

Gutman, Naham 1899(?)-1981, *25:* 129 (Obituary)

Guy, Rosa (Cuthbert) 1928- , *14:* 77

Gwynne, Fred 1926- , *27:* 106 (Brief Entry)

Haas, Irene 1929- , *17:* 76

Habenstreit, Barbara 1937- , *5:* 78

Haber, Louis 1910- , *12:* 90

Hader, Berta (Hoerner) 1891(?)-1976, *16:* 122

Hader, Elmer (Stanley) 1889-1973, *16:* 124

Hadley, Franklin. *See* Winterbotham, R(ussell) R(obert), *10:* 198

Hafner, Marylin 1925- , *7:* 119

Hager, Alice Rogers 1894-1969, *26:* 96 (Obituary)

Haggard, H(enry) Rider
   1856-1925, *16:* 129
Haggerty, James J(oseph) 1920-
   5: 78
Hagon, Priscilla. *See* Allan, Mabel
   Esther, *5:* 2
Hahn, Emily 1905- , *3:* 81
Hahn, Hannelore 1926- , *8:* 74
Hahn, James (Sage) 1947- , *9:* 90
Hahn, (Mona) Lynn 1949- , *9:* 91
Haig-Brown, Roderick (Langmere)
   1908-1976, *12:* 90
Haight, Anne Lyon 1895-1977,
   30: 126 (Obituary)
Haines, Gail Kay 1943- , *11:* 124
Haining, Peter 1940- , *14:* 77
Haldane, Roger John 1945- ,
   13: 75
Hale, Edward Everett 1822-1909,
   16: 143
Hale, Helen. *See* Mulcahy, Lucille
   Burnett, *12:* 155
Hale, Irina 1932- , *26:* 96
Hale, Kathleen 1898- , *17:* 78
Hale, Linda 1929- , *6:* 99
Hale, Lucretia Peabody
   1820-1900, *26:* 99
Hale, Nancy 1908- , *31:* 77
Haley, Gail E(inhart) 1939- ,
   28: 123 (Brief Entry)
Hall, Adam. *See* Trevor, Elleston,
   28: 207
Hall, Adele 1910- , *7:* 120
Hall, Anna Gertrude 1882-1967,
   8: 75
Hall, Borden. *See* Yates, Raymond
   F(rancis), *31:* 189
Hall, Brian P(atrick) 1935- ,
   31: 78
Hall, Donald (Andrew, Jr.)
   1928- , *23:* 92
Hall, Elvajean, *6:* 100
Hall, James Norman 1887-1951,
   21: 54
Hall, Jesse. *See* Boesen, Victor,
   16: 53
Hall, Lynn 1937- , *2:* 130
Hall, Malcolm 1945- , *7:* 121
Hall, Marjory. *See* Yeakley,
   Marjory Hall, *21:* 207
Hall, Rosalys Haskell 1914- ,
   7: 121
Hallard, Peter. *See* Catherall,
   Arthur, *3:* 38
Hallas, Richard. *See* Knight, Eric
   (Mowbray), *18:* 151
Hall-Clarke, James. *See* Rowland-
   Entwistle, (Arthur) Theodore
   (Henry), *31:* 145
Halliburton, Warren J. 1924- ,
   19: 143
Hallin, Emily Watson 1919- ,
   6: 101
Hallman, Ruth 1929- , *28:* 123
   (Brief Entry)

Hall-Quest, Olga W(ilbourne)
   1899- , *11:* 125
Hallstead, William F(inn) III
   1924- , *11:* 126
Hallward, Michael 1889- , *12:* 91
Halsell, Grace 1923- , *13:* 76
Halsted, Anna Roosevelt
   1906-1975, *30:* 126 (Obituary)
Halter, Jon C(harles) 1941- ,
   22: 152
Hamberger, John 1934- , *14:* 79
Hamerstrom, Frances 1907- ,
   24: 125
Hamil, Thomas Arthur 1928- ,
   14: 80
Hamil, Tom. *See* Hamil, Thomas
   Arthur, *14:* 80
Hamilton, Alice. *See* Cromie, Alice
   Hamilton, *24:* 78
Hamilton, Charles Harold St. John
   1875-1961, *13:* 77
Hamilton, Clive. *See* Lewis, C. S.,
   13: 129
Hamilton, Dorothy 1906- , *12:* 92
Hamilton, Edith 1867-1963,
   20: 75
Hamilton, Elizabeth 1906- ,
   23: 94
Hamilton, Robert W. *See*
   Stratemeyer, Edward L., *1:* 208
Hamilton, Virginia 1936- , *4:* 97
Hammer, Richard 1928- , *6:* 102
Hammerman, Gay M(orenus)
   1926- , *9:* 92
Hammond, Winifred G(raham)
   1899- , *29:* 102
Hammontree, Marie (Gertrude)
   1913- , *13:* 89
Hampson, (Richard) Denman
   1929- , *15:* 129
Hamre, Leif 1914- , *5:* 79
Hancock, Mary A. 1923- , *31:* 78
Hancock, Sibyl 1940- , *9:* 92
Hane, Roger 1940-1974, *20:* 79
   (Obituary)
Haney, Lynn 1941- , *23:* 95
Hanff, Helene, *11:* 128
Hanlon, Emily 1945- , *15:* 131
Hann, Jacquie 1951- , *19:* 144
Hanna, Paul R(obert) 1902- ,
   9: 93
Hano, Arnold 1922- , *12:* 93
Hanser, Richard (Frederick)
   1909- , *13:* 90
Hanson, Joan 1938- , *8:* 75
Hanson, Joseph E. 1894(?)-1971,
   27: 107 (Obituary)
Harald, Eric. *See* Boesen, Victor,
   16: 53
Harding, Lee 1937- , *31:* 78
   (Brief Entry)
Hardwick, Richard Holmes, Jr.
   1923- , *12:* 94
Hardy, Alice Dale [Collective
   pseudonym], *1:* 109

Hardy, David A(ndrews) 1936- ,
   9: 95
Hardy, Stuart. *See* Schisgall, Oscar,
   12: 187
Hardy, Thomas 1840-1928,
   25: 129
Hark, Mildred. *See* McQueen,
   Mildred Hark, *12:* 145
Harkaway, Hal. *See* Stratemeyer,
   Edward L., *1:* 208
Harkins, Philip 1912- , *6:* 102
Harlan, Glen. *See* Cebulash, Mel,
   10: 19
Harman, Fred 1902(?)-1982,
   30: 126 (Obituary)
Harmelink, Barbara (Mary), *9:* 97
Harmon, Margaret 1906- , *20:* 80
Harnan, Terry 1920- , *12:* 94
Harnett, Cynthia (Mary), *5:* 79
Harper, Mary Wood. *See* Dixon,
   Jeanne, *31:* 60
Harper, Wilhelmina 1884-1973,
   4: 99; *26:* 101 (Obituary)
Harrell, Sara Gordon. *See* Banks,
   Sara (Jeanne Gordon Harrell),
   26: 33
Harrington, Lyn 1911- , *5:* 80
Harris, Christie 1907- , *6:* 103
Harris, Colver. *See* Colver, Anne,
   7: 54
Harris, Dorothy Joan 1931- ,
   13: 91
Harris, Janet 1932-1979, *4:* 100;
   23: 97 (Obituary)
Harris, Joel Chandler 1848-1908,
   YABC 1: 154
Harris, Lavinia. *See* Johnston,
   Norma, *29:* 116
Harris, Leon A., Jr. 1926- ,
   4: 101
Harris, Lorle K(empe) 1912- ,
   22: 153
Harris, Rosemary (Jeanne), *4:* 101
Harris, Sherwood 1932- , *25:* 139
Harrison, David Lee 1937- ,
   26: 101
Harrison, Deloris 1938- , *9:* 97
Harrison, Harry 1925- , *4:* 102
Harshaw, Ruth H(etzel)
   1890-1968, *27:* 107
Harte, (Francis) Bret(t)
   1836-1902, *26:* 103
Hartley, Ellen (Raphael) 1915- ,
   23: 97
Hartley, William B(rown) 1913- ,
   23: 98
Hartman, Louis F(rancis)
   1901-1970, *22:* 154
Hartshorn, Ruth M. 1928- ,
   11: 129
Harvey, Edith 1908(?)-1972,
   27: 107 (Obituary)
Harwin, Brian. *See* Henderson,
   LeGrand, *9:* 104
Harwood, Pearl Augusta (Bragdon)
   1903- , *9:* 98

Haskell, Arnold 1903- , *6:* 104
Haskins, James 1941- , *9:* 100
Haskins, Jim. *See* Haskins, James, *9:* 100
Hasler, Joan 1931- , *28:* 123
Hassler, Jon (Francis) 1933- , *19:* 145
Hatch, Mary Cottam 1912-1970, *28:* 123 (Brief Entry)
Hatlo, Jimmy 1898-1963, *23:* 100 (Obituary)
Haugaard, Erik Christian 1923- , *4:* 104
Hauser, Margaret L(ouise) 1909- , *10:* 54
Hausman, Gerald 1945- , *13:* 93
Hausman, Gerry. *See* Hausman, Gerald, *13:* 93
Hautzig, Deborah 1956- , *31:* 79
Hautzig, Esther 1930- , *4:* 105
Havenhand, John. *See* Cox, John Roberts, *9:* 42
Havighurst, Walter (Edwin) 1901- , *1:* 109
Haviland, Virginia 1911- , *6:* 105
Hawes, Judy 1913- , *4:* 107
Hawk, Virginia Driving. *See* Sneve, Virginia Driving Hawk, *8:* 193
Hawkesworth, Eric 1921- , *13:* 94
Hawkins, Arthur 1903- , *19:* 146
Hawkins, Quail 1905- , *6:* 107
Hawkinson, John 1912- , *4:* 108
Hawkinson, Lucy (Ozone) 1924-1971, *21:* 63
Hawley, Mable C. [Collective pseudonym], *1:* 110
Hawthorne, Captain R. M. *See* Ellis, Edward S(ylvester), *YABC 1:* 116
Hawthorne, Nathaniel 1804-1864, *YABC 2:* 143
Hay, John 1915- , *13:* 95
Hay, Timothy. *See* Brown, Margaret Wise, *YABC 2:* 9
Haycraft, Howard 1905- , *6:* 108
Haycraft, Molly Costain 1911- , *6:* 110
Hayden, Robert C(arter), Jr. 1937- , *28:* 124 (Brief Entry)
Hayden, Robert E(arl) 1913-1980, *19:* 147; *26:* 111 (Obituary)
Hayes, Carlton J. H. 1882-1964, *11:* 129
Hayes, Geoffrey 1947- , *26:* 111
Hayes, John F. 1904- , *11:* 129
Hayes, Will, *7:* 122
Hayes, William D(imitt) 1913- , *8:* 76
Hays, H(offman) R(eynolds) 1904-1980, *26:* 112
Hays, Wilma Pitchford 1909- , *1:* 110; *28:* 124
Haywood, Carolyn 1898- , *1:* 111; *29:* 103
Hazen, Barbara Shook 1930- , *27:* 107

Head, Gay. *See* Hauser, Margaret L(ouise), *10:* 54
Headley, Elizabeth. *See* Cavanna, Betty, *1:* 54; *30:* 84
Headstrom, Richard 1902- , *8:* 77
Heady, Eleanor B(utler) 1917- , *8:* 78
Heal, Edith 1903- , *7:* 123
Healey, Brooks. *See* Albert, Burton, Jr., *22:* 7
Heaps, Willard (Allison) 1909- , *26:* 113
Heath, Veronica. *See* Blackett, Veronica Heath, *12:* 54
Heaven, Constance. *See* Fecher, Constance, *7:* 83
Hecht, George J(oseph) 1895-1980, *22:* 155 (Obituary)
Hecht, Henri Joseph 1922- , *9:* 101
Hechtkopf, Henryk 1910- , *17:* 79
Heck, Bessie Holland 1911- , *26:* 114
Hedderwick, Mairi 1939- , *30:* 126
Hedges, Sid(ney) G(eorge) 1897-1974, *28:* 127
Hefter, Richard 1942- , *31:* 80
Hegarty, Reginald Beaton 1906-1973, *10:* 54
Heiderstadt, Dorothy 1907- , *6:* 111
Hein, Lucille Eleanor 1915- , *20:* 80
Heinemann, George Alfred 1918- , *31:* 83 (Brief Entry)
Heinlein, Robert A(nson) 1907- , *9:* 102
Heins, Paul 1909- , *13:* 96
Heintze, Carl 1922- , *26:* 116
Heinz, W(ilfred) C(harles) 1915- , *26:* 116
Helfman, Elizabeth S(eaver) 1911- , *3:* 83
Helfman, Harry 1910- , *3:* 84
Hellman, Hal. *See* Hellman, Harold, *4:* 109
Hellman, Harold 1927- , *4:* 109
Helps, Racey 1913-1971, *2:* 131; *25:* 139 (Obituary)
Hemming, Roy 1928- , *11:* 130
Henderley, Brooks [Collective pseudonym], *1:* 113
Henderson, LeGrand 1901-1965, *9:* 104
Henderson, Nancy Wallace 1916- , *22:* 155
Henderson, Zenna (Chlarson) 1917- *5:* 81
Hendrickson, Walter Brookfield, Jr. 1936- , *9:* 104
Henriod, Lorraine 1925- , *26:* 117
Henry, Joanne Landers 1927- , *6:* 112
Henry, Marguerite, *11:* 131

Henry, O. *See* Porter, William Sydney, *YABC 2:* 259
Henry, Oliver. *See* Porter, William Sydney, *YABC 2:* 259
Henry, T. E. *See* Rowland-Entwistle, (Arthur) Theodore (Henry), *31:* 145
Henstra, Friso 1928- , *8:* 80
Hentoff, Nat(han Irving) 1925- , *27:* 110 (Brief Entry)
Herald, Kathleen. *See* Peyton, Kathleen (Wendy), *15:* 211
Herbert, Cecil. *See* Hamilton, Charles Harold St. John, *13:* 77
Herbert, Don 1917- , *2:* 131
Herbert, Frank (Patrick) 1920- , *9:* 105
Herbert, Wally. *See* Herbert, Walter William, *23:* 101
Herbert, Walter William 1934- , *23:* 101
Hergé. *See* Remi, Georges, *13:* 183
Herman, Charlotte 1937- , *20:* 81
Hermanson, Dennis (Everett) 1947- , *10:* 55
Hermes, Patricia 1936- , *31:* 83
Herrmanns, Ralph 1933- , *11:* 133
Herron, Edward A(lbert) 1912- , *4:* 110
Hersey, John (Richard) 1914- , *25:* 139
Hertz, Grete Janus 1915- , *23:* 102
Hess, Lilo 1916- , *4:* 111
Heuman, William 1912-1971, *21:* 64
Hewett, Anita 1918- , *13:* 97
Hext, Harrington. *See* Phillpotts, Eden, *24:* 159
Hey, Nigel S(tewart) 1936- , *20:* 83
Heyduck-Huth, Hilde 1929- , *8:* 81
Heyerdahl, Thor 1914- , *2:* 132
Heyliger, William 1884-1955, *YABC 1:* 163
Heyward, Du Bose 1885-1940, *21:* 66
Hibbert, Christopher 1924- , *4:* 112
Hibbert, Eleanor Burford 1906- , *2:* 134
Hickman, Janet 1940- , *12:* 97
Hickman, Martha Whitmore 1925- , *26:* 119
Hickok, Lorena A. 1892(?)-1968, *20:* 83
Hicks, Eleanor B. *See* Coerr, Eleanor, *1:* 64
Hicks, Harvey. *See* Stratemeyer, Edward L., *1:* 208
Hieatt, Constance B(artlett) 1928- , *4:* 113
Hiebert, Ray Eldon 1932- , *13:* 98

Higdon, Hal   1931- , 4: 115
Higginbottom, J(effrey) Winslow
   1945- , 29: 105
Highet, Helen. See MacInnes,
   Helen, 22: 181
Hightower, Florence Cole
   1916-1981, 4: 115; 27: 110
   (Obituary)
Highwater, Jamake   1942- ,
   30: 128 (Brief Entry)
Hildick, E. W. See Hildick,
   Wallace, 2: 135
Hildick, (Edmund) Wallace
   1925- , 2: 135
Hill, Donna (Marie), 24: 127
Hill, Elizabeth Starr   1925- ,
   24: 129
Hill, Grace Brooks [Collective
   pseudonym], 1: 113
Hill, Grace Livingston   1865-1947,
   YABC 2: 162
Hill, Helen M(orey)   1915- ,
   27: 110
Hill, Kathleen Louise   1917- ,
   4: 116
Hill, Kay. See Hill, Kathleen
   Louise, 4: 116
Hill, Lorna   1902- , 12: 97
Hill, Monica. See Watson, Jane
   Werner, 3: 244
Hill, Robert W(hite)   1919-1982,
   12: 98; 31: 84 (Obituary)
Hill, Ruth A. See Viguers, Ruth
   Hill, 6: 214
Hill, Ruth Livingston. See Munce,
   Ruth Hill, 12: 156
Hillcourt, William   1900- ,
   27: 111
Hillerman, Tony   1925- , 6: 113
Hillert, Margaret   1920- , 8: 82
Hilton, Irene (P.)   1912- , 7: 124
Hilton, Ralph   1907- , 8: 83
Hilton, Suzanne   1922- , 4: 117
Him, George   1900-1982, 30: 128
   (Obituary)
Himler, Ann   1946- , 8: 84
Himler, Ronald   1937- , 6: 114
Hinckley, Helen. See Jones, Helen
   Hinckley, 26: 128
Hinton, S(usan) E(loise)   1950- ,
   19: 147
Hirsch, S. Carl   1913- , 2: 137
Hirsh, Marilyn   1944- , 7: 126
Hiser, Iona Seibert   1901- , 4: 118
Hitchcock, Alfred (Joseph)
   1899-1980, 24: 131 (Obituary);
   27: 112
Hitte, Kathryn   1919- , 16: 158
Hitz, Demi   1942- , 11: 134
Ho, Minfong   1951- , 15: 131
Hoban, Lillian   1925- , 22: 157
Hoban, Russell C(onwell)   1925- ,
   1: 113
Hoban, Tana, 22: 158
Hobart, Lois, 7: 127

Hoberman, Mary Ann   1930- ,
   5: 82
Hobson, Burton (Harold)   1933- ,
   28: 128
Hochschild, Arlie Russell   1940- ,
   11: 135
Hockenberry, Hope. See Newell,
   Hope (Hockenberry), 24: 154
Hodge, P(aul) W(illiam)   1934- ,
   12: 99
Hodges, C(yril) Walter   1909- ,
   2: 138
Hodges, Carl G.   1902-1964,
   10: 56
Hodges, Elizabeth Jamison, 1: 114
Hodges, Margaret Moore   1911- ,
   1: 116
Hoexter, Corinne K.   1927- ,
   6: 115
Hoff, Carol   1900- , 11: 136
Hoff, Syd(ney)   1912- , 9: 106
Hoffman, Phyllis M.   1944- ,
   4: 120
Hoffman, Rosekrans   1926- ,
   15: 133
Hoffmann, E(rnst) T(heodor)
   A(madeus)   1776-1822,
   27: 118
Hoffmann, Felix   1911-1975,
   9: 108
Hofsinde, Robert   1902-1973,
   21: 69
Hogan, Bernice Harris   1929- ,
   12: 99
Hogan, Inez   1895- , 2: 140
Hogarth, Jr. See Kent, Rockwell,
   6: 128
Hogg, Garry   1902- , 2: 142
Hogner, Dorothy Childs, 4: 121
Hogner, Nils   1893-1970, 25: 142
Hogrogian, Nonny   1932- , 7: 128
Hoke, Helen (L.)   1903- , 15: 133
Hoke, John   1925- , 7: 129
Holbeach, Henry. See Rands,
   William Brighty, 17: 156
Holberg, Ruth Langland   1889- ,
   1: 117
Holbrook, Peter. See Glick, Carl
   (Cannon), 14: 72
Holbrook, Stewart Hall
   1893-1964, 2: 143
Holding, James   1907- , 3: 85
Holisher, Desider   1901-1972,
   6: 115
Holl, Adelaide (Hinkle), 8: 84
Holland, Isabelle   1920- , 8: 86
Holland, Janice   1913-1962,
   18: 117
Holland, John L(ewis)   1919- ,
   20: 87
Holland, Marion   1908- , 6: 116
Hollander, John   1929- , 13: 99
Holldobler, Turid   1939- , 26: 121
Holliday, Joe. See Holliday, Joseph,
   11: 137
Holliday, Joseph   1910- , 11: 137

Holling, Holling C(lancy)
   1900-1973, 15: 135; 26: 121
   (Obituary)
Holloway, Teresa (Bragunier)
   1906- , 26: 122
Holm, (Else) Anne (Lise)   1922- ,
   1: 118
Holman, Felice   1919- , 7: 131
Holme, Bryan   1913- , 26: 123
Holmes, Rick. See Hardwick,
   Richard Holmes, Jr., 12: 94
Holmgren, Virginia C(unningham)
   1909- , 26: 124
Holmquist, Eve   1921- , 11: 138
Holt, Margaret   1937- , 4: 122
Holt, Michael (Paul)   1929- ,
   13: 100
Holt, Stephen. See Thompson,
   Harlan H., 10: 177
Holt, Victoria. See Hibbert,
   Eleanor, 2: 134
Holton, Leonard. See Wibberley,
   Leonard, 2: 271
Holyer, Erna Maria   1925- ,
   22: 159
Holyer, Ernie. See Holyer, Erna
   Maria, 22: 159
Holz, Loretta (Marie)   1943- ,
   17: 81
Homze, Alma C.   1932- , 17: 82
Honig, Donald   1931- , 18: 119
Honness, Elizabeth H.   1904- ,
   2: 145
Hoobler, Dorothy, 28: 128
Hoobler, Thomas, 28: 130
Hood, Joseph F.   1925- , 4: 123
Hood, Robert E.   1926- , 21: 70
Hook, Frances   1912- , 27: 126
Hook, Martha   1936- , 27: 127
Hooker, Ruth   1920- , 21: 71
Hooks, William H(arris)   1921- ,
   16: 159
Hooper, Byrd. See St. Clair, Byrd
   Hooper, 28: 177 (Obituary)
Hooper, Meredith (Jean)   1939- ,
   28: 131
Hoopes, Ned E(dward)   1932- ,
   21: 73
Hoopes, Roy   1922- , 11: 140
Hoover, Helen (Drusilla Blackburn)
   1910- , 12: 100
Hope, Laura Lee [Collective
   pseudonym], 1: 119; 29: 26
   (Obituary)
Hope Simpson, Jacynth   1930- ,
   12: 102
Hopf, Alice L(ightner)   1904- ,
   5: 82
Hopkins, A. T. See Turngren,
   Annette, 23: 233 (Obituary)
Hopkins, Joseph G(erard) E(dward)
   1909- , 11: 141
Hopkins, Lee Bennett   1938- ,
   3: 85
Hopkins, Lyman. See Folsom,
   Franklin, 5: 67

Hopkins, Marjorie   1911- , *9:* 110
Horgan, Paul   1903- , *13:* 102
Hornblow, Arthur (Jr.)   1893-1976, *15:* 138
Hornblow, Leonora (Schinasi) 1920- , *18:* 120
Horne, Richard Henry   1803-1884, *29:* 106
Horner, Dave   1934- , *12:* 104
Hornos, Axel   1907- , *20:* 88
Horvath, Betty   1927- , *4:* 125
Horwich, Frances R(appaport) 1908- , *11:* 142
Hosford, Dorothy (Grant) 1900-1952, *22:* 161
Hosford, Jessie   1892- , *5:* 83
Hoskyns-Abrahall, Clare, *13:* 105
Houck, Carter   1924- , *22:* 164
Hough, (Helen) Charlotte   1924- , *9:* 110
Hough, Richard (Alexander) 1922- , *17:* 83
Houghton, Eric   1930- , *7:* 132
Houlehen, Robert J.   1918- , *18:* 121
Household, Geoffrey (Edward West) 1900- , *14:* 81
Houselander, (Frances) Caryll   1900-1954, *31:* 84 (Brief Entry)
Housman, Laurence   1865-1959, *25:* 144
Houston, James A(rchibald) 1921- , *13:* 106
Howard, Elizabeth. *See* Mizner, Elizabeth Howard, *27:* 151
Howard, Prosper. *See* Hamilton, Charles Harold St. John, *13:* 77
Howard, Robert West   1908- , *5:* 85
Howarth, David   1912- , *6:* 117
Howe, Deborah   1946-1978, *29:* 109
Howe, James   1946- , *29:* 110
Howell, Pat   1947- , *15:* 139
Howell, S. *See* Styles, Frank Showell, *10:* 167
Howell, Virginia Tier. *See* Ellison, Virginia Howell, *4:* 74
Howes, Barbara   1914- , *5:* 87
Hoyle, Geoffrey   1942- , *18:* 121
Hoyt, Edwin P(almer), Jr.   1923- , *28:* 132
Hoyt, Olga (Gruhzit)   1922- , *16:* 161
Hubbell, Patricia   1928- , *8:* 86
Hubley, John   1914-1977, *24:* 131 (Obituary)
Hudson, Jeffrey. *See* Crichton, (J.) Michael, *9:* 44
Huffaker, Sandy   1943- , *10:* 56
Huffman, Tom, *24:* 131
Hughes, Langston   1902-1967, *4:* 125

Hughes, Matilda. *See* MacLeod, Charlotte (Matilda Hughes), *28:* 147
Hughes, Monica   1925- , *15:* 140
Hughes, Richard (Arthur Warren) 1900-1976, *8:* 87; *25:* 153 (Obituary)
Hughes, Shirley   1929- , *16:* 162
Hughes, Ted   1930- , *27:* 128 (Brief Entry)
Hughes, Thomas   1822-1896, *31:* 85
Hughes, Walter (Llewellyn) 1910- , *26:* 125
Hull, Eleanor (Means)   1913- , *21:* 74
Hull, Eric Traviss. *See* Harnan, Terry, *12:* 94
Hull, H. Braxton. *See* Jacobs, Helen Hull, *12:* 112
Hull, Katharine   1921-1977, *23:* 103
Hülsmann, Eva   1928- , *16:* 165
Hults, Dorothy Niebrugge   1898- , *6:* 117
Hume, Lotta Carswell, *7:* 133
Hume, Ruth (Fox)   1922-1980, *22:* 165 (Obituary); *26:* 126
Humphrey, Henry (III)   1930- , *16:* 167
Hungerford, Pixie. *See* Brinsmead, H(esba) F(ay), *18:* 36
Hunt, Francis. *See* Stratemeyer, Edward L., *1:* 208
Hunt, Irene   1907- , *2:* 146
Hunt, Joyce   1927- , *31:* 91
Hunt, Mabel Leigh   1892-1971, *1:* 120; *26:* 127 (Obituary)
Hunt, Morton   1920- , *22:* 165
Hunter, Clingham, M.D. *See* Adams, William Taylor, *28:* 21
Hunter, Dawe. *See* Downie, Mary Alice, *13:* 32
Hunter, Edith Fisher   1919- , *31:* 93
Hunter, Evan   1926- , *25:* 153
Hunter, Hilda   1921- , *7:* 135
Hunter, Kristin (Eggleston) 1931- , *12:* 105
Hunter, Mollie. *See* McIllwraith, Maureen, *2:* 193
Hunter, Norman (George Lorimer) 1899- , *26:* 127
Hunter Blair, Pauline   1921- , *3:* 87
Huntington, Harriet E(lizabeth) 1909- , *1:* 121
Huntsberry, William E(mery) 1916- , *5:* 87
Hurd, Clement   1908- , *2:* 147
Hurd, Edith Thacher   1910- , *2:* 150
Hürlimann, Ruth   1939- , *31:* 93 (Brief Entry)
Hurwitz, Johanna   1937- , *20:* 88

Hurwood, Bernhardt J.   1926- , *12:* 107
Hutchens, Paul   1902-1977, *31:* 94
Hutchins, Carleen Maley   1911- , *9:* 112
Hutchins, Pat   1942- , *15:* 141
Hutchins, Ross E(lliott)   1906- , *4:* 127
Hutchmacher, J. Joseph   1929- , *5:* 88
Hutto, Nelson (Allen)   1904- , *20:* 90
Hutton, Warwick   1939- , *20:* 90
Hyde, Dayton O(gden), *9:* 113
Hyde, Hawk. *See* Hyde, Dayton O(gden), *9:* 113
Hyde, Margaret Oldroyd   1917- , *1:* 122
Hyde, Wayne F.   1922- , *7:* 135
Hylander, Clarence J.   1897-1964, *7:* 137
Hyman, Robin P(hilip)   1931- , *12:* 108
Hyman, Trina Schart   1939- , *7:* 137
Hymes, Lucia M.   1907- , *7:* 139
Hyndman, Jane Andrews   1912-1978, *1:* 122; *23:* 103 (Obituary)
Hyndman, Robert Utley   1906(?)-1973, *18:* 123

Iannone, Jeanne, *7:* 139
Ibbotson, Eva   1925- , *13:* 108
Ibbotson, M. C(hristine)   1930- , *5:* 89
Ilowite, Sheldon A.   1931- , *27:* 128
Ilsley, Dent [Joint pseudonym]. *See* Chapman, John Stanton Higham, *27:* 41 (Obituary)
Ilsley, Velma (Elizabeth)   1918- , *12:* 109
Immel, Mary Blair   1930- , *28:* 133
Ingham, Colonel Frederic. *See* Hale, Edward Everett, *16:* 143
Ingraham, Leonard W(illiam) 1913- , *4:* 129
Ingrams, Doreen   1906- , *20:* 92
Inyart, Gene,   1927- *6:* 119
Ionesco, Eugene,   1912- *7:* 140
Ipcar, Dahlov (Zorach)   1917- , *1:* 125
Irvin, Fred   1914- , *15:* 143
Irving, Alexander. *See* Hume, Ruth (Fox), *26:* 126
Irving, Robert. *See* Adler, Irving, *1:* 2; *29:* 26
Irving, Washington   1783-1859, *YABC 2:* 164
Irwin, Constance Frick   1913- , *6:* 119

Irwin, Keith Gordon 1885-1964, *11:* 143
Isaac, Joanne 1934- , *21:* 75
Isaacs, Jacob. *See* Kranzler, George G(ershon), *28:* 143
Isham, Charlotte H(ickox) 1912- , *21:* 76
Ish-Kishor, Judith 1892-1972, *11:* 144
Ish-Kishor, Sulamith 1896-1977, *17:* 84
Ishmael, Woodi 1914- , *31:* 99
Israel, Elaine 1945- , *12:* 110
Israel, Marion Louise 1882-1973, *26:* 128 (Obituary)
Iwamatsu, Jun Atsushi 1908- , *14:* 83

Jackson, C. Paul 1902- , *6:* 120
Jackson, Caary. *See* Jackson, C. Paul, *6:* 120
Jackson, Jesse 1908- , *2:* 150; *29:* 111
Jackson, O. B. *See* Jackson, C. Paul, *6:* 120
Jackson, Robert B(lake) 1926- , *8:* 89
Jackson, Sally. *See* Kellogg, Jean, *10:* 66
Jackson, Shirley 1919-1965, *2:* 152
Jacob, Helen Pierce 1927- , *21:* 77
Jacobs, Flora Gill 1918- , *5:* 90
Jacobs, Frank 1929- , *30:* 128
Jacobs, Helen Hull 1908- , *12:* 112
Jacobs, Joseph 1854-1916, *25:* 159
Jacobs, Leland Blair 1907- , *20:* 93
Jacobs, Linda C. 1943- , *21:* 78
Jacobs, Lou(is), Jr. 1921- , *2:* 155
Jacobs, Susan 1940- , *30:* 129
Jacobs, William Jay 1933- , *28:* 134
Jacobson, Daniel 1923- , *12:* 113
Jacobson, Morris K(arl) 1906- , *21:* 79
Jacopetti, Alexandra 1939- , *14:* 85
Jacques, Robin 1920- , *30:* 129 (Brief Entry)
Jagendorf, Moritz (Adolf) 1888-1981, *2:* 155; *24:* 132 (Obituary)
Jahn, (Joseph) Michael 1943- , *28:* 135
Jahn, Mike. *See* Jahn, (Joseph) Michael, *28:* 135
Jahsmann, Allan Hart 1916- , *28:* 136

James, Andrew. *See* Kirkup, James, *12:* 120
James, Dynely. *See* Mayne, William, *6:* 162
James, Harry Clebourne 1896- , *11:* 144
James, Josephine. *See* Sterne, Emma Gelders, *6:* 205
James, T. F. *See* Fleming, Thomas J(ames), *8:* 64
James, Will(iam Roderick) 1892-1942, *19:* 148
Jane, Mary Childs 1909- , *6:* 122
Janes, Edward C. 1908- , *25:* 167
Janeway, Elizabeth (Hall) 1913- , *19:* 165
Janosch. *See* Eckert, Horst, *8:* 47
Jansen, Jared. *See* Cebulash, Mel, *10:* 19
Janson, Dora Jane 1916- , *31:* 100
Janson, H(orst) W(oldemar) 1913- , *9:* 114
Jansson, Tove 1914- , *3:* 88
Janus, Grete. *See* Hertz, Grete Janus, *23:* 102
Jaques, Faith 1923- , *21:* 81
Jaques, Francis Lee 1887-1969, *28:* 137 (Brief Entry)
Jarman, Rosemary Hawley 1935- , *7:* 141
Jarrell, Randall 1914-1965, *7:* 141
Jauss, Anne Marie 1907- , *10:* 57
Jayne, Lieutenant R. H. *See* Ellis, Edward S(ylvester), *YABC 1:* 116
Jeake, Samuel, Jr. *See* Aiken, Conrad, *3:* 3; *30:* 25
Jefferies, (John) Richard 1848-1887, *16:* 168
Jeffers, Susan, *17:* 86
Jefferson, Sarah. *See* Farjeon, Annabel, *11:* 93
Jeffries, Roderic 1926- , *4:* 129
Jenkins, Marie M. 1909- , *7:* 143
Jenkins, William A(twell) 1922- , *9:* 115
Jennings, Gary (Gayne) 1928- , *9:* 115
Jennings, Robert. *See* Hamilton, Charles Harold St. John, *13:* 77
Jennings, S. M. *See* Meyer, Jerome Sydney, *3:* 129; *25:* 181 (Obituary)
Jennison, C. S. *See* Starbird, Kaye, *6:* 204
Jennison, Keith Warren 1911- , *14:* 86
Jensen, Niels 1927- , *25:* 168
Jensen, Virginia Allen 1927- , *8:* 90
Jeschke, Susan 1942- , *27:* 129 (Brief Entry)
Jessel, Camilla (Ruth) 1937- , *29:* 114

Jewett, Eleanore Myers 1890-1967, *5:* 90
Jewett, Sarah Orne 1849-1909, *15:* 144
Jobb, Jamie 1945- , *29:* 116
Johns, Avery. *See* Cousins, Margaret, *2:* 79
Johnson, A. E. [Joint pseudonym] *See* Johnson, Annabell and Edgar, *2:* 156, 157
Johnson, Annabell Jones 1921- , *2:* 156
Johnson, Benj. F., of Boone. *See* Riley, James Whitcomb, *17:* 159
Johnson, Charles R. 1925- , *11:* 146
Johnson, Chuck. *See* Johnson, Charles R., *11:* 146
Johnson, Crockett. *See* Leisk, David (Johnson), *1:* 141; *26:* 133 (Obituary); *30:* 141
Johnson, D(ana) William 1945- , *23:* 103
Johnson, Dorothy M. 1905- , *6:* 123
Johnson, Edgar Raymond 1912- , *2:* 157
Johnson, Elizabeth 1911- , *7:* 144
Johnson, Eric W(arner) 1918- , *8:* 91
Johnson, Evelyne 1932- , *20:* 95
Johnson, Gaylord 1884- , *7:* 146
Johnson, Gerald White 1890-1980, *19:* 166; *28:* 138 (Obituary)
Johnson, James Ralph 1922- , *1:* 126
Johnson, James Weldon. *See* Johnson, James William, *31:* 101
Johnson, James William 1871-1938, *31:* 101
Johnson, LaVerne B(ravo) 1925- , *13:* 108
Johnson, Lois S(mith), *6:* 123
Johnson, Lois W(alfrid) 1936- , *22:* 165
Johnson, Mary Frances K. 1929(?)-1979, *27:* 129 (Obituary)
Johnson, Milton 1932- , *31:* 107
Johnson, (Walter) Ryerson 1901- , *10:* 58
Johnson, Shirley K(ing) 1927- , *10:* 59
Johnson, Siddie Joe 1905-1977, *20:* 95 (Obituary)
Johnson, William Weber 1909- , *7:* 147
Johnston, Agnes Christine. *See* Dazey, Agnes J., *2:* 88
Johnston, H(ugh) A(nthony) S(tephen) 1913-1967, *14:* 87
Johnston, Johanna, *12:* 115
Johnston, Norma, *29:* 116

Johnston, Portia. *See* Takakjian, Portia, *15:* 273
Johnston, Tony 1942- , *8:* 94
Jones, Adrienne 1915- , *7:* 147
Jones, Diana Wynne 1934- , *9:* 116
Jones, Elizabeth Orton 1910- , *18:* 123
Jones, Evan, 1915- *3:* 90
Jones, Gillingham. *See* Hamilton, Charles Harold St. John, *13:* 77
Jones, Harold 1904- , *14:* 87
Jones, Helen Hinckley 1903- , *26:* 128
Jones, Helen L. 1904(?)-1973, *22:* 167 (Obituary)
Jones, Hettie 1934- , *27:* 129 (Brief Entry)
Jones, Hortense P. 1918- , *9:* 118
Jones, Mary Alice, *6:* 125
Jones, Penelope 1938- , *31:* 108
Jones, Weyman 1928- , *4:* 130
Jonk, Clarence 1906- , *10:* 59
Jordan, E(mil) L(eopold) 1900- , *31:* 109 (Brief Entry)
Jordan, Hope (Dahle) 1905- , *15:* 150
Jordan, Jael (Michal) 1949- , *30:* 130
Jordan, June 1936- , *4:* 131
Jordan, Mildred 1901- , *5:* 91
Jorgenson, Ivar. *See* Silverberg, Robert, *13:* 206
Joseph, Joseph M(aron) 1903-1979, *22:* 167
Joslin, Sesyle 1929- , *2:* 158
Joyce, J(ames) Avery, *11:* 147
Jucker, Sita 1921- , *5:* 92
Judd, Frances K. [Collective pseudonym], *1:* 127
Judson, Clara Ingram 1879-1960, *27:* 129 (Brief Entry)
Jumpp, Hugo. *See* MacPeek, Walter G., *4:* 148; *25:* 177 (Obituary)
Jupo, Frank J. 1904- , *7:* 148
Juster, Norton 1929- , *3:* 91
Justus, May, 1898- *1:* 127

Kabdebo, Tamas. *See* Kabdebo, Thomas, *10:* 60
Kabdebo, Thomas 1934- , *10:* 60
Kabibble, Osh. *See* Jobb, Jamie, *29:* 116
Kadesch, Robert R(udstone) 1922- , *31:* 109
Kakimoto, Kozo 1915- , *11:* 147
Kalashnikoff, Nicholas 1888-1961, *16:* 173
Kalb, Jonah 1926- , *23:* 105
Kaler, James Otis 1848-1912, *15:* 151
Kalnay, Francis 1899- , *7:* 149
Kamen, Gloria 1923- , *9:* 118

Kamm, Josephine (Hart) 1905- , *24:* 133
Kane, Henry Bugbee 1902-1971, *14:* 91
Kane, Robert W. 1910- , *18:* 131
Kanzawa, Toshiko. *See* Furukawa, Toshi, *24:* 117
Kaplan, Bess 1927- , *22:* 168
Kaplan, Boche 1926- , *24:* 134
Kaplan, Irma 1900- , *10:* 61
Kaplan, Jean Caryl Korn 1926- , *10:* 62
Karasz, Ilonka 1896-1981, *29:* 118 (Obituary)
Karen, Ruth 1922- , *9:* 120
Kark, Nina Mary 1925- , *4:* 132
Karlin, Eugene 1918- , *10:* 62
Karp, Naomi J. 1926- , *16:* 174
Kashiwagi, Isami 1925- , *10:* 64
Kästner, Erich 1899-1974, *14:* 91
Katchen, Carole 1944- , *9:* 122
Kathryn. *See* Searle, Kathryn Adrienne, *10:* 143
Katona, Robert 1949- , *21:* 84
Katz, Bobbi 1933- , *12:* 116
Katz, Fred 1938- , *6:* 126
Katz, William Loren 1927- , *13:* 109
Kaufman, Mervyn D. 1932- , *4:* 133
Kaufmann, Angelika 1935- , *15:* 155
Kaufmann, John 1931- , *18:* 132
Kaula, Edna Mason 1906- , *13:* 110
Kavaler, Lucy 1930- , *23:* 106
Kay, Helen. *See* Goldfrank, Helen Colodny, *6:* 89
Kay, Mara, *13:* 111
Kaye, Geraldine 1925- , *10:* 64
Keane, Bil 1922- , *4:* 134
Keating, Bern. *See* Keating, Leo Bernard, *10:* 65
Keating, Lawrence A. 1903-1966, *23:* 107
Keating, Leo Bernard 1915- , *10:* 65
Keats, Ezra Jack 1916- , *14:* 99
Keegan, Marcia 1943- , *9:* 121
Keen, Martin L. 1913- , *4:* 135
Keene, Carolyn [Collective pseudonym]. *See* Adams, Harriet S., *1:* 1; *29:* 26 (Obituary); McFarlane, Leslie, *31:* 133; Stratemeyer, Edward L., *1:* 208
Keeping, Charles (William James) 1924- , *9:* 123
Keir, Christine. *See* Pullein-Thompson, Christine, *3:* 164
Keith, Carlton. *See* Robertson, Keith, *1:* 184
Keith, Harold (Verne) 1903- , *2:* 159
Kelen, Emery 1896-1978, *13:* 114; *26:* 130 (Obituary)

Kelleam, Joseph E(veridge) 1913-1975, *31:* 109
Keller, B(everly) L(ou), *13:* 115
Keller, Charles 1942- , *8:* 94
Keller, Gail Faithfull. *See* Faithfull, Gail, *8:* 55
Kelley, Leo P(atrick) 1928- , *31:* 109 (Brief Entry)
Kellin, Sally Moffet 1932- , *9:* 125
Kellogg, Gene. *See* Kellogg, Jean, *10:* 66
Kellogg, Jean 1916- , *10:* 66
Kellogg, Steven 1941- , *8:* 95
Kellow, Kathleen. *See* Hibbert, Eleanor, *2:* 134
Kelly, Eric P(hilbrook) 1884-1960, *YABC 1:* 165
Kelly, Ralph. *See* Geis, Darlene, *7:* 101
Kelly, Regina Z., *5:* 94
Kelly, Walt(er Crawford) 1913-1973, *18:* 135
Kelsey, Alice Geer 1896- , *1:* 129
Kemp, Gene 1926- , *25:* 169
Kempner, Mary Jean 1913-1969, *10:* 67
Kempton, Jean Welch 1914- , *10:* 67
Kendall, Carol (Seeger) 1917- , *11:* 148
Kendall, Lace. *See* Stoutenburg, Adrien, *3:* 217
Kenealy, James P. 1927- , *29:* 118 (Brief Entry)
Kenealy, Jim. *See* Kenealy, James P., *29:* 118 (Brief Entry)
Kennedy, John Fitzgerald 1917-1963, *11:* 150
Kennedy, Joseph 1929- , *14:* 104
Kennedy, (Jerome) Richard 1932- , *22:* 169
Kennedy, X. J. *See* Kennedy, Joseph, *14:* 104
Kennell, Ruth E(pperson) 1893-1977, *6:* 127; *25:* 170 (Obituary)
Kenny, Ellsworth Newcomb 1909-1971, *26:* 130 (Obituary)
Kenny, Herbert A(ndrew) 1912- , *13:* 117
Kent, Alexander. *See* Reeman, Douglas Edward, *28:* 169 (Brief Entry)
Kent, Jack. *See* Kent, John Wellington, *24:* 135
Kent, John Wellington 1920- , *24:* 135
Kent, Margaret 1894- , *2:* 161
Kent, Rockwell 1882-1971, *6:* 128
Kent, Sherman 1903- , *20:* 96
Kenworthy, Leonard S. 1912- , *6:* 131
Kenyon, Ley 1913- , *6:* 131
Kepes, Juliet A(ppleby) 1919- , *13:* 118

Kerigan, Florence 1896- , *12:* 117

Kerman, Gertrude Lerner 1909- , *21:* 85

Kerr, Jessica 1901- , *13:* 119

Kerr, (Anne) Judith 1923- , *24:* 137

Kerr, M. E. *See* Meaker, Marijane, *20:* 124

Kerry, Frances. *See* Kerigan, Florence, *12:* 117

Kerry, Lois. *See* Arquette, Lois S., *1:* 13

Ker Wilson, Barbara 1929- , *20:* 97

Kessler, Leonard P. 1921- , *14:* 106

Kesteven, G. R. *See* Crosher, G(eoffry) R(obins), *14:* 51

Ketcham, Hank. *See* Ketcham, Henry King, *27:* 129 (Brief Entry); *28:* 138

Ketcham, Henry King 1920- , *27:* 129 (Brief Entry); *28:* 138

Kettelkamp, Larry 1933- , *2:* 163

Kevles, Bettyann 1938- , *23:* 107

Key, Alexander (Hill) 1904-1979, *8:* 98; *23:* 108 (Obituary)

Khanshendel, Chiron. *See* Rose, Wendy, *12:* 180

Kherdian, David 1931- , *16:* 175

Kiddell, John 1922- , *3:* 93

Kiefer, Irene 1926- , *21:* 87

Killilea, Marie (Lyons) 1913- , *2:* 165

Kilreon, Beth. *See* Walker, Barbara K., *4:* 219

Kimbrough, Emily 1899- , *2:* 166

Kimmel, Eric A. 1946- , *13:* 120

Kindred, Wendy 1937- , *7:* 150

Kines, Pat Decker 1937- , *12:* 118

King, Arthur. *See* Cain, Arthur H., *3:* 33

King, Billie Jean 1943- , *12:* 119

King, (David) Clive 1924- , *28:* 142

King, Cynthia 1925- , *7:* 152

King, Frank O. 1883-1969, *22:* 170 (Obituary)

King, Marian, *23:* 108

King, Martin. *See* Marks, Stan(ley), *14:* 136

King, Martin Luther, Jr. 1929-1968, *14:* 108

King, Reefe. *See* Barker, Albert W., *8:* 3

King, Stephen 1947- , *9:* 126

Kingman, (Mary) Lee 1919- , *1:* 133

Kingsland, Leslie William 1912- , *13:* 121

Kingsley, Charles 1819-1875, *YABC 2:* 179

Kinney, C. Cle 1915- , *6:* 132

Kinney, Harrison 1921- , *13:* 122

Kinney, Jean Stout 1912- , *12:* 120

Kinsey, Elizabeth. *See* Clymer, Eleanor, *9:* 37

Kipling, (Joseph) Rudyard 1865-1936, *YABC 2:* 193

Kirk, Ruth (Kratz) 1925- , *5:* 95

Kirkup, James 1927- , *12:* 120

Kirkus, Virginia. *See* Glick, Virginia Kirkus, *23:* 78 (Obituary)

Kirtland, G. B. *See* Joslin, Sesyle, *2:* 158

Kishida, Eriko 1929- , *12:* 123

Kisinger, Grace Gelvin 1913-1965, *10:* 68

Kissin, Eva H. 1923- , *10:* 68

Kjelgaard, James Arthur 1910-1959, *17:* 88

Kjelgaard, Jim. *See* Kjelgaard, James Arthur, *17:* 88

Klaperman, Libby Mindlin 1921-1982, *31:* 110 (Obituary)

Klass, Morton 1927- , *11:* 152

Kleberger, Ilse 1921- , *5:* 96

Klein, Aaron E. 1930- , *28:* 143 (Brief Entry)

Klein, H. Arthur, *8:* 99

Klein, Leonore 1916- , *6:* 132

Klein, Mina C(ooper), *8:* 100

Klein, Norma 1938- , *7:* 152

Klemm, Edward G., Jr. 1910- , *30:* 131

Klemm, Roberta K(ohnhorst) 1884- , *30:* 131

Klimowicz, Barbara 1927- , *10:* 69

Klug, Ron(ald) 1939- , *31:* 110

Knickerbocker, Diedrich. *See* Irving, Washington, *YABC 2:* 164

Knifesmith. *See* Cutler, Ivor, *24:* 80

Knight, Damon 1922- , *9:* 126

Knight, David C(arpenter), *14:* 111

Knight, Eric (Mowbray) 1897-1943, *18:* 151

Knight, Francis Edgar, *14:* 112

Knight, Frank. *See* Knight, Francis Edgar, *14:* 112

Knight, Hilary 1926- , *15:* 157

Knight, Mallory T. *See* Hurwood, Bernhardt J., *12:* 107

Knight, Ruth Adams 1898-1974, *20:* 98 (Obituary)

Knott, Bill. *See* Knott, William Cecil, Jr., *3:* 94

Knott, William Cecil, Jr. 1927- , *3:* 94

Knotts, Howard (Clayton, Jr.) 1922- , *25:* 170

Knowles, John 1926- , *8:* 101

Knox, Calvin. *See* Silverberg, Robert, *13:* 206

Knox, (Mary) Eleanor Jessie 1909- , *30:* 131

Knudson, R. R. *See* Knudson, Rozanne, *7:* 154

Knudson, Rozanne 1932- , *7:* 154

Koch, Dorothy Clarke 1924- , *6:* 133

Kocsis, J. C. *See* Paul, James, *23:* 161

Koehn, Ilse. *See* Van Zwienin, Ilse Charlotte Koehn, *28:* 213 (Brief Entry)

Koerner, W(illiam) H(enry) D(avid) 1878-1938, *21:* 88

Kohler, Julilly H(ouse) 1908-1976, *20:* 99 (Obituary)

Kohn, Bernice (Herstein) 1920- , *4:* 136

Kohner, Frederick 1905- , *10:* 70

Kolba, Tamara, *22:* 171

Komisar, Lucy 1942- , *9:* 127

Komoda, Beverly 1939- , *25:* 171

Komoda, Kiyo 1937- , *9:* 127

Komroff, Manuel 1890-1974, *2:* 168; *20:* 99 (Obituary)

Konigsburg, E(laine) L(obl) 1930- , *4:* 137

Koning, Hans. *See* Koningsberger, Hans, *5:* 97

Koningsberger, Hans 1921- , *5:* 97

Konkle, Janet Everest 1917- , *12:* 124

Koob, Theodora (Johanna Foth) 1918- , *23:* 110

Korach, Mimi 1922- , *9:* 128

Koren, Edward 1935- , *5:* 98

Korinetz, Yuri (Iosifovich) 1923- , *9:* 129

Korty, Carol 1937- , *15:* 159

Kossin, Sandy (Sanford) 1926- , *10:* 71

Kotzwinkle, William 1938- , *24:* 138

Koutoukas, H. M. *See* Rivoli, Mario, *10:* 129

Kouts, Anne 1945- , *8:* 103

Krahn, Fernando 1935- , *31:* 111 (Brief Entry)

Kramer, George. *See* Heuman, William, *21:* 64

Kramer, Nora, *26:* 130

Krantz, Hazel (Newman) 1920- , *12:* 126

Kranzler, George G(ershon) 1916- , *28:* 143

Kranzler, Gershon. *See* Kranzler, George G(ershon), *28:* 143

Krasilovsky, Phyllis 1926- , *1:* 134

Kraus, Robert 1925- , *4:* 139

Krauss, Ruth (Ida) 1911- , *1:* 135; *30:* 134

Krautter, Elisa. *See* Bialk, Elisa, *1:* 25

Kredel, Fritz 1900-1973, *17:* 92

Krementz, Jill 1940- , *17:* 96

Kripke, Dorothy Karp, *30:* 137

Kristof, Jane 1932- , *8:* 104
Kroeber, Theodora (Kracaw) 1897- , *1:* 136
Kroll, Francis Lynde 1904-1973, *10:* 72
Kroll, Steven 1941- , *19:* 168
Krumgold, Joseph 1908-1980, *1:* 136; *23:* 111 (Obituary)
Krush, Beth 1918- , *18:* 162
Krush, Joe 1918- , *18:* 163
Krüss, James 1926- , *8:* 104
Kubinyi, Laszlo 1937- , *17:* 99
Kujoth, Jean Spealman 1935-1975, *30:* 139 (Obituary)
Kumin, Maxine (Winokur) 1925- , *12:* 127
Kunhardt, Dorothy Meserve 1901(?)-1979, *22:* 172 (Obituary)
Künstler, Morton 1927- , *10:* 73
Kupferberg, Herbert 1918- , *19:* 169
Kuratomi, Chizuko 1939- , *12:* 128
Kurelek, William 1927-1977, *8:* 106; *27:* 130 (Obituary)
Kurland, Gerald 1942- , *13:* 123
Kuskin, Karla (Seidman) 1932- , *2:* 169
Kuttner, Paul 1931- , *18:* 165
Kvale, Velma R(uth) 1898- , *8:* 108
Kyle, Elisabeth. *See* Dunlop, Agnes M. R., *3:* 62

Lacy, Leslie Alexander 1937- , *6:* 135
Lader, Lawrence 1919- , *6:* 135
Lady of Quality, A. *See* Bagnold, Enid, *1:* 17; *25:* 23
La Farge, Oliver (Hazard Perry) 1901-1963, *19:* 170
La Farge, Phyllis, *14:* 113
Laffin, John (Alfred Charles) 1922- , *31:* 111
La Fontaine, Jean de 1621-1695, *18:* 166
Lagerlöf, Selma (Ottiliana Lovisa) 1858-1940, *15:* 160
Laimgruber, Monika 1946- , *11:* 153
Laite, Gordon 1925- , *31:* 112
Laklan, Carli 1907- , *5:* 100
la Mare, Walter de. *See* de la Mare, Walter, *16:* 73
Lamb, Beatrice Pitney 1904- , *21:* 92
Lamb, Charles 1775-1834, *17:* 101
Lamb, Elizabeth Searle 1917- , *31:* 113
Lamb, G(eoffrey) F(rederick), *10:* 74
Lamb, Lynton 1907- , *10:* 75

Lamb, Mary Ann 1764-1847, *17:* 112
Lamb, Robert (Boyden) 1941- , *13:* 123
Lambert, Janet (Snyder) 1894-1973, *25:* 172
Lambert, Saul 1928- , *23:* 111
Lamburn, Richmal Crompton 1890-1969, *5:* 101
Lamorisse, Albert (Emmanuel) 1922-1970, *23:* 112
Lamplugh, Lois 1921- , *17:* 116
Lampman, Evelyn Sibley 1907-1980, *4:* 140; *23:* 115 (Obituary)
Lamprey, Louise 1869-1951, *YABC 2:* 221
Lancaster, Bruce 1896-1963, *9:* 130
Land, Barbara (Neblett) 1923- , *16:* 177
Land, Jane [Joint pseudonym]. *See* Borland, Kathryn Kilby, *16:* 54. *See* Speicher, Helen Ross (Smith), *8:* 194
Land, Myrick (Ebben) 1922- , *15:* 174
Land, Ross [Joint pseudonym]. *See* Borland, Kathryn Kilby, *16:* 54. *See* Speicher, Helen Ross (Smith), *8:* 194
Landau, Elaine 1948- , *10:* 75
Landeck, Beatrice 1904- , *15:* 175
Landin, Les(lie) 1923- , *2:* 171
Landshoff, Ursula 1908- , *13:* 124
Lane, Carolyn 1926- , *10:* 76
Lane, John 1932- , *15:* 175
Lane, Rose Wilder 1886-1968, *28:* 144 (Brief Entry); *29:* 118
Lanes, Selma G. 1929- , *3:* 96
Lang, Andrew 1844-1912, *16:* 178
Lange, John. *See* Crichton, (J.) Michael, *9:* 44
Lange, Suzanne 1945- , *5:* 103
Langley, Noel 1911-1980, *25:* 173 (Obituary)
Langner, Nola 1930- , *8:* 110
Langstaff, John 1920- , *6:* 135
Langstaff, Launcelot. *See* Irving, Washington, *YABC 2:* 164
Langton, Jane 1922- , *3:* 97
Lanier, Sidney 1842-1881, *18:* 176
Larom, Henry V. 1903(?)-1975, *30:* 139 (Obituary)
Larrecq, John M(aurice) 1926-1980, *25:* 173 (Obituary)
Larrick, Nancy G. 1910- , *4:* 141
Larsen, Egon 1904- , *14:* 115
Larson, Eve. *See* St. John, Wylly Folk, *10:* 132
Larson, Norita D. 1944- , *29:* 124
Larson, William H. 1938- , *10:* 77
Lasell, Elinor H. 1929- , *19:* 178

Lasell, Fen H. *See* Lasell, Elinor H., *19:* 178
Lasher, Faith B. 1921- , *12:* 129
Lasker, Joe 1919- , *9:* 131
Lasky, Kathryn 1944- , *13:* 124
Lassalle, C. E. *See* Ellis, Edward S(ylvester), *YABC 1:* 116
Latham, Barbara 1896- , *16:* 187
Latham, Frank B. 1910- , *6:* 137
Latham, Jean Lee 1902- , *2:* 171
Latham, Mavis. *See* Clark, Mavis Thorpe, *8:* 27
Latham, Philip. *See* Richardson, Robert S(hirley), *8:* 164
Lathrop, Dorothy P(ulis) 1891-1980, *14:* 116; *24:* 140 (Obituary)
Lattimore, Eleanor Frances 1904- , *7:* 155
Lauber, Patricia (Grace) 1924- , *1:* 138
Laugesen, Mary E(akin) 1906- , *5:* 104
Laughbaum, Steve 1945- , *12:* 131
Laughlin, Florence 1910- , *3:* 98
Laurence, Ester Hauser 1935- , *7:* 156
Laurin, Anne. *See* McLaurin, Anne, *27:* 150
Lauritzen, Jonreed 1902- , *13:* 125
Lavine, David 1928- , *31:* 114
Lavine, Sigmund A. 1908- , *3:* 100
Lawrence, Isabelle (Wentworth), *29:* 125 (Brief Entry)
Lawrence, J. T. *See* Rowland-Entwistle, (Arthur) Theodore (Henry), *31:* 145
Lawrence, John 1933- , *30:* 140
Lawrence, Josephine 1890(?)-1978; *24:* 140 (Obituary)
Lawrence, Louise de Kiriline 1894- , *13:* 126
Lawrence, Mildred 1907- , *3:* 101
Lawson, Don(ald Elmer) 1917- , *9:* 132
Lawson, Marion Tubbs 1896- , *22:* 172
Lawson, Robert 1892-1957, *YABC 2:* 222
Laycock, George (Edwin) 1921- *5:* 105
Lazarevich, Mila 1942- , *17:* 118
Lazarus, Keo Felker 1913- , *21:* 94
Lea, Alec 1907- , *19:* 179
Lea, Richard. *See* Lea, Alec, *19:* 179
Leach, Maria 1892-1977, *28:* 144 (Brief Entry)
Leacroft, Helen 1919- , *6:* 139
Leacroft, Richard 1914- , *6:* 139

Leaf, (Wilbur) Munro 1905-1976, 20: 99

Leaf, VaDonna Jean 1929- , 26: 131

Leander, Ed. See Richelson, Geraldine, 29: 167

Lear, Edward 1812-1888, 18: 182

Leavitt, Jerome E(dward) 1916- , 23: 115

LeCain, Errol 1941- , 6: 141

Lee, Benjamin 1921- , 27: 130

Lee, Carol. See Fletcher, Helen Jill, 13: 36

Lee, Dennis (Beynon) 1939- , 14: 120

Lee, (Nelle) Harper 1926- , 11: 154

Lee, John R(obert) 1923-1976, 27: 130

Lee, Manning de V(illeneuve) 1894-1980, 22: 173 (Obituary)

Lee, Mary Price 1934- , 8: 111

Lee, Mildred 1908- , 6: 142

Lee, Robert C. 1931- , 20: 104

Lee, Robert J. 1921- , 10: 77

Lee, Tanith 1947- , 8: 112

Leekley, Thomas B(riggs) 1910- , 23: 117

Leeming, Jo Ann. See Leeming, Joseph, 26: 132

Leeming, Joseph 1897-1968, 26: 132

Lefler, Irene (Whitney) 1917- , 12: 131

Le Gallienne, Eva 1899- , 9: 133

LeGrand. See Henderson, LeGrand, 9: 104

Le Guin, Ursula K(roeber) 1929- , 4: 142

Legum, Colin 1919- , 10: 78

Lehr, Delorès 1920- , 10: 79

Leichman, Seymour 1933- , 5: 106

Leighton, Margaret 1896- , 1: 140

Leipold, L. Edmond 1902- , 16: 189

Leisk, David (Johnson) 1906-1975, 1: 141; 26: 133 (Obituary); 30: 141

Leister, Mary 1917- , 29: 125

Leitch, Patricia 1933- , 11: 155

LeMair, H(enriette) Willebeek 1889-1966, 29: 127 (Brief Entry)

Lenard, Alexander 1910-1972, 21: 95 (Obituary)

L'Engle, Madeleine 1918- , 1: 141; 27: 131

Lengyel, Cornel Adam 1915- , 27: 140

Lengyel, Emil 1895- , 3: 102

Lens, Sidney 1912- , 13: 127

Lenski, Lois 1893-1974, 1: 142; 26: 134

Lent, Blair 1930- , 2: 172

Lent, Henry Bolles 1901-1973, 17: 119

Leodhas, Sorche Nic. See Alger, Leclaire (Gowans), 15: 1

Leong Gor Yun. See Ellison, Virginia Howell, 4: 74

Lerner, Marguerite Rush 1924- , 11: 156

Lerner, Sharon (Ruth) 1938-1982, 11: 157; 29: 127 (Obituary)

Lerrigo, Marion Olive 1898-1968, 29: 127 (Obituary)

LeShan, Eda J(oan) 1922- , 21: 95

LeSieg, Theo. See Geisel, Theodor Seuss, 1: 104; 28: 107

Leslie, Robert Franklin 1911- , 7: 158

Lesser, Margaret 1899(?)-1979, 22: 173 (Obituary)

Lester, Julius B. 1939- , 12: 132

Le Sueur, Meridel 1900- , 6: 143

Leutscher, Alfred (George) 1913- , 23: 117

Levin, Betty 1927- , 19: 179

Levin, Marcia Obrasky 1918- , 13: 128

Levin, Meyer 1905-1981, 21: 96; 27: 140 (Obituary)

Levine, I(srael) E. 1923- , 12: 134

Levine, Joan Goldman, 11: 157

Levine, Rhoda, 14: 122

Levitin, Sonia 1934- , 4: 144

Levy, Elizabeth 1942- , 31: 115

Lewin, Ted 1935- , 21: 98

Lewis, Alice Hudson 1895(?)-1971, 29: 127 (Obituary)

Lewis, (Joseph) Anthony 1927- , 27: 140

Lewis, C(live) S(taples) 1898-1963, 13: 129

Lewis, Claudia (Louise) 1907- , 5: 107

Lewis, E. M., 20: 105

Lewis, Elizabeth Foreman 1892-1958, YABC 2: 243

Lewis, Francine. See Wells, Helen, 2: 266

Lewis, Hilda (Winifred) 1896-1974, 20: 105 (Obituary)

Lewis, Lucia Z. See Anderson, Lucia (Lewis), 10: 4

Lewis, Paul. See Gerson, Noel B(ertram), 22: 118

Lewis, Richard 1935- , 3: 104

Lewis, Shari 1934- , 30: 144 (Brief Entry)

Lewis, Thomas P(arker) 1936- , 27: 141

Lewiton, Mina 1904-1970, 2: 174

Lexau, Joan M., 1: 144

Ley, Willy 1906-1969, 2: 175

Leydon, Rita (Flodén) 1949- , 21: 100

L'Hommedieu, Dorothy K(easley) 1885-1961, 29: 128 (Obituary)

Libby, Bill. See Libby, William M., 5: 109

Libby, William M. 1927- , 5: 109

Liberty, Gene 1924- , 3: 106

Liebers, Arthur 1913- , 12: 134

Lieblich, Irene 1923- , 22: 173

Lietz, Gerald S. 1918- , 11: 159

Lifton, Betty Jean, 6: 143

Lightner, A. M. See Hopf, Alice L. 5: 82

Lilly, Ray. See Curtis, Richard (Alan), 29: 54

Liman, Ellen (Fogelson) 1936- , 22: 174

Limburg, Peter R(ichard) 1929- , 13: 147

Lincoln, C(harles) Eric 1924- , 5: 111

Linde, Gunnel 1924- , 5: 112

Lindgren, Astrid 1907- , 2: 177

Lindop, Edmund 1925- , 5: 113

Lindquist, Jennie Dorothea 1899-1977, 13: 148

Lindquist, Willis 1908- , 20: 105

Line, Les 1935- , 27: 142

Lingard, Joan, 8: 113

Link, Martin 1934- , 28: 144

Lionni, Leo 1910- , 8: 114

Lipinsky de Orlov, Lino S. 1908- , 22: 174

Lipkind, William 1904-1974, 15: 178

Lipman, David 1931- , 21: 101

Lipman, Matthew 1923- , 14: 122

Lippincott, Joseph Wharton 1887-1976, 17: 120

Lippincott, Sarah Lee 1920- , 22: 177

Lippman, Peter J. 1936- , 31: 119

Lipsyte, Robert 1938- , 5: 114

Lisle, Seward D. See Ellis, Edward S(ylvester), YABC 1: 116

Lisowski, Gabriel 1946- , 31: 120 (Brief Entry)

Liss, Howard 1922- , 4: 145

Lissim, Simon 1900-1981, 28: 145 (Brief Entry)

List, Ilka Katherine 1935- , 6: 145

Liston, Robert A. 1927- , 5: 114

Litchfield, Ada B(assett) 1916- , 5: 115

Litowinsky, Olga (Jean) 1936- , 26: 142

Little, A. Edward. See Klein, Aaron E., 28: 143 (Brief Entry)

Little, (Flora) Jean 1932- , 2: 178

Little, Mary E. 1912- , 28: 145

Littledale, Freya (Lota), 2: 179

Lively, Penelope 1933- , 7: 159

Liversidge, (Henry) Douglas 1913- , 8: 116

Livingston, Myra Cohn 1926- , 5: 116

Livingston, Richard R(oland)
1922- , *8:* 118
Llerena-Aguirre, Carlos Antonio
1952- , *19:* 180
Llewellyn, Richard. *See* Llewellyn
Lloyd, Richard Dafydd
Vyvyan, *11:* 160
Llewellyn, T. Harcourt. *See*
Hamilton, Charles Harold St.
John, *13:* 77
Llewellyn Lloyd, Richard Dafydd
Vyvyan 1906- , *11:* 160
Lloyd, Errol 1943- , *22:* 178
Lloyd, Norman 1909-1980,
23: 118 (Obituary)
Lloyd, (Mary) Norris 1908- ,
10: 79
Lobel, Anita 1934- , *6:* 146
Lobel, Arnold 1933- , *6:* 147
Lobsenz, Amelia, *12:* 135
Lobsenz, Norman M. 1919- ,
6: 148
Lochlons, Colin. *See* Jackson, C.
Paul, *6:* 120
Locke, Clinton W. [Collective
pseudonym], *1:* 145
Locke, Lucie 1904- , *10:* 81
Lockwood, Mary. *See* Spelman,
Mary, *28:* 195
Loeb, Robert H., Jr. 1917- ,
21: 102
Loeper, John J(oseph) 1929- ,
10: 81
Loescher, Ann Dull 1942- ,
20: 107
Loescher, Gil(burt Damian)
1945- , *20:* 107
Löfgren, Ulf 1931- , *3:* 106
Lofting, Hugh 1886-1947, *15:* 180
Lofts, Norah (Robinson) 1904- ,
8: 119
Logue, Christopher 1926- ,
23: 119
Loken, Newton (Clayton) 1919- ,
26: 143
Lomas, Steve. *See* Brennan, Joseph
L., *6:* 33
Lomask, Milton 1909- , *20:* 109
London, Jack 1876-1916, *18:* 195
London, Jane. *See* Geis, Darlene,
7: 101
London, John Griffith. *See* London,
Jack, *18:* 195
Lonergan, (Pauline) Joy (Maclean)
1909- , *10:* 82
Long, Helen Beecher [Collective
pseudonym], *1:* 146
Long, Judith Elaine 1953- ,
20: 110
Long, Judy. *See* Long, Judith
Elaine, *20:* 110
Long, Laura Mooney 1892-1967,
29: 128 (Obituary)
Longfellow, Henry Wadsworth
1807-1882, *19:* 181

Longman, Harold S. 1919- ,
5: 117
Longsworth, Polly 1933- ,
28: 146
Longtemps, Kenneth 1933- ,
17: 123
Longway, A. Hugh. *See* Lang,
Andrew, *16:* 178
Loomis, Robert D., *5:* 119
Lopshire, Robert 1927- , *6:* 149
Lord, Beman 1924- , *5:* 119
Lord, (Doreen Mildred) Douglas
1904- , *12:* 136
Lord, John Vernon 1939- ,
21: 103
Lord, Nancy. *See* Titus, Eve,
2: 240
Lord, Walter 1917- , *3:* 109
Lorenzini, Carlo 1826-1890,
29: 128
Lorraine, Walter (Henry) 1929- ,
16: 191
Loss, Joan 1933- , *11:* 162
Lot, Parson. *See* Kingsley, Charles,
YABC 2: 179
Lothrop, Harriet Mulford Stone
1844-1924, *20:* 110
Lourie, Helen. *See* Storr, Catherine
(Cole), *9:* 181
Love, Katherine 1907- , *3:* 109
Love, Sandra (Weller) 1940- ,
26: 144
Lovelace, Delos Wheeler
1894-1967, *7:* 160
Lovelace, Maud Hart 1892-1980,
2: 181; *23:* 120 (Obituary)
Lovett, Margaret (Rose) 1915- ,
22: 179
Low, Alice 1926- , *11:* 163
Low, Elizabeth Hammond 1898- ,
5: 120
Low, Joseph 1911- , *14:* 123
Lowe, Jay, Jr. *See* Loper, John
J(oseph), *10:* 81
Lowenstein, Dyno 1914- , *6:* 150
Lowitz, Anson C. 1901(?)-1978,
18: 214
Lowitz, Sadyebeth (Heath)
1901-1969, *17:* 125
Lowry, Lois 1937- , *23:* 120
Lowry, Peter 1953- , *7:* 160
Lowther, George F. 1913-1975,
30: 144 (Obituary)
Lozier, Herbert 1915- , *26:* 145
Lubell, Cecil 1912- , *6:* 150
Lubell, Winifred 1914- , *6:* 151
Lucas, E(dward) V(errall)
1868-1938, *20:* 117
Luckhardt, Mildred Corell 1898- ,
5: 122
Ludden, Allen (Ellsworth)
1918(?)-1981, *27:* 143
(Obituary)
Ludlum, Mabel Cleland. *See*
Widdemer, Mabel Cleland,
5: 200

Lueders, Edward (George) 1923- ,
14: 125
Lugard, Flora Louisa Shaw
1852-1929, *21:* 104
Luger, Harriett M(andelay)
1914- , *23:* 122
Luhrmann, Winifred B(ruce)
1934- , *11:* 165
Luis, Earlene W. 1929- , *11:* 165
Lum, Peter. *See* Crowe, Bettina
Lum, *6:* 53
Lund, Doris (Herold) 1919- ,
12: 137
Lunn, Janet 1928- , *4:* 146
Luther, Frank 1905-1980, *25:* 173
(Obituary)
Luttrell, Guy L. 1938- , *22:* 180
Lutzker, Edythe 1904- , *5:* 124
Luzzati, Emanuele 1912- , *7:* 161
Lydon, Michael 1942- , *11:* 165
Lyfick, Warren. *See* Reeves,
Lawrence F., *29:* 166
Lyle, Katie Letcher 1938- ,
8: 121
Lynch, Lorenzo 1932- , *7:* 161
Lynch, Marietta 1947-, *29:* 137
Lynch, Patricia (Nora) 1898-1972,
9: 134
Lynn, Mary. *See* Brokamp,
Marilyn, *10:* 15
Lynn, Patricia. *See* Watts, Mabel
Pizzey, *11:* 227
Lyon, Elinor 1921- , *6:* 154
Lyon, Lyman R. *See* De Camp,
L(yon) Sprague, *9:* 49
Lyons, Dorothy 1907- , *3:* 110
Lyons, Grant 1941- , *30:* 144
Lystad, Mary (Hanemann) 1928- ,
11: 166
Lyttle, Richard B(ard) 1927- ,
23: 123
Lytton, Edward G(eorge) E(arle)
L(ytton) Bulwer-Lytton, Baron
1803-1873, *23:* 125

Maar, Leonard (F., Jr.) 1927- ,
30: 146
Maas, Selve, *14:* 127
Mac. *See* MacManus, Seumas,
25: 175
MacArthur-Onslow, Annette
(Rosemary) 1933- , *26:* 145
Macaulay, David Alexander
1946- , *27:* 144 (Brief Entry)
MacBeth, George 1932- , *4:* 146
MacClintock, Dorcas 1932- ,
8: 122
MacDonald, Anson. *See* Heinlein,
Robert A(nson), *9:* 102
MacDonald, Betty (Campbell Bard)
1908-1958, *YABC 1:* 167
Macdonald, Blackie. *See* Emrich,
Duncan, *11:* 90

Macdonald, Dwight 1906- ,
29: 138
Mac Donald, Golden. *See* Brown,
Margaret Wise, *YABC 2:* 9
Macdonald, Marcia. *See* Hill, Grace
Livingston, *YABC 2:* 162
Macdonald, Shelagh 1937- ,
25: 174
Macdonald, Zillah K(atherine)
1885- , *11:* 167
Mace, Elisabeth 1933- , *27:* 144
MacFarlane, Iris 1922- , *11:* 170
MacGregor, Ellen 1906-1954,
27: 145 (Brief Entry)
MacGregor-Hastie, Roy 1929- ,
3: 111
MacInnes, Helen 1907- , *22:* 181
MacIntyre, Elisabeth 1916- ,
17: 125
Mack, Stan(ley), *17:* 128
MacKellar, William 1914- ,
4: 148
Mackenzie, Dr. Willard. *See*
Stratemeyer, Edward L., *1:* 208
MacKenzie, Garry 1921- ,
31: 120 (Brief Entry)
MacLean, Alistair (Stuart) 1923- ,
23: 131
MacLeod, Beatrice (Beach)
1910- , *10:* 82
MacLeod, Charlotte (Matilda
Hughes) 1922- , *28:* 147
MacLeod, Ellen Jane (Anderson)
1916- , *14:* 129
MacManus, James. *See* MacManus,
Seumas, 25: 175
MacManus, Seumas 1869-1960,
25: 175
MacMillan, Annabelle. *See* Quick,
Annabelle, 2: 207
MacPeek, Walter G. 1902-1973,
4: 148; 25: 177 (Obituary)
MacPherson, Margaret 1908- ,
9: 135
MacPherson, Thomas George
1915-1976, 30: 147 (Obituary)
Macrae, Hawk. *See* Barker, Albert
W., 8: 3
MacRae, Travis. *See* Feagles, Anita
(MacRae), 9: 63
Macumber, Mari. *See* Sandoz,
Mari, 5: 159
Madden, Don 1927- , *3:* 112
Maddison, Angela Mary 1923- ,
10: 82
Maddock, Reginald 1912- ,
15: 184
Madian, Jon 1941- , *9:* 136
Madison, Arnold 1937- , *6:* 155
Madison, Winifred, *5:* 125
Maestro, Betsy 1944- , *30:* 147
(Brief Entry)
Maestro, Giulio 1942- , *8:* 123
Maguire, Gregory 1954- , *28:* 148
Maher, Ramona 1934- , *13:* 149

Mählqvist, (Karl) Stefan 1943- ,
30: 147
Mahon, Julia C(unha) 1916- ,
11: 171
Mahony, Elizabeth Winthrop
1948- , *8:* 125
Mahood, Kenneth 1930- , *24:* 140
Mahy, Margaret 1936- , *14:* 129
Maidoff, Ilka List. *See* List, Ilka
Katherine, 6: 145
Maik, Henri. *See* Hecht, Henri
Joseph, 9: 101
Maitland, Antony (Jasper) 1935- ,
25: 177
Malcolmson, Anne. *See* Storch,
Anne B. von, *1:* 221
Malcolmson, David 1899- ,
6: 157
Malmberg, Carl 1904- , *9:* 136
Malo, John 1911- , *4:* 149
Maltese, Michael 1908(?)-1981,
24: 141(Obituary)
Malvern, Gladys (?)-1962,
23: 133
Manchel, Frank 1935- , *10:* 83
Manfred, Frederick F(eikema)
1912- , *30:* 150
Mangione, Jerre 1909- , *6:* 157
Mangurian, David 1938- ,
14: 131
Maniscalco, Joseph 1926- ,
10: 85
Manley, Deborah 1932- , *28:* 149
Manley, Seon, *15:* 185
Mann, Peggy, *6:* 157
Mannheim, Grete (Salomon)
1909- , *10:* 85
Manniche, Lise 1943- , *31:* 120
Manning, Rosemary 1911- ,
10: 87
Manning-Sanders, Ruth 1895- ,
15: 186
Manton, Jo. *See* Gittings, Jo
Manton, 3: 76
Manushkin, Fran 1942- , *7:* 161
Mapes, Mary A. *See* Ellison,
Virginia Howell, 4:-74
Mara, Barney. *See* Roth, Arthur
J(oseph), 28: 177 (Brief Entry)
Mara, Jeanette. *See* Cebulash, Mel,
10: 19
Marais, Josef 1905-1978, 24: 141
(Obituary)
Marasmus, Seymour. *See* Rivoli,
Mario, 10: 129
Marcellino. *See* Agnew, Edith J.,
11: 3
Marchant, Bessie 1862-1941,
YABC 2: 245
Marchant, Catherine. *See* Cookson,
Catherine (McMulen), 9: 42
Marcher, Marion Walden 1890- ,
10: 87
Marcus, Rebecca B(rian) 1907- ,
9: 138

Margolis, Richard J(ules) 1929- ,
4: 150
Mariana. *See* Foster, Marian Curtis,
23: 73
Marino, Dorothy Bronson 1912- ,
14: 134
Mark, Jan 1943- , *22:* 182
Mark, Pauline (Dahlin) 1913- ,
14: 136
Mark, Polly. *See* Mark, Pauline
(Dahlin), *14:* 136
Markins, W. S. *See* Jenkins, Marie
M., 7: 143
Marko, Katherine D(olores),
28: 151
Marks, J. *See* Highwater, Jamake,
30: 128 (Brief Entry)
Marks, J(ames) M(acdonald)
1921- , *13:* 150
Marks, Margaret L. 1911(?)-1980,
23: 134 (Obituary)
Marks, Mickey Klar, *12:* 139
Marks, Peter. *See* Smith, Robert
Kimmel, 12: 205
Marks, Stan(ley) 1929- , *14:* 136
Markun, Patricia M(aloney)
1924- , *15:* 189
Marlowe, Amy Bell [Collective
pseudonym], *1:* 146
Marokvia, Artur 1909- , *31:* 122
Marokvia, Mireille (Journet)
1918- , *5:* 126
Marriott, Alice Lee 1910- ,
31: 123
Mars, W. T. *See* Mars, Witold
Tadeusz J., *3:* 114
Mars, Witold Tadeusz, J. 1912- ,
3: 114
Marsh, J. E. *See* Marshall, Evelyn,
11: 172
Marsh, Jean. *See* Marshall, Evelyn,
11: 172
Marshall, Anthony D(ryden)
1924- , *18:* 215
Marshall, (Sarah) Catherine
1914- , *2:* 182
Marshall, Douglas. *See* McClintock,
Marshall, 3: 119
Marshall, Evelyn 1897- , *11:* 172
Marshall, James 1942- , *6:* 161
Marshall, Percy. *See* Young, Percy
M(arshall), *31:* 191
Marshall, S(amuel) L(yman)
A(twood) 1900-1977, 21: 107
Marsten, Richard. *See* Hunter,
Evan, 25: 153
Marston, Hope Irvin 1935- ,
31: 124
Martignoni, Margaret E.
1908(?)-1974, 27: 145
(Obituary)
Martin, Eugene [Collective
pseudonym], *1:* 146
Martin, Fredric. *See* Christopher,
Matt, 2: 58

Martin, J(ohn) P(ercival) 1880(?)-1966, *15:* 190

Martin, Jeremy. *See* Levin, Marcia Obransky, *13:* 128

Martin, Lynne 1923- , *21:* 109

Martin, Marcia. *See* Levin, Marcia Obransky, *13:* 128

Martin, Nancy. *See* Salmon, Annie Elizabeth, *13:* 188

Martin, Patricia Miles 1899- , *1:* 146

Martin, Peter. *See* Chaundler, Christine, *1:* 56; *25:* 83 (Obituary)

Martin, Rene (?)-1977, *20:* 123 (Obituary)

Martin, Rupert (Claude) 1905- , *31:* 125

Martin, Vicky. *See* Storey, Victoria Carolyn, *16:* 248

Martineau, Harriet 1802-1876, *YABC 2:* 247

Martini, Teri 1930- , *3:* 116

Marx, Robert F(rank) 1936- , *24:* 142

Marzani, Carl (Aldo) 1912- , *12:* 140

Marzollo, Jean 1942- , *29:* 139

Masefield, John 1878-1967, *19:* 204

Mason, F. van Wyck 1901-1978, *3:* 117; *26:* 146 (Obituary)

Mason, Frank W. *See* Mason, F. van Wyck, *3:* 117; *26:* 146 (Obituary)

Mason, George Frederick 1904- , *14:* 138

Mason, Miriam E(vangeline) 1900-1973, *2:* 183; *26:* 146 (Obituary)

Mason, Tally. *See* Derleth, August (William), *5:* 54

Mason, Van Wyck. *See* Mason, F. van Wyck, *3:* 117; *26:* 146 (Obituary)

Masselman, George 1897-1971, *19:* 214

Massie, Diane Redfield, *16:* 193

Masters, Kelly R. 1897- , *3:* 118

Masters, William. *See* Cousins, Margaret, *2:* 79

Mathiesen, Egon 1907-1976, *28:* 151 (Obituary)

Mathis, Sharon Bell 1937- , *7:* 162

Matson, Emerson N(els) 1926- , *12:* 141

Matsui, Tadashi 1926- , *8:* 126

Matsuno, Masako 1935- , *6:* 161

Matte, (Encarnacion) L'Enc 1936- , *22:* 182

Matthews, Ellen 1950- , *28:* 152

Matthews, Patricia 1927- , *28:* 153

Matthews, William Henry III 1919- , *28:* 155 (Brief Entry)

Matthiessen, Peter 1927- , *27:* 145

Matulka, Jan 1890-1972, *28:* 155 (Brief Entry)

Matus, Greta 1938- , *12:* 142

Maves, Mary Carolyn 1916- , *10:* 88

Maves, Paul B(enjamin) 1913- , *10:* 88

Mawicke, Tran 1911- , *15:* 190

Maxon, Anne. *See* Best, Allena Champlin, *2:* 25; *25:* 48 (Obituary)

Maxwell, Arthur S. 1896-1970, *11:* 173

Maxwell, Edith 1923- , *7:* 164

May, Charles Paul 1920- , *4:* 151

May, Julian 1931- , *11:* 175

May, Robert Lewis 1905-1976, *27:* 146 (Obituary)

Mayberry, Florence V(irginia Wilson), *10:* 89

Mayer, Albert Ignatius, Jr. 1906-1960, *29:* 142 (Obituary)

Mayer, Ann M(argaret) 1938- , *14:* 140

Mayer, Mercer 1943- , *16:* 195

Mayne, William 1928- , *6:* 162

Mays, (Lewis) Victor, (Jr.) 1927- , *5:* 126

Mazer, Harry 1925- , *31:* 126

Mazer, Norma Fox 1931- , *24:* 144

Mazza, Adriana 1928- , *19:* 215

McBain, Ed. *See* Hunter, Evan, *25:* 153

McCaffrey, Anne 1926- , *8:* 127

McCain, Murray (David, Jr.) 1926-1981, *7:* 165; *29:* 142 (Obituary)

McCall, Edith S. 1911- , *6:* 163

McCall, Virginia Nielsen 1909- , *13:* 151

McCallum, Phyllis 1911- , *10:* 90

McCarthy, Agnes 1933- , *4:* 152

McCarty, Rega Kramer 1904- , *10:* 91

McCaslin, Nellie 1914- , *12:* 143

McClintock, Marshall 1906-1967, *3:* 119

McClintock, Mike. *See* McClintock, Marshall, *3:* 119

McClintock, Theodore 1902-1971, *14:* 140

McClinton, Leon 1933- , *11:* 178

McCloskey, Robert 1914- , *2:* 185

McClung, Robert M. 1916- , *2:* 188

McClure, Gillian Mary 1948- , *31:* 131

McCord, David (Thompson Watson) 1897- , *18:* 217

McCormick, Brooks. *See* Adams, William Taylor, *28:* 21

McCormick, Dell J. 1892-1949, *19:* 216

McCormick, (George) Donald (King) 1911- , *14:* 141

McCormick, Edith (Joan) 1934- , *30:* 152

McCourt, Edward (Alexander) 1907-1972, *28:* 155 (Obituary)

McCoy, Iola Fuller, *3:* 120

McCoy, J(oseph) J(erome) 1917- , *8:* 127

McCrady, Lady 1951- , *16:* 197

McCrea, James 1920- , *3:* 121

McCrea, Ruth 1921- , *3:* 121

McCullers, (Lula) Carson 1917-1967, *27:* 146

McCulloch, Derek (Ivor Breashur) 1897-1967, *29:* 142 (Obituary)

McCullough, Frances Monson 1938- , *8:* 129

McCully, Emily Arnold 1939- , *5:* 128

McCurdy, Michael 1942- , *13:* 153

McDearmon, Kay, *20:* 123

McDermott, Beverly Brodsky 1941- , *11:* 179

McDermott, Gerald 1941- , *16:* 199

McDole, Carol. *See* Farley, Carol, *4:* 81

McDonald, Gerald D. 1905-1970, *3:* 123

McDonald, Jill (Masefield) 1927-1982, *13:* 154; *29:* 142 (Obituary)

McDonald, Lucile Saunders 1898- , *10:* 92

McDonnell, Lois Eddy 1914- , *10:* 94

McEwen, Robert (Lindley) 1926-1980, *23:* 134 (Obituary)

McFall, Christie 1918- , *12:* 144

McFarland, Kenton D(ean) 1920- , *11:* 180

McFarlane, Leslie 1902-1977, *31:* 133

McGaw, Jessie Brewer 1913- , *10:* 95

McGee, Barbara 1943- , *6:* 165

McGiffin, (Lewis) Lee (Shaffer) 1908- , *1:* 148

McGill, Marci. *See* Ridlon, Marci, *22:* 211

McGinley, Phyllis 1905-1978, *2:* 190; *24:* 145 (Obituary)

McGovern, Ann, *8:* 130

McGowen, Thomas E. 1927- , *2:* 192

McGowen, Tom. *See* McGowen, Thomas, *2:* 192

McGrady, Mike 1933- , *6:* 166

McGraw, Eloise Jarvis 1915- , *1:* 149

McGraw, William Corbin 1916- , *3:* 124

McGregor, Craig 1933- , *8:* 131

McGregor, Iona 1929- , *25:* 179

McGuire, Edna 1899- , *13:* 155

McGurk, Slater. *See* Roth, Arthur J(oseph), *28:* 177

McHargue, Georgess, *4:* 152

McIlwraith, Maureen 1922- , *2:* 193

McKay, Robert W. 1921- , *15:* 192

McKenzie, Dorothy Clayton 1910-1981, *28:* 155 (Obituary)

McKillip, Patricia A(nne) 1948- , *30:* 152

McKown, Robin, *6:* 166

McLaurin, Anne 1953- , *27:* 150

McLean, Kathryn (Anderson) 1909-1966, *9:* 140

McLeod, Emilie Warren 1926-1982, *23:* 135; *31:* 142 (Obituary)

McLeod, Margaret Vail. *See* Holloway, Teresa (Bragunier), *26:* 122

McMeekin, Clark. *See* McMeekin, Isabel McLennan, *3:* 126

McMeekin, Isabel McLennan 1895- , *3:* 126

McMillan, Bruce 1947- , *22:* 183

McMullen, Catherine. *See* Cookson, Catherine (McMullen), *9:* 42

McMurtrey, Martin A(loysius) 1921- , *21:* 110

McNair, Kate, *3:* 127

McNamara, Margaret C(raig) 1915-1981, *24:* 145 (Obituary)

McNeely, Jeannette 1918- , *25:* 180

McNeer, May, *1:* 150

McNeill, Janet 1907- , *1:* 151

McNickle, (William) D'Arcy 1904-1977, *22:* 185 (Obituary)

McNulty, Faith 1918- , *12:* 144

McPharlin, Paul 1903-1948, *31:* 142 (Brief Entry)

McPherson, James M. 1936- , *16:* 202

McQueen, Mildred Hark 1908- , *12:* 145

McSwigan, Marie 1907-1962, *24:* 146

McWhirter, A(lan) Ross 1925-1975, *31:* 143 (Obituary)

Mead, Margaret 1901-1978, *20:* 123 (Obituary)

Mead, Russell (M., Jr.) 1935- , *10:* 96

Mead, Stella (?)-1981, *27:* 151 (Obituary)

Meade, Ellen (Roddick) 1936- , *5:* 130

Meade, Marion 1934- , *23:* 136

Meader, Stephen W(arren) 1892- , *1:* 153

Meadow, Charles T(roub) 1929- , *23:* 136

Meadowcroft, Enid LaMonte. *See* Wright, Enid Meadowcroft, *3:* 267

Meaker, M. J. *See* Meaker, Marijane, *20:* 124

Meaker, Marijane 1927- , *20:* 124

Means, Florence Crannell 1891-1980, *1:* 154; *25:* 181 (Obituary)

Medary, Marjorie 1890- , *14:* 143

Meddaugh, Susan 1944- , *29:* 144

Medearis, Mary 1915- , *5:* 130

Mee, Charles L., Jr. 1938- , *8:* 132

Meek, S(terner St.) P(aul) 1894-1972, *28:* 155 (Obituary)

Meeker, Oden 1918(?)-1976, *14:* 144

Meeks, Esther MacBain, *1:* 155

Mehdevi, Alexander 1947- , *7:* 166

Mehdevi, Anne (Marie) Sinclair, *8:* 132

Meighan, Donald Charles 1929- , *30:* 153

Meigs, Cornelia Lynde 1884-1973, *6:* 167

Melcher, Frederic Gershom 1879-1963, *22:* 185 (Obituary)

Melcher, Marguerite Fellows 1879-1969, *10:* 96

Melin, Grace Hathaway 1892-1973, *10:* 96

Mellersh, H(arold) E(dward) L(eslie) 1897- , *10:* 97

Meltzer, Milton 1915- , *1:* 156

Melville, Anne. *See* Potter, Margaret (Newman), *21:* 119

Melwood, Mary. *See* Lewis, E. M., *20:* 105

Melzack, Ronald 1929- , *5:* 130

Memling, Carl 1918-1969, *6:* 169

Mendel, Jo [House pseudonym]. *See* Bond, Gladys Baker, *14:* 41

Meng, Heinz (Karl) 1924- , *13:* 157

Menotti, Gian Carlo 1911- , *29:* 144

Mercer, Charles (Edward) 1917- , *16:* 203

Meredith, David William. *See* Miers, Earl Schenck, *1:* 160; *26:* 146 (Obituary)

Meriwether, Louise 1923- , *31:* 143 (Brief Entry)

Merriam, Eve 1916- , *3:* 128

Merrill, Jean (Fairbanks) 1923- , *1:* 158

Metcalf, Suzanne. *See* Baum, L(yman) Frank, *18:* 7

Meyer, Carolyn 1935- , *9:* 140

Meyer, Edith Patterson 1895- , *5:* 131

Meyer, F(ranklyn) E(dward) 1932- , *9:* 142

Meyer, Jean Shepherd 1929- , *11:* 181

Meyer, Jerome Sydney 1895-1975, *3:* 129; *25:* 181 (Obituary)

Meyer, June. *See* Jordan, June, *4:* 131

Meyer, Louis A(lbert) 1942- , *12:* 147

Meyer, Renate 1930- , *6:* 170

Meyers, Susan 1942- , *19:* 216

Meynier, Yvonne (Pollet) 1908- , *14:* 146

Micale, Albert 1913- , *22:* 185

Micklish, Rita 1931- , *12:* 147

Miers, Earl Schenck 1910-1972, *1:* 160; *26:* 146 (Obituary)

Miklowitz, Gloria D. 1927- , *4:* 154

Mikolaycak, Charles 1937- , *9:* 143

Miles, Betty 1928- , *8:* 132

Miles, Miska. *See* Martin, Patricia Miles, *1:* 146

Miles, (Mary) Patricia 1930- , *29:* 146

Milgrom, Harry 1912- , *25:* 181

Milhous, Katherine 1894-1977, *15:* 192

Militant. *See* Sandburg, Carl (August), *8:* 177

Millar, Barbara F. 1924- , *12:* 149

Miller, Albert G(riffith) 1905-1982, *12:* 150; *31:* 143 (Obituary)

Miller, Alice P(atricia McCarthy), *22:* 187

Miller, Don 1923- , *15:* 194

Miller, Doris R. *See* Mosesson, Gloria R(ubin), *24:* 153

Miller, Eddie. *See* Miller, Edward, *8:* 134

Miller, Edna (Anita) 1920- , *29:* 147

Miller, Edward 1905-1974, *8:* 134

Miller, Helen M(arkley), *5:* 133

Miller, Helen Topping 1884-1960, *29:* 149 (Obituary)

Miller, Jane (Judith) 1925- , *15:* 196

Miller, John. *See* Samachson, Joseph, *3:* 182

Miller, Mary Beth 1942- , *9:* 145

Milligan, Spike. *See* Milligan, Terence Alan, *29:* 151

Milligan, Terence Alan 1918- , *29:* 151

Millstead, Thomas Edward, *30:* 156

Milne, A(lan) A(lexander) 1882-1956, *YABC 1:* 174

Milne, Lorus J., *5:* 133

Milne, Margery, *5:* 134

Milonas, Rolf. *See* Myller, Rolf, *27:* 153

Milotte, Alfred G(eorge) 1904- ,
　11: 181
Milton, Hilary (Herbert) 1920- ,
　23: 137
Milton, John R(onald) 1924- ,
　24: 147
Minarik, Else Holmelund 1920- ,
　15: 197
Miner, Lewis S. 1909- , *11:* 183
Minier, Nelson. *See* Stoutenburg,
　Adrien, *3:* 217
Mintonye, Grace, *4:* 156
Mirsky, Jeannette 1903- , *8:* 135
Mirsky, Reba Paeff 1902-1966,
　1: 161
Miskovits, Christine 1939- ,
　10: 98
Miss Francis. *See* Horwich, Francis
　R., *11:* 142
Miss Read. *See* Saint, Dora Jessie,
　10: 132
Mitchell, Cynthia 1922- , *29:* 151
Mitchell, (Sibyl) Elyne (Keith)
　1913- , *10:* 98
Mitchell, Yvonne 1925-1979,
　24: 148 (Obituary)
Mitchison, Naomi Margaret
　(Haldane) 1897- , *24:* 148
Mizner, Elizabeth Howard 1907- ,
　27: 151
Mizumura, Kazue, *18:* 222
Moe, Barbara 1937- , *20:* 126
Moeri, Louise 1924- , *24:* 151
Moffett, Martha (Leatherwood)
　1934- , *8:* 136
Mohn, Peter B(urnet) 1934- ,
　28: 155
Mohn, Viola Kohl 1914- , *8:* 138
Mohr, Nicholasa 1935- , *8:* 138
Molarsky, Osmond 1909- ,
　16: 204
Molloy, Paul 1920- , *5:* 135
Momaday, N(avarre) Scott
　1934- , *30:* 156 (Brief Entry)
Moncure, Jane Belk, *23:* 139
Monjo, F(erdinand) N. 1924-1978,
　16: 206
Monroe, Lyle. *See* Heinlein, Robert
　A(nson), *9:* 102
Monsell, Helen (Albee)
　1895-1971, *24:* 152
Montana, Bob 1920-1975, *21:* 110
　(Obituary)
Montgomerie, Norah Mary
　1913- , *26:* 146
Montgomery, Constance. *See*
　Cappell, Constance, *22:* 65
Montgomery, Elizabeth Rider,
　3: 132
Montgomery, L(ucy) M(aud)
　1874-1942, *YABC 1:* 182
Montgomery, Rutherford George
　1894- , *3:* 134
Montresor, Beni 1926- , *3:* 136
Moody, Ralph Owen 1898- ,
　1: 162

Moon, Carl 1879-1948, *25:* 182
Moon, Grace 1877(?)-1947,
　25: 185
Moon, Sheila (Elizabeth) 1910- ,
　5: 136
Moor, Emily. *See* Deming, Richard,
　24: 83
Moore, Anne Carroll 1871-1961,
　13: 158
Moore, Clement Clarke
　1779-1863, *18:* 224
Moore, Eva 1942- , *20:* 127
Moore, Fenworth. *See* Stratemeyer,
　Edward L., *1:* 208
Moore, Janet Gaylord 1905- ,
　18: 236
Moore, John Travers 1908- ,
　12: 151
Moore, Lamont 1909- , *29:* 153
　(Brief Entry)
Moore, Margaret Rumberger
　1903- , *12:* 154
Moore, Marianne (Craig)
　1887-1972, *20:* 128
Moore, Regina. *See* Dunne, Mary
　Collins, *11:* 83
Moore, Rosalie. *See* Brown, Rosalie
　(Gertrude) Moore, *9:* 26
Moore, Ruth, *23:* 142
Moore, S. E., *23:* 142
Mooser, Stephen 1941- , *28:* 157
Mordvinoff, Nicolas 1911-1973,
　17: 129
More, Caroline. *See* Cone, Molly
　Lamken, *1:* 66; *28:* 65
More, Caroline. *See* Strachan,
　Margaret Pitcairn, *14:* 193
Morey, Charles. *See* Fletcher, Helen
　Jill, *13:* 36
Morey, Walt 1907- , *3:* 139
Morgan, Alison Mary 1930- ,
　30: 157
Morgan, Helen (Gertrude Louise)
　1921- , *29:* 154
Morgan, Helen Tudor. *See* Morgan,
　Helen (Gertrude Louise),
　29: 154
Morgan, Jane. *See* Cooper, James
　Fenimore, *19:* 68
Morgan, Lenore 1908- , *8:* 139
Morgan, Louise. *See* Morgan,
　Helen (Gertrude Louise),
　29: 154
Morgan, Shirley 1933- , *10:* 99
Morrah, Dave. *See* Morrah, David
　Wardlaw, Jr., *10:* 100
Morrah, David Wardlaw, Jr.
　1914- , *10:* 100
Morressy, John 1930- , *23:* 143
Morris, Desmond (John) 1928- ,
　14: 146
Morris, Robert A. 1933- , *7:* 166
Morris, William 1913- , *29:* 155
Morrison, Dorothy Nafus, *29:* 155
Morrison, Gert W. *See* Stratemeyer,
　Edward L., *1:* 208

Morrison, Lillian 1917- , *3:* 140
Morrison, Lucile Phillips 1896- ,
　17: 134
Morrison, Velma Ford 1909- ,
　21: 110
Morrison, William. *See* Samachson,
　Joseph, *3:* 182
Morriss, James E(dward) 1932- ,
　8: 139
Morrow, Betty. *See* Bacon,
　Elizabeth, *3:* 14
Morse, Carol. *See* Yeakley, Marjory
　Hall, *21:* 207
Morse, Dorothy B(ayley)
　1906-1979, *24:* 153 (Obituary)
Morse, Flo 1921- , *30:* 158
Mort, Vivian. *See* Cromie, Alice
　Hamilton, *24:* 78
Morton, Miriam 1918- , *9:* 145
Moscow, Alvin 1925- , *3:* 142
Mosel, Arlene 1921- , *7:* 167
Moser, Don. *See* Moser, Donald
　Bruce, *31:* 143
Moser, Donald Bruce 1932- ,
　31: 143
Mosesson, Gloria R(ubin), *24:* 153
Moskin, Marietta D(unston)
　1928- , *23:* 144
Moskof, Martin Stephen 1930- ,
　27: 152
Moss, Don(ald) 1920- , *11:* 183
Moss, Elaine Dora 1924- ,
　31: 144 (Brief Entry)
Motz, Lloyd, *20:* 133
Mountfield, David. *See* Grant, Neil,
　14: 75
Moussard, Jacqueline 1924- ,
　24: 154
Mowat, Farley 1921- , *3:* 142
Mrs. Fairstar. *See* Horne, Richard
　Henry, *29:* 106
Mueller, Virginia 1924- , *28:* 157
Muir, Frank 1920- , *30:* 159
Mulcahy, Lucille Burnett, *12:* 155
Mulgan, Catherine. *See* Gough,
　Catherine, *24:* 125
Muller, Billex. *See* Ellis, Edward
　S(ylvester), *YABC 1:* 116
Mullins, Edward S(wift) 1922- ,
　10: 101
Mulvihill, William Patrick 1923- ,
　8: 140
Mun. *See* Leaf, (Wilbur) Munro,
　20: 99
Munari, Bruno 1907- , *15:* 199
Munce, Ruth Hill 1898- , *12:* 156
Munowitz, Ken 1935-1977,
　14: 149
Munro, Alice 1931- , *29:* 156
Munson(-Benson), Tunie 1946- ,
　15: 201
Munves, James (Albert) 1922- ,
　30: 161
Munzer, Martha E. 1899- , *4:* 157
Murphy, Barbara Beasley 1933- ,
　5: 137

Murphy, E(mmett) Jefferson
1926- , 4: 159
Murphy, Pat. See Murphy,
E(mmett) Jefferson, 4: 159
Murphy, Robert (William)
1902-1971, 10: 102
Murray, Marian, 5: 138
Murray, Michele 1933-1974,
7: 170
Musgrave, Florence 1902- ,
3: 144
Musgrove, Margaret W(ynkoop)
1943- , 26: 147
Mussey, Virginia T. H. See Ellison,
Virginia Howell, 4: 74
Mutz. See Kunstler, Morton, 10: 73
Myers, Bernice, 9: 146
Myers, Caroline Elizabeth (Clark)
1887-1980, 28: 158
Myers, Hortense (Powner) 1913- ,
10: 102
Myers, Walter Dean 1937- ,
27: 153 (Brief Entry)
Myller, Rolf 1926- , 27: 153
Myrus, Donald (Richard) 1927- ,
23: 147

Namioka, Lensey 1929- , 27: 154
Napier, Mark. See Laffin, John
(Alfred Charles), 31: 111
Nash, Linell. See Smith, Linell
Nash, 2: 227
Nash, (Fridric) Ogden
1902-1971, 2: 194
Nast, Elsa Ruth. See Watson, Jane
Werner, 3: 244
Nathan, Dorothy (Goldeen)
(?)-1966, 15: 202
Nathan, Robert 1894- , 6: 171
Navarra, John Gabriel 1927- ,
8: 141
Naylor, Penelope 1941- , 10: 104
Naylor, Phyllis Reynolds 1933- ,
12: 156
Nazaroff, Alexander I. 1898- ,
4: 160
Neal, Harry Edward 1906- ,
5: 139
Nee, Kay Bonner, 10: 104
Needle, Jan 1943- , 30: 162
Needleman, Jacob 1934- , 6: 172
Negri, Rocco 1932- , 12: 157
Neigoff, Anne, 13: 165
Neigoff, Mike 1920- , 13: 166
Neilson, Frances Fullerton (Jones)
1910- , 14: 149
Neimark, Anne E. 1935- , 4: 160
Nelson, Cordner (Bruce) 1918- ,
29: 156 (Brief Entry)
Nelson, Esther L. 1928- , 13: 167
Nelson, Lawrence E(rnest)
1928-1977, 28: 160 (Obituary)
Nelson, Mary Carroll 1929- ,
23: 147

Nesbit, E(dith) 1858-1924,
YABC 1: 193
Nesbit, Troy. See Folsom, Franklin,
5: 67
Nespojohn, Katherine V. 1912- ,
7: 170
Ness, Evaline (Michelow) 1911- ,
1: 165; 26: 149
Neufeld, John 1938- , 6: 173
Neumeyer, Peter F(lorian) 1929- ,
13: 168
Neurath, Marie (Reidemeister)
1898- , 1: 166
Neville, Emily Cheney 1919- ,
1: 169
Neville, Mary. See Woodrich, Mary
Neville, 2: 274
Nevins, Albert J. 1915- , 20: 134
Newberry, Clare Turlay
1903-1970, 1: 170; 26: 153
(Obituary)
Newbery, John 1713-1767,
20: 135
Newcomb, Ellsworth. See Kenny,
Ellsworth Newcomb, 26: 130
(Obituary)
Newell, Crosby. See Bonsall,
Crosby (Barbara Newell), 23: 6
Newell, Edythe W. 1910- ,
11: 185
Newell, Hope (Hockenberry)
1896-1965, 24: 154
Newfeld, Frank 1928- , 26: 153
Newlon, Clarke, 6: 174
Newman, Daisy 1904- , 27: 154
Newman, Robert (Howard)
1909- , 4: 161
Newman, Shirlee Petkin 1924- ,
10: 105
Newton, James R(obert) 1935- ,
23: 149
Newton, Suzanne 1936- , 5: 140
Nic Leodhas, Sorche. See Alger,
Leclaire (Gowans), 15: 1
Nichols, Cecilia Fawn 1906- ,
12: 159
Nichols, Peter. See Youd,
(Christopher) Samuel, 30: 222
(Brief Entry)
Nichols, (Joanna) Ruth 1948- ,
15: 204
Nickelsburg, Janet 1893- ,
11: 185
Nickerson, Betty. See Nickerson,
Elizabeth, 14: 150
Nickerson, Elizabeth 1922- ,
14: 150
Nicol, Ann. See Turnbull, Ann
(Christine), 18: 281
Nicolas. See Mordvinoff, Nicolas,
17: 129
Nicolay, Helen 1866-1954,
YABC 1: 204
Nicole, Christopher Robin 1930- ,
5: 141

Nielsen, Kay (Rasmus)
1886-1957, 16: 210
Nielsen, Virginia. See McCall,
Virginia Nielsen, 13: 151
Niland, Deborah 1951- , 27: 156
Nixon, Joan Lowery 1927- ,
8: 143
Nixon, K. See Nixon, Kathleen
Irene (Blundell), 14: 152
Nixon, Kathleen Irene (Blundell),
14: 152
Noble, Iris 1922- , 5: 142
Nodset, Joan M. See Lexau, Joan
M., 1: 144
Nolan, Jeannette Covert
1897-1974, 2: 196; 27: 157
(Obituary)
Nolan, William F(rancis) 1928- ,
28: 160 (Brief Entry)
Noonan, Julia 1946- , 4: 163
Norcross, John. See Conroy, Jack
(Wesley), 19: 65
Nordhoff, Charles (Bernard)
1887-1947, 23: 150
Nordlicht, Lillian, 29: 157
Nordstrom, Ursula, 3: 144
Norman, James. See Schmidt,
James Norman, 21: 141
Norman, Steve. See Pashko,
Stanley, 29: 159
Norris, Gunilla B(rodde) 1939- ,
20: 139
North, Andrew. See Norton, Alice
Mary, 1: 173
North, Captain George. See
Stevenson, Robert Louis,
YABC 2: 307
North, Joan 1920- , 16: 218
North, Robert. See Withers, Carl
A., 14: 261
North, Sterling 1906-1974, 1: 171;
26: 155 (Obituary)
Norton, Alice Mary 1912- ,
1: 173
Norton, Andre. See Norton, Alice
Mary, 1: 173
Norton, Browning. See Norton,
Frank R(owland) B(rowning),
10: 107
Norton, Frank R(owland)
B(rowning) 1909- , 10: 107
Norton, Mary 1903- , 18: 236
Nowell, Elizabeth Cameron,
12: 160
Numeroff, Laura Joffe 1953- ,
28: 160
Nurnberg, Maxwell 1897- ,
27: 157
Nussbaumer, Paul (Edmond)
1934- , 16: 218
Nyce, (Nellie) Helene von Strecker
1885-1969, 19: 218
Nyce, Vera 1862-1925, 19: 219
Nye, Harold G. See Harding, Lee,
31: 78 (Brief Entry)
Nye, Robert 1939- , 6: 174

Oakes, Vanya 1909- , *6:* 175
Oakley, Don(ald G.) 1927- , *8:* 144
Oakley, Graham 1929- , *30:* 163
Oakley, Helen 1906- , *10:* 107
Obrant, Susan 1946- , *11:* 186
O'Brien, Esse Forrester 1895(?)-1975, *30:* 166 (Obituary)
O'Brien, Robert C. *See* Conly, Robert Leslie, *23:* 45
O'Brien, Thomas C(lement) 1938- , *29:* 158
O'Carroll, Ryan. *See* Markun, Patricia M(aloney), *15:* 189
O'Connell, Margaret F(orster) 1935-1977, *30:* 166 (Obituary)
O'Connell, Peg. *See* Ahern, Margaret McCrohan, *10:* 2
O'Connor, Patrick. *See* Wibberley, Leonard, *2:* 271
O'Connor, Richard 1915-1975, *21:* 111 (Obituary)
O'Daniel, Janet 1921- , *24:* 155
O'Dell, Scott 1903- , *12:* 161
Odenwald, Robert P(aul) 1899-1965, *11:* 187
Oechsli, Kelly 1918- , *5:* 143
Offit, Sidney 1928- , *10:* 108
Ofosu-Appiah, L(awrence) H(enry) 1920- , *13:* 170
Ogan, George F. 1912- , *13:* 171
Ogan, M. G. [Joint pseudonym]. *See* Ogan, George F. and Margaret E. (Nettles), *13:* 171
Ogan, Margaret E. (Nettles) 1923- , *13:* 171
Ogburn, Charlton, Jr. 1911- , *3:* 145
Ogilvie, Elisabeth 1917- , *29:* 158 (Brief Entry)
O'Hara, Mary. *See* Alsop, Mary O'Hara, *2:* 4; *24:* 26 (Obituary)
Ohlsson, Ib 1935- , *7:* 171
Olcott, Frances Jenkins 1872(?)-1963, *19:* 220
Old Boy. *See* Hughes, Thomas, *31:* 85
Old Fag. *See* Bell, Robert S(tanley) W(arren), *27:* 32 (Brief Entry)
Olds, Elizabeth 1896- , *3:* 146
Olds, Helen Diehl 1895-1981, *9:* 148; *25:* 186 (Obituary)
Oldstyle, Jonathan. *See* Irving, Washington, *YABC 2:* 164
O'Leary, Brian 1940- , *6:* 176
Oliver, John Edward 1933- , *21:* 112
Olmstead, Lorena Ann 1890- , *13:* 172
Olney, Ross R. 1929- , *13:* 173
Olschewski, Alfred 1920- , *7:* 172
Olsen, Ib Spang 1921- , *6:* 177
Olugebefola, Ademole 1941- , *15:* 204

Ommanney, F(rancis) D(ownes) 1903-1980, *23:* 159
O Mude. *See* Gorey, Edward St. John, *27:* 104 (Brief Entry)
Oneal, Elizabeth 1934- , *30:* 166
Oneal, Zibby. *See* Oneal, Elizabeth, *30:* 166
O'Neill, Mary L(e Duc) 1908- , *2:* 197
Opie, Iona 1923- , *3:* 148
Opie, Peter (Mason) 1918-1982, *3:* 149; *28:* 162 (Obituary)
Oppenheim, Joanne 1934- , *5:* 146
Oppenheimer, Joan L(etson) 1925- , *28:* 162
Optic, Oliver. *See* Adams, William Taylor, *28:* 21
Orbach, Ruth Gary 1941- , *21:* 112
Orgel, Doris 1929- , *7:* 173
Orleans, Ilo 1897-1962, *10:* 110
Ormondroyd, Edward 1925- , *14:* 153
Ormsby, Virginia H(aire), *11:* 187
Orth, Richard. *See* Gardner, Richard, *24:* 119
Orwell, George. *See* Blair, Eric Arthur, *29:* 39
Osborne, Chester G. 1915- , *11:* 188
Osborne, David. *See* Silverberg, Robert, *13:* 206
Osborne, Leone Neal 1914- , *2:* 198
Osmond, Edward 1900- , *10:* 110
Ossoli, Sarah Margaret (Fuller) marchesa d' 1810-1850, *25:* 186
Otis, James. *See* Kaler, James Otis, *15:* 151
O'Trigger, Sir Lucius. *See* Horne, Richard Henry, *29:* 106
Ottley, Reginald (Leslie), *26:* 155
Otto, Margaret Glover 1909-1976, *30:* 167 (Obituary)
Ouida. *See* De La Ramée, (Marie) Louise, *20:* 26
Ousley, Odille 1896- , *10:* 111
Owen, Caroline Dale. *See* Snedecker, Caroline Dale (Parke), *YABC 2:* 296
Owen, Clifford. *See* Hamilton, Charles Harold St. John, *13:* 77
Oxenbury, Helen 1938- , *3:* 151

Pace, Mildred Mastin 1907- , *29:* 159 (Brief Entry)
Packer, Vin. *See* Meaker, Marijane, *20:* 124
Page, Eileen. *See* Heal, Edith, *7:* 123
Page, Eleanor. *See* Coerr, Eleanor, *1:* 64

Paget-Fredericks, Joseph E. P. Rous-Marten 1903-1963, *30:* 167 (Brief Entry)
Pahz, (Anne) Cheryl Suzanne 1949- , *11:* 189
Pahz, James Alon 1943- , *11:* 190
Paice, Margaret 1920- , *10:* 111
Paine, Roberta M. 1925- , *13:* 174
Paisley, Tom. *See* Bethancourt, T. Ernesto, *11:* 27
Palazzo, Anthony D. 1905-1970, *3:* 152
Palazzo, Tony. *See* Palazzo, Anthony D., *3:* 152
Palder, Edward L. 1922- , *5:* 146
Pallas, Norvin 1918- , *23:* 160
Pallister, John C(lare) 1891-1980, *26:* 157 (Obituary)
Palmer, Bernard 1914- , *26:* 157
Palmer, C(yril) Everard 1930- , *14:* 153
Palmer, (Ruth) Candida 1926- , *11:* 191
Palmer, Heidi 1948- , *15:* 206
Palmer, Helen Marion. *See* Geisel, Helen, *26:* 83
Palmer, Juliette 1930- , *15:* 208
Panetta, George 1915-1969, *15:* 210
Pansy. *See* Alden, Isabella (Macdonald), *YABC 2:* 1
Panter, Carol 1936- , *9:* 150
Papashvily, George 1898-1978, *17:* 135
Papashvily, Helen (Waite) 1906- , *17:* 141
Pape, D(onna) L(ugg) 1930- , *2:* 198
Paradis, Adrian A(lexis) 1912- , *1:* 175
Paradis, Marjorie (Bartholomew) 1886(?)-1970, *17:* 143
Parish, Peggy 1927- , *17:* 144
Park, Bill. *See* Park, W(illiam) B(ryan), *22:* 188
Park, Ruth, *25:* 190
Park, W(illiam) B(ryan) 1936- , *22:* 188
Parker, Elinor 1906- , *3:* 155
Parker, Lois M(ay) 1912- , *30:* 167
Parker, Nancy Winslow 1930- , *10:* 113
Parker, Richard 1915- , *14:* 156
Parker, Robert. *See* Boyd, Waldo T., *18:* 35
Parkinson, Ethelyn M(inerva) 1906- , *11:* 192
Parks, Edd Winfield 1906-1968, *10:* 114
Parks, Gordon (Alexander Buchanan) 1912- , *8:* 145
Parley, Peter. *See* Goodrich, Samuel Griswold, *23:* 82

Parlin, John. *See* Graves, Charles Parlin, *4:* 94
Parnall, Peter 1936- , *16:* 220
Parr, Lucy 1924- , *10:* 115
Parrish, Anne 1888-1957, *27:* 157
Parrish, Mary. *See* Cousins, Margaret, *2:* 79
Parrish, (Frederick) Maxfield 1870-1966, *14:* 158
Parry, Marian 1924- , *13:* 175
Parsons, Tom. *See* MacPherson, Thomas George, *30:* 147 (Obituary)
Partridge, Benjamin W(aring), Jr. 1915- , *28:* 165
Pascal, David 1918- , *14:* 174
Paschal, Nancy. *See* Trotter, Grace V(iolet), *10:* 180
Pashko, Stanley 1913- , *29:* 159
Patent, Dorothy Hinshaw 1940- , *22:* 190
Paterson, Katherine (Womeldorf) 1932- , *13:* 176
Paton, Alan (Stewart) 1903- , *11:* 194
Paton Walsh, Gillian 1939- , *4:* 164
Patten, Brian 1946- , *29:* 160
Patterson, Lillie G., *14:* 174
Paul, Aileen 1917- , *12:* 164
Paul, James 1936- , *23:* 161
Paul, Robert. *See* Roberts, John G(aither), *27:* 171
Pauli, Hertha (Ernestine) 1909-1973, *3:* 155; *26:* 160 (Obituary)
Paull, Grace A. 1898- , *24:* 156
Paulsen, Gary 1939- , *22:* 192
Paulson, Jack. *See* Jackson, C. Paul, *6:* 120
Pavel, Frances 1907- , *10:* 116
Payson, Dale 1943- , *9:* 150
Payzant, Charles, *18:* 239
Payzant, Jessie Mercer Knechtel. *See* Shannon, Terry, *21:* 147
Paz, A. *See* Pahz, James Alon, *11:* 190
Paz, Zan. *See* Pahz, Cheryl Suzanne, *11:* 189
Peake, Mervyn 1911-1968, *23:* 162
Peale, Norman Vincent 1898- , *20:* 140
Pearce, (Ann) Philippa, *1:* 176
Peare, Catherine Owens 1911- , *9:* 152
Pears, Charles 1873-1958, *30:* 168 (Brief Entry)
Pearson, Susan 1946- , *27:* 161 (Brief Entry)
Pease, Howard 1894-1974, *2:* 199; *25:* 191 (Obituary)
Peck, Anne Merriman 1884- , *18:* 240
Peck, Richard 1934- , *18:* 242

Peck, Robert Newton III 1928- , *21:* 113
Peeples, Edwin A. 1915- , *6:* 181
Peet, Bill. *See* Peet, William B., *2:* 201
Peet, Creighton B. 1899-1977, *30:* 168
Peet, William Bartlett 1915- , *2:* 201
Peirce, Waldo 1884-1970, *28:* 165 (Brief Entry)
Pelaez, Jill 1924- , *12:* 165
Pellowski, Anne 1933- , *20:* 145
Pelta, Kathy 1928- , *18:* 245
Peltier, Leslie C(opus) 1900- , *13:* 177
Pembury, Bill. *See* Groom, Arthur William, *10:* 53
Pendennis, Arthur, Esquire. *See* Thackeray, William Makepeace, *23:* 223
Pender, Lydia 1907- , *3:* 157
Pendery, Rosemary, *7:* 174
Pendle, Alexy 1943- , *29:* 161
Pendle, George 1906-1977, *28:* 165 (Obituary)
Penn, Ruth Bonn. *See* Rosenberg, Ethel, *3:* 176
Pennage, E. M. *See* Finkel, George (Irvine), *8:* 59
Pennington, Eunice 1923- , *27:* 161
Penrose, Margaret. *See* Stratemeyer, Edward L., *1:* 208
Pepe, Phil(ip) 1935- , *20:* 145
Peppe, Rodney 1934- , *4:* 164
Percy, Charles Henry. *See* Smith, Dodie, *4:* 194
Perera, Thomas Biddle 1938- , *13:* 179
Perkins, Al(bert Rogers) 1904-1975, *30:* 169
Perkins, Marlin 1905- , *21:* 114
Perl, Lila, *6:* 182
Perl, Susan 1922- , *22:* 193
Perlmutter, O(scar) William 1920-1975, *8:* 149
Perrault, Charles 1628-1703, *25:* 192
Perreard, Suzanne Louise Butler 1919- , *29:* 162 (Brief Entry)
Perrine, Mary 1913- , *2:* 203
Perry, Patricia 1949- , *30:* 170
Perry, Roger 1933- , *27:* 163
Pershing, Marie. *See* Schultz, Pearle Henriksen, *21:* 142
Peters, Caroline. *See* Betz, Eva Kelly, *10:* 10
Peters, S. H. *See* Porter, William Sydney, *YABC 2:* 259
Petersham, Maud (Fuller) 1890-1971, *17:* 146
Petersham, Miska 1888-1960, *17:* 149
Peterson, Hans 1922- , *8:* 149

Peterson, Harold L(eslie) 1922- , *8:* 151
Peterson, Helen Stone 1910- , *8:* 152
Peterson, Jeanne Whitehouse. *See* Whitehouse, Jeanne, *29:* 239
Petie, Haris 1915- , *10:* 118
Petrides, Heidrun 1944- , *19:* 222
Petrovskaya, Kyra. *See* Wayne, Kyra Petrovskaya, *8:* 213
Petry, Ann (Lane), *5:* 148
Pevsner, Stella, *8:* 154
Peyton, K. M. *See* Peyton, Kathleen (Wendy), *15:* 211
Peyton, Kathleen (Wendy) 1929- , *15:* 211
Pfeffer, Susan Beth 1948- , *4:* 166
Phelan, Josephine 1905- , *30:* 171 (Brief Entry)
Phelan, Mary Kay 1914- , *3:* 158
Philbrook, Clem(ent E.) 1917- , *24:* 158
Phillips, Irv. *See* Phillips, Irving W., *11:* 196
Phillips, Irving W. 1908- , *11:* 196
Phillips, Jack. *See* Sandburg, Carl (August), *8:* 177
Phillips, Leon. *See* Gerson, Noel B(ertram), *22:* 118
Phillips, Loretta (Hosey) 1893- , *10:* 119
Phillips, Louis 1942- , *8:* 155
Phillips, Mary Geisler 1881-1964, *10:* 119
Phillips, Prentice 1894- , *10:* 119
Phillpotts, Eden 1862-1960, *24:* 159
Phipson, Joan. *See* Fitzhardinge, Joan M., *2:* 107
Phiz. *See* Browne, Hablot Knight, *21:* 13
Phleger, Marjorie Temple, *1:* 176
Phypps, Hyacinthe. *See* Gorey, Edward St. John, *29:* 89
Piaget, Jean 1896-1980, *23:* 166 (Obituary)
Piatti, Celestino 1922- , *16:* 222
Picard, Barbara Leonie 1917- , *2:* 205
Pickering, James Sayre 1897-1969, *28:* 166 (Obituary)
Pienkowski, Jan 1936- , *6:* 182
Pierce, Katherine. *See* St. John, Wylly Folk, *10:* 132
Pierce, Ruth (Ireland) 1936- , *5:* 148
Pierik, Robert 1921- , *13:* 180
Pig, Edward. *See* Gorey, Edward St. John, *29:* 89
Pike, E(dgar) Royston 1896- , *22:* 194
Pilarski, Laura 1926- , *13:* 181
Pilgrim, Anne. *See* Allan, Mabel Esther, *5:* 2

Pilkington, Francis Meredyth
  1907- , *4:* 166
Pilkington, Roger (Windle)
  1915- , *10:* 120
Pincus, Harriet 1938- , *27:* 164
Pine, Tillie S(chloss) 1897- ,
  13: 182
Pinkerton, Kathrene Sutherland
  (Gedney) 1887-1967, *26:* 160
  (Obituary)
Pinkwater, Manus 1941- , *8:* 156
Pioneer. *See* Yates, Raymond
  F(rancis), *31:* 189
Piper, Roger. *See* Fisher, John
  (Oswald Hamilton), *15:* 115
Piper, Watty. *See* Bragg, Mabel
  Caroline, *24:* 52
Piro, Richard 1934- , *7:* 176
Pitrone, Jean Maddern 1920- ,
  4: 167
Pitz, Henry C(larence) 1895-1976,
  4: 167; *24:* 162 (Obituary)
Pizer, Vernon 1918- , *21:* 116
Place, Marian T. 1910- , *3:* 160
Plaidy, Jean. *See* Hibbert, Eleanor,
  2: 134
Plaine, Alfred R. 1898(?)-1981,
  29: 162 (Obituary)
Platt, Kin 1911- , *21:* 117
Plimpton, George (Ames) 1927- ,
  10: 121
Plomer, William (Charles Franklin)
  1903-1973, *24:* 163
Plowman, Stephanie 1922- ,
  6: 184
Pluckrose, Henry (Arthur) 1931- ,
  13: 183
Plum, J. *See* Wodehouse, P(elham)
  G(renville), *22:* 241
Plumb, Charles P. 1900(?)-1982,
  29: 162 (Obituary)
Plummer, Margaret 1911- ,
  2: 206
Podendorf, Illa E., *18:* 247
Poe, Edgar Allan 1809-1849,
  23: 167
Pogany, Willy 1882-1955, *30:* 171
  (Brief Entry)
Pohl, Frederik 1919- , *24:* 165
Pohlmann, Lillian (Grenfell)
  1902- , *11:* 196
Pointon, Robert. *See* Rooke,
  Daphne (Marie), *12:* 178
Pola. *See* Watson, Pauline, *14:* 235
Polatnick, Florence T. 1923- ,
  5: 149
Polder, Markus. *See* Krüss, James,
  8: 104
Polhamus, Jean Burt 1928- ,
  21: 118
Politi, Leo 1908- , *1:* 177
Polking, Kirk 1925- , *5:* 149
Polland, Madeleine A. 1918- ,
  6: 185
Pollock, Mary. *See* Blyton, Enid
  (Mary), *25:* 48

Pollowitz, Melinda (Kilborn)
  1944- , *26:* 160
Polseno, Jo, *17:* 153
Pomerantz, Charlotte, *20:* 146
Pomeroy, Pete. *See* Roth, Arthur
  J(oseph), *28:* 177 (Brief Entry)
Pond, Alonzo W(illiam) 1894- ,
  5: 150
Poole, Gray Johnson 1906- ,
  1: 179
Poole, Josephine 1933- , *5:* 152
Poole, Lynn 1910-1969, *1:* 179
Portal, Colette 1936- , *6:* 186
Porter, Katherine Anne
  1890-1980, *23:* 192 (Obituary)
Porter, Sheena 1935- , *24:* 166
Porter, William Sydney
  1862-1910, *YABC 2:* 259
Posell, Elsa Z., *3:* 160
Posten, Margaret L(ois) 1915- ,
  10: 123
Potter, (Helen) Beatrix 1866-1943,
  YABC 1: 205
Potter, Margaret (Newman)
  1926- , *21:* 119
Potter, Marian 1915- , *9:* 153
Potter, Miriam Clark 1886-1965,
  3: 161
Pournelle, Jerry (Eugene) 1933- ,
  26: 161
Powell, Richard Stillman. *See*
  Barbour, Ralph Henry, *16:* 27
Powers, Anne. *See* Schwartz, Anne
  Powers, *10:* 142
Powers, Bill 1931- , *31:* 144
  (Brief Entry)
Powers, Margaret. *See* Heal, Edith,
  7: 123
Poynter, Margaret 1927- , *27:* 165
Prelutsky, Jack, *22:* 195
Preussler, Otfried 1923- , *24:* 167
Prevert, Jacques (Henri Marie)
  1900-1977, *30:* 171 (Obituary)
Price, Christine 1928-1980,
  3: 162; *23:* 192 (Obituary)
Price, Garrett 1896-1979, *22:* 197
  (Obituary)
Price, Jennifer. *See* Hoover, Helen
  (Drusilla Blackburn), *12:* 100
Price, Lucie Locke. *See* Locke,
  Lucie, *10:* 81
Price, Margaret (Evans)
  1888-1973, *28:* 166 (Brief
  Entry)
Price, Olive 1903- , *8:* 157
Price, Susan 1955- , *25:* 206
Priestley, Lee (Shore) 1904- ,
  27: 166
Prieto, Mariana B(eeching)
  1912- , *8:* 160
Prince, Alison 1931- , *28:* 166
Prince, J(ack) H(arvey) 1908- ,
  17: 155
Pringle, Laurence 1935- , *4:* 171
Proctor, Everitt. *See* Montgomery,
  Rutherford, *3:* 134

Professor Zingara. *See* Leeming,
  Joseph, *26:* 132
Provensen, Alice 1918- , *9:* 154
Provensen, Martin 1916- , *9:* 155
Pryor, Helen Brenton 1897-1972,
  4: 172
Pudney, John (Sleigh) 1909-1977,
  24: 168
Pugh, Ellen T. 1920- , *7:* 176
Pullein-Thompson, Christine
  1930- , *3:* 164
Pullein-Thompson, Diana, *3:* 165
Pullein-Thompson, Josephine,
  3: 166
Purdy, Susan Gold 1939- , *8:* 161
Purscell, Phyllis 1934- , *7:* 177
Putnam, Arthur Lee. *See* Alger,
  Horatio, Jr., *16:* 3
Putnam, Peter B(rock) 1920- ,
  30: 172
Pyle, Howard 1853-1911, *16:* 224
Pyne, Mable Mandeville
  1903-1969, *9:* 155

Quackenbush, Robert M. 1929- ,
  7: 177
Quammen, David 1948- , *7:* 179
Quarles, Benjamin 1904- ,
  12: 166
Queen, Ellery, Jr. *See* Holding,
  James, *3:* 85
Quennell, Marjorie (Courtney)
  1884-1972, *29:* 162
Quick, Annabelle 1922- , *2:* 207
Quin-Harkin, Janet 1941- ,
  18: 247
Quinn, Elisabeth 1881-1962,
  22: 197
Quinn, Susan. *See* Jacobs, Susan,
  30: 129
Quinn, Vernon. *See* Quinn,
  Elisabeth, *22:* 197

Rabe, Berniece 1928- , *7:* 179
Rabe, Olive H(anson) 1887-1968,
  13: 183
Rabinowich, Ellen 1946- ,
  29: 165
Rackham, Arthur 1867-1939,
  15: 213
Radford, Ruby L(orraine)
  1891-1971, *6:* 186
Radlauer, David 1952- , *28:* 167
Radlauer, Edward 1921- , *15:* 227
Radlauer, Ruth (Shaw) 1926- ,
  15: 229
Radley, Gail 1951- , *25:* 206
Raebeck, Lois 1921- , *5:* 153
Raftery, Gerald (Bransfield)
  1905- , *11:* 197
Rahn, Joan Elma 1929- , *27:* 167
Raiff, Stan 1930- , *11:* 197

Ralston, Jan. *See* Dunlop, Agnes
M. R., *3: 62*
Ramal, Walter. *See* de la Mare,
Walter, *16:* 73
Ranadive, Gail 1944- , *10:* 123
Rand, Ann (Binkley), *30:* 173
Rand, Paul 1914- , *6:* 188
Randall, Florence Engel 1917- ,
5: 154
Randall, Janet. *See* Young, Janet
Randall and Young, Robert
W., *3:* 268-269
Randall, Robert. *See* Silverberg,
Robert, *13:* 206
Randall, Ruth Painter 1892-1971,
3: 167
Randolph, Lieutenant J. H. *See*
Ellis, Edward S(ylvester),
YABC 1: 116
Rands, William Brighty
1823-1882, *17:* 156
Ranney, Agnes V. 1916- , *6:* 189
Ransome, Arthur (Michell)
1884-1967, *22:* 198
Rapaport, Stella F(read), *10:* 126
Raphael, Elaine (Chionchio)
1933- , *23:* 192
Rappaport, Eva 1924- , *6:* 189
Raskin, Edith (Lefkowitz) 1908- ,
9: 156
Raskin, Ellen 1928- , *2:* 209
Raskin, Joseph 1897-1982,
12: 166; *29:* 166 (Obituary)
Rathjen, Carl H(enry) 1909- ,
11: 198
Rattray, Simon. *See* Trevor,
Elleston, *28:* 207
Rau, Margaret 1913- , *9:* 157
Rauch, Mabel Thompson
1888-1972, *26:* 162 (Obituary)
Raucher, Herman 1928- , *8:* 162
Ravielli, Anthony 1916- , *3:* 169
Rawlings, Marjorie Kinnan
1896-1953, *YABC 1:* 218
Rawls, (Woodrow) Wilson
1913- , *22:* 205
Ray, Deborah 1940- , *8:* 163
Ray, Irene. *See* Sutton, Margaret
Beebe, *1:* 213
Ray, JoAnne 1935- , *9:* 157
Ray, Mary (Eva Pedder) 1932- ,
2: 210
Raymond, James Crossley
1917-1981, *29:* 166 (Obituary)
Raymond, Robert. *See* Alter, Robert
Edmond, *9:* 8
Rayner, Mary 1933- , *22:* 207
Raynor, Dorka, *28:* 169
Rayson, Steven 1932- , *30:* 175
Razzell, Arthur (George) 1925- ,
11: 199
Razzi, James 1931- , *10:* 126
Read, Elfreida 1920- , *2:* 211
Read, Piers Paul 1941- , *21:* 119
Reck, Franklin Mering 1896-1965,
30: 175 (Brief Entry)

Redding, Robert Hull 1919- ,
2: 212
Redway, Ralph. *See* Hamilton,
Charles Harold St. John, *13:* 77
Redway, Ridley. *See* Hamilton,
Charles Harold St. John, *13:* 77
Reed, Betty Jane 1921- , *4:* 172
Reed, Gwendolyn E(lizabeth)
1932- , *21:* 120
Reed, Philip G. 1908- , *29:* 166
(Brief Entry)
Reed, William Maxwell
1871-1962, *15:* 230
Reeder, Colonel Red. *See* Reeder,
Russell P., Jr., *4:* 174
Reeder, Russell P., Jr. 1902- ,
4: 174
Reeman, Douglas Edward 1924- ,
28: 169 (Brief Entry)
Rees, Ennis 1925- , *3:* 169
Reeve, Joel. *See* Cox, William
R(obert), *31:* 53 (Brief Entry)
Reeves, James 1909- , *15:* 231
Reeves, Joyce 1911- , *17:* 158
Reeves, Lawrence F. 1926- ,
29: 166
Reeves, Ruth Ellen. *See* Ranney,
Agnes V., *6:* 189
Reggiani, Renée, *18:* 248
Reid, Barbara 1922- , *21:* 121
Reid, Dorothy M(arion) (?)-1974,
29: 167 (Brief Entry)
Reid, Eugenie Chazal 1924- ,
12: 167
Reid, John Calvin, *21:* 122
Reid, (Thomas) Mayne
1818-1883, *24:* 170
Reid Banks, Lynne 1929- ,
22: 208
Reiff, Stephanie Ann 1948- ,
28: 169 (Brief Entry)
Reig, June 1933- , *30:* 175
Reinach, Jacquelyn (Krasne)
1930- , *28:* 170
Reiner, William B(uck) -
1910-1976, *30:* 176 (Obituary)
Reinfeld, Fred 1910-1964, *3:* 170
Reiss, Johanna de Leeuw 1932- ,
18: 250
Reiss, John J., *23:* 193
Reit, Seymour, *21:* 123
Reit, Sy. *See* Reit, Seymour,
21: 123
Remi, Georges 1907- , *13:* 183
Renault, Mary. *See* Challans, Mary,
23: 33
Rendell, Joan, *28:* 171
Rendina, Laura Cooper 1902- ,
10: 127
Renick, Marion (Lewis) 1905- ,
1: 180
Renken, Aleda 1907- , *27:* 168
Renlie, Frank H. 1936- , *11:* 200
Rensie, Willis. *See* Eisner, Will(iam
Erwin), *31:* 62
Renvoize, Jean 1930- , *5:* 157

Resnick, Seymour 1920- ,
23: 193
Retla, Robert. *See* Alter, Robert
Edmond, *9:* 8
Reuter, Carol (Joan) 1931- ,
2: 213
Rey, H(ans) A(ugusto) 1898-1977,
1: 181; *26:* 162
Rey, Margret (Elizabeth) 1906- ,
26: 165
Reyher, Becky. *See* Reyher,
Rebecca Hourwich, *18:* 253
Reyher, Rebecca Hourwich
1897- , *18:* 253
Reynolds, Dickson. *See* Reynolds,
Helen Mary Greenwood
Campbell, *26:* 169 (Obituary)
Reynolds, Helen Mary Greenwood
Campbell 1884-1969, *26:* 169
(Obituary)
Reynolds, Malvina 1900-1978,
24: 173 (Obituary)
Rhys, Megan. *See* Williams,
Jeanne, *5:* 202
Ribbons, Ian 1924- , *30:* 176
(Brief Entry)
Ricciuti, Edward R(aphael)
1938- , *10:* 110
Rice, Charles D(uane) 1910-1971,
27: 170 (Obituary)
Rice, Elizabeth 1913- , *2:* 213
Rice, Inez 1907- , *13:* 186
Rice, James 1934- , *22:* 210
Rich, Elaine Sommers 1926- ,
6: 190
Rich, Josephine 1912- , *10:* 129
Richard, Adrienne 1921- , *5:* 157
Richards, Curtis. *See* Curtis,
Richard (Alan), *29:* 54
Richards, Frank. *See* Hamilton,
Charles Howard St. John,
13: 77
Richards, Hilda. *See* Hamilton,
Charles Howard St. John,
13: 77
Richards, Kay. *See* Baker, Susan
(Catherine), *29:* 35
Richards, Laura E(lizabeth Howe)
1850-1943, *YABC 1:* 224
Richardson, Frank Howard
1882-1970, *27:* 170 (Obituary)
Richardson, Grace Lee. *See*
Dickson, Naida, *8:* 41
Richardson, Robert S(hirley)
1902- , *8:* 164
Richelson, Geraldine 1922- ,
29: 167
Richler, Mordecai 1931- , *27:* 170
(Brief Entry)
Richoux, Pat 1927- , *7:* 180
Richter, Alice 1941- , *30:* 176
Richter, Conrad 1890-1968,
3: 171
Richter, Hans Peter 1925- ,
6: 191

Ridge, Antonia (Florence)
(?)-1981, *7:* 181; *27:* 170
(Obituary)

Ridley, Nat, Jr. *See* Stratemeyer,
Edward L., *1:* 208

Ridlon, Marci 1942- , *22:* 211

Riedman, Sarah R(egal) 1902- ,
1: 183

Riesenberg, Felix, Jr. 1913-1962,
23: 194

Rieu, E(mile) V(ictor) 1887-1972,
26: 169 (Obituary)

Riggs, Sidney Noyes 1892-1975,
28: 172 (Obituary)

Rikhoff, Jean 1928- , *9:* 158

Riley, James Whitcomb
1849-1916, *17:* 159

Ringi, Kjell Arne Sörensen
1939- , *12:* 168

Rinkoff, Barbara (Jean)
1923-1975, *4:* 174; *27:* 170
(Obituary)

Riordan, James 1936- , *28:* 172

Rios, Tere. *See* Versace, Marie
Teresa, *2:* 254

Ripley, Elizabeth Blake
1906-1969, *5:* 158

Ripper, Charles L. 1929- , *3:* 174

Ritchie, Barbara (Gibbons), *14:* 176

Ritts, Paul 1920(?)-1980, *25:* 207
(Obituary)

Rivera, Geraldo 1943- , *28:* 174
(Brief Entry)

Riverside, John. *See* Heinlein,
Robert A(nson), *9:* 102

Rivoli, Mario 1943- , *10:* 129

Roach, Marilynne K(athleen)
1946- , *9:* 158

Roach, Portia. *See* Takakjian,
Portia, *15:* 273

Robbins, Raleigh. *See* Hamilton,
Charles Harold St. John, *13:* 77

Robbins, Ruth 1917(?)- , *14:* 177

Robbins, Tony. *See* Pashko,
Stanley, *29:* 159

Roberts, Charles G(eorge) D(ouglas)
1860-1943, *29:* 168 (Brief
Entry)

Roberts, David. *See* Cox, John
Roberts, *9:* 42

Roberts, Elizabeth Madox
1886-1941, *27:* 170 (Brief
Entry)

Roberts, Jim. *See* Bates, Barbara
S(nedeker), *12:* 34

Roberts, John G(aither) 1913- ,
27: 171

Roberts, Nancy Correll 1924- ,
28: 175 (Brief Entry)

Roberts, Terence. *See* Sanderson,
Ivan T., *6:* 195

Roberts, Willo Davis 1928- ,
21: 125

Robertson, Barbara (Anne)
1931- , *12:* 172

Robertson, Don 1929- , *8:* 165

Robertson, Dorothy Lewis 1912- ,
12: 173

Robertson, Jennifer (Sinclair)
1942- , *12:* 174

Robertson, Keith 1914- , *1:* 184

Robinet, Harriette Gillem 1931- ,
27: 173

Robins, Seelin. *See* Ellis, Edward
S(ylvester), *YABC 1:* 116

Robinson, Adjai 1932- , *8:* 165

Robinson, Barbara (Webb)
1927- , *8:* 166

Robinson, Charles 1870-1937,
17: 171

Robinson, Charles 1931- , *6:* 192

Robinson, Jan M. 1933- , *6:* 194

Robinson, Jean O. 1934- , *7:* 182

Robinson, Joan (Mary) G(ale
Thomas) 1910- , *7:* 183

Robinson, Maudie (Millian Oller)
1914- , *11:* 200

Robinson, Maurice R. 1895-1982,
29: 169 (Obituary)

Robinson, Nancy
K(onheim) 1942- , *31:* 144
(Brief Entry)

Robinson, Ray(mond Kenneth)
1920- , *23:* 194

Robinson, T(homas) H(eath)
1869-1950, *17:* 178

Robinson, (Wanda) Veronica
1926- , *30:* 177

Robinson, W(illiam) Heath
1872-1944, *17:* 184

Robison, Bonnie 1924- , *12:* 175

Robottom, John 1934- , *7:* 185

Roche, A. K. [Joint pseudonym].
See Abisch, Roslyn Kroop,
9: 3. *See* Kaplan, Boche,
24: 134

Rockwell, Norman (Percevel)
1894-1978, *23:* 195

Rockwell, Thomas 1933- , *7:* 185

Rockwood, Roy [Collective
pseudonym], *1:* 185.
See also McFarlane, Leslie,
31: 133; Stratemeyer, Edward
L., *1:* 208

Rodgers, Mary 1931- , *8:* 167

Rodman, Emerson. *See* Ellis,
Edward S(ylvester),
YABC 1: 116

Rodman, Maia. *See*
Wojciechowska, Maia, *1:* 228;
28: 222

Rodman, Selden 1909- , *9:* 159

Rodowsky, Colby 1932- , *21:* 126

Roe, Harry Mason. *See*
Stratemeyer, Edward L., *1:* 208

Roever, J(oan) M(arilyn) 1935- ,
26: 170

Rogers, (Thomas) Alan
(Stinchcombe) 1937- , *2:* 215

Rogers, Frances 1888-1974,
10: 130

Rogers, Matilda 1894- , *5:* 158

Rogers, Pamela 1927- , *9:* 160

Rogers, Robert. *See* Hamilton,
Charles Harold St. John, *13:* 77

Rogers, W(illiam) G(arland)
1896-1978, *23:* 208

Rojan. *See* Rojankovsky, Feodor
(Stepanovich), *21:* 127

Rojankovsky, Feodor (Stepanovich)
1891-1970, *21:* 127

Rokeby-Thomas, Anna E(lma)
1911- , *15:* 233

Roland, Albert 1925- , *11:* 201

Rolerson, Darrell A(llen) 1946- ,
8: 168

Roll, Winifred 1909- , *6:* 194

Rollins, Charlemae Hill
1897-1979, *3:* 175; *26:* 171
(Obituary)

Rongen, Björn 1906- , *10:* 131

Rood, Ronald (N.) 1920- ,
12: 177

Rooke, Daphne (Marie) 1914- ,
12: 178

Rose, Anne, *8:* 168

Rose, Carl 1903-1971, *31:* 144
(Brief Entry)

Rose, Elizabeth Jane (Pretty)
1933- , *28:* 175 (Brief Entry)

Rose, Florella. *See* Carlson, Vada
F., *16:* 64

Rose, Gerald (Hembdon Seymour)
1935- , *30:* 178 (Brief Entry)

Rose, Wendy 1948- , *12:* 180

Rosen, Sidney 1916- , *1:* 185

Rosen, Winifred 1943- , *8:* 169

Rosenbaum, Maurice 1907- ,
6: 195

Rosenberg, Ethel, *3:* 176

Rosenberg, Nancy Sherman
1931- , *4:* 177

Rosenberg, Sharon 1942- , *8:* 171

Rosenbloom, Joseph 1928- ,
21: 131

Rosenblum, Richard 1928- ,
11: 202

Rosenburg, John M. 1918- ,
6: 195

Ross, Alex(ander) 1909- , *29:* 169
(Brief Entry)

Ross, David 1896-1975, *20:* 147
(Obituary)

Ross, Diana. *See* Denney, Diana,
25: 90

Ross, Frank (Xavier), Jr. 1914- ,
28: 175

Ross, Tony 1938- , *17:* 203

Rossel, Seymour 1945- , *28:* 176

Rossetti, Christiana (Georgina)
1830-1894, *20:* 147

Roth, Arnold 1929- , *21:* 133

Roth, Arthur J(oseph) 1925- ,
28: 177 (Brief Entry)

Rothkopf, Carol Z. 1929- , *4:* 177

Rothman, Joel 1938- , *7:* 186

Roueché, Berton 1911- , *28:* 177

Rounds, Glen (Harold) 1906- ,
   8: 171
Rourke, Constance (Mayfield)
   1885-1941, *YABC 1:* 232
Rowe, Viola Carson 1903-1969,
   26: 171 (Obituary)
Rowland, Florence Wightman
   1900- , *8:* 173
Rowland-Entwistle, (Arthur)
   Theodore (Henry) 1925- ,
   31: 145
Roy, Liam. *See* Scarry, Patricia,
   2: 218
Rubel, Nicole 1953- , *18:* 255
Ruchlis, Hy 1913- , *3:* 177
Rudley, Stephen 1946- , *30:* 179
Rudolph, Marguerita 1908- ,
   21: 133
Rudomin, Esther. *See* Hautzig,
   Esther, *4:* 105
Ruedi, Norma Paul. *See* Ainsworth,
   Norma, *9:* 4
Ruffell, Ann 1941- , *30:* 179
Rugoff, Milton 1913- , *30:* 180
Ruhen, Olaf 1911- , *17:* 204
Rukeyser, Muriel 1913-1980,
   22: 211 (Obituary)
Rumsey, Marian (Barritt) 1928- ,
   16: 236
Runyan, John. *See* Palmer, Bernard,
   26: 157
Rushmore, Helen 1898- , *3:* 178
Rushmore, Robert (William)
   1926- , *8:* 174
Ruskin, Ariane. *See* Batterberry,
   Ariane Ruskin, *7:* 187; *13:* 10
Ruskin, John 1819-1900, *24:* 173
Russell, Charlotte. *See* Rathjen,
   Carl H(enry), *11:* 198
Russell, Franklin 1926- , *11:* 203
Russell, Helen Ross 1915- ,
   8: 175
Russell, Patrick. *See* Sammis, John,
   4: 178
Russell, Solveig Paulson 1904- ,
   3: 179
Russo, Susan 1947- , *30:* 181
Ruth, Rod 1912- , *9:* 160
Ruthin, Margaret, *4:* 178
Rutgers van der Loeff, An(na)
   Basenau 1910- , *22:* 211
Rutz, Viola Larkin 1932- ,
   12: 181
Ruzicka, Rudolph 1883-1978,
   24: 181 (Obituary)
Ryan, Betsy. *See* Ryan, Elizabeth
   (Anne), *30:* 183
Ryan, Cheli Durán, *20:* 154
Ryan, Elizabeth (Anne) 1943- ,
   30: 183
Ryan, John (Gerald Christopher)
   1921- , *22:* 214
Ryan, Peter (Charles) 1939- ,
   15: 235
Rydberg, Ernest E(mil) 1901- ,
   21: 135

Rydberg, Lou(isa Hampton)
   1908- , *27:* 173
Rydell, Wendell. *See* Rydell,
   Wendy, *4:* 178
Rydell, Wendy, *4:* 178
Ryden, Hope, *8:* 176
Rye, Anthony. *See* Youd,
   (Christopher) Samuel, *30:* 222
   (Brief Entry)

Sabin, Edwin Legrand 1870-1952,
   YABC 2: 277
Sabin, Francene, *27:* 174
Sabin, Louis 1930- , *27:* 174
Sabre, Dirk. *See* Laffin, John
   (Alfred Charles), *31:* 111
Sabuso. *See* Phillips, Irving W.,
   11: 196
Sachs, Marilyn 1927- , *3:* 180
Sackett, S(amuel) J(ohn) 1928- ,
   12: 181
Sackson, Sid 1920- , *16:* 237
Sadie, Stanley (John) 1930- ,
   14: 177
Sage, Juniper [Joint pseudonym].
   See Brown, Margaret Wise,
   YABC 2: 9
Sage, Juniper. *See* Hurd, Edith,
   2: 150
Sagsoorian, Paul 1923- , *12:* 183
Saida. *See* LeMair, H(enriette)
   Willebeek, *29:* 127 (Brief
   Entry)
Saint, Dora Jessie 1913- , *10:* 132
St. Briavels, James. *See* Wood,
   James Playsted, *1:* 229
St. Clair, Byrd Hooper
   1905-1976, *28:* 177 (Obituary)
Saint Exupéry, Antoine de
   1900-1944, *20:* 154
St. George, Judith 1931- ,
   13: 187
St. John, Nicole. *See* Johnston,
   Norma, *29:* 116
St. John, Philip. *See* Del Rey,
   Lester, *22:* 97
St. John, Wylly Folk 1908- ,
   10: 132
St. Meyer, Ned. *See* Stratemeyer,
   Edward L., *1:* 208
St. Tamara. *See* Kolba, Tamara,
   22: 171
Saito, Michiko. *See* Fujiwara,
   Michiko, *15:* 120
Salmon, Annie Elizabeth 1899- ,
   13: 188
Salten, Felix. *See* Salzmann,
   Siegmund, *25:* 207
Salter, Cedric. *See* Knight, Francis
   Edgar, *14:* 112
Salzer, L. E. *See* Wilson, Lionel,
   31: 186 (Brief Entry)
Salzmann, Siegmund 1869-1945,
   25: 207

Samachson, Dorothy 1914- ,
   3: 182
Samachson, Joseph 1906- , *3:* 182
Sammis, John 1942- , *4:* 178
Samson, Anne S(tringer) 1933- ,
   2: 216
Samson, Joan 1937-1976, *13:* 189
Samuels, Charles 1902- , *12:* 183
Samuels, Gertrude, *17:* 206
Sanchez, Sonia 1934- , *22:* 214
Sanchez-Silva, Jose Maria 1911- ,
   16: 237
Sandberg, (Karin) Inger 1930- ,
   15: 238
Sandberg, Lasse (E. M.) 1924- ,
   15: 239
Sandburg, Carl (August)
   1878-1967, *8:* 177
Sandburg, Charles A. *See*
   Sandburg, Carl (August),
   8: 177
Sandburg, Helga 1918- , *3:* 184
Sanderlin, George 1915- , *4:* 180
Sanderlin, Owenita (Harrah)
   1916- , *11:* 204
Sanderson, Ivan T. 1911-1973,
   6: 195
Sandin, Joan 1942- , *12:* 185
Sandison, Janet. *See* Cameron,
   Elizabeth Jane, *30:* 73
   (Obituary)
Sandoz, Mari (Susette) 1901-1966,
   5: 159
Sanger, Marjory Bartlett 1920- ,
   8: 181
Sankey, Alice (Ann-Susan)
   1910- , *27:* 174
Santesson, Hans Stefan
   1914(?)-1975, *30:* 183
   (Obituary)
Sarac, Roger. *See* Caras, Roger
   A(ndrew), *12:* 65
Sarg, Anthony Fredrick. *See* Sarg,
   Tony, *YABC 1:* 233
Sarg, Tony 1880-1942,
   YABC 1: 233
Sargent, Pamela, *29:* 169
Sargent, Robert 1933- , *2:* 216
Sargent, Shirley 1927- , *11:* 205
Sari. *See* Fleur, Anne, *31:* 70 (Brief
   Entry)
Sarnoff, Jane 1937- , *10:* 133
Saroyan, William 1908-1981,
   23: 210; *24:* 181 (Obituary)
Sasek, Miroslav 1916-1980,
   16: 239; *23:* 218 (Obituary)
Sattler, Helen Roney 1921- ,
   4: 181
Saunders, Caleb. *See* Heinlein,
   Robert A(nson), *9:* 102
Saunders, Keith 1910- , *12:* 186
Saunders, Rubie (Agnes) 1929- ,
   21: 136
Savage, Blake. *See* Goodwin,
   Harold Leland, *13:* 73

Savery, Constance (Winifred) 1897- , *1:* 186
Saville, (Leonard) Malcolm 1901-1982, *23:* 218; *31:* 146 (Obituary)
Saviozzi, Adriana. *See* Mazza, Adriana, *19:* 215
Savitt, Sam, *8:* 181
Savitz, Harriet May 1933- , *5:* 161
Sawyer, Ruth 1880-1970, *17:* 207
Say, Allen 1937- , *28:* 179
Sayers, Frances Clarke 1897- , *3:* 185
Sazer, Nina 1949- , *13:* 191
Scabrini, Janet 1953- , *13:* 191
Scagnetti, Jack 1924- , *7:* 188
Scanlon, Marion Stephany, *11:* 206
Scarf, Maggi. *See* Scarf, Maggie, *5:* 162
Scarf, Maggie 1932- , *5:* 162
Scarry, Patricia (Murphy) 1924- , *2:* 218
Scarry, Patsy. *See* Scarry, Patricia, *2:* 218
Scarry, Richard (McClure) 1919- , *2:* 218
Schaefer, Jack 1907- , *3:* 186
Schaeffer, Mead 1898- , *21:* 137
Schaller, George B(eals) 1933- , *30:* 184
Schatzki, Walter 1899- , *31:* 146 (Brief Entry)
Schechter, Betty (Goodstein) 1921- , *5:* 163
Scheer, Julian (Weisel) 1926- , *8:* 183
Scheffer, Victor B. 1906- , *6:* 197
Schell, Orville H. 1940- , *10:* 136
Schellie, Don 1932- , *29:* 170
Schemm, Mildred Walker 1905- , *21:* 139
Scherf, Margaret 1908- , *10:* 136
Schermer, Judith (Denise) 1941- , *30:* 184
Schick, Alice 1946- , *27:* 176
Schick, Eleanor 1942- , *9:* 161
Schick, Joel 1945- , *30:* 185 (Brief Entry); *31:* 147
Schiff, Ken 1942- , *7:* 189
Schiller, Andrew 1919- , *21:* 139
Schiller, Barbara (Heyman) 1928- , *21:* 140
Schiller, Justin G. 1943- , *31:* 149 (Brief Entry)
Schisgall, Oscar 1901- , *12:* 187
Schlein, Miriam 1926- , *2:* 222
Schloat, G. Warren, Jr. 1914- , *4:* 181
Schmid, Eleonore 1939- , *12:* 188
Schmiderer, Dorothy 1940- , *19:* 223
Schmidt, Elizabeth 1915- , *15:* 242
Schmidt, James Norman 1912- , *21:* 141

Schneider, Herman 1905- , *7:* 189
Schneider, Nina 1913- , *2:* 222
Schnirel, James R(einhold) 1931- , *14:* 178
Schoen, Barbara 1924- , *13:* 192
Scholastica, Sister Mary. *See* Jenkins, Marie M., *7:* 143
Scholefield, Edmund O. *See* Butterworth, W. E., *5:* 40
Scholey, Arthur 1932- , *28:* 179
Schone, Virginia, *22:* 215
Schoonover, Frank (Earle) 1877-1972, *24:* 182
Schoor, Gene 1921- , *3:* 188
Schraff, Anne E(laine) 1939- , *27:* 177
Schreiber, Elizabeth Anne (Ferguson) 1947- , *13:* 192
Schreiber, Georges 1904-1977, *29:* 171 (Brief Entry)
Schreiber, Ralph W(alter) 1942- , *13:* 194
Schroeder, Ted 1931(?)-1973, *20:* 163 (Obituary)
Schulman, Janet 1933- , *22:* 216
Schulman, L(ester) M(artin) 1934- , *13:* 194
Schultz, Gwendolyn, *21:* 142
Schultz, James Willard 1859-1947, *YABC 1:* 238
Schultz, Pearle Henriksen 1918- , *21:* 142
Schulz, Charles M(onroe) 1922- , *10:* 137
Schurfranz, Vivian 1925- , *13:* 194
Schutzer, A. I. 1922- , *13:* 195
Schuyler, Pamela R(icka) 1948- , *30:* 185
Schwartz, Alvin 1927- , *4:* 183
Schwartz, Anne Powers 1913- , *10:* 142
Schwartz, Charles W(alsh) 1914- , *8:* 184
Schwartz, Daniel (Bennet) 1929- , *29:* 172 (Brief Entry)
Schwartz, Elizabeth Reeder 1912- , *8:* 184
Schwartz, Sheila (Ruth) 1929- , *27:* 178
Schwartz, Stephen (Lawrence) 1948- , *19:* 224
Schweninger, Ann 1951- , *29:* 172
Scoggin, Margaret C. 1905-1968, *28:* 180 (Brief Entry)
Scoppettone, Sandra 1936- , *9:* 162
Scott, Ann Herbert 1926- , *29:* 173 (Brief Entry)
Scott, Cora Annett (Pipitone) 1931- , *11:* 207
Scott, Dan [House pseudonym]. *See* Barker, S. Omar, *10:* 8
Scott, Dan. *See* Stratemeyer, Edward L., *1:* 208

Scott, Jack Denton 1915- , *31:* 149
Scott, John 1912-1976, *14:* 178
Scott, John Anthony 1916- , *23:* 219
Scott, John M(artin) 1913- , *12:* 188
Scott, Tony. *See* Scott, John Anthony, *23:* 219
Scott, Sir Walter 1771-1832, *YABC 2:* 280
Scott, Warwick. *See* Trevor, Elleston, *28:* 207
Scribner, Charles, Jr. 1921- , *13:* 195
Scrimsher, Lila Gravatt 1897-1974, *28:* 180 (Obituary)
Scuro, Vincent 1951- , *21:* 144
Seabrooke, Brenda 1941- , *30:* 186
Seaman, Augusta Huiell 1879-1950, *31:* 153
Seamands, Ruth (Childers) 1916- , *9:* 163
Searight, Mary W(illiams) 1918- , *17:* 211
Searle, Kathryn Adrienne 1942- , *10:* 143
Sears, Stephen W. 1932- , *4:* 184
Sebastian, Lee. *See* Silverberg, Robert, *13:* 206
Sechrist, Elizabeth Hough 1903- , *2:* 224
Sedges, John. *See* Buck, Pearl S., *1:* 36; *25:* 63
Seed, Jenny 1930- , *8:* 186
Seed, Sheila Turner 1937(?)-1979, *23:* 220 (Obituary)
Seeger, Elizabeth 1889-1973, *20:* 163 (Obituary)
Seeger, Pete(r) 1919- , *13:* 196
Seever, R. *See* Reeves, Lawrence F., *29:* 166
Segal, Lore 1928- , *4:* 186
Seidelman, James Edward 1926- , *6:* 197
Seidman, Laurence (Ivan) 1925- , *15:* 244
Seigal, Kalman 1917- , *12:* 190
Seignobosc, Francoise 1897-1961, *21:* 145
Seixas, Judith S. 1922- , *17:* 212
Sejima, Yoshimasa 1913- , *8:* 186
Selden, George. *See* Thompson, George Selden, *4:* 204
Self, Margaret Cabell 1902- , *24:* 191
Selig, Sylvie 1942- , *13:* 199
Selkirk, Jane [Joint pseudonym]. *See* Chapman, John Stanton Higham, *27:* 41 (Obituary)
Selsam, Millicent E(llis) 1912- , *1:* 188; *29:* 173
Seltzer, Meyer 1932- , *17:* 213
Sendak, Jack, *28:* 180

Sendak, Maurice (Bernard)
   1928- , *1:* 190; *27:* 181
Sengler, Johanna   1924- , *18:* 255
Serage, Nancy   1924- , *10:* 143
Seredy, Kate   1899-1975, *1:* 193;
   24: 193 (Obituary)
Seroff, Victor I(lyitch)   1902-1979,
   12: 190; *26:* 171 (Obituary)
Serraillier, Ian (Lucien)   1912- ,
   1: 193
Servello, Joe   1932- , *10:* 143
Service, Robert W(illiam)
   1874(?)-1958, *20:* 163
Serwadda, William Moses   1931- ,
   27: 201
Serwer, Blanche L.   1910- ,
   10: 144
Seton, Anya, *3:* 188
Seton, Ernest Thompson
   1860-1946, *18:* 257
Seuling, Barbara   1937- , *10:* 145
Seuss, Dr. *See* Geisel, Theodor
   Seuss, *1:* 104; *28:* 107
Severn, Bill. *See* Severn, William
   Irving, *1:* 195
Severn, David. *See* Unwin, David
   S(torr), *14:* 217
Severn, William Irving   1914- ,
   1: 195
Seward, Prudence   1926- , *16:* 242
Sewell, Anna   1820-1878, *24:* 193
Sexton, Anne (Harvey)
   1928-1974, *10:* 146
Seymour, Alta Halverson, *10:* 147
Shafer, Robert E(ugene)   1925- ,
   9: 164
Shahn, Ben(jamin)   1898-1969,
   21: 146 (Obituary)
Shahn, Bernarda Bryson. *See*
   Bryson, Bernarda, *9:* 26
Shanks, Ann Zane (Kushner),
   10: 148
Shannon, Monica   (?)-1965,
   28: 186
Shannon, Terry, *21:* 147
Shapp, Martha   1910- , *3:* 189
Sharfman, Amalie, *14:* 179
Sharma, Partap   1939- , *15:* 244
Sharmat, Marjorie Weinman
   1928- , *4:* 187
Sharp, Margery   1905- , *1:* 196;
   29: 176
Sharp, Zerna A.   1889-1981,
   27: 202 (Obituary)
Sharpe, Mitchell R(aymond)
   1924- , *12:* 191
Shaw, Arnold   1909- , *4:* 189
Shaw, Charles (Green)   1892-1974,
   13: 200
Shaw, Evelyn   1927- , *28:* 187
Shaw, Flora Louisa. *See* Lugard,
   Flora Louisa Shaw, *21:* 104
Shaw, Ray, *7:* 190
Shaw, Richard   1923- , *12:* 192
Shay, Arthur   1922- , *4:* 189

Shearer, John   1947- , *27:* 202
   (Brief Entry)
Shecter, Ben   1935- , *16:* 243
Sheedy, Alexandra Elizabeth
   1962- , *19:* 225
Sheehan, Ethna   1908- , *9:* 165
Sheffield, Janet N.   1926- ,
   26: 171
Shekerjian, Regina Tor, *16:* 244
Sheldon, Ann [Collective
   pseudonym], *1:* 198
Sheldon, Aure   1917-1976, *12:* 194
Shelley, Mary Wollstonecraft
   (Godwin)   1797-1851, *29:* 181
Shelton, William Roy   1919- ,
   5: 164
Shemin, Margaretha   1928- ,
   4: 190
Shepard, Ernest Howard
   1879-1976, *3:* 191; *24:* 201
   (Obituary)
Shepard, Mary. *See* Knox, (Mary)
   Eleanor Jessie, *30:* 131
Shephard, Esther   1891-1975,
   5: 165; *26:* 172 (Obituary)
Shepherd, Elizabeth, *4:* 191
Sherburne, Zoa   1912- , *3:* 194
Sherman, D(enis) R(onald)
   1934- , *29:* 192 (Brief Entry)
Sherman, Diane (Finn)   1928- ,
   12: 194
Sherman, Elizabeth. *See* Friskey,
   Margaret Richards, *5:* 72
Sherman, Nancy. *See* Rosenberg,
   Nancy Sherman, *4:* 177
Sherrod, Jane. *See* Singer, Jane
   Sherrod, *4:* 192
Sherry, (Dulcie) Sylvia   1932- ,
   8: 187
Sherwan, Earl   1917- , *3:* 195
Shiefman, Vicky, *22:* 217
Shields, Charles   1944- , *10:* 149
Shimin, Symeon   1902- , *13:* 201
Shinn, Everett   1876-1953, *21:* 148
Shippen, Katherine B(inney)
   1892-1980, *1:* 198; *23:* 221
   (Obituary)
Shipton, Eric   1907- , *10:* 151
Shirreffs, Gordon D(onald)
   1914- , *11:* 207
Shore, June Lewis, *30:* 186
Shortall, Leonard W., *19:* 226
Shotwell, Louisa R.   1902- ,
   3: 196
Showalter, Jean B(reckinridge),
   12: 195
Showers, Paul C.   1910- , *21:* 152
Shub, Elizabeth, *5:* 166
Shulevitz, Uri   1935- , *3:* 197
Shulman, Alix Kates   1932- ,
   7: 191
Shulman, Irving   1913- , *13:* 204
Shumsky, Zena. *See* Collier, Zena,
   23: 41
Shura, Mary Francis. *See* Craig,
   Mary Francis, *6:* 52

Shuttlesworth, Dorothy, *3:* 200
Shyer, Marlene Fanta, *13:* 205
Siberell, Anne, *29:* 192
Sibley, Don   1922- , *12:* 195
Siculan, Daniel   1922- , *12:* 197
Sidjakov, Nicolas   1924- , *18:* 272
Sidney, Margaret. *See* Lothrop,
   Harriet Mulford Stone, *20:* 110
Silcock, Sara Lesley   1947- ,
   12: 199
Silver, Ruth. *See* Chew, Ruth,
   7: 45
Silverberg, Robert, *13:* 206
Silverman, Mel(vin Frank)
   1931-1966, *9:* 166
Silverstein, Alvin   1933- , *8:* 188
Silverstein, Shel(by)   1932- ,
   27: 202 (Brief Entry)
Silverstein, Virginia B(arbara
   Opshelor)   1937- , *8:* 190
Simon, Charlie May. *See* Fletcher,
   Charlie May, *3:* 70
Simon, Hilda (Rita)   1921- ,
   28: 188
Simon, Howard   1903-1979,
   21: 154 (Obituary)
Simon, Joe. *See* Simon, Joseph H.,
   7: 192
Simon, Joseph H.   1913- , *7:* 192
Simon, Martin P(aul William)
   1903-1969, *12:* 200
Simon, Mina Lewiton. *See* Lewiton,
   Mina, *2:* 174
Simon, Norma   1927- , *3:* 201
Simon, Seymour   1931- , *4:* 191
Simon, Shirley (Schwartz)   1921- ,
   11: 210
Simonetta, Linda   1948- , *14:* 179
Simonetta, Sam   1936- , *14:* 180
Simont, Marc   1915- , *9:* 167
Simpson, Colin   1908- , *14:* 181
Simpson, Myrtle L(illias)   1931- ,
   14: 181
Sinclair, Upton (Beall)   1878-1968,
   9: 168
Singer, Isaac. *See* Singer, Isaac
   Bashevis, *3:* 203; *27:* 202
Singer, Isaac Bashevis   1904- ,
   3: 203; *27:* 202
Singer, Jane Sherrod   1917- ,
   4: 192
Singer, Julia   1917- , *28:* 190
Singer, Susan (Mahler)   1941- ,
   9: 170
Sisson, Rosemary Anne   1923- ,
   11: 211
Sitomer, Harry   1903- , *31:* 155
Sitomer, Mindel   1903- , *31:* 157
Sive, Helen R.   1951- , *30:* 187
Sivulich, Sandra (Jeanne) Stroner
   1941- , *9:* 171
Skelly, James R(ichard)   1927- ,
   17: 215
Skinner, Constance Lindsay
   1882-1939, *YABC 1:* 247

Skinner, Cornelia Otis 1901- ,
  2: 225
Skorpen, Liesel Moak 1935- ,
  3: 206
Skurzynski, Gloria (Joan) 1930- ,
  8: 190
Slackman, Charles B. 1934- ,
  12: 200
Slade, Richard 1910-1971, *9:* 171
Slaughter, Jean. *See* Doty, Jean
  Slaughter, *28:* 95
Sleator, William 1945- , *3:* 207
Sleigh, Barbara 1906-1982,
  3: 208; *30:* 188 (Obituary)
Slicer, Margaret O. 1920- ,
  4: 193
Slobodkin, Florence (Gersh)
  1905- , *5:* 167
Slobodkin, Louis 1903-1975,
  1: 199; *26:* 172
Slobodkina, Esphyr 1909- ,
  1: 201
Slote, Alfred 1926- , *8:* 192
Small, Ernest. *See* Lent, Blair,
  2: 172
Smaridge, Norah 1903- , *6:* 198
Smiley, Virginia Kester 1923- ,
  2: 227
Smith, Beatrice S(chillinger),
  12: 201
Smith, Betty 1896-1972, *6:* 199
Smith, Bradford 1909-1964,
  5: 168
Smith, Caesar. *See* Trevor,
  Elleston, *28:* 207
Smith, Datus C(lifford), Jr.
  1907- , *13:* 208
Smith, Dodie, *4:* 194
Smith, Doris Buchanan 1934- ,
  28: 191
Smith, Dorothy Stafford 1905- ,
  6: 201
Smith, E(lmer) Boyd 1860-1943,
  YABC 1: 248
Smith, Elva S(ophronia) 1871-
  1965, *31:* 157 (Brief Entry)
Smith, Eunice Young 1902- ,
  5: 169
Smith, Frances C. 1904- , *3:* 209
Smith, Fredrika Shumway
  1877-1968, *30:* 188 (Brief
  Entry)
Smith, Gary R(ichard) 1932- ,
  14: 182
Smith, George Harmon 1920- ,
  5: 171
Smith, H(arry) Allen 1907-1976,
  20: 171 (Obituary)
Smith, Howard Everett, Jr.
  1927- , *12:* 201
Smith, Hugh L(etcher) 1921-1968,
  5: 172
Smith, Imogene Henderson
  1922- , *12:* 203
Smith, Jean. *See* Smith, Frances C.,
  3: 209

Smith, Jean Pajot 1945- , *10:* 151
Smith, Jessie Willcox 1863-1935,
  21: 155
Smith, Johnston. *See* Crane,
  Stephen (Townley),
  YABC 2: 84
Smith, Lafayette. *See* Higdon, Hal,
  4: 115
Smith, Lee. *See* Albion, Lee Smith,
  29: 32
Smith, Linell Nash 1932- , *2:* 227
Smith, Lucia B. 1943- , *30:* 189
Smith, Marion Hagens 1913- ,
  12: 204
Smith, Marion Jaques 1899- ,
  13: 209
Smith, Mary Ellen, *10:* 152
Smith, Mike. *See* Smith, Mary
  Ellen, *10:* 152
Smith, Nancy Covert 1935- ,
  12: 204
Smith, Norman F. 1920- , *5:* 172
Smith, Pauline C(oggeshall)
  1908- , *27:* 215
Smith, Robert Kimmel 1930- ,
  12: 205
Smith, Robert Paul 1915-1977,
  30: 189 (Obituary)
Smith, Ruth Leslie 1902- , *2:* 228
Smith, Sarah Stafford. *See* Smith,
  Dorothy Stafford, *6:* 201
Smith, Susan Carlton 1923- ,
  12: 207
Smith, Vian (Crocker) 1919-1969,
  11: 213
Smith, Ward. *See* Goldsmith,
  Howard, *24:* 123
Smith, William A., *10:* 153
Smith, William Jay 1918- ,
  2: 229
Smith, Z. Z. *See* Westheimer,
  David, *14:* 242
Smits, Teo. *See* Smits, Theodore
  R(ichard), *28:* 192 (Brief
  Entry)
Smits, Theodore R(ichard) 1905- ,
  28: 192 (Brief Entry)
Smucker, Barbara (Claassen)
  1915- , *29:* 194
Snedeker, Caroline Dale (Parke)
  1871-1956, *YABC 2:* 296
Sneve, Virginia Driving Hawk
  1933- , *8:* 193
Sniff, Mr. *See* Abisch, Roslyn
  Kroop, *9:* 3
Snodgrass, Thomas Jefferson. *See*
  Clemens, Samuel Langhorne,
  YABC 2: 51
Snow, Donald Clifford 1917- ,
  16: 246
Snow, Dorothea J(ohnston)
  1909- , *9:* 172
Snyder, Anne 1922- , *4:* 195
Snyder, Jerome 1916-1976,
  20: 171 (Obituary)

Snyder, Zilpha Keatley 1927- ,
  1: 202; *28:* 192
Snyderman, Reuven K. 1922- ,
  5: 173
Sobol, Donald J. 1924- , *1:* 203;
  31: 157
Soderlind, Arthur E(dwin) 1920- ,
  14: 183
Softly, Barbara (Frewin) 1924- ,
  12: 209
Soglow, Otto 1900-1975, *30:* 189
  (Obituary)
Sohl, Frederic J(ohn) 1916- ,
  10: 154
Solbert, Romaine G. 1925- ,
  2: 232
Solbert, Ronni. *See* Solbert,
  Romaine G., *2:* 232
Solomons, Ikey, Esquire, Jr. *See*
  Thackeray, William
  Makepeace, *23:* 223
Solonevich, George 1915- ,
  15: 245
Solot, Mary Lynn 1939- , *12:* 210
Sommer, Elyse 1929- , *7:* 192
Sommer, Robert 1929- , *12:* 211
Sommerfelt, Aimee 1892- ,
  5: 173
Sonneborn, Ruth (Cantor) A.
  1899-1974, *4:* 196; *27:* 216
  (Obituary)
Sorche, Nic Leodhas. *See* Alger,
  Leclaire (Gowans), *15:* 1
Sorensen, Virginia 1912- , *2:* 233
Sorrentino, Joseph N., *6:* 203
Sortor, June Elizabeth 1939- ,
  12: 212
Sortor, Toni. *See* Sortor, June
  Elizabeth, *12:* 212
Soskin, V. H. *See* Ellison, Virginia
  Howell, *4:* 74
Sotomayor, Antonio 1902- ,
  11: 214
Soudley, Henry. *See* Wood, James
  Playsted, *1:* 229
Soule, Gardner (Bosworth)
  1913- , *14:* 183
Soule, Jean Conder 1919- ,
  10: 154
Southall, Ivan 1921- , *3:* 210
Spanfeller, James J(ohn) 1930- ,
  19: 230
Spangenberg, Judith Dunn 1942- ,
  5: 175
Spar, Jerome 1918- , *10:* 156
Sparks, Beatrice Mathews 1918- ,
  28: 195 (Brief Entry)
Sparks, Mary W. 1920- , *15:* 247
Spaulding, Leonard. *See* Bradbury,
  Ray, *11:* 29
Speare, Elizabeth George 1908- ,
  5: 176
Spearing, Judith (Mary Harlow)
  1922- , *9:* 173
Specking, Inez 1890-196(?),
  11: 217

Speicher, Helen Ross (Smith) 1915- , *8:* 194
Spellman, John W(illard) 1934- , *14:* 186
Spelman, Mary 1934- , *28:* 195
Spence, Eleanor (Rachel) 1927- , *21:* 163
Spencer, Ann 1918- , *10:* 156
Spencer, Cornelia. *See* Yaukey, Grace S. *5:* 203
Spencer, Elizabeth 1921- , *14:* 186
Spencer, William 1922- , *9:* 175
Sperry, Armstrong W. 1897-1976, *1:* 204; *27:* 216 (Obituary)
Sperry, Raymond, Jr. [Collective pseudonym], *1:* 205
Spiegelman, Judith M., *5:* 179
Spier, Peter (Edward) 1927- , *4:* 198
Spilhaus, Athelstan 1911- , *13:* 209
Spilka, Arnold 1917- , *6:* 203
Spink, Reginald (William) 1905- , *11:* 217
Spinossimus. *See* White, William, *16:* 276
Splaver, Sarah 1921- , *28:* 197 (Brief Entry)
Spollen, Christopher 1952- , *12:* 213
Sprague, Gretchen (Burnham) 1926- , *27:* 216
Sprigge, Elizabeth 1900-1974, *10:* 157
Spring, (Robert) Howard 1889-1965, *28:* 197
Spykman, E(lizabeth) C. 19(?)-1965, *10:* 157
Spyri, Johanna (Heusser) 1827-1901, *19:* 232
Squire, Miriam. *See* Sprigge, Elizabeth, *10:* 157
Squires, Phil. *See* Barker, S. Omar, *10:* 8
S-Ringi, Kjell. *See* Ringi, Kjell, *12:* 168
Stadtler, Bea 1921- , *17:* 215
Stafford, Jean 1915-1979, *22:* 218 (Obituary)
Stahl, Ben(jamin) 1910- , *5:* 179
Stalder, Valerie, *27:* 216
Stamaty, Mark Alan 1947- , *12:* 214
Stambler, Irwin 1924- , *5:* 181
Stang, Judit 1921-1977, *29:* 196
Stang, Judy. *See* Stang, Judit, *29:* 196
Stanhope, Eric. *See* Hamilton, Charles Harold St. John, *13:* 77
Stankevich, Boris 1928- , *2:* 234
Stanley, Diana 1909- , *30:* 190 (Brief Entry)
Stanley, Robert. *See* Hamilton, Charles Harold St. John, *13:* 77

Stanstead, John. *See* Groom, Arthur William, *10:* 53
Stapleton, Marjorie (Winifred) 1932- , *28:* 199
Stapp, Arthur D(onald) 1906-1972, *4:* 201
Starbird, Kaye 1916- , *6:* 204
Stark, James. *See* Goldston, Robert, *6:* 90
Starkey, Marion L. 1901- , *13:* 211
Starret, William. *See* McClintock, Marshall, *3:* 119
Stauffer, Don. *See* Berkebile, Fred D(onovan), *26:* 37 (Obituary)
Staunton, Schuyler. *See* Baum, L(yman) Frank, *18:* 7
Stearns, Monroe (Mather) 1913- , *5:* 182
Steele, Chester K. *See* Stratemeyer, Edward L., *1:* 208
Steele, Mary Q., *3:* 211
Steele, (Henry) Max(well) 1922- , *10:* 159
Steele, William O(wen) 1917-1979, *1:* 205; *27:* 217 (Obituary)
Steig, William 1907- , *18:* 275
Stein, Harvé 1904- , *30:* 190 (Brief Entry)
Stein, M(eyer) L(ewis), *6:* 205
Stein, Mini, *2:* 234
Stein, R(ichard) Conrad 1937- , *31:* 159
Steinbeck, John (Ernst) 1902-1968, *9:* 176
Steinberg, Alfred 1917- , *9:* 178
Steinberg, Fred J. 1933- , *4:* 201
Steiner, Barbara A(nnette) 1934- , *13:* 213
Steiner, Stan(ley) 1925- , *14:* 187
Stephens, Mary Jo 1935- , *8:* 196
Stephens, William M(cLain) 1925- , *21:* 165
Stepp, Ann 1935- , *29:* 197
Steptoe, John (Lewis) 1950- , *8:* 198
Sterling, Dorothy 1913- , *1:* 206
Sterling, Helen. *See* Hoke, Helen (L.), *15:* 133
Sterling, Philip 1907- , *8:* 198
Stern, Ellen N(orman) 1927- , *26:* 180
Stern, Madeleine B(ettina) 1912- , *14:* 188
Stern, Philip Van Doren 1900- , *13:* 215
Stern, Simon 1943- , *15:* 248
Sterne, Emma Gelders 1894-1971, *6:* 205
Steurt, Marjorie Rankin 1888- , *10:* 159
Stevens, Carla M(cBride) 1928- , *13:* 217
Stevens, Franklin 1933- , *6:* 206

Stevens, Patricia Bunning 1931- , *27:* 217
Stevens, Peter. *See* Geis, Darlene, *7:* 101
Stevenson, Anna (M.) 1905- , *12:* 216
Stevenson, Augusta 1869(?)-1976, *2:* 235; *26:* 180 (Obituary)
Stevenson, Burton E(gbert) 1872-1962, *25:* 213
Stevenson, Janet 1913- , *8:* 199
Stevenson, Robert Louis 1850-1894, *YABC 2:* 307
Stewart, A(gnes) C(harlotte), *15:* 250
Stewart, Charles. *See* Zurhorst, Charles (Stewart, Jr.), *12:* 240
Stewart, Elizabeth Laing 1907- , *6:* 206
Stewart, John (William) 1920- , *14:* 189
Stewart, George Rippey 1895-1980, *3:* 213; *23:* 221 (Obituary)
Stewart, Mary (Florence Elinor) 1916- , *12:* 217
Stewart, Robert Neil 1891-1972, *7:* 192
Stewig, John Warren 1937- , *26:* 181
Stiles, Martha Bennett, *6:* 207
Still, James 1906- , *29:* 197
Stillerman, Robbie 1947- , *12:* 219
Stilley, Frank 1918- , *29:* 200
Stine, G(eorge) Harry 1928- , *10:* 161
Stine, Jovial Bob. *See* Stine, Robert Lawrence, *31:* 160
Stine, Robert Lawrence 1943- , *31:* 160
Stinetorf, Louise 1900- , *10:* 162
Stirling, Arthur. *See* Sinclair, Upton (Beall), *9:* 168
Stirling, Nora B., *3:* 214
Stirnweis, Shannon 1931- , *10:* 163
Stobbs, William 1914- , *17:* 216
Stoddard, Edward G. 1923- , *10:* 164
Stoddard, Hope 1900- , *6:* 207
Stoddard, Sandol. *See* Warburg, Sandol Stoddard, *14:* 234
Stoiko, Michael 1919- , *14:* 190
Stoker, Abraham 1847-1912, *29:* 202
Stoker, Bram. *See* Stoker, Abraham, *29:* 202
Stokes, Cedric. *See* Beardmore, George, *20:* 10
Stokes, Jack (Tilden) 1923- , *13:* 218
Stolz, Mary (Slattery) 1920- , *10:* 165
Stone, Alan [Collective pseudonym], *1:* 208. *See also*

Svenson, Andrew E., *2:* 238;
26: 185 (Obituary)
Stone, D(avid) K(arl) 1922- ,
9: 179
Stone, Eugenia 1879-1971, *7:* 193
Stone, Gene. *See* Stone, Eugenia,
7: 193
Stone, Helen V., *6:* 208
Stone, Irving 1903- , *3:* 215
Stone, Josephine Rector. *See* Dixon,
Jeanne, *31:* 60
Stone, Raymond [Collective
pseudonym], *1:* 208
Stone, Richard A. *See* Stratemeyer,
Edward L., *1:* 208
Stonehouse, Bernard 1926- ,
13: 219
Storch, Anne B. von. *See* von
Storch, Anne B., *1:* 221
Storey, (Elizabeth) Margaret
(Carlton) 1926- , *9:* 180
Storey, Victoria Carolyn 1945- ,
16: 248
Storme, Peter. *See* Stern, Philip
Van Doren, *13:* 215
Storr, Catherine (Cole) 1913- ,
9: 181
Stoutenburg, Adrien 1916- ,
3: 217
Stover, Allan C(arl) 1938- ,
14: 191
Stover, Marjorie Filley 1914- ,
9: 182
Stowe, Harriet (Elizabeth) Beecher
1811-1896, *YABC 1:* 250
Strachan, Margaret Pitcairn
1908- , *14:* 193
Stranger, Joyce. *See* Wilson, Joyce
M(uriel Judson), *21:* 201
Stratemeyer, Edward L.
1862-1930, *1:* 208
Stratton-Porter, Gene 1863-1924,
15: 251
Strayer, E. Ward. *See* Stratemeyer,
Edward L., *1:* 208
Streano, Vince(nt Catello) 1945- ,
20: 172
Streatfeild, Noel 1897- , *20:* 173
Street, Julia Montgomery 1898- ,
11: 218
Strong, Charles [Joint pseudonym].
See Epstein, Beryl, *31:* 64;
Epstein, Samuel, *1:* 87; *31:* 66
Ströyer, Poul 1923- , *13:* 221
Stuart, David. *See* Hoyt, Edwin
P(almer), Jr., *28:* 132
Stuart, Forbes 1924- , *13:* 222
Stuart, Ian. *See* MacLean, Alistair
(Stuart), *23:* 131
Stuart, (Hilton) Jesse 1907- ,
2: 236
Stuart, Sheila. *See* Baker, Mary
Gladys Steel, *12:* 27
Stubis, Talivaldis 1926- , *5:* 183
Stubley, Trevor (Hugh) 1932- ,
22: 218

Stultifer, Morton. *See* Curtis,
Richard (Alan), *29:* 54
Sture-Vasa, Mary. *See* Alsop,
Mary, *2:* 4
Sturton, Hugh. *See* Johnston,
H(ugh) A(nthony) S(tephen),
14: 87
Sturtzel, Howard A(llison) 1894- ,
1: 210
Sturtzel, Jane Levington 1903- ,
1: 212
Styles, Frank Showell 1908- ,
10: 167
Suba, Susanne, *4:* 202
Subond, Valerie. *See* Grayland,
Valerie, *7:* 111
Suhl, Yuri 1908- , *8:* 200
Suid, Murray 1942- , *27:* 218
Sullivan, George E(dward)
1927- , *4:* 202
Sullivan, Mary W(ilson) 1907- ,
13: 224
Sullivan, Thomas Joseph, Jr.
1947- , *16:* 248
Sullivan, Tom. *See* Sullivan,
Thomas Joseph, Jr., *16:* 248
Sumichrast, Jözef 1948- , *29:* 212
Summers, James L(evingston)
1910- , *28:* 199 (Brief Entry)
Sunderlin, Sylvia 1911- , *28:* 199
Sung, Betty Lee, *26:* 183
Supraner, Robyn 1930- , *20:* 182
Surge, Frank 1931- , *13:* 225
Susac, Andrew 1929- , *5:* 184
Sutcliff, Rosemary 1920- , *6:* 209
Sutherland, Efua (Theodora
Morgue) 1924- , *25:* 215
Sutherland, Margaret 1941- ,
15: 271
Suttles, Shirley (Smith) 1922- ,
21: 166
Sutton, Ann (Livesay) 1923- ,
31: 161
Sutton, Eve(lyn Mary) 1906- ,
26: 184
Sutton, Felix 1910(?)- , *31:* 162
Sutton, Larry M(atthew) 1931- ,
29: 214
Sutton, Margaret (Beebe) 1903- ,
1: 213
Sutton, Myron Daniel 1925- ,
31: 165
Svenson, Andrew E. 1910-1975,
2: 238; *26:* 185 (Obituary)
Swain, Su Zan (Noguchi) 1916- ,
21: 169
Swan, Susan 1944- , *22:* 219
Swarthout, Glendon (Fred)
1918- , *26:* 185
Swarthout, Kathryn 1919- ,
7: 194
Sweeney, James B(artholomew)
1910- , *21:* 170
Swenson, Allan A(rmstrong)
1933- , *21:* 172
Swenson, May 1919- , *15:* 271

Swift, David. *See* Kaufmann, John,
18: 132
Swift, Hildegarde Hoyt
1890(?)-1977, *20:* 184
(Obituary)
Swift, Jonathan 1667-1745,
19: 244
Swift, Merlin. *See* Leeming,
Joseph, *26:* 132
Swiger, Elinor Porter 1927- ,
8: 202
Swinburne, Laurence 1924- ,
9: 183
Sylvester, Natalie G(abry) 1922- ,
22: 222
Syme, (Neville) Ronald 1913- ,
2: 239
Synge, (Phyllis) Ursula 1930- ,
9: 184
Sypher, Lucy Johnston 1907- ,
7: 195
Szasz, Suzanne Shorr 1919- ,
13: 226
Szekeres, Cyndy 1933- , *5:* 184
Szulc, Tad 1926- , *26:* 187

Taber, Gladys (Bagg) 1899-1980,
22: 223 (Obituary)
Tabrah, Ruth Milander 1921- ,
14: 194
Tait, Douglas 1944- , *12:* 220
Takakjian, Portia 1930- , *15:* 273
Takashima, Shizuye 1928- ,
13: 227
Talbot, Charlene Joy 1928- ,
10: 169
Talbot, Toby 1928- , *14:* 195
Talker, T. *See* Rands, William
Brighty, *17:* 156
Tallcott, Emogene, *10:* 170
Tallon, Robert 1940- , *28:* 202
(Brief Entry)
Talmadge, Marian, *14:* 196
Tamarin, Alfred, *13:* 229
Tamburine, Jean 1930- , *12:* 221
Tannenbaum, Beulah 1916- ,
3: 219
Tanner, Louise S(tickney) 1922- ,
9: 185
Tanobe, Miyuki 1937- , *23:* 222
Tapio, Pat Decker. *See* Kines, Pat
Decker, *12:* 118
Tarkington, (Newton) Booth
1869-1946, *17:* 218
Tarry, Ellen 1906- , *16:* 250
Tarshis, Jerome 1936- , *9:* 186
Tashjian, Virginia A. 1921- ,
3: 220
Tasker, James, *9:* 187
Tate, Ellalice. *See* Hibbert, Eleanor,
2: 134
Tate, Joan 1922- , *9:* 188
Tatham, Campbell. *See* Elting,
Mary, *2:* 100

Taves, Isabella 1915- , *27:* 219
Taylor, Barbara J. 1927- ,
   10: 171
Taylor, Carl 1937- , *14:* 196
Taylor, David 1900-1965, *10:* 172
Taylor, Elizabeth 1912-1975,
   13: 230
Taylor, Florance Walton, *9:* 190
Taylor, Florence M(arion
   Tompkins) 1892- , *9:* 191
Taylor, Herb(ert Norman, Jr.)
   1942- , *22:* 223
Taylor, Kenneth N(athaniel)
   1917- , *26:* 187
Taylor, L(ester) B(arbour), Jr.
   1932- , *27:* 219
Taylor, Mark, *28:* 202 (Brief Entry)
Taylor, Mildred D., *15:* 275
Taylor, Robert Lewis 1912- ,
   10: 172
Taylor, Sydney (Brenner)
   1904(?)-1978, *1:* 214; *26:* 189
   (Obituary); *28:* 202
Taylor, Theodore 1924- , *5:* 185
Teague, Bob. *See* Teague, Robert,
   31: 166 (Brief Entry)
Teague, Robert 1929- , *31:* 166
   (Brief Entry)
Teal, Val 1903- , *10:* 174
Teale, Edwin Way 1899-1980,
   7: 196; *25:* 215 (Obituary)
Tebbel, John (William) 1912- ,
   26: 190
Tee-Van, Helen Damrosch
   1893-1976, *10:* 176; *27:* 221
   (Obituary)
Telescope, Tom. *See* Newbery,
   John, *20:* 135
Temkin, Sara Anne (Schlossberg)
   1913- , *26:* 192
Temko, Florence, *13:* 231
Templar, Maurice. *See* Groom,
   Arthur William, *10:* 53
Tenggren, Gustaf 1896-1970,
   18: 277; *26:* 193 (Obituary)
Tennant, Kylie 1912- , *6:* 210
Tenniel, Sir John 1820-1914,
   27: 221 (Brief Entry)
ter Haar, Jaap 1922- , *6:* 211
Terhune, Albert Payson
   1872-1942, *15:* 277
Terlouw, Jan (Cornelis) 1931- ,
   30: 190
Terris, Susan 1937- , *3:* 221
Terry, Luther L(eonidas) 1911- ,
   11: 220
Terry, Walter 1913- , *14:* 198
Terzian, James P. 1915- , *14:* 199
Thacher, Mary McGrath 1933- ,
   9: 192
Thackeray, William Makepeace
   1811-1863, *23:* 223
Tharp, Louise Hall 1898- , *3:* 223
Thayer, Jane. *See* Woolley,
   Catherine, *3:* 265

Thayer, Peter. *See* Wyler, Rose,
   18: 303
Thelwell, Norman 1923- ,
   14: 200
Thieda, Shirley Ann 1943- ,
   13: 233
Thiele, Colin (Milton) 1920- ,
   14: 201
Thistlethwaite, Miles 1945- ,
   12: 223
Thollander, Earl 1922- , *22:* 224
Thomas, Estelle Webb 1899- ,
   26: 193
Thomas, H. C. *See* Keating,
   Lawrence A., *23:* 107
Thomas, J. F. *See* Fleming, Thomas
   J(ames), *8:* 64
Thomas, Joan Gale. *See* Robinson,
   Joan G., *7:* 183
Thomas, Lowell (Jackson), Jr.
   1923- , *15:* 290
Thompson, Christine Pullein. *See*
   Pullein-Thompson, Christine,
   3: 164
Thompson, David H(ugh) 1941- ,
   17: 236
Thompson, Diana Pullein. *See*
   Pullein-Thompson, Diana,
   3: 165
Thompson, George Selden 1929- ,
   4: 204
Thompson, Harlan H. 1894- ,
   10: 177
Thompson, Josephine Pullein. *See*
   Pullein-Thompson, Josephine,
   3: 166
Thompson, Kay 1912- , *16:* 257
Thompson, Stith 1885-1976,
   20: 184 (Obituary)
Thompson, Vivian L. 1911- ,
   3: 224
Thomson, Peggy 1922- , *31:* 166
Thorndyke, Helen Louise
   [Collective pseudonym], *1:* 216
Thorne, Ian. *See* May, Julian,
   11: 175
Thornton, W. B. *See* Burgess,
   Thornton Waldo, *17:* 19
Thorpe, E(ustace) G(eorge)
   1916- , *21:* 173
Thorvall, Kerstin 1925- , *13:* 233
Thrasher, Crystal (Faye) 1921- ,
   27: 221
Thum, Gladys 1920- , *26:* 194
Thum, Marcella, *3:* 226; *28:* 206
Thundercloud, Katherine. *See* Witt,
   Shirley Hill, *17:* 247
Thurber, James (Grover)
   1894-1961, *13:* 235
Thwaite, Ann (Barbara Harrop)
   1932- , *14:* 206
Ticheburn, Cheviot. *See* Ainsworth,
   William Harrison, *24:* 21
Tichenor, Tom 1923- , *14:* 206
Tichy, William 1924- , *31:* 168
Timmins, William F., *10:* 177

Tinkelman, Murray 1933- ,
   12: 224
Titler, Dale Milton 1926- ,
   28: 207 (Brief Entry)
Titmarsh, Michael Angelo. *See*
   Thackeray, William
   Makepeace, *23:* 223
Titus, Eve 1922- , *2:* 240
Tobias, Tobi 1938- , *5:* 187
Todd, Anne Ophelia. *See* Dowden,
   Anne Ophelia, *7:* 69
Todd, Barbara K. 1917- , *10:* 178
Todd, H(erbert) E(atton) 1908- ,
   11: 221
Todd, Loreto 1942- , *30:* 190
Tolkien, J(ohn) R(onald) R(euel)
   1892-1973, *2:* 242; *24:* 201
   (Obituary)
Tolles, Martha 1921- , *8:* 203
Tolmie, Ken(neth Donald) 1941- ,
   15: 291
Tolstoi, Leo (Nikolaevich)
   1828-1910, *26:* 195
Tomalin, Ruth, *29:* 215
Tomes, Margot (Ladd) 1917- ,
   27: 223 (Brief Entry)
Tomfool. *See* Farjeon, Eleanor,
   2: 103
Tomlinson, Jill 1931-1976,
   3: 227; *24:* 201 (Obituary)
Tomlinson, Reginald R(obert)
   1885-1979(?), *27:* 223
   (Obituary)
Tompert, Ann 1918- , *14:* 208
Toner, Raymond John 1908- ,
   10: 179
Toonder, Martin. *See* Groom,
   Arthur William, *10:* 53
Toothaker, Roy Eugene 1928- ,
   18: 280
Tooze, Ruth 1892-1972, *4:* 205
Topping, Audrey R(onning)
   1928- , *14:* 209
Tor, Regina. *See* Shekerjian, Regina
   Tor, *16:* 244
Torbert, Floyd James 1922- ,
   22: 226
Totham, Mary. *See* Breinburg,
   Petronella, *11:* 36
Tournier, Michel 1924- , *23:* 232
Towne, Mary. *See* Spelman, Mary,
   28: 195
Townsend, John Rowe 1922- ,
   4: 206
Toye, Clive 1933(?)- , *30:* 191
   (Brief Entry)
Toye, William E(ldred) 1926- ,
   8: 203
Traherne, Michael. *See* Watkins-
   Pitchford, D. J., *6:* 214
Trapp, Maria (Augusta) von
   1905- , *16:* 260
Travers, P(amela) L(yndon)
   1906- , *4:* 208
Trease, (Robert) Geoffrey 1909- ,
   2: 244

Tredez, Alain   1926- , *17:* 236
Treece, Henry   1911-1966, *2:* 246
Tregaskis, Richard   1916-1973,
  3: 228; *26:* 210 (Obituary)
Trell, Max   1900- , *14:* 211
Tremain, Ruthven   1922- , *17:* 237
Trent, Robbie   1894- , *26:* 210
Trent, Timothy. *See* Malmberg,
  Carl, *9:* 136
Tresselt, Alvin   1916- , *7:* 197
Treviño, Elizabeth B(orton) de
  1904- , *1:* 216; *29:* 216
Trevor, Elleston   1920- , *28:* 207
Trevor, (Lucy) Meriol   1919- ,
  10: 180
Trez, Alain. *See* Tredez, Alain,
  17: 236
Tripp, Eleanor B.   1936- , *4:* 210
Tripp, Paul, *8:* 204
Tripp, Wallace (Whitney)   1940- ,
  31: 169
Trivett, Daphne (Harwood)
  1940- , *22:* 227
Trollope, Anthony   1815-1882,
  22: 229
Trost, Lucille Wood   1938- ,
  12: 226
Trotter, Grace V(iolet)   1900- ,
  10: 180
Tucker, Caroline. *See* Nolan,
  Jeannette, *2:* 196; *27:* 157
  (Obituary)
Tudor, Tasha, *20:* 184
Tully, John (Kimberley)   1923- ,
  14: 212
Tunis, Edwin (Burdett)
  1897-1973, *1:* 217; *24:* 201
  (Obituary); *28:* 208
Tunis, John R(oberts)   1889-1975,
  30: 191 (Brief Entry)
Turkle, Brinton   1915- , *2:* 248
Turlington, Bayly   1919- , *5:* 187
Turnbull, Agnes Sligh, *14:* 213
Turnbull, Ann (Christine)   1943- ,
  18: 281
Turner, Alice K.   1940- , *10:* 181
Turner, Ann W(arren)   1945- ,
  14: 214
Turner, Elizabeth   1774-1846,
  YABC 2: 332
Turner, Josie. *See* Crawford,
  Phyllis, *3:* 57
Turner, Philip   1925- , *11:* 222
Turner, Sheila R. *See* Seed, Sheila
  Turner, *23:* 220 (Obituary)
Turngren, Annette   1902(?)-1980,
  23: 233 (Obituary)
Turngren, Ellen   (?)-1964, *3:* 230
Turska, Krystyna Zofia   1933- ,
  27: 223 (Brief Entry); *31:* 172
Tusan, Stan   1936- , *22:* 236
Twain, Mark. *See* Clemens, Samuel
  Langhorne, *YABC 2:* 51
Tweedsmuir, Baron. *See* Buchan,
  John, *YABC 2:* 21

Tworkov, Jack   1900-1982,
  31: 176
Tyler, Anne   1941- , *7:* 198

Ubell, Earl   1926- , *4:* 210
Uchida, Yoshiko   1921- , *1:* 219
Udall, Jan Beaney   1938- ,
  10: 182
Uden, (Bernard Gilbert) Grant
  1910- , *26:* 211
Udry, Janice May   1928- , *4:* 212
Ullman, James Ramsey
  1907-1971, *7:* 199
Ulm, Robert   1934-1977, *17:* 238
Ulyatt, Kenneth   1920- , *14:* 216
Unada. *See* Gliewe, Unada, *3:* 77
Uncle Gus. *See* Rey, H. A., *1:* 181;
  26: 162
Uncle Mac. *See* McCulloch, Derek
  (Ivor Breashur), *29:* 142
  (Obituary)
Uncle Ray. *See* Coffman, Ramon
  Peyton, *4:* 53
Underhill, Alice Mertie
  1900-1971, *10:* 182
Ungerer, Jean Thomas   1931- ,
  5: 187
Ungerer, Tomi. *See* Ungerer, Jean
  Thomas, *5:* 187
Unkelbach, Kurt   1913- , *4:* 213
Unnerstad, Edith   1900- , *3:* 230
Unrau, Ruth   1922- , *9:* 192
Unstead R(obert) J(ohn)   1915- ,
  12: 226
Unsworth, Walt   1928- , *4:* 215
Untermeyer, Louis   1885-1977,
  2: 250; *26:* 211 (Obituary)
Unwin, David S(torr)   1918- ,
  14: 217
Unwin, Nora S.   1907- , *3:* 233
Usher, Margo Scegge. *See*
  McHargue, Georgess, *4:* 152
Uttley, Alice Jane (Taylor)
  1884-1976, *26:* 212 (Obituary)
Uttley, Alison. *See* Uttley, Alice
  Jane (Taylor), *26:* 212
  (Obituary)
Utz, Lois   1932- , *5:* 189
Uzair, Salem ben. *See* Horne,
  Richard Henry, *29:* 106

Vaeth, J(oseph) Gordon   1921- ,
  17: 239
Valen, Nanine   1950- , *21:* 173
Valens, Evans G., Jr.   1920- ,
  1: 220
Van Abbé, Salaman   1883-1955,
  18: 282
Van Anrooy, Francine   1924- ,
  2: 252
Van Anrooy, Frans. *See* Van
  Anrooy, Francine, *2:* 252

Vance, Eleanor Graham   1908- ,
  11: 223
Vance, Marguerite   1889-1965,
  29: 221
Vandenburg, Mary Lou   1943- ,
  17: 240
Vander Boom, Mae M., *14:* 219
Van der Veer, Judy   1912- ,
  4: 216
Vandivert, Rita (Andre)   1905- ,
  21: 174
Van Duyn, Janet   1910- , *18:* 283
Van Dyne, Edith. *See* Baum,
  L(yman) Frank, *18:* 7
Van Iterson, S(iny) R(ose), *26:* 212
Van Leeuwen, Jean   1937- ,
  6: 212
Van Lhin, Erik. *See* Del Rey,
  Lester, *22:* 97
Van Loon, Hendrik Willem
  1882-1944, *18:* 284
Van Orden, M(erton) D(ick)
  1921- , *4:* 218
Van Rensselaer, Alexander (Taylor
  Mason)   1892-1962, *14:* 219
Van Riper, Guernsey, Jr.   1909- ,
  3: 239
Van Stockum, Hilda   1908- ,
  5: 191
Van Tuyl, Barbara   1940- ,
  11: 224
Van Vogt, A(lfred) E(lton)
  1912- , *14:* 220
Van Woerkom, Dorothy (O'Brien)
  1924- , *21:* 176
Van Wyck Mason. *See* Mason, F.
  van Wyck, *3:* 117
Van-Wyck Mason, F. *See* Mason,
  F. van Wyck, *3:* 117
Van Zwienin, Ilse Charlotte Koehn
  1929- , *28:* 213 (Brief Entry)
Varga, Judy. *See* Stang, Judit,
  29: 196
Varley, Dimitry V.   1906- ,
  10: 183
Vasiliu, Mircea   1920- , *2:* 254
Vass, George   1927- , *31:* 176
  (Brief Entry)
Vaughan, Carter A. *See* Gerson,
  Noel B(ertram), *22:* 118
Vaughan, Harold Cecil   1923- ,
  14: 221
Vaughan, Sam(uel) S.   1928- ,
  14: 222
Vaughn, Ruth   1935- , *14:* 223
Vavra, Robert James   1944- ,
  8: 206
Vecsey, George   1939- , *9:* 192
Veglahn, Nancy (Crary)   1937- ,
  5: 194
Venable, Alan (Hudson)   1944- ,
  8: 206
Vequin, Capini. *See* Quinn,
  Elisabeth, *22:* 197
Verne, Jules   1828-1905, *21:* 178

Verner, Gerald 1897(?)-1980, 25: 216 (Obituary)

Verney, John 1913- , 14: 224

Vernon, (Elda) Louise A(nderson) 1914- , 14: 225

Vernor, D. See Casewit, Curtis, 4: 43

Verral, Charles Spain 1904- , 11: 225

Versace, Marie Teresa Rios 1917- , 2: 254

Vesey, Paul. See Allen, Samuel (Washington), 9: 6

Vestly, Anne-Cath(arina) 1920- , 14: 228

Viator, Vacuus. See Hughes, Thomas, 31: 85

Vicarion, Count Palmiro. See Logue, Christopher, 23: 119

Vicker, Angus. See Felsen, Henry Gregor, 1: 89

Victor, Edward 1914- , 3: 240

Victor, Joan Berg 1937- , 30: 192

Viereck, Ellen K. 1928- , 14: 229

Viereck, Phillip 1925- , 3: 241

Viertel, Janet 1915- , 10: 183

Vigna, Judith 1936- , 15: 292

Viguers, Ruth Hill 1903-1971, 6: 214

Villiard, Paul 1910-1974, 20: 188 (Obituary)

Villiers, Alan (John) 1903- , 10: 184

Vincent, Mary Keith. See St. John, Wylly Folk, 10: 132

Vining, Elizabeth Gray. See Gray, Elizabeth Janet, 6: 93

Vinson, Kathryn 1911- , 21: 193

Vinton, Iris, 24: 202

Viorst, Judith, 7: 200

Visser, W(illiam) F(rederick) H(endrik) 1900-1968, 10: 186

Vlahos, Olivia 1924- , 31: 176

Vo-Dinh, Mai 1933- , 16: 271

Vogel, Ilse-Margret 1914- , 14: 231

Vogel, John H(ollister), Jr. 1950- , 18: 292

Vogt, Esther Loewen 1915- , 14: 231

Voight, Virginia Frances 1909- , 8: 208

von Almedingen, Martha Edith. See Almedingen, E. M., 3: 9

Von Hagen, Victor Wolfgang 1908- , 29: 223

von Klopp, Vahrah. See Malvern, Gladys, 23: 133

von Storch, Anne B. 1910- , 1: 221

Vosburgh, Leonard (W.) 1912- , 15: 294

Voyle, Mary. See Manning, Rosemary, 10: 87

Waddell, Evelyn Margaret 1918- , 10: 186

Wagenheim, Kal 1935- , 21: 196

Wagner, Sharon B. 1936- , 4: 218

Wagoner, David (Russell) 1926- , 14: 232

Wahl, Jan 1933- , 2: 256

Waide, Jan 1952- , 29: 225

Waitley, Douglas 1927- , 30: 194

Walden, Amelia Elizabeth, 3: 242

Waldman, Bruce 1949- , 15: 297

Waldron, Ann Wood 1924- , 16: 273

Walker, Alice 1944- , 31: 177

Walker, Barbara K. 1921- , 4: 219

Walker, David Harry 1911- , 8: 210

Walker, Diana 1925- , 9: 193

Walker, Holly Beth. See Bond, Gladys Baker, 14: 41

Walker, Mildred. See Schemm, Mildred Walker, 21: 139

Walker, (Addison) Mort 1923- , 8: 211

Walker, Pamela 1948- , 24: 203

Walker, Stephen J. 1951- , 12: 228

Wallace, Barbara Brooks, 4: 221

Wallace, Beverly Dobrin 1921- , 19: 258

Wallace, John A. 1915- , 3: 243

Wallace, Nigel. See Hamilton, Charles Harold St. John, 13: 77

Waller, Leslie 1923- , 20: 188

Wallis, G. McDonald. See Campbell, Hope, 20: 19

Wallner, John C. 1945- , 10: 189

Wallower, Lucille, 11: 226

Walsh, Jill Paton. See Paton Walsh, Gillian, 4: 164

Walter, Villiam Christian. See Andersen, Hans Christian, YABC 1: 23

Walters, Audrey 1929- , 18: 293

Walters, Hugh. See Hughes, Walter (Llewellyn), 26: 125

Walther, Thomas A. 1950- , 31: 179

Walther, Tom. See Walther, Thomas A., 31: 179

Walton, Richard J. 1928- , 4: 223

Waltrip, Lela (Kingston) 1904- , 9: 194

Waltrip, Rufus (Charles) 1898- , 9: 195

Walworth, Nancy Zinsser 1917- , 14: 233

Wannamaker, Bruce. See Moncure, Jane Belk, 23: 139

Warbler, J. M. See Cocagnac, A. M., 7: 52

Warburg, Sandol Stoddard 1927- , 14: 234

Ward, Lynd (Kendall) 1905- , 2: 257

Ward, Martha (Eads) 1921- , 5: 195

Ward, Melanie. See Curtis, Richard (Alan), 29: 54

Ward, Dean. See Prince, J(ack) H(arvey), 17: 155

Ware, Leon (Vernon) 1909- , 4: 224

Warner, Frank A. [Collective pseudonym], 1: 222

Warner, Gertrude Chandler 1890- , 9: 195

Warner, Lucille Schulberg, 30: 195

Warner, Oliver 1903-1976, 29: 226

Warren, Billy. See Warren, William Stephen, 9: 196

Warren, Elizabeth. See Supraner, Robyn, 20: 182

Warren, Joyce W(illiams) 1935- , 18: 294

Warren, Mary Phraner 1929- , 10: 190

Warren, William Stephen 1882-1968, 9: 196

Warsh. See Warshaw, Jerry, 30: 196

Warshaw, Jerry 1929- , 30: 196

Warshofsky, Fred 1931- , 24: 203

Warshofsky, Isaac. See Singer, Isaac Bashevis, 3: 203; 27: 202

Wa-sha-quon-asin. See Belaney, Archibald Stansfeld, 24: 39

Washburne, Heluiz Chandler 1892-1970, 10: 192; 26: 213 (Obituary)

Washington, Booker T(aliaferro) 1858(?)-1915, 28: 213

Waters, John F(rederick) 1930- , 4: 225

Watkins-Pitchford, D. J. 1905- , 6: 214

Watson, Clyde 1947- , 5: 196

Watson, Helen Orr 1892-1978, 24: 205 (Obituary)

Watson, James 1936- , 10: 192

Watson, Jane Werner 1915- , 3: 244

Watson, Pauline 1925- , 14: 235

Watson, Sally 1924- , 3: 245

Watson, Wendy (McLeod) 1942- , 5: 198

Watt, Thomas 1935- , 4: 226

Watts, Bernadette 1942- , 4: 226

Watts, Ephraim. See Horne, Richard Henry, 29: 106

Watts, Franklin (Mowry) 1904-1978, 21: 196 (Obituary)

Watts, Mabel Pizzey 1906- , 11: 227

Waugh, Dorothy, 11: 228

Wayland, Patrick. See O'Connor, Richard, 21: 111

Wayne, Kyra Petrovskaya 1918- , *8:* 213

Wayne, Richard. *See* Decker, Duane, *5:* 53

Waystaff, Simon. *See* Swift, Jonathan, *19:* 244

Weales, Gerald (Clifford) 1925- , *11:* 229

Weary, Ogdred. *See* Gorey, Edward St. John, *27:* 104 (Brief Entry); *29:* 89

Weaver, Ward. *See* Mason, F. van Wyck, *3:* 117; *26:* 146 (Obituary)

Webb, Christopher. *See* Wibberley, Leonard, *2:* 271

Webber, Irma E(leanor Schmidt) 1904- , *14:* 237

Weber, Alfons 1921- , *8:* 215

Weber, Lenora Mattingly 1895-1971, *2:* 260; *26:* 213 (Obituary)

Weber, William John 1927- , *14:* 239

Webster, Alice (Jane Chandler) 1876-1916, *17:* 241

Webster, David 1930- , *11:* 230

Webster, Frank V. [Collective pseudonym], *1:* 222

Webster, Gary. *See* Garrison, Webb B(lack), *25:* 119

Webster, James 1925-1981, *17:* 242; *27:* 223 (Obituary)

Webster, Jean. *See* Webster, Alice (Jane Chandler), *17:* 241

Wechsler, Herman 1904-1976, *20:* 189 (Obituary)

Weddle, Ethel H(arshbarger) 1897- , *11:* 231

Wegner, Fritz 1924- , *20:* 189

Weihs, Erika 1917- , *15:* 297

Weik, Mary Hays 1898(?)-1979, *3:* 247; *23:* 233 (Obituary)

Weil, Ann Yezner 1908-1969, *9:* 197

Weil, Lisl, *7:* 202

Weilerstein, Sadie Rose 1894- , *3:* 248

Weiner, Sandra 1922- , *14:* 240

Weingarten, Violet (Brown) 1915-1976, *3:* 250; *27:* 223 (Obituary)

Weingartner, Charles 1922- , *5:* 199

Weir, LaVada, *2:* 261

Weir, Rosemary (Green) 1905- , *21:* 196

Weisberger, Bernard A(llen) 1922- , *21:* 198

Weisgard, Leonard (Joseph) 1916- , *2:* 263; *30:* 198

Weiss, Adelle 1920- , *18:* 296

Weiss, Ann E(dwards) 1943- , *30:* 205

Weiss, Harvey 1922- , *1:* 222; *27:* 225

Weiss, Malcolm E. 1928- , *3:* 251

Weiss, Miriam. *See* Schlein, Miriam, *2:* 222

Weiss, Renee Karol 1923- , *5:* 199

Weissenborn, Hellmuth 1898-1982, *31:* 179 (Obituary)

Welber, Robert, *26:* 214

Welch, D'Alte Aldridge 1907-1970, *27:* 227 (Obituary)

Welch, Jean-Louise. *See* Kempton, Jean Welch, *10:* 67

Welch, Pauline. *See* Bodenham, Hilda Esther, *13:* 16

Welch, Ronald. *See* Felton, Ronald Oliver, *3:* 67

Weller, George (Anthony) 1907- , *31:* 179

Welles, Winifred 1893-1939, *27:* 227 (Brief Entry)

Wellman, Manly Wade 1903- , *6:* 217

Wellman, Paul I. 1898-1966, *3:* 251

Wells, H(erbert) G(eorge) 1866-1946, *20:* 190

Wells, Helen 1910- , *2:* 266

Wells, J. Wellington. *See* DeCamp, L(yon) Sprague, *9:* 49

Wells, Rosemary, *18:* 296

Wels, Byron G(erald) 1924- , *9:* 197

Welty, S. F. *See* Welty, Susan F., *9:* 198

Welty, Susan F. 1905- , *9:* 198

Wendelin, Rudolph 1910- , *23:* 233

Werner, Jane. *See* Watson, Jane Werner, *3:* 244

Werner, K. *See* Casewit, Curtis, *4:* 43

Wersba, Barbara 1932- , *1:* 224

Werstein, Irving 1914-1971, *14:* 240

Werth, Kurt 1896- , *20:* 213

West, Barbara. *See* Price, Olive, *8:* 157

West, Betty 1921- , *11:* 233

West, C. P. *See* Wodehouse, P(elham) G(renville), *22:* 241

West, James. *See* Withers, Carl A., *14:* 261

West, Jerry. *See* Stratemeyer, Edward L., *1:* 208

West, Jerry. *See* Svenson, Andrew E., *2:* 238; *26:* 185 (Obituary)

West, Ward. *See* Borland, Hal, *5:* 22; *24:* 51 (Obituary)

Westall, Robert (Atkinson) 1929- , *23:* 235

Westerberg, Christine 1950- , *29:* 226

Westervelt, Virginia (Veeder) 1914- , *10:* 193

Westheimer, David 1917- , *14:* 242

Weston, John (Harrison) 1932- , *21:* 199

Westwood, Jennifer 1940- , *10:* 194

Wexler, Jerome (LeRoy) 1923- , *14:* 243

Wharf, Michael. *See* Weller, George (Anthony), *31:* 179

Wheatley, Arabelle 1921- , *16:* 275

Wheeler, Captain. *See* Ellis, Edward S(ylvester), *YABC 1:* 116

Wheeler, Janet D. [Collective pseudonym], *1:* 225

Wheeler, Opal 1898- , *23:* 236

Whelan, Elizabeth M(urphy) 1943- , *14:* 244

Whistler, Reginald John 1905-1944, *30:* 206

Whistler, Rex. *See* Whistler, Reginald John, *30:* 206

Whitcomb, Jon 1906- , *10:* 195

White, Anne Terry 1896- , *2:* 267

White, Dale. *See* Place, Marian T., *3:* 160

White, Dori 1919- , *10:* 195

White, E(lwyn) B(rooks) 1899- , *2:* 268; *29:* 227

White, Eliza Orne 1856-1947, *YABC 2:* 333

White, Florence M(eiman) 1910- , *14:* 244

White, Laurence B., Jr. 1935- , *10:* 196

White, Ramy Allison [Collective pseudonym], *1:* 225

White, Robb 1909- , *1:* 225

White, T(erence) H(anbury) 1906-1964, *12:* 229

White, William, Jr. 1934- , *16:* 276

Whitehead, Don(ald) F. 1908- , *4:* 227

Whitehouse, Arch. *See* Whitehouse, Arthur George, *14:* 246; *23:* 238 (Obituary)

Whitehouse, Arthur George 1895-1979, *14:* 246; *23:* 238 (Obituary)

Whitehouse, Jeanne 1939- , *29:* 239

Whitinger, R. D. *See* Place, Marian T., *3:* 160

Whitlock, Pamela 1921(?)-1982, *31:* 181 (Obituary)

Whitman, Walt(er) 1819-1892, *20:* 215

Whitney, Alex(andra) 1922- , *14:* 249

Whitney, David C(harles) 1921- , *29:* 239 (Brief Entry)

Whitney, Phyllis A(yame) 1903- , *1:* 226; *30:* 209

Whitney, Thomas P(orter) 1917- , 25: 216

Wibberley, Leonard 1915- , 2: 271

Widdemer, Mabel Cleland 1902-1964, 5: 200

Widenberg, Siv 1931- , 10: 197

Wier, Ester 1910- , 3: 252

Wiese, Kurt 1887-1974, 3: 254; 24: 205 (Obituary)

Wiesner, Portia. See Takakjian, Portia, 15: 273

Wiesner, William 1899- , 5: 200

Wiggin, Kate Douglas (Smith) 1856-1923, YABC 1: 258

Wilbur, C. Keith 1923- , 27: 227

Wilbur, Richard (Purdy) 1921- , 9: 200

Wilde, Gunther. See Hurwood, Bernhardt J., 12: 107

Wilde, Oscar (Fingal O'Flahertie Wills) 1854-1900, 24: 205

Wilder, Laura Ingalls 1867-1957, 29: 239

Wildsmith, Brian 1930- , 16: 277

Wilkie, Katharine E(lliott) 1904-1980, 31: 181

Wilkins, Frances 1923- , 14: 249

Wilkins, Marilyn (Ruth) 1926- , 30: 212

Wilkins, Marne. See Wilkins, Marilyn (Ruth), 30: 212

Wilkinson, Brenda 1946- , 14: 250

Wilkinson, Burke 1913- , 4: 229

Wilkoń, Józef 1930- , 31: 182

Will. See Lipkind, William, 15: 178

Willard, Barbara (Mary) 1909- , 17: 243

Willard, Mildred Wilds 1911- , 14: 252

Willard, Nancy 1936- , 30: 213 (Brief Entry)

Willey, Robert. See Ley, Willy, 2: 175

Williams, Barbara 1925- , 11: 233

Williams, Beryl. See Epstein, Beryl, 1: 85; 31: 64

Williams, Charles. See Collier, James Lincoln, 8: 33

Williams, Clyde C. 1881-1974, 8: 216; 27: 229 (Obituary)

Williams, Eric (Ernest) 1911- , 14: 253

Williams, Ferelith Eccles 1920- , 22: 237

Williams, Frances B. See Browin, Frances Williams, 5: 30

Williams, Garth (Montgomery) 1912- , 18: 298

Williams, Guy R. 1920- , 11: 235

Williams, Hawley. See Heyliger, William, YABC 1: 163

Williams, J. R. See Williams, Jeanne, 5: 202

Williams, J. Walker. See Wodehouse, P(elham) G(renville), 22: 241

Williams, Jay 1914-1978, 3: 256; 24: 221 (Obituary)

Williams, Jeanne 1930- , 5: 202

Williams, Maureen 1951- , 12: 238

Williams, Michael. See St. John, Wylly Folk, 10: 132

Williams, Patrick J. See Butterworth, W. E., 5: 40

Williams, Selma R(uth) 1925- , 14: 256

Williams, Slim. See Williams, Clyde C., 8: 216; 27: 229 (Obituary)

Williams, Ursula Moray 1911- , 3: 257

Williams-Ellis, (Mary) Amabel (Nassau) 1894- , 29: 249

Williamson, Henry 1895-1977, 30: 214 (Obituary)

Williamson, Joanne Small 1926- , 3: 259

Willson, Robina Beckles (Ballard) 1930- , 27: 229

Wilma, Dana. See Faralla, Dana, 9: 62

Wilson, Beth P(ierre), 8: 218

Wilson, Carter 1941- , 6: 218

Wilson, Charles Morrow 1905-1977, 30: 214

Wilson, Dagmar 1916- , 31: 186 (Brief Entry)

Wilson, Dorothy Clarke 1904- , 16: 283

Wilson, Ellen (Janet Cameron) (?)-1976, 9: 200; 26: 214 (Obituary)

Wilson, Forrest 1918- , 27: 230

Wilson, Gahan 1930- , 27: 231 (Brief Entry)

Wilson, (Leslie) Granville 1912- , 14: 257

Wilson, Hazel 1898- , 3: 260

Wilson, John 1922- , 22: 239

Wilson, Joyce M(uriel Judson), 21: 201

Wilson, Lionel 1924- , 31: 186 (Brief Entry)

Wilson, Tom 1931- , 30: 215 (Brief Entry)

Wilson, Walt(er N.) 1939- , 14: 258

Wilton, Elizabeth 1937- , 14: 259

Wilwerding, Walter Joseph 1891-1966, 9: 201

Winchester, James H. 1917- , 30: 215

Winders, Gertrude Hecker, 3: 261

Windham, Basil. See Wodehouse, P(elham) G(renville), 22: 241

Windham, Kathryn T(ucker) 1918- , 14: 259

Windsor, Claire. See Hamerstrom, Frances, 24: 125

Windsor, Patricia 1938- , 30: 216

Winfield, Arthur M. See Stratemeyer, Edward L., 1: 208

Winfield, Edna. See Stratemeyer, Edward L., 1: 208

Winter, Milo (Kendall) 1888-1956, 21: 202

Winter, R. R.. See Winterbotham, R(ussell) R(obert), 10: 198

Winterbotham, R(ussell) R(obert) 1904-1971, 10: 198

Winterton, Gayle. See Adams, William Taylor, 28: 21

Winthrop, Elizabeth. See Mahony, Elizabeth Winthrop, 8: 125

Wirtenberg, Patricia Z. 1932- , 10: 199

Wise, William 1923- , 4: 230

Wise, Winifred E., 2: 273

Wiseman, Ann (Sayre) 1926- , 31: 186

Wiseman, B(ernard) 1922- , 4: 232

Withers, Carl A. 1900-1970, 14: 261

Witt, Shirley Hill 1934- , 17: 247

Wittels, Harriet Joan 1938- , 31: 187

Wittman, Sally (Anne Christensen) 1941- , 30: 218

Witty, Paul A(ndrew) 1898-1976, 30: 219 (Obituary)

Wizard, Mr. See Herbert, Don, 2: 131

Wodehouse, P(elham) G(renville) 1881-1975, 22: 241

Wodge, Dreary. See Gorey, Edward St. John, 27: 104 (Brief Entry)

Wohlrabe, Raymond A. 1900- , 4: 234

Wojciechowska, Maia 1927- , 1: 228; 28: 222

Wolcott, Patty 1929- , 14: 264

Wold, Jo Anne 1938- , 30: 219

Wolfe, Burton H. 1932- , 5: 202

Wolfe, Louis 1905- , 8: 219

Wolfenden, George. See Beardmore, George, 20: 10

Wolff, Diane 1945- , 27: 231

Wolff, Robert Jay 1905- , 10: 199

Wolitzer, Hilma 1930- , 31: 188

Wolkstein, Diane 1942- , 7: 204

Wondriska, William 1931- , 6: 219

Wood, Edgar A(llardyce) 1907- , 14: 264

Wood, Esther. See Brady, Esther Wood, 31: 35

Wood, James Playsted 1905- , 1: 229

Wood, Kerry. See Wood, Edgar A(llardyce), 14: 264

Wood, Nancy 1936- , 6: 220

Wood, Phyllis Anderson 1923- , *30:* 221 (Brief Entry)
Woodard, Carol 1929- , *14:* 266
Woodburn, John Henry 1914- , *11:* 236
Woodford, Peggy 1937- , *25:* 218
Woodrich, Mary Neville 1915- , *2:* 274
Woods, George A(llan) 1926- , *30:* 221
Woods, Margaret 1921- , *2:* 275
Woods, Nat. *See* Stratemeyer, Edward L., *1:* 208
Woodson, Jack. *See* Woodson, John Waddie, Jr., *10:* 200
Woodson, John Waddie, Jr., *10:* 200
Woodward, Cleveland 1900- , *10:* 201
Woody, Regina Jones 1894- , *3:* 263
Wooldridge, Rhoda 1906- , *22:* 249
Woolley, Catherine 1904- , *3:* 265
Woolsey, Janette 1904- , *3:* 266
Worcester, Donald Emmet 1915- , *18:* 301
Worline, Bonnie Bess 1914- , *14:* 267
Wormser, Sophie 1896- , *22:* 250
Worth, Valerie 1933- , *8:* 220
Wortis, Avi 1937- , *14:* 269
Wosmek, Frances 1917- , *29:* 251
Wriggins, Sally Hovey 1922- , *17:* 248
Wright, Dare 1926(?)- , *21:* 206
Wright, Enid Meadowcroft 1898-1966, *3:* 267
Wright, Esmond 1915- , *10:* 202
Wright, Frances Fitzpatrick 1897- , *10:* 202
Wright, Judith 1915- , *14:* 270
Wright, Kenneth. *See* Del Rey, Lester, *22:* 97
Wright, R(obert) H. 1906- , *6:* 220
Wrightson, Patricia 1921- , *8:* 220
Wronker, Lili Cassel 1924- , *10:* 204
Wuorio, Eva-Lis 1918- , *28:* 228 (Brief Entry)
Wyeth, N(ewell) C(onvers) 1882-1945, *17:* 249
Wyler, Rose 1909- , *18:* 303
Wylie, Laura. *See* Matthews, Patricia, *28:* 153

Wymer, Norman George 1911- , *25:* 219
Wynants, Miche 1934- , *31:* 189 (Brief Entry)
Wyndham, Lee. *See* Hyndman, Jane Andrews, *1:* 122; *23:* 103 (Obituary)
Wyndham, Robert. *See* Hyndman, Robert Utley, *18:* 123
Wynter, Edward (John) 1914- , *14:* 271
Wynyard, Talbot. *See* Hamilton, Charles Harold St. John, *13:* 77
Wyss, Johann David Von 1743-1818, *27:* 232 (Brief Entry); *29:* 252
Wyss, Thelma Hatch 1934- , *10:* 205

Yamaguchi, Marianne 1936- , *7:* 205
Yang, Jay 1941- , *12:* 239
Yashima, Taro. *See* Iwamatsu, Jun Atsushi, *14:* 83
Yates, Elizabeth 1905- , *4:* 235
Yates, Raymond F(rancis) 1895-1966, *31:* 189
Yaukey, Grace S(ydenstricker) 1899- , *5:* 203
Yeakley, Marjory Hall 1908- , *21:* 207
Yensid, Retlaw. *See* Disney, Walt(er Elias), *28:* 70
Yeo, Wilma (Lethem) 1918-, *24:* 221
Yeoman, John (Brian) 1934- , *28:* 228
Yep, Laurence M. 1948- , *7:* 206
Yerian, Cameron John, *21:* 208
Yerian, Margaret A., *21:* 209
Yolen, Jane H. 1939- , *4:* 237
York, Andrew. *See* Nicole, Christopher Robin, *5:* 141
Yonge, Charlotte Mary 1823-1901, *17:* 272
York, Carol Beach 1928- , *6:* 221
Yost, Edna 1889-1971, *26:* 215 (Obituary)
Youd, (Christopher) Samuel 1922- , *30:* 222 (Brief Entry)
Young, Bob. *See* Young, Robert W., *3:* 269
Young, Clarence [Collective pseudonym], *1:* 231
Young, Dorothea Bennett 1924- , *31:* 191

Young, Ed 1931- , *10:* 205
Young, Edward. *See* Reinfeld, Fred, *3:* 170
Young, Jan. *See* Young, Janet Randall, *3:* 268
Young, Janet Randall 1919- , *3:* 268
Young, Lois Horton 1911-1981, *26:* 215
Young, Margaret B(uckner) 1922- , *2:* 275
Young, Miriam 1913-1934, *7:* 208
Young, (Rodney Lee) Patrick (Jr.) 1937- , *22:* 251
Young, Percy M(arshall) 1912- , *31:* 191
Young, Robert W. 1916-1969, *3:* 269
Young, Scott A(lexander) 1918- , *5:* 204

Zalben, Jane Breskin 1950- , *7:* 211
Zallinger, Jean (Day) 1918- , *14:* 272
Zappler, Lisbeth 1930- , *10:* 206
Zei, Alki, *24:* 223
Zellan, Audrey Penn 1950- , *22:* 252
Zemach, Harve 1933- , *3:* 270
Zemach, Margot 1931- , *21:* 209
Ziemienski, Dennis 1947- , *10:* 206
Zillah. *See* Macdonald, Zillah K., *11:* 167
Zim, Herbert S(pencer) 1909- , *1:* 231; *30:* 222
Zim, Sonia Bleeker. *See* Bleeker, Sonia, *26:* 37 (Obituary)
Zimmerman, Naoma 1914- , *10:* 207
Zindel, Paul 1936- , *16:* 283
Ziner, (Florence) Feenie 1921- , *5:* 204
Zion, (Eu)Gene 1913-1975, *18:* 305
Zollinger, Gulielma 1856-1917, *27:* 232 (Brief Entry)
Zolotow, Charlotte S. 1915- , *1:* 233
Zonia, Dhimitri 1921- , *20:* 233
Zurhorst, Charles (Stewart, Jr.) 1913- , *12:* 240
Zweifel, Frances 1931- , *14:* 273